ISBN 978-1-331-68831-0
PIBN 10221634

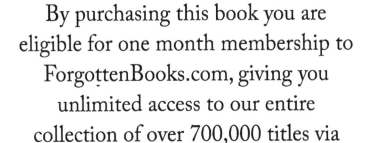

ACKNOWLEDGMENT.

The compiler of this Digest acknowledges his obligations to the judges of the U. S. District Courts throughout the Union for the numerous decisions in Bankruptcy Cases which they so courteously and promptly forwarded to him in manuscript, and for correct copies of the Rules of their several Courts.

He also tenders his thanks to R. A. Fisher, Esq., of Essex Court, Temple, London, for the professional courtesy manifested in his interesting letter of the seventeenth of February, 1871. (See preceding page.)

Valuable assistance has also been freely rendered by Wm. A. Shinn and John V. Kernan, Esqs., of the New York Bar, which places the compiler under obligations to both those gentlemen, which it is becoming that he should thus, with thanks, publicly acknowledge.

AUDLEY W. GAZZAM.

DIGEST

OF

BANKRUPTCY DECISIONS

IN THE

UNITED STATES AND ENGLAND, TOGETHER WITH UNITED STATES BANKRUPT ACTS OF 1800, 1841 AND 1867.

QUALIFICATION OF PETITIONERS.

1. The fact that a person becomes a petitioning creditor of an insolvent for the nominal amount of a debt purchased by him at a discount rather than the amount paid by him will not per se vitiate the discharge. Small v. Graves, 7 Barb. 576.

QUESTIONS.

1. Arising in progress of case. A question arising in the progress of a case in bankruptcy will be heard by petition and not by an appeal in the circuit court, and such petitions will be heard and acted upon in chambers or elsewhere. In re Reed, (Ohio,) 2 N. B. R. 2.

2. A question in order to be properly certified to the judge, must arise regularly in the course of proceedings before the register, and between parties having the legal right to raise it. In re Wright, (Ky.) 1 N. B. R. 91.

3. Certifying. Where the questions certified to a district judge in bankruptcy are merely questions in the abstract, not arising in the course of bankruptcy proceedings or upon the result of such proceedings, and are certified in behalf of a person who

is not a party to the proceedings in the bankrupt court, they will be returned undecided, for the reason that a decision would be of no force or effect. In re Haskell, 4 N. B. R. 181.

4. Of fact. A witness is not bound to answer a question that does not relate to any matter of fact in issue, or to any matter contained in his direct testimony. Especially if a truthful answer to it would tend to degrade him. In re Lewis, (S. D. N. Y.) 3 N. B. R. 153.

5. Whether a departing the dwelling house is accompanied with an intent to delay a creditor, is a question of fact for a jury to decide upon all the circumstances. Aldridge v. Ireland, 1 Taunt. 273, n. (Eng.)

6. To render a mortgage void under the 35th section of the bankrupt act, it is not necessary that the debtor knew or believed himself insolvent; the section treats of insolvency as a matter of fact, not of belief, and with knowledge of which and its consequences he is chargeable in law. It follows, as a logical sequence, that when a man, insolvent in fact, gives a mortgage to one existing creditor, he does so with a view to give him a preference. The bankrupt law of 1841, and the Massachusetts insolvent law and decisions commented upon. The act of 1841 declares void preferences made by a party contem-

plating bankruptcy; the act of 1867 includes those made by a party being insolvent, and the decisions under the former act are not always applicable to the present statute. The question whether the debtor knew or did not know of his insolvency, is unimportant in determining as to him; and the purpose of the act being to enforce the equal distribution of the estate. Every act of an insolvent that tends to defeat that purpose, should be construed strictly against him, and courts should indulge every presumption permissible by the well settled rule of law, to secure the full benefit of this cardinal principle of the law. The strict definition of insolvency, usually given in commercial centers, should not be applied in country places. A party should be held insolvent only when he fails to meet his debts according to the usages and customs of the place of his business; the rule should be in harmony with the general custom of the place. If an insolvent give a mortgage to a creditor, who has reasonable cause to believe him insolvent, the fraud upon the bankrupt act. is complete as to both. The question as to the creditor, is whether he had reasonable cause to believe the debtor insolvent, not what he did believe, the latter is immaterial. The creditor is not constituted the sole judge of the sufficiency of the evidence of his debtor's insolvency; that is for the court to determine, the security being attached. Where a debtor had, during two years, paid off only a small portion of an overdue debt, had sold out the stock of goods for which the account was made, and transferred a part of the paper received therefor, had applied for extensions and been refused, had previously declined to execute a mortgage on the ground that it would injure his credit, and had been pressed by his different creditors. These facts constituted reasonable cause for belief of insolvency, and the creditor cannot escape from the consequences of knowledge of them. *In re* Wager & Fales, 5 *N. B. R.* 181.

7. Of fact and of law. A. wishing to purchase a lot of sheep from B. and they not able to agree on the terms, the sheep were placed on A.'s farm by mutual agreement. They remained there five days and before the price was agreed on, A. became bankrupt. In an action by B. against the assignees of A. for taking the sheep, it was held, that the question whether the sheep were in A.'s possession as reputed owner, was a matter of fact for the jury, and the assignees, having put it as a matter of law at the trial; could not afterwards contend that the judge should have left the question to the jury. Trismall *v.* Lovegrove, 10 *W. R.* 527; 6 *L. T., N. S.* 329. (Eng.)

8. Of insolvency, how to be construed. What is insolvency? It is true that "insolvency and inability to pay" are synonymous, but solvency does not mean ability to pay at all times, under all circumstances, and everywhere on demand, nor does it require that a person shall have in his possession the amount of money necessary to pay all claims against him. Difficulty in · paying particular demands is not insolvency. *Held*, that the insolvency of the partnership was not so clearly made out as to warrant any interference by the court. Walkenshaw *v.* Perzel, 32 *How. Pr. R.* 233.

9. Of practice. The circuit court will not review an incidental question of practice arising in the district court. *In re* Robinson, 2 *N. B. R.* 108; s. c. 6 *Bl. C. C.* 253.

10. On examination. As to relevancy or irrelevancy; see *in re* Carson & Hard. (*S. D. N. Y.*) 2 *N. B. R.* 41.

11. Relative to property. When a bankrupt testifies that the owner of certain property, questions relating to the identity of the owner, duration, extent and character of the ownership of that property, are irrelevant; likewise all questions, which on their face relate to property that does not belong to the bankrupt, are irrelevant. *In re* Van Tuyl, 1 *N. B. R.* 193.

12. A bankrupt must answer questions in relation to property, in which it is shown that he might possibly have an interest. *In re* Bonesteel, (*S. D. N. Y.*) 2 *N. B. R.* 106.

RAILROAD COMPANIES.

1. A corporation carrying on and pursuing any lawful business defined and clothed by its charter, with power to do so, is clearly a business corporation, and amenable to the provisions of the bankrupt act; therefore the objection to the adjudication of a railroad company, because it is not a monied business, or commercial corporation, or a joint stock company, is not well taken. For it seems to be the clear intent of the thirty-seventh section, to bring within the scope of the bankrupt act, all corporations except those organized for religious, charitable, literary, educational, municipal or political purposes. Where the bankruptcy proceedings against the Alabama & Chattanooga railroad company are based on the ninth clause of the thirty- ninth section of the bankrupt act of eighteen hundred and sixty-seven, as amended, it is necessary to aver and prove that the debtor was either a banker, broker, merchant, manufacturer, miner or trader, and as the charter of the Alabama & Chattanooga railroad company does not authórize it to carry on either of these pursuits, it does not come within the provisions of the ninth clause of section thirty-nine, as amended. As the petition upon which the adjudication of this railroad company was made, did not allege that it was either a banker, broker, merchant, manufacturer, miner or trader, and as no proof thereof was offered to this effect, the irresistible conclusion is, that upon that petition, this railroad company should not have been adjudicated a bankrupt upon the petition and proofs presented to the court. *In re* The Alabama & Chattanooga R. R. Co., 5 *N. B. R.* 97.

2. Railroad corporations are created to transport passengers and freight, and it is that precise business in which they are employed. They must therefore be held to be commercial corporations. Undoubtedly the word "business," as applied to corporations, has a broader meaning than the word "commercial," as used in the same clause, but it was not the intention of congress, in the opinion of the court, to give such a scope to the word "business" as to supersede the words "monied and commercial," and leave them without any practical signification. Harris *v.* Amery, 1 *Law Rep.*, *C. P.* 154 ; Sweatt *v.* The Boston, Hartford & Erie R. R. Co. *et al.* 5 *N. B. R.* 234.

3. Assignees of in several districts. Where a corporation holding property and carrying on business in three seve-

ral states is adjudicated bankrupt, and assignees are appointed, who are · respectively citizens of two states in which proceedings in bankruptcy are pending; but an assignee is not appointed who resides in the third state in which proceedings in bankruptcy are also pending. *Held*, that as three assignees were to be chosen, and proceedings were pending in three different districts, it ought to have been so arranged that each of the districts could have an assignee within it a resident thereof; and that in the district in which no assignee has been appointed, the court there declines to approve the election of assignees. *In re* Boston, Hartford & Erie Railway Co. (*S. D. N. Y.*) 5 *N. B. R.* 233.

4. Bonds of. Railroad corporations from their character as branches of the great system of internal improvements do not come within the *regime* of the bankrupt law. The fact that the bonds of a road are at a mere nominal value does not show that the road should be considered insolvent. Bonds and coupons of a railroad are not commercial paper within the meaning of the U. S. bankrupt act of 1867, and the paying of its coupons after suit brought is not preferring one creditor over another. *In re* Opelusa & Great Western R. R. *Ex parte* Tucker, *et al.* (*La.*) 3 *N. B. R.* 31.

5. Not subject to the provisions of bankrupt act. A railroad corporation is not within the purview of the bankrupt law. *Ex parte* Opelusa & Great Western R. R. Co., 3 *N. B. R.* 31; *contra, in re* Rankin *v.* Florida, Atlantic & G. C. R. R. Co., 1 *N. B. R.* 96; *in re* The Boston, Hartford & Erie R. R. Co., 4 *N. B. R.* 99; *in re* Alabama & Chattanooga R. R. Co., 5 *N. B. R.* 97.

6. Property in the hands of receiver. Property in the hands of the receiver of the company must be regarded as being in the possession of the several state courts which appointed such receivers, and where their appointment was prior. to the commencement of proceedings in bankruptcy, the U. S. district court will not interfere until their title is impeached. Alden *v.* The Boston, Hartford & Erie R. R. C., 5 *N. B. R.* 231.

7. Subject to provisions of bankrupt act. The grantee of the franchise of a corporation to operate a railroad can acquire no greater rights than the corporation itself has by the terms of its charter. The purchaser must take his title subject to all the creditors of the original grant, and subject to all duties and liabilities to the state; the public and individuals, none of whose rights can be impaired by the transfer. Hence, there are no such inherent difficulties in the way of the sale and transfer of the property and franchises of a railroad as would require such a construction of the U. S. bankrupt act of 1867, as to exclude railroad corporations from the operation of that clause of the act, the literal construction of which clearly renders them liable to be dealt with under its provisions. Adams v. Boston, Hartford & Erie R. R. Co., (*Mass.*) 4 *N. B. R.* 99, (citing Dartmouth College v. Woodward, 4 *Wheat.* 701; Harris v. Amery, 1 *L. R., C. P.* 154; Hall v. Sullivan R. R. Co., 21 *Law R.* 138.)

8. Moneyed business and commercial corporations are certainly within the words of the bankrupt act of 1867, as the 37th section enacts that the provisions of the act shall apply to such corporations and to joint stock companies. Whenever the word person is used in the act, it must doubtless be construed as including corporations as the 48th section of the act so provides; but that section cannot be construed as including any corporation within the provisions of the bankrupt act, except such as are mentioned in the 37th section of the act, as the rules therein prescribed regulating the proceedings in such cases, do not apply *to any other* corporations than those previously named in the same section. Railroads being engaged in commercial pursuits, such as the transportation of passengers and freight, and as auxiliaries of commerce & trade are commercial corporations, and are subject to the provisions of the U. S. bankrupt act of 1867. Sweatt v. The Boston, Hartford & Erie R. R. Co., et al. 5 *N. B. R.* 234.

9. Railroad corporations may be declared bankrupt under the proper construction of the U. S. bankrupt act of 1867. Adams v. Boston, Hartford & Erie R. R. Co. (*Mass.*) 4 *N. B. R.* 99.

RATES.

1. Parochial. One year's parochial rates due at the date of bankruptcy may be paid in full. *In re* Saberton, 9 *L. T., N. S.* 267. (Eng.)

2. A sum assessed by way of poor rate, was a claim or demand provable under a commission of bankrupty under 5 & 6 Vict. c. 122, s. 7; and a certificate was, therefore, a bar to any subsequent proceedings under 43 Eliz. c. 2, to levy the amount by distress and sale of the bankrupt's goods. *Ex parte* Bunvash, (Churchwardens, &c.) 1 *L. M. & P.* 60; 19 *L. J., M. G.* 115. (Eng.)

RATIFICATION.

1. Of previous assignment. When persons indebted made a voluntary assignment for the benefit of creditors which was voidable, and afterwards executed an assignment to trustees under the insolvent laws, none but creditors or their representatives (the trustees) can avoid the voluntary assignment. And an action brought by the insolvent trustees, upon the bonds given for the purchase money to the voluntary assignees, after the securities had been transferred to the former, under a decree in equity accompanied with an offer to ratify the purchase, is a direct ratification of the title of the purchaser, which removes all ground of defence founded upon a defect of title. Moss & Hanson, 17 *Penn. R.* 379.

REAL ESTATE.

1. Distribution of proceeds of. A creditor of a bankrupt whose claim is in the form of a judgment, will share with the other creditors in the distribution of the assets of real estate, derived from the collection of a promissory note. *In re* Erwin & Hardee, (*Ga.*) 3 *N. B. R.* 142.

2. Dower right in. The widow of a bankrupt, where petition in bankruptcy was filed after the act by the legislature of North Carolina, repealing the statutory provisions and restoring the common law right of dower, the bankrupt dying after the issuing of the warrant in bankruptcy, is entitled to dower in the land owned by the bankrupt at the time of filing his petition. The act referred to repealed the statutory provisions in regard to dower which, in effect, restored *eo instante* the common law. The legislature by the act attempted to create additional exemptions to those theretofore allowed by law; those exemptions are void as to creditors whose debts are contracted previous to the passage of the act. The widow of a bankrupt is not entitled to the personal property exempted by the provisions of the 14th section of the act of 1867, nor is the assignee in bankruptcy. No title to exempt property passes to the assignee by the assignment, it remains in the bankrupt; at his death it passes to his legal representatives. *In re* Hester, (*N. C.*) 5 *N. B. R.* 285.

3. Equitable interest in. Though a petitioner in bankruptcy may have had an equitable interest in land, which has been sold by the legal owner, who had taken a note payable to himself for the purchase money, it would not certainly follow that the petitioner in bankruptcy had any interest in the note, nor would an omission to specify the note in the schedule be conclusive evidence of fraud on his part, such as to invalidate his certificate of discharge. Carey *v.* Esty, 29 *Maine R.* 154.

4. Insolvency of demandant. The insolvency of the demandant in a real action, and the assignment of his estate under the insolvent laws after the commencement of the action can only be pleaded in abatement, and at the first term after the assignment. Gerrish *v.* Gary, 1 *Allen,* (*Mass.*) 213.

5. Joint purchase of. The plaintiff and defendant gave their bond upon a joint purchase of real estate. The plaintiff afterwards conveyed his share of the land to the defendant; who thereupon agreed to pay the bond and indemnify the plaintiff against the same. Subsequently the defendant was discharged as a bankrupt under the late act of congress, and after that instalments fell due on the bond, which the plaintiff was obliged to pay. *Held,* that the plaintiff was to be regarded as standing in the relation of surety for the defendant, and, therefore,

that his right to recover further instalments so paid was barred by the discharge. Craft *v.* Mott, 4 *Comstock,* (*N. Y.*) 60.

6. Levy on, after publication of notices. If a judgment creditor of an insolvent debtor has levied his execution upon the debtor's reversion of real estate after the first publication of notice of the issuing of the warrant, the assignee in insolvency may maintain a bill in equity to set aside the levy. Hall *v.* Whiston, 5 *Allen,* (*Mass.*) 126.

7. Levy on, subsequent to proceedings. A levy of an execution by a judgment creditor upon the real estate of an insolvent debtor, made after the first publication of notice of the issuing of a warrant, is not valid against the title of the assignee, although the assignee has not recorded the assignment in the county where the land lies, and although the creditor has no actual notice of the insolvency. Hall *v.* Whiston, 5 *Allen,* (*Mass.*) 126.

8. Lien on. Where a creditor having a judgment against a bankrupt, which is a lien upon his real estate, proves his debt in bankruptcy and comes in upon the bankrupt's estate for the whole debt, the assignee in bankruptcy is entitled to be subrogated to the rights of the judgment creditor, as regards its lien upon the real estate. Wallace *v.* Conrad, 3 *N. B. R.* 10; citing McLean *v.* Meline, 3 *McLean,* 200.

9. A creditor having a lien on bankrupt's real estate cannot prove his debt in bankruptcy for the whole amount without relinquishing the lien to the assignee for the benefit of the bankrupt estate. Wallace *v.* Conrad, (*Pa.*) 3 *N. B. R.* 10; citing McLean *v.* Meline, 3 *McLean,* 200.

10. Lien on, when not discharged. Where a judgment creditor is not one of the petitioning creditors in insolvent proceedings, under article 3d of the insolvent debtors' act, the discharge does not subvert the judgment as a lien upon the insolvent's real estate, although it extinguishes it as a personal debt against the insolvent. Kelly *v.* Thayer, 34 *How. P. R.* 163.

11. Vendor's equitable lien upon the land sold is not discharged by the subsequent taking of a mortgage upon the same land, and takes precedence over a judgment lien obtained prior to the mortgage. *In re* Bryan, (*Ga.*) 3 *N. B. R.* 28; citing Mieur *v.* M. & M. & H. R. R. Co., 3 *Kelley*, 342; Mieur *et al. v.* Lockett, 23 *Ga.* 241; Schenk *v.* Arrowsmith, (*N. J.*) 1 *Stock.* 314; Ewing, 17 *Ohio*, 500.

12. Sale of. Allegations upon information and belief, unsupported by other proof, are not sufficient to sustain an injunction to restrain the sale of real estate, although the affidavits fail to make out a proper case, if sufficient appears *aliunde* upon a hearing, the injunction will be retained until the further order of the court. *In re* Bloss, (*Mich.*) 4 *N. B. R.* 37.

13. Title to. A decree in bankruptcy, passed in 1843 by the district court of the United States for the eastern district of Louisiana, did not pass to the assignee the title to a house and lot in the city of Galveston and state of Texas, which house and lot were the property of the bankrupt. Texas was then a foreign state, and whatever difference of opinion there may be with respect to the extra territorial operation of a bankrupt law upon personal property, there is none as to its operation upon real estate. This court concurs with Sir William Grant in 14 Vesey, 537, that the validity of every disposition of real estate must depend upon the law of the country in which that estate is situated. Besides the deed made by the assignee in bankruptcy to one of the parties in the present case was not made conformably with the laws of Texas; and letters of administration upon the estate of the bankrupt had been taken out in Texas before the fact of the bankruptcy was known there, and the creditors of the estate in Texas had a better lien upon the property than the assignee in Louisiana. Oakey *v.* Bennett *et al.* (*U. S. S. Ct.*) 11 *How.* 33.

14. Transfer of. Where a petitioning creditor alleges in his petition as an act of bankruptcy, that on the 29th day of October, 1870, the debtor made certain transfers of real and personal property with intent to delay his creditors, and the debtor, in his answer (which was supported by the proof), showed that the transfers were by way of mortgages. That both mortgages were given to secure the sum ($1,080) borrowed by the debtor on the 29th day of October, 1870, from the mortgagee, in order to relieve the debtor's stock in business from a contested attachment and thus enable the debtor to go on in his business of manufacturing shingles. That the loan was specifically to settle this attachment suit, and also to pay the only overdue paper of the debtor known by the mortgagee to be outstanding, except only such secured paper as the mortgagee already had. *Held*, that as the mortgages were based upon a present consideration and were neither given nor received with any intent to delay creditors, they did not constitute an act of bankruptcy. Petition dismissed at cost of petitioning creditors. *In re* Sanford, Unreported.

15. What a charge on. A. wrote word to B. that he had inclosed the particulars of title deeds of property which he had deposited with B. for the security of a debt, and in the schedule inclosed among other entries was the following: "9,000*l.*, buildings, houses, etc., at Titherington." A. sent B. a box containing the deeds and other securities, which B. did not examine until after A.'s bankruptcy, when he found that the only deed relating to the Titherington estate was an old paid off mortgage. *Held*, nevertheless, that the letter and schedule taken together, created an equitable charge on the Titherington estate. *Ex parte* Arkwright, 3 *Mont.*, *D. & D.* 129. (Eng.)

REASONABLE CAUSE.

1. A firm had notes past due and falling due, without available means to meet them, and obtained loans for the purpose from parties liable on certain of the firm notes and private notes of the members, giving two new notes for the loans so obtained, and securing payment thereof by executing a mortgage of all the firm property. The firm was subsequently adjudged bankrupt, on the petition of a creditor in involuntary bankruptcy, and an assignee in bankruptcy brought action in equity to set aside said mortgage as constituting a fraudulent preference under section thirty-five of the bankrupt act. The mortgagees swore that they believed the firm to be solvent at the time such mortgage was executed, and a member of the firm swore that he believed the same, and had not then contemplated insolvency or bankruptcy. *Held*, that as the firm was actually insolvent when the mortgage was executed, and the mortgagees as well as the mortgagor had reasonable cause to believe that the mortgagee was insolvent and on the eve of a state of bankruptcy, mortgage must be set aside as void. Scammon *et al. v.* Cole *et al.* 3 *N. B. R.* 100.

2. The defendant sued the bankrupt to recover a debt when he knew or had reasonable cause to believe his debtor was insolvent. Judgment having been rendered upon the default of the debtor, who did not appear or answer to the action, the execution creditor seized the real estate of the debtor, which was attached to the writ, and proceeded to complete his levy. After rendition of the judgment, and before the levy was completed, the debtor filed his petition in bankruptcy, and his assignee applied to the bankrupt court for an injunction to restrain further proceedings under the seizure, and the sale of the estate of the bankrupt on the execution, the attachment being within four months of the commencement of the proceedings in bankruptcy. *Held*, that the relief prayed for should be granted, and injunction made perpetual. Cases Black & Secor, 1 *N. B. R.* 81; Beattie *v.* Gardner, 4 *N. B. R.* 106, approved. Haskell *v.* Ingalls, (*Maine*,) 5 *N. B. R.* 205.

3. Upon the issue whether a debtor who asked an extension from his creditors at a particular time was then insolvent and had reasonable cause to believe himself so, evidence is competent to show that persons engaged in the same line of business at that time generally obtained an extension; that it was the general understanding among the trade that asking for an extenston at that time was no sign of inability to pay debts; and that all persons in that line of business, either temporarily suspended payment or asked for an extension at that time. Vennard *v.* McConnell, 11 *Allen*, (*Mass.*) 555.

4. If at the time of the entry of judgment the creditor has knowledge of his debtor's insolvency or notice of such facts, as make it reasonable to believe him insolvent, he is guilty of intending a fraud upon the bank-

rupt law. Golson *et al. v.* Neihoff *et al.* 5 *N. B. R.* 56.

5. Under the Massachusetts insolvent act of 1841, c. 124, the mere fact that the assignment was made about two months before the insolvency of the assignor was published, and that the assignee received as collateral security nearly double the amount due to him in debts apparently due to the assignor, were held not to be sufficient to authorize the conclusion that the assignee " had reasonable cause to believe such debtor was insolvent. Porter *v.* Bullard, 26 *Me. R.* 448.

6. Creditors who have accounts over due seven or eight months and have finally to resort to legal measures for their collection must be considered as having reasonable cause to believe their debtor insolvent, and money received under such circumstances must be paid to the debtor's assignee in bankruptcy, together with interest and costs of the proceedings instituted by said assignee for the recovery of the money. Stranahan *v.* Gregory *et al.* (*Vermont*,) 4 *N. B. R.* 142.

7. Whenever a creditor is in possession of such facts and circumstances in reference to his debtor as arouses his suspicion with regard to his ability to meet his indebtedness, he may be said to have reasonable cause to believe him to be insolvent. *In re* Driggs, (*Mich.*) 3 *N. B. R.* 149.

8. A creditor has reasonable cause to believe his debtor to be insolvent when he knows that his debtor cannot pay all his debts in the ordinary course of business. Wilson *v.* Brinkman *et al.* (*Mo.*) 2 *N. B. R.* 149.

9. Although a register may have no authority to take a particular deposition he has full authority to administer oaths and when by the assets of parties he has taken such deposition to be used in evidence in a cause the same becomes a sworn statement made in the case to be used as evidence therein to which the party causing the deposition to be so taken, cannot object. It is not error to direct the attention of the jury to the distinction between " reasonable

cause to believe" and "actual belief." If a father-in-law when his son-in-law is known by him to be insolvent and within a few days of his voluntary application to be adjudged a bankrupt buys out of the usual course of trade a large portion of the insolvent property, and gives notes payable at long dates, cashes the notes and pays to his own son as mortgagee the money thus furnished in discharge of mortgage on the property of his daughter, who is the wife of the bankrupt son-in-law, that is certainly a transfer of the bankrupt's property to his wife in fraud of his creditor's, through the agency of the wife's father and therefor fraudulent and void. Lawrence v. Graves, (*Mo.*) 5 *N. B. R.* 279.

10. Evidence of. The sale of a dwelling house for a fair price for cash by the owner, within six months prior to his going into insolvency, will not be deemed to be out of the usual and ordinary course of his business, without further proof, and will not afford *prima facie* evidence under Gen. Sts. c. 118, s. 91, that the purchaser had reasonable cause to believe him insolvent. Pearson v. Goodwin, 9 *Allen*, (*Mass.*) 482.

11. Evidence that an insolvent debtor had the reputation of neglecting and mismanaging his business at the time when a conveyance by him was made, is admissible upon the issue whether the grantee had reasonable cause to believe him insolvent. Bartholmew v McKinstry, 6 *Allen*, (*Mass.*) 567.

12. Evidence of the pecuniary standing of an insolvent debtor among his neighbors, creditors, and all others having business with him, is competent for the purpose of showing that a preferred creditor had no reasonable cause to believe him insolvent. Bartlett v. Decreet, 4 *Gray*, (*Mass.*) 141; Heywood v. Reed, *id.* 574.

13. Sufficient to make judgment a fraud. If at the time of the entry of judgment the creditor has knowledge of his debt's insolvency or notice of such facts as make it reasonable to believe him insolvent he is guilty of intending a fraud upon the bankrupt act. Golson *et al.* v. Neihoff *et al.* 5 *N. B. R.* 56.

REASONABLE TIME.

1. Question of. A bankrupt, at the time of his bankruptcy in 1847, had deposited the lease of a house with the plaintiff as security for advances. In 1859, a year and half after the bankrupt's death, the plaintiff obtained an order from the court of bankruptcy for a sale of the house, and that if the amount of his debt was not realized at the sale, the assignees should assign the lease to the plaintiff. The amount was not realized, and in 1860 the assignees, in pursuance of the order, assigned the lease to the plaintiff. In ejectment by him against the widow of the bankrupt, *held*, that, assigning the lease to the plaintiff was an acceptance of the lease by the assignees; but that it was a question for a jury whether they had accepted it within a reasonable time. Mackley v. Pattenden, 7 *Jur.*, *N. S.* 1056; 30 *L. J., Q. B.* 235; 9 *W. R.* 601; 4 *L. T., N. S.* 285. (Eng.)

REBELLION.

1. Effect on statutes of limitations. Statutes of limitations exist in all the states, and with few exceptions have been copied from the one brought here by our ancestors in colonial time. They are regarded as statutes of repose arising from the lapse of time, and proceed upon the presumption that claims are extinguished whenever they are not litigated in the proper forum within the prescribed period. Exceptions are to be found in all such statutes, but cases where the courts of justice were closed in consequence of insurrection or rebellion are not within the express terms of any such exception contained either in the original act or any other of later date, and if no exception can be applied, then all debts due from one belligerent to another as well as executory contracts involving commercial intercourse with the enemy, are practically discharged, as if the war is of much duration prior claims will be barred by the local statute of limitations. Enemy creditors cannot prosecute their claims subsequent to the commencement of hostilities, as the rule is universal and per emptory that they are totally incapable of sustaining any contract in the tribunals of the other belligerent. The time during which the courts of the states in rebellion were closed to the citizens of the rest of the Union is to be excluded in the suits since brought, from the computation of the time fixed by the statutes of limitation within which suits may be brought, though no such exception is expressly admitted in the limitation act. Neither laches nor fraud can be imputed to the creditor in such a case, as the liability to sue becomes absolute by the declaration of war wholly irrespective of his consent or opposition. His remedy is suspended by the two governments and the law of nations, which come into operation in consequence of an event over which he has no control. The former decisions of the federal supreme court and the supreme court of Louisiana upon the questions involved commented on, and the court as now constituted adheres to the former. Creditor's debts due from belligerents are suspended during the war, but the debts are not annulled; the right to sue revives when peace is restored, and the restoration of peace returns to the creditor both the remedy and the right. Levy *v.* Stewart, 4 *N. B. R.* 193; s. c. 3 *C. L. N.* 274.

RECEIPT FOR MONEY.

1. Does not constitute fiduciary debt. A deposit of money by A. with B. for which B. has given the following receipt: "Received from A. $5,000 for the purchase of stocks, for which I agree to account for on demand," is not shown by said receipt to be such a trust as to constitute a fiduciary debt which would not be barred by a discharge in insolvency. Halpine *v.* May, 100 *Mass. R.* 498.

RECEIVER.

1. Appointment of. Where an assignee under an assignment made under state laws had given security by order of a state court, but had been enjoined from action in the premises by the bankruptcy court, the bankruptcy court decided that a receiver should be appointed and that he must give

adequate security for the faithful discharge of his duties, the amount to be fixed on notice to all parties. *In re* Sedgwick, (*S. D. N. Y.*) 3 *N. B. R.* 35.

2. Appointed by state court cannot be dispossessed by bankruptcy proceedings. Where the property of a bankrupt is lawfully in the custody of a receiver appointed by a state court the court of bankruptcy cannot interfere with his possession. *In re* Clark & Bininger, 3 *N. B. R.* 130.

3. In chancery. The difference between a receiver in chancery and an assignee in bankruptcy explained. Booth *v.* Clark, (*U. S. S. Ct*) 17 *Howard*, 322.

4. In state court. Where a bankrupt made a fraudulent assignment and his assignee filed a bill and obtained an injunction restraining a receiver in a state court from all proceedings in the court of appeals, and from interfering or meddling with the assignee's property or the proceeds thereof. Upon argument of the motion to modify or vacate the injunction, the judge decided that it must be sustained, and denied the motion to vacate or modify the same. *In re* Sedgwick, (*S. D. N. Y.*) 1 *N. B. R.* 108.

5. Obtaining possession of property. When creditors' bills were filed and a receiver appointed, who obtained possession of the property of the debtor, an assignee in bankruptcy has no right to the property thus secured by law, to the payment of debts of judgment creditors. *In re* Sedgwick, (*S. D. N. Y.*) 1 *N. B. R.* 204.

6. Of a bank, recovery from. Where a receiver of a bank who was appointed by a state court, has possession of the assets of the bank, of which the bankrupt was in fact the sole owner, the assets of the bank are not liable to distribution in the debtor's bankruptcy, according to the rules which govern these proceedings. Goodrich *v.* Rennington, 6 *Bl. C. C.* 515.

7. Of corporations. Where an application is made to an officer by a receiver of an insolvent corporation for a warrant to bring a debtor before such officer for examination, pursuant to the statute, the petition for that purpose should state the facts upon which the application is founded positively, and not in the alternative. If the petition states that the person proceeded against has in his possession, either individually or as administrator, &c., some property belonging to the petitioner ; that such person, for the estate of his intestate, is indebted to the petitioner, and that he, either individually or as such administrator, has in his hands a large amount of money belonging to the petitioner which he has not accounted for or delivered over to him, such petition will be defective and will not authorize the issuing of a warrant. If the person against whom an application of this nature is made, is indebted only as an administrator, he is not a person liable to be proceeded against under the statute. Halliday v. Noble, 1 Barb. 137.

8. Taking of property by. Allowing a receiver appointed by order of a state court to take property, is suffering property to be taken under legal process, within the meaning of section 39 of the U. S. bankrupt act of 1867. In re Clark & Bininger, (S. D. N. Y.) 3 N. B. R. 99 ; citing Denny v. Dana, 2 Cush. 160, 172 ; Beals v. Clark, 13 Gray, 18, 21 ; in re Smith, 3 N. B. R. 98.

RECITALS.

1. In bond. The omission of the words " and generally to abide all orders of the said court," prescribed as part of the condition of the bond, to be given by a petitioner for the benefit of the insolvent laws, by the supplemental act of the 28th of March, 1820, does not vitiate the bond, as respects the principal or sureties, and it is immaterial that the parties recite, in the introduction of the condition, that the bond was given to comply with the requisition of an act of assembly which has been repealed. Farmers' Bank of Reading v. Boyer, 16 S. & R., Pa. R. 48.

RECOGNITION.

1. Of foreign laws granting contracts. Where the decree of a court of another government is interposed to judicial proceedings in this state, the jurisdiction of

such court may properly become a matter of inquiry. And where a person residing in this state petitions a court of bankruptcy in the province of New Brunswick, and obtains a discharge from all his debts, under the decree of that court, such discharge is invalid and can have no effect, even upon a contract entered into in that province; but where such court of bankruptcy has jurisdiction of the persons applying for the benefit of the bankrupt act of that province, and a decree is made in conformity with the requirements of their law, it operates to discharge the contracts of the applicant, and cannot be *impeached* in a subsequent action upon such contracts prosecuted in this state by a citizen of that province. The laws of a foreign country in their effect upon contracts made under them are recognized not as having any binding force in our courts but on the principle of international comity. As the bankrupt act of New Brunswick gives no *liens* upon property attached, the attachment of the property of a petitioner for their benefit before his petition is filed, cannot operate to hold the property after he has obtained his discharge from the contract on which the seizure was made. Long v. Hammond, 40 Me. R. 204.

RECOGNIZANCE.

1. Action on. A discharge in insolvency is no bar to an action upon a recognizance taken upon an arrest of a debtor on an execution issued upon a judgment recovered upon a claim for necessaries, and, if it only appears that the claim was for clothing furnished to the debtor, the presumption is that such clothing was necessary. Smith v. Randall, 1 Allen, (Mass.) 456.

2. Bankrupt's exoneration from. If commissioners of bankruptcy, in their declaring a man a bankrupt specify the day when he became so, it is not conclusive as to the time, they having no authority to decide it. If a man go to prison on the first of the month, continue there sixty days, in the course of which he is fixed as bail for another, and at the expiration of that priod be declared a bankrupt on a commission duly sued out, he will be exonerated from his recognizance, and an execution taken out upon it be set aside. In such a case the plaintiff may prove his debt under the commission. Rathbone *v.* Blackford, 1 *Caines' Cases*, 587.

RECORD.

1. The certificate of appointment of a creditor's assignee, under 24 & 25 Vict. c. 134, s. 123, is a record of the court of bankruptcy, and conclusive evidence of the appointment, and may be used as such in an action by the assignee, though signed and sealed after the action was commenced. Kelly *v.* Morray, 1 *H. & R.* 684; 35 *L. J., C. P.* 667; 12 *Jur., N. S.* 769; 14 *L. J., N. S.* 624. (Eng.)

2. **Of judgment.** When the record of a judgment in a state court showed that the suit was one to recover a debt created by fraud, a court of bankruptcy will not go behind that record to call in question its verity before that court. *In re* Robinson, (*S. D. N. Y.*) 2 *N. B. R.* 108.

RECORDING.

1. Where a creditor claims a lien by virtue of a judgment against the bankrupt, recovered on the 5th of November, 1866, but which was not recorded in the clerk's office until October 16th, 1867, and another creditor holds a mortgage executed by the bankrupt and recorded April 7th, 1867, the court decided that the mortgage lien has priority over the judgment. *In re* Lacy, (*Texas*,) 4 *N. B. R.* 15.

2. The recording acts do not apply to insolvent assignment. A sale of lands, therefore, by the insolvent after his discharge, but before his trustees have given bond according to law, is invalid, although none of the proceedings under the insolvent law have been recorded in the county where such lands lie. Ruby *v.* Glenn, 5 *Watts' Pa. R.* 77.

3. **Chattel mortgage.** An unrecorded mortgage of personal property which has not been delivered to and retained by the mortgagee is valid against the assignees in bankruptcy of the mortgagor. *In re* Grif-

fiths, (*Mass.*) 3 *N. B. R.* 179; citing Conrad *v.* Atlantic Insurance Company, 1 *Pet.* 449; De Wolf *v.* Harris, *Mason*, 515.

4. **Mortgages on vessels.** In the bankrupt court, mortgages on vessels recorded under the act of congress of July, 1850, in the office of collector of customs, in the home port, of a prior date, shall receive a preference over domestic claims. *In re* Scott, (*Ohio*,) 3 *N. B. R.* 181; citing Tug Eagle *v.* Brig General Worth, 2 *C. L. N.* 205; General Buel *v.* Long, 18 *Ohio S. Rep.* 521.

5. **Of deed of assignment.** A deed of assignment must be recorded in the county where the property is located, upon a certificate of the clerk of the U. S. district court, that the same is a copy of the assignment on file in his office, and a tender to the clerk or other officer of the state court of the fees allowed by the laws of the state. *In re* Neale, (*N. C.*) 3 *N. B. R.* 43.

6. **Of mortgage.** An unregistered personal mortgage is not valid in the state of Kansas as against creditors. The Second National Bank of Leavenworth *et al. v.* Hunt *et al.* 4 *N. B. R.* 198.

7. Where a mortgage is valid under state law as between grantor and grantee, though not recorded, it must be held valid between the grantor's trustee and the grantee. Potter, Dennison & Co. *v.* Coggswell, (*R. I.*) 4 *N. B. R.* 19; citing *in re* Grffiths, 3 *N. B. R.* 179.

8. An unrecorded mortgage of personal property, which has not been delivered to and retained by the mortgagee, is valid against the assignees in bankruptcy of the mortgagor. *In re* Griffiths, (*Mass.*) 3 *N. B. R.* 179; citing Bingham *v.* Jordan, 1 *Allen*, 373; Conrad *v.* Atlantic Ins. Co. 1 *Pet.* 449; De Wolf *v.* Harris, 4 *Mason*, 515; Travis *v.* Bishop, 13 *Met.* 304

9. **Of trust deed.** The recording of a trust deed within four months before the commencement of bankruptcy proceedngs is not an act of bankruptcy, when the deed was executed and delivered some months prior to the recording. If the beneficiaries in a deed or mortgage are satisfied with the security afforded by an unrecorded instru-

ment, there is neither necessity or obligation to record it. Recording is only necessary to make an instrument valid against creditors under state laws, and the bankrupt act recognizes and respects such validity, if it be made six months prior to the bankruptcy proceedings. *In re* Wynne, (*Va.*) 4 *N. B. R.* 5; citing Gardner *v.* Collector, 6 *Wall,* 511; Windsor *v.* Kendall, 3 *Story,* 515.

10. When necessary. A chattel mortgage not valid as against creditors under the state law, and under which the mortgagee has taken possession, having at the time reasonable cause to believe his debtor insolvent, is invalid as against the assignee in bankruptcy. Though the mortgage be good as between the parties, and given to secure a *bona fide* loan, the mortgagee not having it acknowledged and recorded as required by the state statute, but retaining it until the insolvency of the debtor, loses his lien. He cannot by then taking possession be remitted to his rights as of the date of the mortgage. Though possession was taken before commencement of proceedings in bankruptcy, and was in accordance with the provisions of the mortgage, yet being within the time limited by the bankrupt act, it operated as a preference, void as against creditors, and is equally void as against the assignee. Harvey, assignee, *v.* Crane, 5 *N. B.R.* 218. s. c. 3 *C. L. N.* 341.

RECOVERY.

1. Of balance on account current. In an action to recover the balance upon an account current, a verdict for the plaintiff was taken by consent, subject to a reference to an arbitrator, who was empowered to direct that a verdict should be entered for the plaintiff or the defendant, and the costs were to abide the result of the award. After the award, which was in favor of the plaintiff, and before judgment, the defendant committed an act of bankruptcy, of which notice was given to the plaintiff in an action, but judgment was nevertheless entered up upon the award. On the defendant being adjudicated a bankrupt, *held,* that the amount for which the judgment was entered up, with interest and costs, constituted a provable debt. *Ex parte* Harding, 5 *De G. Mac. & G.* 367. (Eng.)

2. Of goods fraudulently sold. No offer to return the consideration received by an insolvent debtor for goods sold by him in violation of the provisions of St. 1856, c. 284, c. 27, is necessary to enable his assignees to sustain an action against the purchaser to recover the value of the goods. Tapley *v.* Forbes, 2 *Allen,* (*Mass.*) 20.

3. Of judgment after commencement of bankruptcy proceedings. A discharge in bankruptcy does not bar a *judgment* recovered *after* the defendant's application to be decreed a bankrupt, although it be founded upon a note which *might have* been proven in bankruptcy Pike *v.* McDonald, 42 *Maine R.* 418

4. Of judgment against failing debtor. The defendant sued the bankrupt to recover a debt, when he knew or had reasonable cause to believe his debtor was insolvent. Judgment having been rendered upon the default of the debtor, who did not appear or answer to the action, the execution creditor seized the real estate of the debtor, which was attached to the writ, and proceeded to complete his levy. After rendition of the judgment, and before the levy was completed, the debtor filed his petition in bankruptcy, and his assignee applied to the bankrupt court for an injunction to restrain further proceedings under the seizures, and the sale of the estate of the bankrupt on the execution, the attachment being within four months of the commencement of the proceedings in bankruptcy. *Held,* that the relief prayed for should be granted, and injunction made perpetual. Cases Black & Secor, 1 *N. B. R.* 81; Beattie *v.* Gardner, 4 *N. B. R.* 106, approved. Haskell *v.* Ingalls, (*Maine,*) 5 *N. B. R.*

5. Of judgment assignment previous to. When a creditor is about to recover a judgment against his debtor, and the debtor makes a general assignment of all his property for the benefit of all his creditors before the judgment is rendered, such conveyance is not necessarily a conveyance with intent to delay, defraud or hinder creditors. Langley *v.* Perry, (*Ohio,*) 2 *N. B. R.* 180.

6. Of judgment before discharge.
A discharge under the bankrupt act of 1841, may be pleaded in bar to an action upon a judgment founded on debt existing when the bankrupt filed his petition, but which judgment was recovered before the discharge was granted, so that the defendant had no opportunity of pleading such discharge in the suit. Pox v. Woodruff, 9 Barb. 498.

7. Judgment by creditor of decedent. A creditor of a deceased person recovered judgment and levied execution on the land of the deceased, after which the estate was represented insolvent, and proved to be so ; the same creditor filed her claim with the commissioner, had it allowed, and received of the administrator nearly the whole of the dividend awarded her ; her title to the land was sustainsd. Ramsdell v. Creasey, 10 Mass. R. 170.

8. Of judgment by default. A plaintiff recovered judgment by default, the defendants having at the time an equitable defence to the action, upon which the court of chancery, upon an application, would have granted an injunction to restrain the action, the defendant having afterwards become bankrupt, held, that the jurisdiction in bankruptcy, being both legal and equitable, the court would not admit a proof tendered by the plaintiff upon the judgment. Ex parte Mudie, 6 Jur. 1093. (Eng.)

9. Of judgment subsequent to bankruptcy. A judgment against the defendant recovered after his petition, but before the decree of his bankruptcy, is not barred by the bankruptcy discharge subsequently obtained. Fisher v. Foss, 30 Me. 459.

10. Of money paid to creditor. In an action brought by the assignee of an insolvent debtor, to recover back money paid by the debtor to a creditor by way of preference, it is incumbent on the plaintiff to establish by competent and sufficient evidence, that the defendant at the time of recovering the money had reasonable cause to believe the debtor insolvent, and if there is no evidence to show that the defendant was aware of any fact indicating the debtor's insolvency, such a failure to meet debts which had fallen due, in an excess of liabilities, over the means of meeting them, the judge may properly direct a verdict for the defendant. Everett v. Stowell, 14 Allen, (Mass.) 32.

11. Of pre-existing debt. In an action for tort for the conversion by the assignee of an insolvent debtor, of property claimed by the plaintiff under a conveyance from the debtor, if the jury find the conveyance void as a preference made in payment of a pre-existing debt, the plaintiff cannot recever cash paid by him to the debtor for the difference in value between such property and the debt which the conveyance was made to secure. Bartlett v. Decreet, 4 Grays' (Mass.) 111.

12. Of property. After committing an act of bankruptcy, one of two partners handed over a bank post bill and some silver to the agent of the drawer of a bill of exchange, accepted by the partners, and which was just about to become due, for the purpose of protecting such bill. Such handing over was found to be a fraudulent preference, and to have been in contemplation of bankruptcy. On the same day, but a few hours after the delivery of the post bank bill and note, the other partner committed an act of bankruptcy. It was held that the act of the partner, who had committed the act of bankruptcy before he handed over the property, was not binding, and that the assignees of the two partners might recover the value of the property. Burt v. Moult, 1 C. & M. 525 ; 3 Tyr. 564. (Eng.)

13. On judgment in another state. In an action on a judgment, rendered in this court, the plaintiff is not estopped to show that the judgment here was rendered on another judgment in a neighboring state, which latter judgment was rendered on a contract made and to be performed there, before the passage of our insolvent law, and thus to avoid the operation of a discharge under that law, which is pleaded here to an action on the last judgment. Wyman v. Mitchell, 1 Cowen, 316.

RE-EXAMINATION.

1. Of state court decisions. It is not competent for a court of bankruptcy to re-examine a question which has passed *in rem* jurisdiction in a state court. McKenzie *v.* Harding, 4 *N. B. R.* 10.

REDEMPTION.

1. Creditors right of. The right of a judgment creditor to redeem premises which have been sold upon a prior execution against the property of his debtor, cannot be defeated by the act of the purchaser in paying the judgment under which the creditor claims to redeem without his consent, especially where such payment is not made until after the redeeming creditor has actually paid to the sheriff the amount of the purchase bid with interest, and has commenced delivering to the sheriff the papers required by the statute to be presented to and left with him. A stranger to a judgment has no right to pay the same for the purpose of extinguishing the lien thereof and preventing the holder from redeeming by virtue thereof. The People *v.* Beebe, 1 *Barb.* 379.

2. Of mortgaged property. If a bankrupt, since his application in bankruptcy, has purchased an equity of redeeming mortgaged land, the mortgagee (though he has also bought the bankrupt's right to the land by a sale in bankruptcy), cannot bar the bankrupt's right to redeem by merely showing that, at the time of such application the bankrupt had a conditional bond for a conveyance to him of the equity, *unless* the *mortgagee* shall have performed the condition of the bond. Before such purchaser from the assignee in bankruptcy can be treated as the owner of the right of redemption, he must have established the right by a suit in equity, in which all opposing interests had opportunity to be examined. Kittridge *v.* McLaughlin, 33 *Maine* R. 327.

3. Property. Whenever it may be deemed for the benefit of the estate of a bankrupt to redeem and discharge any mortgage or other pledge, or deposit, or lien upon any property, real or personal, or to relieve said property from any conditional contract, and to render performance of the conditions thereof, or to compound any debts, or other claims or securities due or belonging to the estate of the bankrupt, the assignee, or the bankrupt, or any creditor who has proved his debt, may file his petition therefor in the office of the clerk of the district court, and thereupon the court shall appoint a suitable time and place for the hearing thereof, notice of which shall be given in some newspaper, to be designated by the court, at least ten days before the hearing, so that all creditors and other persons interested may appear and show cause, if any they have, why an order should not be passed by the court upon the petition, authorizing such act on the part of the assignee. *General Order No. 17, Sup. Ct. U. S.—In bankruptcy.*

4. Release of. If the value of the property exceeds the sum for which it is so held as security, the assignee may release to the creditor the bankrupt's right of redemption therein on receiving such excess; or he may sell the property subject to the claim of the creditors thereon; and in either case the assignee and creditor respectively, shall execute all deed and writings necessary or proper to consummate the transaction. If the property is not so sold or released or delivered up, the creditor shall not be allowed to prove any part of his debt. *Section 20 U. S. bankrupt act,* 1867.

REFERENCE.

1. Where a reference is necessary to ascertain the value of mortgaged goods taken it must be made to the register in charge of the case. *In re* Rosenberg, (*S. D. N. Y.*) 3 *N.B.R.* 33.

2. Of petition to annul fiat on bill of cost. Upon a petition by a bankrupt to annul a fiat issued by an attorney for the amount of his bill of costs, on the ground that the chief part of the bill consisted of charges for the prosecution of an action on the part of the bankrupt, in which he was nonsuited by reason of the gross negligence of the attorney, the court referred it to the registrar to inquire and report as to the *quantum* of negligence. *Ex parte* Southall, 4 *Deac.* 91; *Mont. & Chit.* 346. (Eng.)

REFUNDING MONIES.

1. Where a party made a purchase of the assignee in bankauptcy for much less than the property was actually worth, the court declared the sale void, but decided that the money paid therefor to the assignee could not be refunded, inasmuch as the conveyances had not been delivered up to be canceled. *In re* Mott, (*S. D. N. Y.*) 1 *N. B. R.* 9. Act of 1841.

REFUSAL.

1. **By assignee to comply with leave.** A bankrupt agreed in writing to take a lease of a manufactory for a term of years, and the landlord agreed to erect at his own expense certain buildings upon the bankrupt paying an additional rent upon the amount so expended. The buildings, however, were subsequently erected by the bankrupt, on the verbal assurance of the landlord that the bankrupt might deduct the amount expended from the rent. The assignees elected not to adopt the agreement for the lease, but refused to deliver up possession to the landlord unless he allowed them the sum which the bankrupt had expended on the buildings. *Held,* that as both the written and verbal agreement between the landlord and the bankrupt contemplated a continuance of the tenancy, which the assignees had themselves repudiated, they had no lien on the premises for the money expended by the bankrupt. *Ex parte* Ladd, 3 *Deac & Chit.* 647. (Eng.)

2. **To admit proof.** W. claimed to prove against a bankrupt's estate for a bill of exchange which he had taken up for the honor of the acceptor. The bankrupt was not a party to the bill, and it was not protested. By agreement between W. and the assignees, the right to prove was referred to arbitration, but without the leave of the court, as required by 12 and 13 Vict. c. 106, s. 153. The arbitrator decided against the

right to prove. The claimant insisted upon such right, notwithstanding the award. The commissioner, however, refused to admit the proof. *Held,* that although the award was not made pursuant to the statute, W., having agreed to the arbitration, and not having taken any abjection to the validity of the submission before the commissioner was bound by it. *Ex parte* Wyle, 2 *De G., F. & J.* 641; 7 *Jur., N. S.* 294; 30 *L. J., Bank.* 10; 9 *W. R.* 421; 3 *L. T., N. S.* 934. (Eng.)

3. **To approve of assignees out of district.** Where a corporation holding property and carrying on business in three several states, is adjudicated bankrupt, and assignees are appointed who are respectively citizens of two states in which proceedings in bankruptcy are pending, but an assignee is not appointed who resides in the third state, in which proceedings in bankruptcy are also pending. *Held,* that as three assignees were to be chosen and proceedings were pending in three different districts, it ought to be so arranged that each of the districts could have an assignee within it, a resident thereof, and that in the district in which no assignee has been appointed, the court there declines to approve the election of assignees. *In re* Boston & Hartford & Erie Railroad, (*S. D. N. Y.*) 5 *N.B.R.* 233.

4. **To hear objections.** A discharge of an insolvent debtor will not be set aside on *certiorari* because the officer, before whom the proceedings was had, refused to hear the objections of a creditor who appeared to show cause thirty minutes after the hour appointed; the order of assignment executed and the discharge signed, but not delivered when the creditor appeared. *In re* Pulver, 6 *Wend.* 632.

5. **To testify.** Parties and witnesses summoned before a register shall be bound to attend in pursuance of such summons at the place and time designated therein, and shall be entitled to protection and be liable to process of contempt in like manner as parties and witnesses are now liable thereto in case of default in attendance, made under any writ of subpœna. And all persons wilfully and corruptly swearing or affirming falsely before a register, shall be liable to all the penalties, punishment and consequences

of perjury. If any person examined before a register shall refuse or decline to answer or to swear to or sign his examination when taken, the register shall refer the matter to the judge, who shall have power to order the person so acting to pay the costs thereby occasioned, if such person be compelled by law to answer such question or to sign such examination; and such person shall also be liable to be punished for contempt. *Sec. 7 U. S..bankrupt act*, 1867.

REFUSAL OF DISCHARGE.

1. Where the debtor was adjudicated a bankrupt on voluntary petition on the 17th of February, 1868, but neglected to make application for final discharge until the 3d of May, 1869. It appearing to the court that no assets had come to the hands of the assignee, and that the discharge was not made within one year from the date of adjudication, a discharge was therefore refused. *In re* Farrell, (*N. J.*) 5 *N. B. R.* 125.

2. If the examination of the record upon an application for a final discharge discloses the fact that the bankrupt has done any act which, under the statute, would be a bar to the granting of a certificate, it will refuse to make the order for a discharge, although no creditors appear in opposition. *In re* Schoo, (*Mo.*) 3 *N. B. R.* 52; *in re* Wilkinson, (*Mo.*) 3 *N. B. R.* 74.

3. A discharge will not be refused because of an act of bankruptcy committed a long time before the passage of the U. S. bankrupt act of 1867. A specification in opposition to a discharge to conform to the requirements of section 29 of said bankrupt act, must allege wilful false swearing, as well as a wilful omission in the bankrupt schedules. *In re* Keefer, (1 *Mich.*) 4 *N. B. R.* 126.

4. In a specification in opposition to a bankrupt's discharge setting forth that he has concealed his effects, or has wilfully sworn falsely in his affidavit annexed to his inventory, it is required that these acts should be shown to be intentional to preclude the granting of a discharge. *In re* Wyatt, (*Ky.*) 2 *N. B. R.* 94.

5. Where a professional singer declined to exercise her musical talents for the benefit of her creditors, the commissioners refused her an order of discharge, and withheld protection. On appeal the decision was reversed. *Ex parte* Ellison, 8 *L. T., N. S.* 407. (Eng.)

6. A discharge will be refused until the bankrupt's schedule is so amended as to include an interest in an estate in expectancy under a will. *In re* Carnell, (*S. D. N. Y.*) 3 *N. B. R.* 113.

7. A bankrupt will be refused his discharge where he has made an assignment although for the benefit of all his creditors without preferences. *In re* Goldschmidt, (*S. D. N. Y.*) 3 *N. B. R.* 41.

8. A discharge will be refused where a bankrupt has, by an assignment to a private assignee, placed all his property where it can be administered only by the tribunals of the state. *In re* Brodhead, (*E. D. N. Y.*) 2 *N. B. R.* 93.

9. A discharge will not be refused because the bankrupt made an assignment, without preference, for the benefit of creditors, within six months of his bankruptcy, where he did so to prevent a creditor from obtaining a judgment. *In re* Pierce & Holbrook, (*Penn.*) 4 *N. B. R.* 61.

10. **Because assets are insufficient.** Where an appraisement is exaggerated, although there is no evidence of any depreciation, the proceedings having been commenced after January 1, 1869, and the debtors not having shown that their assets are or have been at any time since they filed their petition equal to fifty per cent. of the claim proved against their estate, upon which they are or were liable as principal debtors, and not having filed the assent in writing of a majority in number and value of their creditors, to whom they are or have become liable as principal debtors, and who have proved their claims, a discharge must be refused to the debtors. *In re* Borden & Geary, (*S. D. N. Y.*) 5 *N. B. R.* 125.

11. **Concealment.** A bankrupt is guilty of concealment and false swearing in stating in the affidavit annexed to his

inventory that he has no assets, where he is the real partner in a firm, though the interest ostensibly appears to belong to his wife, and a discharge will be refused. *In re* Rathbone, 1 *N. B. R.* 145 ; 2 *N. B. R.* 89.

12. A bankrupt having in his possession joint estate and joint books of account which he wilfully fails to disclose to his assignee cannot receive his discharge. *In re* Beale, (*Mass.*) 2 *N. B. R.* 178.

13. Where it was shown that the bankrupt had concealed his money by attempting to prove that he owed it to his brother, the discharge was refused. *In re* Goodridge, 2 *N. B. R.* 105.

14. A discharge was refused where a bankrupt failed to disclose his interest in goods, that he had sold fraudulently before the commencement of bankruptcy proceedings. *In re* Hussman, (*Ky.*) 2 *N. B. R.* 140.

15. The withholding of the title to property intentionally by the bankrupt, is such a concealmnnt as will preclude a discharge. *In re* O'Bannon, 2 *N. B. R.* 6.

16. A bankrupt's omission to disclose his interest in property must be construed as a concealment where, owing to a sale, it had apparently changed hands, and a discharge will not be granted. *In re* Hussman, 2 *N. B. R.* 140.

17. Where a bankrupt conceals books of account of a firm of which he was a member, a discharge must be refused. *In re* Beal, 2 *N. B. R.* 178.

18. Where property has been conveyed before bankruptcy to a debtor, though without consideration, and for the purpose of preventing the grantor's creditors from seizing and selling it, said debtor is nevertheless guilty of concealment, if he neglect to return it in his inventory, and a discharge must be refused. *In re* O'Bannon, 2 *N. B. R.* 6.

19. Delay to apply. The discharge is in a favor granted upon compliance with conditions prescribed, and not a right. Therefore, a discharge will be refused where the application is made more than a year after the adjudication, and no sufficient reason is shown for the delay. *In re* Martin, (*S. D. N. Y.*) 2 *N. B. R.* 169.

20. Different district. A discharge cannot be granted to a bankrupt in another district from that in which he carries on business. *In re* Little, (*S. D. N. Y.*) 2 *N. B. R.* 97.

21. Failure to file schedule. The failure of one member of a firm to file a schedule of his personal property is not sufficient ground for refusing the other members of said firm their discharge. *In re* Scofield *et al.* (*S. D. N. Y.*) 2 *N. R. R.* 137.

22. Failure to keep books of account. Where it appears from the evidence that a bankrupt tradesman has failed to keep proper books of account, a discharge will not be granted to him. *In re* Bound, (*S. D. N. Y.*) 4 *N. B. R.* 164.

23. A discharge will not be granted a bankrupt merchant or trader, who has omitted to keep proper books of account, although he may have been entirely innocent of any intention of thus defrauding his creditors. *In re* Solomon, (*Pa.*) 2 *N. B. R.* 94; *in re* Newman, (*S. D. N. Y.*) 2 *N. B. R.* 99.

24. A discharge cannot be granted to bankrupts where the books of account are not properly kept. *In re* Mackey *et al.* (*S. D. N. Y.*) 4 *N. B. R.* 17.

25. For want of jurisdiction. Want of jurisdiction is ground for the refusal of a discharge. That is the time for urging such objection in behalf of creditors. *In re* Penn, 3 *N. B. R.* 145.

26. Where the bankrupt resided at Boston, Mass., from May, 1st, 1867, to December 7th, 1867, and from December 7th, 1867, to January 21st, 1868, he resided at New York, therefore he did not reside in the latter district for the six months next immediately preceding the time of filing the petition, or for the longest period during such six months; nor did he carry on business in this district for such six months, or for the longest period during that period. He did not carry on business any where

within the meaning of the act during any part of such six months, certainly not in the southern district of New York, and if he did carry on business any where during any part of such six months, the place where he did so carry it on must have been Boston. A discharge therefore refused in the southern district of New York for want of jurisdiction. *In re* Leighton, (*S. D. N. Y.*) 5 *N. B. R.* 95.

27. Fraud. Fraud contrary to the true intent of the bankrupt act is such as will prevent a discharge. *In re* Locke, 2 *N. B. R.* 123.

28. A discharge will be refused where the creditors establish a *prima facie* case of fraud. *In re* P. A. Doyle, (*R. I.*) 3 *N. B. R.* 190.

29. The fair and reasonable construction of section 29 of the U. S. bankrupt act is, that it refuses a discharge on the ground of preference only, when the act is brought within the definition of section 35 or of section 29 itself. Under the latter it must be proved that bankruptcy was in contemplation, and under the former that the creditor was a party to the fraud. *In re* Locke, (*Mass.*) 2 *N. B. R.* 123.

30. Fraudulent preference. A discharge will be refused if creditors opposing shall show that the bankrupt has made any fraudulent preference. *In re* L. J. Doyle, (*R. I.*) 3 *N. B. R.* 158.

31. A bankrupt will be refused a discharge if he has been guilty of fraudulently preferring certain creditors over others in violation of the provisions of the U. S. bankrupt act of 1867. *In re* Gay, (*Me.*) 2 *N. B. R.* 114.

32. An assignment of a claim due to a debtor to secure a pre-existing indebtedness made when he was insolvent, and not as a pledge of security made at the time the indebtedness was contracted, and not as a part of the transaction is a fraudulent preference and a good ground for refusing a discharge. *In re* Foster, (*S. D. N. Y.*) 2 *N. B. R.* 81.

33. Unless preferences are fraudulent within the meaning of the 29th section of

the U. S. bankrupt act of 1867, they will not be considered sufficient to prevent a discharge. *In re* Rosenfield, 2 *N. B. R.* 49; s. c. *L. T. B.* 100; s. c. 8 *A. L. Reg.* 44.

34. Where debtors knowing themselves to be insolvent pay certain of their creditors, it is a fraudulent preference with intent, and the discharge will be refused. *In re* Lewis *et al.* 1 *N. B. R.* 145.

35. Fraudulent sale. A sale by a bankrupt of his stock of goods to his father-in-law without any real change of possession is fraudulent, and will be sufficient cause for refusing a discharge. *In re* Hussman, (*Ky.*) 2 *N. B. R.* 140.

36. On account of mortgage. A mortgaging of the right to redeem personal property which is already subject to a mortgage for more than its value, if given within six months before going into insolvency, to secure a pre-existing debt by a person who is not able to meet his engagements in the ordinary course of business, and knows that he is not, but has the intention and expectation of paying the first mortgage and all other debts at some future time is such preference as will prevent a discharge. Barnard *v.* Crosby, 6 *Allen*, (*Mass.*) 327.

37. Omission of creditor's names. Where it is not shown that the omission of creditor's names from the schedules has been by fraudulent intent, a discharge will not be refused. Where it does not appear that there has been a fraudulent intent in the omission of certain creditor's names from the schedules, but it appears it was with their assent expressed or implied. Other creditors who are not injured thereby cannot prevent a discharge on account of such omissions. *In re* Needham, 2 *N. B. R.* 24.

38. Omission of entries. The burden of proof rests with creditors to show that at the time of making a preference, bankruptcy was intended, unless the creditors succeed in such proof a discharge will not be refused. An accidental omission of entries in books of account will not prevent a discharge. *In re* Burgess, (*Mass.*) 3 *N. B. R.* 47.

39. Omission to publish notice.

A discharge will not be refused simply for the reason that the publication of the notice of the assignees appointment was omitted. *In re* Strachan, (*New Mexico*,) 3 *N. B. R.* 148.

40. Payment to attorney. Payment to a bankrupt's attorney is not a preference and will not prevent the discharge of the bankrupt. *In re* Sidle, (*Ohio*,) 1 *N. B. R.* 77.

41. Necessary expenditures incurred by the bankrupt while insolvent in support of his family ought not to prejudice his right to a discharge. Payment made by a bankrupt without fraud to counsel for services rendered and to be rendered, is not a ground for the refusal of a discharge. *In re* Rosenfeld, jr. (*N. J.*) 2 *N. B. R.* 49.

REGISTER.

1. The list made by the register under sections 23 and 29 of the U. S. bankrupt act of 1867, is to be given to the assignee by the register. Anon. 1 *N. B. R.* 2; 2 *N. B. R.* 21.

2. Where parties waive the adjournment into court of question, they must abide the decision of the register if they argue the same before him. *In re* Patterson, *N. B. R. Sup.* xxii.

3. See sections 3 and 5 of the U. S. bankrupt act of 1867.

4. When questions are objected to, the register will pass upon the same and permit the parties to take formal exception to his ruling, and at the close of the examination, a motion to strike out specified points or to have excluded questions answered will be entertained, and the questions be certified for the decision of the judge, and proceedings to be had thereafter, must be had in accordance with such decision. *In re* Levy, (*S. D. N. Y.*) *N. B. R. Sup.* xxiii; *in re* Lyon, (*S. D. N. Y.*) *N. B. R. Sup.* xxiv.

5. It shall be the duty of the judges of the *district* court of the United States within and for the several districts to appoint in each congressional district in said districts, upon the nomination and recommendation of the chief justice of the supreme court of the United States one or more *registers* in bankruptcy, to assist the judge of the district court in the performance of his duties under this act. No person shall be eligible to such appointment unless he be a councellor of said court, or of some one of the courts of record of the state in which he resides. Before entering upon the duties of his office, every person so appointed a register in bankruptcy shall give a *bond* to the United States with condition that he will faithfully discharge the duties of his office, in a sum not less than one thousand dollars, to be fixed by said court with sureties satisfactory to said court or to either of the said justices thereof; and he shall in open court, take and subscribe the oath prescribed in the act entitled " An act to prescribe an oath of office and for other purposes," approved July 2d, 1862, and also that he will not, during his continuance in office, be directly or indirectly interested in, or benefited by the fees or emoluments arising from any suit or matter pending in bankruptcy in either the district or circuit court in his district. *Section 3 U. S. bankrupt act,* 1867.

6. Account of for services. Every register shall keep an accurate account of his traveling and incidental expenses, and those of any clerk or other officer attending him in the performance of his duties in any case or number of cases which may be referred to him ; and shall make return of the same under oath, with proper vouchers (when vouchers can be procured), on the first Tuesday in each month, and the marshal shall make his return under oath, of his actual and necessary expenses in the service of every warrant addressed to him ; and for custody of property, publication of notices, and other services, and other actual and necessary expenses paid by him, with the vouchers therefor whenever practicable, and also with a statement that the amounts charged by him are just and reasonable. *General Order No.* 12, *Sup. Ct. U. S.—In bankruptcy.*

7. Appointment of assignees, &c. The register should state to the creditors at a meeting held for the purpose of choosing an assignee, that in case of their failure to make a choice the judge would appoint an assignee if there was an opposing interest. *In re* Pearson, 2 *N. B. R.* 151.

8. If a register is satisfied that any reasons exist why an assignee elected or appointed should not act, it is his duty to certify the same to the judge giving his reasons therefor at length. *In re* Bliss, *N. B. R. Sup.* xvii; *In re* Noble, 3 *N. B. R.* 25.

9. The register has power to appoint an assignee where there is no choice by the creditors, either from failure to appear and prove their debts or from other causes, where there does not appear to be an opposing interest. *In re* Cogswell, *N. B. R. Sup.* xiv.; s. c 2 *Pitts, L. J.* 626.

10. An opposed motion to remove an assignee, appointed by the court, cannot be entertained by the register. *In re* Stokes, (*S. D. N. Y.*) 1 *N. B. R.* 130.

11. As embrio judges. See opinion of register John Fitch. *In re* Heller, (*S. D. N. Y.*) 5 *N. B. R.* 46.

12. As regulated by general orders. The time when and the place where the registers shall act upon the matters arising under the several cases referred to them shall be fixed by special order of the district court or by the register, acting under the authority of a general order in each case, made by the district court; and at such times and places the registers may perform the acts which they are empowered to do by the act, and conduct proceedings in relation to the following matters when uncontested, viz., making adjudication of bankruptcy on petition of the debtor, directing, unless otherwise ordered by the court, the newspapers in which the notices shall be published by the messenger, administering oaths, receiving the surrender of a bankrupt, granting protection thereon, giving requisite directions for notices, advertisements and other ministerial proceedings, taking proofs of claims, ordering payment of rates and taxes and salary or wages of persons in the employment of the assignee ; ordering amendments or inspection, or copies or extracts of any proceedings, taking accounts of proceeds of securities held by any creditor, taking evidence concerning expenses and charges against the bankrupt's estate, auditing and passing accounts of assignees,

proceedings for the declaration and payment of dividends, and taxing costs in any of the proceedings, all of which shall be subject to the control of the court. *General Order No.* 5, *Sup. Ct. U. S.—In bankruptcy.*

13. Special custodian. A register may be appointed by the bankruptcy court a special custodian of property which is advertised for sale under a mortgage, and be directed to sell the same under general orders 19 & 21; with the authority to make other advertisements than those required by the rules of court. The order should designate the bank in which the money preceeds of the sale shall be deposited as a separate fund subject to the further orders of the court. The register may also be directed to make the deed to the purchaser, and to convey title under the order of the court free from certain liens in pursuance to sec. 20 of the act, and the lien of the mortgage will be transferred from the property so sold to the proceeds of the sale. If advisable in order to obtain a better price for the property, an injunction already granted may be removed or modified so that a sale may be had under a judgment, and the referee may make out the deed. *In re* Hanna, (*S. D. N. Y.*) Unreported.

14. Depositions before. Although a register may have no authority to take a particular deposition he has full authority to administer oaths and, when by the assent of parties he has taken such a deposition to be used in evidence in a cause, the same becomes a sworn statment made *in* the case to be used as evidence therein to which the party causing the deposition to be so taken cannot object. It is not error to direct the attention of the jury to the distinction between " reasonable cause to believe" and " actual belief." If a father-in-law ,when his son-in-law is known by him to be insolvent and within a few days of his voluntary application to be adjudged a bankrupt, buys out of the usual course of trade a large portion of the insolvent's property, and gives notes payable at long dates, cashes the notes and pays to his own son as mortgagor the money thus furnished in discharge of a mortgage on the property of his daughter who is the wife of the bankrupt son-in-law, that is certainly a transfer of the bankrupt's property to his wife in fraud of his creditors, through the agency of the wife's father, and, therefore, fraudulent and void. Lawrence v. Graves, (*Mo.*) 5 *N. B. R.* 279.

15. Fees of. When a register in bankruptcy had control and custody for twenty-five days of bankrupt's stock of goods, and made sales of the same, the court decided that he might be allowed $5 per day and a commission of $250 for the custody of the money, by way of compensation, payable out of the assets. *In re* Loder *et al.* (*S. D. N. Y.*) 2 *N. B. R.* 162.

16. A register is not entitled to a fee of $5 upon an adjournment as for a days' service. *In re* Clark, (*E. D. N. Y.*) *N. B. R. Sup.* xli.

17. Have control over postponements and adjournments. Registers have control over postponements and adjournments, and must exercise this power with discretion. Where a party unreasonably refuses to proceed in a matter, the same may go on without him under the supervision of the register. *In re* Hyman, (*S. D. N. Y.*) 2 *N. B. R.* 107.

18. May postpone debts. Debts proved and filed with the register, may be postponed for investigation before the assignee, and not allowed to be voted upon for the assignee. *In re* Frank, (*N. D. N. Y.*) 5 *N. B. R.* 194.

19. Must not be interested in proceedings. No register shall be of counsel or attorney, either in or out of court, in any suit or matter pending in bankruptcy in either the circuit or district courts of his district, nor in an appeal therefrom, nor shall he be executor, administrator, guardian, commissioner, appraiser, divider or assignee, of or upon any estate within the jurisdiction of either of said courts of bankruptcy, nor be interested in the fees or emoluments arising from either of said trusts. *Sec.* 4 *U. S. bankrupt act,* 1867.

20. Must reject claims not duly proved. A register is, under section 22 of the U. S. bankrupt act of 1867, to reject all claims not duly proved; but if an issue of fact or law is raised, it must be adjourned

into court for decision by the judge. *In re* Loder, (*S. D. N. Y.*) 3 *N. B. R.* 162.

21. Oath administered by. Where there is no opposition to the bankrupt's discharge, the register may administer to the bankrupt the oath provided by section 29 of the U. S. bankrupt act of 1867. It is also the register's duty, after a careful examination, to certify that the bankrupt has conformed to all the requirements of said act. *In re* Bellamy, (*S. D. N. Y.*) *N. B. R. Sup.* xxi.

22. Oath of allegiance to be taken before. The oath of allegiance required to be annexed to the debtor's petition may be taken before a register. *In re* Walker, 1 *N. B. R.* 67.

23. Orders by. Whenever an order is made by a register in any proceeding in which notice is required to be given to either party before the order can be made, the fact that the notice was given, and the substance of the evidence of the manner in which it was given, shall be recited in the preamble to the order; and the fact also stated that no adverse interest was represented at the time and place appointed for the hearing of the matter upon such notice; and whenever an order is made where adverse interests are represented before the register, the fact shall be stated that the opposing parties consented thereto, or that the adverse interest represented made no opposition to the granting of such order. *General Order No. 8, Sup. Ct. U. S.—In bankruptcy.*

24. Powers and duties of. The register has power to order the payment of fees and expenses incurred in a case out of the assets in the hands of the assignee, on application of the attorney for the bankrupt. *In re* Lane, (*S. D. N. Y.*) 2 *N. B. R.* 100.

25. A register cannot allow payment to the petitioning creditor's attorney in the first instance. *In re* Dibblee, (*S. D. N. Y.*) 3 *N. B. R.* 185.

26. A register has power under sections 12 and 42 of the U. S. bankrupt act of 1867, to adjourn a meeting of creditors where notice to the creditors has not been given as required in the warrant. *In re* Schepler, (*S. D. N. Y.*) 3 *N. B. R.* 42.

27. A register on the examination of a witness has no power to decide on the materiality or relevancy of questions. *In re* Bond, (*S. D. N. Y.*) 3 *N. B. R.* 2; affirming *in re* Levy *et al. N. B. R. Sup.* xxiii; citing *in re* Rosenfield, 1 *N. B. R.* 61.

28. A register cannot inquire into the authority of an attorney or counselor of the district court to appear for creditors. The certificate of the register to the sufficiency of the inventory of the debtor's debts is not so conclusive as to prevent inquiry when the question is raised by a proper party at a proper time. *In re* Hill, (*S. D. N. Y.*) *N. B. R. Sup.* iv.

29. A register has no power to order a bankrupt to execute deeds of release of his property. Hence, if the bankrupt refuses to sign such deeds, application must be made to the court. Anon. (*Me.*) 3 *N. B. R.* 58.

30. A register may make the order to show cause if the judge so directs, specially or generally. *In re* Bellamy, (*S. D. N. Y.*) *N. B. R. Sup.* xiv ; s. c. *id.* 21.

31. Whenever a register is satisfied that reasons exist why the appointment of an assignee should not be approved by the judge, it is his duty to state such reasons fully in submitting the question of the approval to the judge. *In re* Bliss, (*S. D. N. Y.*) *N. B. R. Sup.* xiv.

32. A register cannot make any binding decision, or compel a witness to answer if he refuses. It is his duty to report the testimony if required. *In re* Koch, (*N. D. N. Y.*) 1 *N. B. R.* 153.

33. A register may, if he deems it proper, allow a bankrupt on his examination to consult with counsel before answering interrogatories. *In re* Collins, (*Ky.*) 1 *N. B. R.* 153 ; citing Tanner, 1 *N. B. R.* 59 ; *in re* Judson, 1 *N. B. R.* 82 ; *in re Patterson*, *N. B. R. Sup.* xxxiii.

34. A register is not bound to receive and file a deposition for proof of debt taken and certified before another register as correct, especially if it appear defective to the register to whom the matter has been referred. *In re* Loder, (*S. D. N. Y.*) 3 *N. B. R.* 162.

35. A resgister, to whom bankruptcy proceedings have been referred, is not bound to receive and file " as of course," depositions for proofs of debt taken and certified before another register. The register acting as the court is, under section 22 of the U. S. bankrupt act of 1867, to reject all claims not duly proved. His proper course is to return claims with defective proofs for amendment. *In re* Loder, 3 *N. B. R.* 162.

36. A bankrupt under examination may consult with his counsel in the discretion of the register. *In re* Patterson, (*S. D. N. Y.*) *N. B. R. Sup.* xxxiii.

37. A register has no power to decide as to the relevancy of questions put to the bankrupt on his examination. *In re* Levy *et al.* (*S. D. N. Y.*) *N. B. R. Sup.* xxx.

38. A register had no power prior to November, 1867, to take affidavits in involuntary bankruptcy. Anon. (*N. D. N. Y.*) *N. B. R. Sup.* xxxix.

39. The fixing of the time for the first meeting of creditors is a matter of discretion with the register. *In re* Heys, (*S. D. N. Y.*) *N. B. R. Sup.* v.

40. The register may appoint a watchman, if necessary, to take charge of and guard the bankrupt's property, which has been surrendered to him. *In re* Shafer *et al.* 2 *N. B. R.* 178.

41. Registers must see that proper notice is given to the creditors by the assignee, including both those who have and have not previously proved their debts. *In re* Bushey, 3 *N. B. R.* 167.

42. Registers are charged with the general care and supervision of cases referred to them, and must act impartially between all parties. *In re* Orne, *N. B. R. Sup.* xviii.

43. For power of registers to administer oaths, see amendment to U. S. bankrupt act, approved July 25th, 1868.

44. A register has power to take affidavits and depositions in cases not before him at any time after a petition has been filed. *In re* Dean *et al.* (*Mo.*) 2 *N. B. R.* 29.

45. A register may issue an order for the wife of the bankrupt to attend and be examined as a witness. *In re* Van Tuyl, (*S. D. N. Y.*) 2 *N. B. R.* 177.

46. The oath required by section 29 of the U. S. bankrupt act of 1867, to be taken by the bankrupt, is to be produced to the register, who is then to certify conformity or non-conformity by the bankrupt to the requirements of the law. If specifications in opposition to his discharge are filed, and the bankrupt has conformed in the judgment of the register to all the requirements of law and to all his duty under the act, the register is to certify that he has so conformed, except in the particulars covered by the specifications. *In re* Pulver, (*S. D. N. Y.*) 2 *N. B. R.* 101.

47. The register has power to permit a bankrupt to amend his schedules, such amendment being on an *ex parte* application. No notice to creditors is necessary. *In re* Watts, (*S. D. N. Y.*) 2 *N. B. R.* 145 ; *in re* Orne, (*S. D. N. Y.*) *N. B. R. Sup.* xviii ; *in re* Morford, (*S. D. N. Y.*) *N. B. R. Sup.* xlvi.

48. It is the right and duty of the register to permit and require amendment of deficient deposition. *In re* Elder, (*Nevada*,) 3 *N. B. R.* 165.

49. Under section 22 of the U. S. bankrupt act of 1867, the register is empowered to pass upon the satisfactory or unsatisfactory character of proofs of debts ; but all matters of fact or of law are to be reserved for the decision of the court. *In re* Bogert & Evans, (*S. D. N. Y.*) 2 *N. B. R.* 139.

50. A register has no power to decide on the competency, materiality or relevancy of a question under G. O. No. 10. *In re* Rosenfeld, (*N. J.*) 1 *N. B. R.* 60.

51. A register has no power to decide the validity of objections nor the admissibility of questions. *In re* Patterson, (*S. D. N. Y.*) *N. B. R. Sup.* xxxii.

52. A register may act at chambers in aid of the judge of the U. S. district court. *In re* Brandt, 2 *N. B. R.* 76.

53. A register should see that the bankrupt summoned to attend before him shall be protected from arrest during such attendance. As regards such attendance, the bankrupt is to be treated as a witness in U. S. courts. *In re* Kimball, (*S. D. N. Y.*) *N. B. R.* xlii.

54. A register in bankruptcy cannot fulfil the requirements of his official duty for any county in which business must wait his convenience. Nor does he fill the requirement of his official duty when the books and papers of any county are not so open to inspecton at the local seat of justice, as those in the office of the clerk of a court should be. *In re* Sherwood, 1 *N. B. R.* 74. He will be required to show cause why not. *In re* Leland, unreported.

55. In exceptional cases, with the leave of court, registers may appoint a commissioner to act in their place for certain purposes. *In re* Sherwood, 1 *N. B. R.* 74.

56. The register must cause the question or issue to be stated by the opposing parties in writing, and adjourn the same into court for decision by the judge. *In re* Bogert & Evans, 2 *N. B. R.* 139.

57. The register being prohibited from hearing questions as to the allowance of an order of discharge intrudes upon the exclusive jurisdiction of the court when he makes a certificate and requests the opinion of the court as to whether the bankrupt is entitled to a discharge. *In re* Mawson, 1 *N. B. R.* 33

58. The register may refuse to certify a question raised by a witness or person other than a " party to the proceedings before him ;" the word " party " means the bankrupt or a creditor, it does not mean a witness who is not a bankrupt or creditor to the proceedings. A witness is not entitled to counsel when he appears before a register. Where there is no point or matter within the meaning of section 6 of the U. S. bankrupt act of 1867, to be certified by the register, he ought to decline to trouble the court with irrelevant matter. *In re* Fredenburgh, 1 *N. B. R.* 34.

59. A register is not authorized under the U. S. bankrupt act of 1867 to determine questions of allowance, or supension of an order of discharge, but he must adjourn into court all contested matters where a

question of law or fact is raised in proceedings before him. *In re* Brandt, 2 *N. B. R.* 76; *In re* Lanier, 2 *N. B. R.* 59.

60. It is the duty of the register to see that proper notice is given by the assignee to the creditors. *In re* Bushey, (*Pa.*) 3 *N. B. R.* 167.

61. A creditor, who was also the assignee in bankruptcy employed counsel in proceedings before the adjudication of his debtor, and asked the register for an order for payment of the same out of the bankrupt's estate. The court decided that a register could not entertain such an application in the first instance, but that the creditor must petition to the court setting out the facts and asking the relief desired. *In re* Dibble, (*S. D. N. Y.*) 3 *N. B. R.* 185; *in re* New York Mail Steamship Co. 3 *N. B. R.* 155.

62. A register has power to postpone proof of a claim until an assignee is chosen where there are doubts as to the validity of the claim or to the right of the creditor to prove it, and the register ought to exclude from voting for an assignee all persons, who are inhibited from proving their debts by the provisions of sections 23, 39 and 35 of the U. S. bankrupt act of 1867. *In re* Stevens (*S. D. N. Y.*) 4 *N. B. R.* 122.

63. The register is a part of the court, his duties are of a judicial character and his action should, under all circumstances, be free from reproach; hence any attempt on his part to influence the choice of an assignee is unauthorized and improper. *In re* Smith, (*S. D. N. Y.*) 1 *N. B. R.* 25; *in re* Pearson, (*N. D. N. Y.*) 2 *N. B. R.* 151.

64. A register has no authority to issue an order to a creditor to show cause why his proof of debt should not be vacated and the record canceled. Such order should be made by the court. *In re* Comstock & Wheeler, (*S. D. N. Y.*) 2 *N. B. R.* 171.

65. A register has the power to postpone the proof of a claim until after the choice of an assignee, if a case is made out for such postponement within rule 6 of this court, but he has no power to institute the inquiry provided for by the last clause of section 22

of the U. S. bankrupt act of 1867. *In re* Herrman *et al.* (*S. D. N. Y.*) 3 *N. B. R.* 153.

66. As an officer of the court acting in the place of the judge, the register is authorized where there is no opposing interest or no contest, to "sit in chambers," and act on and dispatch there such part of the administrative business of the court, in accordance to general rule and orders, and particular instructions received from the judge. *In re* Gettleston, 1 *N. B. R.* 170.

67. Section 5 of the U. S. bankrupt act, of 1867, clothes the register with certain powers, but does not authorize him to commit for contempt. *In re* Lanier, 2 *N. B. R.* 59.

68. A register has power to order an assignee to submit and file the account required by sec. 28. *In re* Bellamy, *N. B. R. Sup.* xiv; s. c. *L. T. B.* 22.

69. The register has no authority to sanction a prospective payment by the assignee, unless the matter is specially referred to him. *In re* Bellamy, *N. B. R. Sup.* xiv.

70. Proofs of debt must be referred to. All proofs of debt under section 22 of the U. S. bankrupt act of 1867, should go to the assignee, and when he has made his register, they must be returned to the register. Anon. (*S. D. N. Y.*) 1 *N. B. R.* 2.

71. Surrendering property to. After an adjudication of voluntary bankruptcy, the bankrupt will not be permitted to plead as an excuse for not surrendering his property to the register, that there is a prospect of settlement with bankrupt's creditors. *In re* Shafer & Hamilton, (*S. D. N. Y.*) 2 *N. B. R.* 178.

72. Where a debtor has been adjudged a bankrupt on his own petition, the register is authorized and required to receive a surrender of the bankrupt's property, and keep it safely until it can be turned over to the assignee. *In re* Hasbrouck, *N. B. R. Sup.* xvii.

73. Title to property. The title to the property of a bankrupt by operation of law, vests in the register as register, although the property may be in possession of the U.

S. marshal as messenger, it is still in the possession of the court, and the register is by the bankrupt law the court. *In re* Carow, 4 *N. B. R.* 178.

74. To investigate question of validity of claim. When a question is raised as to the validity of a claim, the register ought, before proceeding further in the case, to investigate the question and not allow the claim merely because the creditor has sworn to it. *In re* Orne, (*S. D. N. Y.*) *N. B.'R. Sup.* xiii.

75. Traveling expenses. Although a non-resident register may only be allowed for the expenses of three journeys in a case, he will not be allowed to procrastinate his visits to a remote county until there has been an accumulation of business there, whereby he can distribute his expenses and receive a more liberal allowance for travel. *In re* Sherwood, (*Pa.*) 1 *N. B. R.* 74.

REGISTRARS.

1. Proceedings held in goal before a registrar, upon the examination of a debtor in custody, are judicial and in a public court. Ryalls *v.* Leader, 1 *L. R., Exch.* 296; 35 *L. J., Exch.* 185. (Eng.)

2. The registrar sitting for the commissioner, extended the time for shewing cause against an adjudication to a specified day. When the time arrived the parties attended, and the registrar (who has not the power of reversing an adjudication,) again sat for the commissioner, and further adjourned the time for shewing cause beyond the extended time authorized by the act. *Held*, that the registrar sitting for the commissioner could so adjourn it. *Ex parte* Washbourne, 4 *De G. & S.* 193. (Eng.)

3. Bankrupts gave a notice on the 27th December, of their intention to show cause on the 29th of that month against an adjudication. On the 29th December, in the absence of the commissioner, the registrar made an order extending the time for shewing cause, and in the *interim* suspending advertisements. *Held*, that such order was not *ultra vires* the registrar. *Ex parte* Jacobson, 7 *Jur.*, *N. S.* 322; 4 *L. T.*, *N. S.* 102. (Eng.)
Gaz.

4. An order made by a registrar acting as the deputy of a commissioner, should show upon the face of it that he was appointed by and duly authorized to act for the commissioner. *Ex parte* Morgan, 9 *Jur.*, *N. S.* 881; 32 *L. J., Bank.* 61; 11 *W. R.* 1048; 7 *L. T.*, *N. S.* 778. (Eng.)

5. A registrar acting as deputy of the commissioner, has power to grant orders of discharge in unopposed cases. The order of discharge in such cases ought to be signed by the registrar and by the commissioner. *Ex parte* Lees, 33 *L. J.*, *Bank.* 25; 12 *W. R.* 697, c. (Eng.)

6. A registrar appointed to act in the place of a commissioner, under 17 & 18 Vict. c. 119, s. 6, had no jurisdiction after the death of the commissioner. *Ex parte* Corliss, 3 *De G. & J.* 484; 5 *Jur.*, *N. S.* 110; 28 *L. J.*, *Bank.* 15; 17 *W. R.* 220; 32 *L. T.*, *N. S.* 326. (Eng.)

7. B. gave notice to dispute an adjudication which had been made against him, the notice being signed by D. & L. as his solicitors. When the validity of the adjudication came on for argument before the commissioner, R., who was the managing clerk of D. & L., and who was himself a solicitor of the court, appeared for the bankrupt. The commissioner, however, declined to hear him, and, although the bankrupt, who was in court, said that he wished R. to be heard on his behalf, the commissioner confirmed the adjudication with costs against the bankrupt. *Held*, that the commissioner was right in refusing to hear R., so long as he appeared in the character of clerk to D. & L.; but that the bankrupt ought to have been more fully informed of the position in which he stood, and to have had an opportunity of constituting R. his solicitor if he desired to do so. *Ex parte* Broadhouse, 2 *L. R.*, *Ch.* 655; 36 *L. J.*, *Bank.* 29; 15 *W. R.* 126; 17 *L. T.*, *N. S.* 126. (Eng.)

8. A commissioner in bankruptcy is not bound to hear a person who, although a duly admitted solicitor of the court, does not appear as the solicitor of the party for whom he appears, but only as the clerk of such solicitor. Broadhouse, *ex parte*, 2 *L. R.*, *Ch.* 655; 36 *L. J.*, *Bank.* 29; 15 *W. R.* 126; 17 *L. T.*, *N. S.* 126.

96

9. The registrar, when holding a meeting in a district court of bankruptcy, had no jurisdiction to make an order for the delivery up by the creditors' assignee of documents of the bankrupt in his custody. *Ex parte* Thwaites, 16 *W. R.* 660. (Eng.)

10. The examination of a prisoner in gaol by a registrar was a public judicial proceeding, and, therefore, a fair and correct report, without comment, of the examination was privileged, even though it may have contained statements, which injuriously affected the character of a third person. Ryalls *v.* Leader, 1 *L. R., Exch.* 296; 12 *Jur., N. S.* 503; 35 *L. J., N. S. Exch.* 185; 14 *W. R.* 838; 14 *L. T., N. S.* 562. (Eng.)

REIMBURSEMENT BY ASSIGNEES.

1. B. deposited India bills with her bankers specially indorsed by her, to receive the amount when due; the balance of her banking account (exclusive of the amount of the bills) being then in her favor, and continuing so up to the bankruptcy of the bankers. The bankers charged discount on the bills in their account with B., who might have drawn on them for the amount; it being the custom of bankers to consider ordinary bills so deposited as cash. The bankers paid the bills away to a creditor, with whom the assignees afterwards settled an account, charging him with the amount of the bills, and receiving from him the balance due the estate. *Held*, that B. was entitled to be reimbursed the whole amount of the bills from the assignees. *Ex parte* Bond, 1 *Mont., D. & D.* 10. (Eng.)

REJECTED CLAIMS.

1. A supposed creditor, who takes an appeal to the circuit court from the decision of the district court, rejecting his claim in whole or in part shall, upon entering his appeal in the circuit court, file in the clerk's office thereof a statement in writing of his claim, setting forth the same substantially as in a declaration for the same class of action at law and the assignee shall plead or

answer thereto in like manner, and like proceedings shall thereupon be held in the pleadings, trial and determination of the cause, as in an action at law commenced and prosecuted in the usual manner, in the court of the United States, except that no execution shall be awarded against the assignee for the amount of a debt found due to the creditor. The final judgment of the court shall be conclusive, and the list of debts shall, if necessary, be altered to conform thereto. The party prevailing in the suit shall be entitled to costs against the adverse party, to be taxed and recovered as in suits at law; if recovered against the assignee, they shall be allowed out of the estate *Section 24 U. S. bankrupt act*, 1867.

RELATIONSHIP.

1. Relationship in the ninth or less degree on the part of a proposed trustee to a bankrupt or to a creditor, even the largest in amount of the bankrupt, or to the proposed member of the committee to such creditor or to the bankrupt, cannot be regarded as a disqualification. Other facts may concur with relationship which would make confirmation improper. *In re* Zinn, (*S. D. N. Y.*) 4 *N. B. R.* 145.

RELEASE.

1. Of bail. A voluntary surrender of himself by one who has given bond to take the benefit of the insolvent laws, will not relieve his bail from the obligation contained in his bond. Wolfram *v.* Strickhouser, 1 *W. & S. Pa. R.* 379.

2. Covenant not to. A lessee covenants not to lease or underlet, nor permit any person to occupy the premises without the consent of the lessor, affords no defence to the lessee in an action to recover the premises by one holding an assignment from the lessee's assignee appointed in voluntary proceedings in insolvency. Bemis *v.* Wilder, 100 *Mass. R.* 446.

3. Of Mortgage property. If the value of the property exceeds the sum for which it is so held as security, the assignee

may release to the creditor the bankrupt's right of redemption therein on receiving such excess; or he may sell the property, subject to the claim of the creditors therein; and in either case the assignee and creditor, respectively, shall execute all deeds and writings necessary or proper to consummate the transaction. If the property is not so sold or released and delivered up, the creditor shall not be allowed to prove any part of his debt. *Section* 20 *U. S. bankrupt act,* 1867.

RELINQUISHMENT OF JUDGMENT.

1. It is no objection to a commission, when the petitioning creditor's debt is on a judgment, that, prior to presenting a petition for a commission, the petitioning creditor had not relinquished his judgment. Bryant *v.* Withers, 2 *Rose,* 8; 2 *M. & S.* 123. (Eng.)

REMAINING ABSENT.

1. *And be it further enacted,* That any persons residing and owing debts as aforesaid, who, after the passage of this act, shall depart from the state, district or territory of which he is an inhabitant, with intent to defraud his creditors; or, being absent, shall, with such intent, remain absent, shall be deemed to have committed an act of bankruptcy, and subject to the conditions hereinafter prescribed, shall be adjudged a bankrupt, on the petition of one or more of his creditors, the aggregate of whose debts provable under this act amount to at least two hundred and fifty dollars, *provided,* such petition is brought within six months after the act of bankruptcy shall have been committed. *Section* 39 *U. S. bankrupt act,* 1867.

REMAINING SECURITIES.

1. A firm in Ceylon employed a firm in England as their agents and factors, the course of business being that the Ceylon firm consigned cargoes to the English firm for sale on their account, and drew bills on the English firm against the consignments

Consignments of coffee having been made in this manner, and bills accepted by the English firm against them, the English firm pledged the coffee, together with securities of their own, with T., their broker, to secure a large debt due from them to him. The English firm became insolvent and executed a creditor's deed under the English bankruptcy act of 1861, and then T. sold the coffee (which produced more than sufficient to cover the bills drawn against it) and enough of the other securities to satisfy the debt. *Held,* that the Ceylon firm was entitled, as against the English firm in liquidation, to have the remaining securities in T.'s hands marshaled and to have a lien thereon for the balance due to them upon the coffee transaction. *Ex parte* Alston, *in re* Holland, 4 *L. R., Ch.* 168; 17 *W. R.* 266; 19 *L. T., N. S.* 542. (Eng.)

REMEDIES.

1. **District.** A master having sued for his wages at law, and recovered judgment, which judgment remained unsatisfied in consequence of the owner's bankruptcy, and having proved his debt under the owner's bankruptcy, is entitled to sue the ship in the admiralty court, notwithstanding the ship has changed hands. The Bengal, *Swabey,* 468. (Eng.)

REMEDY.

1. **Assignee can take advantage of.** An assignee in bankruptcy represents the creditors of the bankrupt as well as the bankrupt himself, and can take advantage of any remedy which would have been open to an attaching creditor. Beers *v.* Place, 4 *N. B. R.* 158.

2. **At law does not bar remedy by court of equity.** A court of equity will not refuse to take jurisdiction of a cause merely on the ground that complainant has a complete remedy at law, where the parties have submitted their rights to the jurisdiction of the court without objection, especially where proofs have been taken and a hearing upon the merits

has been entered upon. Post v. Corbin, 5 *N. B. R.* 11; 4 *Cowen*, 727; 11 *Paige*, 569; 4 *J. Ch. R.* 399; 2 *Caines' Cases*, 57; 1 *Atk. Ch. R.* 126.

3. Of Lessor.

Assignees of a bankrupt are not liable as assignees of a term, unless they have done some act which unequivocally indicates to the lessor that they have elected to take the benefit of the lease. The remedy of the lessor is by application to the court of bankruptcy under 12 & 13 Vict. c. 106, s. 145. Goodwin v. Noble, 8 *El. & Bl.* 587; 4 *Jur.*, *N. S.* 208; 27 *L. J.*, *Q. B.* 204. (Eng.)

4. In actions by and against assignees, form of.

Assignees cannot at first affirm the act of a creditor interfering with the bankrupt's effects as a contract, and afterward disaffirm it as a tort; although such act if disaffirmed in the first instance, would have amounted to a conversion of the bankrupt's goods, and would have rendered the creditor liable to the assignees in trover. But trover will not lie in an action by assignee, against a person who had wrongfully cantinued the bankrupt's business, where, by accepting the proceeds, thev had either affirmed his acts as their agent, or had received them as a satisfaction for the wrongful act. Brewer v. Sparrow, 1 *M. & R.* 2; 7 *B. & C.* 310; *S. P.*, Lythgoe v. Vernon, 5 *H. & N.* 180. (Eng.)

5. Where S. was indebted to the defendant, an attorney, who had a lien on a lease relating to premises belonging to S., as a security for his debt. A commission of bankruptcy issued against S. and an assignee being appointed, the defendant acted as a solicitor to the commission; a petition was presented to supersede the commission, on the ground that there was no valid petitioning creditor's debt, and the defendant with notice of the fact, joined the assignee in an assignment of the lease to a purchaser; the assignee paid the defendant the debt due from the bankrupt out of the purchase money, and also a part of the amount of his bill as solicitor to the commission; by authority of the assignee the defendant also received certain sums of money accruing from the rents of the premises, in part liquidation of the

debts due him; after these things happened the commission was superseded, and assignees were appointed under a new fiat. It was held, that the new assignees could recover the sums so received by the defendant in an action for money had and received, for by parting with the lease the defendant was guilty of a conversion, and the plaintiffs were therefore entitled to waive the tort and sue in assumpsit, and that as to the rents received by the defendants, it was money received to the use of the assignees after notice of an act of bankruptcy, and as the first assignee was not assignee *de jure*, his assent to the payments made no difference. Clark v. Gilbert, 2 *Scott*, 520 ; 2 *Bing.*, *N. C.* 343; 1 *Hodges*, 347. (Eng.)

6. Where the defendant demised a fulling mill for fourteen years to two persons who during the continuance of the lease, became bankrupt, the lease after reciting that the machinery had been valued at a certain sum, contained covenants, that at the end, or other sooner determination of the term, the machinery should be again valued by two disinterested persons, chosen by the lessor and the lessees. Upon the bankruptcy of the lessees, their assignees declined to take the lease, but they required the defendant to appoint a person to value the machinery, and on his refusal so to do, appointed one themselves, who valued the machinery then in the mill at a sum exceeding the original valuation, most of which machinery had been placed there by the bankrupts. The assignees then delivered possession of the premises to the defendant, and demanded the difference between the two valuations which he refused to pay. It was held, that the assignees, having demanded the machinery were entitled to recover it in trover; and that their remedy was not by an action on the covenants, which had been determined by the bankruptcy, and by their refusal to take the lease. Fairburn v. Eastwood, 6 *M. & W.* 679. (Eng.)

7. Where a person fraudulently procures a bill from A. and afterwards becomes bankrupt, and his assignee receive the money for the bill, A. may recover from them in an action for money had and received. Harrison v. Walker, *Peake*, 111; see Willis v. Freeman, 12 *East*, 656; Glad-

stone *v.* Hadwen, 1 *M. & S.* 517; 2 *Rose,* 131; Milward *v.* Forbes, 4 *Esp.* 171; Haswell *v.* Hunt, 5 *T. R.* 231. (Eng.)

REMOVAL OF ASSIGNEE.

1. The court after due notice and hearing may remove an assignee for any cause which in the judgment of the court render such removal necessary or expedient. At a meeting called by order of the court, in its discretion, for the purpose, or which shall be called upon the application of the creditors in number and value, the creditors may, with consent of court, remove any assignee by such a vote as is hereinbefore provided for the choice of assignee. *Section* 18 *U. S. bankrupt act,* 1867.

REMOVAL OF PROPERTY.

1. *And be it further enacted,* That any person residing and owing debts as aforesaid, who, after the passage of this act shall conceal or remove any of his property to avoid its being attached, taken or sequestered on legal process shall be deemed to have committed an act of bankruptcy, and subject to the conditions hereinafter prescribed, shall be adjudged a bankrupt, on the petition of one or more of his creditors, the aggregate of whose debts, provable under this act, amount to at least two hundred and fifty dollars; *provided,* such petition is brought within six months after the act of bankruptcy shall have been committed. And if such person shall be adjudged a bankrupt, the assignee may recover back the money, or other property so paid, conveyed, sold, assigned or transferred contrary to this act. *Provided,* the person receiving such payment or conveyance had reasonable cause to believe that a fraud on this act was intended, and that the debtor was insolvent. And such creditor shall not be allowed to prove his debt in bankruptcy. *Section* 39 *U. S. bankrupt act,* 1867.

RENEWAL.

1. Where a debtor is continually renewing his checks or notes the rights of those holding such renewals will date back to the date of the execution of a fraudulent conveyance to a bankrupt's wife, where he was indebted at the time he made such conveyance if that indebtedness is now represented by renewals or new commercial paper. Antrims, assignee, *v.* Kelly *et al.* (*Mo.*) 4 *N. B. R.* 189. *In re* Case, 5 *N. B. R.*

2. **Assignees, right of.** The court cannot sanction the renewal of a lease by the assignees for the purpose of carrying on the bankrupt's business if any creditors object to that arrangement, notwithstanding it may have been determined upon by a majority of the creditors present at a meeting duly called for that purpose. *Ex parte* Miller, 1 *Mont., D. & D.* 39. (Eng.)

RENDITION OF JUDGMENT.

1. **Subsequent to bankruptcy proceedings.** A judgment rendered after the defendant had presented his petition to be declared a bankrupt, is not affected by the bankrupt discharge subsequently obtained in that proceeding. Kellogg *v.* Schuyler, 2 *Denio,* 73.

RENT.

1. Before the statute a certificate discharged a bankrupt from an action on the reddendum in a lease, whether the rent accrued due before or after the bankruptcy. Wadham *v.* Marlowe, 2 *Chit.* 600; 4 *Dougl.* 54; 1 *H. Bl.* 437, n; 1 *T. R.* 91; 8 *East,* 314, n; see Gill *v.* Scrivens, 7 *T R.* 27. (Eng.)

2. But the bankruptcy of the lessee could not be pleaded in bar of an action of covenant for rent. Mills *v.* Aurial, 1 *H. Bl.* 433; 4 *T. R.* 94. (Eng.)

3. A parol lease was within 6 Geo. 4, c. 16, s. 75. *Ex parte* Hopton, 2 *Mont., D. & D.* 347; 5 *Jur.* 804. (Eng.)

4. A claim for rent of a house under a lease executed by several persons as joint lessees, cannot be excepted from operation of a certificate of discharge in insolvency, granted to a portion of them on the

ground that the rent was within the class of "necessaries." Pylmptom v. Roberts, 12 (Mass.) 366.

5. A discharge in bankruptcy taking effect on the 28th of June, 1842, is not a bar to the recovery of a quarters' rent falling due upon the 9th of July following, the bankrupt having occupied the premises to the end of the quarter. Savory v. Stocking, 4 Cush. (Mass.) 607.

6. A debtor promised in writing to deliver 6,400 lbs. of cotton to pay for rent, mules, fodder and corn bought from landlord. The debtor assigned cotton and farm stock to his brother, to pay his just debts, with his own and his brother's knowledge of his insolvency. The court decided that, under the state law, the landlord could not distrain, and had no lien on the cotton raised as against general creditors. In re Brock, (Miss.) 2 N. B. R. 190.

7. Where bankrupt's exempt property has been seized and sold under a warrant of distress for rent, the assignee cannot pay any money to the bankrupt except what may be exempted from levy and sale upon execution by the state laws. In re Lawson, (Md.) 2 N. B. R. 19.

8. When no distress warrant has been issued prior to the filing of the petition in bankruptcy, a landlord has no priority or preference over the general creditors for his rent, and he must prove this debt like any other general creditor of the bankrupt. In re Joslyn et al. (Ill.) 3 N. B. R. 118; citing O'Hare v. Jones, 46 Ill. Rep. 288; Rogers v. Dickey; 1 Gilman, 636.

9. Assignees, when liable for. Where the assignees of a bankrupt coachmaker, who was a tenant from year to year, entered upon the premises to keep the coaches in repair, in pursuance of the bankrupt's contracts, and in August sold the bankrupt's effects and delivered the key of the premises to the bankrupt, but paid the. rent up to the Michaelmas following. It was held, in an action by the landlord for a quarters' rent due the Christmas following, that the assignees were liable. Ansell v. Robson, 2 C. & J. 610. (Eng.)

10. In an action by a landlord against the assignees of a bankrupt for rent, the latter may plead that the term did not rest in them, or that it did rest, but that they abandoned it and were not therefore liable. Thompson v. Bradbury, 3 D. C. P. 147; 1 Scott, 279; 1 Bing., N. C. 327. (Eng.)

11. Where the mortgagor and mortgagee of one undivided moiety and the owner of the other, joined in a demise of the whole premises to G. for twenty-one years, he covenanting with the three jointly and severally to pay (without mentioning to whom) the reserved rent, and G. entered and then became bankrupt, and his assignees accepted the lease, it was held, that the assignees were liable in an action at the suit of the three lessors, for rent due since their acceptance of the lease. Magnay v. Edwards, 13 C. B. 479; 17 Jur. 839; 22 L. J., C. P. 171. (Eng.)

12. A landlord's claim for rent can only be enforced against assignees after a seizure under a fi. fa. by distress. Gethin v. Wilks, 2 D. P. C. 189. (Eng.)

13. Where an assignee in bankruptcy elects to accept a lease held by the bankrupt, he renders himself liable on behalf of the estate for rent, from the date of the petition. In re Laurie et al. (Mass.) 4 N. B. R. 7; citing in re Merrifield, 3 N. B. R. 25.

14. The debtors, before proceedings in bankruptcy were commenced, rented a storehouse under a written lease; after bankruptcy the assignees retained possession with the bankrupt's goods therein, but finally surrendered the premises to the lessor. The court decided that the lessor had a preferred claim for the rent, that after the filing of the petition in bankruptcy, rent for the occupation of the store should be paid as a part of the expenses of the custody of bankrupt's estate. In re Rose, Lyon & Co. (Md.) 3 N. B. R. 63.

15. By distress after bankruptcy. After a petition has been presented for the benefit of the bankrupt law, and before the applicant has been declared a bankrupt, his goods found upon demised premises may be distrained and sold by his landlord for the payment of his rent. Butter *v.* Morgan, 8 *W. & S.*, *Pa. R.* 183.

16. A ground rent coming due after the discharge of the debtor as a bankrupt, is not extinguished by the certificate. Bosler *v.* Kerhon, 8 *W. & S.*, *Pa. R.* 183.

17. Distress for. A., being tenant from year to year to B. of a mill, at the rent of 1,400*l.*, payable quarterly, assigned to C. the machinery and effects in the mill, by way of mortgage, to secure 14,900*l.*, with a power of entering and taking possession of the machinery and selling the same in default of payment. In July, 1856, C. took possession of the machinery and effects, and afterwards A. became bankrupt. At the time of the bankruptcy, 1,948*l.* was due from A. to B. for rent of the mill, including the quarter's rent due on the 16th July, 1856. And A. had become bankrupt, and while the machinery and effects remained in the possession of C., B. gave notice to C. that he intended to distrain for the 1,948*l.*, and C., for the purpose of preventing the distress, paid B. 1,306*l.*, the amount of one year's rent, deducting the property tax. On the 5th September, 1856, an order was made that the assignees of A. should elect to accept or decline the tenancy of the mill, and they declined it, but neither A. nor C., nor the assignee, ever offered to surrender the possession of the mill to B., and C. continued in possession of the mill, machinery and effects, until the same were sold. *Held*, first, the 12 & 13 Vict. c. 106, s. 129, by which no distress for rent levied upon the goods or effects of any bankrupt shall be available for more than one years' rent, did not prevent B. from distraining for more than a years' rent, due on the 16th July, 1856, as the machinery and effects had ceased to be the goods of the bankrupt, and the object of the section was to protect the property of the creditors. Brocklehurst *v.* Lowe, 7 *El. & Bl.* 176; 3 *Jur.*, *N. S.* 436; 26 *L. J.*, *Q. B.* 107. (Eng.)

18. *Held*, secondly, that the tenancy not having been put an end to on the 16th October, 1856, the machinery and effects were liable to be distrained for the quarter's rent then due. *Ib.*

19. Covenant for rent. Plea, that before the rent became due, the defendants, by deed, assigned all their interest in the demised premises to A., subject to the payment of the rent, and performance of the covenants contained in the lease; that A. covenanted to pay the rent and perform the covenants contained in the lease; that the defendants delivered the lease to him, and he accepted the same, and entered on the premises by virtue of the assignment. The plea then stated, that A. became bankrupt, and that the arrears of rent accrued after the date of the commission; that the assignee of his estate declined the lease, and that the bankrupt within fourteen days after notice of that fact delivered up such lease to the plaintiffs' devisees of the reversion. *Held*, that the plea was bad, inasmuch as the 6 Geo. 4, c. 16, s. 75, did not put an end to the lease, but merely discharged the bankrupt from any subsequent payment of the rent or observance of the covenants. Manning *v.* Flight, 3 *B. & Ad.* 211. (Eng.)

20. A landlord may distrain for rent after an act of bankruptcy; therefore, money paid to him by a bankrupt tenant to avoid a threatened distress, is a protected payment, and cannot be recovered back by the assignees. Stevenson *v.* Wood, 5 *Esp.* 200; and see Mavor *v.* Croome, 8 *Moore*, 171; 2 *Bing.* 261. (Eng.)

21. If goods are distrained for rent, and replevied by the tenant, and afterwards (the tenant becoming a bankrupt) they are sold by the assignees, the landlord succeeding in the replevin, and obtaining a *retorno habendo*, cannot recover the amount of the rent against the assignees as money had and received. Boddyll *v.* Jones, 4 *Doug.* 52. (Eng.)

22. The assignees of a bankrupt having entered into possession of land in the middle of a quarter, which the bankrupt had agreed to take upon a building lease, upon the terms of paying the rent half-yearly. *Held*, that an action for use and occupation would lie against them for the whole year, though they had not occupied during all the time. Gibson *v.* Courthrope, 1 *D. & R.* 205. (Eng.)

23. When a bankrupt holds under a

lease, rendering rent, the assignees are not liable for rent becoming due after the bankruptcy, if they have never taken possession of the premises occupied by the bankrupt. Bourdillon v. Dalton, 1 Esp. 223; Peake, 238. (Eng.)

24. A landlord levied a distress for rent, and, before he sold, the tenant was adjudicated a bankrupt, and then the sale took place under the distress. The commissioner decided that the landlord was only entitled to retain one year's rent; but on appeal, held, that the landlord was, under the 3 and 4 Will. 4, c. 27, s. 42, (the statute of limitations,) entitled to six year's rent out of the proceeds of the sale. Ex parte Bayley, 22 L. J., Bank. 26. (Eng.)

25. A landlord, who had distrained, and to whom, in addition to arrears of rent, a sum was due from the tenant exceeding 50l. for goods sold and delivered, petitioned for adjudication in bankruptcy against him. Held, that the landlord was not bound to forego his distress. Ex parte Bell, 4 De G. & S. 597. (Eng.)

26. A landlord having distrained and levied for four years' rent on the 11th October, 1861, the tenant, a non-trader, was adjudicated a bankrupt on his own petition on the 17th October, 1861, under 24 and 25 Vict. c. 134, ss. 86, 87. In March, 1861, he had committed a previous act of bankruptcy, he being then a vendee. Held, that the landlord was entitled to the whole of the rent, and was not limited to one year's rent only by 12 and 13 Vict. c. 106, s. 129, for the act of bankruptcy mentioned therein means one to which the title of the assignee could not relate to the act of bankruptcy in March. Paull v. Best, 32 L. J., Q. B. 96; 3 B. & S. 537; 7 L. T., N. S. 738.

27. Where a landlord distrained the goods of a bankrupt before a sale by the assignee the court decided that the landlord had a claim for the rent but without the costs of distress. In re Appold, (Pa.) 1 N. B. R. 178.

28. For occupation of premises by assignee. A bankrupt held his store on a verbal lease, terminating May 1st, 1869, for $1,600 per annum and taxes. On December 26th, 1868, he surrendered his stock of goods to the register and delivered to him the key of the store. The register turned the same over to the assignee March 2d, 1869, and on the 25th of March the goods therein were sold by the assignee's order. On the 1st of February the landlord executed another lease to a store company. Toward the end of April application was made to the assignee for the key which he immediately delivered up. The store had been unoccupied by the assignee after the 1st of April, and he was ignorant as to who was the owner of the store and of the second lease. The landlord claimed rent from December 26th, 1868, to February 1st, 1869, and the store company claimed rent at the rate of $2,000 per annum from February 1st, 1869, to May 1st, 1869. The court decided that the assignee should only pay rent at the rate of $1,600 per annum to April 1st, 1869. In re Merrifield, (S. D. N. Y.) 3 N. B. R. 25

29. The assignees of a bankrupt having allowed his effects to remain on the premises occupied by him nearly a twelvemonth after the bankruptcy, for the purpose of preventing a distress, paid the arrears of rent due, at the same time intimating to the landlord that they did not mean to take the lease unless it could be advantageously disposed of; the effects were soon after sold, and removed from the premises; the lease at the same time was put up for sale by order of the assignee, but there were no bidders for it; they omitted to return the key to the landlord for nearly four months after; however they were not asked for it, and they in no wise made use of the premises. Held, that they were not, under these circumstances, liable to the landlord as assignees of the lease. Wheeler v. Bramah, 3 Camp. 340; 1 Rose, 363. (Eng.)

30. For occupation by marshal of premises. Upon the application of a landlord for an allowance of rent for the time during which his premises were occupied by the goods which were in the hands of the marshal, the court held that the landlord ought to have applied to it for possession of the premises immediately after the marshal took possession of them, and that it would have ordered a removal of the goods and furniture therefrom, and the premises vacated by the marshal. If the landlord

had an opportunity to rent the premises during the time they were occupied by the marshal he should have so represented to the court and he would then have received an allowance for rent or immediate possession of his premises. *Application for* payment of rent by the marshal denied. *In re* McGrath & Hunt, (*S. D. N. Y.*) 5 *N. B. R.*

31. Liability of assignee for. An assignee in insolvency does not become liable for rent of premises demised to his insolvent debtor merely by accepting the trust and receiving a deed of assignment of the debtor's estate. Hoyt *v.* Stoddard, 2 *Allens' (Mass.)* 442.

32. Lien of landlord for. A landlord has a lien in the state of South Carolina on the personal property of the tenant, which is good for one year as against executors and other creditors. Under the statute of Ann, a landlord has a secured lien for his rent in the state of South Carolina, and that law is still in force, having been repealed by the military order of General Sickles. An assignee in bankruptcy is bound to respect the landlord's lien for rent. *In re* Trim & Purcell; Wagner *et al. v.* Wagner *et al.* (*S. C.*) 5 *N. B. R.* 23.

33. Where a landlord has a lien for rent under the state laws, it will be upheld in a bankruptcy court, and the assignee must take title subject thereto. A landlord will be entitled to prove his claim in bankruptcy for the unexpired term of a lease beyond one year, even though he has been preferred under a state law for his rent up to the end of the year. *In re* Wynne, 4 *N. B. R.* 5.

34. May be proved. Where the bankrupt is liable to pay rent, or other debts falling due at fixed and stated periods, the creditor may prove for a proportionate part thereof up to the time of the bankruptcy, as if the same grew due from day to day, and not at such fixed and stated periods. *Section* 19 *U. S. bankrupt act,* 1867.

35. Prior to mortgage sale. In general an equitable mortgagee is not entitled to his rents prior to the date of the order for sale. But where, prior to the bankruptcy, the mortgagor absconded, and the equitable mortgagee of part of the property

took possession of that part from an agent, and a fiat issued against the mortgagor, and then the solicitor to the commission on behalf of the creditors and the equitable mortgagee, jointly appointed the same agent to manage the whole property, which agent was subsequently adopted by the assignees. *Held,* that the mortgagee, though he was also petitioning creditor, was entitled to the rents from his first taking possession. *Ex parte* Bignold, 4 *Deac. & Chit.* 259; 2 *Mont. & Ayr.* 16. (Eng.)

36. Subsequent to order of sale. Where there has been an order for the sale of mortgaged property, and the sale afterwards deferred, the mortgagee is entitled to apply the rents and profits in reduction of the interest accruing subsequently to the order of sale, and up to the time of taking the account. *Ex parte* Ramsbottom, 4 *Deac. & Chit.* 198; 2 *Mont. & Ayr.* 79. (Eng.)

37. Suit for, by assignee. In 1840, A., being lessee of a warehouse and cellar, under a demise from B., and also lessee, under C., of other adjoining property, comprising a vault, D. became tenant from year to year of the warehouse and cellar and vault, at an annual rent of 185*l.*, made up of 140*l.* for the warehouse and cellar, and 45*l.* for the vault. On the 27th of October, 1845, A. became bankrupt, 92*l.* 10*s.* being at the time due as rent from D. to the bankrupt. The assignees, upon being appointed, elected to take the property held under B., and on the 26th February, 1846, elected not to take the property held under C. At Christmas, 1845, rent to the amount of 114*l.* 7*s.* and 6*d.* became due from A. to C., for which amount, on the 19th of February, 1846, C. distrained upon the goods in the vault held by D., who to relieve himself of that distress, paid that sum to C. An action having subsequently been brought by the assignees of A. against D. to recover the 92*l.* 10*s.* and 35*l.* for a quarter's rent due at Christmas, for the warehouse and cellar, *held,* that they could well sue for the quarter's rent due since the bankruptcy in their representative character as assignees. Graham *v.* Allsopp, 3 *Exch.* 186; 18 *L. J., Exch.* 85. (Eng.)

38. Unpaid and accruing. Upon

the dissolution of a partnership, one of the partners took an assignment of the other's interest in the joint property and afterwards agreed with their lessor that the lessor should release him from the lease at a future day and receive his rent until that day, and afterwards receive the rents of his under-tenants. *Held*, that the unpaid rent accruing after the dissolution of the partnership, and before that day was due from him to the lessor, and might be proved against* his separate estate in insolvency under a warrant subsequently issued. Dwight *v.* Mudge, 12 *Grays' (Mass.)* 23.

39. When landlord entitled to. A landlord is entitled to compensation for the use and occupation of his premises, while they have been actually used for the benefit of the estate of the bankrupt, and the rent should be paid by the assignee and charged as part of his expenses. *In re* Walton, *(Mo.)* 1 *N. B. R.* 154.

40. When not discharged. Where the plaintiff, prior to May 1, 1842, demised a house to the defendant for one year from that day, for a certain rent, payable quarterly, and the defendant occupied during the term, but on the 12th day of December, 1842, petitioned to be declared a bankrupt, and obtained his certificate in August, 1843. *Held*, that the discharge was not a bar to an action on the lease for the last quarter's rent falling due May 1, 1843. Stinmets *v.* Ainslie, 4 *Denio*, 573.

RENTING.

1. With proviso to be void in case of bankruptcy. Property may be limited or leased to a man to go over or revert back in the event of his bankruptcy. Brandon *v.* Robinson, 1 *Rose*, 197; s. c. nom. *ex parte* Brandon, 18 *Ves.* 429.

REPAYMENT TO MESSENGER.

1. An assignee was not liable under 5 Geo. 2, c. 30, s. 25, to repay the messenger the costs incurred by him previously to the appointment of the assignee. Burwood *v.* Felton, 4 *D. & R.* 62; 3 *B. & C.* 43. (Eng.)

REPEAL.

1. Of act. The saving clause contained in the act repealing the bankrupt act extended to all the proceedings necessary to consummate the relief intended by the provisions of the act repealed, until the final distribution and settlement of the bankrupt's estate, in any case commenced previous to the repeal. By the repeal of the bankrupt act the jurisdiction of the district courts to entertain a plenary suit in equity commenced by bill of complaint in matters relating to a case in bankruptcy, was taken away, but the powers to entertain summary proceedings on petition in a case commenced previous to the repeal, was retained. Under the latter power the district court might dismiss a bill of complaint, and direct that it be retained as a petition, and further proceedings be had thereupon. Chemung Canal Bank *v.* Judson, 4 *Selden*, (*N. Y.*) 254.

2. Of bankrupt act vitiates discharge. A petition filed, after the repeal of the bankrupt act for the benefit of said act, the district court had no jurisdiction, although it was made, signed and sworn to prior to said repeal, for the purpose of being filed. A discharge of the petitioner, granted afterwards, upon such petition, is not a bar to a suit against him, on a contract debt due before the signing of such petition. Wells *v.* Brackett, 30 *Me.* 61.

3. Of U. S. bankrupt act of 1841. Since the state insolvent law went again into operation by the repeal of the United States bankrupt act of 1841, the creditors of one who was decreed a bankrupt under that act, but whose discharge was refused by the court of the United States, may prove their debts against his estate under that insolvent law. And if they so prove their debts, it seems that they will be bound by his discharge under that law. But such discharge will not bar those creditors whose claims arose before the debtor was decreed a bankrupt, unless they voluntarily prove them according to the provisions of the insolvent law. Fisher *v.* Currier, 7 *Met.* (*Mass.*) 424.

REPLEADER.

1. A repleader will be awarded where, in pleading an insolvent discharge, the defendant omits to aver that he was an inhabitant, or imprisoned in the county where his discharge was granted. Where a repleader is awarded, neither party is entitled to costs. Otis v. Hitchcock, 6 *Wend.* 433.

REPLEVIN.

1. A plaintiff in replevin cannot maintain his action simply by showing that since it was commenced the defendant has gone into insolvency, although the assignee does not appear and take upon himself the defence. Hallett v. Fowler, 8 *Allen*, (*Mass.*) 93.

2. An officer who holds as messenger in insolvency goods which are claimed by persons to whom the insolvent debtor has undertaken to sell them after a demand by those persons for the delivery of the goods, may set up their title in defence to an action of replevin brought against him by other persons to whom the insolvent debtor has also assumed to sell the goods. Ropes v. Lane, 9 *Allen*, (*Mass.*) 502.

3. Replevin suits cannot be maintained under the 25th section of the U. S. bankrupt act of 1867. *In re* Vogel, (*S. D. N. Y.*) 2 *N. B. R.* 138; citing *in re* Barrow, 1 *N. B. R.* 125.

4. Creditors replevied certain goods of the bankrupt in a state court after a petition filed against him, but an application of the assignees in bankruptcy, the U. S. district court ordered the goods to be delivered to said assignees, deciding that the title to all property in the actual possession of the bankrupt at the commencement of bankruptcy proceedings passed to the assignees. *In re* Vogel, (*S. D. N. Y.*) 3 *N. B. R.* 49.

5. Action by bailee. Where the messenger of the commissioners of a bankrupt had delivered goods of the bankrupt to a stranger, taking his obligation to keep them safely and to re-deliver them on demand, it was held, that the bailee could not maintain replevin against one who had taken them. Property, either general or special, being required to be shown in replevin, though possession is sufficient to maintain trover. Waterman v. Robinson, 5 *Mass.* 303.

REPLEVIN BOND.

1. Action on. When the original debtor has received a discharge in bankruptcy, and his assignee has discharged all claim against the officer for the property attached, the damages to be recovered in an action upon the replevin bond, are to be retained for the plaintiff's own use; the amount of the judgment for costs recovered in the action of replevin with interest from the time of judgment, his reasonable expenses incurred in that action and interest for the same time, and his reasonable expenses incurred in the suit upon the bond, and also to recover for the use of the creditor interest at the rate of twelve per cent. per annum on the value of the goods as alleged in the bonds, from the time of the recovery of his judgment to the time when the attachment was dissolved. Howe v. Handley, 28. *Me. R.* 241.

2. When claim cannot be made. Where the purchaser of the debtor's right to the property attached at a sale in bankruptcy has released to the attaching officer all claim thereto, the latter cannot recover anything on the replevin bond for the use of such debtor or his assignee, although it did not appear that the assignee had observed all the rules prescribed in making the sale. Howe v. Handley, 28 *Me. R.* 241.

REPLICATION.

1. To plea of discharge. A replication to a plea of the defendant's discharge under the bankrupt act, averring fraud in obtaining the discharge, must specify the particular acts of the defendant, which the plaintiff will give in evidence, and claim to be fraudulent. Dresser v. Brooks, 3 *Barb.* 429.

REPORT OF EXEMPTED PROPERTY.

1. The rule requiring assignees to make report of exempt property to the court within twenty days after receiving the articles set off to the bankrupt by him is to receive such a construction as will prevent injustice to the bankrupt. *In re* Shields, (*Pa.*) 1 *N. B. R.* 170.

REPUTED OWNER.

1. Where property is assignable by transfer tickets, the reputed owner is the possessor of the tickets. Ridout *v.* Lloyd, 1 *Mont.* 103. (**Eng.**)

2. If A. lets a house to B. with a covenant that the lease shall determine on B. committing an act of bankruptcy, on which a commission should issue ; and by another deed of the same date A. grants the use of the furniture to B. in like manner, and with a similar covenant to allow A. to resume the possession of the furniture on the commission of an act of bankruptcy. If B. becomes bankrupt and the jury find that B. was the reputed owner of the furniture it will pass to the assignees, notwithstanding these covenants. Hickenbotham *v.* Graves, 2 *C. & P.* 492. (**Eng.**)

REPUTED OWNERSHIP.

1. Where the custom of country tea dealers in purchasing teas from wholesale houses in London, was to leave the warrants, after payment, in the hands of the London dealers, to pass the entries and make the necessary arrangements with the dock authorities for the delivery of the teas so purchased, and to deliver the teas in portions as the country dealers required them ; and teas were purchased in the usual course from the bankrupts, who credited the purchasers in their books with the moneys so paid to them and indorsed the names of the purchasers on the warrants. *Held*, that the teas so purchased were not the subject of reputed ownership. *In re* Burt, 15 *L. T.*, *N. S.* 368. (**Eng.**)

2. Where sub-mortgagees of shipments at Ceylon and Hong Kong sent there directed to the parties in possession, by the next direct mail, notices of their security, there being another and earlier mail by a different route; by which notices might possibly have sooner reached their destination, but the sub-mortgagors became bankrupt before notice could have reached them by either mode of transmission, it was held, that the notice was sufficient to take the goods out of their reputed ownership. *Ex parte* Kalsall, *De Gex,* 352. (**Eng.**)

3. The fact of a business being carried on in the name of one ostensible partner does not make a reputed ownership in the partner whose name is used. A secret partnership is not within the meaning of the law as to reputed ownership, and no true owner as distinct from an apparent owner. Reynolds *v.* Bowley, 8 *B. S.* 406 ; 36 *L. J.*, *Q. B.* 247 ; 2 *L. R.*, *Exch.* 474 ; 15 *W. R.* 813 ; 16 *L. T.*, *N. S.* 532; overruling *ex parte* Enderby, 2 *B. & C.* 389. (**Eng.**)

RESIDENCE.

1. One who had resided and carried on business in New York for twenty years prior to June, 1866, and removed to New Jersey in that year, was held to be properly an applicant for the benefit of the bankrupt law in New York. *In re* Belcher, *N. B. R.* 202; s. c. 2 *Bt.* 468.

2. A non-resident of a judicial district having a fixed place of business within it will be appointed assignee in a proper case. *In re* Loder et al. (*S. D. N. Y.*) 2 *N. B. R.* 161.

3. Neither the actual nor the alleged residence or place of business can be directly made the ground of opposition to a bankrupt's discharge. *In re* Burk, (*Oregon,*) 3 *N. B. R.* 76.

4. Creditors residing out of the jurisdiction of the state at the time the debt is contracted are not to be affected in their rights by the insolvent laws of this state. The fact that they seek to avail themselves of the courts of this state to enforce their rights under such extraterritorial contracts, does not render them amenable under the insolvent laws of this state. Soule *v.* Chase, 12 *Tiffany,* (39 *N. Y.*) 342.

5. The term "residence" refers to the abode of the creditor, whose post-office address should be stated also in the schedules. When the residence is stated therein as unknown, proof of due inquiry to ascertain the same must be produced by the bankrupt. *In re* Pulver, (*S. D. N. Y.*) *N. B. R. Sup.* xi.

6. For the longest part of six months. Where the bankrupt resided at Boston, Mass., from May 1, 1867, to December 7, 1867, and from December 7, 1867, to January 21, 1868, he resided at New York, therefore he did not reside in the latter district for the six months next immediately preceding the time of filing the petition, or for the longest period during such six months, and he did not carry on business in the latter district for such six months, or for the longest period thereof, and a discharge must be refused in the latter district for want of jurisdiction. *In re* Leighton, (*S. D. N. Y.*) 5 *N. B. R.* 95.

7. Of copartners in different districts. Where one member of a firm files his petition in one state and asks his copartners to join him in the proceedings which they refuse to do, but subsequently appear by attorney, and consent to an adjudication, whereupon all the members of said firm are adjudicated bankrupt, and upon the application for the discharge of the bankrupts, specifications are filed in opposition to their discharge, on the grounds of a want of jurisdiction of the court, that the petition of the petitioning debtor upon which the adjudication was made, does not show that the members of the copartnership as such, carried on business in the district where said adjudication was made, at any time *within six months* next immediately preceding the filing of the petition, or that the copartnership had any assets either at the time of filing the petition, or at any time within the six months next immediately preceding such filing, and that in point of fact such copartnership was dissolved prior to such commencement of proceedings—and that it has not since that time carried on business anywhere. That no assets of the copartnership have come to the hands of the assignee in bankruptcy. That neither one of the two copartners who did not file their petition, resided or carried on business within said district at any time within six months next immediately preceding the filing of the petition by the other partner, and that neither when that petition was filed, nor within six months next immediately preceding the filing thereof, did such copartnership exist, nor did it at any time within such period possess any copartnership assets. *Held,* that the averment of the petitioning partner that he resided within the district where the proceedings were commenced, is a sufficient allegation to satisfy the requirements of section 36 of the bankrupt act in regard to adjudging two or more persons who are copartners in trade; also *held,* that as to the allegation of fact as to the dissolution of copartnership, and that no assets have come to the hands of the assignee, and that no such assets existed when the petition was filed, or at any time within the six months next immediately preceding the filing thereof, is in itself sufficient to say that the proof shows satisfactorily that assets of the copartnership have come to the hands of the assignee, a portion of such assets being the proceeds of an item mentioned in the schedule of copartnership assets annexed to the petition of the petitioning copartner, and that such assets existed when such petition was filed. That this existing of copartnership assets at the time makes the copartnership a subsisting copartnership at the time *quoad,* creditors then existing for the purpose of bankruptcy proceedings. *In re* Penn & Culver, (*S. D. N. Y.*) 5 *N. B. R.* 30.

8. Proof of. The statute of (2 R. S. 35, s. 2) requiring proof that an insolvent whose discharge is petitioned for, resides or is imprisoned in the county in which resides the officer to whom the petition is presented, such proof is an essential preliminary to the jurisdiction of the officer. It will not be assumed in favor of the insolvent's discharge that proper proof as to the insolvent's residence, which is not suggested by the record, was on fact given. People *v.* Machad, 16 *Abb.* 460.

9. Statement of requisite. The plea of an insolvent discharged under the act of April 12th, 1813, (sess. 46, ch. 38, R.

L. 460) must expressly aver, that the defendant at the time he applied for the discharge, was an inhabitant of the county in which his application was made. This is essential to give the judge jurisdiction. The want of proper averments to give jurisdiction, cannot be supplied by the recital in the discharge. Wyman *v.* Mitchell, 1 Cowen, 316.

10. Subjects to jurisdiction. A creditor who has proved his debt is subject to the jurisdiction of the court without regard to his place of residence. *In re* Kyler, 3 *N. B. R.* 11; s. c. 2 *Bt.* 414.

11. When not domicil. Debtor being a resident of St. Louis, bought a stock of goods in Montana in July, 1869, went to Montana in August, 1869, leaving his family in St. Louis, remained in Montana except a few weeks, when on a business trip to St. Louis, until June, 1870; petition in bankruptcy filed against him in eastern district of Missouri, July 8th, 1870. *Held,* that Montana was his place of residence within the meaning of the bankrupt act during the six months preceding the filing of the petition; the word "residence" in section 11 not synonymous with the word "domicil." Petition dismissed for want of jurisdiction. *In re* Watson, 4 *N. B. R.* 197.

RESIDENT OF KANSAS.

1. Not subject to jurisdiction of other states. A debtor residing in Kansas was adjudged bankrupt on the petition of creditors by the United States district court of Kansas, and assignees appointed. After the bankruptcy proceedings were instituted a mortgage creditor commenced suit to foreclose in one of the state courts of Indiana, without permission of the bankrupt court, making the assignees defendants. The mortgagee was a resident and citizen of Minnesota. The assignees in bankruptcy filed a bill in the circuit court of the United States for the district of Minnesota against the mortgagee, charging that the mortgage was fraudulent, both in fact and under the bankrupt law, and asking a decree to have it declared void, and for an injunction to restrain the defendant from further prosecuting his foreclosure suit in

Indiana. *Held,* that in this case the circuit court for the Minnesota district had no bankruptcy jurisdiction, and could exercise only its ordinary equity powers, and for this reason the injunction asked for was refused, but the court intimated that the question might be presented by a bill similar to the one before it in the circuit court for the district of Kansas. Markson *et al. v.* Heaney, (*Minn.*) 4 *N. B. R.* 165.

RESIGNATION OF ASSIGNEE.

1. An assignee may, with the consent of the judge, resign his trust, and be discharged therefrom. *Sec.* 18 *U. S. bankrupt act,* 1867.

RESTRAINING PROCEEDINGS.

1. An injunction may be issued to restrain proceedings upon the foreclosure of a mortgage where independent proceedings are commenced after bankruptcy. *In re* Snedaker, (*Utah,*) 3 *N. B. R.* 155. *In re* Sachi E. *D. N. Y.*

2. Under the insolvent act. An injunction will not be granted to restrain a defendant in a creditor's suit from proceeding under the insolvent act, to obtain his discharge, unless special cause is shown for restraining him. Shanck *v.* Sniffen, 1 *Barb.* 35.

RESTRAINING TRANSFER OF PROPERTY.

1. And may also, by its injunction, restrain the debtor, and any other person in the meantime from making any transfer or disposition of any part of the debtor's property not excepted by this act from the operation thereof, and from any inference therewith. *Section* 40 *U. S. bankrupt act,* 1867.

RETIRING ASSIGNEE.

1. Any former assignee, his executors or administrators, upon request, and at the expense of the estate, shall make and execute to the new assignees all deeds, conveyances and assurances, and do all other lawful acts requisite to enable him to recover and receive all the estate. And the court may make all orders which it may deem expedient to secure the proper fulfilment of the duties of any former assignee, and the rights and interest of all persons interested in the estate. *Section* 18 *U. S. bankrupt act,* 1867.

RETURN DAY.

1. The publication of the notices required in the warrant, to be published by the marshal, should be completed more than ten days prior to the return day. *In re* Devlin *et al.* (*S. D. N. Y.*) *N. B. R. Sup.* viii.

RETURN OF GOODS TO SELLER.

1. Where, by the course of dealing between a trader and the defendants, the trader could return wool for which he had no call, though previously ordered, and in December the trader ordered a lot of wool, which was not, however, delivered till the 19th February following. The trader, being absent at the time the bags of wool were delivered, on his return the same day, he gave directions not to have them opened or entered in his books, but only weighed off to see if they agreed with the invoice, he being then in embarrassed circumstances, and intending not to take them into the account of his stock, if he found himself unable to carry on his business. On the 4th and 5th of March, being then insolvent, he returned the bags, with a letter declaring his situation, and hoping that they would not object to take back the wool, and requesting a line of approbation, which approbation was given, after an act of bankruptcy committed the same day the letter was sent. It was held that the trader ought to have exercised his option to keep or return the goods on the receipt of the same, and not having done so, the option became lost; that being in a state of insolvency and on the eve of bankruptcy, he could not return the goods to the seller, and that the assignees were entitled to the property. Ncate *v.* Ball, 2 *East,* 117. (*Eng.*)

2. Where a trader ordered goods from the country, to be sent to another place for the purpose of being afterwards sent to his correspondent abroad, which was the usual course of his dealings, it was held, that it was competent for him upon his becoming insolvent, but before an act of bankruptcy, to agree *bona fide* to give up the goods to the defendants from whom they were ordered upon a claim of a right of stoppage *in transitu* ; and the circumstances of the trader having called a meeting of his creditors, and taken legal advice, and being encouraged by . the result of such meeting and advice to give up the goods, was evidence for the jury to find that they were given up *bona fide,* and not from any motive of voluntary and undue preference to the defendants, though done by him in the situation of impending bankruptcy at the time. Dixon *v.* Baldwin, 5 *East,* 175. (Eng.)

3. A., having purchased goods from B. for the purpose of exporting the same, and finding that he could not apply them to the purpose for which he bought them, and that he must stop payment, returned them eight days after the purchase to B. On the following day A. stopped payment, but expecting remittances from abroad more than sufficient to pay his debts, he had no doubt that his creditors would give him time ; they however refused, and he was made bankrupt. In an action by the assignees against B. for the value of the goods, it was held, that the jury were warranted in finding that the return of the goods to B. was not made in contemplation of bankruptcy. Fidgen *v.* Sharp, 1 *Marsh,* 196 ; 2 *Rose,* 153; 5 *Taunt.* 539. (Eng.)

4. Where there has been an actual delivery of goods to the buyer, who becomes insolvent before they are paid for, he cannot rescind the contract, and return the goods with the consent of the seller, so as to give the seller a preference over his other creditors. Barnes *v.* Freeland, 6 *T. R.* 80. (Eng.)

RETURN OF MESSENGER.

1. Although the return of the messenger may not be conclusive for all purposes, it is authority sufficient for the register to pro-

ceed in the matter ; and if from such return it appears that the notices have been duly served and published, as directed in the warrant, the creditors served should proceed to prove their claims, and elect the assignee. The notices to be published and served should contain the same language as that of the warrant. *In re* Pulver, *N. B. R. Sup.* xi ; *in re* Hill, *N. B. R. Sup.* iv.

RETURN OF NOTE.

1. Used as proof. A bill of exchange, promissory note, or other instrument used in evidence upon the proof of a claim, and left in court, or deposited in the clerk's office, may be delivered by the register or clerk having the custody thereof, to the person who used it, upon his filing a copy thereof, attested by the clerk of the court, who shall indorse upon it the name of the party against whose estate it has been proved, and the date and amount of any dividend declared thereon. *Section* 24 *U. S. bankrupt act,* 1867.

RETURN OF WARRANT.

1. At the meeting held in pursuance of the notice, one of the registers of the court shall preside, and the messenger shall make return of the warrant and of his doings thereon, and if it appears that the notice to the creditors has not been given as required in the warrant, the meeting shall forthwith be adjourned and a new notice given as required. If the debtor dies after the issuing of the warrant the proceedings may be continued and concluded in like manner as if he had lived. *Section* 12 *U. S. bankrupt act,* 1867.

RETURN OF WRITTEN INSTRUMENT OR OBLIGATION.

1. Used as proof. A bill of exchange, promissory note, or other instrument used in evidence upon the proof of a claim, and left in court, or deposited in the clerk's office, may be delivered by the register or clerk having the custody thereof, to the person who used it, upon his filing a copy thereof, attested by the clerk of the court, who shall indorse upon it the name of the party against whose estate it has been proved, and the date and amount of any dividend declared thereon. *Section* 24 *U. S. bankrupt act,* 1867.

REVERSAL.

1. Of adjudication. Where an order of adjudication has been made adjudging a debtor a bankrupt on the grounds that he permitted a judgment to be entered against him, (having forgotten about the suit), and because he had not forthwith filed a petition in bankruptcy, it will be reversed. *In re* Wright, (*Mo.*) 4 *N. B. R.* 197.

2. Of bankruptcy adjudication. A bill in equity may be brought in the circuit court, to reverse an adjudication in involuntary bankruptcy by the bankrupt. Farrin *v.* Crawford *et al.* 2 *N. B. R.* 181 ; Langley *v.* Perry, 2 *N. B. R.* 180; s. c. *A. L. Reg.* 427 ; 4 *Pitts. L. J.* 117.

3. Of rulings of U. S. district court. The circuit court, under the second section of the bankrupt act, has jurisdiction to revise, correct and reverse the rulings and judgment of the district court in proceedings in bankruptcy. Langley *v.* Perry, 2 *N. B. R.* 180.

REVERSION AND REMAINDER.

1. Property previously conveyed should be set forth in the bankrupt's schedules under the head of property in reversion, remainder and expectancy. *In re* Arledge, (*Ga.*) 1 *N. B. R.* 195.

REVERSIONARY INTEREST.

1. If a bankrupt has a lease of premises, and also a reversionary interest in the premises, and his assignees sell his estate and reversionary interest in the premises, it amounts to an acceptance of the lease by the assignees. Page v. Godden, 2 *Stark*, 309. (Eng.)

REVERSIONARY INTERESTS IN PERSONAL PROPERTY.

1. Vesting in and not vesting in assignees. The assignee of a share in a reversionary fund obtained a stop order and afterwards mortgaged the share to A. and became bankrupt before the fund was distributable. A. presented a petition for payment to him but obtained no stop order, the assignees of the bankrupt also claimed the share, as being within his order and disposition, with the consent of the true owner. It was held that the assignees in bankruptcy were entitled to the share of the fund, discharged of the mortgage. Bartlett v. Bartlett, 1 *De G. & J.* 127; 3 *Jur.*, *N. S.* 705; 26 *L. J.*, *Chanc.* 577. (Eng.)

2. A mortgagee of a reversionary fund in court, who had obtained no stop order, became insolvent before the interest became reducible to possession. *Held*, that the reversionary interest was not in the order and disposition of the insolvent so as to vest in his assignees. *In re* Grainge, 13 *W. R.* 833; 12 *L. T.*, *N. S.* 564. (Eng.)

3. When in the order and disposition of bankrupt. Notice of an assignment of a reversionary interest given to the solicitor of the trustees is notice to the trustees, so as to take it out of the order and disposition of the assignor on his insolvency. Richards v. Gledstanes, 2 *Giff.* 298; 8 *Jur.*, *N. S.* 455; 5 *L. T.*, *N. S.* 416; affirmed on appeal, 5 *L. T.*, *N. S.* 568. (Eng.)

4. The mere fact af an interest in a legacy being reversionary at the time of the act of bankruptcy does not take it out of the rule as to the order and disposition; but where the true owner has no knowledge, nor any means of knowing of the bankrupt's interest, it cannot be said to be in the order and disposition of the bankrupt with the consent of the true owner. *In re* Rawbone, 3 *K. & J.* 476; 3 *Jur.*, *N. S.* 837; 26 *L. J.*, *Chanc.* 588. (Eng.)

REVESTING OF PROPETY IN ASSIGNEE.

1. An assignment in fraud of creditors, being valid as between the parties, the assignee cannot take a judgment and execution, which shall bind the subject of the assignment until this is annulled, released or abandoned, so as to revest the property in the assignee. The intention to use a judgment confessed by a fraudulent assignor to a fraudulent assignee, only in case the assignment should be adjudged invalid, connects the judgment, and infects it with the vices of the assignment. Mackie v. Cairns, 5 *Cow.* 547.

REVIEW.

1. By circuit court. If the petitioner prosecutes his review in due form, and be without fault therein, the circuit court will hear it, although an action be pending between the parties in a state court. The circuit court will not compel the petitioner to make an election, under pain of a dismissal of his proceedings, as to which of the suits he will prosecute. *In re* Bininger & Clark, 3 *N. B. R.* 121.

2. Of decision of a U. S. district court by a U. S. circuit court. The mode of review by petition bill, etc., under section 2 of the act is expressly confined to cases in which no special provision is otherwise made, and does not apply to cases where an appeal may be taken. Claimants cannot be permitted to treat the petition for a review, as such a statement as the statute requires upon an appeal. *In re* Place and Sparkman, (*S. D. N. Y.*); also see 1 *N. B. R.* 204; 3 *N. B. R.* 35; 3 *N. B. R.* 78; 4 *N. B. R.* 178.

3. Of sale by bill of equity. In all sales under deeds of trust outstanding, when such deeds have been given by bankrupts, the party holding claims secured by deed of trust must come in and prove his claim. A bill in equity will lie to review all sales made under deeds of trust subsequent to bankruptcy. Davis et al. v. Carpenter et al. (*Mo.*) 2 *N. B. R.* 125.

4. What court has power. The

power of review is conferred by the bankrupt act on the circurt court, in term time, or a judge in vacation. *In re* Alabama & Chattanooga R. R. Co. 5 *N. B. R.* 97.

REVIEWING PROCEEDINGS.

1. The court of bankruptcy has power to review an order refusing the discharge of a bankrupt, although it has no power to review an order granting or suspending the discharge. *Ex parte* Atherton, 3 *L. R.*, *Ch.* 142; 37 *L. J.*, *Bank.* 6; 16 *W. R.* 294; 17 *L. T.*, *N. S.* 485. (Eng.)

REVISION OF BANKRUPTCY PROCEEDINGS.

1. The revision contemplated by the first clause of section 2 of the U. S. bankrupt act of 1867, is of a special and summary character, as sufficiently appears from the words, "general superintendence," preceding and qualifying the word jurisdiction, and more clearly from the fact that the power to revise as conferred extends to mere questions, as well as to cases and to every interlocutory order in the case pending the proceedings, and also from the language of the second clause of the same section that the powers and jurisdiction therein granted may be exercised by said court or by any justice thereof in term time or vacation. Morgan c. Thornhill, 11 *Wall*, 80; Sweatt v. The Boston, Hartford & Erie R. R. Co. *et al.* (*Mass.*) 5 *N. B. R.* 234.

2. Circuit courts within and for the district. Where the proceedings in bankruptcy are pending, have a general superintendence and jurisdiction of all cases and questions arising under the bankrupt act, and except when special provision is otherwise made, may, upon bill petition or other proper process of any party aggrieved, hear and determine the case as in a court of equity. 14 *Stat. at Large*, 518; *Gazzam's Treatise on the Bankrupt Law, Appendix; American and English Bankruptcy Digest, Appendix.* Sweatt v. The Boston, Hartford and Erie R. R. Co., *et al.*, 5 *N. B. R.* 234.

3. Delay in filing petition for.

Where in the light of attending circumstances there is sufficient cause for the delay in filing the application for revision, the petitioner will be heard upon the merits. *In re* Alexander, 3 *N. B. R.* 6; Littlefield v. Del. & Hud. Canal Co. 4 *N. B. R.* 77; Sweatt v. The Boston, Hartford & Erie R. R. Co. *et al.* 5 *N. B. R.* 234.

REVISORY JURISDICTION.

1. The revisory jurisdiction of the U. S. circuit court as to questions arising in the progress of the cause is not exercised by appeal but by petition. *In re* Reed, 2 *N. B. R.* 2.

2. Of U. S. circuit court. The appellate jurisdiction of the U. S. circuit court is limited to controversies between assignees and the claimants of adverse interests, and to controversies between assignees and creditor claimants touching the allowance of claim. The general revisory jurisdiction of the U. S. circuit court extends to all decisions of the district court of district judge at chambers, which cannot be reviewed upon appeal or writ of error under the provision of said section. *In re* Alexander, (*Va.*) 3 *N. B. R.* 6.

REVISORY POWER.

1. The court has no revising power over the decrees of the district court sitting in bankruptcy; nor is it authorized to issue a writ of prohibition to it in any case except when the district court is proceeding as a court of admiralty and maritime jurisdiction. The district court when sitting in bankruptcy has jurisdiction over liens and mortgages existing upon the property of a bankrupt, so as to inquire into their validity and extent and grant the same relief which the state court might or ought to grant. *Ex parte* Christy, (*U. S. S. Ct.*) 3 *Howard*, 292.

REVIVAL OF JUDGMENT.

1. In the case of *scire facias*, to revive a judgment of revival, a plea that the defendant was discharged as a bankrupt at a time

which was after the original judgment, but, before the judgment of revival, was bad, though a demurrer to such evidence might have been properly overruled, as the evidence was in accordance with the plea, yet on the whole record the plaintiff was entitled to judgment. Stewart *v.* Colwell, 24 *Penn. R.* 67.

REVIVAL OF DEBTS.

1. By new promise to pay. If a debtor on the eve of bankruptcy promises to pay the debt when he shall be able, his certificate of discharge under the act of April 4th, 1800, is no bar to a suit brought upon the new promise. It seems that if the creditor proves the original debt under the commission and receives a dividend, he may recover the balance in a suit brought after the bankruptcy founded upon such a promise. Kingston *v.* Wharton, 2 *S. & R. Pa. R.* 208.

RIGHTS.

1. Of bail. The bail of an insolvent is entitled to every part of the condition of the bond prescribed by the act of the assembly, and if it do not contain the alternatives of a procurement of a discharge or a surrender to jail no recovery can be had upon it. Hutton *v.* Helme, 5 *Watts' Pa. R.* 346.

2. Of bankrupt to discharge. Jurisdiction of a bankrupt court does not depend upon the right of a bankrupt to obtain a discharge. Van Nostrand *v.* Barr, *et al.* (*Md.*) 2 *N. B. R.* 154.

3. Of creditors. Any creditor considering himself aggrieved by the discharge of the bankrupt, has a right to be heard in that matter in the circuit court. Ruddick *v.* Billings, (*Iowa,*) 3 *N. B. R.* 14.

4. Of debtor. A debtor or defendant has the right to know what are the allegations which are made against him, and may insist that he shall not be tried on charges not made against him in the original proceedings upon which he has joined issue, and especially that he shall not be called upon just before trial to meet an entirely distinct cause of action. *In re* Leonard, 4 *N. B. R.* 182.

5. Of indorser to prove claim. Where the holder of a note receives part of the amount of the same from the indorser, he is entitled to prove for the whole amount against the estate of the bankrupt maker, and holds any surplus he may receive over and above the amount of the note in trust for the indorser. If the creditor omits to prove his debt, thus showing he looks to the indorser alone for payment, the indorser is entitled to come in and prove the note against the bankrupt's estate, and receive dividends upon its whole amount. *In re* Ellerhorst & Co. (*Cal.*) 5 *N. B. R.* 144.

6. Of landlord. A debtor promised in writing to deliver 6,400 pounds of cotton to pay for rent and for mules, fodder and corn bought from the landlord. Debtor assigned cotton and farm stock to his brother to pay just debts with his own and his brother's knowledge of his insolvency. The court decided that under the state law, the landlord could not distrain and had no lien in cotton raised against general creditors. *In re* Brock, 2 *N. B. R.* 100.

7. Where assignees of a bankrupt lessee, chosen on the 15th of November, kept the bankrupt in the premises, carrying on the business for the benefit of the creditors until April following, and himself occasionally superintended; but on the 23d December, disclaimed the lease by letter to the landlord. *Held,* that notwithstanding such disclaimer, he had elected to accept the lease by using the premises for the benefit of the creditors. Clarke *v.* Hume, *R. & M.* 207. (Eng.)

8. Of materialman. The lien created by the statute of Wisconsin, attaches from the time the work was commenced, or the materials furnished for the building upon which it was done or used. Any mechanic who had a lien at the filing of the publication in bankruptcy, would have a right to file a petition under section 4 of the act so as to continue it, notwithstanding the commencement or pendency of bankruptcy proceedings. The bankrupt act provides for the protection of legal liens against the bankrupt's estate instead of destroying them, and that where a party has a lien when the petition in bankruptcy is filed; but it is necessary under the state law, to file a petition in the clerk's office, in order to continue it beyond a certain period; that such party has the right to file such petition, and thereby continue the lien thereon. When a party has a lien or interest in the property, in the hands of an assignee in bankruptcy, he should apply to the U. S. court for relief, and it would grant the relief, or allow a suit to be brought in such court or state court to determine the same; but without such consent parties have no right to sue, and are guilty of a contempt of the authority of the court if they do. Parties commencing suits in the state courts without such consent, must give them up before they can be paid by order of the bankruptcy court. *In re* Cook & Gleason, 3 *C. L. N.* 410.

9. Under the lien act of Oregon, the lien of a mechanic or materialman, arises from the doing of the work or the furnishing the material, and attached to the building from that time, upon the condition subsequent that the lien creditor file a notice of his intention to hold such lien within three months from the completion of the building. The notice required to be filed does not create the lien, but is necessary to preserve or continue it beyond three months after the completion of the building; and, therefore, the commencement of proceedings in bankruptcy between the doing of the work or furnishing of material and the filing of such notice, does not impair or affect the lien or the right of the lien creditor to continue it by filing the notice. The lien given by the local act to mechanics or materialmen is not opposed to the terms or policy of the bankrupt act, as it in no way prefers one creditor at the expense of another or diminishes the general assets of the debtor, otherwise applicable to the payment of his general creditors. *In re* Coulter, (*Oregon,*) 5 *N. B. R.* 64.

10. Of mortgagees. Mortgage and other liens that have been obtained fairly and in good faith, are recognized and protected by the U. S. bankrupt act of 1867, when the mortgagor or lawful holder thereof conforms to its provisions for the purpose of establishing and realizing upon such security, but he must come into the bankrupt court for his rights under said act, and if the creditor commences proceedings to foreclose he may be restrained by injunction. *In re* Snedaker, (*Utah T.*) 3 *N. B. R.* 155; citing Davis, assignee, *v.* Bittel, 2 *N. B. R.* 125.

11. Of wife. The wife of the owner of an estate subject to a mortgage valid against her, has no rights as against her husband or his assignees in bankruptcy, in the proceeds of sale of the estate made by the mortgagee for breach of condition and under a power in the mortgage deed. Newhall *v.* Lynn Five Cents Savings' Bank, 101 *Mass.* 428.

———

RIGHTS OF ACTION.

1. Vesting in assignees. A right of action for the seduction of the bankrupt's daughter, does not pass to the assignees. Howard *v.* Crowther, 8 *M. & W.* 601; 5 *Jur.* 91. (Eng.)

2. A right of action for damages for the taking of bankrupt's goods on an unfounded claim, by which he was injured in his business, and on account of which his lodgers left him and his customers believes him to be insolvent, does not pass to and vest in his assignees. Brewer *v.* Drew, 11 *M. & W.* 625; 1 *D. & L.* 383; 7 *Jur.* 953; 12 *L. J., Exch.* 448. (Eng.)

3. Where the defendant entered the plaintiff's dwelling house, created a noise and disturbance, damaged the doors, seized the plaintiff's goods and exposed the same for sale without his permission, and thereby greatly annoyed and disturbed his family and prevented him from carrying on his business, and afterwards the plaintiff became bankrupt, *held*, that the primary personal injury to the bankrupt being the principal and essential cause of action, did not pass to and vest in the assignees. Rogers *v.* Spence, (in error,) 12 *C. & F.* 700; s. c. in *Exch. Cham.* 12 *M. & W.* 571; 15 *L. J., Exch.* 49; and in *Exch.* 2 *D., N. S.* 999; 11 *M. & W.* 191; 12 *L. J., Exch.* 252. Affirmed. (Eng.)

4. Where a bankrupt averred that, by the fraudulent representations of the defendant he was induced to pay a sum of money, and sustained great loss, was adjudicated a bankrupt, suffered personal annoyance and was injured in his character and credit, and the defendant pleaded that the loss sustained was pecuniary, and the right to sue passed to his assignees, *held*, that the only damage recoverable was a direct pecuniary loss, the right to sue for which passed to and vested in the assignees. Hodgson *v.* Sidney, 1 *L. R.*, *Exch.* 313; 35 *L. J.*, *Exch.* 182; 14 *W. R.* 923. (Eng.)

5. The right of action for a debt due to the bankrupt is vested upon the death of the assignee in his executor. Richards *v.* Md. Ins. Co. 8 *Cranch*, (*U. S. S. Ct.*) 85.

6. A right of entry, which was vested in a husband and wife in the right of the wife before the husband's bankruptcy, passes to and vests in the assignees. Mitchell *v.* Hughes, 6 *Bing.* 689: 4 *M. & P.* 577. (Eng.)

7. The right of action for unliquidated damages, which have accrued before bankruptcy by the non-performance of a contract, passes to and vests in the assignees. Wright *v.* Fairfield, 2 *B. & Ad.* 727. (Eng.)

8. Where the goods of an under-tenant are seized, under a distress for rent, by the superior landlord, the injury, resulting to the under-tenant from such distress; gives a right of action to the under-tenant's assignees against the lessee, where there is an implied duty on the part of such lessee to indemnify his under-tenant from the consequences of the non-performance of his covenants with the superior landlord, for breach of which an action would lie. Hancock *v.* Coffger, 1 *M. & Scott*, 521; 8 *Bing.* 359. (Eng.)

9. An action of trespass *quare clausum fregit*, is maintainable by a tenant from year to year, who has become bankrupt after the trespass, and before the commencement of the suit; and the right of action does not pass to the assignees, unless they interfere; as the bankrupt may sue as a trustee for, and has a good title against all but them Clark *v.* Calvart, 3 *Moore*, 96; 8 *Taunt.* 742. (Eng.)

10. A bankrupt before his bankruptcy, hired a carriage of M., and let it to the defendant, who returned it to the bankrupt damaged; M., with the consent of the bankrupt, had it repaired and proved the amount due for repairs against the bankrupt. *Held*, that although the bankrupt's estate paid no dividend, still his assignee had a right of action against the defendant for nominal damages. Porter *v.* Vorley, 9 *Bing.* 93; 2 *M. & Scott*, 141. (Eng.)

11. Where a British vice-counsel interfered with and obtained an order of suspension of a suit, theretofore commenced by Y. for the recovery of goods, and Y. afterwards became bankrupt, it was held, that the claim was not for a mere personal wrong, but affected the right of property, and therefore passed to and vested in the assignees. *In re* Young, 12 *W. R.* 537. (Eng.)

12. Where A. agreed to serve two partners and the survivor for a certain specified time and at a fixed salary, and one of the partners became bankrupt, it was held, that as the right of action for damages or penalty under the contract accrued before the bankruptcy, and the damages related rather to the property than to the person, feelings or character of the bankrupt, such right of action passed to and vested in the assignees. Beckham *v.* Drake, (in error,) 2 *H. L.*, *Cas.* 579; 13 *Jur.* 921; 8 *M. & W.* 845; 11 *M. & W.* 315; 7 *Jur.* 204; 12 *L. J.*, *Exch.* 486. (Eng.)

RIGHTS AND DUTIES OF PARTNERS.

1. Where one of two partners becomes bankrupt, the solvent partner may, for a valuable consideration and without fraud, dispose of the partnership effects; and if he afterwards fail, the assignees under a joint commission against both, cannot maintain trover against the *bona fide* vendee of such partnership effects. Fox *v.* Hanbury, *Cowp.* 445. (Eng.)

RIGHT OF DOWER.

1. The widow of a bankrupt where petition in bankruptcy was filed after the act

passed by the legislature of North Carolina repealing the statutory provisions, and restoring the common law right of dower, the bankrupt dying after the issuing of the warrant in bankruptcy, is entitled to dower in the land owned by the bankrupt at the time of the filing of his petition. The act referred to, repealed the statutory provisions in regard to dower which, in effect, restored *eo instanti*, the common law. The legislation by that act attempted to create additional exemptions to those theretofore allowed by law; those exemptions are void as to creditors whose debts were contracted previous to the passage of the act. The widow of a bankrupt is not entitled to the personal property exempted by the provisions of the 14th section of the act of 1867, nor is the assignee in bankruptcy. No title to exempt property passes to the assignee by the assignment; it remains with the bankrupt; on his death it passes to the legal representatives. *In re* Hester, (*N. C.*) 5 *N. B. R.* 46.

2. **Divesting of.** The dower right of the wife of a bankrupt, is not divested by proceedings under U. S. bankrupt act of 1867. *In re* Angier, 4 *N. B. R.* 199.

3. **In suits by husband and wife.** In May, 1863, a *femme sole*, being the owner in her own right of a chose in action, marries and a suit is instituted shortly thereafter to recover from the debtor in the name of the husband and wife. This suit continues pending until 1868, when the husband upon his own petition, was declared a bankrupt, and an assignee was appointed and an assignment executed in the usual form. Thereafter the assignee was, upon his own motion. by order of the court, made party plaintiff, with the wife, and a judgment was recovered in favor of the plaintiffs. *Held*, that the assignee may proceed to enforce the payment of such judgment by execution, and receive the money when collected; if this be done in the lifetime of the husband and wife, and if collected by him must distribute the same to creditors, as the law directs. The assignee is deprived of no right because the bankrupt has failed to schedule such chose in action, nor by the provisions of the constitution of North Carolina, adopted in 1868. *In re* Boyd, (*N. C.*) 5 *N. B. R.*

RULES.

1. **Regulating bankruptcy proceedings.** The justice of the supreme court of the United States subject to the provisions of this act, shall frame general orders for the following purposes : For regulating the practice and procedure of the district courts in bankruptcy and the several forms of petitions, orders, and other proceedings to be used in said courts in all matters under the act; for regulating the duties of the various officers of said courts; for regulating the fees payable and the charges and costs to be allowed except such as are established by this act or by law with respect to all proceedings in bankruptcy before said courts not exceeding the vote of fees now allowed by law for similar services in other proceedings ; for regulating the practice and procedure upon appeals; for regulating the filing, custody and inspection of records, and generally for carrying the provisions of this act into effect. After such general orders shall have been so framed, they or any of them may be rescinded or varied, and other general orders may be framed in manner aforesaid, and all such general orders so framed shall, from time to time, by the justice of the supreme court be reported to Congress, with such suggestions as said justices may think proper. *Sec.* 10 *U. S. bankrupt act*, 1867.

2. **Of course.** The rule to discontinue, on receiving a plea of an insolvent discharge, is not a rule of course. Fifield *v.* Brown, 2 *Cowen*, 503.

SALE.

1. A sale made out of the ordinary course of business is void under the U. S. bankrupt act of 1867, where the purchaser had good reason to believe that the debtors were insolvent. *In re* Kahley, (*Wis.*) 4 *N. B. R.* 124.

2. **Avoidance of.** An attaching creditor cannot avoid a sale and delivery of personal property simply on the ground that they were made with intent to prefer another creditor in violation of the provisions

of the insolvent law. Gardner v. Lane, 9 Allen, (Mass.) 492.

3. By marshal. A sale by the marshal as messenger under a special order of the court prior to the appointment of an assignee is to be considered as in the nature of a sale made by a provisional assignee. In a sale so made of the lease, good will and fixtures of a grocery store, only such things (or their accessories) as are actually or constructively fastened to the freehold, will pass to the purchaser of the fixtures. A purchaser of the fixtures at such a sale may make a claim upon the funds in the hands of the assignee for the sale by the messenger of such articles as were properly included under the sale of the fixtures. In re Hitchings, (E. D. Pa.) 4 N. B. R. 125.

4. The marshal, like a sheriff, can only sell and convey such right or interest in property, as the process in his hands will warrant. In re Jordan, (N. C.) 3 N. B. R. 45.

5. A private transfer or sale by the marshal to a friend of the bankrupt is good in the absence of proof of collusion. Marsh v. Heaton, et al. (Mass.) 2 N. B. R. 66.

6. By sheriff, dissolution of injunction. Where judgments were obtained in good faith against a bankrupt, and levies on executions issued under them were made prior to the filing of his petition in bankruptcy, after which injunctions were granted by the bankruptcy court, which court held on a motion to dissolve them, that as it did not appear that the property levied upon was worth more than the amount of the judgments, nor that a sale by the assignee would realize any more than a sale by the sheriff, and as there was no proof that any advantage would result to any creditor by continuing the injunctions, they must be dissolved. In re Wilbur, (E. D. N. Y.) 3 N. B. R. 71.

7. Costs of. Where a party having an equitable mortgage by deposit of title deeds, with a written memorandum, has lost the memorandum, he will, on his presenting a petition for the usual order for sale, have to pay any costs occasioned by such loss.

Ex parte Rogers, 3 Mont., D. & D. 297 ; 7 Jur. 406. (Eng.)

8. The costs of an application of a mortgagee for leave to bid at the sale will not be allowed out of the proceeds unless the assignees consent. Anon. 3 Mont., D. & D 339. (Eng.)

9. Practice as to costs of equitable mortgagee's petition for sale. Ex parte Barclarg, 5 De G., Mac. & G. 403. (Eng.)

10. Equitable mortgagee, by deposit of shares in a public company without written memorandum, is entitled to his costs on evidence of custom not to give a written memorandum. Ex parte Moss, 3 De G. & S. 299 ; 13 Jur. 866 ; 18 L. J., Bank. 17. (Eng.)

11. A letter written after the deposit, and referring in general terms to it, and to a bond, in which the purpose of the deposit was stated, is a sufficient memorandum to entitle to costs. Ex parte Bisdee, 1 Mont., D. & D. 333. (Eng.)

12. A letter noticing that certain deeds had been deposited to secure a particular debt, together with a subsequent letter requesting further accommodation, on the ground that the depositary held ample security for the amount of the depositor's account, constitutes together a sufficiently definite memorandum in writing of an equitable mortgage for the whole amount due, so as to entitle the depositary to his costs. Ex parte Corlett, 1 Mont., D. & D. 689 ; 5 Jur. 555. (Eng.)

13. Where a legal mortgagee petitions for leave to bid and not for sale, it is not the practice to give him costs. Ex parte Smith, 13 Jur. 1044 ; S. P., ex parte Martelli, 6 Jur. 352. (Eng.)

14. An order was made, with the consent of the mortgagee, of an estate of the bankrupt with a power of sale, that it should be sold in the bankruptcy. A petition was presented by the mortgagee for liberty to bid at the sale, and for payment of the costs of the application out of the purchase money, to which the assignee assented. Held, that he was not entitled to such costs, unless the assignees would state that the petition was presented at their request. *Ex parte* Danks, 12 *L. J., Bank.* 45. (Eng.)

15. Where the mortgagee of a bankrupt's estate called on the commissioner to dirict a sale, under Lord Loughborough's order of March, 1794, and became the purchaser at such sale. *Held*, in an action for money paid, brought by the solicitors to the assignees, that he was liable to reimburse them the expenses of advertisements, and the commissioners for their attendance to perfect such sale, although the estate sold was insufficient to cover the sum originally advanced by such mortgagee. Bowles *v.* Perring, 5 *Moore*, 290; 2 *B. & B.* 457. (Eng.)

16. If a legal mortgage is ordered to be sold, the assignees are entitled to the rents to the time of sale, unless the mortgagee makes an actual entry, or gives notice to the tenants to pay the rents to him. *Ex parte* Living, 2 *Mont. & Ayr.* 223; 1 *Deac.* 1. (Eng.)

17. A bankrupt executed a mortgage with a power of sale, subject to a proviso that the power was not to be exercised for five years, if the interest was regularly paid. *Held*, that the mortgagee might have the common order for sale, with liberty to prove for the residue. *Ex parte* Bignold, 3 *Deac.* 151; 3 *Mont. & Ayr.* 477. (Eng.)

18. Both freehold and leasehold may be included in an order of sale. *Ex parte* Leathes, 3 *Deac. & Chit.* 112. (Eng.)

19. A legal mortgagee obtained the usual order for the sale of the property, previous to which it was arranged between himself and the assignee that he should be placed in the same situation as if he had given notice to the tenants. *Held*, that the mortgagee was, under these circumstances, entitled to the crops growing on the estate at the time of the order of the sale. *Ex parte* Barnes, 3 *Deac.* 223; 3 *Mont. & Ayr.* 497; 2 *Jur.* 329. (Eng.)

20. And to the same rents due since the bankruptcy and to the crops. *Id.*

21. Evidence. Public statements by the owner of property, of his intent and purpose to dispose of it, are competent evidence that a subsequent sale of the property by him was made in good faith and without intent to defraud creditors. The statements of an insolvent debtor, whether made before or after a sale alleged to be fraudulent, as to the value of the property and of his other property, are admissible against his assignee in insolvency to show that the sale was in good faith. Heywood *v.* Reed, 4 *Grays'* (*Mass.*) 574.

22. Fraudulent. A fraudulent sale of property by a bankrupt before the passage of the U. S. bankrupt act of 1867, is void, and will preclude his discharge. *In re* Hussman, (*Ky.*) 2 *N. B. R.* 140.

23. Of bankrupt's estate under act of 1841. Sales of a bankrupt's estate by his assignee in bankruptcy under the late law of the United States, were valid only when authorized by the court of bankruptcy. The conveyances *of land* in which, by the 15th section of that law, the assignee was bound to recite a copy of the decree of bankruptcy, and of the appointment of the assignee, included *transfers of mortgages of land.* Warren *v.* Homestead, 33 *Me. R.* 256.

24. Bankrupt's real estate only passes his title at time of commencement of proceedings. The sale of a bankrupt's right in real estate made by his assignee in bankruptcy, conveys only the right in law and equity which the *bankrupt* had in the land at the *time* of the filing of *his petition* to be decreed a bankrupt. A right which, after the filing of a petition to be decreed a bankrupt, may be yielded to the bankrupt by the waiver of a previous forfeiture, does not pass by the sale in bankruptcy. Kittridge *v.* McLaughlin, 33 *Me. R.* 327.

25. Of exempt property. A marshal cannot sell the property of a debtor that is exempt from levy and sale, both by the state law and the U. S. bankrupt law, although levied on at the time a petition in bankruptcy is filed. *In re* Griffin, (*Ga.*) 2 *N. B. R.* 85.

26. Of goods. Where A. sold goods

to B., by which the latter was to pay by a bill at three months, B. gave a check on his bankers (who were also the bankers of A.), requiring them to pay A. on demand in a bill at three months. A. paid the check to the bankers, and took no 'bill from them; but the amount was transferred in the bankers' books from B.'s account to A.'s, with the knowledge of both. The bankers failed before the checks became due. It was held, that A. could not recover the value of the goods against B. Bolton v. Richard, 6 T. R. 139 ; 1 Esp. 106. (Eng.).

27. A., after having received information of the insolvency of his debtor, accepted a chattel mortgage on his stock, subject to a prior mortgage, and the possession of the latter mortgagee. Debtor, having been declared a bankrupt, the court decided that A.'s mortgage was fraudulent, and could not be paid out of the sale of the goods it purported to convey. In re Palmer, (Wis.) 3 N. B. R. 74.

28. Sale by the vendee of goods purchased with his own promissory note at sixty days, and left in the possession of the vendor, who shows them as the vendee's, is good against one, by the vendor subsequently made, in consequence of the bankruptcy of the vendee, whose vendee may maintain trover for them, as the showing the goods by the vendor operated in favor of a bona fide purchaser as a delivery, and put an end to the transit. Hunn v. Bowne, 2 Caines' Cases, 38.

29. Of goods, giving a preference. If the purchaser of goods sold by an insolvent debtor, with a view to give an unlawful preference, has reasonable cause to believe that such is the intention of the seller, the sale is void, although the benefit of the preference is to enure to a creditor who, by reason of his innocence of the fraud, can retain the payment so made upon his debt. Crafts v. Belden, 99 Mass. Reports, 535.

30. Of goods, when and when not void. A fraudulent sale of goods by a bankrupt to a creditor, in order to keep up his sinking credit, to prefer this one and cheat others, is void. Martin v. Pentress, 4 Burr, 2477. (Eng.)

31. Of goods, when property
GAZ.   99

vested in vendee on. Where the bankrupt bought a parcel of tobacco to be paid for in ready money, and the same day absconded, leaving word at his house to receive the goods, and they were left there without the money having been demanded therefor, it was held, that the sale was complete and vested the property in the bankrupt. Haswell v. Hunt, 5 T. R. 231. (Eng.)

32. Of land, execution of agreement made previous to knowledge of insolvency. If an agreement for the purchase and sale of real estate has been made in good faith, and the purchase money paid, but the giving of the deed postponed merely for the convenience of the parties, the subsequent insolvency of the vendor will not prevent him from conveying a good title to the purchaser by a deed executed before the institution of proceedings in insolvency, although the agent of the latter who received the deed had reason to believe that the vendor was then insolvent. Nickerson v. Baker, 5 Allens' (Mass.) 142.

33. Of leasehold premises. Under 12 & 13 Vict. c. 106, s. 145, a bankrupt's interest in leasehold property remains in the assignees until they elect not to take the demise. Therefore, where assignees allowed a bankrupt to remain in possession of leasehold premises, and pay rent to the lessor, but afterwards sold without his knowledge, held, that the sale was valid. Cartwright v. Glover, 2 Giff. 620; 7 Jur., N. S. 857; 30 L. J., Chanc. 324 ; 9 W. R. 408 ; 3 L. T., N. S. 880. (Eng.)

34. Of lumber. A sale of lumber by an instrument in writing on condition that the vendor may repurchase it at the same price on or before a certain day, is not a mortgage and need not be recorded, and the right of property, as between vendor and purchaser, passes without delivery ; and possession of part, taken by the purchaser, though opposed by the vendor, before notice to the purchaser or publication of notice of proceedings in insolvency, will complete the purchaser's title to all the lumber sold, as against the assignee in insolvency of the vendor, if the lumber sold was not part of a larger lot. Lee v. Kilburn, 3 Gray, (Mass.) 594.

35. Of mortgaged premises. Mortgage creditors have a right to ask that the property mortgaged shall be sold, and the proceeds applied to the payment of their debts, and the assignee on the other hand may contest their claim. *Ex parte* Christy, (*U. S. S. Ct.*) 3 *How.* 292.

36. An injunction will be granted to restrain a mortgagee from selling property of the bankrupt where there is a doubt as to the amount due, and a prospect of making a more advantageous sale. Foster *et al. v.* Ames, (*Mass.*) 2 *N. B. R.* 147.

37. Where no notice of the application to the court for leave to foreclose has been given to the assignee, and no proof is made of the existence of the debt or its amount, to grant permission for a sale without previous proof of the claim, would be to assume as proved the facts upon which the right to the order is dependent. *Held,* that the mortgage debt must be first proved in the usual manner before the register in the bankruptcy proceedings. It must be proved as a secured claim. After thus proven the creditor may, on notice to the assignee, apply to court to have the mortgaged premises sold. *In re* Frizelle, (*Mich.*) 5 *N. B. R.* 119.

38. Of mortgaged property. The district court has power to authorize the sale of mortgaged property discharged of the incumbrances, but such a sale should not be ordered when the substantial rights of the mortgagee will be injuriously affected by it. Dwight *v.* Ames, 2 *N. B. R.* 147.

39. The district court of the United States sitting in bankruptcy had power to decree a sale of the mortgaged property of a bankrupt, and if there are more mortgages than one, and the proceeds of sale are sufficient to discharge the eldest mortgage, the purchaser will hold the property free and clear of all incumbrances arising from the junior mortgage. Houston *v.* City Bank of New Orleans, (*U. S. S. Ct.*) 6 *How.* 486.

40. The district court in bankruptcy may authorize the assignee to sell mortgaged property discharged of the incumbrances, and the mortgagees will then have their liens transferred to the proceeds of sale. The power of this court to order such a sale does not depend on section 25 of the U. S. bankrupt act of 1867, and is not limited to the proviso of that section, but may be exercised notwithstanding the mortgagee asserts a right of immediate possession of the goods, and intends to bring or does bring an action for the recovery of possession. Such a sale however, ought not to be ordered when the substantial rights of the mortgagee are to be thereby injuriously affected. It was the intention of congress to confer on the U. S. district court power to dispose of the incumbered property of the bankrupt in any manner it might in its discretion deem best for the interest of all concerned, and the purchaser will ordinarily, take the property when sold, free from all incumbrances, the lien being transferred from the property to the fund. *In re* Salmon, (*Ga.*) 2 *N. B. R.* 19.

41. A register may be appointed by the bankruptcy court, a special custodian of property which is ad ertised for sale under a mortgage, and be directed to sell the same under general orders 19 and 21, with the authority to make other advertisements than those required by the rules of court. The order should designate the bank in which the money proceeds of the sale shall be deposited, as a separate fund subject to the further orders of the court. The register may also be directed to make the deed to the purchaser, and to convey title under the order of the court, free from certain liens in pursuance to section 20 of the act, and the lien of the mortgage will be transferred from the property so sold to the proceeds of the sale. If advisable in order to obtain a better price for the property, an injunction already granted may be removed or modified, so that a sale may be had under a judgment, and the referee may make out the deed. *In re* Hanna, (*S. D. N. Y.*) 5 *N. B R.* 292.

42. Of necessaries to a firm. A claim for articles delivered to a firm cannot be excepted from the operation of a certificate of discharge in insolvency on the ground that the articles were necessaries actually used in the families of the debtors. Drake *v.* Bailey, 5 *Allen,* (*Mass.*) 210.

43. Of personal property. A colorable sale and transfer of personal property, although void as against the creditors of the vendor, do not amount to an act of bankruptcy within the bankrupt law of the United States, unless executed by a fraudulent deed or conveyance. Livermore, assignee, v. Bagley, 3 *Mass.* 487.

44. Mortgaged personal property must be sold in such a manner as to realize the largest possible amount. *In re* Rosenberg, (*S. D. N. Y.*) 3 *N. B. R.* 33.

45. Of property. When a judgment is taken against one who has taken the benefit of the insolvent laws, after his discharge, and a sale is made of land which was his when he was discharged, under such judgment the sale is only of what interest, if any, that remains in him and the judgment creditor, and not his assignee or trustee, is entitled to the proceeds of the sale. Ebright *v.* The Bank, 1 *Watts' (Pa.) R.* 397.

46. During the pending of an appeal by an equitable mortgagee from a decree of the court, it was agreed between him and the assignees, that the property should be sold, and the proceeds invested by the assignees to abide the result of the appeal, which was accordingly done. Three years elapsed before a final order was made in favor of the mortgagee. It was held, that although he was entitled to the interest made by the assignees from the investment of the proceeds of the sale of the property, he was not entitled to have interest calculated on his debt subsequently to the date of the fiat. *Ex parte* Pollard, 1 *Mont., D. & D.* 264. (Eng.)

47. Of property after commencement of proceedings. A sale by a debtor of his property made by him, after proceedings have been commenced by creditors to have him adjudged a bankrupt, will be valid if the purchaser has acted in good faith and without notice of such proceedings. *In re* Pratt, (*Mo.*) Unreported.

48. Of property, distribution of proceeds. The proceeds of sale by execution of the resulting interest of an insolvent in his assigned estate, under a judgment subsequent to his discharge, go to the execution creditor, and not to the assignor of such debtor for the property of his general creditors. Shaffer *v.* Child, 7 *Metts, Penn. Reports,* 84.

49. Of property not in possession of marshal. The U. S. district court has no power to order the sale of the property as perishable, unless it is in the possession of the marshal. *In re* Metzler & Cowperthwaite, (*S. D. N. Y.*) *N. B. R. Sup.* ix.

50. Of property, pending suit for. Where the assignee had commenced suit in the U. S. district court against lien creditors, the court ordered a sale jointly by the assignee and the referee of certain mortgaged property and the deposit of the proceeds in the treasury of the court, to await the determination of the suit against the said lien creditors. *In re* Columbian Metal Works, (*S. D. N Y.*) 3 *N. B. R.* 18.

51. Of real estate. The jurisdiction of the U. S. district court to sell real estate and pay off liens is not exclusive. *In re* Bowie, (*Md.*) 1 *N. B. R.* 185, citing *Ex parte* Christie, 3 *How.* 292; Norton's assignee *v.* Doyd *et al.* 3 *How.* 434; McLean *v.* Rockey, 3 *McLean's Rep.* 235.

52. Of stock of goods. A sale of a stock of goods not made in the usual and ordinary course of business of the debtor is *prima facie* evidence of fraud, and void by section 35 of the U. S bankrupt act of 1867. *In re* Deane, (*Mo.*) 2 *N. B. R.* 29.

53. The sale of property cannot be ordered until it is in the possession of the marshal. *In re* Metzler, (*S. D. N. Y.*) *N. B. R. Sup.* ix.

54. Where a levy on goods has been made after the filing of a voluntary petition by the debtor, the title being vested in the assignee; he must make sale of such goods and deposit the proceeds subject to whatever claims may be determined by the court to be a lien on the fund. *In re* Pennington & Sale, (*Miss.*) 1 *N. B. R.* 157.

55. On credit. An assignment for the benefit of creditors which directs that the assignees are to convert the assigned estate into money "within such convenient time as to them shall seem meet, and as shall be most conducive to all parties concerned," is bad because it undoubtedly authorizes a sale on credit. Murphy *v.* Bell, 8 *Howard's P. R.* 468,

56. *Contra.* An assignment for the benefit of creditors, which authorizes the assignees to sell and dispose of property upon such terms and conditions as in their judgment shall appear best, &c. *Held,* good, for it merely authorizes the assignees to do what the law imposes upon them as a duty. And a provision which directs that the surplus after paying the preferred debts shall be paid *pro rata* to all the other creditors, does not render the assignment invalid. Southworth *v.* Sheldon, 7 *How· P. R.* 414.

57. A provision in an assignment, authorizing the assignees to take possession of the assigned property "and sell and dispose of the same," upon such terms and conditions as in their judgment may appear best, and most for the interest of the parties concerned, and convert the same into money, does not authorize a sale upon credit, and will not therefore render the assignment void as hindering or delaying creditors. Kellogg *v.* Slawson, 12 *Barb.* 56.

58. Stoppage in transitu. Where goods are forwarded under a contract for their sale with an agreement that if, on arrival, they prove unsatisfactory, they may be returned by the consignee, and a bill of sale thereof is sent by mail and received by him, but he, before he knows of the arrival of the goods, or pays their price or the freight thereon, ascertaining that he is insolvent, executes a bill of sale thereof to the consignor, and delivers it to a third person for him; this operates as a stoppage *in transitu* of the goods, or a refusal to complete the contract of sale; and the assignee in insolvency of the consignee cannot recover the goods or their value from the consignor, nor from such third person claiming under subsequent purchase from him, although such person supposed the bill of sale back to be made by way of preference. Grout *v.* Hill, 4 *Grays'* (*Mass.*) 361.

59. A vendor of cotton in America, by direction of the purchasers in England, shipped the cotton on board a vessel belonging to the latter, who became bankrupt before its arrival. A mortgagee of the ship, who happened to be an agent of the vendor, took possession of the ship under his mortgage, and sold the cotton under·a supposed right, on the part of the principal, to stop it *in transitu,* and the principal sanctioned the transaction, as between himself and his agent, by accepting a credit in account for the proceeds of the cotton. The assignees of the purchaser then brought an action against the mortgagee for the seizure, and he paid them, under a compromise, the amount for which the cotton sold. *Held,* that the contract was not rescinded by seizure of the cotton, but that the vendor was entitled to prove for the purchase money. *In re* Humberston, *De Gex,* 262; 8 *Jur.* 675. (Eng.)

60. When fraudulent. A retention of the possession and use and ostensible ownership of movable property after an absolute voluntary sale is a fraud conclusive and not traversable against *bona fide* creditors. *In re* Hussman, (*Ky.*) 2 *N. B. R.* 140.

61. The title of a second vendee can only be impeached when it is shown that he participated in the fraudulent sale to the first vendee, or if this is not shown then it must appear that he purchased with the knowledge that the sale to the first vendee was fraudulent. The mere fact that the second vendee knew that the vendor had disposed of his entire stock of goods to the first vendee out of the ordinary course of business, will not alone defeat the title of the second vendee to the goods. Babbitt *v.* Walbrun & Co. (*Mo.*) 2 *C. L. N.* 285 ; s. c. 4 *N. B. R.* 30.

62. When not void. A sale made by a person contemplating bankruptcy is not *ipso facto,* void ; but if made out of the usual course of trade, or if it is unusal in the time, place, price, character or quantity of the goods sold, such facts as against the vendee are held to be *prima facie* evidence of fraud. Sales involving all the elements of fraud so far as the vendor is concerned, may still stand on account of the good faith of the vendee. *In re* Hunt, (*R. I.*) 2 *N. B. R.* 166.

63. Without delivery, goods in the reputed ownership of bankrupt. Where a party having goods in his own warehouse at Liverpool sold them and gave to the vendee a warehouse receipt therefor in the words following, "We hold to your order 39 pipes &c., rent free, to the 29th November next." The goods remained unpaid for and in the warehouse up to the time the vendee became bankrupt. In an action of trover by the assignee it was shown to be the usage at Liverpool, that goods for which such warehouse receipts was so given were considered as delivered. It was held, that the bankrupt had not possession of the goods as reputed owner, with the consent of the true owner, within 6 Geo. 4, c. 16, s. 72. Townley *v.* Crump, 4 *A. & E.* 58 ; 5 *N. & M.* 606 ; 1 *H. & W.* 564. (Eng.)

64. Without delivery, goods vesting in and not vesting in assignees. Where wine which had been sold by the bankrupt, remained in the bankrupt's cellar, set apart in a particular bin, and marked with the purchasers seal, and entered in the bankrupt's books as belonging to the purchaser, it was held, that it did not pass to the assignees of the bankrupt as being in his order and disposition. *Ex parte* Marrable, 1 *Glyn & J.* 402. (Eng.)

65. Where farming produce has been purchased and the price paid before bankruptcy, but it appeared to be the custom of farmers to leave such produce upon the farm of the seller until it was convenient for the buyer to take it away, it was held, that this custom exempted such produce from passing to the assignees under the law of reputed ownership. *In re* Terry, 11 *W. R.* 113 ; 7 *L. T., N. S.* 370. (Eng.)

66. Where there was a custom that purchasers of hops should leave them for the purpose of re-sale in the warehouse of the hop merchant, but such custom was not clear, distinct and precise enough to enable others to know that the hops so left were not the property of the hop merchant, it was held, that on the bankruptcy of the hop merchant the hops would pass to his assignees as being in his possession, order and disposition. Thackwaite *v.* Cock, 3 *Taunt.* 487 ; 2 *Rose*, 105 ; see White *v.* Wilks, 5 *Taunt.* 176 ; 1 *Marsh*, 2. (Eng.)

67. A., a spirit merchant, sold to B., a wine merchant, several casks of brandy, some of which, at the time of the sale, were in A.'s own vaults, and others in the vaults of a warehouse keeper. It was agreed between the parties that the brandies snould remain where they were until the vendee could conveniently remove them. Immediately after the sale the vendee marked the several casks with his initials. It was well known among persons engaged in the wine trade at the place where the parties resided, that this sale had taken place, but no notice had been given to the warehouse keeper. A. became bankrupt while the brandies still remained where they were at the time of the purchase. It was held, that all the brandies passed to the assignees of A., as being in his possession, order and disposition, by the consent and permission of the true owner. Knowles *v.* Horsfall, 5 *B.* & *A.* 134. (Eng.)

68. Where A. had been accustomed to draw bills of exchange on consignments made by him to his agent in a foreign country, to be paid out of the proceeds of such consignments, and C. was in the habit of indorsing such bills. After some of the bills so indorsed had been dishonored, C. requested A. to direct his agent, in case he did not pay the drafts, to immediately hand over to C.'s agent enough of A.'s goods to cover the amount of the drafts unpaid. A. agreed to do so, but became bankrupt before the order to transfer the goods reached his agent. It was held, that the bargain between A. & C. did not operate as a legal or equitable assignment of the goods, but that they remained the property of A. at the time of his bankruptcy, and passed to his assignees. Carvalho *v.* Burn, 4 *B. & Ad.* 382 ; 1 *N. & M.* 700 ; s. c. (in error) 4 *N. & M.* 889 ; 1 *A. & E.* 883 ; see s. c. in chancery, 4 *Mylne & C.* 690 ; 3 *Jur.* 1141. (Eng.)

SCAVENGER.

1. *Semble.* That a scavenger is not a trader. *Ex parte* Collins, 1 *Rose*, 373. (Eng.)

SCHEDULES.

1. Money returned in bankrupt's schedules as "cash on hand," must be paid to the assignee in voluntary bankruptcy, or to the marshal as messenger in involuntary cases, and a bankrupt who refuses to do so will be adjudged guilty of contempt. *In re* Dresser, (Me.) 3 *N. B. R.* 138.

2. A creditor who does not appear in person or by duly constituted attorney, and has proved no debt, cannot file a protest against being named as a creditor in bankrupt's schedules. *In re* Altenheim, (*S. D. N. Y.*) *N. B. R. Sup.* xix.

3. In involuntary bankruptcy, if bankrupt is not ready to file his schedules on the return day, there must be an adjournment, or if this is not done, a new warrant must be issued. *In re* Schepeler, (*S. D. N. Y.*) 3 *N. B. R.* 42.

4. Where a debtor files his petition and schedules during the pendency of a creditor's petition upon the adjudication of bankruptcy, the schedules filed with the debtor's petition will be held and regarded as if filed under the adjudication of creditor's petition. *In re* Stewart, (*Texas,*) 3 *N. B. R.* 28.

5. A debt barred by the statute of limitation where the bankrupt resides is not revived by being entered in the bankrupt's schedules. *In re* Kingsley, (*Mass.*) 1 *N. B. R.* 66.

6. A bankrupt must include in his schedules, property belonging to an assignee under an earlier assignment under the laws of the state of his residence. *In re* Beal, (*Mass.*) 2 *N. B. R.* 178.

7. A bankrupt is bound to state upon his schedule the nature of the debt if it be a fiduciary one. Should he omit to do so he would be guilty of a fraud, and his discharge will not avail him, but if a creditor in such case proves his debt and receives a dividend from the estate he is estopped from afterwards saying that his debt was not within the law. Chapman *v.* Forsyth, (*U. S. S. Ct.*) 2 *Howard*, 202.

8. A party who owed another two distinct debts, was discharged as an insolvent debtor, having inserted only one of these debts in his schedule. It was held, that he was not discharged from the other debt and might be sued for it. Leonard *v.* Baker, 15 *M. & W.* 202; 10 *Jur.* 226; 15 *L. J., Exch.* 177; *S. P.*, Tyers *v.* Stunt, 7 *Scott*, 349. (Eng.)

9. The discharge is of no avail to the plaintiff in an action against a set-off, unless he explains the difference between the amount of the debt inserted in his schedules and the amount claimed as set off. Maile *v.* Bays, 2 *D. & S.* 964; 9 *Jur.* 1108; 14 *L. J., Q. B.* 231. (Eng.)

10. An insolvent in his schedule described a debt as being due to "Messrs. Brown & Janson, bankers, 32 Clement's-lane-city." The correct address of Messrs. Brown & Janson was No. 32 Abchurch lane, and the notice of hearing had been duly served at that place. It was held, that though Messrs. Brown & Janson denied having received it, that the description in the schedule was sufficient. Brown *v.* Thompson, 17 *C. B.* 245; 25 *L. J., C. P.* 55. (Eng.)

11. A debtor was protected from paying a bill if he described it substantially in his schedule, though inaccurately as to the amount or length of time for which it was drawn provided such misdescription was not intentional or fraudulent. Booth *v.* Coldman,.1 *El. & El.* 414; 5 *Jur., N. S.* 844; 28 *L. J., Q. B.* 137; *S. P.*, Romillio *v.* Halahan, 1 *B. & S.* 279; 8 *Jur., N. S.* 11; 30 *L. J., Q. B.* 231; 9 *W. R.* 737; 4 *L. T., N. S.* 402; 2 *F. & F.* 418. (Eng.)

12. The final order was only a bar to actions brought in respect of debts mentioned in the schedule. Phillips *v.* Pickford, 1 *L. M. & P.* 134; 9 *C. B.* 459; 14 *Jur.* 272; 19 *L. J., C. P.* 171. (Eng.)

13. It is sufficient if judgment debts due to firms are scheduled in the name of the firm without specifying the individual members thereof. Anon. *N. B. R. Sup.* xxvii.

14. A petitioner is required to use such only of the forms as are appropriate to and descriptive of the debts and property he is required to schedule. Anon. *N. B. R. Sup.* xxvii.

15. Amendment of. Where a bankrupt amended his schedules by inserting the names of creditors (omitted under the impression that their debts were barred by the statute of limitations), the court decided that a new warrant should issue for a first meeting of creditors to choose an assignee. *In re* Perry, (*N. D. N. Y.*) 1 *N. B. R.* 2.

16. Material additions to the bankrupt's schedules of debts or of property are not allowable by way of amendment after the first meeting of creditors, except upon such conditions as may prevent injustice. *In re* Ratcliffe, (*Pa.*) 1 *N. B. R.* 98.

17. A bankrupt may amend his schedules even after the consideration of specifications in opposition to his discharge by order of court. *In re* Preston, (*S. D. N. Y.*) 3 *N. B. R.* 27.

18. A creditor has the right after his claim has been duly proved to ask that petitioner amend any defect in his petition or schedule. *In re* Jones, (*Va.*) 2 *N. B. R.* 20.

19. A debtor's schedules containing the names of several newspapers should be so amended as to show who are the owners of the papers, they being the real creditors. Anon. (*N. D. N. Y.*) 2 *N. B. R.* 53.

20. The application of a bankrupt to amend his schedules is an *ex parte* one and the register is authorized to allow him to do so. *In re* Watts, (*S. D. N. Y.*) 2 *N. B. R.* 145.

21. The sign "do," dots or inverted commas, cannot be used in the schedules by way of reference to indicate anything necessary to be stated. The register may order a bankrupt to amend his schedules, but the order ought to specify the respects in which they are defective. *In re* Orne, (*S. D. N. Y.*) *N. B. R. Sup.* xviii.

22. It is a sufficient statement in the bankrupt's schedules to give the sum and date of the contracting of the debt. Schedules are defective if they do not set forth the separate items of the bankrupt's personal estate, but they may be remedied by amendment at the instance of the bankrupt. *In re* Hill, (*S. D. N. Y.*) *N. B. R. Sup.* iv.

23. Where the bankrupt omitted to include in schedule B. the statement of an interest in an estate in expectancy under a will; the court decided that a discharge must be refused until the schedule was amended, *In re* Connell, (*S. D. N. Y.*) 3 *N. B. R.* 113.

24. The register may allow an amendment to the bankrupt's schedules of property and liabilities when the amendment is uncontested. *In re* Morford, (*S. D. N. Y.*) *N. B. R. Sup.* xlvi.

25. Amendment of — effect of choice of assignee. Where a bankrupt (after an assignee has been chosen), with leave, has amended his schedules so as to include a new creditor it is not necessary to call a new meeting of creditors for the purpose of choosing an assignee. This would be contrary to the spirit and intent of the bankrupt act. The new creditor should receive full notice of the state of the case and he has an opportunity under the U. S. supreme court orders to petition for the removal of the assignee for cause. *In re* Carson, (*S. D. N. Y.*) 5 *N. B. R.* 291.

26. And forms. The several forms specified in the schedules annexed to these orders for the several purposes therein stated, shall be observed and used with such alteration as may be necessary to suit the circumstances of any particular case. In all cases, where, by the provisions of the act, a special order is required to be made in any proceeding, or in any case instituted under the act in a district court of the United States, such order shall be framed by the court to suit the circumstances of the particular case, and the forms hereby prescribed shall be followed as nearly as may be, and so far as the same are applicable to the circumstances requiring such special order. In proceedings in equity, instituted for the purpose of carrying into effect the provisions of the act, or of enforcing the rights and remedies given by it, the rules of the equity practice established by the supreme court of the United States, shall be followed as nearly as may be. In proceedings at law instituted for the same purpose, the rules of the circuit court regulating the practice and procedure in cases at law, shall be followed as nearly as may be. But the court, or the judge thereof, may, by special rule in any case, vary the time allowed for return of process, for appearance and pleading, and for taking testimony and publication, and may otherwise modify the rules for the preparation of any particular case so as to facilitate a speedy hearing. *General Order No. 32, Sup. Ct. U. S.—In bankruptcy.*

27. Description of debt in. As to what is an insufficient description of debt arising on bills of exchange in a particular instance. Symons *v.* May, 6 *Exch.* 707; 20 *L. J., Exch.* 414. (Eng.)

28. Excepted property. An insolvent seeking to except his wearing apparal, bedding, and other necessaries, and his working tools and implements, under the value of 20*l.*, from the operation of 7 & 8 Vict. c. 96, s. 9, must in his schedule have specified each article and its value. Taylor *v.* Roberts, 1 *H. & M.* 96. (Eng.)

29. Under 1 & 2 Vict. c. 110, s. 37, it was not a condition on the non vesting in the assignee of the excepted articles of the insolvent, not exceeding the value of 20*l.*, that those articles should be specified by him in his schedule. Willsmer *v.* Jacklin, 1 *B. & S.* 641; 8 *Jur., N. S.* 96; 31 *L. J., Q. B.* 1.; 10 *W. R.* 12; 5 *L. T., N. S.* 252. (Eng.)

30. Fictitious insertion in. On an indictment against a bankrupt for fraudulently concealing and disposing of goods, and fraudulently omitting transactions and inserting fictitious transactions in his schedules, the jury is to judge of the intent, in such instances, from the general character of the transactions, as disclosed in the whole of the evidence, and to consider whether it indicates a scheme and design on the part of the debtor to obtain the benefit of the bankruptcy law, and relieve himself from his liabilities, without making an honest disclosure and surrender of his property for the benefit of his creditors. Reg. *v.* Manser, 4 *F. & F.* 45. (Eng.)

31. Imperfect. If it be apparent from the papers that the true cause and consideration of the alleged indebtedness of an insolvent debtor to a creditor are not set forth in the schedule annexed to his petition as the statute requires, this is a matter proper for the consideration and determination of the judge who hears the petition. The People *ex rel.* Stryker *v.* Stryker, 24 *Barb.* 649.

32. S. & F. made an assignment for the benefit of creditors, giving preferences according to schedule B. of " all and singular the lands, tenements, &c." situate within the state of New York, and all the goods,

chattels, &c., and property of every name and nature of the said S. & F. more particularly enumerated and described in the schedule hereto annexed, marked "Schedule A," in trust that the assignees should take possession and sell and dispose of the same, upon such terms and conditions as in their judgment they may think meet, &c., " and convert the same into money." The assignment consisted of separate sheets not attached together when it was executed. S. himself drew schedule A, which was on a separate sheet; and there was no evidence that F. ever saw it. Afterwards the several sheets, excepting schedule A, were wafered together, and sent to the clerk's office to be recorded; the attorney who drew the papers still retaining schedule A. After the making of a contract for the sale of the assigned property, by the assignees, and a levy thereon by a creditor, and the commencement of a suit by the purchasers against the sheriff, schedule A. was attached to the assignment. *Held,* that the schedule, containing a specification of the property conveyed would have controlled and limited the general words of the assignment; that such schedule not being annexed, the assignment was insensible, and as against creditors, did not convey the property to the assignees. Moir *et al. v.* Brown, 14 *Barb.* 39.

33. An insolvent debtor inserted a creditor in his schedule, but by mistake and without fraud stated the debt to be 3*l.*, whereas, in fact, it was 7*l.* It was held, that inasmuch as the creditor was thereby deprived of notice to be given to creditors for 5*l.*, and upwards, under 1 & 2 Vict. c. 110, s. 71, this was not a case within the protection of the 3d section, and the debtor's discharge was no bar to an action for this debt. Hoyles *v.* Blore, 14 *M. & L.* 387; 15 *L. J., Exch.* 28. (Eng.)

34. A party having become security for another person to the plaintiffs, became insolvent and obtained his discharge. In the list of creditors in his schedule, he described the plaintiffs as Birchring & Parmeter, brewers, Runham, Norfolk, their names and descriptions being Bircham & Parmeter, brewers, Reepham, Norfolk. Runham is a small village thirty-five miles distant from Reepham, and in another post delivery. The plaintiffs never received any notice whatsoever of the insolvency. It was held, that the inaccuracy was substantial misdescription ; and therefore there was no full and true description of the plaintiffs in the schedules as required by the act, and that the debtor was not discharged from the debt. Bircham v. Walker, 1 *L. T., N. S.* 191. (Eng.)

35. Omissions in. Creditors names omitted from the bankrupt's schedules with their consent does not prevent him from obtaining his discharge. *In re* Needham, (*Mass.*) 2 *N. B. R.* 124.

36. Where a d ed of real estate was made in fraud of creditors, prior to the passage of the bankrupt act, and such estate omitted from the schedule, the fraud upon the act consisted not in making the deed, but in omitting to return the property. Peterson v. Speer, 29 *Penn. R.* 478.

37. An omission by an insolvent debtor of a large proportion of his creditors from his schedule, if not done wilfully and fraudulently, will not of itself avoid a discharge. Williams v. Coggeshall, 11 *Cush.* (*Mass.*) 442.

38. A shareholder in a company, in respect to which a winding up order was made, applied for his discharge in India under the Indian insolvent act, but did not name the company in his schedule. After he had obtained his discharge, his name was placed on the list of contributories, and a call was made. It was held, that his name must be removed from the list, and that he was not liable to the call. *Ex parte* Parbring, 7 *Jur., N. S.* 503 ; 30 *L. J., Chanc.* 513 ; 4 *L. T., N. S.* 62 ; 9 *W. R.* 470. (Eng.)

39. Where a certificate of discharge was duly granted to a bankrupt, and within the limited term of two years, creditors whose debts were provable against the bankrupt's estate applied to have his discharge anulled and set aside on the grounds that he had wilfully sworn falsely in his affidavit annexed to his schedules, and knowing the residence of those creditors and his liability to them, he did not include their names and claims therein. *Held*, that the court finding the act as charged fully proven, and that the

same was a material fact concerning the debt, and that the creditors had no knowledge of the commission thereof until after the granting of the discharge, judgment should be granted in favor of the creditors, and, therefore, the discharge annulled and set aside. *In re* Herrick, (*S. D. N. Y.*) 5 *N. B. R.*

40. Where one who petitioned for protection had omitted a debt from his schedule, with the knowledge and consent and through the contrivance and procurement of the party to whom it was owing, the debt was barred. Wilkin v. Manning, 9 *Exch.* 575 ; 2 *C. L. R.* 573 ; 18 *Jur.* 271 ; 23 *L. J., Exch.* 174. (Eng.)

41. The omission of a creditor's name from the bankrupt's schedules, does not discharge the debt of that creditor, if bankrupt does obtain his discharge. Barnes v. Moore, (*Ohio*,) 2 *N. B. R.* 174.

42. Showing claim makes discharge good. The discharge of an insolvent debtor from a debt in respect of which he had accepted a bill of exchange, was no discharge as to the bills in the hands of a third person, unless the holder's name was inserted in the schedule, or stated therein that he was unknown. Beck v. Beverly, 11 *M. & W.* 745 ; *S. P.,* Lambert v. Smith, 11 *C. B.* 358 ; 2 *L., M. & P.* 446; 28 *L. J., C. P.* 195. (Eng.)

SCHOOLMASTER.

1. A schoolmaster buying books and shoes, and selling them at an advanced price to his scholars, is not a trader. Valentine v Vaughan, *Peake,* 76. (Eng.)

SCRIVENERS.

1. A scrivener within the bankrupt law is one who, with an intention thereby to get a living, receives into his custody other men's money, to be laid out on their account according to the purpose for which it is deposited. The mode of his remuneration, whether by procuration fees, by a charge for commission or otherwise is a circumstance immaterial; the actual deposit of, and complete control over the money of others till invested, and the intention thereby to get a living, being the essence of this species of trading. *Ex parte* Malkin, 2 *Rose*, 27; 2 *Ves. & B.* 31. (Eng.)

2. Again, a scrivener has been held to be a person entrusted with the money of his employer, and who, for commission, finds a borrower. *Ex parte* Bath, 1 *Mont.* 82; *S. P.*, Feo *v.* Allen, 3 *Dougl.* 214. (Eng.)

3. An attorney is not necessarily a scrivener. *Ex parte* Malkin, 2 *Ves. & B.* 175. (Eng.)

4. Unless he has been in the habit of having money deposited with him for the purpose of laying it out on securities. Adams *v.* Malkin, 3 *Camp.* 534; see Hurd *v.* Brydges, *Holt*, 654. (Eng.)

5. An attorney does not become a scrivener, liable to be made a bankrupt by lending the money of clients and charging a procuration fee to the borrowers. Lott *v.* Millville, 3 *N. & G.* 40; 3 *Scott, N. R.* 346; 9 *D. P. C.* 882; 5 *Jur.* 436. (Eng.)

6. A transaction in which an attorney calls in and receives the money of a client, and retains the money in his possession, paying interest to that client upon the amount, is not a trading as a money scrivener. A scrivener is one whose trade is to procure loans for such persons as want to borrow money, and investments for those who wish to lend, who charge procuration fees for his work. But in order to bring him within the statutes, so as to be liable to be a bankrupt, he must be one whose business is (as a general means of obtaining a livelihood) to receive other men's monies or estates, for the purpose of so laying them out in securities. Where an attorney was in the habit of having the money of his clients deposited with him to lay out for them upon mortgage, and received from others a compensation or gratuity for procuring loans of money for them, besides his charge for preparing the mortgage securities, he was held to be a trader as a money broker and a person receiving other men's monies into his trust or custody, whether or not he might be considered liable to the bankrupt law as a banker or scrivener. *Ex parte* Gem, 2 *Mont., D. & D.* 99; 5 *Jur.* 683. (Eng.)

7. A partner in a firm of two solicitors received monies belonging to the sister of the other for investment and in a few instances without any special security having been arranged. The usual charges of an attorney or solicitor were alone made upon the transactions. *Held*, not to amount to trading as a scrivener. *Ex parte* Dufour, 2 *De G., Mac. & G.* 246; 21 *L. J., Bank.* 38; see Hannan *v.* Johnson, 2 *El. & Bl.* 61; 3 *C. & K.* 272; 17 *Jur.* 1096; 22 *L. J., Q. B.* 297. (Eng.)

8. An attorney employed to receive money and pay it to the clients account, paid it to his own, and on the client bringing an action vexatiously defended it, and filed a bill (which was dismissed) to restrain execution. He was afterwards found bankrupt as a scrivener. *Held*, that the conduct of the bankrupt was not conduct as a scrivener so as to be capable of being regarded in reference to the allowance of his certificate. *Ex parte* Spicer, 3 *De G. & S.* 601; 14 *Jur.* 30. (Eng.)

9. On an indictment against an attorney for not surrendering to the fiat. *Held*, that he was liable to be made a bankrupt as a scrivener, it being shown that in one or more instances he had acted as such in procuring loans of and lending other persons' money out on interest, and that one such instance being shown, it might be presumed that he carried on business until the contrary was shown. Reg. *v.* Hughes, 1 *F. & F.* 726. (Eng.)

SECOND BANKRUPTCY.

1. The debtor, on voluntary petition, was adjudicated a bankrupt on the 17th of February, 1868, but neglected to make application for final discharge until the 3d of May, 1869. It appearing to the court that no assets had come to the hands of the assignee, and that the application for discharge was not made within one year from the date of adjudication, his discharge was refused. The debtor afterwards filed a new petition in bankruptcy, and was adjudged a bankrupt, and on motion of the creditors to vacate the adjudication and strike the petition from the file, *held*, that the refusal of the court to grant a discharge upon that ground was no bar to the new proceedings. *In re* Farrell, (*N. J.*) 5 *N. B. R.* 125.

SECOND MEETING OF CREDITORS.

1. And the assignee shall then report, and exhibit to the court and to the creditors, just and true accounts of all his receipts and payments, verified by his oath; and he shall also produce and file vouchers for all payments for which vouchers shall be required by any rule of the court; he shall also submit the schedule of the bankrupt's creditors and property, as amended, duly verified by the bankrupt, and a statement of the whole estate of the bankrupt, as then ascertained, of the property recovered, and of the property outstanding, specifying the cause of its being outstanding, also what debts or claims are yet undetermined, and stating what sum remains in his hands. *Section 27 U. S. bankrupt act,* 1867.

2. Whenever any bankrupt shall apply for his discharge within three months from the date of his being adjudged a bankrupt, under the provisions of the 29th section of the act, the court may direct that the second and third meetings of creditors of said bankrupt, required by the 27th and 28th sections of said act, shall be had on the day which may be fixed in the order of notice for the creditors to appear and show cause why a discharge should not be granted such bankrupt; and the notices of such meeting shall be sufficient if it be added to the notice to show cause, that the second and third meetings of said creditors shall be had before the register upon the same day that cause may be shown against the discharge, or upon some previous day or days. *General Order No. 25, Sup. Ct. U. S.—In Bankruptcy.*

[In the southern district of New York second and third meetings are required only where there are assets. 1 *N. B. R.* 26.]

SECRETING DEBTOR.

1. And if it shall appear that there is probable cause for believing that the debtor is about to leave the district, or to remove or conceal his goods and chattels or his evidence of property, or make any fraudulent conveyance or disposition thereof, the court may issue a warrant to the marshal of the district, commanding him to arrest the alleged bankrupt and him safely keep, unless he shall give bail, to the satisfaction of the court, for his appearance from time to time, as required by the court, until the decision of the court upon the petition, or the further order of the court, and forthwith to take possession provisionally of all the property and effects of the debtor, and safely keep the same until the further order of the court. *Section 40 U. S. bankrupt act,* 1867.

SECURITY.

1. After a valid inspectorship deed had been executed and registered, the court ought not, at the instance of a non-assenting creditor, taking out a trader debtor summons, to require the debtor to enter into a bond for payment of the amount of the debt. *Ex parte* Watson, 35 *L. J., Bank.* 41; 14 *L. T., N. S.* 243. (Eng.)

2. A trader and a firm of traders, having agreed to assist by mutual advances, the following dealings took place between them: The trader delivered to the firm several acceptances and a quantity of wool, and procured bills of exchange, drawn by the firm, to be accepted by strangers, on the trader's indemnity. He also made payments on account of the firm. The firm, on their part, advanced to him cash to the amount of 5,000*l.*, and delivered to him several acceptances, exceeding the amount of the acceptances delivered and procured by the trader, as above mentioned. By a contemporaneous memorandum, signed by the trader, he stated that he had consigned the wool, in consideration of the advance of 5,000*l.*, and that the firm was to be at liberty to sell it, if he should, when called upon, reimburse their advances. The acceptances were chiefly those of strangers. It appeared that the wool was deposited, in pursuance of an agreement, that it was to be a security for all the advances made by the firm, and there was nothing to show that the cash received by the firm upon the discount of the acceptances received by them from and on the indemnity of the trader did not exceed

the cash advance of 5,000*l*. On the affairs of the firm and of the trader being wound up, under arrangements analogous to the bankrupts of law, *held*, that the holders of the bills, delivered by the firm to the trader, were entitled ratably to the proceeds of the wool according to the principle of *ex parte* Waring, 19 *Ves.* 345. *Ex parte* Ackroyd, 3 *De G., F. & J.* 726. (Eng.)

3. M. borrowed money from a company, for which he accepted and gave to them bills of exchange, and deposited shares as a collateral security. When the bills became due, M. wished the loan continued, and the managing director of the company sent him for acceptance fresh bills, with a letter stating them to be in place of those falling due. M. accepted the new set of bills on that footing. After this M. died insolvent, and the company was ordered to be wound up, and was admitted to be utterly insolvent. Both set of bills had been negotiated, and were outstanding. The holders of the first set of bills applied to have such first set paid by means of the deposited shares, on the principle of *ex parte* Waring, 19 *Ves.* 345. *Held*, that *ex parte* Waring did not apply in favor of the holders of the first set of bills, for that the company, after receiving the new bills in place of the old ones, were bound to indemnify M. against the old ones, and had no right to apply his shares in payment of them. *In re* General Rolling Company, *ex parte* Alliance Bank, 4 *L. R., Ch.* 423 ; 38 *L. J., Chanc.* 714. (Eng.)

4. At time of bankruptcy. Judgment was entered up on a warrant of attorney given by two joint traders, and a *fi. fa.* issued returnable on the 2d May. On the first of that month the sheriff's officer received from the defendant the money directed to be levied. On the 2d May, one of them committed an act of bankruptcy, and the other on the 5th. On the 11th a commission of bankruptcy issued ; and on the 19th the sheriff paid over the money to the execution creditor. In an action by the assignees, it was held, that the creditor was entitled to return it, not being a creditor having a security at the time of the bankruptcy. Morland *v.* Pellatt, 8 *B. & C.* 722 ; 2 *M. & R.* 411. (Eng.)

5. Bills as collateral. A. owed B.

217*l.*, and to secure the amount deposited with him bills to the amount of 1,158*l* drawn by A. and accepted by C. A. and C. ; both became bankrupt. *Held*, that B. might prove the full amount of the bills under the fiat against C., but not to receive dividends beyond 227*l*. *Ex parte* Philips, 1 *Mont., D. & D.* 232. (Eng.)

6. By assignee. An assignee chosen by a majority in number and amount of the creditors of a bankrupt, may be required to give reasonable security on application of a creditor in a proper case. *In re* Fernberg, (*S. D. N. Y.*) 2 *N. B. R.* 114.

7. By attachment. A creditor's lien by attachment is good if the attachment was levied more than four month's prior to the commencement of bankruptcy proceedings by or against the debtor. Bowman *v.* Harding, (*Me.*) 4 *N. B. R.* 5.

8. An attachment of property on *mesne* process, is a lien or security on property valid by the laws of this state, and is therefore within s. 2 of the U. S. bankrupt act of 1841, which provides that such lien or security shall not be destroyed or impaired by anything in that act contained. Davenport *v.* Tilton, 10 *Met.* (*Mass.*) 320.

9. By chattel mortgage. A chattel mortgage given to secure the payment of borrowed money, even though part of the consideration was for money loaned sometime previous to the giving of the security, will be held to be valid where no suspicion of complicity or knowledge of insolvency of debtor rests upon mortgagee. *In re* Rosenberg, 3 *N. B. R.* 33.

10. By deed, when not a fraudulent preference. A trader being indebted to the defendant upon a balance of account for goods, and being pressed for payment, as an inducement for forbearance, executed a deed by which he mortgaged to the defendant the public house in which he carried on his business, and assigned to him his trade and other fixtures, with a covenant for payment with interest by instalments, the period of payment extending over several months, and a proviso that, on payment of the instalments, the deed was to be void, but on default the defendant might enter and sell. He continued his business, receiving supplies of goods and advances from the defendant, and making various payments to creditors, until he became bankrupt. It was held, that the deed was not void as a fraudulent preference, for even if made in contemplation of bankruptcy, it was not voluntary, but procured by pressure on the part of the defendant. Hale *v.* Allmitt, 18 *C. B.* 505; 2 *Jur., N. S.* 904; 25 *L. J., C. P.* 267. (Eng.)

11. By delivery of goods, when and when not a fraudulent preference. Where a trader delivered goods as security to the defendant, who was under acceptances for him not yet due, and it appeared that such delivery was not voluntary on the trader's part, but made in consequence of the urgency of the defendant, it is immaterial to consider whether or not the trader had his bankruptcy in contemplation at the time; nor will the transaction, if *bona fide* and not colorable, be impeached by the secrecy with which the delivery was made by the trader, in order to save his own credit in the view of the world. Crosby *v.* Crouch, 11 *East,* 256; 2 *Camp.* 166. (Eng.)

12. By deposit. An agreement was entered into for the purchase of 4,000 tons of iron rails, at 12*l.* 12*s.* 6*d.* per ton, according to a section, to be delivered by the 1st of November, 1846; and 11,500*l.* was to be paid by the purchaser by way of deposit. According to the custom of the trade, this deposit was to be retained by the seller as a security against any damages from the non-performance of the contract. The deposit was paid in bills of exchange. In June, 1846, the purchaser became bankrupt. On the bills becoming due, they were dishonored. *Held,* that the vendors were entitled to prove upon two of the bills remaining in their hands. *Ex parte* Bolckow, 3 *De G. & S.* 656. (Eng.)

13. Where a bankrupt, seven days before his bankruptcy, deposited a bill by way of security with a party, without indorsing it, for a valuable consideration, an order was made that the bankrupt should indorse it, no question being raised as to its being a fraudulent preference. *Ex parte* Rhodes, 2 *Deac.* 394; 3 *Mont. & Ayr.* 207. (Eng.)

14. By garnishee. A garnishee was

ordered under 17 & 18 Vict. c. 125, s. 63, to pay a plaintiff's judgment debt forthwith, or execution to issue. The order was served and payment demanded, but subsequently and before payment or execution, the judgment debtor became bankrupt. *Held,* that the plaintiff was only a creditor having security for his debt within 12 & 13 Vict. c. 125, s. 184; that such security was not such a lien as was protected by the exception in that section, and that he was not entitled to the amount of his judgment debt in the garnishee's hands as against the assignees in bankruptcy of the judgment debtor. Filbury *v.* Brown, 6 *Jur., N. S.* 1151; 9 *W. R.* 147; 3 *L. T., N. S.* 380. (Eng.)

15. By judgment. A confession of judgment given by a debtor as security for borrowed money given before he became insolvent is valid. Judgments obtained against an insolvent debtor by creditors who were not fully aware of his condition are good against his assets. *In re* Wright, (*N. J.*) 2 *N. B. R.* 155; citing Buckingham *v.* McLean, 13 *How.* 150; Merchants' Nat. Bank of Hastings *v.* Truax, 1 *N. B. R.* 141.

16. By mortgage, when void. To render a mortgage void under the 35th section of the bankrupt act, it is not necessary that the debtor knew or believed himself insolvent; the section treats of insolvency as a condition of fact, not of belief, and with knowledge of which and its consequences he is chargeable in law. It follows, as a logical sequence, that when a man insolvent in fact gives a mortgage to one existing creditor, does so with a view to give him a preference. The bankrupt law of 1841 and the Massachusetts insolvent law and decisions commented upon. The act of 1841 declares void preference made by a party *contemplating* bankruptcy; the act of 1867 includes those made by a party *being insolvent,* and the decisions under the former act are not always applicable to the present statute. The question whether the debtor knew or did not know of his insolvency is unimportant in determining as to him, and the purpose of the act being to enforce the equal distribution of the estate. Every act of an insolvent that tends to defeat that purpose should be construed strictly as against him, and courts should indulge every presumption permissible by the well-settled rules of law to secure the full benefit of this cardinal principle of the law. The strict definition of insolvency usually given in commercial centers should not be applied in country places. A party should be held insolvent only when he fails to meet his debts according to the usages and customs of the place of his business; the rule should be in harmony with the general custom of the place. If an insolvent give a mortgage to a creditor who has reasonable cause to believe him insolvent, the fraud upon the bankrupt act is complete as to both. The question as to the creditor is, whether he "had reasonable cause to believe" the debtor insolvent, not what he *did* believe; the latter is immaterial. The creditor is not constituted the sole judge of the sufficiency of the evidence of his debtor's insolvency; that is for the court to determine, the security being attached. Where a debtor had, during two years, paid off only a small portion of an overdue debt, had sold out the stock of goods for which the account was made, and transferred a part of the paper received therefor, had applied for extension and been refused, and had previously declined to execute a mortgage, on the ground that it would injure his credit, and had been pressed by his different creditors — these facts constituted cause for belief of insolvency, and the creditor cannot escape from the consequences of knowledge of them. *In re* Wager & Fales, 5 *N. B. R.* 181, s. c. 3 *C. L. N.* 401.

17. By mortgage deed. An equitable mortgage may be created on deeds in the hands of a third party, and by a memorandum of agreement on the part of the mortgagor to assign his interest in the property comprised in the deeds, and that such assignment, when made, and the agreement, in the meantime, should be a security for the amount due on an account current. *Ex parte* Heathcoate, 2 *Mont., D. & D.* 711. (Eng.)

18. Where a grantee had no reasonable cause to believe that the grantor meditated an actual fraud, or that such a fraud was intended, the court will decree a deed a mortgage, where given to secure the payment of moneys advanced by the grantee to the grantor. *In re* Gaffney's assignee, 5 *N. B. R.*

19. By mortgage only covers certain property. A trader (being solvent) mortgaged his furniture, shop fittings and stock in trade and book debts, for securing a debt due and a new advance. The bankrupt being permitted to have possession of those goods, and being in possession also of other personal chattels to which the creditor's security did not extend, the bankrupt's landlord distrained for rent, not upon the former only, but upon both sets of goods. The person in possession under this distress was requested by the mortgagee, and consented, to hold possession of the goods for him, as well as for the landlord, without prejudice to the landlord's rights. A sale took place under the distress. The goods which were the subject of the distress were not all sold, but they included some of those which were the subject of the mortgagee's security, while the goods to which the security did not extend, remained unsold. A fiat having issued against the mortgagor, the mortgagee petitioned to have his security declared as against the remaining furniture, the stock in trade at present existing and the book debts. *Held,* that the mortgagee's security extended only to such of the furniture, fixtures and stock in trade and property purporting to be in the assignment as were in the house and shop at its date, and remained at the time of the bankruptcy. *Ex parte* Stephenson, 1 *De Gex,* 586; 14 *Jur.* 6; 17 *L. J., Bank.* 5 (Eng.)

20. By mortgage, when not an act of bankruptcy. Where a petitioning creditor alleges in his petition as an act of bankruptcy, that on the 27th day of October, 1870, the debtor made certain transfers of real and personal property, with intent to delay his creditors, and the debtor in his answer (which was supported by the proof) showed that the transfers were by way of mortgages, that both mortgages were given to secure the same sum ($1,080) borrowed by the debtor on the 29th day of October, 1870, from the mortgagee, in order to relieve the debtor's stock in business from a contested attachment, and thus enable the debtor to go on in his business of manufacturing shingles; that the loan was specifically to settle this attachment suit, and also to pay the only overdue paper of the debtor known by the mortgagee to be outstanding, except any such secured paper as the mortgagee already had. *Held,* that as the mortgages were based upon a present consideration, and were neither given nor received with any intent to delay creditors, they did not constitute an act of bankruptcy. Petition dismissed at cost of petitioning creditors. *In re* Sanford, (*Wis.*) 5 *N. B. R.*

21. Collateral. A note executed and delivered by a firm as collateral security for a guarantee, on which the guarantor is still responsible, may be proved against the insolvent estate of the makers. A note executed by a partner in name of his firm, as a substitute for a note of the same amount previously executed by them, and delivered prior to the institution of proceedings in insolvency by the makers, may be proved against their estate, there being nothing to show that in making and delivering the same he exceeded his authority. Moseley *v.* Ames, 5 *Allen,* (*Mass.*) 163.

22. Confession of judgment as. When a debtor confessed a judgment within four months before the filing of the petition against him, being at the time insolvent, and his creditors have reason to believe him to be so, the court decided such confession of judgment was in fraud of the U. S. bankrupt act of 1867, and further that such judgment being taken for the security of several other judgments, regular and valid, and to facilitate their collection does not effect their validity. Vogle *v.* Lathrop, (*Pa.*) 4 *N. B. R.* 146.

23. Double. The rule in bankruptcy that a joint and separate creditor must elect, does not apply to a contract for double security against distinct firms, viz., bills drawn by all the partners upon a distinct firm constituted of some of them ; proof therefore is allowed against both estates. *Ex parte* Adam, 1 *Ves. & B.* 493 ; 2 *Rose,* 36. (Eng.)

24. Where parties are indebted jointly, and enter into a covenant by which they promise on demand jointly and severally to pay, no demand is necessary, in order to entitle the creditor to proceed severally against the parties; but when it was expressly stipulated by three partners, that, until a demand was made, an existing debt should

remain a joint debt, and no demand was made previously to the bankruptcy, the debt is provable against the joint estate, but not against the separate estates of the three. *Ex parte* Fairlie, 1 *Mont.* 17. (Eng.)

25. Where a debt of 27,620*l*. 19*s*. 10*d*. was due from the bankrupts at the bankruptcy to their bankers 'on a balance of account, and such balance was covered by joint promissory notes of the bankrupts, to the extent of 18,000*l*.. and also by mortgage of some property belonging to one of the bankrupts, with joint and several covenants from each of them for the payment of the whole balance ; and part of the debt to the amount of 17,000*l*. had been permitted to be proved by the bankers against the joint estate, on their petition, for the purpose of their commanding the choice of assignees. *Held,* that the bankers were entitled to a proof of the 18,000*l*. against the joint estate, and to prove the residue against the separate estate of one of the bankrupts. *Ex parte* Ladbroke, 2 *Glyn & J.* 81. (Eng.)

26. A creditor, by a joint and several bond, must elect whether he will go against the joint or separate estate ; but is not bound by taking a joint security. *Ex parte* Hay, 15 *Ves.* 14. (Eng.)

27. A joint note of A. and B. is given for goods sold to A. only, and a receipt given as for money paid. A joint commission issued against A. and B. The seller may still prove his debt for goods sold against the separate estate of A. *Ex parte* Seddon, 2 *Cox,* 49. (Eng.)

28. On a separate commission against one of a firm, a joint and separate creditor, who, in respect of his joint debt, has taken a warrant of attorney, and sued out a separate execution against the bankrupt, is entitled to prove his separate debt, without giving up his execution. *Ex parte* Stanborough, 5 *Madd.* 89. (Eng.)

29. B. and C., being indebted to A., gave a joint and several bond ; A. took as part of the same security a joint warrant of attorney, and entered up a joint judgment. B. and C. became bankrupts. *Held,* that the bond was merged in the judgment, and that A. could only prove against the joint estate

of B. and C. *Ex parte* Christie, 2 *Deac.*
& Chit. 155 ; *Mont. & Bligh,* 352. (Eng.)

30. A firm consisting of two persons, D.
& T., carrying on business as D., T. & Co.,
at Liverpool, and of three persons, D., T. &
Y., carrying on business at Pernambuco,
were adjudicated bankrupts, in 1854, at
Liverpool. A creditor of both firms proved
for a debt under this bankruptcy, and received a dividend, after which receipt the
house at Pernambuco also became bankrupt,
and the creditor proved the same debt
against the estate there, and received a dividend in respect of it. In 1861, an order was
made by the commissioner in England, that
the proof in this country should be expunged,
unless the creditor paid to the assignee the
dividend received by him at Pernambuco.
This order was varied by the lords' justices,
who declared that the creditor was not entitled to any dividend in England, except the
first which had received, but without prejudice to any question as to that dividend, or
as to any question under the foreign bankruptcy. The assignees presented a petition
that the creditor might be ordered to refund such first dividend. *Held,* that in the
absence of all evidence to show that the law
of Brazil would not have given the creditor
the right to receive the dividend there, he
was under no obligation as to that which he
received here ; but that, as he had rightfully
received, he was entitled to retain it. *Ex
parte* Smith, 31 *L. J., Bank.* 60 ; 10 *W. R.*
276 ; 6 *L. T., N. S.* 268. (Eng.)

31. Where two of a firm of bankers had
drawn out a balance standing to the account
of customers in the character of executors, and had invested it in the names
of themselves and two trustees, upon an unauthorized security. *Held,* on the bankruptcy of the bankers, not to be a case for
double proof against the joint estate and the
separate estates of the two parties. *Ex
parte* Barnewall, 6 *De. G., Mac. & G.* 795.
(Eng.)

32. For indorsements. A debtor
gave a chattel mortgage upon the fixtures
and tools in his factory to a creditor, which
mortgage recited that said creditor had indorsed notes for him on a promise of security. The condition was, that the bankrupt,
his executors, administrators and assigns,

should, at or before the expiration of nine
months from the date of the mortgage, pay
certain promissory notes, and save the creditor harmless from payment of the same.
One note was then described, and the condition proceeded "and any and all notes given
and indorsed by said creditor for the accommodation of the said bankrupt during the
pendency of this deed." The note described
in the deed, and all other notes given or indorsed within nine months after the date of
the deed, were paid ; but the parties continued in their course of dealing, and there
were outstanding at the time of the bankruptcy of the debtor, notes of like description to a greater amount than the value of
the mortgaged chattels. The court decided
that the mortgage deed secured the notes
made and indorsed after nine months from
its date, and that the notes outstanding at
the time of bankruptcy were thereby secured. *In re* Griffiths, (*Mass.*) 3 *N. B. R.*
179 ; citing Bingham *v.* Jordan, 1 *Allen,*
373 ; Winser *v.* McClellan, 2 *Story ;* Travis
v. Bishop, 13 *Met.* 304.

33. From father to son, not registered. Where M., a trader, engaged in
extensive business, was in embarrassed circumstances, and likely to become bankrupt,
although not suspected from January, 1831,
to January, 1832, when he actually became
bankrupt. Among others, he owed his son
12,000*l.,* which debt, upon his son's marriage, was settled on his son's wife. In
May, 1831, some of M.'s property was released from mortgage, and M. at the request
of his son, on the 1st of July, 1831, conveyed it to trustees under his son's marriage
settlement, as a security for or in discharge
of the debt due from him to his son. The
transfer was not registered or otherwise
made public till after M.'s bankruptcy. A
jury having found that it was not made
voluntarily by way of fraudulent preference,
or in contemplation of bankruptcy, the court
refused to grant a new trial. Belcher *v.*
Prittie, 4 *M. & Scott,* 295 ; 10 *Bing.* 408
(Eng.)

34. Held by creditor. When a creditor has a mortgage or pledge of real or personal property of the bankrupt, or a lien
thereon for securing the payment of a debt
owing to him from the bankrupt, he shall
be admitted as a creditor only for the balance

of the debt after deducting the value of such property, to be ascertained by agreement between him and the assignee, or by a sale thereof, to be made in such manner as the court shall direct. *Section* 20 *U. S. bankrupt act*, 1867.

35. In Kentucky. In Kentucky the creditor obtains a lien upon the property of his debtor by the delivery of a *fi. fa.* to the sheriff, and this lien is as absolute before the levy as it is afterwards; therefore a creditor is not deprived of his lien by an act of bankruptcy on the part of the debtor, committed before the levy is made, but after the execution is in the hands of the sheriff. *Savage's assignee*, (*U. S. S. Ct.*) 3 *How*. 111.

36. Of fees. The fees of the register, marshal and clerk shall be paid or secured in all cases before they shall be compelled to peform the duties required of them by the parties requiring such service; and in the case of witnesses, their fees shall be tendered or paid at the time of the service of the summons or subpœna, and shall include their traveling expenses to and from the place at which they must be summoned to attend. The court may order the whole or such portion of the fees and costs in each case to be paid out of the fund in court in such case, as shall seem just. *General Order No.* 29, *Sup. Ct. U. S.—In bankruptcy.*

37. On appeal bond. A security on an appeal bond under the Georgia code only binds himself for the payment of the debt or damages for which judgment may be entered in the cause; hence, if no judgment is ever entered against the principal in the cause, no liability attaches to security, nor if the principal is discharged in bankruptcy, as a discharge terminates the case pending in a state court, if the debt is a provable one, and prevents any judgment. *Odell v. Wootten* (*Georgia*,) 4 *N. B. R.* 46.

38. On goods at sea. Where the owner of goods on ship board assigned the property to the owner of the ship, to secure a debt, the ship, at the time of the assignment, was abroad, and under the command of the mate; before she arrived in England the owner of the goods committed an act of bankruptcy. It was held, that the goods were virtually in the possession of the

GAZ. 101

owner at the time of the assignment, and that he retained his lien as against the assignees of the bankrupt. *Belcher v.* Oldfield, 8 *Scott*, 231; 6 *Bing., N. C.* 102; 3 *Jur.* 1194. (Eng.)

39. On separate estate of bankrupt. The joint and separate estates in bankruptcy are considered distinct estates. A joint creditor having security on the separate estate may prove against the joint estate, without relinquishing his security; may prove his whole claim against both estates, and be entitled to a dividend from each to an amount equal to the entire claim, but not to exceed that from all sources. *In re Howard, Cole & Co.* (*Md.*) 4 *N. B. R.* 185.

40. Only covers what is subject to its lien. A., an uncertificated bankrupt, having been employed as a manager of one hotel, agreed to purchase the stock and good will from B., who knew of the bankruptcy, and who agreed to lend A. money to purchase stock and other trade effects, but on the understanding that the effects were to be assigned to B. as security for the debt. Accordingly B. lent A. the money, taking A.'s bond for the amount, and the same day A. purchased the effects, and assigned the same as security to B The official assignee knew that A. was carrying on business on his own account, but did not know of the transaction. It was held that the loan, purchase and mortgage were one transaction, and nothing passed to the official assignee except what was subject to the lien. *Kerakorse v.* Brooks, 3 *L. T., N. S.* 712. (Eng.)

41. Out of the ordinary course. Security given to a creditor by mortgage, though out of the usual course of business, will be valid if the creditor was ignorant at the time such security was given of his debtor's insolvency. *In re Lee et al.* 3 *N. B. R.* 53.

42. Postponement of. The owner of a public house agreed to grant a lease of it at a premium. The intended lessee deposited the agreement with M. & Co., brewers, to secure repayment of an advance. The lease was executed, and was deposited by the lessee with the landlord's solicitor, to secure the premium. The lessee obtained it from them for the purpose, as he alleged, of producing it to the magistrate, to enable him to procure a license. He undertook to return it forthwith, but, instead of doing so, he instructed an auctioneer to obtain an advance upon it from other brewers, R. & Co. The auctioneer produced to R. & Co.'s agent an order from the lessee for the delivery of the lease to R. & Co., noticing that the advance was for the purpose of enabling the lessee to pay M. & Co. The agent objected to recognize this memorandum, and inquired whether the lessee owed anything to M. &. Co. He was informed by the lessee's agent that there was nothing due to M. & Co., except for goods supplied. He had previously obtained from the lessee himself an order for the delivery of the lease, not mentioning M. & Co. at all, and he obtained the lease on delivering the order. R. & Co. advanced money in the deposit. *Held,* that their security must be postponed to those of the landlord, and of M. & Co. *Ex parte* Reid 1 *De Gex*, 600; 12 *Jur*. 533; 17 *L. J., Bank.* 19. (Eng.)

43. Present passing. The bankrupt act does not prohibit a person from loaning money at legal rates to one whom he has reason to believe to be insolvent, and taking security for such loan, provided it be made *bona fide* and without any intent or participation in any intent to defraud creditors or defeat the bankrupt act. Advances made in good faith to an indebted person to enable him to carry on his business, upon security taken at the time do not violate either the terms or policy of the bankrupt act, since the debtor gets a present equivalent for the new debt he creates and the security he gives. Darby's trustees *v.* Boatman's Saving Institution, 4 *N. B. R.* 195.

44. Release of. In proceedings for the discharge of an insolvent from his debts, under 2 Revised Statutes, 35, the omission of a petition creditor to relinquish a security held by him, does not affect the jurisdiction of the officer nor avoid the discharge even though his petition discloses the existence of such security. Soule *v.* Chase, 1 *Robb.* 222.

45. A firm in Charleston applied to a firm in Liverpool to raise the necessary funds for the purchase of cotton in America for sale in England, at the risk of certain speculators for whom they acted, and the Liverpool firm applied to an English bank for an advance for that purpose. An arrangement was accordingly made, under which the Charleston firm drew upon an American branch of the bank for the amount required, purchased the cotton, consigned it to the Liverpool firm, drew bills upon that firm, and indorsed them to the bank. At the same time the cotton was consigned to the Liverpool firm who accepted the bills drawn upon them by the Charleston firm, and the bills of lading were indorsed by the Charleston firm, to the bank as security for their advance. Afterwards the Liverpool and Charleston firms became insolvent. The value of the property was insufficient to cover the acceptances of the Liverpool firm. *Held,* that the transaction was a joint adventure of the Charleston and Liverpool firm, and that they were jointly interested in the cotton, and consequently that the bank could prove against the Liverpool firm for the amount advanced without giving up their security. *Ex parte* English and American Bank, 19 *L. T., N. S.* 302; 4 *L. R., Ch.* 49. (Eng.)

46. To an indorser. A partnership note having been indorsed by the payee to a third person, and by him indorsed to and discounted at a bank of which he was president and one of the promisers having afterwards become insolvent, the bank proved the note as a claim against his estate. The solvent promisor afterwards at the urgent request of the second indorser and for the purpose of securing him and the bank, but without the knowledge of the bank, gave him security applicable to the note in question and also to another note held by the bank, such indorser promising to account to the promisor for the surplus of the security, if any. It was held, that the security was not given to the bank but was a personal one to the second indorsee, and to indemnify him as such; and that a subsequent order of the commissioner, on the motion of the assignee, directing the note to be struck out of the list of claims proved, and disallowing the same on the ground that the bank held collateral security therefor which had not been surrendered or applied, was erroneous. Agawam Bank *v.* Morris, 4 *Cush.* (*Mass.*) 99.

47. Void. If the consideration of a contract is partly legal and partly illegal the security is void, but that part of the debt which is upon good consideration may be proved. *Ex parte* Mather, 3 *Ves.* 373. (Eng.)

48. When held by solicitor. A solicitor paid off with his own money a mortgage debt on a client's property, which was thereupon reconveyed to the client. The solicitor took the title deeds by an equitable mortgage, with a written memorandum. Afterwards he induced another client to advance a smaller sum on a proposed mortgage of the property. The money was paid to the solicitor by the second client, and a mortgage was prepared for execution by the first client, who, however, never executed it, nor was aware of the intended security. The title deeds were kept by the solicitor apart from other deeds of the mortgagor, but were not placed in any box of the proposed mortgagee. On the solicitor becoming bankrupt, and the property having been sold by arrangement, it was held, that the second client had a valid security on the property as against the assignees; and that he was entitled to be paid his principal and interest and costs, prior to any claim on the part of the assignees in respect to the residue of the sum secured. *Ex parte* Heitzel, 3 *De G. & J.* 464. (Eng.)

———

SECURITIES.

1. Creditors holding. A security for a separate demand does not extend to a joint demand. *Ex parte* Freen & Morrice, 2 *Glyn & J.* 246. (Eng.)

2. Of bankrupt and others. A creditor has a right to prove and avail himself of all collateral securities from third persons, to the extent of 20*s.* in the pound; therefore, where bills are drawn and accepted by the same persons as constituting distinct firms, proof may be made against the acceptor without deducting the value of a security from the drawer. *Ex parte* Parr, 18 *Ves.* 65; 1 *Rose,* 76. (Eng.)

3. A bankrupt previously to the commission against him, procured persons to assign an interest in the copyhold premises, as a security to a creditor of his. The creditor may prove under the commission without delivering up such security. *Ex parte* Goodman, 3 *Madd.* 373. (Eng.)

4. An obligee of a bond given by a principal and surety for payment by instalments, who has proved against the principal the whole debt, and received a dividend of 2*s.* 7*d.* in the pound, may recover against the surety an instalment due, making a deduction of 2*s.* 7*d.* on the amount of such instalment; and the surety is not entitled to have the whole dividend applied in discharge, but only ratably in part payment of each instalment as it becomes due. Martin *v.* Bucknell, 2 *Rose,* 156; 2 *M. & S.* 39. (Eng.)

5. The holder of a bill may be compelled to prove against the acceptor for the benefit of the drawer. Wright *v.* Simpson, 6 *Ves.* 734. (Eng.)

6. The deduction of a security is never made in bankruptcy, except where it is the property of the bankrupt. *Ex parte* Parr, 1 *Rose,* 76; 18 *Ves.* 65. (Eng.)

7. Security is not to go in reduction of proof, unless the property of the estate against which the proof is ordered. *Ex parte* Adams, 3 *Mont. & Ayr.* 265. (Eng.)

8. A security given by the bankrupt to a creditor on an expectancy as next of kin, in the event of a person dying intestate, must be noticed by the creditor in the proof. *Ex parte* M'Turk, 2 *Deac.* 58; 3 *Mont. & Ayr.* 1. (Eng.)

9. A claim of proof cannot be resisted because the creditor has property belonging to the estate in his possession; that is only a ground to retrain payment of the dividends. *Ex parte* Dobson, 1 *Mont. & Ayr.* 666; 4 *Deac. & Chit.* 69. (Eng.)

10. The mere circumstance of a creditor coming in under the commission to prove or claim a debt, only gives the court jurisdiction as to the proof or claim, and not over any property in his possession, of which he claims the legal ownership. *Id.*

11. A creditor having a joint and several security for his debt, is not entitled to double proof against the joint and separate estates, although his debt is secured by two independent instruments. *Ex parte* Hill, 2 *Deac.* 249. (Eng.)

12. A debt cannot be expunged because a creditor holds a security not disclosed on proving; so doing is an election to abandon his lien thereon. *Ex parte* Rolfe, 3 *Mont. & Ayr.* 305. (Eng.)

13. Where shares in a company stood in separate names of two partners, and the company's deed provided that no shares should be held jointly, but the two partners agreed that the shares should be partnership property, the company cannot prove a joint debt against the partners without deducting the amount of such shares as they hold as security. *Ex parte* Connell, 3 *Mont. & Ayr.* 581; 3 *Deac.* 201. (Eng.)

14. W. & T., partners, being indebted to A. in 10,000*l.* on bills, T. alone assigned to A. certain securities to secure the 10,000*l.*, under which 8,414*l.* was received, on the bankruptcy of W. & T. *Held,* that A. might prove for 10,000*l.*, without deducting the 8,414*l.* from the proof. *Ex parte* Adams, 3 *Mont. & Ayr.* 157. (Eng.)

15. The principle of Lord Eldon's decision in *ex parte* Waring, 19 *Ves.* 345, namely, that where A. & B. are acceptor and drawer of bills of exchange, and property of one comes to the hands of the other, to be held as security against the bills, and then both become bankrupt, the bill holders have a right to have the property applied exclusively, in the first instance, in payment of the bills, is applicable as well to the cases of double insolvency as of double bankruptcy; and the principle is applicable although the property held as an indemnity is not sufficient to pay the bills in full. Powles *v.* Hargreaves, 17 *Jur.* 1083. (Eng.)

16. The general doctrine is, that a creditor holding a security is entitled to apply it in discharge of whatever liability of a bankrupt debtor he may think fit. *Ex parte* Johnson, 3 *De G., Mac. & G.* 218; 22 *L. J., Bank.* 65. (Eng.)

17. Where two firms deal together, one making payments for and accepting bills for the accommodation of the other, and receiving cash and bills for the accommodated firm, by way of payment and security for the outlay and liabilities made and incurred, the question how the proceeds of the bill so remitted are to be applied, must depend on the contract of the parties, expressed or implied. *Id.*

18. Of others than bankrupts. Creditors having securities of third persons to a greater amount than the debt may prove and receive dividends upon the full amount of the securities, to the extent of 20*s.* in the pound upon the actual debt. *Ex parte* Bloxham, 6 *Ves.* 449, 800. (Eng.)

19. A joint creditor, having separate security from one of his codebtors, was admitted to prove his debt against the joint estate, without surrender or sale of his security. *Ex parte* Peacock, 2 *Glyn & J.* 27. (Eng.)

20. N. accepted bills of exchange for 3,069*l.* and 9,431*l.* against goods shipped on his account, which bills, together with bills of lading, were held by a bank. The plaintiffs, at the request of N., obtained the bills of lading from the bank upon guaranteeing to show the payment of the bills of exchange. The cargo having fallen in value, and the plaintiffs having ascertained that the defendants were interested in it to the extent of one-half, the defendants, at their request, signed the following undertaking: "The produce held on account of N., to be sold to the best advantage by the brokers in whose hands it is now placed, and under advice of L. & Co. (the defendants) as far as practicable, and after the current sales are made up, and the amount guaranteed deducted, L. & Co. will bear one-half of whatever loss may appear on the transaction." The plaintiffs paid the bills of exchange, and on the sale of the cargo there was a deficiency of 4,215*l.* N. became bankrupt, and the plaintiffs proved against his estate for the whole loss, and received dividends thereon, amounting to 1,137*l.* *Held,* that the defendants were not entitled to credit for the dividends received from the estate of N. Liverpool Borough Bank *v.* Logan, 5 *H. & N.* 464; 29 *L. J., Exch.* 249. (Eng.)

21. Relinquishment of. An equitable mortgagee of an estate, of which a bankrupt is legally the owner, may prove, without giving up his security, if the estate which is subject to the mortgage, is so encumbered that the bankrupt would have no beneficial interest in it, if the mortgage was removed. *Ex parte* Turner, 3 *Mont., D. & D.* 576. (Eng.)

22. A partnership, consisting of a father and son, was dissolved. The father equitably mortgaged an estate of his own, to secure a debt due from the son separately, and afterwards died indebted jointly with his son, to an amount more than sufficient to exhaust his assets, including the mortgaged estate, even if the mortgage were removed. The estate descended to the son who became bankrupt. *Held*, that the mortgagee might prove and keep his security. *Id.*

23. A creditor, whose debt was secured by the joint and several covenants of two partners in trade, and also by a mortgage on part of the joint property, admitted to prove his debt against the separate estate of each, without surrendering or realizing his mortgage security. *In re* Plummer, 1 *Ph.* 56. (Eng.)

24. One of three partners deposited with a joint creditor a bond belonging to himself, to secure the partnership debt. *Held*, on the bankruptcy of the partners, that the creditor could prove the amount of his debt against the joint estate, without giving up the bond. *Ex parte* Halifax, 1 *Mont., D. & D.* 544. (Eng.)

25. A creditor, to whom a bankrupt has made an assignment, to secure a debt with interest, cannot, with giving up the security, prove upon a promissory note, part of the consideration for which consists of arrears of interest upon the secured debt. *Ex parte* Clark, 1 *Mont., D. & D.* 622. (Eng.)

26. Where a bankrupt and his wife executed a power of appointment of the wife's estate to a creditor as a security for a debt due from the bankrupt. *Held*, that the creditor might prove for the whole debt without giving up the security, it being incumbent on him, however, to recover what he could from the bankrupt's estate before he resorted to the property of the wife. *Ex*

parte Hedderley, 2 *Mont., D. & D.* 487 (Eng.)

27. Where parties have proved their debts on the footing of holding no security, they will not generally be permitted to withdraw their proof and set up a security; but ignorance of the existence of a security may be ground for granting relief to a party who has so proved. Grugeon *v.* Gerrard, 4 *Y. & C.* 119. (Eng.)

28. A creditor who has obtained an order for sale of a security, with liberty to prove for the deficiency, cannot afterwards abandon that order, and claim to prove for his whole debt, retaining his security, although the order may not have been acted on, and he was not aware of his rights when the order was obtained. *Ex parte* Davenport, 1 *Mont., D. & D.* 313. (Eng.)

29. A. and B., copartners, executed a mortgage upon their joint property, for securing payment of a sum of money due by them to C., and by the mortgage deed they entered into a joint and several covenant for payment of the debt to C. Upon the bankruptcy of A. and B., *held*, that C. was entitled to prove his debt against the separate estates of A. and B. respectively without giving up his joint security. *Ex parte* Sheppard, 3 *Jur.* 1147. (Eng.)

30. A composition creditor, who receives an assignment of a debt as a security for the composition, is not, when the old debt revives, entitled to retain the debt on a question of proof. *Ex parte* Ellis, 2 *Mont. & Ayr.* 370. (Eng.)

31. If a creditor, who has an additional security for his debt, takes the bankrupt's acceptances, it is his duty when he proves the debt, to state that fact; and where a creditor had not done so, the proof was ordered to be expunged, with liberty for him to go again before the commissioners and tender his proof. *Ex parte* Hossack, *Buck,* 390. (Eng.)

32. Separate creditors who had taken a joint security permitted, on giving it up, to resort under a commission of bankruptcy to their original debts. *Ex parte* Lobb, 7 *Ves* 598. (Eng.)

33. Proof is equivalent to payment; therefore, where solicitors obtained an order to have their bill taxed, and to prove for the amount, *held*, that they had relinquished their lien upon the papers in their hands belonging to the bankrupt. *Ex parte* Hornby, *Buck*, 351. (Eng.)

34. A creditor, who has obtained goods of his debtor, just before bankruptcy, cannot prove for the residue without accounting for the goods so obtained. *Ex parte* Smith, 3 *Bro.*, *C. C.* 46. (Eng.)

35. Sale of. No permission should be granted to creditors to sell securities, which they may hold until their right to do so is shown in the manner prescribed in the 22d section of the U. S. bankrupt act of 1867. *In re* Bigelow, (*E. D. N. Y.*) 1 *N. B. R.* 186.

36. Surrender of. The payment of a dividend in bankruptcy is not the payment of the debt, except as against the debtor himself, and confers no right on the bankrupt or his assignee to call upon the creditor to surrender any collateral securities. Ewart *v.* Latta, 4 *Macy, H. L. Cas.* 983. (Eng.)

37. With respect to discharge. Where one creditor signs a petition for annulling the discharge of the bankrupt only on the guarantee of the defendant, it was held, in an action on the guarantee, that the same was not in contravention of 12 & 13 Vict. c. 106, s. 268, and was not fraudulent. Smith *v.* Saltzmann, 9 *Exch.* 535 ; 23 *L. J., Exch.* 177. (Eng.)

38. A guarantee for the payment of goods to be supplied to a bankrupt by a creditor, given with intent to persuade the creditor to sign the certificate was void by 6 Geo. 4, c. 16, s. 125. Hankey *v.* Cobb, 1 *G. & D.* 47; 1 *Q. B.* 490; 5 *Jur.* 891. (Eng.)

39. A security given by a bankrupt to a creditor, with intent to persuade such creditor to forbear opposing the granting of the bankrupt's certificate, was only void as between the immediate parties to it, under 12 & 13 Vict. c. 106, s. 202; in the hands of a *bona fide* indorsee for value, it was an avail-

able instrument. Goldsmid *v.* Hampton, 5 *C. B., N. S.* 94; 4 *Jur.*, *N. S.* 1108; 27 *L. J., C. P.* 286. (Eng.)

40. The repeal of section 202 of 12 & 13 Vict. c. 106, by 24 & 25 Vict. c. 134, does not make available, even in the hands of a *bona fide* holder for value, without notice, a negotiable instrument declared void by the repealed section, where the indorsement was made and the instrument became due after the latter act went into operation. Reeves *v.* Hawkes, 6 *L. T., N. S.* 53. (Eng.)

41. A contract or security made or given in trust for a creditor for securing the payment of money due by a bankrupt, as a consideration or with intent to persuade him to forbear opposing the final examination of the bankrupt, was not rendered void by 12 & 13 Vict. c. 106, s. 202. Taylor *v.* Wilson, 5 *Exch.* 251; 14 *Jur.* 366; 19 *L. J., Exch.* 241. (Eng.)

SEIZURE.

1. By marshal. Where the warrant to a marshal transcends the power conferred in a United States district court by section 40 of the U. S. bankrupt act of 1867, property taken possession of by a marshal from a person other than the bankrupt, cannot be held by the assignee in bankruptcy. Such property, or its proceeds, is the proper subject of a petition by the person from whom it is taken, and such person will not be held to be a party to the bankruptcy proceedings. Upon filing a petition for the restitution of the property, the proceeds or the property must be given to the person from whose hands the marshal made an improper seizure. *In re* Harthill, (*S. D. N. Y.*) 4 *N. B. R.* 131.

2. Of property. Where personal property has been fraudulently assigned by the bankrupt, the court may assume the custody of it on a summary application, but will not do so where the vendees have purchased in good faith, and are able to respond to an adverse judgment at the suit of the assignee. *In re* Hunt, 2 *N. B. R.* 166 ; s. c. 1 *C. L. N.* 169.

3. The messenger is to enter and seize, at his own hazard, the property of the bankrupt; but if he enters the house and seize the property of another, acting under authority, he cannot be turned out, but the party must take his remedy at law. Obstructing a messenger in the execution of his warrant is a contempt. *Ex parte* Page, 1 *Rose*, 1; 17 *Ves*. 59. (Eng.)

SEPARATE ASSETS.

1. How divided. The assignee shall be chosen by the creditors of the company, and shall also keep separate accounts of the joint stock or property of the copartnership, and of the separate estate of each member thereof. And, after deducting out of the whole amount received by such assignee the whole of the expenses and disbursements, the net proceeds of the joint stock shall be appropriated to pay the creditors of the copartnership, and the net proceeds of the separate estate of each partner shall be appropriated to pay his separate creditors. And if there shall be any balance of the separate estate of any partner, after the payment of his separate debts, such balance shall be added to the joint stock for the payment of the joint creditors. And if there shall be any balance of the joint stock after payment of the joint debts, such balance shall be divided and appropriated to and among the separate estates of the several partners, according to their respective right and interest therein, and as it would have been if the partnership had been dissolved without any bankruptcy. And the sum so appropriated to the separate estate of each partner shall be applied to the payment of his separate debts. *Section 36 U. S. bankrupt act*, 1867.

SEPARATE DEBT.

1. Judgment of outlawry against two or three joint debtors does not make the debt a separate one, as against the third debtor, and it cannot be proved under his separate commission. *Ex parte* Dunlop, *Buck*, 253. (Eng.)

2. Of copartner. In order to entitle a creditor to prove on the joint estate of a partnership firm, for a debt which was originally the separate debt of one of the partners, there must be either a positive agreement to adopt the debt as that of the firm, or facts from which the court will be justified in deducing an agreement or consent to the adoption. It is not sufficient that the money lent to one partner has been ultimately applied to the purpose of the firm. *In re* Ferras, 2 *Jur.*, *Chan. Rep.* 11. (Eng.)

SEPARATE ESTATE.

1. Where a bank held notes of a firm indorsed by the individual members thereof, the court decided that the bank had a right to dividends against the joint and separate estates of the bankrupts, according as its interest might be proven. *In re* Mead assignee, (*N. D. N. Y.*) 2 *N. B. R.* 65; citing *ex parte* Brown, 1 *Atkins*, 225; *ex parte* Emrly, 1 *Rose*, 61; Marwick, 8 *Boston Law R.* 169; Colling & Son *v.* Hood, 3 *McLean*, 186, 188; Ingall's case, 5 *Boston Law R.* 401.

2. In bankruptcy the joint and separate estates are considered as distinct estates. A joint creditor having security on the separate estate, may prove against the joint estate without relinquishing his security, may prove his whole claim against both estates and recover a dividend from each,' but so as not to receive more than the full amount of his debt from both sources. *In re* Howard, Cole & Co. 4 *N. B. R.* 185.

3. Claim against. When a party files his proof of debt for the same amount against two members of the same firm, the claims stand as proven, and the motion of the assignee that the claims be stricken from the list will be overruled, and the claim must stand allowing the creditors to prove their claims against the separate estates of each partner. *In re* Beers *et al.* (*Ohio*,) 5 *N. B. R.*

SEPARATE LIABILITY.

1. Discharge of. A New York house accepted bills for the accommodation of a Virginia house, on an agreement for reimbursement, entered into by a London merchant, the correspondent of the Virginia house. Afterwards the London merchant entered into partnership, and by letter desired the New York house to consider all credits, advices and instructions then in force from him, as extending to the new firm. The New York house replied that they would make up and transfer to the new firm the open accounts in joint exchange transactions, but that they hoped to have the account current made up before they carried the old account to the new firm. They afterwards paid the accommodation bills and drew on the new firm for the amount. The new firm became bankrupt. *Held*, that under the circumstances, the separate liability was discharged, and that the New York house were only joint creditors. *Ex parte* Jackson, 2 *Mont., D. & D*. 146. (Eng.)

SEQUESTRATION.

1. A sequestration issued by a judgment creditor of a beneficied clergyman, who became bankrupt, is entitled to a priority over a subsequent sequestration issued by his assignees under the bankruptcy, notwithstanding that the first of such sequestration was not published until after the commission of the act of bankruptcy, Hopkins *v.* Clark, 4 *B. & S.* 836; 10 *Jur., N. S.* 439; 33 *L. J., Q. B.* 93; 12 *W. R.* 370; affirmed on appeal, 5 *B. & S.* 753; 10 *Jur., N. S.* 1071; 33 *L. J., Q. B.* 334; 12 *W. R.* 1029. (Eng.)

SERVICE.

1. Notice of petition. Where notice of the petition had been served on the attorney in the suit, the plaintiff, the creditor residing *out of the state*. *Held*, that the service was sufficient. *In re* Williamson, *Coleman's Cases*, 64; Coleman & Caines' *Cases*, 174.

2. Of order. A judgment creditor, H., having by leave of a judge proceeded against a garnishee, who was an auctioneer, and P. sent him goods for sale for ready money, not to be recovered until payment. The auctioneer sold them on those terms, stated in the conditions of sale, and received part

of the price from some of the purchasers; but H., who had purchased part, took them away without payment, and without the consent of the auctioneer or of P. H. refused to pay, offering to set off a debt due to him from P.; this was declined. A. having obtained judgment against P., obtained an order to attach the price of the goods remaining in the auctioneer's hands, under 17 & 18 Vict. c. 125, s. 61, which was served on the garnishee. On the same day, but after the service, P. became bankrupt. His assignees claimed the money from the garnishee, and also demanded payment from A. of the price of the goods taken away by him. *Held*, that the service of the order bound the debt, so as to render the judgment creditor a creditor having security for his debt, within 12 & 13 Vict. c. 106, s. 184, but did not give a lien, so as to bring him within the exception in that section; and, consequently, that the judgment creditor could not prevail against the assignees. Holmes *v.* Tutton, 5 *El. & Bl.* 65; 1 *Jur., N. S.* 975; 24 *L. J., Q. B.* 346. (Eng.)

3. Of notice. The notice provided by the 18th section of the act, shall be served by the marshal, or his deputy, and notices to the creditors of the time and place of meeting provided by the section, shall be given through the mail by letter, signed by the clerk of the court. Every envelope containing a notice sent by the clerk or messenger shall have printed on it a direction to the postmaster at the place to which it is sent, to return the same within ten days unless called for. *General Order No. 53, Sup. Ct. U. S.—In bankruptcy.*

4. Of papers. If such debtor cannot be found, or his place of residence ascertained, service shall be made by publication, in such manner as the judge may direct. *Section 40, U. S. bankrupt act*, 1867.

5. Of petition. A non-trader, much indebted, left the realm, and an order had been made under the English bankruptcy act of 1861, s. 70, for service of a petition for adjudication on him abroad. His solicitor, with whom he was in communication was present when the order was made, but gave no information, and declined to accept service. The petitioner sent a clerk abroad, who was unable to find and serve the debtor. Service of the petition was then ordered to be made on the solicitor, and the debtor was thereupon adjudged bankrupt. *Held*, that, under the circumstances, the adjudication was good. *In re* Calthrop, 3 *L. R., Ch.* 252; 37 *L. J., Bank.* 17; 18 *L. T., N. S.* 166; 16 *W. R.* 446. (Eng.)

6. Of petition and order to show cause. The fortieth section of the bankrupt act does not intend that if the debtor "cannot be found" within the district where the proceedings are pending, or have been commenced, that the marshal as messenger, even if cognizant of the whereabouts of the debtor, without the district shall then prove him absent to effect service, such service is invalid. *In re* Alabama & Chattanooga R. R. Co., 5 *N. B. B.* 97.

SERVICES OF COUNSEL.

1. Services rendered by counsel, in proceedings to obtain an adjudication of bankruptcy, will not in general be allowed out of the bankrupt's estate. *In re* N. Y. Mail Steamship Co. (*S. D. N. Y.*) 2 *N. B. R.* 137.

SET-OFFS.

1. A creditor of an insolvent is not entitled to a set-off in an action brought by the insolvent debtors' factor for goods sold to the creditor. Borwood *v.* Pelosi, 2 *Dallas' Pa. Rep.* 43.

2. A commission of bankruptcy is legal notice to affect the subsequent assignee of a promissory note with the stated right of set-off. Humphries *v.* Blight, assignee, 4 *Dallas' Pa. Rep.* 370.

3. In an action by an assignee of an insolvent debtor, on a debt due to the insolvent; debts due and payable from the insolvent more than six years before the commencement of the action, but less than six years before the commencement of the proceedings in insolvency may be set off. Parker *v.* Sanborn, 7 *Grays' (Mass.)* 191.

GAZ. 102

4. A right of set-off between an insolvent debtor and his creditor accrues at the time of the first publication of the notice of the insolvency, and the account is to be stated, and the balance ascertained as of that day. Demmon *v.* Boylston Bank, 5 *Cushing, (Mass.)* 194.

5. Where B., a debtor of an insolvent, who has assigned all his estate to his trustees, for the benefit of his creditors, purchased a promissory note of the insolvent's after the assignment, it was held, that B could not set off the note purchased by him against a debt due by him to the insolvent, in a suit brought by the trustees. Johnson *v.* Bloodgood, 1 *Johnson*, 51.

6. In an action by assignees of a bankrupt, for money due their bankrupt as supercargo, the defendant cannot set off a claim against the bankrupt for not keeping his vessel fully insured, the same being then unliquidated. Brown *v.* Carning, 2 *Caines' Cases*, 33.

7. And mutual debts and credits. Where A. before executing a deed of inspectorship, which was afterwards registered, deposited bills of exchange with a bank for collection when due, and the authority to collect and receive the money on the bills remained unrevoked up to the execution of such deed, *held*, that there was a credit given by A. to the bank within the meaning of the mutual credit clause of the English bankrupt act of 1849, s. 171; and that the bank, therefore, was entitled to set off the amount collected on such bills against a debt due from A. to the bank. Naoroji *v.* Chartered Bank of India, Australia and China, 37 *L. J., C. P.* 221; 16 *W. R.* 791; 3 *L. R., C. P.* 444; 18 *L. T., N. S.* 358. (Eng.)

8. An executor proving against the estate of a bankrupt for a debt due to his testator's estate extinguishes the debt as effectually as if due to him in his own right; he cannot, therefore, set it off against a claim of the bankrupt to a share in the residuary estate of the testator. Stammers *v.* Elliott, 37 *L. J., Chanc.* 353; 3 *L. R., Ch.* 195; 18 *L. T., N. S.* 1; 16 *W. R.* 489. (Eng.)

9. A. sued B., C. and D. on a joint debt.

They pleaded a set-off. A. replied that before plea D. had become bankrupt. *Held*, a good replication. New Quebrada Company *v.* Carr, 4 *L. R.*, *C. P.* 651; 38 *L. J.*, *C. P.* 283; 17 *W. R.* 859. (Eng.)

10. A shareholder of a company in course of winding up, being also a creditor of the company, assigned his estate and effeets to trustees for his creditors. *Held*, that inasmuch as a set-off of mutual credits was allowed by the English bankruptcy law act of 1849, though n..t allowed in respect of calls by the companies' act of 1862, the court of chancery sitting as the court of appeal in bankruptcy, was bound to allow the claim upon the company to be set off against the calls. *In re* Duckworth, *ex parte* Cooper, 36 *L. J.*, *Bank.* 28; 2 *L. R.*, *Ch.* 578; 15 *W. R.* 858; 16 *L. T.*, *N. S.* 580. (Eng.)

11. The defendants accepted two bills of exchange drawn by J. & Co., who undertook to provide funds before maturity, and as collateral security deposited with the defendants cotton, coffee, and certain bills of exchange. The defendants discounted away the bills so deposited, and obtained the assent of J. & Co. to their selling the goods and receiving the proceeds, and acted thereon. But after the cotton was sold, and before the coffee was sold, J. & Co. became bankrupt. The proceeds of the deposited goods and bills left a balance in the hands of the defendants after payment of the two bills accepted by them, but a larger balance was owing by J. & Co. to the defendants on other matters. The assignees in bankruptcy of J. & Co. brought an action to recover the balance of the proceeds of the deposited bills and goods. *Held*, that they were not entitled to succeed, inasmuch as the only question was whether at the time of the bankruptcy of J. & Co. there was such a mutual credit between them and the defendants as to entitle the latter to retain the proceeds of the coffee against the larger balance owing to them, and that after the arrangement authorizing the sale of the cotton and coffee, there was such a mutual credit. Astley *v.* Gurney, 38 *L. J.*, *C. P.* 357; 4 *L. R.*, *C. P.* 714; 18 *W. R.* 44. (Eng.)

12. Where a bank holds a protested acceptance of one of its regular depositors and he has a balance to his credit in the bank, which the bank applies as a credit on the protested acceptance, and the depositor within a month afterwards is adjudged a bankrupt. *Held*, that the bank has a right to set off the amount of the draft against the deposit, thereby reducing the amount of the draft, and that the bank should not pay over to the assignee the amount of said deposit. *In re* Petrie *et al.* (*S. D. N. Y.*) 5 *N. B. R.*

13. **Balance in bank.** If the maker of a promissory note, which has been discounted at a bank, becomes insolvent, having money on deposit in such bank, the amount of the note may be set off against the amount of the deposit, and the balance only of the latter paid to the assignees, provided the note is due absolutely, although not payable until afterwards. Demmon *v.* Boylston Bank, 5 *Cush.* (*Mass.*) 194.

14. **Plea of.** To an action by assignees of a bankrupt for 48*l.*, the price of phæton which the defendant had purchased from the plaintiffs for cash on delivery, the defendant pleaded that before and at the time of the delivery of the phæton and of the bankruptcy, the bankrupt was indebted to the defendant in 48*l.* upon a bill of exchange drawn by Elves and accepted by the bankrupt, payable to Harland, indorsed to the defendant; the plaintiffs replied that the bankrupts had accepted the bill for a debt due from him to Harland, and that after the bill became due and was dishonored, Harland indorsed it to the defendant without consideration, in order that the defendant might purchase the phæton, setting off the amount of the bill, and then hand over the phæton to Harland. It was held, that the replication was a good answer to the claim of set-off. Lackington *v.* Combes, 8 *Scott*, 312; 6 *Bing.*, *N. C.* 71. (Eng.)

15. In an action by the assignees of a bankrupt to recover the price of machinery supplied by the bankrupt, the court allowed the defendant to plead an equitable plea of set-off for unliquidated damages arising out of the same contract. Makeham *v.* Crow, 18 *C. B.*, *N. S.* 847. (Eng.)

16. A plea of mutual credit by way of set-off, cannot be pleaded to a declaration by

assignees, charging the defendant with having received a sum of money from the bankrupt for the purpose of meeting an acceptance, and neglecting so to apply it, whereby the bankrupt's estate sustained damage, the claim being for unliquidated damages. Bell v Carey, 8 C. B. 887; 19 L. J., C. P. 103. (Eng.)

17. A plea of set-off to an action by assignees of a bankrupt must show that it is pleaded to a debt to which it is strictly applicable. Groom v. Mealey, 2 Scott, 171; 2 Bing., N. C. 138; 1 Hodges, 212; see Wood v. Smith, 4 M. & W. 522. (Eng.)

18. To an action by a trustee of a Scotch bankrupt for money received by the defendant for the use of the plaintiff as trustee, after the bankruptcy, and for interest upon money due from the defendant to the plaintiff as trustee, foreborne to the defendant at his request, it is good defence that there were mutual credits between the bankrupt and the defendant, and that by the Scotch law, the trustee is only entitled to sue for the balance. Macfarlane v. Norris, 2 B. & S. 783; 3 L. J., Q. B. 245; 6 L. T., N. S. 492; 9 Jur., N. S. 374. (Eng.)

19. In an action by assignees, it is not sufficient proof of a set-off that the commissioners permitted the defendant to prove the debt proposed to be set off. Pirie v. Mennett, 3 Camp. 279; 1 Rose, 359. (Eng.)

20. What and what not allowed as. Where a bankrupt, on the eve of bankruptcy, fraudulently delivers goods to one of his creditors, the assignees may disaffirm the contract, and recover the value of the goods in trover, but if they bring assumpsit, they affirm the contract and then the creditor may set off his debt. Smith v. Hodson, 4 T. R. 211. (Eng.)

21. Where A. first purchased one and afterwards another parcel of goods of B., each on a six months' credit when the first sum was due, he left with B. a bill of exchange for a larger amount than the value of the goods, in order to pay for them, B. agreeing to return to A. the overplus when he was paid the bill. B. received the amount of the bill and then A. became bankrupt, not having paid for the second parcel. It was held, in

an action by A.'s assignees, that B. might retain such overplus to satisfy his demand for the second parcel of goods. Atkinson v. Elliott, 7 T. R. 378. (Eng.)

22. A tradesman undertook to do work upon an article delivered to him, for a person to whom he was indebted, and it was agreed that the work should be paid for in ready money. He afterwards became bankrupt. It was held, that the assignees were not liable in trover for refusing to deliver such article to the creditor on his offering to set off the price of the work against his own demand. Clark v. Fell, 4 B. & Ad. 404; 1 N. & M. 244. (Eng.)

23. An agreement for a lease of a mill provided that the machinery of the mill at the commencement and expiration of the tenancy should be valued, and the increase or diminution in value paid by the lessor or lessee, as the case might be. The lessee became bankrupt, having improved the machinery. The assignees elected not to continue the tenancy, and the value of the improvements were ascertained. It was held, that against this amount the landlord might set off the rent, and also a demand for goods sold and delivered. Ex parte Hanson, 3 De G. & J., 92; 4 Jur. N. S. 464; 27 L. J., Bank. 40. (Eng.)

24. A. & Co., merchants at Liverpool, remitted a bill to B. & Co. in London, with directions to get it discounted, and apply the proceeds in a particular way. B. & Co. did not have it discounted, but received the money when it became due. Before that time, A. & Co. had stopped payment, and desired to have the bill returned to them. A commission of bankruptcy was issued against them before the money was received on the bill of B. & Co. It was held, that the latter were liable to be sued for the amount by the assignees of A. & Co. for money received to their use; and that B. & Co. could not set off a debt due to them from A. & Co. Buchanan v. Findley, 9 B. & C. 738; 4 M. & R. 593. (Eng.)

25. A creditor of a partnership having made further advances on the security of a bill deposited with him for that purpose by the partners, and having undertaken to receive the amount when due and return the

surplus, the bill having been discharged and remaining in his hands unpaid, is not entitled, on the bankruptcy of the partners, to set off his prior advances against a demand by the assignees of the bill. *Ex parte* Flint, 1 *Swans.* 30. (Eng.)

26. The defendants were the holders of a bill of exchange, accepted by M., for 760*l.*, which was indorsed to them by the commercial bank of Scotland, and they were also the acceptors of a bill drawn by the commercial bank in favor of M. The former bill became due on the 6th of January, and was dishonored, M. having stopped payment. On the 7th, the defendants debited the commercial bank in their account with the 760*l.*, and wrote a receipt on the back of the bill, and returned it protested to the commercial bank. The latter, hearing of the failure of M., on the 6th wrote to the defendants, requesting them to keep the 760*l.* bill, and set off the amount against the 1,000*l.*, their acceptance, which would become due on the 12th. In an action by the assignees of M., who had become bankrupt, against the defendants, as acceptors of the 1,000*l.* bill, it was held, that they were not entitled to set off the 760*l.* Belcher *v.* Lloyd, 3 *M. & Scott,* 822. (Eng.)

27. Where a regimental agent, under authority of a power of attorney from the colonel, had received monies from the paymaster-general of the forces and then became bankrupt, it was held, in an action by the assignees for goods sold and delivered by the agent for the use of the regiment, that the colonel might set off the money, which the agent had received from the paymaster-general remaining unaccounted for, in reduction of the demand. Knowles *v.* Maitland, 6 *D. & R.* 312; 4 *B. & C.* 173. (Eng.)

28. Where bankers receive pay, money on account of a bankrupt, after notice of an act of bankruptcy, all the sums received are to the use of the estate; and they cannot set off the payments made, or be allowed to come in as creditors, and claim dividends on debts paid, which were owing before the act of bankruptcy. Hankey *v.* Vernon, 3 *Bro., C. C.* 313. (Eng.)

29. In an action by assignees of a bankrupt, the defendant is entitled to set off a debt due to him from the bankrupt, if when he gave credit to the bankrupt, he had no notice of a prior act of bankruptcy, though he had notice that the bankrupt had stopped payment. Hawkins *v.* Whitten, 5 *M. & R.* 219; 10 *B. & C.* 217. (Eng.)

30. Where a person indebted to his sister became a bankrupt, shortly afterwards the sister made her will, and thereby gave certain sums to trustees and executors, as pecuniary provisions for the benefit of the bankrupt, in a form apparently intended to exclude the claims of creditors. She never proved her debt against the bankrupt's estate, and died before he obtained his certificate. On a bill in equity by the assignee against her executors for payment of the money bequeathed for the use of the bankrupt, it was held, that the executors were not entitled to set off the amount of the unproved debt against the demand of the assignees. Cherry *v.* Boultbee, 4 *Mylne & C.* 422. (Eng.)

31. Where assignees brought an action of trover to recover a policy of insurance, the defendent pleaded a custom for insurance brokers to have a general lien upon policies of insurance in their possession for their general balance; that mutual dealings and accounts existed between the bankrupt and the defendant, and that at the time of the conversion the bankrupt was indebted to the defendant in 200*l.* Replication, that the 200*l.* was the price of goods sold to the bankrupt upon twelve month's credit, and that a bill of exchange was drawn and accepted in payment, which bill was not due at the time of the conversion. It was held, first that by taking the security the lien was gone; secondly, that the defendant could not rest his defence upon 6 Geo. 4, c. 16, s. 50, without specially pleading the facts; thirdly, that if the plea of mutual credits was set up, then it could not succeed, because it did not appear that the balance was due at the time of the bankruptcy. Hewison *v.* Gutherie, 2 *Hodge,* 51; 2 *Bing., N. C.* 755; 3 *Scott,* 298. (Eng.)

32. Where D. and another purchased goods of two London houses, and shipped them upon speculation to a foreign port in the name of C., and not wishing to appear as principles in the transaction, represented

to the London houses, and to the consignees abroad, that C. was the principal, and that they acted merely as his agents; and after the shipment, the London houses made advances to D. and his partner, as agents of C. on account of the goods, the proceeds of which remained in the hands of the consignees abroad; and C. also advanced money to D. and his partner, who afterwards became bankrupts, and at the date of the commission were indebted to C. for such advances. It was held, in an action by the assignees for money had and received, that C. had a right to retain the proceeds of the goods as a set-off for money advanced to the bankrupts, it being a case of mutual credit. Easum *v.* Cato, 1 *D. & R.* 530; 5 *B. & A.* 860. (Eng.)

33. Though in general after bankruptcy an assignment cannot be taken of a debt of the bankrupt, in order to set it off against a debt due the bankrupt, yet if such assignment is taken in consequence of any arrangement for that purpose made before the bankruptcy, or by reason of any equity, to have such assignment arising from matters, which have occurred before the bankruptcy, then a set-off will be allowed in respect to the debt so assigned. So a surety before bankruptcy, paying off the debt of the principal after bankruptcy, and taking an assignment of securities, among which is a security of the bankrupt, is entitled to set it off against a debt due from him to the bankrupt. *Ex parte* Barrett, 13 *W. R.* 559; 34 *L. J., Bank.* 41. (Eng.)

34. Where a policy to a broker acting under a *del credere* commission was underwritten by the bankrupt, and a loss upon the policy happens before the bankruptcy, the broker may deduct the amount of the loss from the debt which he owes to the bankrupt's estate. Bize *v.* Dickason, 1 *T. R.* 285. (Eng.)

35. Where assignees bring an action for a debt due to the bankrupt's estate, the defendant may set off notes in his possession issued by the bankrupt before his bankruptcy. Moore *v.* Wright, 2 *Rose,* 470; 2 *Marsh,* 209; 6 *Taunt.* 517. (Eng.)

36. Where there are cross acceptances and the right of set-off clear, the court of

bankruptcy will restrain the assignees from bringing an action. *Ex parte* Clegg, 1 *Mont. & Ayr.* 91; 3 *Deac. & Chit.* 505. (Eng.)

37. If a debtor of the bankrupt's estate obtains a bill with the bankrupt's name upon it, which he knows forms no demand upon the estate, after notice of the bankrupt's insolvency, and with a view to a set-off, he is not a *bona fide* holder. *Ex parte* Stone, 1 *Glyn & J.* 191. (Eng.)

38. Acceptances not due till after the bankruptcy of the acceptor, may be set off. *Ex parte* Wagstaff, 13 *Ves.* 65. (Eng.)

39. Where, previously to October 24th, 1842, the defendants, who were bankers, had discounted bills to a large amount for certain customers, who had become bankrupts on that day, at which time the defendants had in their hands a balance belonging to the bankrupts. The bills were indorsed by the bankrupts in blank, and two of them were paid by the acceptors before the bankruptcy; the others far exceeded the amount of the balance in the defendants' hands, did not become due till the 16th of November and on other subsequent days. The action, which was for money lent, was commenced on the 2d of November; and on the 8th of the same month, the defendants proved against the bankrupt's estate the whole of the bills, except the two which had been paid, deducting the balance in their hands. It was held, that the defendants, as indorsers of the bills, were entitled to set them off in the action. Alsager *v.* Currie, 12 *M. & W.* 751; 13 *L. J., Exch.* 203. (Eng.)

40. Where bankers advanced to C. 500*l.* on his promissory note, and subsequently, without notice to him, deposited the same, with other securities, with W. & Co. as security for a debt. The bankers having become bankrupt, W. & Co. compelled C. to pay them the amount due on his note. Prior to the bankruptcy C. had obtained possession of bank and interest notes of the bankers to an amount more than sufficient to have paid the amount due on his promissory note. Credit was given to the assignees of the bankrupt by W. & Co. for the amount paid to them by C., and the assignees having paid them the balance of

their debt, they delivered over o them the securities then in their hands, which were more than sufficient to secure them the repayment of their debt. It was held, that C. was entitled to set off against the amount due on his note a sufficient portion of bank and interest notes of the bankrupts in his hands and to prove the balance due on such notes against the estate. *Ex parte* Staddon, 3 *Mont., D. & D.* 256; 7 *Jur.* 358; 12 *L. J., Bank.* 39. (Eng.)

41. In an action by assignees to recover the value of goods sold and delivered to the defendants by the bankrupt, the defendants cannot set off the bankrupt's acceptance, which they do not hold in their own right, but in effect for other persons. Fair *v.* McIver, 16 *East*, 130. (Eng.)

42. In an action by assignees of a bankrupt underwriter against insurance brokers for premiums due to the bankrupt, the brokers are entitled to set off, by reason of mutual credit, a loss which occurred before the bankruptcy upon a policy underwritten by the bankrupt and effected by the brokers in their own name, for a principal for whom they were acting on a *del credere* commission. Lee *v.* Bullen, 4 *Jur. N. S.*, 557; 27 *L. J. B.* 161; 8 *El. & Bl.* 692 *n.* (Eng.)

43. Where insurance brokers effected several policies of insurance, some in the name and on account of their own firm, others in the name of their own firm but on account of principals, and others in the name and on account of their principals, for which principals they acted under a *del credere* commission, without the knowledge of the underwriters, it was held, that in an action against them for premiums by the assignees of one of the underwriters upon those policies, who had become bankrupt, the brokers might set off losses and returns due on all of those policies which were effected in the name of their own firm, but not on such as were effected in the names of their principals, such losses and returns having become due on those policies before the time when the bankrupt stopped payment, though they had not been adjusted by the bankrupt, but only by the other underwriters, between the time of his stopping payment and committing an act of bankruptcy, on

which adjustment the brokers had given their principals credit for the amount. Koster *v.* Eason, 2 *M. & S.* 112. (Eng.)

44. A party has a right to set off notes of a firm of bankers, taken by him after he knew that they had stopped payment, but before he knew that either of the partners had committed an act of bankruptcy; but he is not entitled to set off notes of such bankers, taken by him after he knew that either of the partners of the bank had committed an act of bankruptcy. Dixon *v.* Cass, 1 *B. & Ad.* 343. (Eng.)

45. P. & Co., having borrowed a large sum from the bank of Bengal, deposited company's paper with the bank to a greater amount, as a collateral security, accompanied with a written agreement authorizing the bank, in default of non-payment by a given day, " to sell the company's paper for the disbursement of the bank, rendering to P. & Co. any surplus." Before default P. & Co. were declared insolvents, under the Indian insolvent act, 9 Geo. 4, c. 73. At the time of the adjudication of insolvency the bank were holders of two promissory notes of P. & Co., which they had discounted for them before the loan. The time for repayment having expired, the bank sold the company's paper, the proceeds of which, after satisfying the principal and interest, produced a considerable surplus. In an action by the assignees of P. & Co. against the bank, to recover the surplus, it was held, that the bank could not set off the two promissory notes, and that the case did not come within the mutual credit clause in bankruptcy act. Young *v.* Bank of Bengal, 1 *Moore, P. C. C.* 150; 1 *Deac.* 622. (Eng.)

46. In October, 1825, G. applied to the bankrupt to discount the note, and took as part payment the proceeds of a bill accepted by the bankrupt, payable to G.'s order. G. indorsed this bill for value to the defendant, and he got it discounted by H., who was the holder when it became due. A commission of bankruptcy issued against the bankrupt on the 23d December, and the bill became due on the 24th, when it was presented and dishonored. On the 26th, H. received the amount from the defendant, and returned the bill to him. It was held, that he

had a right to set off the bill against the demand of the assignees on the note. Collins v. Jones, 10 B. & C. 777. (Eng.)

47. An insurance broker who is indebted to the assignees of a bankrupt underwriter for premiums, cannot, without an especial authority, set off against that debt sums due from the underwriter for returns of premium, whether the returns became due before the bankruptcy or after the bankruptcy. Minett v. Forrester, 4 Taunt. 541. (Eng.)

48. Although a discharge did not operate as a complete extinguishment of a scheduled debt, the creditor was not entitled to plead such debt by way of set-off to an action against him by the insolvent for a demand accruing subsequently to his discharge. Francis v. Dodsworth, 4 C. B. 202; 17 L. J., C. P. 185. (Eng.)

49. Where the defendant kept cash with M. & W., bankers, and accepted a bill drawn by one of the partners in the house, and indorsed by the partner to the house, who discounted and afterwards indorsed it for value to S. Before the bill became due M. & W. had become bankrupts, having funds in the hands of S. more than sufficient to meet the bill, and having in their hands money belonging to the defendant. When the bill became due, S. presented it for payment to the defendant, who having refused to pay, S. paid himself out of the funds of M. & W. remaining in his hands, and delivered the bill to their assignees. It was held, in an action by the assignees against the defendant as acceptor of the bill, that there had been before the bankruptcy a mutual credit between the bankrupt and the defendant, and that the latter was entitled to set off against the sum due to the bankrupts on the bill, the debt due to him by them at the time of their bankruptcy. Rolland v. Nash, 8 B. & C. 105; 2 M. & R. 189 (Eng.)

50. A debt from a bankrupt to a married woman dum sola cannot be set off against a debt from her husband to the bankrupt. Ex parte Blagden, 19 Ves. 465. (Eng.)

51. Set-off is allowed of a separate debt due from the estate against the joint debt

due to it, and liberty given to prove the balance. Ex parte Hanson, 12 Ves. 346. (Eng.).

52. A., on entering into partnership with B., applied to his bankers for a loan, to constitute his capital. They consented, upon a condition that B. joined in a security for the repayment of the loan, which was complied with. The partnership opened an account with the bankers, who also continued the private bankers of A. On the bankruptcy of the bankers, the balance on the joint account, arising from this loan, was against A. and B., but A.'s private account was in his favor. A. and B. were allowed to set off this private balance against the joint debt, it being but a security for the separate debt. A. and B., soon after the partnership commenced, took in another partner, but it was understood that the account with the bankers was to continue as before. The new partner drew checks in the firm name, and paid them into his private accounts. The assignees were held not to be entitled to charge the checks so transferred against the partnership account. Ex parte Hanson, 18 Ves. 233; 1 Rose, 156. (Eng.)

53. debtor, by bond to the separate estate of a deceased partner, is not allowed in equity to set off his bond debt, in respect to acceptances for which he had become liable to the partnership estate, and which were proved by him under a joint commission of bankruptcy. Addis v. Knight, 2 Mer. 117. (Eng.)

54. Part owners of a ship cannot set off their proportions of a debt due to the bankrupt on that account against debts due by the bankrupt to them individually. Ex parte Christie, 10 Ves. 105. (Eng.)

55. The debt of the bankrupt to one partner is allowed to be set off against the joint debt of him and his partner on their bond to secure the separate debt of the former. Ex parte Hanson, 18 Ves. 233; 1 Rose, 156. (Eng.)

56. A building society borrowed a sum of money from its bankers, upon a joint and several promissory note of two of its trustees and a director. The bankers, at the time of their bankruptcy, held the note, and

there was also a balance in their hands, to the credit of the society upon a current account. It was held, that the society was entitled to set off the amount of the balance against the sum due upon the note. *Ex parte* Clennel, 9 *W. R.* 380; s. c. nom. *In re* Penfold, 4 *L. T., N. S.* 6. (Eng.)

57. Under a separate commission, relief in the nature of a set-off was refused to a separate creditor of the bankrupt, indebted to the partnership in a greater amount. *Ex parte* Twogood, 11 *Ves.* 517. (Eng.)

58. An underwriter cannot set off, as a mutual credit, against a loss accruing after bankruptcy of the assured, premiums of the same and other policies due before the bankruptcy from the assured, who was himself his own insurance broker in effecting those policies. Neither can he set off returns of premiums upon voyages not complete before the bankruptcy, although the underwriter must, upon the conclusion of the adventure, necessarily become debtor to the assured, either for a loss or a return of premium. Glennie *v.* Edmunds, 4 *Taunt.* 775. (Eng.)

59. Where, under an agreement, the plaintiffs and defendants were jointly entitled to the benefits of a charter party and the plaintiffs assigned their interest in it, by indorsement to D., their creditor, at the same time giving the defendant notice of the assignment and afterwards became bankrupt. The assignees of the charter party having sued on it in the names of the plaintiffs, the defendants pleaded the bankruptcy of the plaintiffs, by which the right to their choses in action vested in their assignees in bankruptcy. Replication setting forth the assignment by the plaintiffs of their interest in the charter party to D., and notice to the defendants of that assignment given by them before the bankruptcy of the plaintiffs, and that the plaintiffs sued on account of D. Rejoinder setting up the previous agreement between the plaintiffs and defendants, to share the benefits of the charter party, by way of a mutual credit between the parties, on which an account should be stated and one demand set off against the other. It was held bad in substance, for at the time of the bankruptcy no mutual credit existed between the plaintiffs and defendants. Boyd *v.* Mangles, 16 *M. & W.* 337. (Eng.)

60. A., B. & C., traders in partnership, were indebted to H. in 51,981*l.* 12*s.* Upon the dissolution of the firm, it was found C., the retiring partner, was indebted to the firm in 6,817*l.* 9*s.* 6*d.*, supposing all the debts of the firm (including that of H.) to be paid; whereupon it was agreed between them that C. should pay to A. & B. the 6,817*l.* 9*s.* 6*d.*, and should assign to them all the assets and effects of the firm, they undertaking to pay the partnership debts. A. & B. subsequently becoming bankrupts, leaving unpaid the debts due to H., a balance of 47,000*l.* It was held, that C.'s liability to H. did not constitute a debt or mutual credit, which could be set off under 6 Geo. 4, c. 16, s. 50 in an action by the assignees of A. & B. against him for the recovery of the 6,817*l.* 9*s.* 6*d.* due from him to the firm. Abbott *v.* Hicks, 7 *Scott*, 715; 5 *Bing. N. C.* 578; 3 *Jur.* 871. (Eng.)

61. The defendant advanced the money to purchase a string of pearls on joint account of himself and C., and agreed that the profit and loss thereon should be equally divided, C. paying his share of interest till the pearls were sold. C. being indebted to the defendant at the time became bankrupt. The pearls were afterwards sold, and the money received by the defendant. In an action by the assignees of C., for his share of the money received, it was held, that the defendant was entitled to set off the debt due from C. to himself, this being a case of mutual credit within 5 Geo. 2, c. 30, s. 28. French *v.* Fenn, 3 *Dougl* 257. (Eng.)

62. The defendant pleaded to a declaration by assignees for goods sold and delivered by the bankrupt that, before notice of any act of bankruptcy, and before the issuing of the fiat, and before action, the defendant gave credit to the bankrupt, by accepting bills of exchange for his accommodation, without any consideration or value, which bills were, before notice of the bankruptcy, negotiated by the bankrupt for his own use and benefit; that the credits so given were likely to end in debts from the bankrupt to the defendant, and that afterwards and before action, the defendant paid the bills. It was held, a good set-off, under 6 Geo. 4, c. 16, s. 50, on the ground that a mutual credit was shown. Russell *v.* Bell, 8 *M. & W.* 277 · 1 *D. N. S.* 107. (Eng.)

63. A declaration by assignees, that, in consideration that R. before his bankruptcy would sell goods to the defendant, the defendant agreed to pay for them prompt two months or by an acceptance ; containing an averment of delivery of the goods, and of the defendant's refusal to pay by an acceptance or otherwise, whereby R., before he became bankrupt, was deprived of the use and benefit of the acceptance, and of the benefit which would have resulted from discounting the acceptance, and was put to great loss and inconvenience, and his estate applicable to the discharge of his just debts was, by reason of the non-payment of the goods, much diminished in value, does not sound in unliquidated damages so as to deprive the defendant of his set-off. *Groom v. West,* 1 *P. & D.* 19; 8 *A. & E.* 758 ; 2 *Jur.* 940; 8 *L. J., Q. B.* 25. (Eng.)

64. A defendant may set off a debt due to him from a bankrupt for money lent against a claim by the bankrupt's assignees on him for not accepting pursuant to agreement, a bill of exchange by way of part payment for goods sold and delivered by the bankrupt to himself. *Gibson v. Bell,* 1 *Scott,* 712; 1 *Bing., N. C.* 743 ; 1 *Hodges,* 136. (Eng.)

65. Where an action was brought by the assignees of S., a bankrupt, for money had and received to the use of the assignees since bankruptcy. The plea was, that before the bankruptcy, and before notice of any act of bankruptcy, the defendant gave credit to the bankrupt to the amount of 50*l.*, by indorsing for his accommodation, and without consideration, a bill of exchange for that amount, drawn by him and payable to the bankrupt's order, and that such credit was of a nature extremely likely to end in a debt. The plea then alleged that the amount of the bill was paid by the defendant on its dishonor after the bankruptcy, but before the commencement of the action; and the bankrupt thereupon became indebted to the defendant; that before the bankruptcy, S. drew a bill of exchange on a bank, and delivered it to the defendant by way of loan, that he might raise the amount, and thereby give credit to the defendant to that amount; and that afterwards, before the bankruptcy, the defendant obtained the amount of the bill from the bank, and that he was ready

and willing to set off the two sums against each other. It was held, that the plea showed such a giving of credit to the bankrupt within the 6 Geo. 4, c. 16, s. 50, as might be the subject of a set-off in an action brought by the assignees. Hulme *v.* Muggleston, 3 *M. & W.* 31; 6 *D., P. C.* 112; *M. & H.* 344. (Eng.)

66. The defendant, in consideration of having received A.'s acceptance 'for 20*l.*, undertook to indorse to A. a bill drawn by the defendant on E., payable to the defendant's order. He gave the bill, but would not indorse it. On an action by the assignees of A., who had become bankrupt, and whose acceptance was dishonored, it was held, that the contract to indorse was not a subject of mutual credit within 6 Geo. 4, c. 16, s. 50, and could not have been set off by the assignees against the 20*l.* due from A. to the defendant. Rose *v.* Sims, 1 *B. & Ad.* 521. (Eng.)

67. The defendant being indebted for money lent to them by their bankers, who afterwards became bankrupt, received from their customers on the day of stoppage of payment by the bankers, but without notice of an act of bankruptcy, certain notes of the bankrupts in part payment of antecedent debts, on condition of debiting themselves with so much only as they should receive from the assignees on the notes. They also received from other parties other notes of the bankrupts for which they were to pay so much only as they should receive from the assignees for such notes. An action for for money loaned having been brought by the assignees of the bankrupts against the defendants, it was held, that the defendants had a beneficial interest in the first description of notes, and might therefore set them off, but that they could not set off the second description of notes, as they held them merely as trustees for others. Foster *v.* Wilson, 12 *M. & W.* 191; 13 *L. J.,* *Exch.* 209. (Eng.)

68. Where three partners delivered bills to D. for a special purpose. Two of the partners became bankrupts. In an action by their assignees against D. for the proceeds of the bill, it was held, that one of the partners not having been made, this was not a case of mutual credits, within 5 Geo. 2, c

30, s. 28, so as to entitle the defendant to set off the bills against a debt due to him from the partners. Stainforth *v.* Fellows, 1 *Marsh,* 184; 2 *Rose,* 151. (Eng.)

69. Where brokers effected policies on goods on account of their principals, in their own names, and accepted bills on account of the goods which were consigned to them and lost before arrival. It was held, that they might set off such losses in an action by the assignees of the underwriter for premiums, although they had not any *del credere* commission, and the losses were not adjusted. Parker *v.* Beasley, 2 *M. & S.* 423. (Eng.)

70. A broker, who is indebted to assignees for premiums due to them upon policies subscribed by the bankrupt before his bankruptcy, is not entitled to set off returns of premium due upon the arrival of ships which have arrived since bankruptcy. Goldschmidt *v.* Lyon, 4 *Taunt.* 534. (Eng.)

SETTING ASIDE ADJUDICATION OF BANKRUPTCY.

1. There is no party to a creditor's petition except the petitioning creditor and the bankrupt. An injunction may be served under it on any person or number of persons, but such service does not make them parties to the proceedings there. Any one served may himself, upon motion or by petition, have a wrongful injunction dissolved, but he would obtain no right to control or vacate the adjudication, that being a matter in which he shall not be permitted to interfere. No one has a right to contest an adjudication and pray for its vacation without some priority of interest. Karr *v.* Whittaker, (*Tenn.*) 5 *N. B. R.* 123.

SETTING ASIDE JUDGMENT.

1. The exacting of a high rate of interest is not a sufficient cause for setting aside a judgment, especially when at the time of entering up the judgment, valuable collateral securities were surrendered to debtor by plaintiff for a large part of the judgment. Shaffer *v.* Fritchery *et al.* 4 *N. B. R.* 179.

SETTING ASIDE MORTGAGE.

1. If land has been conveyed by an insolvent debtor in fraud of creditors to one who has thereafter mortgaged it to a third person by a mortgage, which is also void, the assignee of the insolvent debtor may maintain a bill in equity to set aside the conveyances. If, however, the mortgage has been assigned to an innocent purchaser for a valuable consideration, it cannot be declared void, but the parties to the fraud will be held responsible for the amount thereof. Hubbell *v.* Currier, 10 *Allen,* (*Mass.*) 333.

SETTING UP THE ACT.

1. **Who estopped from.** Parties who were privies, and had assented to a deed of assignment, could not set it up as an act of bankruptcy. Bamford *v.* Baron, 2 *T. R.* 594; *S. P.,* Marshall *v.* Barkworth, 1 *N. & M.* 279; 4 *B. & A.* 508. (Eng.)

2. A commission being sued out upon the petition of a creditor, who had not concurred in a deed of conveyance, and who, together with others who had so concurred, was chosen assignee. *Held,* that it was no objection to an action by them as assignees, that some of them had concurred in such deed. Tappenden *v.* Burgess, 4 *East,* 230; 1 *Smith,* 33. (Eng.)

3. The assignees of a bankrupt, though neither of them are petitioning creditors, cannot avail themselves of an act of bankruptcy of which the petitioning creditor would be estopped from availing himself. Tope *v.* Hockin, 9 *D. & R.* 881; 7 *B. & C.* 101. (Eng.)

4. Execution by a trader of a deed of assignment of all his estate and effects for the benefit of his creditors, although purporting to be made under the arrangement clauses of the 12 and 13 Vict. c. 106, s. 224, was an act of bankruptcy, of which any creditor who had not executed or acceded to the deed might, prior to its execution by the required majority of six-sevenths in number and value of the creditors, avail himself in support of his petition for adjudication against the trader. *Ex parte* Alsop, 1 *De G., F. & J*

289; 29 *L. J., Bank.* 7 ; 6 *Jur., N. S.* 282. (Eng.)

5. But where a creditor had advised the trader respecting a sale under such a deed, he had acquiesced in it so as to be precluded from treating it as an act of bankruptcy. *Id.*

6. A bankrupt, previous to the fiat, having called a meeting of his creditors at Manchester, H. & Co., creditors at Halifax, wrote to G., an attorney at Manchester, to attend the meeting on their behalf, saying, "we will leave our interest in your hands." In pursuance of the resolutions passed at the meeting, which were communicated to H. & Co., a trust deed was prepared by G. and executed by the bankrupt and many of the creditors, but not by H. & Co. A dividend was afterwards declared by the trustees, of which H. & Co. were also informed, without making any objection to the arrangement. *Held,* that they could not afterwards set up his deed as an act of bankruptcy. *Ex parte* Tealdi, 1 *Mont., D. & D.* 210. (Eng.)

7. Traders executed an assignment of all their effects in trust for their creditors, and afterwards sued out a fiat against themselves, but did not apply for adjudication. Two creditors, who could have sued out a fiat against the bankrupts, and who could, under it, have impeached the deed, applied for and obtained an adjudication. *Held,* that the assignees could successfully impeach the deed, *Ex parte* Jackson, 1 *De Gex,* 609 ; 19 *Jur.* 770 ; 17 *L. J , Bank.* 19. (Eng.)

SETTLEMENTS.

1. **By marriage contract.** Where by a marriage settlement, the trustees covenant to permit the husband to receive, during his life, the dividends arising from bank stock vested in their names; if the husband becomes bankrupt and the trustees authorize a third person to receive the dividends and pay them over to the bankrupt's wife, they are liable to his assignees in an action for money had and received, Allen *v.* Impett, 2 *Moore,* 240 ; 8 *Taunt.* 263 ; *Holt,* 641. (Eng.)

2. **Family.** A solicitor and money scrivener, being in insolvent circumstances, upon his marriage with a woman with whom he had for seven years previously cohabited, by a deed of settlement and articles of agreement executed prior to the marriage, conveyed and assigned his real and personal estate to trustees, for his wife, with a joint power of appointment among the children of the marriage, (including an illegitimate daughter,) by reserving no interest to himself; immediately after the marriage the power was exercised in favor of the illegitimate daughter. The property remained under the control of the husband, and within two months after the marriage, a fiat issued against him. *Held,* that the settlement was itself an act of bankruptcy, and void as against the assignees. Colombine *v.* Penhall, 1 *Sm. & G.* 228. (Eng.)

3. A trader, previously to and in consideration of his marriage, which was solemnized in pursuance of an engagement of several years' standing, the fulfilment of which had been delayed by circumstances not connected with the state of his affairs, made a settlement of part of his property. After his marriage he was adjudged bankrupt. Before the execution of the settlement he had, to the knowledge of the intended wife, committed acts of bankruptcy subsequently to his contracting the debt due to the petitioning creditor, and within twelve months before the adjudication. *Held,* that the settlement was invalid as against the assignees. Praser *v.* Thompson, 4 *De G. & J.* 659. (Eng.)

4. **Of controversies.** He may, under the direction of the court, submit any controversy arising in the settlement of demands against the estate or of debts due to it, to the determination of arbitrator to be chosen by him and the other party to the controversy, and may, under such direction, compound and settle any such controversy, by agreement with the other party, as he thinks proper and most for the interest of the creditor. *Section* 17 *U. S. bankrupt act,* 1867.

5. **Of estates.** In the settlement of insolvent estates, equity allows the creditor, to prove and take a dividend on his whole debt, without regard to any collateral security he may hold. Jervis *v.* Smith, (*N. Y.*)

3 *N. B. R.* 147; citing Cheesebrough *v.* Millard, 1 *Johns. Ch.* 409; Brinckerhoff *v.* Marvin, 5 *id.* 320; Evertson *v.* Booth, 19 *Johns.* 468; Van Mater *v.* Ely, 1 *Beas.* 271; Bell *v.* Fleming, *id.* 13; Allston *v.* Mumford, 1 *Brock & Marsh*, 265; Aldrich *v.* Cooper, 2 *Leading Cases in Equity*, 56; Mason *v.* Bogg, 2 *Mylne & C.* 443; Amory *v.* Francis, 16 *Mass.* 208; Farnum *v.* Boutelle, 13 *Met.* 159; Routz *v.* Hart, 13 *Iowa*, 515; Putnam *v.* Russell, 17 *Vt.* 54; West *v.* Bank of Rutland, 19 *id.* 403.

6. Of property by voluntary act.
If an individual being in debt shall make a voluntary conveyance of his entire property, it would be a clear case of fraud, but this would not apply, if such conveyance be made by a person free from all embarrassments and without reference to future responsibilities. Between these extremes, however, numberless cases arise under facts and circumstances, which must be minutely examined to ascertain their true character. To hold that a settlement of a small amount by an individual in independent ' circumstances, which, if known to be public, would not affect his credit, if fraudulent would be a perversion of the statute, (13 Elizabeth.) It did not intend thus to disturb the ordinary and safe transaction in society, made in good faith, and which at the time subjected the creditors to no hazard. If the debt of the creditor, by whom the voluntary settlement is impeached, existed at the date of the settlement, and if it is shown that the remedy of the creditor is defeated or delayed by the existence of the settlement, it is immaterial whether the debtor was or was not solvent after making the settlement. But if a voluntary settlement or deed of gift be impeached by subsequent creditors, whose debts had not been contracted at the date of the settlement, then it is necessary to show either that the settler made the settlement with the express intent to delay, hinder or defraud creditors, or that after the settlement, the settlor had not sufficient means or reasonable expectations of being able to pay his then existing debts, that is to say was reduced to a state of insolvency, in which case the law infers that the settlement was made with intent to delay, hinder or defraud creditors, and therefore fraudulent and void. It is obvious, that the fact of a voluntary settlement, re-taining money enough to pay the debts which he owed at the time of making the settlement, but not actually paying them, cannot give a different character to the settlement, or take it out of the statute. It still remains a voluntary alienation or deed of gift whereby in the event the remedies of creditors are delayed, hindered, and defrauded, is void as against the plaintiff seeking, as a creditor, to set such settlement aside. Spirett *v.* Willows, quoted in Freeman *v.* Pope, 9 *Eng. Law Rep.* 206; Sedgwick *v.* Place *et al.* 5 *N. B. R.* 168.

SHARES.

1. Acceptance by assignees of.
After a shareholder in a railway company had become bankrupt, but before he had obtained his certificate, calls were made. The assignees took possession of the scrip, and a correspondence was carried on between the official assignee and the trade assignee, in the course of which the latter sent the former a statement of the bankrupt's property, including the value of the shares and with an estimate of the probable amount forthcoming, to carry on the bankrupt proceedings and pay dividends. The trade assignee subsequently wrote to the official assignee, suggesting that the shares, which continued in the possession of the assignees, should be sold. *Held*, that there was not sufficient evidence to warrant a finding by a jury, that the assignees had accepted the shares. South Staffordshire Railway Company *v.* Burnside, 6 *Railw. Cas.* 611; 5 *Exch.* 129; 20 *L. J., Exch.* 120. (Eng.)

2. A shareholder at the time of his bankruptcy held shares in an incorporated company standing in his own name on the company's books, but which were of no value at the time and on which only 25*l.* per share had been paid. The certificates were handed over to his assignees by the bankrupt, but nothing further was done in respect thereto by either the assignees, the bankrupt or the company for over five years thereafter, when the shares having risen in the market, the assignees claimed them and demanded to be registered in the company's books as the owners, which, however, the company refused to do. *Held*, that, assuming an acceptance of the shares was necessary to prove the assignees' title, and that the acceptance ought to be within a reasonable time, still that the facts proved more evidence of their title, and that the question of reasonable time was one for the jury; but that the judge ought to direct the jury that the reasonable time for accepting them did not begin to run until some party interested in the shares had taken some step respecting them. Graham *v.* Van Diemen's Land Company, 11 *Exch.* 101; 3 *C. L. R.* 887; 1 *Jur.*, *N. S.* 806; 24 *L. J. Exch.* 213. (Eng.)

3. In companies, vesting in and not vesting in assignees. Where the act of incorporation of a company declares that the "shares shall be deemed personal estate, and shall be transmissible as such," it was held, that though the profits arose out of the land, the shares were personal property, passing as such to the assignees, on the bankruptcy of the owner and holder theeof. *Ex parte* Lancaster Canal Company, 1 *Deac. & Chit.* 411; 1 *Mont.* 116; 1 *Mont. & Bligh*, 94; *S. P., ex parte* Lawrence, 1 *De Gex*, 269. (Eng.)

4. But shares in the Vauxhall bridge company are real estate and not within 21 Jac., 1, c. 19, s. 11. *Ex parte* Vauxhall bridge company, 1 *Glyn & J.* 101. (Eng.)

5. A. purchased shares in the name of the bankrupt, who verbally declared that he held them as trustee for A., and the certificates of shares were in A.'s possession, but no notice was given to the company of the trust, nor did the bankrupt sign a written declaration of the trust until seven days before the fiat was issued against him. According to the rules of the company only prin:ipals could become subscribers. It was held, that the shares were in the order and disposition of the bankrupt as reputed owner and therefore passed to his assignees. *Ex parte* Orde, 1 *Deac.* 166. (Eng.)

6. Where it was stipulated by a clause in the deed of settlement of a banking company, that it should have a lien on the shares of such proprietors as were customers for balances due the bank, and that no share should be transferred without the con-sent of the directors, and there was indorsed on each certificate of shares a memorandum of such provisions. A person being largely indebted to the bank for advances and being the proprietor of thirty shares of the company, a certificate of which so indorsed he held at the time, became bankrupt. It was held, that the shares did not pass to his assignees under the clause of reputed ownership, so as to defeat the lien of the bank, which had been provided for in the deed. *Ex parte* Plant, 4 *Deac. & Chit.* 160. (Eng.)

7. In companies, when in the order and disposition of bankrupt, and when not. A. borrowed money from B. in 1846, to purchase the requisite amount of shares in two companies to qualify him for the office of director in each; and having purchased the shares and become a director in both companies, A. assigned all the shares to B., as security for the loan. In one of the companies the qualification for the office of director would be lost by the disposal or reduction of the amount of that qualification, and the other company required that its directors should be possessed of, or entitled to, the requisite amount of shares in their own right. In 1854 A. signed a declaration of insolvency, upon which he was adjudicated a bankrupt, the shares at the time standing in his name; five days previously, however, B. gave notice to the directors of both companies of the assignment to him. At the time of his bankruptcy A. was actually a director in one of the companies, and out of office by rotation in the other, with a probability of a re-election. It was held, that the shares in neither company were in the possession, order or disposition of A. at the time of his bankruptcy, with the consent of the true owner. *Ex parte* Littledale, 6 *De G., Mac. & G.* 714; *Jur.*, *N. S.* 385; 24 *L. J., Bank.* 9. (Eng.)

8. By the rules of an insurance company, no person, except a director, was permitted to hold more than two shares in his own name; but there was no rule preventing a person from being beneficially entitled to more than two shares, by holding them in the name of another party. A proprietor who was already a holder of two shares, having purchased two others, caused them to be entered in the name of the bankrupt in the company's books, with the knowledge of one of the directors and the actuary. The bankrupt signed a declaration of trust, that he held the shares as trustee for the proprietor; but no notice of the trust was entered in the books of the company, and the bankrupt held the certificates of shares, and continued to receive the dividends thereon, accounting for them from time to time to the proprietor, up to the time of his bankrcptcy, at which time the shares were still standing in his name, during all which time he was treated as owner by the company, had notice of meetings served on him, attended the meetings of the shareholders, and voted as a shareholder. It was held, that this was such a secret trust as was not within 6 Geo. 4, c. 16, s. 79, and that the shares were in the order and disposition of the bankrupt, as reputed owner. *Ex parte* Burbridge, 1 *Deac.* 131. (Eng.)

9. Where the secretary of a company, with the knowledge of its directors, but without any formal notice to them, deposits certificates of shares of the company with a bank, as security for money advanced for the use of the company, it was held, on the bankruptcy of the secretary, that, the directors having knowledge of the transaction, no further notice was necessary, and that the shares were not therefore within the order and disposition of the secretary at the time of his bankruptcy. *Ex parte* Stewart, 11 *Jur.*, *N. S.* 25; 34 *L. J.*, *Chanc.* 6; 13 *W. R.* 356; 11 *L. T.*, *N. S.* 554. (Eng.)

10. Where, on the day on which a transfer of shares was executed with the name of the transferee and the date left blank, the assistant secretary of the company certified, on the application of the purchaser, on the instrument of transfer, that the certificates for the shares were at the company's office, the certificates not having yet been issued to the shareholders. Before the name of the purchaser was inserted in the transfer, the transferor became bankrupt. The assistant secretary testified, that after the certificate which he had indorsed on the instrument of transfer, no transfer of the shares would have been permitted, except under that transfer, or upon the production of that transfer canceled. It was held, that

the shares were neither in the order and disposition, nor in the reputed ownership of the transferor, at the time of his bankruptcy. Morris *v.* Cannan, 8 *Jur.*, *N. S.* 653; 31 *L. J.*, *Chanc.* 425; 10 *W. R.* 589; 6 *L. T.*, *N. S.* 521. (Eng.)

11. Where a solicitor was the holder of shares in a railway company, which was subject to the companies clauses act, 8 & 9 Vict. c. 16, and was one of the secretaries of the company, and borrowed money from his client on a deposit of the certificates of shares, but no further notice of the deposit was given to the company, and the solicitor became bankrupt, it was held, that the shares were in the order and disposition of the solicitor at the time of his bankruptcy, with the consent of the client. *Ex parte* Boulton, 1 *De G. & J.* 163; 3 *Jur.*, *N. S.* 425; 26 *L. J.*, *Bank.* 45. (Eng.)

12. Where a person at the time of his bankruptcy holds shares in a company, which stand in his own name on the books thereof, both as trustee and in his own right, and the shares are not numbered and there is nothing in the mode of entry or transfer by which they could be distinguished. After the investment of the trust monies in the shares and before his bankruptcy, the bankrupt bought and sold several shares, but he always had sufficient in his name to cover the trust monies. It was held, that so many of the shares standing in his name as equaled the number in which the trust monies had been invested, were not in his order and disposition at the time of his bankruptcy. Pinkett *v.* Wright, 2 *Hare*, 120; 6 *Jur.* 1102; 12 *L. J.*, *Chanc.* 119. (Eng.)

13. In companies, when in the reputed ownership of bankrupt and when not. Where the bankrupt had possession of the certificates of shares of a company, which shares stood in his name, and he was on all occasions the only apparent owner of the same, but the shares really belonged to another person, in whose favor there existed a secret declaration of trust, it was held that the shares were not in the reputed ownership of the bankrupt. *Ex parte* Watkins, 2 *Mont. & Ayr.* 349; 4 *Deac. & Chit.* 87. (Eng.)

SHERIFF.

1. Where a sheriff executed processes in certain replevin suits instituted by creditors of a bankrupt, and took property in the possession of said bankrupt and set forth in his inventory, and delivered the same to the several claimants, the court held that the action of the sheriff was unauthorized and ordered claimants to deliver the property to the assignee in bankruptcy, or if the same had been sold, to pay the value thereof to the said assignee, and in default so to do, attachment to issue against them. *In re* Vogel, (*S. D. N. Y.*) 2 *N. B. R.* 138.

2. The sheriff having seized, notice was given of a prior act of bankruptcy by the debtor, and a petition was filed under which he was adjudicated bankrupt, the goods remaining unsold, and the messenger took possession of them. It was held, that the sheriff was not entitled to a rule calling upon the assignees to pay him the expenses of preparing for a sale of the goods. Searle *v.* Blaise, 14 *C. B., N. S.* 856. (Eng.)

3. On the 22d of November, a *fi. fa.* issued upon a judgment obtained against A., the partner of B., and on the same day was lodged with the sheriff. On the following day the officer entered under a warrant granted thereon, and seized the whole of the partnership effects. On the 2d of December another *fi. fa.* issued upon a judgment against A. and B., directed to the same sheriff, who thereupon granted a warrant to different officers; no actual seizure was made under the second writ. On the 7th of December each of the partners committed an act of bankruptcy; on the 9th a fiat issued against them, under which they were duly declared bankrupts. The sheriff afterwards sold the whole of the partnership effects, in satisfaction of the two writs. It was held, that the sheriff was not justified in selling any part of the goods to satisfy the second writ, such writ not having been served or levied by seizure upon the property of the bankrupts before the issuing of the fiats, within 6 Geo. 4, c. 16, s. 108. Johnson *v.* Evans, 7 *M. & G.* 240; 7 *Scott, N. R.* 1035; 1 *D. & L.* 935; 13 *L. J., C. P.* 117. (Eng.)

4. **Actions by and against.** No action will lie against a sheriff for taking in execution under a *fi. fa.* the bedding and other articles of an insolvent debtor, who had petitioned under 5 & 6 Vict., c. 116, and 7 & 8 Vict. c. 96; but if the goods were protected from seizure the remedy was by application to the court for an order to the sheriff to restore them. Rideal *v.* Fort, 11 *Exch.* 847; 25 *L. J., Exch.* 204. (Eng.)

5. **And creditors liable for illegal acts.** Judgment creditors who direct the sheriff to sell property which has been assigned by the judgment debtor in trust for the benefit of creditors, and who indemnify him for so doing, are jointly liable with the sheriff to the assignee for such illegal act. Ball *v.* Loomis, 2 *Tiffany,* (29 *N. Y.*) 412.

6. **Bill of sale by.** An execution is *bona fide* completed by sale if there is a bill of sale to the execution creditor for the full value and the amount is actually paid over. Loader *v.* Hiscock, 1 *F. & F.* 132. (Eng.)

7. **Injunction against, when to be dissolved.** Where no advantage will be derived from interfering with the proceedings upon the execution in the hands of the sheriff, an injunction previously granted will be dissolved. *In re* Wilbur, (*E. D. N. Y.*) 3 *N. B. R.* 71.

8. **Levy before proceedings in bankruptcy.** Before the filing of a voluntary petition execution was issued on a docketed judgment and came into the hands of the sheriff who had levied on and held personal property of the bankrupt under a prior execution. The court decided that liens against the real estate by the New York law were perfected in both cases within the saving clause of sections 14 and 20 of bankrupt act. *In re* Smith, (*S. D. N. Y.*) 1 *N. B. R.* 169.

9. **Costs of.** Where the question at issue was whether the claim of a sheriff for costs on attachment suit against property of bankrupt which has been claimed as exempt is such a claim as can be proved in bankruptcy against the bankrupt's estate.

The assignee objecting to the proof and allowance of such claim on the ground that the claim of one of the plaintiffs in the attachment suit has never been proven against the bankrupt's estate, *held*, that the debt or principal must be proven and allowed before the costs made before the commencement of proceedings in bankruptcy can be proven and allowed. Where the principal debt has been duly proved against the bankrupt's estate, the costs can be proved if made in good faith before commencement of proceedings in bankruptcy and without knowledge of the insolvency of the defendant and without intention of defeating the provisions of the bankrupt law. Where, however, a portion of the costs have been made after the commencement of the bankruptcy proceedings, that portion will be disallowed. *In re* Preston, (*Washington Ter.*) 5 *N. B. R.* 293.

10. Levy by. A levy made by a sheriff in Ohio by obtaining a description in person at the recorder's office of the defendant's lands and indorsing the fact of a levy and a description of the lands on the back of the execution is a good levy, even though the sheriff was never on, near, or in sight of said lands. Armstrong *v.* Rickey Bros. (*Ohio*,) 2 *N. B. R.* 150.

11. Levy by, when to be satisfied by marshal. Where there is no dispute as to the validity of judgment under which executions were issued and levy made, the execution creditors are entitled to satisfaction out of the proceeds of the goods levied on by the sheriff and afterwards seized by the United States marshal, under a warrant in bankruptcy. Swope, Levy *et al. v.* Arnold, (*Mo.*) 5 *N. B. R.*

12. Liability under execution. No action will lie against a sheriff for taking in execution under a *fi. fa.* the bedding and other artices of an insolvent debtor, who had petitioned under 5 & 6 Vict. c. 116, and 7 and 8 Vict. c. 96, but if the goods were protected from seizure, the remedy was by application to the court for an order to the sheriff to restore them. Rideal *v.* Fort, 11 *Exch.* 847 ; 25 *L. J., Exch.* 204. (Eng.)

13. Return. The truth or falsity of a sheriff's return cannot be inquired into by

the U. S. district court, on a petition filed by the assignee of a bankrupt, for the purpose of ascertaining the validity of a certain judgment. Armstrong *v.* Rickey Brothers, (*Ohio*,) 2 *N. B. R.* 150.

14. When, and when not liable for seizure and sale under execution. Trover will lie against a sheriff, who, having seized goods after an act of bankruptcy, under a *fi. fa.* issued on a judgment, founded on a warrant of attorney, sold the goods after the fiat. Cheston *v.* Gibbs, 12 *M. & W.* 111; 1 *D. & L.* 420; 13 *L. J., Exch.* 53. (Eng.)

15. 1 Will. 4, c. 7, s. 7, did not extend to a judgment on a warrant of attorney though given without collusion or fraudulent preference, and a sheriff, having seized and sold the goods on an execution issued upon such judgment, and paying over the proceeds after notice of an act of bankruptcy committed by the defendant, was held to be answerable to the assignees for money had and received. Crossfield *v.* Stanley, 4 *B. & Ad.* 87 ; 1 *N. & M.* 668. (Eng.)

15. When liable to assignees. Where the goods of a debtor were seized by the sheriff under a *fi. fa.*, and sold and delivered by him to the judgment creditor in satisfaction of the debt, after a secret act of bankruptcy committed by the debtor, but before the commission, it was held, that the seizure and sale of the goods were a wrongful conversion, for which the sheriff was liable in trover at the suit of the assignees subsequently chosen. Balme *v.* Hutton, 3 *M. & Scott*, 1; 9 *Bing.* 471; 1 *C. & M.* 262; 2 *Tyr.* 630 ; reversing s. c. *Tyr.* 17; 2 *C. & J.* 19 ; 2 *T. & J.* 101. (Eng.)

17. A sheriff who, after an act of bankruptcy committed by a defendant, but without notice thereof, and before the issuing of the commission, seized and sold the goods of the defendant under a *fi. fa.* is liable in trover to the assignees. Garland *v.* Carlisle, 3 *M. & W.* 152; 4 *Bing., N. C.* 7; 5 *Scott*, 587; 9 *Bligh, N. S.* 421. (Eng.)

18. Where a creditor obtained judgment by *nil dicit* against a trader, and thereupon issued a *fi. fa.*, under which the sheriff seized the goods of the trader, who afterwards, and before the goods were sold, committed an act of bankruptcy, upon which a commission issued, and he was duly declared a bankrupt, of which the sheriff had notice, but nevertheless sold the goods, and paid over the proceeds to the execution creditor, it was held, that he was not justified in paying over the money, and was liable to be sued for it by the assignees in an action for money had and received. Notley v. Buck, 2 M. & R. 68; 6 B. & C. 160. (Eng.)

19. If a sheriff takes goods of a bankrupt in execution, after the act of bankruptcy, and before the commission issued, and sold them after the commission issued, he was liable for the goods to the assignees in trover. Cooper v. Chitty, 1 W. Bl. 65; 1 Burr, 20. (Eng.)

SHIPS.

1. Joint property in. Where the names of two partners in trade appeared (among others) on the certificate of registry, as owners of a ship, the registry acts did not prevent the showing how and in what proportions the several owners were respectively entitled; and though the title of the partners might be derived under different conveyances, yet if their shares were purchased with the partnership funds, and treated by them as partnership property, and the partners became bankrupt, these shares were considered as the joint property. Ex parte Jones, 4 M. & S. 450. (Eng.)

2. Mortgage on. Where the mortgage deeds of three fishing boats were deposited with bankers, as security for a debt, by the registered mortgagees, who afterwards became bankrupt, it was held, that the statutory form assignment being by indorsement, the mortgages could not be dealt with by the bankrupts, and, therefore, were not in their order and dispensation. Lacon v. Liffen, 4 Giff. 75; 9 Jur., N. S. 13; affirmed on appeal, 9 Jur., N. S. 477; 32 L. J., Chanc. 315; 11 W. R. 474; 7 L. T., N. S. 774. (Eng.)

3. Right of one partner to deal with partnership. Where a ship is owned and registered in the name of a part-

nership firm, one partners has a right to deal with her as with any other partnership property, consequently can sell or mortgage her without any power of attorney from his partner. Ex parte Hawden, 2 Mont., D. & D. 574. (Eng.)

4. Title to as between assignees. An absolute bill of sale of a ship to C. & D. was executed by A. & B., the owners thereof, for a nominal consideration. There was also a parol agreement between them that C. & D. should accept bills for the accommodation of A. & B., and that the ship should be security for any advances they should make on such acceptances, and that until default made by A. &. B. in providing for the acceptances, the ship should remain in their possession and management. The ship was registered in the names of C. & D., but A. & B. remained in the possession and management of her, appeared to the world as owners, and obtained credit thereby. Before default by A. & B. in providing for the acceptances, C. & D. became bankrupts, and their assignees immediately seized and sold the ship. A. & B. afterward became bankrupts. Held, that trover for the ship could not be maintained by the assignees of A. & B. against the assignees of C. & D.; for the parol agreement could not be set up against the bill of sale, and the case did not come within the 21 Jac. 1, c. 19, s. 11, the ship having been seized before the bankruptcy of A. & B.; and though the bill of sale, unaccompanied by possession, might be void as against creditors, it was binding upon A. & B. and their assignees. Robinson v. McDonnell, 2 B. & A. 134. (Eng.)

5. Unregistered bill of sale of. Where a person purchases and takes possession of a ship, for which he has paid the purchase money, and the ship is transferred by a bill of sale in proper form but not registered, and the seller afterwards becomes bankrupt. Held, that the purchaser has, under 17 and 18 Vict. c. 104, a good legal title against the bankrupt and all who claim under him. And by 25 and 26 Vict. c. 63, he has an equitable title, which will entitle him to maintain trover against any one not having both a legal and equitable title. Stapleton v. Hayman, 2 H. & C. 918; 10

Jur., *N. S.* 497; 33 *L. J.*, *Exch.* 170; 12 *W. R.* 317. (Eng.)

6. Vesting in and not vesting in assignees. Where the mortgagee, under a bill of sale, of the greater part of a ship, does not take possession, but allows the mortgagors and the other part owners to have the management and act as the visible owners of the vessel. The mortgagor having become bankrupt, it was held, that his share in the ship passed to his assignees, under 21 Jac. 1, c. 19. Hall *v.* Gurney, 3 *Dougl.* 356. (Eng.)

7. Where M., as security for money borrowed from S. gave him a bill of sale of a ship and cargo at sea, and the policy thereon, and indorsed over to him the bills of lading; but S. neglected up to the time of the bankruptcy of M., after notice of the arrival of the ship, to take possession of the ship and cargo, or to do any act to show the transfer of them to him, it was held, that the ship and cargo passed to the assignees of M., as being in his possession, order and disposition at the time of his bankruptcy within 21 Jac. 1, c. 19. Mair *v.* Glennie, 4 *M. & S.* 240. (Eng.)

8. Where three-fourth shares of a ship are secretly mortgaged by the owner of the ship to a creditor as security for a debt, and the creditor permits the mortgagor to retain sole possession, management and control of her until he becomes bankrupt, it was held, that, although the requisites of the registry acts had been complied with, the whole ship passed to and vested in the assignees of the bankrupt under 21 Jac. 1, c. 19, s. 11, and that they could bring an action of trover against the mortgagee, who had taken possession of the ship upon the bankruptcy of the mortgagor. Kirkley *v.* Hodgson, 2 *D. & R.* 848; 1 *B. & C.* 588. (Eng.)

9. Where a firm, consisting of A., B. and C., purchased a ship, on which there was a lien in favor of D. and E., and which was then registered in the names of B., C., D. and E.; afterwards the firm made an agreement to assign the ship to third parties, as security, without any notice thereof being given to D. and E. The firm subsequently became bankrupt. It was held, that if the agreement had not been void under 17 and 18 Vict. c. 104, the interest of the mortgagees

would not have passed to the assignees under the order and disposition clause in 12 and 13 Vict. c. 106, s. 125. Liverpool Borough Bank *v.* Turner, 1 *Johns. & H.* 159; 30 *L. J., Chanc.* 879. (Eng.)

10. Where an unfinished ship was assigned to a creditor by a ship builder, who agreed to complete it at his own expense, the value of the finished ship to be set off against an equal amount of the pre-existing indebtedness. The course of trade of the ship builder was to build ships on his own account, and sell them when finished. Before the ship was finished the builder became bankrupt. It was held, that the ship did not pass to his assignees as being in his order and disposition at the time of the bankruptcy. Holderness *v.* Rankin, 2 *De G., F. & J.* 258; 29 *L. J., Chanc.* 753; 6 *Jur., N S.* 928; s. c. 28 *Beav.* 180; 6 *Jur., N. S.* 903, affirmed. (Eng.)

11. Where mortgagees of a ship, under a bill of sale in writing, which was executed before, but not registered until after, the bankruptcy of the mortgagor, had not taken possession of the ship; and the bankrupt's assignees claimed to hold the ship on the ground, that the bankrupt was the owner at the time of his bankruptcy, or that it was then in his order and disposition, it was held, that under 3 and 4 Will. 4, c. 55, ss. 31, 34 and 35, the operation of the bill of sale commenced not from the time of execution, but only from the time of registration; and that, therefore, the ship passed to and vested in the assignees as part of the property of the bankrupt, and not as the property of the mortgagee in the order and disposition of the bankrupt. Boyson *v.* Gibson, 4 *C. B.* 121; 16 *L. J., C. P.* 147; 3b *L. J., Chanc.* 379. (Eng.)

SIGNATURE.

1. A creditor's usual signature to the particulars of a demand is sufficient. *Ex parte* Roche, 37 *L. J., Bank.* 16. (Eng.)

SIX MONTHS.

1. Under the former English bankrupt law no person was liable to become bankrupt by reason of any act of bankruptcy committed more than *twelve* months prior to the issuing of any fiat or the filing of any petition. Six months is now the limit. *Williams & Williams English Bankrupt Law, p.* 10; also *see Am. and English Bankruptcy Digest Appendix,* 942.

2. A judgment given more than six months before the filing of the petition by the bankrupt is not void, although taken contrary to the bankrupt act. *In re* Fuller, 4 *N. B. R.* 29; s. c. 2 *C. L. N.* 373.

3. Where a debtor makes an assignment of all his estate in trust, for distribution among all his creditors within *six months* of the commencement of bankruptcy proceedings, even in the absence of actual fraud, the same is an act of bankruptcy, and voidable by the assignee in bankruptcy. Barnes *v.* Rettew (*Pa.*), unreported.

4. The fraud cannot exist if the preference was not obtained in contemplation of bankruptcy, and within the specified time (six months); the preference in such case becomes merely the payment of a just debt Forsaith *v.* Merritt *et al.* (*Mass.*) 3 *N. B. R.* 11.

5. Longest period during. A partnership will be declared bankrupt in the district in which proceedings are first commenced, provided it has carried on business in that district for as great a part of the six months next preceding the filing of the petition as in any other district. The longest period of the six months next preceding the filing of the petition does not necessarily imply three months and one day, or any greater part of the six months, but intends to fix the district in which bankrupts have been doing business for the longest period within the six months. *In re* Foster *et al.* (*S. D. N. Y.*) 3 *N. B. R.* 57.

6. Residence and place of business. Where the bankrupt resided at Boston, Mass., from May 1, 1867, to December 7, 1867, and from December 7, 1867, to January 21, 1868, he resided at New York, therefore he did not reside in the latter district for the six months next immediately preceding the time of filing the petition, or for the longest period during such six months, and he did not carry on

business in the latter district for such six months or for the longest period thereof; and a discharge must be refused in the latter district, for want of jurisdiction. *In re* Leighton *et al.* (*S. D. N. Y.*) 5 *N. B. R.* 95.

SMELTING.

1. A., who held a lease of mines of coal and iron-stone, and carried on the business of smelting, adding to the iron ore produced from his own mines from 65 to 70 per cent. of ore which he bought elsewhere, and smelted the whole into pig iron, which he sold in market, is a trade within the 12 and 13 Vict., c. 106, s. 65. Turner *v.* Hardcastle, 11 *C. B., N. S.* 683; 31 *L. J., C. P.* 193. (Eng.)

SOLICITORS.

1. A non-trader, much indebted, left the realm, and an order had been made under the English bankruptcy act of 1861, s. 70, for service of a petition for adjudication on him abroad. His solicitor, with whom he was in communication, was present when the order was made, but gave no information, and declined to accept service. The petitioner sent a clerk abroad, who was unable to find and serve the debtor. Service of the petition was then ordered to be made on the solicitor, and the debtor was thereupon adjudged bankrupt. *Held,* that, under the circumstances, the adjudication was good. *In re* Calthrop, 3 *L. R., Ch.* 252; 38 *L. J., Bank.* 17; 18 *L. T., N. S.* 166; 16 *W. R.* 446. (Eng.)

2. An attachment will not lie against an attorney for non-payment of money pursuant to the master's allocation after his bankruptcy. Baron *v.* Martelt, 9 *D. & R.,* 390. (Eng.)

3. A solicitor may sue out a commission upon his debt for costs, without, as in the case of an action, having delivered his bill one month previous thereto. *Ex parte* Sutton, 11 *Ves.* 162. (Eng.)

4. A commissioner in bankruptcy is not bound to hear a person who, although a duly admitted solicitor of the court, does not appear as the solicitor of the party for whom he appears, but only as the clerk of such solicitor. *Ex parte* Broadhouse, 2 *L. R., Ch.* 655 ; 36 *L. J., Bank.* 29 ; 15 *W. R.* 126 ; 17 *L. T., N. S.* 126. (Eng.)

5. The solicitor is not liable in the first instance to the messenger whom he nominated for his bill of fees, but if the solicitor agree with the petitioning creditor to work a commission for a sum certain, and receives a great part of that sum, he will be liable to such messenger. Hartop *v.* Inckes, 2 *M. & Scott,* 438 ; 2 *Rose,* 263. (Eng.)

6. **Frauds committed by.** Where a solicitor did an act which was irregular and censurable, but which did not amount to a wilful fraud, the court granted him a second-class certificate with a suspension for two years but with protection in the meantime, as he had undergone an imprisonment of nearly three months. *In re* Freston, 7 *Jur., N. S.* 1173 ; 10 *W. R.* 25 ; 5 *L. T., N. S.* 267 ; 31 *L. J., Bank.* 1. (Eng.)

7. Where a solicitor committed a gross breach of duty towards his client, it is something which the interests of society require should be severely visited and that a certificate should be refused to the solicitor on becoming bankrupt, even though the client received interest from the solicitor after the discovery of his misconduct. *Ex parte* Selby, 2 *Jur., N. S.* 29 ; 25 *L. J., Bank.* 13. (Eng.)

8. Where a solicitor who had no defence removed from one court to another an action brought against him by his client and in which judgment was recovered against him. He was adjudicated a bankrupt on the petition of his brother. It was held, that his petition was properly suspended for twelve months. *Ex parte* Blackhartt, 3 *De G. & J.* 39 ; 4 *Jur., N. S.* 1065 ; 27 *L. J., Bank.* 24. (Eng.)

9. Where an attorney, employed by both vendor and purchaser, receives the purchase money and omits to pay it over, and afterwards becomes bankrupt and obtains his certificate, the court will not make a rule compelling him to pay the amount unless fraud is shown ; otherwise if there is fraud. *In re* Bonnor, 1 *N. & M.* 555 ; 4 *B. & Ad.* 811. (Eng.)

SOUTH CAROLINA.

1. **Insolvent law of.** One discharged by the insolvent laws of South Carolina, and held to bail here, in a suit on a judgment in that state, an exoneratur ordered to be entered. Archibod's executor *v.* Moultrie, 2 *Yates' Pa. R.* 435.

SPECIAL ATTORNEY.

1. **Verification of creditors' petition by.** It is not sufficient that a creditor's petition be signed in the firm name by a special attorney and verified by him. *In re* Steere & Pooke, (*R. I.*) 5 *N. B. R.* 161.

SPECIAL PARTNER.

1. **By omission, becomes liable as a general partner.** One who has entered a firm as a special partner, without complying with the provisions of the statute respecting limited partnership, is liable to be included as a general partner in the firm in proceedings in insolvency. Lancaster *v.* Choate, 5 *Allens' (Mass.)* 530.

SPECIAL PLEA.

1. **Substitution of.** Plaintiff may have leave (on terms) to substitute a special plea for a notice subjoined to a replication, where he wishes to introduce testimony to show fraud in the discharge and certificate of the defendant, which has been pleaded specially to plaintiff's declaration. It seems that testimony going to show fraud, etc., in a defendant's discharge and certificate in bankruptcy cannot be given under a notice ; it must be pleaded specially. Dresser *v.* Brooks, 1 *How. Pr. R.* 169.

SPECIFIC APPROPRIATION.

1. Business transactions were carried on between R. & Co., of London, and B. & Co., of Barbadoes, on a general account between the two houses. The course of business was for B. & Co. to draw bills of exchange upon R. & Co., and sell them in Barbadoes; and in order to keep R. & Co. in funds to meet the bills so drawn upon them, and repay them for any monies expended on behalf of B. & Co., B. & Co. were in the habit of buying bills in Barbadoes and remitting them to R. & Co. The proceeds of such remittances were carried to the general account between the two firms. Between the time of certain remittances being posted in Barbadoes for transmission to R. & Co., and of the same being received by R. & Co., the London firm became bankrupt. Subsequently B. & Co. also failed. *Held,* that, under the circumstances, there was no specific appropriation of the remittances, but that so far as the remittances were in specie at the time of R. & Co.'s bankruptcy, the assignees of B. & Co. were entitled to have the same appropriated to the purposes of the general account, subject to the right of appropriation by the London firm to items in such account; and that, on R. & Co. submitting to appropriate the proceeds of such remittances to outstanding acceptances, the order in *ex parte* Waring, 19 *Ves.* 345, must be followed, and Powles *v.* Hargreaves, 3 *De G., M. & G.* 430, must apply. Trimingham *v.* Maud, 38 *L. J., Chanc.* 207; 7 *L. R., Eq.* 201; 19 *L. T., N. S.* 554; 17 *W. R.* 313. (Eng.)

2. L. deposited certain securities with a company, upon an agreement that the company might sell them and apply the proceeds in reimbursing themselves and money owing by L. to them. Subsequently the company accepted bills for L.'s accommodation. Afterwards, before the bills were paid, the company went into liquidation, and L. made an assignment for the benefit of his creditors. The only liability of L. to the company was in respect to these bills. *Held,* that *ex parte* Waring, 19 *Ves.* 345, did not apply, and that neither the bill holders nor L. were entitled to have the proceeds of the sale of the securities applied in payment of the bills. *In re* New Zealand Banking Corporation, *ex parte* Levi, 7 *L. R., Eq.* 449; 17 *W. R.* 565; 20 *L. T., N. S.* 296. (Eng.)

SPECIFIC PERFORMANCE.

1. A., before his bankruptcy, agreed to take a lease of a cotton mill, and entered into possession. After his bankruptcy, one of his assignees took possession, and agreed to accept the lease, a draft of which was sent to the assignees, containing covenants personally binding on them during the whole of the term, and one in particular to prevent them from assigning without the license of the lessor. *Held,* that the assignees were not bound to accept of such a lease, and even if they were, that the court of review had no jurisdiction to compel specific performance of the agreement. *Ex parte* Lucas, 3 *Deac. & Chit.* 144; 1 *Mont. & Ayr.* 83. (Eng.)

SPECIFIC PROPERTY.

1. Where, under a fiduciary employment, money is received by the attorney or agent, it is the specific money of the employer, and not merely a debt owing him by the attorney or agent. White *v.* Platt, 5 *Denio* 269.

SPECIFICATIONS.

1. **Opposing discharge.** It is not necessary to state in specifications that the persons named to whom fraudulent payments are stated to have been made were creditors of the bankrupt. *In re* Smith & Bickford, (*N. D. N. Y.*) 5 *N. B. R.* 20.

2. *And be it further enacted,* That any creditor opposing the discharge of any bankrupt may file a specification in writing of the grounds of his opposition, and the court may in its discretion order any question of fact so presented to be tried at a stated session of the district court. *Section* 31 *U. S. bankrupt act,* 1867.

3. A creditor opposing the application of a bankrupt for discharge, shall enter his appearance in opposition thereto on the day when the creditors are required to show cause, and shall file his specification of the grounds of his opposition, in writing, within ten days thereafter, unless the time shall be enlarged by order of the district court in the case, and the court shall thereupon make an order as to the entry of said case for trial on the docket of the district court, and the time within which the same shall be heard and decided. *General Order No. 24, Sup. Ct. U. S.—In bankruptcy.*

4. A specification that a bankrupt has concealed his effects, or that he has wilfully sworn falsely in his affidavit annexed to his inventory require that these acts should be shown to be intentional to preclude a discharge. *In re* Wyatt, (*Ky.*) 2 *N. B. R.* 94.

5. Incomplete specifications in opposition to a discharge in bankruptcy may be amended upon an application to the court before a discharge is granted. An averment that the bankrupt has a large amount of personal property, which he has not put in his schedule of assets or passed over to the assignee, is too vague to found any action of the court upon, and insufficient to vacate a certificate of discharge. *In re* McIntire, (*S. D. N. Y.*) 1 *N. B. R.* 115.

6. A specification in opposition to a discharge in bankruptcy " that the bankrupt has influenced the action of certain creditors by a pecuniary consideration and obligation," may be held sufficient under certain circumstances. Specifications as to the concealment or transfer of property should specify with some particularity what property has been concealed or transferred. *In re* Mawson, (*S. D. N. Y.*) 1 *N. B. R.* 115.

7. Where the omission to file specifications in opposition to the bankrupt's discharge within ten days from the return day, to show cause, was inadvertent. Creditors may file the same with permission *nunc pro tunc. In re* Grefe, (*S. D. N. Y.*) 2 *N. B. R.* 106.

8. Where specifications in opposition to the discharge of the bankrupt are filed by a creditor, if the bankrupt has, in the judgment of the register, conformed to all the requirements of law and to all his duty under the U. S. bankrupt act of 1867, the register is to certify that he has so conformed except in the particulars covered by the specifications. *In re* Pulver, (*S. D. N. Y.*) 2 *N. B. R.* 101.

9. Creditors are bound by the specifications filed. Failing in these to oppose successfully bankrupt's discharge, they cannot allege new or different grounds not contained in the specifications. *In re* Rosenfeld, Jr. (*N. J.*) 2 *N. B. R.* 49.

10. Specifications opposing a discharge must be precise and definite and must particularize facts. A specification containing a reference to facts supposed to be shown on an examination of the bankrupt by the register is faulty. The facts showing a ground under the 29th section of the U. S. bankrupt act of 1867, for resisting the discharge should be set forth without reference to any matter *aliunde. In re* Eidom, (*Tex.*) 3 *N. B. R.* 61.

11. On filing the specifications in opposition to a bankrupt's discharge, the hearing upon the petition is at once transferred into court by section four of the bankrupt act of 1867; therefore there cannot be any examination of the bankrupt by the creditors before a register, on the application by the bankrupt before the discharge. If creditors desire a further examination of the bankrupt before the register, to be used by them in opposing his discharge, they must proceed under section twenty-six of the act. *In re* S. F. & C. S. Frizelle, (*Mich.*) 5 *N. B. R.* 119.

12. Vague and general specifications will not be allowed in opposition to a discharge. *In re* Hansen, (*S. D. N. Y.*) 2 *N. B. R.* 73; *in re* Tyrrell, (*S. D. N. Y.*) 2 *N. B. R.* 73; *in re* Dryer, (*S. D. N. Y.*) 2 *N. B. R.* 76.

13. A creditor, who has proved his debt may file specifications in opposition to the discharge of the bankrupt at any time before the period fixed by G. O. XXIV. *In re* Baum, (*S. D. N. Y.*) *N. B. R. Sup.* ii.

SPECULATIONS.

1. **Rash and hazardous.** The bankruptcy of a share broker, who has met with losses on time bargains, is to be attributed to rash and hazardous speculation, and by increasing the balance against him at two banks, shortly before his failure, he is guilty of contracting debts without reasonable expectation of being able to pay the same. *In re* Wilson, 14 *L. T., N. S.* 492. (Eng.)

2. Where a bankrupt had entered into contracts from which he was to derive pecuniary advantages, on the foundation of a company, of which he was the promoter, but which company became defunct, by reason of the necessary capital not having been subscribed. It was held that he had not been guilty of embarking in a rash and hazardous speculation. *Ex parte* Dowman, 9 *Jur., N. S.* 811 ; 32 *L. J., Bank.* 49 ; 11 *W. R.* 577 ; 8 *L. T., N. S.* 225. (Eng.)

3. A trader bought goods for home trade, as he alleged to the seller, he was at the time perfectly solvent, though he shortly afterwards became bankrupt. The goods were sent to America and disposed of at a loss. His discharge was opposed on the ground of his misrepresentations, and that the consignment of the goods to America was a rash and hazardous speculation. It was held, that his discharge should not be refused, as the bankrupt at the time of the venture possessed property beyond the amount of his liabilities, and the representations, though erroneous, were not fraudulent. *Ex parte* Evans, 31 *L. J., Bank.* 63 ; 6 *L. T., N. S.* 519. (Eng.)

4. A country banker accepted, to a large amount, bills drawn upon him by a person who failed to remit other good bills, according to his agreement, without any security whatever. He afterwards became bankrupt. *Held*, that his insolvency was attributable to rash and hazardous speculation, and that his order of discharge was properly made conditional on the setting aside part of his subsequent earnings for the benefit of his creditors. *Ex parte* Bragington, 14 *W. R.* 593 ; 14 *L. T., N. S.* 276. (Eng.)

5. A merchant, at the end of 1865, held invoices for 800 bales of cotton, of the value of 29,000*l.*, for which he had accepted bills. At that time he knew himself to be, if not insolvent, at all events in a critical position, having nothing but the cotton to meet the bills. He stopped payment in June, 1866, and became bankrupt, having in the meantime given or confirmed orders for 1,100 more bales of cotton, of the value of 35,000*l.* He had scarcely any assets besides his cotton, which was pledged beyond its value, and his unsecured debts were 58,000*l.* *Held*, that although dealing in cotton was within the limits of legitimate commerce, still, as such dealing was notoriously hazardous, the bankrupt, having regard to the state of his affairs, at the end of 1865, was bound to exercise the greatest caution as to extending his liabilities for cotton, and that the subsequent orders for 1,100 bales, which appear not to have been requisite for keeping his business together, must be considered as having been given in order to take the chances of a rise in the price, with a certainty that the loss, in case of a fall, would have to be borne by his creditors, and that this was rash and hazardous speculation. *Ex parte* Heyn, 2 *L. R. Ch.* 650; 17 *L. T., N. S.* 91; 15 *W. R.* 1185. (Eng.)

STAMP.

1. An agreement by a debtor to transfer certain accounts to his creditor is void and of no effect without a stamp, and therefore such an agreement cannot be made the basis of an involuntary petition in bankruptcy. *In re* Dunham, (*S. D. N. Y.*) 2 *N. B. R.* 9.

2. A deed of assignment for the benefit of creditors, not registered through want of the necessary assents, may be used, even though unstamped, as evidence of an act of bankruptcy. *In re* Gouldwell, *ex parte* Squire, 38 *L. J., Bank.* 13 ; 4 *L. R. Ch.* 47 ; 17 *W. R.* 40 ; 19 *L. T., N. S.* 272, overruling, *ex parte* Potter, 11 *Jur., N. S.* 49 ; 34 *L. J., Bank.* 46 ; 3 *De G., J. & S.* 240 ; 13 *W. R.* 189 ; 11 *L. T., N. S.* 435 (Eng.)

3. The want of a stamp to an insolvent's discharge cannot be urged as a reason to show it was not duly obtained, and prevent the exoneration of his bail. Fraud only can

effect it. Oole v. Stafford, 1 *Caines' Cases*, 249.

4. Inventory under state law must be stamped. Baker *ads*. Burns, *Colemans' Cases*, 73 ; s. c. *Coleman & Caines' Cases*, 78.

5. A power of attorney to represent a creditor in bankruptcy does not need a stamp. *In re* Myrick, (*Ga.*) 3 *N. B. R.* 38.

___

STAMPED PAPER.

1. In July, 1846, the defendant having been arrested under a *ca. sa.* in order to obtain his discharge, gave to the attorney of the execution creditor 5*l.* and a blank promissory note stamp, with his name written on it. In 1851, the defendant obtained a certificate in bankruptcy, and in 1852 the attorney filled up the blank stamped paper by making it a promissory note for 24*l.* 18*s.* 6*d.* at one month s date, and indorsed it to the plaintiff for value. *Held*, that it was properly left to the jury to say whether the stamped paper was filled up within a reasonable time, considering the circumstances of the defendant and his ability to pay the note. Finple v. Pullen, 8 *Exch.* 389 ; 22 *L. J., Exch.* 151. (Eng.)

___

STATE.

1. Claim of. A claim of the commonwealth upon an insolvent estate, entitled, under other circumstances, to a preference over other creditors, is not entitled to payment at all, if it be not presented to the auditors appointed to marshal the estate among the creditors, until after their report be made, although it be not confirmed by the orphan's court. Mitchell's Estate, 2 *Watts' Pa. R.* 87.

2. Exemptions. A merchant residing in Kansas, is not entitled to the speeial exemptions allowed mechanics, miners and other persons, for the purpose of carrying on their trade or business. Such exemptions made by an assignee will be disallowed. *In re* Schwartz, 4 *N. B. R.* 189.

3. Jurisdiction. This court has jurisdiction in equity upon a proper case being made to enjoin a citizen of this commonwealth from availing himself of an attachment of personal property in another state in an action against a debtor who is insolvent under the laws of this commonwealth, and thus preventing the same from coming to the hands of the assignee ; and it is no objection that the action was commenced before the institution of proceedings in insolvency, if this was done with knowledge that such proceedings were about to be instituted, and with a view to obtain a preference. Dehan v. Foster, 4 *Allen*, (*Mass.*) 545.

4. An insolvent discharge obtained in this state cannot be pleaded in bar of a suit brought in a court of this state, on a contract made in another state subsequent to the passage of the act under which the discharge is obtained, between parties not inhabitants of this state at the time of the contract, although previous to the presenting the petition for the discharge, they become such inhabitants. Witt v. Follett, 2 *Wendell*, 457.

5. Liens. A state in its sovereign capacity has a lien on all its realty for taxes. Such lien has priority over any claim of one of its citizens, no matter when such claim may have been acquired. *In re* Brant, (*W. Va.*) 3 *N. B. R.* 85.

6. Officers cannot take proof of debt. Notaries are state officers and responsible alone to their respective states ; hence a creditor residing in another judicial district from that in which proceedings in bankruptcy are pending cannot make proof of his claim before a notary public. *In re* Strauss, (*Ohio*,) 2 *N. B. R.* 18.

7. Other than where contract is made. The constitutional and legal rights of a citizen of the United States to sue in the circuit court of the United States do not permit an act of insolvency, completely executed under the authority of a state, to be a good bar against a recovery upon a contract made in another state ; hence the plea that the estate of the said decedent is insolvent, is not sufficient to vote the plaintiff a claim. Suydam *et al.* v. Broudwax, (*U. S. S. C.*) 14 *Peters*, 67.

STATE COURT.

1. Where there is a state court and the amount due is in dispute, the court of bankruptcy may allow the suit to proceed for the purpose of ascertaining the amount due which amount may be proved in bankruptcy. *In re* Rundle & Jones, (*S. D. N. Y.*) 2 *N. B. R.* 49.

2. The process of state courts can no longer be used successfully to thwart or defeat the equal distribution of an insolvent debtor's estate among all his creditors. *In re* McDonough, (*Mo.*) 3 *N. B. R.* 53.

3. A bankrupt court will not go behind the record of a state court which has been made according to the practice and course of proceeding in such court. *In re* Robinson, (*S. D. N. Y.*) 2 *N. B. R.* 108.

4. **Attacking discharge in.** The authority to set aside and annul a discharge in bankruptcy conferred upon the federal court by section 34 of the U. S. bankrupt act of 1867, is incompatible with the exercise of the same power by a state court, and the former is paramount. Corey *et al. v.* Ripley, (*Me.*) 4 *N. B. R.* 163.; citing Chadwick *v.* Starrett, 27 *Me.* 138 ; Coates *v.* Bush, 1 *Cush.* 564 ; Humphrey *v.* Sweat, 31 *Me.* 192 ; Dudley *v.* Mayhew, 3 *N. Y.* 10 ; Stephens *v.* Evans, 2 *Barr.* 1157 ; City of Boston *v.* Shaw, 1 *Met.* 130 ; Sturges *v.* Crowninshield, 4 *Wheat.* 196 ; Stetson *v.* City of Bangor, 56 (*Me.*) 286.

5. **Cannot interfere with distribution of bankrupt's assets.** A state court cannot interfere with the distribution of assets of a bankrupt. Money awarded under a rule of court cannot be attached. *In re* Bridgman, (*Ga.*) 2 *N. B. R.* 84.

6. **Costs in.** A creditor cannot be held in custody on account of a judgment obtained against him for costs in an action in a state court, if he has been declared a bankrupt in the United States court. *In re* Borst, 2 *N. B. R.* 92.

7. **Interference by U. S. courts.** The U. S. district court will not interfere with suits pending in state courts, it appearing that the amount of valid liens is greater

than the assets, and by no possibility can there be anything for distribution amongst the general creditors. *In re* Bowie, (*Md.*) 1 *N. B. R.* 185.

8. **Judgment of conclusive and binding.** The judgment of a state court is conclusive and binding on all the courts, both state and federal, whether erroneous or not, until reversed in due course of law. *In re* Hussman, (*Ky.*) 2 *N. B. R.* 140.

9. **Jurisdiction of.** The jurisdiction of state courts is not extinguished, except in cases where the creditor proves his debts or claims in a bankruptcy court. A petition or prayer to a United States district court to take such claims under its own jurisdiction must be denied. The bankrupt and a creditor, on the eve of a debtor's bankruptcy, will not be permitted to enter into any arrangement by which they can control the course of litigation in state courts in suits pending in such courts to which the bankrupt is a party. Samson *et al. v.* Burton, 4 *N. B. R.* 1.

10. State courts having once acquired jurisdiction, a U. S. court has no authority by which it may oust the jurisdiction of the state court. *In re* Clark & Bininger, 3 *N. B. R.* 129 ; citing *in re* Campbell, *N. B. R. Sup.* xxxvi; *in re* Burns, *N. B. R. Sup.* xxxviii; *in re* Donaldson, *N. B. R. Sup.* xxxix; Houseberger *v.* Zibelien, 2 *N. B. R.* 32.; Sedgwick, assignee, *v.* Minck, *et al.* 1 *N. B. R.* 204 ; *in re* Smith, 1 *N. B. R.* 169 ; *in re* Hill, 2 *N. B. R.* 108 ; Farrin *v.* Crawford, 2 *N. B. R.* 181 ; *in re* Marks, 2 *N. B. R.* 175 ; *in re* Hazleton, 2 *N. B. R.* 12.

11. **May entertain petition to enforce mechanics' lien.** A state court may entertain a petition to enforce a mechanics' lien, without necessarily conflicting or interfering with the jurisdiction of the bankruptcy court. *In re* Clifton, (*Mass.*) 3 *N. B. R.* 162 ; citing Nugent *v.* Boyd, 3 *How.* 426 ; Wiswal *v.* Sampson, 14 *How.* 52 ; Taylor *v.* Carryl, 20 *How.* 583 ; Peale *v.* Phipps, 14 *How.* 368 ; Foster *v.* The Richard Busteed, 100 *Mass.* 411 ; Hilliard *v.* Allen, 4 *Cush.* 532 ; *in re* Day, 3 *N. B. R.* 81 ; *in re* Bininger, 3 *N. B. R.* 121 ; *in re* Pacific Mail Steamship Co., 2 *N. B. R.*

170; Houston v. City Bank, 6 How. 486; Fowler v. Herst, 13 How. 373; Pulliam v. Osborne, 17 How. 476; in re Barrow, 1 N. B. R. 125; Foster v. Ames, 2 N. B. R. 147; Briggs v. Stephens, Law Rep. 281; in re McClellan, 1 N. B. R. 91.

12. Of Maryland. The court of appeals of Maryland has appellate jurisdiction from the court of common pleas in insolvent cases under a proper construction of section 28 of the 4th article of the state constitution. The United States courts have exclusive jurisdiction in the case of an insolvent debtor as to his right to a discharge in bankruptcy. Van Nostrand v. Barr, et al. (Md.) 2 N. B. R. 154; citing Sturgis v. Crowninshield, 4 Wheat. 122; Ogden v. Saunders, 12 Wheat. 213; ex parte Eames, 2 Story, 522; Larrabee v. Talbot, 5 Gill. 426; Commonwealth v. O'Hara, N. B. R. Sup. xix; Perry v. Langley, 1 N. B. R. 155.

13. Proceedings in. No creditor can, by instituting proceedings in a state court after the commission of an act of bankruptcy by his debtor, obtain a valid lien upon the property conveyed by such fraudulent deeds, if he has notice of the commission of an act of bankruptcy by the debtor. It passes to the assignee of the bankrupt for the benefit of all the creditors. Shawhan v. Wherritt, (U. S. S. Ct.) 7 How. 627.

14. Restraining proceedings in. An application for an injunction to restrain proceedings under a state court, will be denied where there is no allegation made impeaching the validity of the state court proceedings. In re Clark & Bininger, (S. D. N. Y.) 3 N. B. R. 130.

15. Stay of proceedings. Proceedings in an action in a state court will not be stayed simply on the ground that the plaintiffs have taken proceedings to have the defendants declared involuntary bankrupts. In such case an order of the court of bankruptcy adjudging the defendants bankrupts, must be made before they are entitled to a stay of proceedings in the state court. Maxwell et al. v. Faxton, et al. 4 N. B. R. 60.

16. Withdrawal of cases from. The United States district courts have no authority to withdraw cases from state courts, and proceed to their trial. Congress, although having the right to have directed that suits should be taken out of state courts and be transferred to a United States court in bankruptcy, did not do so in the bankrupt act of 1867. "It not only has not deprived the state courts of jurisdiction over such cases, but it has provided for their prosecution and defence in these courts by the assignee. See sections 14 and 16 U. S. bankrupt act of 1867. Samson et al. v. Burton et al. 4 N. B. R. 1; in re Marks, 2 N. B. R. 175.

STATE INSOLVENT LAW.

1. A state insolvent or bankrupt law (which not only liberates the person of the debtor but discharges him from all liability for the debt) so far as it attempts to discharge the contract, is repugnant to the constitution of the United States, and it makes no difference in the application of the principle whether the law was passed before or after the debt was contracted. McMillan v. McNeill, 4 Wheat. (U. S. S. Ct.) 209; Sturges v. Crowninshield, 122, 192.

2. The act of a state legislature which discharges a debtor from all liability for debts contracted previous to his discharge, on his surrendering his property for the benefit of his creditors is a law imposing the obligation of contracts within the meaning of the constitution of the United States, so far as it attempts to discharge the contract, and it makes no difference in such a case that the suit was brought in a state court, of the state of which both parties were citizens where the contract was made, and the discharge obtained, and where they continued to reside until the suit was brought. Farmers' & Mechanics' Bank v. Smith, 6 Wheat. (U. S. S. Ct.) 131.

3. The effect and operation of the insolvent laws of one state upon contracts to which citizens of other states are parties, considered. Van Hook v. Whitlock, 26 Wendell, 43.

4. Since the adoption of the constitution of the United States, a state has authority to pass a bankrupt law, provided such law does not impair the obligation of contracts within the meaning of the constitution art. 1, s. 10, and provided there be no act of congress in force to establish a uniform system of bankruptcy conflicting with such law. Sturges v. Crowninshield, 4 *Wheat.* 122,192.

5. An insolvent discharge of a neighboring state which exempts the person from imprisonment, but leaves the future acquisitions of the debtor liable to execution, relates to the remedy merely, not the contract, and is not of any force in the state of New York. Imprisonment is no part of the contract. The *lex fori* governs the remedy. An insolvent law does not operate as a part of the *lex loci contractus*, unless it discharge the contract. Whittimore v. Adams, 2 *Cowen*, 626.

6. Constitutionality of. An insolvent law of one of the United States, which discharges the person and further acquisitions of a debtor, is constitutional and valid as to contracts made between citizens of such state subsequent to the passing of the law. Sebring v. Mersereau, 9 *Cowen*, 344.

7. Superseding of. The U. S. bankruptcy act of 1867, so far as it operated to supersede the state insolvent laws, did not take effect until June 1, 1867; hence proceedings commenced prior to that date would be unaffected by its operation. Martin v. Berry, (*Cal.*) 2 *N. B. R.* 188; citing Sturgis v. Crowninshield, 4 *Wheat.* 122; Ogden v. Saunders, 12 *Wheat.* 213; Blanchard v. Russell, 13 *Mass.* 12; Adams v. Story, 1 *Paines' C. C. R.* 79; Mathews v. Zani, 7 *Wheat.* 164; *ex parte* Emes, 2 *Story*, 326.

8. The act of congress passed March 2, 1867, supersedes the state insolvent laws even where the plaintiff are both citizens of the same state. Cassard *et al.* v. Kroner, 4 *N. B. R.* 185.

9. The insolvent laws of the commonwealth were not superseded until June 1, 1867, by the U. S. bankrupt law, approved by the president March 2d, 1867. Day v. Bardwell, (*Mass.*) 3 *N. B. R.* 115.

10. The state insolvent laws were super-

seded on the 1st June, 1867, by the bankrupt act. Thornhill v. Bank of Louisiana 3 *N. B. R.* 110; s. c. 2 *C. L. N.* 157.

STATEMENT OF ACCOUNTS.

1. If a creditor who proves his debt by declaration files a statement of account which is not full, true and complete, his proof ought to be rejected. *Ex parte* Barnett, 4 *L. R.*, *Ch.* 68; 19 *L. T.*, *N. S.* 406; 17 *W. R.* 88. (Eng.)

STATUTES.

1. The bankrupt statutes do not bind the crown. *Ex parte* Russell, 19 *Ves.* 165. (Eng.)

2. The 12 & 13 Vict. c. 106, does not interfere with rights accruing under any of the acts repealed by the first section, notwithstanding such rights may have accrued after the passing of the act. *In re* Bissell, 2 *Kay & J.* 328; 2 *Jur.*, *N. S.* 370; 25 *L. J.*, *Chanc.* 323. (Eng.)

3. A bankrupt had been guilty of an offence against 12 & 13 Vict. c. 106, s. 251, in not surrendering himself to the court, and an information had been laid before a magistrate, who had issued a warrant for his apprehension. Subsequently the 24 & 25 Vict. c. 134, came into operation, which, by sec. 230, repeals 12 & 13 Vict. c. 106, s. 251, subject to the exceptions therein contained. The bankrupt was afterwards indicted and convicted under the repealed enactment. *Held,* that this was a proceeding pending within 24 & 25 Vict. c. 134, s. 230; and secondly, that the word penalty in that section, extends to any penal consequences whatsoever, and is not restricted to a pecuniary penalty only. Reg. v. Smith, 1 *L. & C.*, *C. C.* 131; 9 *Cox*, *C. C.* 110; 8 *Jur.*, *N. S.* 199; 31 *L. J.*, *M. C.* 105; 10 *W. R.* 273; 5 *L. T.*, *N. S.* 761. (Eng.)

STATUTES OF LIMITATION.

1. State statutes of limitation are applied to controversies in the courts of the United

States, unless congress has otherwise provided, with the same effect as they would be if the controversy were pending in the courts of the state. In case of fraud the statute will in equity begin to run as against the plaintiff when he has knowledge or information of facts which creates the belief that the transaction is fraudulent and can be proved to be so; and if, under all the circumstances, the plaintiff has been guilty of negligence in discovering or attacking the fraud, the statute will begin to operate against him from the period his laches commenced. Martin, assignee *v.* Smith, (*Mo.*) 4 *N. B. R.* 83; citing Hovenden *v.* Lord Annesby, 2 *Sch. & Lef.* 624; Troup *v.* Smith, 20 *Johns. R.* 33, 47, 48; Stearns *v.* Paige, 7 *How.* 819, 829; Carr *v.* Hilton, 1 *Cur.*, *C. C. R.* 230; s. c. *Id.* 399; McLain *v.* Ferrell, 1 *Swan*, (*Tenn.*) 48; Bucknor *v.* Calcote, 28 *Miss.* 432.

2. The third section of the act of congress of March 30th, 1803, for the relief of insolvent debtors in the district of Columbia, does not create any express or implied exception to the operation of the statute of limitations, by making the insolvent a trustee for his creditors in respect to his future property, or by making any demand included in the schedule of his debts, a debt of record. The including of a demand in the schedule of the insolvent's debt is sufficient evidence to sustain an issue on a replication of a new promise to the plea of the statute of limitations, if the period of limitation has not elapsed after the date of schedule. Brown *v.* Henderson, 6 *Wheat.* 514.

3. Acknowledgment of debt. Statements made by a legatee in his balance or on his examination under his bankruptcy, will not constitute an acknowledgment of the debt within the statute of limitations, but such statements are evidence to show the character of the advances made to the legatee by the testator, namely, whether made as gifts or as loans. Courtnay *v.* Williams, 3 *Hare*, 539; 13 *L. J., Chanc.* 461. (Eng.)

4. Debts barred by. Debts barred by the statute of limitation are not provable. *Ex parte* Dewdney, 15 *Ves.* 479; *ex parte* Ross, 2 *Gl. & J.* 330.

5. A debt barred by the statute of limitations of the state where the bankrupt resides, cannot be proved against his estate in bankruptcy. The entry of a debt upon the schedule by a bankrupt is not such an acknowledgment or new promise as will revive a debt thus barred. *In re* Kingsley, (*Mass.*) 1 *N. B. R.* 66; citing *ex parte* Dewdney, 15 *Ves.* 479; *ex parte* Roffey, 19 *Ves.* 468; Gregory *v.* Hurrill, 3 *B. & C.* 341; Taylor *v.* Hyrkins, 5 *B. & C.* 489; Hunter *v.* Potts, 4 *T. R.* 182; Potter *v.* Brown, 5 *East*, 124; May *v.* Breed, 7 *Cush.* 15; *Story Conflict of Laws*, 335; Richardson *v.* Thomas, 13 *Gray*, 381; Roscoe *v.* Hale, 7 *Gray*, 274; Stoddard *v.* Doane, 7 *Gray*, 274.

6. A debt barred by the statute of limitations of Maine, where the bankrupt resides, cannot be proved against his estate in bankruptcy by a creditor, resident in another state, notwithstanding such demand is not barred by the statute of limitations in the state where the creditor resides. An entry of such debt in bankrupt's schedules does not revive it. *In re* Haden, (*Me.*) 1 *N. B. R.* 97; citing Bell *v.* Morrison, 1 *Peters*, 362.

7. *Contra.* Although a debt may be barred by the statute of limitations of the state where the bankrupt resides, it may nevertheless be proven against his estate in bankruptcy. *In re* Shepherd, (*N. D. N. Y.*) 1 *N. B. R.* 115; citing Rawls *v.* Am. Life Ins. Co. 36 *Barb.* 357; McElmoyle *v.* Cohn, 13 *Peters*, 312; Townsend *v.* Jemison, 9 *How.* 407; Gares *v.* Frank, 36 *Barb.* 320; Power *v.* Hathaway, 42 *Barb.* 214; Ruggles *v.* Keeler, 3 *Johns. R.* 263; Bulger *v.* Roche, 11 *Pick.* 39; Dwight *v.* Clark, 7 *Mass.* 515; Decouche *v.* Savolier, 3 *Johns. Ch. R.* 190; Lincoln *v.* Battile, 6 *Wend.* 472; Byrne *v.* Crowningshill, 17 *Mass.* 55; Medbury *v.* Hopkins, 3 *Conn. R.* 472.

8. In repose during the rebellion. Statutes of limitations exist in all the states and have, with few exceptions, been copied from the statute of limitations brought to this country by our colonial ancestors. Absolute suspension of the right to sue and prohibition to exercise it, exist during war by the law of nations, but the disability is removed upon the restoration of peace. An enemy creditor cannot prosecute his claims after the commencement of hostilities, and these statutes are not to be construed as prohibiting the prosecution of those claims after the lapse of the limited period, when the pendency of hostilities precludes the use of the legal remedies during the designated time. *Held,* that creditors debts due from belligerents, are not annulled, but are only suspended during the war; when peace is restored they are revived, and the remedy in favor of the creditors is renewed. Levy *v.* Stewart & Co. 4 *N. B. R.* 193.

9. Pennsylvania. The statute of limitations does not run against debts due by an insolvent debtor. Lapse of time, much greater than that allowed by the statutes, may raise the presumption of the payment of such debts, but where a debtor returns no fund but a debt to become due on a future contingency, no presumption of payment would arise before the fund came to hand. Feather's Appeal, 1 *R. P & W. Pa. R.* 322.

10. By the express provisions of the insolvent law, the statute of limitations does not run against debts due by an insolvent debtor. *Id.*

11. A discharge under the insolvent law does not take from the debtor the protection of the statute of limitations. Shornberger *v.* Adams, 4 *Watts' Penn. R.* 430.

12. Plea of. Where a bill in equity was brought to recover from the defendant money alleged to be due to the plaintiff on an agreement made by defendant with the bankrupts to pay them, as salaries for their services as clerks, certain portions of the net profits realized from the business carried on by the defendant and for an accounting, the court decided that a plea as to the statute of limitations was not warranted by the 2d section of the U. S. bankrupt act of 1867, in the above case. Sedgwick *v.* Casey, (*S. D. N. Y.*) 4 *N. B. R.* 161.

13. What will and what will not take debt out of. An admission by a bankrupt in his balance sheet will not take a debt out of the statute of limitations as against his assignees; nor will an admission in an unsigned letter, written and sent by

direction of the assignees by an accountant employed by them to wind up the affairs of the bankrupt's estate. Pott *v.* Clegg, 16 *M. & W.* 321; 11 *Jur.* 289; 16 *L. L.,* *Exch.* 310. (Eng.)

STATUTORY FORFEITURE.

1. Assignee in bankruptcy cannot maintain action for. There is not in the bankrupt act any grant of a power or right to institute proceedings for the recovery of a statutory forfeiture not claimed by the bankrupt, either before or after the proceedings in bankruptcy. The assignee may require the creditor to prove his debt, reciting the security and setting forth the consideration, and contest the claim for any usurious surplus. Although neither of the mortgagors united in the petition nor were parties to the record, yet under the act of congress of March 3, 1865, they are not competent witnesses against the executors of the opposite party as to transactions with or statements made by the testator. Brombey *v.* Smith *et al.* (*Wis.*) 3 *C. L. N.* 298; s. c. 5 *N. B. R.*

STAY OF FORECLOSURE.

1. The mortgagees of certain realty assets of a bankrupt corporation brought suit in a state court to foreclose, and made assignee in bankruptcy a defendant. The assignee filed a petition in the U. S. district court, praying that proceedings in the foreclosure suit be stayed, and the mortgage be set aside as invalid. Further proceedings were accordingly enjoined, whereupon mortgagees petitioned for review, denying the jurisdiction of the district court upon the petition of the assignee aforesaid. The court decided that the district court had jurisdiction under section 1 of the U. S. bankrupt act of 1867, and that the proceedings by the assignee should have been by a bill in equity and not by petition; accordingly leave was granted for the petition to be amended and filed as a bill in equity. *In re* N. Y. Kerosene Oil Co. (*E. D. N. Y.*) 2 *N. B. R.* 31.

STAY OF PROCEEDINGS.

1. A stay of proceedings to await the question of discharge will not be granted where parties have become sureties for the costs of bankrupt in a judgment obtained against him (bankrupt) from which an appeal was taken to the general term, but all proceedings on any judgment that may be obtained against him must be stayed until the further order of the court. A stay of proceedings in this class of actions would permit one defendant by filing a petition in bankruptcy to stay proceedings against all others, and thus subject the creditor to the delay of a year or two and the other defendants in the meantime might themselves become insolvent. *In re* Hoyt *et al. v.* Freel *et al.* superior court N. Y., 4 *N. B. R.* 34.

2. It is the duty of the U. S. district court to continue an injunction staying a proceeding in a state court until the bankrupt has had reasonable time to obtain his discharge. *In re* Metcalf, (*S. D. N. Y.*) *N. B. R. Sup.* xliii ; *in re* Reed, (*S. D. N. Y.*) *N. B. R. Sup.* i.

3. A U. S. district court has no power to grant an injunction to stay proceedings in a state court by reason of bankruptcy proceedings pending in another state, and before another district court. *In re* Richardson *et al.* (*S. D. N. Y.*) 2 *N. B. R.* 74.

4. A creditor of a debt which is provable in bankruptcy, who has commenced a suit in a state court for the recovery of his debt, may be enjoined to stay all proceedings in such suit, whether such debt be one to which the bankrupt's discharge would be a bar or not. *In re* Rosenberg, 2 *N. B. R.* 81.

5. Where a defendant has become bankrupt, after verdict and before judgment, and the plaintiff had proved for the debt but had not been permitted to prove for the costs, upon summary application, under 6 Geo. 4, c. 16, s. 59, stayed proceedings in the action for the recovery of the costs. Wardward *v.* Meredith, 2 *D. & L.* 136 ; 8 *Jur.* 1136; 13 *L. J., Q. B.* 322. (Eng.)

6. A bankrupt, who has omitted to apply for a stay of proceedings in an action against him pending the question of his discharge may nevertheless apply after judgment when he has his discharge, to have supplementary proceedings on such judgment stayed on the ground that he has been discharged, if plaintiffs demand be one that is affected by the discharge. The World Company *v.* Brooks, 3 *N. B. R.* 146.

7. Proceedings supplementary to execution commenced by an order of a judge of a state court on a judgment recovered therein, will be stayed on application to a court in bankruptcy to await the final decision of that court relative to a bankrupt's discharge. *In re* Reed, *N. B. R. Sup.* i.

8. Creditors will not be allowed to prove their debt where they refuse to surrender bankrupt's property until after the assignee has obtained a decree against them. *In re* Tonkin & Trewartha, (*Mich.*) 4 *N. B. R.* 13.

9. Where a defendant in an action for the recovery of a debt has become bankrupt, and the plaintiff has tendered his claim for proof of the debt under the bankruptcy, and the claim is not allowed, but adjourned, the defendant is not entitled to stay of proceedings in the action. To entitle him to such stay of proceedings the debt must be proved under the bankruptcy, or the claim entered upon the proceedings. Ball *v.* Bowden, 22 *L. J., Exch.* 249.

10. A bankruptcy court has no authority to issue process to any other marshal than that of the district over which said court has jurisdiction, directing such marshal to arrest and bring before such court any person named in such attachment. No action of a creditor against a bankrupt not seeking to enforce any demand against him, or to deprive his assignees of any property or right will be stayed by injunctions under the 21st section of the U. S. bankrupt act of 1867. *In re* Hirsch, 2 *N. B. R.* 1.

11. Any suit or proceeding shall, upon the application of the bankrupt, be stayed to await the determination of the court in bankruptcy, on a question of the discharge *Provided,* There be no unreasonable delay on the part of the bankrupt in endeavoring to obtain his discharge. *Section* 21 *U. S. bankrupt act,* 1867.

STOCK.

1. Claim of exemptions from. Where the assignee only set aside as exempt property to a householder, certain things which were exempt under the law of the bankrupt's domicil, to the amount of sixteen dollars and fifty cents, and there was amongst the bankrupt's assets a stock of dry and fancy goods, which stock sold for thirteen hundred and thirty-three dollars and forty-two cents, a portion of which had been claimed as exempt property under the various provisions of the bankrupt act, to an amount which would equal five hundred dollars, but which was disallowed by the assignee, and on a case stated between the assignee and the bankrupt as to the above facts, a reference is made by the register to the court for its decision as to whether any money allowance should be made to the bankrupt out of the proceeds of the sale. *Held*, that until it appears what articles of the stock of dry and fancy goods were claimed as exempt, it is not possible to decide on that point, but that under the term *article* or *necessaries*, money cannot be set apart unless such money is the proceeds of specified things which ought to have been set apart under the head of "other articles and necessaries" of the bankrupt. *In re* Welch, (*S. D. N. Y.*) 5 *N. B. R.* 348.

2. In fictitious names. Where a bankrupt had invested money in the purchase of stock in a fictitious name for the purpose of defrauding creditors, the court in an action by the assignees, will order the bank to erase from their books the fictitious names, and insert that of the bankrupt. Green *v.* Bank of England, 3 *T. & C.* 722. (Eng.)

3. Mortgaged. A chattel mortgage of a stock of goods executed by one copartner under seal, and assented to by the other partner by parol, is valid, and the seal is a matter of indifference where such mortgages are not required by law to be under seal. When mortgagors in such mortgage had stipulated to retain possession of goods, to sell and dispose of them as agents of the mortgagee of a national bank, the court decided, in an action brought by the assignee in bankruptcy, to set the mortgage aside and recover the amount of deposits made by the mortgagor with the mortgagee, that the matter must be referred to an assignee, with instructions to ascertain the amount of sales, giving the mortgagee on his report a decree for the deficiency, if any should be found. Hawkins, assignee, etc. *v.* First National Bank of Hastings, (*Minn.*) 2 *N. B. R.* 108; citing 1 *Met.* 515; 4 *Metcalf*, 548; 3 *Comstock*, 144; 41 *T.* 313; 19 *Johnson R.* 513; 11 *Pick.* 400; 4 *Minn.* 553; *Wend.* 492; 9 *N. Y.* 213; 13 *N. Y.* 577; 19 *N. Y.* 124; 58 *N. Y. Rep.* 390.

4. A mortgage upon a stock of goods, which authorizes the mortgagor to sell them and replace them with others, at such times and in such manner as he may determine, and use the proceeds generally as he sees fit, is void as to such goods as the power of sale relates to. *In re* Kahley *et al.* (*Wis.*) 4 *N. B. R.* 124; citing Houston *v.* Bank of N. O., 6 *How.* 486; Foster *et al. v.* Ames, 2 *N. B. R.* 147; *ex parte* Christy, 3 *How.* 308; Place *v.* Lingworthy, 13 *Wis.* 629; Gardner *v.* McEvans, 19 *N. Y.* 123; Collins *v.* Meyer, 16 *Ohio*, 547; Jordan *v.* Turner, 3 *Blackford*, 309; Edgesell *v.* Hart, 5 *Seldon*, 213.

5. Where a stock of goods which had been mortgaged was taken possession of by the assignee, and was sold by order of court and the proceeds held subject to its order, the mortgagee claiming it by petition and the assignee opposing, on the ground that the mortgage was voidable under the second clause of the 33d section of the U. S. bankrupt act of 1867, the mortgagor being a trader, and the loan one made out of the ordinary course of business; the court decided that the mortgagor being a retail dealer, a mortgage of the whole of his stock was out of the ordinary course of business, and a confession of insolvency, and mortgagor's petition dismissed. If made directly to the creditor it would have been an act of bankruptcy, and in this case both parties seem to have considered it injurious to the mortgagor's credit, and agreed that it should not be recorded until some necessity should arise therefor. *In re* Butler, 4 *N. B. R.* 91.

6. Where the record before the court does not show that a precedent agreement existed it is not to be assumed. A mere promise does not constitute an agreement. Any agreement by an insolvent debtor with a creditor (a bank) to create a preference in favor of that creditor if he has cause to believe the debtor insolvent, is void if the debtor is afterwards proceeded against under the bankrupt act. Transfers of personal property of an insolvent consisting of a stock of goods only take effect from its delivery to the purchaser. An unregistered personal mortgage is not valid in Kansas as against creditors. Where the mortgagor remained in possession of a stock of goods, the property mortgaged, and continued to make sales of the same, with consent of the mortgagee, the mortgage could not constitute a valid lien. The 2nd Nat. Bank of Leavenworth *et al. v.* Hunt, assignee, 4 *N. B. R.* 198.

7. Notice of assignment of. Where stock stands in the name of and is vested in three trustees for the benefit of A., who assigns his equitable life interest therein to B., to secure advances, and B. subsequently mentions to one of the trustees, who was not the acting trustee, that he was secured by the assignment, it was held, that this was sufficient notice to prevent the interest of A. vesting in his assignees in bankruptcy, as property in his order and disposition. Smith *v.* Smith, 2 *C. & M.* 231; 4 *Tyr.* 52. (Eng.)

8. Sale of. A creditor cannot insist on an immediate sale of the bankrupt's stock in trade unless he prove some particular damage which would be sustained. *Ex parte* Hall, 2 *Deac.* 263; *ex parte* Kendall, 17 *Ves.* 514. (Eng.)

9. If a sale takes place on the premises of the stock in trade, and the house and shop fixtures, and the catalogue states that on the same day will be sold the valuable lease of the premises, with commanding shop, held for an unexpired term of sixteen years from Ladyday preceding, at the low rent of 20*l.* per annum, and the catalogue describes the sale to be made without reserve, and contains a list of fixtures, some of them belonging to the landlord, and some put up by the bankrupt, and the lease is bought in, but all the fixtures are sold, and the premises much injured by their being taken down and carried away, it is taking possession. Carter *v.* Warne, 4 *C. & P.* 191 (Eng.)

10. Vesting in assignees. A firm of two solicitors held a mortgage for 600*l.* upon a share of an estate in Kent, which was sold, and to indemnify the purchasers against certain claims, the purchase money was invested in consols in the name of one of the solicitors and another party, upon trust for indemnity, and subject thereto to secure the debt due the firm. After this the firm, having money of a client in their hands, wrote to her a letter, offering to give her a charge for the amount on a mortgage for 600*l.* on a share of the estate in Kent. Upon the bankruptcy of the firm, *held*, that the letter created a valid charge upon the interest of the firm in the consols; and that as one of the firm was a trustee of the stock, there was sufficient notice of the transaction to prevent the charge being defeated on the ground that the stock was in the order and disposition, or reputed ownership of the bankrupts. *Ex parte* Rogers, 2 *Jur., N. S.* 480; 25 *L. J., Bank.* 41. (Eng.)

11. Stock standing in the name of the bankrupt in trust for other persons, did not pass to his assignees under 6 Geo. 4, c. 16, s. 72, although it was not entered in the name of the bankrupt as trustee in the bank books. *Ex parte* Witham, 1 *Mont., D. & D.* 624. (Eng.)

STOCK COMPANIES.

1. *And be it further enacted,* That the provisions of this act shall apply to all monied, business or commercial corporations, and joint stock companies; and that upon the petition of any officer of any such corporation or company, duly authorized by a vote of a majority of the corporators present at any legal meeting called for the purpose, or upon the petition of any creditor or creditors of such corporation or company, made and presented in the manner hereinafter provided in respect to debtors, the like proceedings shall be had and taken as are hereinafter provided in the case of debtors; and all the provisions of this act which apply to the debtor, or set forth his duties in regard to furnishing schedules and inventories, executing papers, submitting to examinations, dissolving, making over, secreting, concealing, conveying, assigning, or paying away his money or property, shall in like manner and with like force, effect, and penalties, apply to each and every officer of such corporation or company in relation to the same matters concerning the corporation or company, and the money and property thereof. All payments, conveyances and assignments declared fraudulent and void by this act, when made by a debtor, shall in like manner and to the like extent, and with like remedies, be fraudulent and void when made by a corporation or company. No allowance or discharge shall be granted to any corporation or joint stock company, or to any person, or officer or member thereof. *Provided,* That whenever any corporation, by proceedings under this act, shall be declared bankrupt, all its property and assets shall be distributed to the creditors of such corporations in the manner provided in this act in respect to natural persons. *Section 37 U. S. bankrupt act,* 1867.

STOPPAGE AND SUSPENSION OF COMMERCIAL PAPER.

1. *And be it further enacted,* That any persons residing and owing debts as aforesaid, who, after, the passage of this act, being a banker, broker, merchant, trader, manufacturer or miner, has fraudulently stopped payment, or who has stopped or suspended and not resumed payment of his commercial paper within a period of fourteen days, shall be deemed to have committed an act of bankruptcy, and subject to the conditions hereinafter prescribed, shall be adjudged a bankrupt, on the petition of one or more of his creditors, the aggregate of whose debts provable under this act amount to at least two hundred and fifty dollars, provided such petition is brought within six months after the act of bankruptcy shall have been committed, and if such person shall be adjudged a bankrupt, the assignee may recover back the money or other property so paid, conveyed, sold, assigned or transferred contrary to this act; *provided,* the person receiving such payment or conveyance had reasonable cause to believe that a fraud on this act was intended,

and that the debtor was insolvent; and such creditor shall not be allowed to prove his debt in bankruptcy. *Sec.* 39 *U. S. bankrupt act,* 1867.

2. The allegation of stoppage and suspension of payment on a certain day, upon commercial paper which was made and dated within six months next preceding the actual filing of the petition connected with the allegation that payment of the commercial paper (a due bill) had been demanded at different times, and that the respondent had failed to make such payment, was equivalent to an allegation of a demand for payment on that day. Order of adjudication granted. *In re* Chappel, 4 *N. B. R.* 176.

3. In a mercantile community the nonpayment of a note of maturity by the maker who is a merchant or trader, is *prima facie* evidence of insolvency, and warrants a decree in bankruptcy. In an agricultural country the rule is different, and there no man is suspected of being insolvent from the fact alone that his notes are not paid promptly at maturity. Shafer *v*. Fritchery *et al.* 4 *N. B. R.* 179.

4. The suspension of payment of a piece of commercial paper, when there is a defence or other good cause, is not to be counted an act of bankruptcy, but if there is a chronic or habitual suspension, although not continued for a perion of fourteen days, the nonpayment of one piece of commercial paper for that period will be deemed an act of bankruptcy. *In re* Brown, Waler & Co. (*E. D. Mo.*) Unreported.

5. Where drafts made and dated at Neuremberg, Bavaria, drawn or purporting to be drawn on a house at Leipzic, accepted by authorized agents in the United States by merely writing the words "accepted," with date and drawee's name across the face of the draft are over due and the payment thereof is suspended for a period of fourteen days, the drawee having a place of business in the United States (within the southern district of New York,) at which the acceptors were executed, will be ordered to show cause why he shall not be adjudicated a bankrupt upon the petition of the maker or owner of the draft. Geyer *v.* Bombard & Beyrick, (*S. D. N. Y.*) Unreported.

5. The non-payment of a single piece of commercial paper is not an act of bankruptcy in itself, for the reason that there may be a good defence to the payment of it, but when such suspension is chronic or there is an inability to meet and pay checks and notes as they mature, then that is such a suspension as the law contemplates, and even though there may be but a single piece of paper fourteen days past due, the maker may be adjudged bankrupt. McLean *et al. v.* Brown *et al.* 4 *N. B. R.* 188.

6. A suspension of payment of his commercial paper by a solvent trader and non-resumption of such payment within a period of fourteen days is *per se* fraudulent, and is an act of bankruptcy. Hardy, Blake & Co. *v.* Bininger & Co. (*S. D. N. Y.*) 4 *N. B. R.* 77.

7. A dissolution of a copartnership cannot be set up to disprove an act of bankruptcy, by merchants or traders, whose paper has remained unpaid for fourteen days. It is of no avail that when a firm is dissolved that there was an agreement by one member that he should assume and pay all the firm obligations. *In re* Weikert & Parker, (*S. D. N. Y.*) 3 *N. B. R.* 5.

8. The non-payment at maturity of promissory notes that are not commercial paper is no ground for an adjudication of the debtors as bankrupts, on the petition by a creditor in involuntary bankruptcy. Katzenberg *v.* Lowenstein *et al.* (*S. D. N. Y.*) 2 *N. B. R.* 99.

9. It is not necessary to show the stoppage of payment to have been fraudulent. The view of the act which presents uniformity of decision is that a suspension of payment and non-resumption within fourteen days are all that is contemplated by that provision. *In re* Cowles, (*Minn.*) 1 *N. B. R.* 42.

10. If a debtor is guilty of fraudulently suspending the payment of his commercial paper, proceedings may be immediately taken by his creditors to have him adjudged a bankrupt without waiting for the lapse of fourteen days The U. S. bankrupt act of 1867, sec. 39, provides for two classes of cases, a fraudulent suspension and a suspension of payment for fourteen days without

resumption, for either of which a merchant or trader may be adjudged a bankrupt. *In re* Schoo, (*Mo.*) 3 *N. B. R.* 52.

11. A suspension for fourteen days of his commercial paper by a trader is an act of bankruptcy which can only be rebutted by showing a resumption or accident, which prevented such resumption. Where nothing of the kind is claimed, the honest trader is entitled to the fourteen days and no more in which to meet his commercial paper. Claffin & Co. *v.* Wells, (*N. D. N. Y.*) *N. B. R. Sup.* xxxvii.

12. Suspension of payment of commercial paper by a merchant is *prima facie* evidence of fraud, and casts the burden of proof on the bankrupt; and being unexplained, decree of bankruptcy adjudged on petition of creditors. *In re* Ballard & Parsons, (*Conn.*) 2 *N. B. R.* 84.

13. The words "fourteen days," as used in sec. 39 of the U. S. bankrupt act of 1867, do not necessarily apply to the case of a fraudulent stoppage of payment of commercial paper. When a man declines to pay solely because he is not liable, or because he has a valid claim or set-off against the paper, this is not a stoppage or suspension within the meaning of the bankrupt law. When the paper is due and it is not paid, because without adequate legal excuse the maker will not or is not able to pay, and it is continued for the period of fourteen days, the court has held that this constitutes an act of bankruptcy. *In re* Thompson & McClallen, (*Illinois*,) 3 *N. B. R.* 45.

14. The stopping of the payment of commercial paper mentioned in sec. 39, of the bankrupt act, must be fraudulent, and must continue for fourteen days in order to be an act of bankruptcy. Such suspension or non-resumption is fraudulent (supposing the liability to be undisputed) when it is done purposely, and not by accident or mistake. *In re* Hollis, (*Mass.*) 3 *N. B. R.* 82.

15. Failure on the part of the banker, merchant or trader to honor his commercial paper is so far deemed evidence of fraud, as to necessitate an explanation on his part disproving insolvency or intention of fraud. Heinsheimer *v.* Shea *et al.* (*Indiana,*) 3 *N.*

B. R. 47. *In re* Smith, (*N. D. N. Y.*) 3 *N. B. R.* 98.

16. A merchant, banker or trader, who in the course of his business shall execute notes, bills or other instruments, which circulate as commercial paper, and who fails to pay the same within fourteen days after maturity, or the same shall become due and payable, without a sufficient excuse for such failure, shall be deemed to have fraudulently suspended payment, and shall be declared a bankrupt. Davis & Green *v.* Armstrong, (*Miss.*) 3 *N. B. R.* 7.

17. Mere stoppage and non-resumption of payment of commercial paper for fourteen days is not sufficient ground on which to have a debtor declared a bankrupt, nor is fraud inferable therefrom. Gillies v. Cone *et al.* (*S. D. N. Y.*) 2 *N. B. R.* 10.

18. *Contra*, amendments of July 14th, 1870, to U. S. bankrupt act.

19. The suspension of payment of commercial paper, unless fraudulent, is not an act of bankruptcy. *In re* W. Leeds, (*E. D. Pa.*) 1 *N. B. R.* 138 ; citing *in re* Jersey City Window Glass Co. 1 *N. B. R.* 113.

20. A protested note on which a bankrupt was principal debtor held by a bank that had discounted it, was taken up by a new note made by the same parties and accepted by the bank after adjudication of bankruptcy. The court decided that the original debt was thereby extinguished, and the liability ceased to be a claim on the estate. A second indorser might have proved his claim on the original note before extinguishment, but could have received dividends only on the amount he could show that he had personally paid. *In re* Montgomery, (*S. D. N. Y.*) 3 *N. B. R.* 108.

21. Suspension of commercial paper is an act of bankruptcy if continued for fourteen days. 16 *U. S. Stat.* 276.

STRIKING OUT CLAIM.

1. Insufficient testimony. Where the testimony does not show material facts, and the testimony does not admit of rebut-

ting evidence, the prayer of a petitioner to strike out the proof of a claim, will be denied with costs. *In re* Willard & Millward, (*S. D. N. Y.*) 5 *N. R. R.*

SUBPŒNA.

1. It is not necessary, in the courts of the United States, that the subpœna for witnesses should be served by the marshal. Gordon, McMillan & Co. *v.* Scott, (*Pa.*) 2 *N. B. R.* 28.

SUBSEQUENT CONVERSATION

1. Not admissable as to date of act of bankruptcy. Upon an issue directed to try whether P. had committed an act of bankruptcy on a given day, it appeared that on the preceding day he sent a letter from his dwelling house at Greenwich to his place of business, addressed to his son, stating that he was unable to meet his engagements, and desiring that he might be denied to any creditor who might call ; and immediately after dispatching this letter he left him, and remained absent during the whole of that and the following day. A witness proved that P. called on the day in question at her brother's house in London, that he expressed to her an apprehension of being sent to the Fleet, and stated that he was in no hurry to get home, and would not go very early, as he had creditors who would lay hold of him, and that he did not leave till after dark. The jury were told, that if they believed the statements made by the witness, P. on that occasión committed an act of bankruptcy ; they said they did believe the witness, but they did not think P. spoke *bona fide*. *Held*, that P. had committed an act of bankruptcy, and that evidence of his conduct and conversation, on the day subsequent to the date mentioned in the issue, was not admissable to explain his conduct on that day. Johnson *v.* Woolf, 2 *Scott*, 372. (Eng.)

SUBSEQUENT COSTS.

1. Where the question at issue was whether the claim of a sheriff for costs on at-

tachment suit against property of the bankrupt, which has been claimed as exempt, is such a claim as can be proved in bankruptcy against the bankrupt's estate. The assignee objecting to the proof and allowance of such claim, on the grounds that the claim of one of the plaintiffs in the attachment suit has never been proven against the bankrupt's estate. *Held*, that the debt or principal must be proven and allowed before the costs made before the commencement of proceedings in bankruptcy can be proven and allowed. Where the principal debt has been duly proved against the bankrupt's estate, the costs can be proved if made in good faith before ₜₕₑ commencement of proceedings in bankruptcy, and without a knowledge of the insolvency of the defendant, and without intention of defeating the provisions of the bankrupt law. Where, however, a portion of the costs have been made after the commencement of the bankruptcy proceedings, that portion will be disallowed. *In re* Preston, (*Washington Ter.*) 5 *N. B. R.* 293.

SUBSEQUENT INTEREST.

1. Interest on a debt stops at the date of the fiat, and a creditor cannot apply his security in the first place in payment of subsequent interest, and then prove for his debt, which he otherwise might, namely, his original debt and interest up to the date of the fiat, but must, in the absence of a contract entitling him thereto, apply the scourity in reduction of the provable debt. *Ex parte* Pollard, 4 *Jur.* 1018. (Eng.)

SUBSEQUENT PAYMENTS.

1. Reducing indebtedness. The district court has no jurisdiction of an involuntary case in bankruptcy, unless it appears on the trial that the debtor at that time owed debts, provable under the act, exceeding the sum of three hundred dollars, and is indebted to the petitioning creditors in the amount of two hundred and fifty dollars. This is true, even though the debtor was at the time of the filing of the petition indebted to exceed these sums. Where his indebtedness, by subsequent payments, is reduced below those sums, the court loses jurisdiction. *In re* Skelley, (*Ill.*) 5 *N. B. R.* 215.

SUBSEQUENT PROMISE.

1. A subsequent promise to pay a debt, as to which the debtor has been discharged from imprisonment, under the act of 1819, (sess. 42, ch. 101) will not take away the effect of such discharge. Hubert *v.* Williams, 5 *Cowen*, 537.

SUBSEQUENTLY ACQUIRED PROPERTY.

1. And if the complainant wishes to protect and preserve his lien upon the defendants' subsequently acquired real estate, as against those who may become *bona fide* purchasers thereof, without notice of the alleged invalidity of the defendant's discharge, he should file a notice in the county clerk's office, of the pendency of such supplemental suit. Alcott *v.* Avery, 1 *Barb. C. R.* 347.

SUBSTITUTION.

1. A petitioning creditor had sold a bankrupt's goods, in payment of which he took three bills of exchange, accepted by the bankrupt, which the creditor negotiated, and which were not in his hands, nor due at the time he issued the fiat. The commissioner expunged the proof of his debt, on the ground that the bills were not in his possession at the time of the bankruptcy. *Held*, than an order might be made under 6 Geo. 4, c. 16, s. 18, for the substitution of the debt of another creditor. *Ex parte* Smith, 3 *Mont., D. & D.* 341 ; 7 *Jur.* 364. (Eng.)

2. The court of bankruptcy might, under 5 & 6 Vict. c. 122, s. 4, admit another creditor to prosecute the fiat, after an unsuccessful attempt to prove his debt by the original petitioning creditor. Kynaston *v.* Davis, 15 *M. & W.* 705; 10 *Jur.* 620; 15 *L. J., Exch.* 336. (Eng.)

3. When, after admitting a debt under a trader debtor summons, the debtor obtained protection under the arrangement clauses of the bankruptcy act of 1849, and the creditor petitioned for adjudication in bankruptcy, but did not obtain adjudication, and adjudication was obtained on the petition of another creditor. *Held*, that the adjudication was valid. *Ex parte* Dales, 2 *De G. & J*. 206 ; 28 *L. J., Bank*. 13. (Eng.)

4. When a petitioning creditor's debt is insufficient, and the court orders the commission to be proceeded with on proof of a sufficient debt by any other creditor, the debt of the second may be added to that of the first, to make up the requisite amount. Byers *v*. Southwell, 6 *Bing., N. C*. 39 ; 8 *Scott*, 238. (Eng.)

5. The petition on which the order is made, cannot be used to explain an ambiguity on the order. Christie *v*. Unwin, 3 *P. & D*. 204 ; 11 *A. & E*. 373 ; 4 *Jur*. 363. (Eng.)

6. Costs on. On a petition for substitution of a debt, in lieu of the petitioning creditor's debt, the cost of the proceeding must be paid by the petitioning creditor, and not out of the bankrupt's estate. *Ex parte* Hayne, 4 *Deac. & Chit*. 403; *S. P., ex parte* Lloyd, *id*. 306. (Eng.)

7. Where the petitioning creditor's debt was on a bill of exchange, which was not in his hands when the fiat issued, the debt of another creditor was substituted at the cost of the petitioning creditor. *Ex parte* Cottley, 4 *Deac*. 138; 1 *Mont. & Chit*. 360. (Eng.)

SUFFERING PROPERTY TO BE TAKEN ON LEGAL PROCESS.

1. *And be it further enacted*, That any person residing and owing debts as aforesaid, who, after the passage of this act, being bankrupt or insolvent or in contemplation of bankruptcy or insolvency, shall make any payment, gift, grant, sale, conveyance or transfer of money or other property, estate rights or credits, or give any warrant to confess judgment or pro-

cure or suffer his property to be taken on legal process, with intent to give a preference to one or more of his creditors, or to any person or persons who are or may be liable for him as indorsers, bail sureties, or otherwise, or with the intent by such disposition of his property to defeat or delay the operation of this act, shall be deemed to have committed an act of bankruptcy, and, subject to the conditions hereinafter prescribed, shall be adjudged a bankrupt, on the petition of one or more of his creditors, the aggregate of whose debts, provable under this act, amount to at least two hundred and fifty dollars ; *provided*, such petition is brought within six months after the act of bankruptcy shall have been committed. And if such person shall be adjudged a bankrupt, the assignee may recover back the money or other property so paid, conveyed, sold, assigned or transferred contrary to this act. *Provided*, the person receiving such payment or conveyance had reasonable cause to believe that a fraud on the act was intended, and that the debtor was insolvent. And such creditor shall not be allowed to prove his debt in bankruptcy. *Section 39 U. S. bankrupt act*, 1867.

2. Suffering property to be taken on legal process. This was added for a purpose and with an intent. To say that there cannot be a suffering where there is a pressure by a creditor is to destroy the plain meaning of the words. To suffer or permit implies pressure and action from without. Pressure being thus an inherent element of sufferance, to say that where there is pressure there can be no sufferance, is to utter a fallacy. Where a person permits what he can prevent, he suffers or allows the thing to be done, whether he is threatened, or pressed, or not. A debtor who is threatened, or pressed, can prevent the taking of his property on legal process by going into voluntary bankruptcy. If he does not, he clearly suffers, or allows, or permits the taking. In Gore *v*. Loyd, 12 *M. & W*. 480, it was held, that giving under pressure a warrant of attorney to confess a judgment, under which goods were taken on execution, was not procuring, but was suffering the goods to be taken on execution ; and in Gibson *v*. King, 1 *C. & M*. 458, it was held, that allowing a judgment to go by default was suffering goods to be taken in execution which

were taken under the judgment, and was not procuring them to be taken. Extract from opinion of Judge Blatchford. *In re* Craft, (*S. D. N. Y.*) 1 *N. B. R.* 89.

3. Where the only act of bankruptcy charged was " that the bankrupt suffered his property to be taken on legal process with intent to give a preference," the order for adjudication will be reversed on bill in chancery filed in the circuit court for review. Wright *v.* Filley, 4 *N. B. R.* 197.

4. A creditor, having knowledge of his debtor's insolvency, obtained judgment by default, issued execution, and sheriff levied on his property ; other creditors petitioned to have the debtor declared a bankrupt in that he had thereby committed an act of bankruptcy. Before trial, bankrupt filed voluntary petition, and thereupon was adjudged bankrupt. The judgment creditor proved his claim for the full amount of his judgment, less what he would receive from the execution, if that should be deemed a valid payment. Assignee petitioned to have the said judgment set aside and declared void, and that said creditor and sheriff be ordered to pay over to him, less the sheriff's fees, the amount they severally held and received upon said execution, and further, that the judgment creditor's proof of claim be rejected. *Held*, that the bankrupt committed an act of bankruptcy in so suffering his property to be so taken by a creditor on legal process, and also that the judgment creditor had received a preference, and not having surrendered what property was received under it, on proving his claim in bankruptcy, the proof thereof must be rejected, and himself and the sheriff ordered to pay the assignee the amounts in their hands received on such execution, less the sheriff's fees. *In re* Davidson, 3 *N. B. R.* 106.

5. The word "suffer" in the 39th section of the U. S. bankrupt act of 1867, means an act of volition on the part of the debtor; hence where debtor gives a warrant of attorney to confess judgment, it must be held, that he intended to suffer his property to be taken on legal process. *In re* Campbell, (*Ill*) 3 *N. B. R.* 124.

6. If a firm be insolvent or in contemplation of insolvency at the time of a levy by a sheriff on their property, and refrain from going into voluntary bankruptcy, it *suffers* its property to be taken on legal process. *In re* Dibblee, (*S. D. N. Y.*) 2 *N. B. R.* 185.

7. Legal distinction between procuring and suffering. The act of 6 Geo. 4, c. 16, s. 3, provided that if any trader should *suffer* himself to be arrested for any debt not due, or *suffer* himself to be outlawed, or *procure* himself to be arrested, or his goods, money or chattels to be attached, sequestered or taken in execution, he might be brought into bankruptcy. In Gibson *v.* King, 1 Carr. & Marsh, 458, a creditor had brought an action against the bankrupt for a debt, and judgment had been suffered to go by default, and an execution had been issued on it, on which the bankrupt's goods had been taken, and the question arose whether *suffering* the judgment to go by default in the action, and *suffering* the goods to be taken on the execution on the judgment, was *procuring* the goods to be taken in execution, within the statute. The court held that the bankrupt had *suffered* the goods to be taken in execution, but had not *procured* them to be so taken. The same view of the distinction between the two words in the English act was taken in Gore *v.* Loyd, 12 Mee. & W. 463. The distinction there maintained by Baron Alderson was, that the bankrupt *procured* his goods to be taken in execution, when the initiation of the proceeding came from him, when he was the person who began to procure, when he caused the thing to be done, in the ordinary sense of the word, but that the signing reluctantly and under strong pressure from a creditor, of a warrant to confess a judgment, under a stipulation that the warrant should not be unnecessarily put in force, was *suffering* and not *procuring* goods to be taken in execution, which were taken on an execution issued on a judgment entered upon the warrant. The English and other decisions as to pressure by a creditor, and as to what it is to *procure*, have no application to the question of *suffering*. *In re* Black *v.* Secor, (*S. D. N. Y.*) 2 *N. B. R.* 65.

SUFFERING A REMOVAL.

1. When a conversion. If the messenger shows his warrant to a person supposed to be in possession of some bacon, the property of the bankrupt, and the person says, " I have it not. I have some that came from a shop in Exeter," (which was that of the son and daughter of the bankrupt) ; and the messenger desires him to take care of it and not to part with it, as more would be heard about it, and he afterwards suffers it to be removed, this is a conversion. Hawkes *v.* Dunn, 1 *Tyr.* 413 ; 1 *C. & J.* 519. (Eng.)

SUFFERING RECOVERY OF JUDGMENT.

1. The entering up of a judgment, even though prior to the commencement of bankruptcy proceedings, is void if the debtor suffered, not procured, recovery of the judgment, and the subsequent execution and levy, and the creditor had reasonable cause to believe his debtor insolvent. Beattie, assignee, etc. *v.* Gardner *et al.* (*N. D. N. Y.*) 4 *N. B. R.* 106 ; citing, Shawhan *v.* Wherritt, 7 *Howard*, 627 ; Black & Secor, 1 *N. B. R.* 81 ; *in re* Belden, 2 *N. B. R.* 14 ; *in re* Black & Secor, 2 *N. B. R.* 65 ; Fitch *et. al. v.* McGee, 2 *N. B. R.* 164 ; *in re* Wells, 3 *N. B. R.* 95.

2. Suffering a judgment to be recovered is not an act of bankruptcy where there is no intention on the part of the debtor to permit a preference of one creditor over another. *in re* Wright, (*Mo.*) 4 *N. B. R.* 197.

SUFFICIENCY OF ASSETS.

1. The jurisdiction of the bankrupt court does not depend upon the right of the party ultimately to obtain his discharge, hence it is a mistaken construction of the law to assume that because bankrupt's estate is not sufficient to pay fifty per cent. of the liabilities, U. S. courts have no jurisdiction. Van Nostrand *v.* Barr *et al.* 2 *N. B. R.* 154.

SUFFICIENT ALLEGATION.

1. Necessary to support adjudication. Where, in an indictment against a bankrupt for feloniously removing, concealing and embezzling part of his personal estate, it was alleged that he committed an act of bankruptcy by being unable to meet his engagements, and by filing his petition to the court of bankruptcy ; it was held, that as it was not alleged that he did file a declaration that he was unable to meet his engagements, as required by 12 & 13 Vict. c. 106, s. 70, there was no sufficient allegation of an act of bankruptcy, and the indictment could not be supported. Reg. *v.* Massey, 8 *Jur. N. S.* 1183 ; 32 *L. J., M C.* 21 ; 11 *W. R.* 42 ; 7 *L. T., N. S.* 391 ; 1 *L. & C., C. C.* 206 ; 9 *Cox, C. C.* 234. (Eng.)

SUITS.

1. Against a bankrupt. In cases of that kind the court will not relieve the bankrupt, when he has lost the benefit of his discharge by his own negligence. But where a judgment or decree obtained subsequently to the discharge will be binding on the defendant, or his after acquired property, and where he has had no opportunity to set up such discharge, the court will grant him relief, upon a summary application. Alcott *v.* Avery, 1 *Barb. C. R.* 347.

2. By assignee. The limitation provided by section 2, applies to proceedings whether in the bankruptcy court, the district or circuit courts. A proceeding by an assignee for the recovery of property fraudulently assigned is a suit at law. *In re* Krogman, (*Mich.*) 5 *N. B. R.* 116.

3. By creditor, before act of bankruptcy. Until the debtor commits an act of bankruptcy, any creditor may lawfully sue him, and proceed to judgment, execution, levy and sale ; but if the debtor suffers the plaintiff to obtain an advantage by judgment or otherwise over the other creditors, that will be of itself an act of bankruptcy. Smith *v.* Buchanan (*N. D. N. Y.*) 4 *N. B. R.* 133.

4. By creditor, believing debtor insolvent. Where a judgment is regularly recovered under the laws of a state, and execution and levy have duly followed the entering of a judgment, the same is void, even though entered prior to the commencement of bankruptcy proceedings, if the debtor suffered the recovery of the judgment and the subsequent execution and levy, provided the creditor had reasonable cause to believe the debtor insolvent. Beattie, assignee, *v.* Gardner *et al.* (*N. D. N. Y.*) 4 *N. B. R.* 106; citing Williams *v.* Bacon, 11 *Wend.* 636; Rusa *v.* Cooper, 2 *Cowp.* 629; Foster *v.* Goulding, 9 *Gray*, 50, 52; Shawhan *v.* Wherritt, 7 *How.* 627; Black & Secor, 1 *N. B. R.* 81; *id.* 2 *N. B. R.* 65; *in re* Belden, 2 *N. B. R.* 14; Fitch *et al. v.* Magie, 2 *N. B. R.* 164; *in re* Wells, 3 *N. B. R.* 95.

5. By executor, in his representative capacity. The court of queen's bench, in Abbot *et al.* (executors,) *v.* Parfitt, laid it down as a rule that an executor may sue, in his representative character, on contracts made with himself, while the money, when recovered, would be assets. And *held*, therefore, where one D., by his will, directed his executors to continue his business of a baker, and they did so, employing D.'s widow as their agent for the purpose, and, having supplied the defendant with goods, sued him in their representative capacity, that as the amount to be recovered would be assets of the testator, they were entitled to sue in their representative capacity. 24 *L. T., N. S.* 469, *& s. c.* 3 *C. L. N.* 292.

6. By foreign assignee. Although the right of a foreign assignee in bankruptcy must, as respects assets situate in the United States, yield to the claims of domestic creditors, yet such foreign assignee may maintain suits in our courts to collect the assets of the bankrupt's estate. Hunt *v.* Jackson, 5 *Bl. C. C.* 349.

7. By wife and bankrupt husband. In May, 1863, a *femme sole* being the owner, in her own right, of a chose in action, marries, and a suit is instituted shortly thereafter to recover from the defendant in the name of the husband and wife. This suit continues pending until 1868, when the husband, upon his own petition, was declared a bankrupt, and an assignee was appointed and an assignment executed in the usual form. Thereafter the assignee was, upon his own motion, by order of the court, made party plaintiff with the wife, and a

judgment was recovered in favor of the plaintiffs. *Held*, that the assignee may proceed to enforce the payment of such judgment by execution, and receive the money when collected; if this be done in the lifetime of the husband and wife, and if collected by him, must distribute the same to creditors, as the law directs. The assignee is deprived of no right because the bankrupt has failed to schedule such chose in action, nor by the provisions of the constitution of North Carolina, adopted in 1868. *In re* Boyd, (*N. C.*) 5 *N. B. R.*

8. Commencement of. Application for leave to commence a suit against a bankrupt will be entertained and leave granted to begin an action for a debt to which the bankrupt's discharge would not be a bar, if it appears that if not commenced forthwith the statute of limitations might run against it, or that service might not be obtained upon the bankrupt afterwards, or that testimony might be lost, and the court will then stay the suit to await the determination of the question of the debtor's discharge, or the expiration of a reasonable time to make application therefor. Where no such reasons are set forth in an application for leave to commence a suit such application will be denied by the court. *In re* Ghirardelli, (*California*,) 4 *N. B. R.* 42.

9. Commenced after discharge. To excuse from trial and costs, on account of the defendant's insolvency, the plaintiff must show that he was discharged under the insolvent act after suit brought, and move to discontinue without costs. Case *v.* Belknap, 5 *Cowen*, 432.

10. Foreclosure. The U. S. district court has jurisdiction over a foreclosure suit in the supreme court, under section one of the U. S. bankrupt act of 1867, if commenced after the debtor has been declared a bankrupt. *In re* N. Y. Kerosene Oil Co. (*E. D. N. Y.*) 3 *N. B R.* 31.

11. For libel. To charge a commissioner of bankruptcy, with being a misanthrope, a partisan, stripping the unfortunate debtors of every cent, and then depriving them of the benefit of the act, &c., is libellous, and to make out a justification of the charge, the defendant must show that the plaintiff, as commissioner, wilfully perverted the law to such oppressive purposes. Riggs *v.* Denison, 3 *Johns.* 198.

12. In another state. A discharge under the insolvent laws of another state is no bar to a suit here by a citizen of this state for a debt contracted within it, and who has not come in under the proceedings under the insolvent act. Van Raugh *v.* Van Arsdale, 3 *Caines' Cases,* 154.

13. In state court. The district court in bankruptcy may enjoin the further prosecution of a suit in a state court on which an appeal is pending. *In re* Metcalf, 2 *Bt.* 78; 5 *N. B. R.*

14. Jurisdiction of circuit court over. The circuit court has not jurisdiction of suits by the assignee of a bankrupt simply for the collection of the assets. Woods *v.* Forsyth, 16 *Pitts. L. J.* 234; s. c. 2 *W. Jur.* 348.

15. May proceed to judgment. If the amount due the creditor is in dispute, the suit, by leave of the court in bankruptcy, may proceed to judgment for the purpose of ascertaining the amount due, which amount may be proved in bankruptcy, but execution shall be stayed as aforesaid. *Section* 21 *U. S. bankrupt act,* 1867.

15. Pending bankruptcy proceedings. Where a bankrupt must set up a discharge, in a suit pending against him at the time it is obtained, as a bar to the further continuance of such suit, to obtain satisfaction of the debt from him personally or out of the future acquisitions, provided the situation of the suit, at the time of obtaining such discharge, is such as to enable him to set up his discharge as a defence. Alcott *v.* Avery, 1 *Barb. C. R.* 347.

17. Stay of. Any suit or proceeding shall, upon the application of the bankrupt, be stayed to await the determination of the court in bankruptcy on the question of the discharge. *Provided,* there is no unreasonable delay on the part of the bankrupt in endeavoring to obtain his discharge. *Section* 21 *U. S. bankrupt act,* 1867.

SUMMARY PROCESS.

1. Non-interference by bankruptcy court. Where there is no conflict of jurisdiction between the officers of the state courts and those of the court of bankruptcy the latter will not interfere with its summary process. *In re* Davidson, 2 *N. B. R.* 49.

SUMMONS.

1. And particulars. In particulars served by a fruit merchant on a grocer, together with a summons under 12 & 13 Vict. c. 106, s. 78, the word "goods," describes the wares supplied sufficiently to prevent an adjudication from being annulled on the ground of uncertainty in the particulars. *Ex parte* Bower, 1 *De. G. Mac. & G.* 468; 16 *Jur.* 734; 21 *L. J., Bank.* 61.

2. An affidavit filed as the foundation of an act of bankruptcy, states the demand to be for goods sold and delivered, but by the particulars, the greater portion of the debt was stated merely as due on bills of exchange, which, however, it afterwards turned out were given in respect of goods sold and delivered. *Held,* that the proceedings was irregular, and an insufficient foundation for an act of bankruptcy. *Ex parte* Greenstock, *De Gex,* 230; 10 *Jur.* 122; 15 *L. J., Bank.* 5. (Eng.)

3. A debtor on being served with the summons, called on a creditor's solicitor, and saw his clerk, at whose instance the debtor signed a memorandum, promising to pay at a certain time, or that, if he did not, the creditor might proceed on the summons. The debtor was attended by no solicitor on his behalf, and was not aware of the irregularity in the proceedings. *Held,* that neither the signature of the memorandum nor his failure to attend the summons prevented his impeaching the regularity of the proceedings, but that the fiat ought to be annulled with costs. *Id.*

4. A plaintiff filed an affidavit under 5 & 6 Vict. c. 122, s. 11, and in the form specified that the defendant was indebted to him in 99*l.* 19*s.* 7*d.*, and that an account of particulars of demand, amounting to that sum, was thereunto annexed. The particulars purported to be for 99l. 19s. 7d., and after setting out the items, exhibited the following figures:

Total.			£100 14 7
Cr. balance for coats supplied..			10 15 0

£99 19 7

The defendant appeared to the summons issued thereupon, and deposed that he had a good defence to the amount of 54l. 15s. 10d. The plaintiff subsequently brought an action for 100l. 14s. 7d., to which the defendant pleaded a set-off, and the plaintiff recovered 86l. *Held*, that the defendant was not entitled to costs, inasmuch as by reference to the account of the particulars, the affidavit was in substance for 89l. 19s. 7d., and not for 99l. 19s. 7d. Wilding v. Temperley, 11 *Q. B.* 987; 12 *Jur.* 417; 17 *L. J., Q. B.* 184. (Eng.)

5. Where the signature of the commission to an original summons shown to a trader on serving him with the summons, was omitted in the copy of such summons left with him, *held*, that this was not a personal service of the summons upon the trader, and that his not appearing before the commissioners after such service, did not constitute an act of bankruptcy, upon which an adjudication against him could be found. *Ex parte* Jindall, 1 *Jur., N. S.* 858; 24 *L. J., Bank.* (Eng.)

6. On judgment debtor. A judgment debtor summons under section 76, cannot properly be issued against a member of the House of Commons. *Ex parte* Nesbitt, 11 *W. R.* 552; 8 *L. T., N. S.* 812; *S. P., ex parte* Wright, 12 *W. R.* 59; 9 *L. T., N. S.* 349; *ex parte* Gibbon, 8 *L. T., N. S.* 552; 14 *W. R.* 135; 13 *L. T., N. S.* 447. (Eng.)

7. To surrender. A fiat issued against J. D., directed to a district court of bankruptcy, where there were two commissioners, Mr. J. and Mr. S., to whom the fiats were allotted in rotation. The fiat in ques-was allotted to Mr. J. The court was all in one building, and the name of the commissioner to whom each fiat was allotted was posted up at the court. The summons granted by Mr. J. for the surrender of J. D. called on him to surrender "at the district court of bankruptcy." It was proved that

he did not surrender to Mr. J., either at the district court or anywhere else. It was held sufficient proof of non-surrender to Mr. J., either at the district court or anywhere else; also, that the summons was good, although it did not expressly inform the bankrupt that the fiat had been referred to the district court of bankruptcy, and did not contain an allegation that be had been adjudged a bankrupt at that court. Reg. *v.* Dealtry, 2 *C. & K.* 521; 1 *Den. C. C.* 287. (Eng.)

SUPERINTENDENCE OF BANKRUPTCY PROCEEDINGS.

1. Circuit courts within and for the districts where the proceedings in bankruptcy are pending have a general superintendence and jurisdiction of all cases and questions arising under the bankrupt act, "and except when special provision is otherwise made may, upon bill, petition, or other proper process of any party aggrieved, hear and determine the case as in a court of equity." 14 *Stat. at Large*, 518; *Gazzam's Treatise on the Bankrupt Law, Appendix; American and English Bankruptcy Digest, Appendix;* Sweatt *v.* The Boston, Hartford and Erie R. Co. *et al.* 5 *N. B. R.* 234.

SUPERSEDEAS.

1. Where the defendant below became a bankrupt this court will not award a supersedeas to stay an execution because the assignee has his remedy in the circuit court. Black *v.* Zacharie, (*U. S. S. Ct.*) 3 *How.* 483.

SUPERVISORY JURISDICTION OF U. S. COURTS.

1. The decision of a district court sitting in bankruptcy, upon an application to confirm a sale made of a bankrupt's estate, is not a matter within the general supervisory jurisdiction conferred by section two of the U. S. bankrupt act of 1867, upon the circuit court. When it occurs pending the proceedings, that the assignee or creditor is driven to file a bill in equity or bring an

action at law, the circuit court has no supervisory jurisdiction of the proceedings had therein; nor in a case where the claim of a supposed creditor has been rejected in whole or in part, nor where the assignee is dissatisfied with the allowance of a claim. Such cases must be commenced upon writ of error or appeal. Other questions, however, arising in the district court in the progress of a case in bankruptcy, whether of legal or equitable cognizance, fall within the supervisory jurisdiction of the court, and may upon bill petition or other proper process of any party aggrieved, be heard and determined in the circuit court, as a court of equity. *In re* York & Hoover, (*La.*) 4 *N. B. R.* 156.

2. The circuit court cannot exercise its supervisory jurisdiction, except by petition addressed to it, stating clearly and specifically the point or question decided in the district court, and that the petitioner is aggrieved thereby, and praying the circuit court to review and reverse the decision of the court below. *In re* Reed, (*Ohio*,) 2 *N. B. R.* 2.

3. The superintendence and jurisdiction of the U. S. circuit court is revisory in its nature and purpose, and it was not intended that parties should have the option to come to this court for original orders in the nature of a specific execution of the decrees of the district court. *In re* Clark & Bininger, (*S. D. N. Y.*) 3 *N. B. R.* 122.

―――

SUPPLEMENTAL BILL.

1. The appropriate remedy of a complainant, in the court of chancery where he wishes to contest the validity of a defendant's discharge under the bankrupt act, and to obtain satisfaction of the decree out of the defendant's subsequently acquired property, is to file a supplemental bill, stating the obtaining of the decree, the alleged or pretended discharge of the defendant, and the fraud which renders it invalid; and praying that the decree may be carried into full effect against the defendant and his property, notwithstanding his illegal discharge Alcott *v.* Avery, 1 *Barb. Cr.* 347.

SURETIES.

1. **Execution of bond by.** It is not essential to the validity of an insolvent's bond that the insolvent himself shall be bound in it. It is sufficient if it be executed by the sureties alone, and allowed by the judge. Goodrich *v.* Tracy, 3 *P. & W.*, *Pa. R.* 64.

2. **Of a bankrupt.** Sureties to a bond for the payment of money who have been fully indemnified for their responsibility cannot avail themselves of an insolvent discharge granted their principal, although such discharge was obtained by the concurrence of the creditor, and without such concurrence would not have been granted. It seems that a discharge to a principal debtor, under such circumstances, would be a bar to an action against sureties not indemnified. Moore *v.* Paine, 12 *Wendell*, 123.

3. **On bonds.** Where the surety in a custom-house bond, have paid the debt to the United States, and the principal is afterwards discharged by the bankrupt law of 4th April, 1800, the surety is merely entitled to preference out of the estate of the bankrupt, and cannot resort to an action against him for the recovery of the money. Reed *v.* Emory, 1 *S. & R.*, *Pa. R.* 339.

4. The preference given by the act of March 1, 1799, to sureties on custom-house bonds is not taken away by the bankrupt act. Champneys *v.* Lyle, 1 *Binneys' Penn. Reports*, 327.

5. **Who are.** The acceptor of an accommodation bill is a surety, and must prove his debt under a commission against the drawer. Van Sandan *v.* Corsbie, 3 *B. & A.* 13; 1 *Chit.* 16. (Eng.)

6. So an accommodation indorser is a person liable to pay a bill for the party accommodated, against whom, therefore, if he becomes bankrupt, such indorser, though not called on to pay the bill till after the bankruptcy, may prove the amount. Bassett *v.* Dodgin, 9 *Bing.* 653; 2 *M. & Scott*, 777. (Eng.)

7. The plaintiff accepted two bills drawn

upon him by the defendant for value; before they arrived at maturity, the plaintiff being unable to meet them, it was agreed that he should accept other two bills in lieu of them, on consideration of which the defendant undertook to provide for the first two, which he had negotiated. The defendant, however, failed to perform his engagement, and the plaintiff was ultimately compelled to pay all the bills. The two first mentioned bills became due before, but were not taken up by the plaintiff until after the fiat against the defendant. In an action against him for the breach of indemnity; held, that the bills constituted a debt of the bankrupt, for which the plaintiff was liable at the time of the fiat issued, within the 6 Geo. 4, c. 16, s. 52, and consequently that the certificate was a bar. Filby v. Lawford, 4 Scott, N. R. 208; 3 M. & G. 468. (Eng.)

8. Action for money paid. Plea, the defendant's certificate, under a fiat that the money was paid for a debt of the defendant due before his bankruptcy, for which the plaintiff was surety, and that the plaintiff paid the money without request supposed to arise by law. Replication, that before the payment, the defendant had obtained his certificate, and that a final dividend had been made of his estate, and that there was not any debt in respect of the payment of which the plaintiff could have proved, or for which he could have received any dividends. Held, that the certificate was a discharge from the claim, as the principal creditor might have proved, and if he had, the plaintiff would have been entitled to the benefit of that proof, either in reduction of his liability to the creditor, if the creditor received the dividends, or by receiving the dividends himself if he paid the whole debt to the creditor, or the plaintiff might have paid the debt at once to the creditor, and have himself proved before any dividends was declared; or, if the creditor would not take the debt, the plaintiff might have compelled him to prove for the plaintiff's benefit. Jackson v. Magee, 3 Q. B. 48; 2 G. & D. 402; 6 Jur. 1107. (Eng.)

9. The plaintiff having accepted a bill payable at a future day for the accommodation of the defendant, the latter afterwards and before the bill became due, committed an act of bankruptcy, followed by a com-

mission, which was afterwards suspended, and time was given to the bankrupt by his creditors, and the plaintiff thereupon accepted another bill for the same debt with the addition of the interest and stamp. Held, that this was a continuation of the suretyship by the plaintiff for the defendant, which existed before the act of bankruptcy, and the first commission; and a second effectual commission having afterwards issued upon the same act of bankruptcy, before the plaintiff's second acceptance became due which was paid when due. Held, that the amount was provable as a debt under such commission. Stedman v. Martinmaut, 13 East, 664; 1 Rose, 106. (Eng.)

10. A., in consideration of 1l. 10s. 7d. received of B., undertook in writing, to make himself liable for the payment of a note upon which H. was then indebted to B., and B. thereupon consented to furnish H. with more goods; and then A., before the note was due, became bankrupt. Held, that A.'s undertaking was intended as a collateral engagement only, in case H. should not pay the note when due; consequently, as it rested on a contingency whether it would ever become a debt or not, it could not be proved as under A.'s commission. Ex parte Adney, Comp. 460; see Hoffman v. Fendrimere, 5 M. & S. 21. (Eng.)

11. Where the plaintiff who was surety for the defendant for the payment of an annual rent, sued the defendant for money paid and stated in the replication that he had paid it for rent due by the defendant after the bankruptcy. Held, that he could recover, as he was not a surety within the statute. M'Dougal v. Paton, 2 Moore, 644; 8 Taunt. 580. (Eng.)

12. A declaration alleged that the defendant occupied premises of W. at a certain rent, and in consideration that the plaintiff, at the request of the defendant, had become tenant to him at a certain rent, the defendant promised the plaintiff to indemnify him against the rent payable to W., and against any distress or action, costs, charges, damages, or expenses, by reason of non-payment, alleging as a breach that the defendant did not indemnfy the plaintiff by reason whereof a distress was made by W. on his goods for rent in arrear by the defendant,

and that they were sold to satisfy that rent, and the costs of the distress. The defendant pleaded 'that, before distress, he petitioned the court of bankruptcy, was adjudged bankrupt and obtained his certificate, and that the rent distrained for was due at the time of filing the petition, and that the plaintiff was the tenant of the defendant, and by reason of that tenancy was liable to W. for the rent due from the defendant. *Held*, that the plea was bad, as the facts therein stated did not render the plaintiff a surety or liable for debt of the defendant, within 12 & 13 Vict. c. 106, s. 173. Horie *v.* White, 3 *Jur.*, *N. S.* 445. (Eng.)

13. If A. and B. give a joint and several promissory note for the debt of C., and B. becomes bankrupt, and A. pays the amount, he cannot prove against B. as a surety. *Ex parte* Porter, 2 *Mont. & Ayr.* 281. (Eng.)

14. A., as surety to a firm, signed a joint and several bill of exchange, on the faith that B. would join as co-surety. B. never signed it but A. was afterwards compelled to pay it, by proceedings at law, at the suit of an indorsee. One of the firm died, and the others became bankrupt. *Held*, first, that the firm was not entitled to avail itself of the bill, and was liable to repay the amount, and the costs of proceedings, both at law and equity ; and secondly, that the claim was of such a nature as not to be provable under the bankruptcy and therefore not barred by the certificate. Rice *v.* Gordon, 11 *Beav.* 265. (Eng.)

15. The plaintiff, the defendant, and another party, were co-sureties for A., by a joint and several promissory note payable on demand. The defendant afterwards became bankrupt, at which time the plaintiff had not paid his share of the debt, but subsequently he had paid more than his proportion. *Held*, in an action for contribution, that the bankruptcy of the defendant was no answer, as the case was not within 6, Geo. 4, c. 16, s. 52, the plaintiff not being a person liable for the bankrupt's debt within the meaning of that section. Wallis *v.* Swinburne, 1 *Exch.* 203 ; 11 *Jur.* 781 ; 17 *L. J.*, *Exch.* 169. (Eng.)

16. A. and B., his surety, entered into a bond for payment by instalments, of a debt

of A., and also of interest and premiums on a policy. As part of the same arrangement, A. and C. (his partner,) entered into a counter security to B. by way of joint covenant of indemnity. A. and C. became bankrupt, and the condition of the bond having been fulfilled up to the date of the fiat, was afterwards broken. *Held*, that B. who paid the amount could not prove against the joint estate of A. & C. on the counter security. *Ex parte* Mayer, 6 *De G. Mac. & G.* 775 ; 12 *Jur.* 447. (Eng.)

17. Where A., and B. and C. entered into a bond to the king, the condition of which was, that A., as sub-distributor of stamps, should truly account for all stamped vellum which he should receive, and should pay to the commissioners the duties payable for the same, and also the price of such vellum, together with all moneys which he should receive on account of the duties on personal legacies and stage coaches ; and A., being indebted to the king in a certain sum, became bankrupt, and afterwards obtained his certificate ; and a *sciri facias* having afterwards issued on the bond, B., one of the sureties, paid a sum of money to compromise the suit, and a certain other sum in defending the same. *Held*, in an action by the surety to recover these sums from the bankrupt, that B. was a person surety for or liable for a debt of the bankrupt, within the 49 Geo. 3, c. 12, s. 8, and consequently, that the latter was protected by his certificate. Westcott *v.* Hodges, 5 *B. & A.* 12. (Eng.)

18. Where A. became surety for B. for a debt due to C., and after a commission of bankruptcy issued against B., paid part of the debt to C., and obtained from him an indemnity against personal liability for the remainder, the whole of the debt having been proved under the commission by C. *Held*, that A. might maintain an action against B. for the money so paid, as having been paid to his use, notwithstanding the 49 Geo. 3, c. 121, s. 8. Soutter *v.* Soutten, 1 *D. & R.* 521 ; 5 *B. & A.* 852. (Eng.)

SURETY.

1. Where two persons give their joint obligation upon a consideration received by them jointly, each stands in the relation of

surety for the other in respect to one-half the debt. And if an agreement, as afterwards made between them, by which one of them assumes the whole obligation, the other from thenceforth becomes his surety in respect to the whole, and as such may prove his claim under the bankruptcy of his principal, although he has paid nothing on the joint obligation and the same is not yet due. Crafts *v.* Mott, 4 *Comstock,* (4 *N. Y.*) 604.

2. **Actions by and against.** To an action by a surety against his principal, for money paid upon a judgment recovered against them jointly for the debt, a discharge is no defence, if the judgment was recovered subsequent to such discharge, although the note had become payable prior to the commencemet of the proceedings in bankruptcy. Leighton *v.* Atkins, 35 *Me.* 118.

3. A defendant having transferred to the plaintiff's name shares in a mine conducted on the cost book principle as security for a debt, covenanted with him to indemnify him from all calls which might be made upon such shares, and all charges, liabilities and costs that might attach to the said shares. The defendant became bankrupt, and the plaintiff was afterwards compelled to pay in respect to such shares certain debts of the mine, which accrued before the bankruptcy. *Held,* in an action on this covenant for not indemnifying the plaintiff against such payment, that the defendant's liability was not to pay money upon a contingency within 12 & 13 Vict. c. 106, s. 178, nor did the plaintiff stand in the position of surety for the defendant, within the meaning of s. 173; and that therefore his bankruptcy was no bar to the action. Bettely *v.* Stainsby, 36 *L. J., C. P.* 293 ; 2 *L. R., C. P.* 568; 16 *L. T., N. S.* 701; 15 *W. R.* 1047. (Eng.)

4. **Claim of.** The claim of a surety against his principal before payment of the debt by the former is contingent, and is in terms provided for by the bankrupt act. On payment by the surety his claim becomes absolute. It is then a debt, and the relation of principal and surety no longer exists. Such debt is provable under a commission of bankruptcy against the former principal, and will be barred by his certificate. Where

A. agrees with B. to pay and satisfy a bond and mortgage given by them jointly, payable in instalments at future periods, and to save B. harmless therefrom, the equitable relation between the parties is that of principal and surety ; and the claim of B. against A. under the contract to indemnify, is, within the terms, as well as the spirit and design of the bankrupt act, provable against the estate of A. as a contingent claim, to be allowed when it shall become absolute, and will be discharged by A.'s certificate in bankruptcy. Crafts *v.* Mott, 5 *Barb.* 305.

5. **Liability of.** If the bankrupt shall be bound as drawer, indorser, surety, bail, or guarantor upon any bill, bond, note, or any other specialty or contract, or for any debt of another person, and his liability shall not have become absolute until after the adjudication in bankruptcy, the creditor may prove the same after such liability shall have become fixed, and before the final dividend shall have been declared. *Section* 19 *U. S. bankrupt act,* 1867.

6. The liability of an indorser, or other surety, is contingent only if, therefore, the principal pay the debt at maturity, so that the contingent liability of the surety never becomes fixed. In the absence of action by the surety, personally, he is not liable to pay to the assignees the money paid by the principal in discharge of his obligation. The bankrupt act is not to be construed as subversive of the general principal of the law merchant, or of the general law of contracts. Where the bankrupt on becoming embarrassed in his business effected a compromise with his creditors and procured an extension after the compromise, and he, as principal, and two parties executed their joint note to enable him to procure money with which to continue his business. This note the bankrupt, without consultation with his sureties, paid at maturity. Being unable to carry on his business proceedings were instituted against him and he was adjudged a bankrupt. The assignee brought suit to compel the sureties to refund the amount paid by the bankrupt in discharge of the note. One of the sureties was charged with having reasonable cause to believe that the bankrupt was insolvent. At the time he paid the note the other sureties had not this

knowledge. Under the instructions of the court the jury found a verdict against the surety with knowledge and in favor of the other one. Kintzing's assignee *v.* Laflin, (*Mo.*) 5 *N. B. R.* 333.

7. One who has been arrested for debt prior to the passage of the act of 12th of July, 1842, and given bond and filed his petition for the benefit of the insolvent laws, is not relieved from his obligation to appear and prosecute his application at the time appointed by the court by the passage of that act before that time arrived; and upon his failure to appear, he and his surety are liable upon their insolvent bond. Lilley *v.* Torbet, 8 *W. & S. Pa. R.* 89.

8. **Liability on lease after bankruptcy of lessee.** A term remains vested in the bankrupt lessee until either the assignees elect to take it or he delivers it up, and his surety is liable for all breaches of covenant, which accrue after the date of the commission but before the delivery up of the lease by the bankrupt, as such surrender of the lease does not operate by relation back to the date of the commission. Tuck *v.* Tyson, 6 *Bing.* 321; *M. & P.* 715. (Eng.)

9. **Must have satisfied debt.** A., surety with B., for C., was compelled to pay the debt after the bankruptcy of B. The certificate of B. is no answer to the action of A. for contribution. Clements *v.* Langley, 2 *N. & M.* 269; 5 *B. & Ad.* 372. (Eng.)

10. Where one of two assignees of a lease gave a bond to the lessee, by whom the assignment was made, conditioned for the payment of the rent to the lessor and the performance of the other covenants in the lease, and for indemnifying the lessee against the non-performance of the covenants, both the assignees of the lease having become bankrupt, and the bond having been forfeited before the bankruptcy; *held*, that the lessee could not prove for the damages which had accrued previously to the bankruptcy, not having paid them to the lessor. Taylor *v.* Young, (in error) 3 *B. & A.* 521; 2 *Moore*, 326; 8 *Taunt.* 315. (Eng.)

11. If A. is bound with B. as a surety for the payment of a sum certain, and takes

an absolute bond from B., payable the day before the original bond will become due, and B. becomes a bankrupt before the day of payment, A. may prove his debt under the commission, and B.'s certificate will be a bar to an action by A. on the counter bond, though A. does not pay the original bond till after B. has committed an act of bankruptcy. Martin *v.* Court, 2 *T. R.* 640; see Touissant *v.* Martinnant, 2 *T. R.* 100. (Eng.)

12. A bond executed by the defendant, as surety for I., March 1st, 1832, was conditioned for payment of 5*l.* interest on a principal sum of 200*l.*, on the 1st March, 1833; 5*l.* on the 1st March, 1834, and 205*l.* on the 1st March, 1835. The first year's interest was not paid till March 30th, 1833. In June, 1833, the defendant became bankrupt. *Held*, that the bond had been forfeited, and was therefore provable under his commission, and consequently that his certificate was a bar to the action. Skinner's company *v.* Ames, 3 *Bing.* (*N. C.*) 481; 4 *Scott*, 271. (Eng.)

13. X. became bound as surety in a bond with Y. to A., on the 10th of August, 1778, conditioned for payment in six months; on the 1st of March, 1780, he became bound with Y. to B., conditioned for payment in six months; on the 4th of March, 1780, Y. became bound to X. also, in a bond conditioned for payment of the two former bonds, and likewise to indemnify X. against those two bonds. The money secured by the second bond not being paid on the day when it became due, *held*, that the lost bond was thereby forfeited, though X. was not called on to pay the money in the second bond until afterwards, and that X. might prove it as a debt under the commission of bankruptcy that issued against Y. after the forfeiture, and before payment. Hodgson *v.* Bell, 7 *T. R.* 97. (Eng.)

14. In 1855, R., and H. as his surety, gave to Y. a bond for 2,000*l.* R. gave to H., by way of indemnity, a warrant of attorney. In 1858, G., without the knowledge of R., gave up the bond to H., and received, in satisfaction for it, a promissory note of H. for the sum remaining due; R., at the same time, assigned all his property to H., in satisfaction of the liabilities under which H.

had come for him. Afterwards R. became bankrupt, and the warrant of attorney and the assignment became void as against the assignees. *Held*, that the dealings between H. and G. had not taken away the rights of H. against R., and that H., having paid the debt, was entitled to prove against R.'s estate. *Ex parte* Allen, 3 *De G. & J.* 447. (Eng.)

15. Not barred by discharge. A surety in a bond, who pays the debts after his principal has been discharged by the bankrupt law of Maryland, is not barred by the chancellor's certificate. Hadden *v.* Chambers, 1 *Yates' Pa. R.* 529.

16. Of insolvent when not bound by discharge. A surety who pays the bond after the discharge of an insolvent debtor is not bound by the discharge. Hadden *v.* Chambers, 2 *Dallas' Penn. Reports*, 236.

17. On appeal. A judgment was obtained in a state court upon a debt provable in bankruptcy, against a debtor who appealed therefrom and thereafter petitioned and was adjudicated a bankrupt. One of his sureties on the appeal becoming insolvent, judgment creditors gave notice to bankrupt to furnish new security or abandon the appeal. Bankrupt applied for injunction to restrain judgment creditors in the premises, which was granted. On hearing of a motion to dissolve the injunction, the court decided that it was properly granted and would not be dissolved until bankrupt had reasonable time to obtain his discharge. *In re* Metcalf & Duncan, (*E. D. N. Y.*) *N. B. R. Sup.* xliii.

18. On insolvent's bond. If one illegally arrested, with surety conditioned for his appearance to take the benefit of the insolvent law, instead of suing out a *habeas corpus*, the surety will be bound by his obligation. Johnson *v.* Coleman, 8 *W. & S. Pa. R.* 69.

19. On replevin bond. To an action against a surety in a replevin bond it is no sufficient answer that the principal has since become bankrupt and has obtained a certificate of discharge, and that the property in the chattels having by force of the commis-sion of bankruptcy vested in the commissioners, it had become by the act of law impossible to fulfil the condition of the bond. Flagg *v.* Tyler, adm., 6 *Mass.* 33.

20. Payment by. A surety who after the discharge of his principal as a bankrupt, pays instalments of a debt of the principal, which became payable since the discharge, but for which the surety was bound before the application of the bankrupt, is not entitled to recover the same from the principal. Fulwood *v.* Bushfield, 14 *Penn. Reports*, 90.

21. A surety paying after bankruptcy to a creditor who has proved, can only stand in his place upon the bankrupt's estate ; and in case of a surplus can claim interest, which the creditor could not have claimed. *Ex parte* Houston, 2 *Glyn & J.* 36. (Eng.)

22. A surety on a bond who pays the bond after the discharge of an insolvent debtor, is not barred by the discharge. Haddens *v.* Chambers, 2 *Dallas' Pa. Rep.* 236.

23. By the fifth section of the United States bankruptcy act, (3 Stat. at Large, 444) the surety upon a promissory note has a right to prove the demand against the maker, who became a bankrupt, and by the fourth section the bankrupt was discharged from all debts which were provable under the act. Therefore the surety paid the note to the creditor after the discharge of the bankrupt, and brought suit against the bankrupt, he was not entitled to recover it. Mace *v.* Wells, (*U. S. S. Ct.*) 7 *How.* 272.

24. Property assigned to insolvent. Where a trustee in insolvency held certain property which the debtor had equitably assigned to a surety who was insolvent, but the surety had not paid the debt for which he was holden, and it was neither alleged nor found that certain security already held by him was not adequate, the court refused to decree the property to him. Marvin *v.* Bushnell, 36. *Conn.*

25. Release of on insolvent's bond. A surety in an insolvent bond is not released from liability upon it by the conviction and sentence to imprisonment of the principal for a criminal offence, before the condition of the bond is broken. Smith *v.* Barker, 6 *Watts' Pa. R.* 508.

26. Set-offs by. Though in general, after bankruptcy, an assignment cannot be taken of a debt of the bankrupt in order to set it off against a debt due the bankrupt, yet if such assignment is taken in consequence of any arrangement for that purpose made before the bankruptcy, or by reason of any equity to have such assignment, arising from matters which have occurred before the bankruptcy, then a set-off will be allowed in respect to the debt so assigned. So a surety, before bankruptcy, paying off the debt of the principal, after bankruptcy, and taking an assignment of securities, among which is a security of the bankrupt, is entitled to set it off against a debt due from him to the bankrupt. *Ex parte* Barrett, 13 *W. R.* 559.; 34 *L. J., Bank.* 41. (Eng.)

27. When discharged. Where bankers made advances to one of their customers upon a guarantee, and at the same time took from the principal debtor a warrant of attorney to cover the debt, and at the same time agreed with the guarantor that they would, at any time, at his request, enter up judgment and levy execution on the warrant of attorney; but by their neglect to file the warrant of attorney, or a true copy thereof, the warrant became void. It was held, that this neglect on the part of the bankers operated as a discharge of the surety. Watson *v.* Alcock, 4 *De G., Mac. & G.* 247; 17 *Jur.* 568; 22 *L. J., Chanc.* 858; see Parker *v.* Watson, 8 *Exch.* 404; 22 *L. J., Exch.* 167. (Eng.)

———

SURGEONS.

1. A surgeon who dispenses and is paid for medicines administered to his own patients, is an apothecary within the meaning of the bankrupt laws, and liable as such to become bankrupt. *Ex parte* Crabb, 8 *De G., Mac. & G.* 227; 2 *Jur., N. S.* 628; 24 *L. J., Bank.* 45. (Eng.)

2. Retailing of drugs by a surgeon apothecary makes him a trader. Selling drugs, as
Gaz.

ancillary to the business of a surgeon, is not a trading. *Ex parte* Danberry, 3 *Mont. & Ayr.* 16, 17; *Deac.* 72. (Eng.)

———

SURPLUS.

1. Where there is a surplus upon an estate of three, which is indebted to two, the creditors of the three are entitled to interest before the surplus is carried to the estate of the two. *Ex parte* Ogle, 1 *Mont.* 350. (Eng.)

2. Interest out of a surplus is given to a judgment creditor, from the date of the commission to the time when the principal sums were paid, notwithstanding the securities were at the time delivered up to the assignees, with receipts in full indorsed on them, the creditors apprehending the estates would not produce a surplus, which proved to be a mistake. *Ex parte* Day, 2 *Rose,* 148. (Eng.)

3. Funds. Insolvent debtors conveyed their property to assignees for the payment of their debts, the assignees issued certificates to the creditors of the amount of their claims, and after payment of certain dividends the assigneees and creditors agreed that the remaining assets should be specifically valued so as to equal in all the sums remaining due to the creditors, and should be sold by auction in lots to the creditors at such valuations as minimum prices, and be taken by the purchasers in payment of their claims, and any surplus obtained should constitute a fund for a future dividend among the creditors according to the amount of their original claims. One of the creditors indorsed on the certificate of his claim a memorandum addressed to the assignees by which he assigned, "my demands on you for the debt within named to A. without recourse to me in any event, and authorize you to make all settlements with him," and by a similar paper assigned to "A." "all my right, title, or interest in and to a certain portion of a certified claim to K. now held by me, said portion amounting to $1,335, and authorize you to make settlement of above sold portion of said claim with him," and A. rendered an account to this creditor in which he credited him with "balance of your claim on estate,"

108

of the debtor " and for $1,335 of claim of K." each fifty per cent. of the original claim. *Held*, that A., by these transfers, acquired the interest of this creditor in the surplus fund belonging to the transferred debts as well as in the debts themselves; that oral evidence was inadmissible to vary the terms of these written transfers; that a demurrer to a bill by this creditor against A. and the trustees, which set forth the written transfers, and alleged that the plaintiffs reserved all right in the surplus fund did not admit such reservation, and that the plaintiff, after the demurrer had been sustained, could not amend his bill by alleging a mistake in the terms of the transfers, notice thereof to A. and his reply that he claimed only a part of the surplus fund proportionate to the portions of the claims which were unpaid at the time of the assignment. Lea *v.* Robeson, 12 *Grays' (Mass.)* 280.

4. Of individual assets. If there shall be any balance of the separate estate of any partner, after the payment of his separate debts such balance shall be added to the joint stock for the payment of the joint creditors. *Section* 36 *U. S. bankrupt act*, 1867.

5. Of joint assets. If there shall be any balance of the joint stock after payment of the joint debts, such balance shall be divided and appropriated to and among the separate estates of the several partners according to their respective right and interest therein, and as it would have been if the partnership had been dissolved without any bankruptcy. And the sum so appropriated to the separate estate of each partner shall be applied to the payment of his separate debts. *Section* 36 *U. S. bankrupt act*, 1867.

6. To whom paid. A certificated bankrupt, who shows the probability of a surplus is entitled to an account against the assignees. *Ex parte* Malachy, 1 *Mont., D. & D.* 353 ; 4 *Jur.* 1092. (Eng.)

7. Where a man is a partner in separate firms, each of which becomes bankrupt, the surplus of his separate estate will be applied in discharging the joint debts of the firms, in proportion to the whole amount of debts proved against each firm respectively. *Ex parte* Franklyn, *Buck*, 332. (Eng.)

8. A joint commission issued against A. & B., A. being a dormant partner ; the joint creditors resorted to the separate estate of B., thereby diminishing that separate estate, and exonerating the joint estate of A. & B., so as to produce a surplus of it. It was held, that the separate creditors of B. had a lien upon that surplus to the extent which their funds had been diminished by the resort of the joint creditors. *Ex parte* Reid, 1 *Rose*, 84. (Eng.)

9. Where a commission issues against three, and the joint estate is insufficient, and one partner pays the deficiency from his private estate, and there is a surplus on the separate estate of each of the others, the partner who paid the deficiency is entitled to such surplus before interest is paid to the separate creditors. *Ex parte* Rix, 1 *Mont.* 237. (Eng.)

10. Under a separate commission against one of two partners, the bankrupt, having paid 20s. in the pound to all his creditors, obtained an order for the payment of the surplus to him, and the same was accordingly paid. It was held, that his partner was entitled to apply by petition for an account of such surplus, and for payment of his proportion of it, and that the court had jurisdiction to make the order required. *Ex parte* Lanfear, 1 *Rose*, 442. (Eng.)

11. Under a separate commission, the joint property is administered as if both partners were bankrupts, viz: in satisfaction of the joint debts, in the first instance, in order to ascertain the surplus, which alone constitutes the separate interest. Everett *v.* Backhouse, 10 *Ves.* 98. (Eng.)

SUPREME COURT.

1. Jurisdiction of. Where the question is whether an assignment, made by an insolvent debtor in trust for the benefit of his creditors, is fraudulent in fact, the finding of the referee, upon conflicting evidence, that it is not fraudulent, cannot be legally disturbed by the supreme court. Notwithstanding the supreme court may reverse on a question of fact. Such reversal must be consistent with the rules of law. Ball *v.* Loomis, 29 *N. Y. Rep.* 412.

SURRENDER.

1. Although any lien obtained by reason of a judgment for a debt provable in bankruptcy is surrendered and given up by the act of proving the debt the lien of such a suit or judgment is not surrendered so far as it may affect after acquired property in case a discharge is not granted. Hoyt *et al. v.* Freel *et al.* 4 *N. B. R.* 34; citing Haxton *v.* Corse, 2 *Barb.*, *Chanc.* 508.

2. **Discharges from covenants.** Where a lessor covenanted in a lease, to take certain fixtures, on the expiration or other sooner determination of the term, at a price to be fixed by appraisement, and the lessee became bankrupt, and the assignee declined to take the lease, which was delivered up by the bankrupt. It was held, that as the bankrupt, on surrendering the lease, was discharged from all covenants to take the fixtures, could not be enforced by the assignees against the lessor. Kearsey *v.* Carstairs, 2 *B. & Ad.* 716. (Eng.)

3. **Of assets of bank.** A bank incorporated under the laws of the state of Louisiana, became insolvent, and the attorney general of the state, in 1868, proceeded in a state court at the instance and by request of the bank, and thereupon a decree was rendered, forfeiting its charter and directing its affairs to be wound up, in accordance with the insolvent laws of the state. In 1869, creditors of the bank petitioned to have its assets surrendered and administered upon in bankruptcy, and were opposed by the state insolvent commissioners. The court decided that the state laws relating to insolvency, insolvent debtors, etc., were superseded on the 1st June, 1867, by the U. S. bankruptcy act, and further that it was the duty of the directors of the bank, upon learning its insolvency, to have taken proceedings to surrender its assets to be administered upon under the U. S. bankruptcy act. Thornhill *et al. v.* The Bank of Louisiana, (*La.*) 3 *N. B. R.* 110.

4. **Of bankrupt discharges bond.** In those counties where the term of the court is not limited in duration, and there is no order or rule made by the court under the tenth section of the insolvent act of June, 1836, appointing a time for the hearing, an insolvent may present his petition, or surrender himself, in discharge of his bond, at any time while the court is in session, before the succeding term, and if he died during that time his bail will be exonerated. Bailie *v.* Wallace, 10 *Watts' Penn. R.* 228.

5. **Of copyholds.** Previous to 12 & 13 Vict. c. 106, s. 67, this was not an act of bankruptcy, because it was said it could not be done with intent to defeat or delay creditors, as they could not have execution of copyhold lands. *Ex parte* Cockshot, 3 *Bro. C. C.* 502. (Eng.)

6. **Of lease.** In an action for breach of covenant in a lease, a plea under 12 & 13 Vict. c. 106, s. 145, that the assignees declined to take the lease, that within fourteen days after notice thereof, the lessee executed a surrender, and offered to deliver up possession of the premises, is bad, because it does not show the impossibility of a literal compliance with the conditions of the sections, as for instance that the lease was lost or destroyed or the like. Colles *v.* Evanson, 19 *C. B.*, *N. S.* 372; 34 *L. J.*, *C. P.* 320; 13 *W. R.* 1017; 12 *L. T.*, *N. S.* 672. (Eng.)

7. **Of property.** Under the laws of Louisiana after an insolvent debtor has surrendered his property to his creditors and a syndic appointed by them has taken charge thereof, if any of the property be lost the creditors are to sustain the loss, and a creditor cannot sue the debtor until it appears that the creditor will realize nothing from the property so surrendered. In an action by a surety residing in New Orleans against his co-surety for contribution for money paid on account of their principal, it appeared in evidence that the principal in New Orleans had surrendered his property to his creditors, that a syndic had been appointed and that the property surrendered was apparently more than sufficient to pay all his debts, including the claim of the plaintiff, who was named among the creditors. It was held, that it would be presumed that the plaintiff knew of the surrender of the property, and that it being a public proceeding, conducted according to the provisions of law, he was bound by it; that the evidence was *prima facie*, a bar to the action, and

that to rebut it the plaintiff must show what disposition had been made of the property surrendered, and that upon settling the accounts he would receive nothing from it. Cockayne *v.* Lumner, 22 *Pick.* (*Mass.*) 117.

8. A register may appoint a watchman of bankrupt's property surrendered to him. *In re* Bogert and Evans, 2 *N. B. R.* 178.

9. See section 42 U. S. bankrupt act of 1867.

10. An assignee taking property not belonging to the bankrupt should surrender the same to the owners. *In re* Noakes, (*Md.*) 1 *N. B. R.* 164.

11. A register must, on surrender by bankrupt of his property, accept the same. *In re* Hasbrouck, *N. B. R. Sup.* xvii.

12. The register, if requested by the bankrupt after an adjudication, must receive a surrender of the bankrupt's property, and safely keep it until it can be turned over to the assignee. A register is required to receive surrender of the bankrupt. *Rule* 5, *G. O.*

13. The register must safely keep bankrupt's property surrendered to him. *In re* Hasbrouck, *N. B. R. Sup.* xvii.

14. **Previous to passage of bankrupt act.** The U. S. bankrupt law does not divest the state courts of the jurisdiction necessary to the final administration of the estate of an insolvent who had made a surrender previous to its passage. Meekins *et al. v.* Creditors, 19 *La.* 497; s. c. 3 *N. B. R.* 126; citing Sturges *v.* Crowninshield, 4 *Wheat.* 122; Clark *v.* Rosenda, 5 *Rob.* 27; Beach *v.* Miller, 15 *An.* 702; Anceaux *v.* Creditors, 3 *La.* 38.

15. **Under section 23.** Until a recovery has been had by judgment or decree, a preferred creditor may surrender under section 23 any property or security received by him and his right to prove his debt against the bankrupt's estate, and to receive dividends thereupon, will, by such surrender, be revived and become binding on all concerned, regardless of the question whether a suit shall or shall not have been commenced against him by the assignee, and be pending at the time of such surrender. *In re* Kipp, 4 *N. B. R.* 190.

16. Section 23 of the U. S. bankrupt act of 1867, prohibits the proof of claims therein specified without a surrender. Such prohibition continues until such surrender is made. No surrender can be made after a recovery under section 35 of said act. The payment by creditors of the decree obtained against them by the assignee, is not a surrender to the assignee within the true intent and meaning of the said bankrupt act. *In re* Tonkin & Trewartha, (*Mich.*) 4 *N. B. R.* 13; citing *in re* Montgomery, 3 *N. B. R.* 97; *in re* Davidson, *id.* 107; *in re* Princeton, 1 *N. B. R.* 178.

SURVIVING PARTNER.

1. **May commence bankruptcy proceedings on behalf of late firm.** A. who was the remaining partner of a manufacturing firm which had been dissolved said to B. that as his business was so extensive, it was necessary for him to have a partner, so that in case of his decease there would be some one who could go on and close up the concern without the delay arising from an administration of his estate, and proposed to B. to take him as such partner saying that he should have $1,500 the first year, and the next an interest in the business, to which B. assented; and thereupon an agreement was drawn and signed by them as follows: " Copartnership. The subscribers have this day formed a copartnership under the style of A. & Co., and will hereafter carry on the business formerly conducted by A. & C." Public notice of this agreement was given. Subsequently, and until the death of A., which occurred before the expiration of the first year, all purchases, sales and consignment of goods were made, and all drafts were drawn, and promissory notes given by A. & B. in the name of A. & Co., and each of them exercised the full power of a partner in relation to all their business. *Held*, that they were partners, and that after A.'s death, B., as surviving partner, had power to commence proceedings in insolvency which should include the estate of the firm. President, Directors, &c. of the Adams Bank *v.* Rice, 2 *Allen*, 480.

2. Procedings instituted by. The question whether, under proceedings in insolvency instituted by a surviving partner, money found upon the person of a deceased partner and mingled with other money which is admitted to be his own, is partnership or private property, is a question of fact which, if a dispute arises in reference to it, must be submitted to the jury. Durgin *v.* Coolidge, 3 *Allen,* (*Mass.*) 554.

SUSPENSION OF PROCEEDINGS.

1. A bankrupt, the proceedings in whose bankruptcy have been suspended by a resolution, is entitled to apply for an order of discharge, but the bankrupt is not exempt from such a reasonable examination as to conduct as may be had in other cases. *In re* Petrie, 37 *L. J., Bank.* 20; 3 *L. R., Ch.* 610; 16 *W. R.* 817. (Eng.)

2. It is not the course of the court of bankruptcy to suspend proceedings before itself, because a proceeding which may give information as to the bankrupt's estate is pending in another court. *Ex parte* Lee, 3 *L. R., Ch.* 150. (Eng.)

3. Where the creditors of a bankrupt have passed a resolution, under the English bankruptcy act of 1861, s. 110, that the proceedings in bankruptcy shall be suspended, the jurisdiction of the court of bankruptcy to order a sale of the bankrupt's property on the petition of his equitable mortgagee is at an end, unless preserved by the resolutions themselves. *Ex parte* Wood, 1 *L. R., Ch.* 170; 12 *Jur., N. S.* 304; 35 *L. J., Bank.* 34; 14 *W. R.* 320; 14 *L. T., N. S.* 38. (Eng.)

4. A bankrupt proposed, at a meeting of his creditors that the bankruptcy should be suspended under 24 and 25 Vict. c. 134, s. 110, and that he should receive back his estate and pay a composition of 2*s.* 6*d.* in the pound. The creditors, by a resolution duly confirmed, accepted the proposal. The resolution did not purport to revest the estate in the bankrupt until after the payment of the composition. The messenger of the court of bankruptcy then went out

of possession, but the creditors' assignee, who had guaranteed the messenger his fees, retained the keys of the premises. Subsequently and before payment of the composition, a judgment creditor, who was not present at the meeting and had not assented to the resolution, issued execution and seized goods belonging to the bankrupt's estate. *Held,* that the fact of the bankruptcy being suspended under s. 110 did not revest the estate in the bankrupt, and the assignee was therefore entitled to the goods. Macdonald *v.* Thompson, 4 *L. R., C. P.* 747; 38 *L. J., C. P.* 364; 17 *W. R.* 919; 20 *L. T. N. S.* 666. (Eng.)

SUSPICION.

1. In cases of mere suspicion or conjecture, prosecutions are not to be ordered; the court should be satisfied that there is sufficient evidence to establish the guilt of the bankrupts. *Ex parte* Still, 9 *Jur., N. S.* 7; 32 *L. J., Bank.* 12. (Eng.)

TAKING LEASE.

1. By assignee. Assignees of a bankrupt lessee of a hotel, upon the bankruptcy closed the hotel, with the exception of the tap, which was occupied by a third party, tenant to the bankrupt before bankruptcy. He was supplied by order of the assignees with beer and spirits, at a slight advance over cost price, he keeping the proceeds of the business for himself, and the profit on the sale to him being credited to the bankrupt's estate. The license of the tavern was renewed in the bankrupt's name by the assignees. A distress was put in on the premises on two occasions by the lessor, and the assignees, after asking for time, paid rent and costs of distress, for the purpose, as they stated, of saving the furniture, which was afterwards removed from the premises by their order. On their being threatened with ejectment for breaches of covenant, their attorney said they would resist ejectment. The tap was afterwards closed by their order. *Held,* that these facts did not show an election to take the lease. Goodwin *v.* Noble, 8 *El. & Bl.* 587; 4 *Jur., N. S.* 208; 27 *L. J., Q. B.* 204. (Eng.)

2. Time allowed assignee to make election. Assignees allowed ten days to make election to take lease. *Ex parte* Scott, 1 *Rose*, 446, *n.* (Eng.)

3. Thirteen days were decided to be a reasonable time for the assignees of a bankrupt to accept or refuse to take a lease. *Ex parte* Fletcher, 1 *Deac. & Chit.* 356. (Eng.)

TAKING PROPERTY.

1. When a receiver takes possession of property of an insolvent, who makes no attempt to prevent such seizure, there is a taking within the meaning of sec. 39 of the bankrupt act. *In re* Hardy, 3 *N. B. R.* 99.

2. The taking of the property of insolvent traders by a receiver appointed by a state court is a taking under legal process within the meaning of section 39 of the U. S. bankrupt act of 1867. Hardy, Blake & Co. *v.* Bininger & Co. (*S. D. N. Y.*) 4 *N. B. R.* 77; citing 3 *N. B. R.* 99; Denny *v.* Dana, 2 *Cush.* 160, 172; Beale *v.* Clarke, 13 *Gray*, 18, 21.

TAXES.

1. Collection of. A warrant issued by assessors for the collection of a tax justifies an arrest by the collector of a party on whom a tax is assessed, although he may have received a certificate of discharge under the United States bankrupt act of 1841. The question whether such certificate releases the party from the tax cannot be tried in an action against the collector. Aldrich *v.* Aldrich, 8 *Met.* (*Mass.*) 102.

2. Due to the United States. A discharge in bankruptcy obtained under the U. S. bankrupt act of 1867, will discharge debts due to the government of the United States by the bankrupt at the time of the commencement of his bankruptcy proceedings. *In re* Waggenner 5 *N. B. R.*

3. Payment by assignee. The assignees of an insolvent debtor are entitled to be allowed in their account the amount of taxes assessed upon real estate held by them

as such, and paid by them after their removal, even if such payment is made at the request of one who has purchased the land from the new assignee with notice that he must pay the taxes and who has given a bond of indemnity to the first assignees. Loud *v.* Holden 14 *Grays'* (*Mass.*) 154.

TAX WARRANT.

Although a warrant of the commissioners of the land-tax is not equal to an extent, so as to bind the goods of the bankrupt from the date, yet if a collector become bankrupt, and his goods are afterwards seized under a warrant from the commissioners before the actual execution of the assignment, the king's debt must be satisfied. Rex *v.* Jones 8 *Price*, 108. (Eng.)

TEMPORARY INSOLVENT LAWS.

1. Of foreign country. A temporary insolvent law of a foreign country by which debtors were released from all demands against them, on surrendering their effects for the benefit of their creditors, and the same effects were to be distributed among such creditors as should apply within thirty days after public notice of such surrender, was holden not to have been intended to operate beyond the jurisdiction of the government where it was made, and to have no respect to such debts as might be due to persons living in other countries. Prentiss *et al. v.* Savage, 13 *Mass. R.* 20.

TEMPORARY INVESTMENTS.

1. By assignees under order of court. The assignee shall, as soon as may be, after receiving any money belonging to the estate, deposit the same in some bank in his name, as assignee, or otherwise keep it distinct and apart from all other money in his possession, and shall, as far as practicable, keep all goods and effects belonging to the estate separate and apart from all other goods in his possession or designated by appropriate marks so that they may be easily and clearly distinguished, and may not be exposed or liable to be taken as his property or for the payment of his debts. When it appears that the distribution of the estate may be delayed by litigation or other cause, the court may direct the temporary investment of the money belonging to such estate in securities to be approved by a judge or a register of said court, or may authorize the same to be deposited in any convenient bank, upon such interest, not exceeding the legal rate, as the bank may contract with the assignee to pay thereon. *Section* 17 *U. S. bankrupt act*, 1867.

TENANT.

1. Where a lease contained covenants not to assign or underlet, with a proviso that, in case the tenant should voluntarily or otherwise lose possession of the farm, the lessor might re-enter, *held*, that the assignees in bankruptcy of the tenant (the lessor having accepted the assignees) were in by contract with the lessor, and not by operation of law, and were, therefore, bound by the covenants in the lease. Dyke *v.* Taylor, 2 *Giff.* 566; 6 *Jur., N. S.* 1329; 3 *L. T., N. S.* 530; affirmed on appeal, 7 *Jur., N. S.* 583; 30 *L. J., Chanc.* 281; 9 *W. R.* 408; 3 *L. T., N. S.* 717.

2. Where the assignees of a bankrupt coachmaker, who was a tenant from year to year, entered upon the premises to keep the coaches in repair, in pursuance of the bankrupt's contracts, and in August sold the bankrupt's effects, and delivered the key of the premises to the bankrupt, but paid the rent up to the Michaelmas following, it was *held*, in an action by the landlord for a quarter's rent, due the Christmas following, that the assignees were liable. Ansell *v.* Robson, 2 *C. & J.* 610. (Eng.)

3. Fixtures of. A lessee annexed tenant's fixtures, and then deposited the lease by way of mortgage, with a memorandum not noticing the fixtures. *Held*, on his becoming bankrupt, that the security extended to the fixtures. *Ex parte* Tagert, 1 *De Gex*, 531. (Eng.)

4. Leases were deposited by way of equitable mortgage, accompanied by a memorandum of deposit. Tenant's fixtures were included in the security, although they were not mentioned in the memorandum. *Ex parte* Cowell, 12 *Jur.* 411; 17 *L. J., Bank.* 16. (Eng.)

5. A memorandum of deposit, accompanying an equitable mortgage, stated that the bankrupt had deposited the "deeds and documents under which I hold the steammills, cottages, land, buildings and premises at L." *Held*, that the equitable mortgagee had a lien on the fixtures, whether erected before or after the time of the deposit, and including those that were removable as between landlord and tenant. *Ex parte* Price, 2 *Mont., D. & D.* 518. (Eng.)

TERM.

1. The word "marshal" shall include the marshal's deputies, and word "messenger" shall include his assistant or assistants. *Section* 48 *U. S. bankrupt act*, 1867.

2. Insolvency, within the meaning of the U. S. bankrupt act of 1867, means the inability to pay debts in the ordinary course of business as merchants in trade usually do. Where a party cannot pay his debts in the ordinary course of business, and knows that he cannot, he will be held to have had knowledge of his insolvency. Martin *v.* Toof *et al.* (*Ark.*) 4 *N. B. R.* 158; citing Rison *v.* Knapp, 4 *N. B. R.* 114; Black & Secor, 1 *N. B. R.* 81; Merchants' Nat. Bank *v.* Truax, 1 *N. B. R.* 146; *in re* Arnold, 2 *N. B. R.* 61; *in re* Gay, 2 *N. B. R.* 114; Haughey *v.* Albin, 2 *N. B. R.* 129; Wilson *v.* Stortz *et al.* 2 *N. B. R.* 149; Farrin *v.* Crawford *et al.* 2 *N. B. R.* 181; *in re* Randall & Sunderland, 3 *N. B. R.* 4; Ahl *et al. v.* Thorner, 3 *N. B. R.* 29; McDonough *et al. v.* Raferty, 3 *N. B. R.* 53; *in re* Kingsbury *et al.* 3 *N. B. R.* 84; Graham *v.* Stark *et al.* 3 *N. B. R.* 93; Scammon *v.* Cole, 3 *N. B. R.* 100; Campbell *v.* Traders' Nat. Bank, 3 *N. B. R.* 124.

3. In whom vested after bankruptcy. A term remains vested in the bankrupt lessee until either the assignees elect to take it, or he delivers it up, and his surety is liable for all breaches of covenant which accrue after the date of the commission, but before the delivery up of the lease by the bankrupt, as such surrender of the lease does not operate by relation back to the date of the commission. Tuck *v.* Tyson, 6 *Bing.* 321 ; 3 *M. & P.* 715. (Eng.)

TERMINATION OF PROCEEDINGS.

1. Injunction must abide. An injunction issued at the instance of one of the creditors to restrain proceedings under an assignment, and upon confessions of judgment, will not be dissolved until the question of the bankruptcy of the debtor is determined. *In re* Metzler, (*S. D. N. Y.*) *N. B. R. Sup.* ix.

TERRITORIES.

1. Courts of. *And be it further enacted,* That all the jurisdiction, power and authority conferred upon and vesting in the district court of the United States by this act in cases of bankruptcy, are hereby conferred upon and vested in the supreme court of the district of Columbia ; and in and upon the supreme courts of the several territories of the United States, when the bankrupt resides in the said district of Columbia, or in either of the said territories ; and in those judicial districts which are not within any organized circuit of the United States, the power and jurisdiction of a circuit court in bankruptcy may be exercised by the district judge. *Section* 49 *U. S. bankrupt act,* 1867.

2. That the jurisdiction conferred upon the supreme courts of the territories by the act to which this is an amendment, may be exercised upon petitions regularly filed in that court, by either of the justices thereof, while holding the district court in the district in which the petitioner or the alleged bankrupt resides, and said several supreme courts shall have the same supervisory jurisdiction over all acts and decisions of each justice thereof, as is conferred upon the circuit courts of the United States over proceedings in the district courts of the United States, by the second section of said act.

3. *And be it further enacted,* That in case of a vacancy in the office of district judge in any district, or in case any district judge shall, from sickness, absence, or other disability, be unable to act, the circuit judge of the circuit in which such district is included may make, during such disability or vacancy, all necessary rules and orders preparatory to the final hearing of all causes in bankruptcy, and cause the same to be entered or issued, as the case may require, by the clerk of the district court. *Amendment of June* 30, 1870.

TESTATOR.

1. A testator was in the habit of selling land to builders, and of advancing them money for building on it, and on the statement of an account between the parties for the balance of unpaid purchase money and money lent, the builders, by a memorandum in writing, acknowledged that the balance agreed upon was a charge upon the land. The testator by his will authorized his executors to make such agreement with the purchasers of any part of his real estate, and to advance money to them for building in the same manner as he had been accustomed to do. The executors accordingly sold a portion of the land for this purpose, leaving the purchase money to remain a charge upon the land ; and they also made advances to the purchaser to enable him to build thereon, but without taking a memorandum in writing, expressly declaring that the advances were to be charged upon the land. The purchaser became bankrupt. *Held,* that the executors had a lien on the land so sold, for the advances made by them since the death of the testator. *Ex parte* Linden, 1 *Mont., D. & D.* 428 ; 5 *Jur.* 57. (Eng.)

TESTIMONY.

1. As to property in several states. Where bankrupt, a business corporation, made a chattel mortgage of goods, part of which were in New York and part in New Jersey, and filed the mortgage in New York state alone, the court decided that the mortgage was valid against creditors in New York only, and ordered testimony to be taken to show the portion of the property in the respective states at the time of delivery of mortgage. *In re* The Soldiers' Business Messenger and Despatch Company, (*S. D. N. Y.*) 2 *N. B. R.* 162.

2. Taking of. The examination of witnesses before a register in bankruptcy, may be conducted by the party in person, or by his counsel or attorney, and the witnesses shall be subjected to examination and cross-examination, which shall be had in conformity with the mode now adopted in courts of law. The depositions upon such examination shall be taken down in writing by the register in the form of narrative, unless he determine that the examination shall be by question and answer, in special instances, and when completed, shall be read over to the witness and signed by him in the presence of the register. Any question or questions which may be objected to shall be noted by the register upon the deposition, but he shall not have power to decide on the competency, materiality or relevance of the question ; and the court shall have power to deal with the costs of incompetent, immaterial or irrelevant depositions, or parts of them, as may be just. In case of refusal of a witness to attend or to testify before a register, the same proceedings may be had as are now authorized with respect to witnesses to be produced on examination before any examiner of any of the courts of the United States on written interrogatories. *General Order No.* 10, *Sup. Ct. U. S.—In bankruptcy.*

3. To strike out claim. Where the testimony does not show material facts, and the testimony does not admit of rebutting evidence, the prayer of a petitioner to strike out the proof of a claim will be denied with costs. *In re* Willard & Millward, (*S. D. N. Y.* Unreported.

THIRD MEETING OF CREDITORS.

1. Whenever any bankrupt shall apply for his discharge within three months from the date of his being adjudged a bankrupt under the provisions of the 29th section of the act, the court may direct that the sec-

ond and third meetings of creditors of said bankrupt, required by the 27th and 28th sections of said act, shall be had on the day which may be fixed in the order of notice for the creditors to appear and show cause why a discharge should not be granted such bankrupt ; and the notices of such meeting shall be sufficient if it be added to the notice to show cause, that the second and third meetings of said creditors shall be had before the register upon the same day that cause may be shown against the discharge, or upon some previous day or days. *General Order No.* 25, *Sup. Ct. U. S.—In bankruptcy.*

[In the southern district of New York, second and third meetings are required only where there are assets. 1 *N. B. R.* 26.]

2. And after the third meeting of creditors no further meeting shall be called unless ordered by the court. *Sec.* 28 *U. S. bankrupt act,* 1867.

THIRD PERSONS.

1. The examination of a prisoner in gaol by a registrar was a public judicial proceeding ; and therefore a fair and correct report, without comment, of the examination was privileged, even though it may have contained statements which injuriously affected the character of a third person. Ryalls *v.* Leader, 1 *L. R.*, *Exch.* 296 ; 12 *Jur.*, *N. S.* 503 ; 35 *L. J.*, *N. S.*, *Exch.* 185 ; 14 *W. R.* 838 ; 14 *L. T.*, *N. S.* 562. (Eng.)

THIRTY-THIRD SECTION OF UNITED STATES ACT OF 1867, AS AMENDED.

1. Is applicable to both voluntary and involuntary bankruptcy. An involuntary bankrupt who has complied with all the provisions of the bankrupt act, can apply for and receive a discharge the same as a voluntary bankrupt. The thirty-third section of the bankrupt act, as amended July 27, 1868, and July 14, 1870, is applicable to proceedings in involuntary bankruptcy. An insolvent, although having assets, and those assets having been duly surrendered to the assignee, but not amounting to the required fifty per cent. of the claims proven against his estate, is not entitled to a certificate of conformity, unless the bankrupt before, on, or at the time of hearing of the application for discharge, tender or file the assent in writing of a majority in number and value for his creditors, to whom he shall have become liable as principal debtor, and who shall have proved their claims as required by section 33 of the bankrupt act. In case any involuntary bankrupt does not tender or file the assent of his creditors, or show payment of his debts by the return of the assignee, or that his property and effects equal or will pay fifty per cent., so as to comply with the requirements of section 33 of the bankrupt act as amended, the certificate of conformity cannot be granted. *In re* Bunster, 5 *N. B. R.* 82.

THIRTY-NINTH SECTION U. S. BANKRUPT ACT, 1867.

1. Wife may petition under. If a wife is a creditor in her own right to amount of two hundred and fifty dollars, and the debtor (her husband) is owing debts to amount of three hundred dollars and suffers or permits acts denounced as acts of bakruptcy by the 39th section of the bankrupt act of 1867, she may petition for his adjudication as a bankrupt. *In re* Overton, (*N. D. N. Y.*) 5 *N. B. R.* 366.

TIME.

1. Judgment was signed and execution issued against the defendant on the 29th of February, at which time notice was given to the sheriff that the judgment would be disputed. A fiat issued on the 15th of March; the official assignee was appointed on the 4th, and the other assignee on the 12th of April; and the motion to set aside the judgment was made, on the part of the assignees, on the 25th of April. It was held, that the motion was made in time. Brooks *v.* Hodson, 2 *D. & L.* 256; 8 *Scott, N. R.* 223; 7 *M. & G.* 529; 13 *L. J., C. P.* 203. (Eng.)

2. Prescribed by the act must be alleged in the creditor's petition.

Proceedings in insolvency instituted upon the petition of a creditor, which does not allege that the acts of bankruptcy charged were committed within the time prescribed by the insolvent laws before the filing of the petition will be vacated by this court under the equity jurisdiction conferred by those laws. Gross *v.* Potter, 15 *Gray, (Mass.)* 556.

TITLE.

1. Deeds. The title deeds of property belonging to one of two partners in trade, were deposited with a banking firm, to secure the balance on the account current between the banking firm and the partnership. On a particular advance being afterwards made by the former to the latter, the partner to whom the deed belonged, wrote a letter to the effect that the object of the deposit was to secure that as well as any future advances. An alteration took place in the members of the banking firm, but the new firm retained the deeds and continued to advance money to the partnership. *Held,* that the existing banking firm was entitled to the benefit of the secureties. *Ex parte* Smith, 2 *Mont., D. & D.* 314. (Eng.)

2. Where the bankrupt deposited title deeds with his bankers to secure future advances, and after a change in the partnership continued for six years the same mode of dealing with them, and the same running account. *Held,* that this was a tacit recognition of the deposit of the deeds with the new firm, upon the same terms as with the old. *Ex parte* Oakes, 2 *Mont., D. & D.* 234.

3. Deeds, action to recover. In April, 1826, A. having contracted to purchase an estate from B., and having had the title deeds delivered to him, agreed to deposit the same with C. as a security for the loan of 5,000*l.* and to give him the mortgage as soon as the legal estate was conveyed to him. B. afterwards conveyed the estate to A., but before such conveyance was made, and after the title deeds had been deposited with C., the latter refused to complete the mortgage, unless A. would agree to pay usurious interest upon the sum of 5,000*l.* A. having so agreed, delivered to C. the deed of conveyance of the estate from B. to A.

A. afterwards became bankrupt, and in an action of trover brought to recover the deeds, it was held, that the original possession of the title deeds being perfectly good, gave C. a right to the estate whenever B. should have conveyed that estate to A.; and that he and not A.'s assignees had a right therefore to the deed of conveyance from B. to A. Wood *v.* Grimwood, 10 *B. & C.* 679. (Eng.)

4. Deeds deposited as security. Among the effects of a testatrix were title deeds belonging to a trader, and a letter written by the testatrix to her agent, directing him to advance a certain sum to the trader, stating that the advances were made on the security of certain title deeds and documents therein described; and at the foot of this letter the trader signed a receipt for the advances. The title deeds found among the testatrix's effects did not answer the description in the letter; but it did not appear any others were deposited with her on the occasion of the loan. The trader became bankrupt, and the usual petition of an equitable mortgagee was presented by the testatrix's personal representatives. *Held,* that there was a good lien on the property comprised in the title deeds found in the testatrix's possession for the amount of the advances, but that there was no sufficient memorandum to entitle the petitioner to costs. *Ex parte* Powell, 6 *Jur.* 490. (Eng.)

5. Subsequently acquired. Debtors having executed a voluntary assignment, which was afterwards declared fraudulent and void, subsequent to the assignment, petitioned for the benefit of the insolvent laws and were discharged, but, through mistake, failed at the time to execute an assignment to the trustees appointed by the court, which was, however, afterwards done, a judgment having been obtained against the insolvents, *after their discharge, but before their assignment,* on which their real estate was sold. On an ejectment by the purchaser against one claiming by conveyance from the assignees on the voluntary assignment, the defendant may defend under the title existing in the assignees under the insolvent laws, and is not estopped from interposing that title because notice had been given at the sheriff's sale by the voluntary assignees, and of the title claimed under the

voluntary assignment. Muncure *v.* Houston, 15 *Pa. R.* 385.

6. Of assignees, relation of. An adjudication on a petition *in forma pauperis* of a debtor in custody, has relation back to the time of the bankrupt's commitment or detainer, under the above provision, and therefore the title of his assignees will prevail against that of a creditor who, under a bill of sale, seized the bankrupt's goods subsequently to the commitment or detainer. Bramwell *v.* Eglinton, 5 *B. S.* 39; 10 *Jur., N. S.* 583; 33 *L. J., Q. B.* 130; 12 *W. R.* 551; 10 *L. T., N. S.* 295. (Eng.)

7. As section 103 makes the adjudication relate to the commitment or detention absolutely, and not merely as an act of bankruptcy, section 133 of the 12 and 13 Vict. c. 106, affords no protection in such a case. *Id.*

8. To bank stock. Where a bill in chancery was filed by the assignee of a bankrupt claiming certain shares of bank stock, the same being also claimed by the bank and by other persons, who were all made defendants, and the answer of the bank set forth apparently valid titles to the stock, which were not impeached by the complainant in the subsequent proceedings in the cause, nor impeached by the other defendants, the circuit court decreed correctly in conferring the title to the bank. Buckingham *v.* McLean, (*U. S. S. Ct.*) 13 *How.* 152.

9. To estate of insolvent. By the act of 1814, an insolvent's estate invested immediately in his discharge in the trustees, not by virtue of his assignment, but by the provisions of the act. In case a change of trustees, they take not by transfer, but by the mere act of substitution. Ruby *v.* Glenn, 5 *Watts' Pa. R.* 77.

10. To exempt property. The widow of a bankrupt is not entitled to the personal property exempted by the provisions of the 14th section of the act of 1867, nor is the assignee in bankruptcy. No title to exempt property passes to the assignee by the assignment, it remains in the bankrupt. At his death it passes to his legal representatives. *In re* Hester, (*N.C.*) 5 *N.B.R.* 285.

11. To land fraudulently encumbered by bankrupt. The purchaser of a bankrupt's land, at an authorized sale by the assignee, takes the land freed from any incumbrances therein made by the bankrupt in fraud of creditors. Thus if a mortgage of land be made, in fraud of creditors, and the mortgagor afterwards become bankrupt, the purchaser of the assignee's rights holds the fee, unincumbered by the mortgage. Devinel v. Perley, 32 *Maine Reports*, 197.

12. To property. A married woman on her own petition, in which she stated herself to be a widow, was adjudicated a bankrupt, and she was afterwards indicted for concealment and embezzlement of her property, with intent to defraud her creditors, and two other persons were also indicted on account of aiding her. The examinations and answers of the three in bankruptcy were given in evidence in support of the prosecution. No caution was given to them by the commissioner on such examination, and they did not object to answer on the grounds that their answers might criminate them. *Held*, that although the wife was adjudicated a bankrupt, the property belonged to her husband, and the property was not proved as laid in the indictment. Reg. v. Robinson, 16 *L. T., N. S.* 605; 15 *W. R.* 966; 10 *Cox, C. C.* 467; 1 *L. R., C. C.* 80; 36 *L. J., M. C.* 78. (Eng.)

13. A bankrupt proposed at a meeting of his creditors, that the bankruptcy should be suspended under 24 and 25 Vict. c. 134, s. 110, and that he should receive back his estate and pay a composition of 2s. 6d. in the pound. The creditors, by a resolution duly confirmed, accepted the proposal. The resolution did not purport to revest the estate in the bankrupt until after the payment of the composition. The messenger of the court of bankruptcy then went out of possession, but the creditor's assignee who had guaranteed the messenger his fees, retained the keys of the premises. Subsequently and before payment of the composition, a judgment creditor, who was not present at the meeting, and had not assented to the resolution, issued execution and seized goods belonging to the bankrupt's estate. *Held*, that the fact of the bankruptcy being suspended under s. 110 did not revest the estate in the

bankrupt, and the assignee was, therefore, entitled to the goods. Macdonald v. Thompson, 4 *L. R., C. P.* 747; 38 *L. J., C. P.* 364; 17 *W. R.* 919; 20 *L. T., N. S.* 666. (Eng.)

14. A joint debtor cannot execute an assignment of joint property so as to keep the title. Gates v. Andrew, 10 *Tiffany*, (37 *N. Y.*) 657.

15. Vesting in trustee. The real, as well as the personal property of an insolvent debtor, vests in his trustees at the time of his discharge; a formal assignment is not necessary to prove it. McAlister v. Samuel, 17 *Pa. R.* 114.

16. An adjudication under the U. S. bankrupt act of 1867, vests in the assignee the title to all the bankrupt's property, although the same is attached on mesne process. This provision, however, of the said act, does not prevent the enforcement of a judgment against the bankrupt on a portion of his property attached more than four months before he commenced proceedings in bankruptcy. Bates v. Tappan, 3 *N. B. R.* 159; s. c. 99; *Mass. R.* 376.

TORT.

1. Actions for. An action for a tort committed upon a bankrupt, cannot be maintained by his assignee, as torts are to be considered the mere personal concern of the bankrupt. Scott v. Crosdall, 2 *Dallas, Pa. R.* 127.

2. Where a bankrupt is held under arrest upon state process in an action of tort in the nature of deceit, evidence cannot be received in the U. S. district court to contradict the declaration, and to show that no such cause of action really exists as is therein set forth. *In re* Devoe, (*Mass.*) 2 *N. B. R.* 11.

3. An action of tort for fraud and deceit, is not a claim within the description in the 14th section of the U. S. bankrupt act of 1867, of the assets which pass to the assignee in bankruptcy. *In re* Crockett, (*S. D. N. Y.*) 2 *N. B. R.* 75.

4. The forms of the courts in a complaint do not in all cases furnish the court the best evidence of the real nature of the plaintiff's claim. The facts out of which they originated must be ascertained, in order to comprehend the real ground of the action. When the first cause of action mentioned in the plaintiff's complaint is what would have been called (when it had a name) trover; and the second cause of action ceases to recover damages for fraudulently certifying bank checks by means whereof a large sum of money was fraudulently extracted from the plaintiff, *held*, that both causes of action are in tort and not on contract. Grocers' Nat. Bank v. Clark, 31 *How: Pa. R.* 115.

5. The plaintiff might have waived the fraudulent conversion, and sued the defendant for so much money had and received to its use; but not having done so, the discharge of the defendant does not apply to his imprisonment upon the plaintiff's claim. His discharge applies only to debts arising on contract. *Id.*

6. Actions for, by assignee. An action for a tort committed upon a bankrupt cannot be maintained by his assignees. Shoemaker, assignee, v. Kelly, 2 *Dallas' Pa. R.* 213.

7. Actions for, when discharged. A discharge under the act to abolish imprisonment for debt in certain cases, (sess. 42, ch. 101,) extends to judgments in actions for wrongs. *Ex parte* Thayer, 4 *Cowen*, 66.

8. Liability for. The defendant's liability for a tort is not affected by his discharge under the bankrupt law, unless, before the petition in bankruptcy was presented, the demand had become a debt by being converted into judgment. Cranch v. Gridley, 5 *Hill*, 250.

9. A verdict or report of referees obtained by a plaintiff in an action for a tort, merely liquidates the damages, but the nature of demand remains unchanged until judgment is perfected. *Id.*

10. Suit for by bankrupt or his assignee. A bankrupt can, after his bankruptcy, maintain in his own name a suit for a wrong done, brought before he was declared a bankrupt, unless his assignee should interpose an objection. And if there has been an equitable assignment of the cause of action before the bankruptcy, the suit may be prosecuted afterwards in the name of the bankrupt, for the benefit of the party in interest. Sawtelle v. Rollins, 23 *Maine R.* 196.

11. Unliquidated damages for not discharged. An unliquidated claim for damages arising out of a tortious act, is not to be regarded as a debt within the provisions of the statutes authorizing the discharge of insolvent debtors. Ziner v. Ritteman, 2 *Abb. N. S.* 261.

TRADE.

1. Legality of trade immaterial. Saunderson v. Rowles, 4 *Burr*, 2066 ; Martin v. Nightingale, 11 *Moore*, 305. (Eng.)

2. Assignee. A trade assignee under a fiat is not personally liable to the messenger for work done in his time, unless there is either an express contract or an express employment of the messenger by the trade assignee. Stubbs v. Troynand, 7 *C. B., N. S.* 719; 30 *L. J., C. P.* 8. (Eng.)

3. The trade assignee in insolvency was not liable under the 5 & 6 Vict. c. 116, and 7 & 8 Vict. c. 96, s. 4, as such, to pay for the messenger's charge for keeping possession of the insolvent's goods under the petition. Hamber v. Hall, 10 *C. B.* 780 ; 15 *Jur.* 682 ; 20 *L. J., C. P.* 157. (Eng.)

4. Carried on under will. A testator directed that it should be lawful for his wife to retain in her hands, and employ any sum not exceeding 6,000*l.* in carrying on the trades in which he might be engaged at his decease, and he appointed his wife and son executrix and executor. The widow carried on the testator's trade, taking the son into partnership, and the moneys received were placed with the bankers to their joint stock. *Held*, on their bankruptcy, that the employment of 6,000*l.* of the assets in the trade so carried on was authorized by the will, and gave no right of proof in competition with other creditors, and that the circumstances

of the son being taken into partnership made no difference. *Ex parte* Butterfield, *De Gex*, 570; 11 *Jur.* 955; 17 *L. J., Bank.* 10. (Eng.)

5. Party ceasing to. A man who has retired from business may become a bankrupt in respect of debts contracted during the period of his trading. Willoughby *v.* Thornton, 1 *Selw. N. P.* 175; *S. P., Doe d.* Barnard *v.* Lawrence, 2 *C. & P.* 134; Dawe *v.* Holdsworth, *Peake*, 64; *ex parte* Dewdney, 15 *Ves.* 495. (Eng.)

6. So, if a trader ceases to manufacture, but still continues to solicit orders and execute them, and holds himself out to the world as capable of executing them. Wharam *v.* Routledge, 5 *Esp.* 235. (Eng.)

7. A person who had formerly taken in goods on pledge, and had ceased to do so, but continued to sell the unredeemed pledges, is still a trader as a pawnbroker. Rawhuson *v.* Pearson, 5 *B. & A.* 124. (Eng.)

8. Whether or not a trader has ceased his trading does not depend upon the mere discontinuance of it, or the absence of any specific act of trading, but whether there is an intention to exercise or resume it, and that is a question for a jury. *Ex parte* Patterson, 1 *Rose*, 402; *S. P. ex parte* Cundy, 2 *Rose*, 357; Dance *v.* Wyatt, 4 *M. & P.* 201.

9. Where a party having manufactured goods for sale, discontinues the sale almost entirely, and uses all his produce himself, but occasionally allows parties applying to have small quantities on payment, it is a question for the jury whether the sales are within the intention of continuing trade, or for the accommodation of the applicants, and in the latter case he ceases to be a trader. Paul *v.* Dowling, *M. & M.* 263; 3 *C. & P.* 500. (Eng.)

TRADER.

1. An annuity given by will to a trader, and payable to him on his own separate receipt alone, and to cease immediately upon alienation does not pass by the assignment,

as by that act it ceased. Dommett *v.* Bedford, 6 *T. R.* 648; 3 *Ves., Jur.* 149. (Eng.)

2. Money given by a father, who is a trader, to his son, to advance in a partnership trading concern, was not within 1 *Jac.* 1, c. 15, s. 5, and could not be recovered from the son by the assignees of the father, who afterwards became bankrupt. Kensington *v.* Chantler, 2 *M. & S.* 36. (Eng.)

3. If a lease to a trader contains a proviso that it shall be void if he becomes bankrupt, the term does not pass to his assignees but determine altogether upon that event taking place. Roe *d.* Hunter *v.* Galliers, 2 *T. R.* 133. (Eng.)

4. A trader as well as a merchant or banker, who gives notes in the course of his business, and fails to pay the same within fourteen days after maturity cannot set up the claim that he has ceased to be a trader before the notes became due, as that would be no defence against bankruptcy. Davis *et al. v.* Armstrong, 3 *N. B. R.* 7.

5. Absenting himself. A trader in embarrassed circumstances, absented himself from his house from the 16th of February, till the 9th of March. Upon an issue whether he had committed an act of bankruptcy on or before the 5th of March, two letters written by him on the 16th of January preceding, asking for time on two bills of exchange, payable by him in February, were receivable to show the motive of his absence. Smith *v.* Cramer, 1 *Scott*, 541; 1 *Bing., N. C.* 1; 1 *Hodges*, 124. (Eng.)

6. Declarations of. The declarations of a trader, made shortly after an absence, are not admissible to prove such an act of bankruptcy. Lees *v.* Martin, 1 *M. & R.* 210. (Eng.)

7. Definition of. The commercial definition of a trader is one who makes it his business to buy merchandise or things, ordinarily the subject of commerce and traffic. *In re* Cowles, *N. B. R.* 42; s. c. 1 *W. Jur.* 367.

8. Insolvency of. A trader is insolvent when he cannot pay his debts in the ordinary course of trade and business. Wilson *v.* Brinckman, 2 *N. B. R.* 149 ; s. c. 1 *C. L. N.* 193.

9. Insolvency, within the meaning of the U. S. bankrupt act of 1867, when applied to traders, means inability to pay debts in the ordinary course of business, as persons carrying on trade usually do. Merchants' National Bank of Hastings *v.* Truax, (*Minn.*) 1 *N. B. R.* 146.

10. Irish. The time of a "trader's residing or carrying on business in Ireland," within 20 and 21 Vict. c. 607, s. 31, means the time of presenting the petition. *In re* Sanderson, 11 *Jur., Chanc. R.* 421. (Eng.)

11. The Irish court has exclusive jurisdiction over such trader, though he owes debts contracted in England while he was residing and trading there. *Id.* (Eng.)

12. Who is and who is not. A trader is one who makes it his business to buy merchandise or things ordinarily the subjects of commerce and traffic. *In re* Cowles, 1 *N. B. R.* 42.

13. A person dealing in shares of a joint stock company, but not as a general broker, is not a trader within the meaning of the English bankrupt laws. *In re* Cleland, 36 *L. J., Bank.* 33 ; 2 *L. R., Ch.* 466 ; 15 *N. R.* 681 ; 16 *L. T., N. S.* 403. (Eng.)

14. A person who works a slate quarry in the ordinary way, upon lease from the owner, is not a trader within the meaning of the bankrupt laws ; and purchasing a stock of tools and materials and selling them again to the quarrymen, which appears to be the custom in the quarries, does not constitute a trading on the part of such a person. *In re* Cleland, 36 *L. J., Bank.* 33 ; 2 *L. R., Ch.* 466 ; 15 *W. R.* 681 ; 16 *L. T., N. S.* 403. (Eng.)

15. An assignment by a trader of all his property to secure a present advance is not necessarily fraudulent and an act of bankruptcy, unless the lender knew that the object of the loan was to defeat and delay creditors ; and the law does not impose on the lender the obligation of showing the

bona fides of the loan. *In re* Colemere, 1 *L. R., Ch.* 128 ; 12 *Jur., N. S.* 38 ; 35 *L. J., Bank.* 8 ; 13 *L. T., N. S.* 621. (Eng.)

———

TRADING.

1. The trading out of any district will support an adjudication in the district. *In re* Cleland, 36 *L. J., Bank.* 33 ; 2 *L. R., Ch.* 466 ; 15 *W. R.* 681 ; 16 *L. T., N. S.* 403. (Eng.)

2. Trading need not continue till bankruptcy. Anon. 1 *Vent.* 5 ; Willoughby *v.* Thornton, 1 *Sel. U. P.* 175 ; Doe *v.* Lawrence, 2 *C. & P.* 134. (Eng.)

3. By means of fictitious capital. When a trader raised money by discounting accommodation bills, but did not negotiate the bills in the course of his trade, this was not trading by means of fictitious capital, within sec. 159 of the English bankruptcy act of 1861. *Ex parte* Harrison, *in re* Baillie, 2 *L. R., Ch.* 195. (Eng.)

4. Illegal. A smuggler dealing in contraband goods by buying and selling is a trader, and therefore liable to a commission, although such buying and selling are illegal. Cobb *v.* Symonds, 1 *D. & R.* 111 ; 5 *B. & H.* 516. (Eng.)

5. A trader may be a bankrupt although he may not have taken out a license necessary to legalize his trade. Sanderson *v.* Bowles, 4 *Burr,* 2064. (Eng.)

6. But a buying in connection with others, to carry on a system of fraud, is not a trading. Milliken *v.* Brandon, 1 *C. & P.* 380. (Eng.)

7. Proof of. A fiat issued on the 7th of March, 1842, and in an action by the assignee, for goods pledged by the bankrupt on the 28th of February, the trading was disputed. The bankrupt was a boarding-house keeper, and sold wine to her boarders. *Held,* that a paper in the handwriting of the bankrupt, purporting to be an account between her and one of her boarders, from December, 1840, to May, 1841, was not receivable to prove the trading, unless it could be shown to have been written before the bankruptcy. Gibson v. King, *C. & M.* 458. (Eng.)

8. *Held*, also, that a book containing accounts between the bankrupt and one of her boarders, of dates all antecedent to the bankruptcy, and to which the word "settled" was added in the bankrupt's handwriting, was also not receivable, unless it was shewn that the entries were written before the bankruptcy. *Id.*

9. A. carries on trade in a colony, and there becomes insolvent. His estate was distributed according to the laws there in force, but he never obtained a legal discharge, (similar to a certificate.) He afterwards came to reside in England, but carried on no trade or business. *Held*, he was not a trader. *Ex parte* Frith, 1 *Forb. N. R.* 233. (Eng.)

10. The declarations of a bankrupt to a party with whom he is dealing, respecting his transactions in trade, are not evidence to prove the trading of such bankrupt. Brinley v. King, *C. & P.* 646; *S. P., nom.* Bromley v. King, *R. & M.* 228, *Best.* (Eng.)

11. But declarations made by a party, of his object in buying a particular article, are admissible in evidence to prove his intentions, and whether he thereby became a trader. Tale v. Halfknight, 3 *Stark.* 56. (Eng.)

12. An acknowledgment by a person that he was in partnership with another as a trader, who afterwards became bankrupt, is sufficient to constitute a trading, although no acts of buying or selling were proved to have taken place during the partnership. Parker v. Parker, 3 *Moore,* 226; 1 *B. & B.* 9. (Eng.)

13. Whether a man is a trader within the bankrupt law is a question of law, and not of fact. Hankey v. Jones, *Cowp.* 752. (Eng.)

14. A trading to support a commission depends not upon the quantity but upon the intention; and it is a question for a jury whether there is enough to evidence that intention. *Ex parte* Maginnis, 1 *Rose,* 84; *S. P.*, Patman v. Vaughan, 1 *T. R.* 572. (Eng.)

15. Requisites of trading in England. One who has traded in England, whether native, denizen, or alien, though never a resident trader in England, but comes over here occasionally, and commits an act of bankruptcy, is an object of the bankrupt laws. Alexander v. Vaughan, *Cowp.* 398 See *ex parte* Smith, *Cowp.* 402. (Eng.)

16. A person residing in the Isle of Man, but coming from time to time to this country, and buying goods here, which were afterwards sold in that island, is a trader against whom a commission of bankruptcy may issue in this country, although he only bought and never sold any goods here. Allen v. Cannon, 4 *B. & A.* 418. (Eng.)

17. A person residing in India, and trading there, and in the course of that trading drawing bills upon England for the value of other bills sent thither, upon which he got a profit by the exchange, and in the course of that sort of dealing contracting debts in England, is a trader. Ingliss v. Grant, 5 *T. R.* 530. (Eng.)

18. A trader in London purchases goods to be sold by A. & B., partners in trade in Dublin, and charges them to A. & B. at prime cost; this creates a debt due from B. in England, and makes him a trader here. Williams v. Nunn, 1 *Taunt.* 270; 1 *Camp.* 152. (Eng.)

19. What is not. A., in conjunction with T., took a lease of salt works and brine pits, for the purpose of manufacturing and selling salt, which was made by them chiefly from the springs and rock salt upon the premises demised; but some of the brine they obtained by channels from adjoining premises. *Held*, that this was not a trading as a workmanship of goods and commodities within 6 Geo. 4, c. 16, s. 2. *Ex parte* Atkinson, 1 *Mont., D. & D.* 300. (Eng.)

TRANSCRIPTS.

1. Transcripts of judgments filed in the office of the clerk of the county where the debtor resides before the filing of a petition by bankrupt are valid, and if the sale of the personal property does not realize enough

to pay the judgments, the execution will continue a lien on the bankrupt's real estate. *In re* Smith *et al.* (*S. D. N. Y.*) 1 *N. B. R.* 169. Citing Cresson *v.* Stone, 17 *Johns.* 116; Van Winkle *v.* Udall, 1 *Hill*, 559.

TRANSFER OF PROCEEDINGS.

1. From one register to another. Bankruptcy proceedings may be transferred from one register to another by the court if it appear that the register to whom the proceedings have been referred has improperly interfered in the choice of an assignee. *In re* Smith, *N. B. R. Sup.* xlvi; s. c. 2 *Bt.* 113.

TRANSFER AND CONVEYANCES.

1. Fraudulent. The word "fraudulent" applies to each of the words gift, delivery and transfer. Cook *v.* Caldecott, 4 *C. & P.* 315; *M. & M.* 522. (Eng.)

2. The word "delivery" is of very general signification; but, being connected with the words "gift or transfer," it seems that in interpretation, it must be confined to transactions of the same nature. Cotton *v.* James, *M. & M.* 373; 3 *C. & P.* 505. (Eng.)

3. Where, on the eve of bankruptcy, the bankrupt, upon being pressed for payment by a creditor, executed to him an assignment of so much of his estate and effects as to render it impossible for him to continue carrying on his trade, constitutes an act of bankruptcy, and is void as against the general body of his creditors. *Ex parte* Bailey, 3 *De G., Mac. & G.* 534; 17 *Jur.* 475; 22 *L. J., Bank.* 45. (Eng.)

4. Of real estate. Where a petitioning creditor alleges in his petition as an act of bankruptcy that on the 29th day of October, 1870, the debtor made certain transfers of real and personal property with intent to delay his creditors, and the debtor in his answer (which was supported by the proof)

showed that the transfers were by way of mortgages; that both mortgages were given to secure the same sum ($1,080) borrowed by the debtor on the 29th day of October, 1870, from the mortgagee in order to relieve the debtor's stock in business from a contested attachment and thus enable the debtor to go on in his business of manufacturing shingles; that the loan was specifically to settle this attachment suit and also to pay the only overdue paper of the debtor known by the mortgagee to be outstanding except only such secured paper as the mortgagee already had. *Held*, that as the mortgages were based upon a present consideration and were neither given nor received with any intent to delay creditors they did not constitute an act of bankruptcy. Petition dismissed at cost of petitioning creditors. *In re* Sanford, (*Wis.*) 5 *N. B. R.*

5. Within four months not void if in pursuance to previous agreement. Where a transfer of real estate is made in pursuance to a verbal agreement for the purpose of liquidating a debt, if there was no circumstance to impeach it as an intended fraud on the bankrupt act, and when the parties were acting on good faith, even though the transfer was made within four months of the bankruptcy proceedings, the same will be sustained, and an application of an assignee to set the deed aside dismissed. *In re* Wood (*Tenn.*) 5 *N.B.R.* 421.

TRESPASS.

1. Not affected by discharge. A cause of action on trespass is not affected by a discharge in bankruptcy even though a verdict had been rendered before the presentment of the petition to be declared a bankrupt. Kellogg *v.* Schuyler, 2 *Denio*, 73.

2. By marshal. There is nothing in the mere fact that a writ issued from a federal court to estop an action in a state court against a marshal "in trespass to his own tort" for making a levy upon property not liable to the writ, belonging to a person against whom the writ did not run. Buck *v.* Colbath, 3 *Wall*, 334.

TRIAL BY JURY.

1. A trial by jury will not be granted unless the respondents deny their insolvency. *In re* Grady, 3 *N. B. R.* 54.

2. **Demand for.** In involuntary bankruptcy a response to the rule to show cause which denies the acts of bankruptcy charged in the petition, and a demand for trial by jury is sufficient without a formal answer to the petition. *In re* Phelps, (*Minn.*) 3 *N. B. R.* 22.

TROVER.

1. Where the bankrupts had knowledge of facts sufficient to bring home to the minds of reasonable men knowledge of their insolvency, they (the bankrupts) must be held to have had that knowledge, and the mortgaging and transfer to a creditor with knowledge of those facts of their stock of goods, is in fraud of the U. S. bankrupt act of 1867, and an assignee in bankruptcy can maintain an action of trover to recover the value of the property. Rison *v.* Knapp, 4 *N. B. R.* 114; citing Merchants' National Bank of Hastings *v.* Truax, 1 *N. B. R.* 146.

TRUST.

1. **Bill in equity by ward.** If the guardian of a minor does not settle his accounts upon his ward's coming of age, and then being largely indebted to him and being insolvent, executes to him in the presence of an attesting witness and with the intention to set it apart as the property of the ward, an assignment of a mortgage of real estate made to secure a less sum than his indebtedness to his ward, and retains possession thereof until after the institution of proceedings in insolvency by him more than a year afterwards, when the same is taken by the assignee in insolvency, the ward may maintain a bill in equity against such assignee in insolvency, to compel the delivery of the assignment of the mortgage to him, although he was ignorant of its existence until after the commencement of the proceedings in insolvency. Leron *v.* Wilmarth, 9 *Allen*, (*Mass.*) 382.

TRUST DEEDS.

1. **Registration of.** The registration of trust deeds under 24 and 25 Vict. c. 134, ss. 192, 194, although in practice performed by the same officer, are distinct and have different operations; and where, for the want of the papers required by the orders, registration under the former section had been refused by the officer, and the applicant had registered the deed under s. 194. *Held*, that the registration did not prevent the deed, which was an assignment of all the debtor's property, from being an act of bankruptcy. *Ex parte* Morgan, 1 *De G., J. & S.* 288. (Eng.)

2. Deed purporting to assign all a debtor's property for the benefit of his creditors, if unstamped, cannot be relied on as an act of bankruptcy. *Ex parte* Potter, 11 *Jur., N. S.* 49; 34 *L. J., Bank.* 46; 13 *W. R.* 189; 1 *L. T., N. S.* 435. (Eng.)

3. **Sale under.** In a sale under a trust deed the proceeds will be applied by the bankrupt court to the payment of the second debt, and if there be a surplus, said surplus will form part of the general assets for distribution among the general creditors. In case of a deficiency the second creditor will be, for that deficiency, a general creditor, to share *pro rata* in the distribution of the general assets. *In re* Ruehl, (*Mo.*) 2 *N. B. R.* 175.

4. A creditor of a bankrupt holding security by a deed of trust or mortgage, cannot enforce his security after the commencement of proceedings in bankruptcy until he first prove his debt and receive permission of the court. If he proceed without authority of court the sale will be invalid and will be set aside, or upon application for good cause the court may confirm the sale upon terms after the debt is properly proved. *In re* Lee, assignee, (*Mo.*) 3 *N. B. R.* 53.

5. A creditor of a bankrupt holding the security of a deed of trust in the nature of a mortgage with a power of sale, in a third party as trustee, must prove his debt as a creditor holding a security and obtain the permission of the court to have the security sold. If he direct a sale without this per-

mission, the court, upon application of the assignee, will set aside the sale. Davis v. Bittel, (*Mo.*) 2 *N. B. R.* 125.

TRUST FUNDS.

1. Right to recover not affected by discharge. The plaintiff, resident in Ireland, drew a bill of exchange in favor of the defendant, resident in New York, for money, to be employed in building a vessel and prosecuting a particular adventure, pursuant to a previous agreement. The defendant received the bill May 27, 1813, and the money was paid to him upon it July 29, 1818. The defendant built the vessel, but employed her in a different adventure from the one agreed on. On the 22d June, 1818, he petitioned for his discharge under the act for giving relief in cases of insolvency (1 *R. L.* 460), which was granted, his property being assigned, etc., on the 12th August, 1818. *Held*, that the money was recoverable as money had and received to the plaintiff's use ; and the debt (not accruing till after the defendant petitioned) was not affected by the discharge. McNeilly v. Richardson, 4 *Cowen*, 607.

TRUST MONEY.

1. Trust money is not entitled to any special preference when the banker with whom such money was deposited becomes insolvent, and where the trustee of the fund by collusion with the banker obtains a preference over the other creditors; having reasonable cause to believe that the banker was insolvent the trustee will be obliged to refund the amount thus secured although a part of it may have been spent in litigation. Street v. Dawson. (*Md.*) 4 *N. B. R.* 60.

TRUST PROPERTY.

1. Property held in trust does not pass to the assignee by the proceedings in bankruptcy. When, however, the trust property does not remain *in specie* but has been made way with by the trustee the *cestui que trusts* have no longer a specific remedy

against the estate and must come in *pari passu* with the other creditors. *In re* Jane way, (*N. J.*) 4 *N. B. R.* 26 ; citing Kip v Bank of N. Y. 10 *Johnson*, 65.

TRUSTEE.

1. Accounting by. The trustee under an assignment of land which is declared fraudulent at the suit of a creditor, is not bound to account for rents received and applied according to the terms of the trust before the commencement of the suit, or the attaching of any specific lien on the lands. Columb *et al.* v. Read *et al.* 10 *Smith*, 24 (*N. J.*) 505.

2. Appointment of. Where three-fourths in value of the creditors who have proved their debts designate the trustee and the committee, and it does not appear that they are acting in the interest of the bankrupt, their choice will be sustained. The claim of any creditor may be investigated under section 22 of the U. S. bankrupt act of 1867, and the examination of any person had under section 26 of said act, notwithstanding the appointment of a trustee and the assignment of the estate to him. *In re* Quin, (*S. D. N. Y.*) 4 *N. B. R.* 145.

3. Bond of. The trustee of an insolvent debtor cannot maintain an action, in right of the insolvent, without having first given bond. A bond executed with security, and filed upon the trial of the cause is not sufficient. Immel v. Stoerer, 1 *R., P. & W., Pa. R.* 262.

4. Where creditors of a bankrupt had adopted a resolution appointing trustees under section 43 of the U. S. bankrupt act of 1874, the confirmation of which was opposed, the court decided that the parties desiring the confirmation of the resolution were the moving parties, and should send them papers on the opposing parties that they might answer them. *In re* American Waterproof Cloth Company, (*E. D. N. Y.*) 3 *N. B. R.* 74.

5. In insolvency. Trustees in insolvency are clothed with all the power of the creditors of the insolvent, for the purpose of setting aside a fraudulent conveyance or assignment. Tams v. Bullitt, 85 *Penn. R.* 308.

6. **Another branch of the cases arising under the Mexican Company of Baltimore,** formed in 1816. This court decided in 17th Howard, 274, that the interest in one of these shares did not pass to a trustee in insolvency in 1819, the contract with General Mina having been declared by the court of appeals of Maryland, to be utterly null and void, so that no interest could pass to the trustee of an insolvent. But in 1824, Mexico assumed the debt as one of national obligation, and the United States made it the subject of negotiation, until it was finally paid. A second insolvency having taken place in 1829, there was a right of property in the insolvent, which was capable of passing to his trustee. The claim of the latter is, therefore, better than that of the administration of the insolvent. Mayer, trustee, v. White adm. (*U. S. S. Ct.*) 24 *How.* 317, referring to 11 *How.* 529; *id.* 111; 14 *id.* 610; 17 *id.* 234; 20 *id.* 535.

7. **Not qualified.** If the court appoint more than one trustee under the second section of the act of 26th of March 1814, and only one give bond agreeably to the 3d section, he cannot exercise the duties of his trust, and consequently an action brought by him alone cannot be maintained. Park v. Graham, 4 *S. & R. Pa. R.* 549.

8. **Of insolvent.** The trustees of an insolvent debtor, having in his own name sued a mortgage given to the insolvent, obtained a judgment and issued a *sci. fas.* thereupon by virtue of which the sheriff sold the mortgaged premises, and received the purchase money. *Held,* that in a suit brought against the sheriff to recover the money from him, he cannot set up as a defence, that the trustee had never given bond as required by the act of assembly. Dean v. Patton, 1 *P. & W., Pa. R.* 437.

9. **It is not material** when the appointment of a trustee of an insolvent debtor be made, the estate of the insolvent vests in the trustee upon his being duly qualified, whether the appointment be made at the date of the discharge or years afterwards. Keating v. Willams, 5 *Watts' Penn. R.* 382.

10. **The trustee of an insolvent debtor** in the District of Columbia represents the creditors of the insolvent and can take advantage of a defect in a mortgage, of which the insolvent himself could not. Bank of Alex. v. Herbert, 8 *Cranch*, 36.

11. **Of insolvent, when to give bond.** The trustees of an insolvent debtor cannot sustain an action in right of the insolvent, without having first given bond. Nor can an insolvent debtor who has made a general assignment of his property, maintain suit upon a cause of action which accrued previously to the assignment. Power v. Hollman, 2 *Watts' Pa. R.* 218.

12. **Report of.** Where an application was made in behalf of the debtor that the trustees be laid under the rule to report within eight days. *Held,* the debtor as well as his creditors has an interest in the account to be rendered by his trustees, and is equally entitled with them to demand it. It is therefore ordered, that they account within eight days after service of a copy of this rule. *In re* Cascadier, *Coleman's Cases,* 116; *Coleman & Caines' Cases,* 117.

13. **Sale of property.** The insolvent law of 1814 requires that the estate of the debtor should be sold at public sale; a private sale of land by a trustee within this act will confer no title. Robins v. Bellas, 4 *Watts' Pa. R.* 255.

14. **When liable to assignee.** Where an assignment by a debtor of all his property to a trustee for the benefit of his creditors is avoided by one of the creditors, the trustee is liable to an assignee subsequently appointed under proceedings in insolvency for all the property and the proceeds thereof, in money or notes in his hands, and has no right to set off any debt due him from the debtor, nor to deduct any compensation for his own services in executing the trust but is entitled to deduct the necessary expenses of collection. Bartlett v. Bramhell 3 *Gray,* (*Mass.*) 257.

15. **When liable on a judgment.** One who has been charged as the trustee of H. by a judgment in the trustee process, and has paid to the judgment creditor, on execution, the sum with which he has been so charged, will not be protected against H.'s

assignee in insolvency, if the first publication of the warrant in insolvency against H. was before the rendition of the judgment in the trustee process, though he had no actual notice of H.'s insolvency until after payment. Butler *v.* Mullen, 100 *Mass. R.* 453.

TWO-THIRD ACT.

1. Discharge under. A discharge under insolvent proceedings commonly called the two-third act, is personal and does not operate to discharge a joint obligor with the insolvent. Therefore where the plaintiff, the owner of a joint judgment against the defendants, obtained for a partnership debt, relinquishes or assigns the payment to the assignees of one of the defendants, by petition in insolvent proceedings under the statute, and such defendant subsequently obtained his discharge in such proceedings, the plaintiff cannot afterwards enforce his judgment against such insolvent. Ellsworth *v.* Caldwell, 27 *How. Pa. R.* 188.

2. But such proceedings do not affect the liability of the other joint judgment debtors, and the judgment may be enforced against them notwithstanding such discharge of the co-defendant. In case, however, the remaining defendant should subsequently pay the judgment, they could enforce contribution from the insolvent defendant, such judgment creating a demand arising after discharge. *Id.*

3. A discharge under the insolvent laws of this state (known as the two-third act) granted to a citizen of this state, is a bar to an action against him by a citizen of another state, upon a contract made in that state to be recalled within this state. (This appears to be adverse to the case of Baldwin against Hale, and cases there cited. United States supreme court. A. L. Rev. June, 1864, CLIFFORD, J.) Pratt *v.* Chase, 1 *Robt.* 296.

TWO YEARS' LIMITATION.

1. Where a suit is merely to collect a debt, or enforce payment of money due on a contract, and the plaintiff does not claim an interest adverse to the defendant in touching any property or right of property of the bankrupts, transferable to or vested in the plaintiff, as their assignee, and the defendant does not claim any interest adverse to the plaintiff in or touching any such property, the defendant claiming no ownership or title to the debt or contract which the plaintiff is seeking to enforce against the defendant, nor does the plaintiff make any such claim of property or right of property as having passed to him by virtue of his appointment as assignee, nor does the defendant claim any ownership of or title to any specific property which belonged to the bankrupt. The limitation of two years does not apply to this case, but only to such controversies of which by the second section the circuit court of the district has concurrent jurisdiction with the district court of the same district. Plea overruled. Sedgwick, assignee, *v.* Casey, (*S. D. N. Y.*) 5 *N. B. R.*

2. The limitation of two years contained in the 8th section of the bankrupt law of 1841, has no reference to suits growing out of the dealings of the assignee with the estate after it comes into his hands; it only applies to suits growing out of disputes in respect of property and right of property of the bankrupt which come to the hands of the assignee, and to which adverse claims existed while in the hands of the bankrupt, and before the assignment. *In re* Conant, 5 *Bl. C. C.* 54.

UNASCERTAINED DAMAGES.

1. If any bankrupt shall be liable for unliquidated damages arising out of any contract or promise, or on account of any goods or chattels wrongfully taken, converted, or withheld, the court may cause such damages to be assessed in such mode as it may deem best, and the sum so assured may be proved against the estate. No debts other than those above specified shall be proved or allowed against the estate. *Section* 19, *U. S. bankrupt act,* 1867.

UNCLAIMED DIVIDENDS.

1. At their bankers, assignees had two accounts, one general and the other a separate account. To the latter account, sums of a corresponding amount to that required for payment of dividends declared on the bankrupt's estate, were paid. Dividends on the amount of the debts proved had been declared to the extent of 20s. on the pound. Interest accumulated on the amount standing in the separate account for unclaimed dividends. It was held, that such interest belonged to the creditors entitled to the dividends, and not the bankrupt. *Ex parte* Woodford, 3 *De G. & S.* 666; 14 *Jur.* 948; 19 *L. J., Bank.* 8. (Eng.)

UNCOLLECTABLE CLAIMS.

1. If at any time there shall be in the hands of the assignee any outstanding debts or other property, due or belonging to the estate, which cannot be collected and received by the assignee without unreasonable or inconvenient delay or expense, the assignee may under the direction of the court, sell and assign such debts or other property in such manner as the court shall order. *Sec.* 28 *U. S. bankrupt act*, 1867.

UNDERLETTING.

1. Where assignees of a bankrupt, who was possessed of a term, part of which he had underlet to another, released such undertenant, and on being afterwards asked by the lessor to elect, refused to take the original lease. *Held*, that this did not amount to an acceptance by them, and that they were not liable, as assignees of the term. *Hill v.* Dobie, 2 *Moore*, 342; 8 *Taunt.* 325. (Eng.)

2. **No forfeiture of lease.** A. granted a lease to B., which contained a covenant that B., his executors or administrators (without mentioning assigns,) should not underlet without the consent of the lessor; B. became bankrupt, and his assignees assigned the premises to C.; B. obtained his certificate, and C. reassigned the premises to him, after which he underlet them to another person. *Held*, that B. having been discharged at the time of his bankruptcy from the covenants in the lease, by 49 Geo. 3, c. 121, s. 19, the underletting by him which was in character of assignee, was no

forfeiture of the lease. Doe *d.* Cheere *v.* Smith, 1 *Marsh*, 359; 5 *Taunt.* 795; 2 *Rose*, 280. (Eng.)

UNDIVIDED MOIETY.

1. Where the mortgagor and mortgagee of any undivided moiety, and the owner of the other, joined in a demise of the premises to G. for twenty-one years, he covenanting with the three jointly and severally to pay (without mentioning to whom) the reserved rent, and G. entered and then became bankrupt, and his assignees accepted the lease, it was held, that the assignees were liable in an action, at the suit of the three lessors, for rent due since their acceptance of the lease. Magnay *v.* Edwards, 13 *C. B.* 479; 17 *Jur.* 839; 22 *L. J., C. P.* 171. (Eng.)

UNFINISHED CHATTELS.

1. The district court may authorize the assignee to expend money in furnishing chattels which he finds in an incomplete and unsaleable condition. Dwight *et al. v.* Ames, 2 *N. B. R.* 147.

UNITED STATES.

1. **Has no priority over partnership creditors.** The United States has no priority over partnership creditors, where it holds an internal revenue bond, the conditions of which have been broken, and which is signed by the members of the bankrupt firm individually. *In re* Webber *et al.* (*Ohio*,) 2 *N. B. R.* 183.

2. **Lien of.** The United States have no lien on the real estate of their debtor until suit brought or a notorious insolvency has taken place. The United States *v.* Hool, (*U. S. S. Ct.*) 3 *Cranch*, 73.

U. S. COMMISSIONER.

1. A U. S. commissioner may take proof of debt although the bankrupt and creditor both reside in the same judicial district. *In re* Sheppard, (*N. D. N. Y.*) 1 *N. B. R.* 115.

UNITED STATES COURTS.

1. Jurisdiction over insolvents.

The United States courts have exclusive jurisdiction in the case of an insolvent debtor, whether or not he can obtain a discharge in bankruptcy. Van Nostrand v. Barr et al. (Md.) 2 N. B. R. 154; citing Sturgis v. Crowninshield, 4 Wheat. 122; Ogden v. Saunders, 12 Wheat. 213; ex parte Eames, 2 Story, 512; Larrabee v. Talbot, 5 Gill. 426; Commonwealth v. O'Hara, N. B. R. Sup. xix; Langley v. Perry, 1 N. B. R. 155.

UNITED STATES CIRCUIT COURT.

1. The United States circuit court in some cases where it has jurisdiction of the parties, and under some circumstances acting as a court of equity, may interpose to require a citizen of its district to do or forbear something out of the district. In re Hazleton, (Mass.) 2 N. B. R. 12; citing Devon v. Foster.

2. Jurisdiction of. Circuit courts within and for the districts where the proceedings in bankruptcy are pending, have a general superintendence and jurisdiction of all cases and questions arising under the bankrupt act, "except when special provisions is otherwise made, may upon bill, petition or other proper process of any party aggrieved here, and determine the case as in a court of equity." 14 Stat. at Large, 518; Gazzam's Treatise on the Bankrupt Law, Appendix; American and English Bankruptcy Digest, Appendix; Sweatt v. The Boston, Hartford and Erie R. R. Co. et al. 5 N. B. R.

3. Jurisdiction over fraud. The circuit court has not the power under its general jurisdiction over fraud to give relief either at law or in equity in a suit brought by a creditor who had proved his debt under the commission, had assented to the bankrupt's discharge and certificate, and had taken a dividend out of the bankrupt's estate. Commercial Bank of Manchester v. Buckner, (U. S. S. Ct.) 20 How. 108.

UNITED STATES DISTRICT COURTS.

1. The U. S. district court will prevent interference with the property of the bankrupt after he has filed his petition by injunction. In re Wallace, (Oregon,) 2 N. B. R. 52.

2. Control of. The control of the district court over proceedings in the state courts upon liens, etc., is exercised not over the state courts themselves, but upon the parties through an injunction or other appropriate proceedings in equity. Ex parte Christy, (U. S. S. Ct.) 3 How. 292.

3. Jurisdiction of. The jurisdiction of the United States district courts, is limited by the judiciary act to their respective districts, and it has no authority to issue process to the marshal of any other district. In re Hirsch, (E. D. N. Y.) 2 N. B. R. 1.

4. U. S. district courts have original jurisdiction in their respective districts in all matters and proceedings in bankruptcy. In re Glaser, (S. D. N. Y.) 1 N. B. R. 73.

5. For the purpose of instituting proceedings in bankruptcy, the jurisdiction of the U. S. district court is conclusive. In re Bininger et al. (S. D. N. Y.) 3 N. B. R. 121.

6. Equity jurisdiction of. Jurisdiction in equity is conferred upon the district courts in certain cases by the act of congress, establishing a uniform system of bankruptcy, and the eighth section of the act provides that appeals may be taken from the district to the circuit courts, in all such cases where the debt or damages claimed amount to more than five hundred dollars, provided the appeal is claimed within ten days after the entry of the decree, and the appellant complies with the other conditions specified in that section of the bankrupt act. Scammon v. Cole et al. (Me.) 5 N. B. R. 257.

7. Not courts of inferior jurisdiction. The jurisdiction of any court exercising authority over a subject may be inquired into in any court where the proceed-

ings of the former are brought by a party claiming the benefit of them. The district courts of the United States are not courts of inferior jurisdiction in the sense that renders it necessary within their jurisdiction in the face of their records. If jurisdiction do not appear on the face of their proceedings their judgment may be reversed on writ of error, but they are not nullities which in a collateral suit may be disregarded. In such a suit their jurisdiction is presumed until the contrary is shown. The jurisdiction of the district court over the person of one decreed a bankrupt will be presumed, although the decree does not show affirmatively that the court had acquired jurisdiction. The district court had, under the bankrupt act, jurisdiction in all matters and proceedings arising under it, and of all suits in law or equity to be brought by an assignee of the bankrupt and any persons claiming any adverse interest. It might entertain a proceeding in equity by the assignee, although an action at law could have been maintained upon the case made. Chemung Canal Bank *v.* Judson, 4 *Selden,* (8 *N. Y.*) 254.

8. Powers of. The U. S. district court claims power to restrain parties litigant in state courts, when it becomes necessary to give force and effect to the jurisdiction and powers conferred upon it under the U. S. bankrupt law of 1867. *In re* Pennington, (*Mass.*) 1 *N. B. R.* 157.

9. Supervisory jurisdiction. The decision of a district court sitting in bankruptcy, upon an application to confirm a sale made of a bankrupt's estate, is not a matter within the general supervisory jurisdiction, conferred by section 2 of the U. S. bankrupt act of 1867, upon the circuit court. When it occurs pending the proceedings, that the assignee or creditor is driven to file a bill in equity, or bring an action at law, the circuit court has no supervisory jurisdiction of the proceedings had therein; nor in a case where the claim of a supposed creditor has been rejected in whole or in part, nor where the assignee is dissatisfied with the allowance of a claim. Such cases must be commenced upon writ of error or appeal. Other questions, however, arising in the district court, in the progress of a case in bankruptcy whether of legal or equitable cogui-

zance, fall within the supervisory jurisdiction of the court, and may upon a bill, petition or other proper process of any party aggrieved, be heard and determined in the circuit court, as a court of equity. *In re* York & Hoover, (*La.*) 4 *N. B. R.* 156.

10. The circuit court cannot exercise its supervisory jurisdiction except by petition addressed to it stating clearly and specifically the point or question decided in the district court, and that the petitioner is aggrieved thereby, and praying the circuit court to review and reverse the decision of the court below. *In re* Reed, (*Ohio,*) 2 *N. B. R.* 2.

11. The superintendence and jurisdiction of the U. S. circuit court is revisory in its nature and purpose, and it was not intended that parties should have the option to come to this court for original orders in the nature of a specific execution of the decrees of the district court. *In re* Clark & Bininger, (*S. D. N. Y.*) 3 *N. B. R.* 122.

UNRECORDED ASSIGNMENT OF LEASE.

1. An assignment of a ten years' lease by the assignee in insolvency of the lessee, is valid against such lessee, though not recorded. Bemis *v.* Wilder, 100 *Mass. R.* 446.

UNRECORDED CONVEYANCE OF CHATTELS.

1. No mortgage of any vessel, or of any other goods or chattels made as security for any debt or debts in good faith, and for present consideration, *and otherwise valid and duly recorded,* pursuant to any statute of the United States, or of any state, shall be invalidated or affected thereby. *Section* 14 *U. S. bankrupt act,* 1867; *Gazzams' Treatise on the Bankrupt Law,* 332.

2. A bankrupt in July, 1867, gave D. a mortgage upon the fixtures and tools in his factory, which recited that D. had indorsed notes for him on a promise of security. The condition was that the bankrupt, his executors, administrators and assigns should, at or before the expiration of nine months from the date of the mortgage, pay certain promissory notes, and save D. harmless from the payment of the same. One note was then described, and the condition proceeded : "And any and all notes given and indorsed by said D., for the accommodation of the said bankrupt during the pendency of this deed." The note described in the deed, and all other notes given and indorsed within nine months after the date of the deed were paid, but the parties continued in their course of dealing, and there were outstanding at the time of the bankruptcy in January, 1869, notes of the like description to a greater amount than the value of the mortgaged chattels. *Held*, that the mortgaged deed secured the notes made and indorsed after nine months from its date, and that the notes outstanding at the time of bankruptcy were secured thereby. An unrecorded mortgage of personal property which has not been delivered to and retained by the mortgagee, is valid against the assignee in bankruptcy of the mortgagor. *In re* Griffiths, (*Mass.*) 3 *N. B. R.* 179.

3. Where bankrupt was charged, on petition of creditors, with having, in December, 1867, executed a mortgage with intent to prefer other creditors, and in April, 1868, with having suspended and not resumed payment within fourteen days. The court granted an injunction on said mortgage, and in July the debtor was adjudicated bankrupt. The bankrupt leased a spacious mansion and converted it into an infirmary and bathing establishment, and was supplied with wares and merchandise for fitting up the same by the mortgagees upon an agreement of credit. *Held*, there is not sufficient ground in the evidence for adjudging that debtor was insolvent or contemplated insolvency, or that in making the mortgage he even thought of the bankrupt act, much less intended to violate any of its provisions. The mortgagees wisely asked for security, and the debtor had a right to give it. They are not shown to have violated any law, nor, so far as appears in the proofs, any private pledge or stipulation, or any wholesome custom of trade. Judgment in their favor with costs of suit. Potter *v.* Coggeshall, (*R. I.*) 4 *N. B. R.* 19.

4. When a sale or conveyance by the

bankrupt before bankruptcy is void as to creditors, under the local statute of the state where he resides and the sale or conveyance is made, the assignee of the bankrupt who represents in this respect the rights of the creditors, may impeach the same and bring suit for or in respect to property sold or conveyed. The statute of the state of Missouri as to fraudulent conveyances, construed and applied, by Dillion, circuit judge. Allen *v.* Massey, (*Mo.*) 4 *N. B. R.* 75.

5. Where bankrupt, a business corporation, made a mortgage held valid, of goods and chattels, part in New York and part in New Jersey, and filed the mortgage in the first named but not in the latter state. *Held*, that the mortgage was operative against creditors in New York, but not in New Jersey, and testimony to show the portion of the property in the respective states at the time of delivery of the mortgage ordered to be taken. *In re* Soldiers' Business Messenger and Dispatch Co. 2 *N. B. R.* 114.

6. The assignee in bankruptcy represents the whole body of creditors, and it is his right and duty to contest the validity of any mortgage by which one creditor has obtained a preference over another. *In re* Metzger, 2 *N. B. R.* 114.

7. Debtor promised in writing to deliver 6,400 lbs. cotton to pay for rent, and for mules, corn and fodder bought from landlord. Debtor assigned cotton and farm stock to his brother to pay just debts with his own and brother's knowledge of his insolvency and subsequently was adjudged voluntary bankrupt. *Held*, landlord could not distrain under the statutes of Mississippi, and had no lien on cotton raised as against general creditors. The debtor's transfer to his brother was an act of bankruptcy.

8. A deed of trust executed December 8th, 1866, by a bankrupt who did not file his petition till June 8th, 1867, was not recorded until March 2d, 1867. *Held*, that the recording (which was within four months previous to the commencement of bankruptcy proceedings) was not an act of bankruptcy, for the deed was operative from its date and the act of the creditors in recording it cannot be construed as the act of the bankrupt.

If the beneficiaries in a conveyance or mortgage are satisfied with the security offered by the instrument unrecorded there is neither necessity nor obligation to record it. The recording is only necessary to make an instrument valid against creditors under state laws, and the bankrupt act recognizes and respects such validity if it be prior to bankruptcy proceedings. Where, under state laws the landlord has a lien for rent the same will be upheld and respected in a bankruptcy court and the assignee must take title subject thereto. The landlord will be entitled to prove his claim in bankruptcy for the unexpired term of a lease beyond one year even though he has been preferred under a state law, for his rent up to the end of the year. A mortgage or other conveyance made as security for a debt evinced by a note or bond will be upheld as a security for the same continuing debt though the evidence of it may be changed by renewal or otherwise but where the security is changed the same will not be. The assignee takes the property of the bankrupt "in the same plight in which it was held by the bankrupt when his petition was filed." The assignee represents the creditor's rights as well as those of the bankrupt and any incumbrance which would be void as against creditors, would be void as against him. *In re* Wynne, (*Va.*) 4 *N. B. R.* 5.

9. *Held*, that a mortgage of personal property being, under the laws of Wisconsin, ineffectual to pass after acquired property, the assignee in bankruptcy is entitled, in the case stated, to such property, as against the mortgagee who had taken possession. That, though a mortgage be valid as to property then in possession, in a case where a mortgage subsequently given to cover the property afterwards acquired would have been void under the bankrupt laws, the authority given in the mortgage does not enable the mortgagee, by taking possession of such property, to hold it as against the assignee. This would be, in effect, a preference, and against the spirit of the act. That a mortgagee in possession being entitled to retain all property upon which his mortgage was valid, the expenses of a sale of such property by order of the district court should not be paid out of the funds in court *pro rata*, with other expenses in bankruptcy. A chattel mortgage "of all

the goods and merchandise " in a store here, *held* not to include fixtures. *In re* Eldridge, (*Wis.*) 4 *N. B. R.* 162.

10. Unrecorded chattel mortgages are void in bankruptcy. Bank of Leavenworth v. Hunt, 11 *Wallace*, 391; s. c. 4, *A. L Rev.* 54; 4 *N. B. R.* 198.

UNRECORDED MORTGAGE.

1. An unrecorded mortgage of personal property, which is not delivered to and retained by the mortgagee, in not valid against the assignee is insolvency of the mortgagor. Bingham *v.* Jordan, 1 *Allens' (Mass.)* 373.

2. **Recovery of chattels or proceeds of.** Where certain chattels had been transferred, as the assignee claimed, in fraud of the bankrupt act, the insolvency of the debtor who made the transfer being known to the grantees, it appearing also that the mortgage was unrecorded, *held*, that unrecorded chattel mortgages are void in bankruptcy. Bank of Leavenworth *v.* Hunt *et al.* 11 *Wallace*, 54 ; 4 *N.B.R.* 198.

UNSATISFIED JUDGMENT.

1. Where a judgment has been rendered for a debt by a justice of the peace previous to the adjudication of bankruptcy, and still remains unsatisfied, the debt is not so merged in the judgment as to deprive the creditor of the right to prove it. *In re* Vickery, (*Mich.*) 3 *N. B. R.* 171.

UNSOUND MIND.

1. A person who is so unsound in mind as to be wholly incapable of managing his affairs cannot commit an act for which he can be forced into bankruptcy by his creditors against the objections of his guardian. *In re*   6 *N. B. R.*

2. Where the insanity of the bankrupt is alleged in defence of a judgment, the proper mode of redress is by a writ *coram robis* in the court where the judgment was rendered,

the jurisdiction of the U. S. district court would then attach to the whole subject. McKinsey & Brown *v.* Hurt, *et al.* (*Va.*) 4 *N. B. R.* 10.

USURY.

1. The reservation of a greater rate of interest than six per centum by a national bank, or discounting a promissory note, does not render the debt for the principal thereof, one not provable in bankruptcy on the ground of usury. Moore *v.* National Exchange Bank of Columbus, (*Ohio,*) 1 *N. B. R.* 122.

2. A stipulation in a judgment that the interest on it shall bear interest if not paid annually, is void, and does not make such judgment usurious. *In re* Fuller, (*Oregon,*) 4 *N. B. R.* 29.

3. **Action by assignee for.** The assignee in bankruptcy of one of two joint makers of a note and mortgage, cannot maintain a petition to declare the securities void for usury. The assignee is not a borrower within the meaning of the statute of Wisconsin concerning usury, and the power to institute proceedings to obtain a forfeiture is a privilege conferred by the act upon the borrower alone. The assignee, to obtain relief, must tender the money actually borrowed. Brombey *v.* Smith *et al.* (*Wis.*) 3 *C. L. N.* 298 ; s. c. 5 *N. B. R.* 152.

4. An insolvent debtor's right of action for the recovery of threefold, the amount of interest paid by him on a usurious contract, passes by an assignment of his estate, &c., under St. 1838, c. 163, s. 5, and his assignee may maintain a bill in equity to recover it. Gray *v.* Bennett, 3 *Met.* (*Mass.*) 522.

USURIOUS DEBT.

1. A general assignment, by an insolvent debtor of his property to a trustee for the payment of his debts is not void on account of its providing for the payment of an irregular and usurious judgment, giving it priority of other debts, if it be in other respects free from objection. In such case, if the judgment were held void, the indebtedness

would remain, which in the absence of actual fraud would uphold the assignment. It is not a fraud upon other creditors for a debtor to pay or provide for the payment of a usurious debt. Murray *v.* Judson, 9 *N Y. Rep.* 73.

USURIOUS INTEREST.

1. Usurious interest should not be included in proof of claim, even though there has been a judgment on a warrant given by the bankrupt to enter the same. Shaffer *v.* Fritchery *et al.* 4 *N. B. R.* 179.

2. **Right to recover for.** A right of action of an insolvent debtor, on the gen. stats. c. 53, sec. 5, whether absolute or contingent to recover three-fold the amount of usurious interest paid by him, passes by an assignment of his estate in insolvency. Tamplin *v.* Wentworth, 99 *Mass. R.* 63.

VACANCIES.

1. Vacancies caused by death or otherwise in the office of assignee may be filled by appointment of the court or at its discretion by an election by the creditors in the manner hereinbefore provided at a regular meeting or at a meeting called for the purpose with such notice thereof in writing to all known creditors and by such person as the court may direct. *Sec.* 18 *U. S. bankrupt act,* 1867.

2. **In U. S. district court, of judge.** In a case of a vacancy in the office of a district judge the circuit judge may make all necessary rules and orders preparatory to the final hearing, and cause the same to be entered or issued as the case may require by the clerk of the district court. Morgan *et al. v.* Thornhill *et al.* 5 *N. B. R.* 1; see 14 *Stat. at Large,* 517 ; 16 *id.* 174.

3. *And be it further enacted,* that in case of a vacancy in the office of district judge in any district, or in case any district judge shall, from sickness, absence or other disability, be unable to act, the circuit judge of the circuit in which such district is included may make, during such disability or vacancy

all necessary rules and orders preparatory to the final hearing of all causes in bankruptcy, and cause the same to be entered or issued as the case may require, by the clerk of the district court. *Amendment to U. S. bankrupt act of* 1869. Approved June 30, 1870.

VACATION OF A RULE BY MANDAMUS.

1. A motion for a mandamus to compel the judges of the inferior court to vacate a rule opening a judgment to enable a defendant to plead a bankrupt discharge will not be entertained, though it was urged that the order interfered with vested rights. Elkins *v.* Athearn, 2 *Denio*, 191.

VALID MORTGAGES.

1. Based upon a present consideration. Where a petitioning creditor alleges in his petition as an act of bankruptcy that on the 29th day of October, 1870, the debtor made certain transfers of real and personal property with intent to delay his creditors, and the debtor in his answer, which was supported by the proof, showed that the transfers were by way of mortgages; that both mortgages were given to secure the same sum $1,080, borrowed by the debtor on the 29th day of October, 1870, from the mortgagee, in order to relieve the debtor's stock in business from a contested attachment, and thus enable the debtor to go on in his business of manufacturing shingles; that the loan was specifically to settle this attachment suit, and also to pay the only overdue paper of the debtor known of by the mortgagee to be outstanding, except only such secured paper as the mortgagee already had. *Held*, that as the mortgages were based upon a present consideration; and were neither given or secured with any intent to delay creditors, they did not constitute an act of bankruptcy. Petition dismissed at cost of petitioning creditors. *In re* Sanford, (*Wis.*) 5 *N. B. R.*

VALID BILL OF SALE.

1. On the 9th of December, 1865, in consideration of the defendant having agreed to lend to J. 107*l.* to pay an acceptance then about to fall due, J. agreed to give a mortgage of all his goods and chattels as security for that sum, and also for any further advances he might make. On the 6th of January, 1866, the defendant made a further advance of 64*l.* to J., who, on the 27th of January, executed a bill of sale in pursuance of the agreement reciting the total amount then due, and assigning all his personal property to the defendant as security for it. On the 31st December, 1866, J. was adjudicated a bankrupt. *Held*, that the bill of sale being partly in respect of the original agreement and partly in respect of the subsequent advance, which was actually made to such an amount as to constitute a substantial equivalent for the assignment, was a valid bill of sale against the assignee in bankruptcy. Mercer *v.* Peterson, 37 *L. J., Exch.* 54; 3 *L. R. Exch.* 104; 16 *W. R.* 486; 18 *L. T., N. S.* 30. (Eng.)

VALID LIENS.

1. Under the U. S. bankrupt law of 1867, the U. S. district court is bound to recognize and enforce all valid liens. In the case of a vessel or steamboat navigating the lakes, strictly maritime liens have the preference, next statutory liens according to the priority of their dates, and lastly mortgage liens. As a state has full authority to discriminate by law and create preferable liens upon property, so far as these liens are created or given validity to by the state legislature. *In re* Scott, (*Ohio*,) 3 *N. B. R.* 181; citing 10 *Wheat.* 428; 11 *Peters*, 1756; Brig Eagle *v.* Brig General Worth, 2 *C. L. N.* 205; Genesee Chief, 12 *How.* 459; The Moses Taylor *v.* The Hine and Moore, 4 *Wall.*; Belfast, 7 *Wall.*; General Buell *v.* Long, 18 *Ohio S. Rep.* 521; *N. Y.* 36 *Tiff.* 19; 12 *Min. Rep.* 565; 28 *Ind.* 341; *Ky.* 3; *Barb. Rep.* 438; 7 *Wall*, 646; 14 *Ohio R.* 72; 17 *Ohio Rep.* 359.

2. A creditor who had obtained judgment in Georgia against a bankrupt in 1858, ·sought to prove his claim in bankruptcy. The court decided that his judgment was entitled to no priority as by the laws of Georgia he had no lien, and further that the U. S. bankrupt law of 1867 recognizes as liens only those that are valid and binding in the state where the property is situated. *In re* Cozart, (*Ga.*) 3 *N. B. R.* 126.

3. Liens can be respected and allowed by the bankruptcy court only when they are valid at the time of the filing of the petition in bankruptcy. *In re* Dey, (*S. D. N. Y.*) 3 *N. B. R.* 81; citing *in re* Bernstein, *N. B. R. Sup.* xliii; *in re* Smith, 1 *N. B. R.* 169; Pennington *v.* Sale, 1 *N. B. R.* 157; Jones *v.* Leach, 1 *N. B. R.* 165; *in re* Ellis, 1 *N. B. R.* 154; *in re* Houseberger, 2 *N. B. R.* 33.

VALIDITY OF A MORTGAGE.

1. **Question of.** If the validity of a mortgage made by an insolvent debtor upon his homestead, to secure a pre-existing debt within six months previous to the commencement of proceedings in insolvency, is questioned on the ground that it was not made in the usual and ordinary course of his business, and the evidence simply shows that he was a millwright, and had no other occupation or business, the jury should be instructed that the mortgage was not made in the usual and ordinary course of his business. Nary *v.* Merrill, 8 *Allen,* (*Mass.*) 451.

VALIDITY OF DISCHARGE MAY BE CONTESTED.

1. *Always provided,* That any creditor or creditors of said bankrupt whose debt was proved or provable against the estate in bankruptcy, who shall see fit to contest the validity of said discharge on the ground that it was fraudulently obtained, may, at any time within two years after the date thereof, apply to the court which granted it to set aside and annul the same. Said application shall be in writing, shall specify which, in particular, of the several acts mentioned in section twenty-nine it was intended to give evidence of against the bankrupt, setting forth the grounds of avoidance, and no evidence shall be admitted as to any other of the said acts; but said application shall be subject to amendment at the discretion of the court. The court shall cause reasonable notice of said application to be given to said bankrupt, and order him to appear and answer the same within such time as to the court shall seem fit and proper. If, upon the hearing of said parties, the court shall find that the fraudulent acts, or any of them, set forth as aforesaid by said creditor or creditors against the bankrupt are proved, and that said creditor or creditors had no knowledge of the same until after the granting of said discharge, judgment shall be given in favor of said creditor or creditors, and the discharge of said bankrupt shall be set aside and annulled. But if said court shall find that said fraudulent acts and all of them, set forth as aforesaid, are not proved, or that they were known to said creditor or creditors before the granting of said discharge, then judgment shall not be affected by said proceedings. *Section* 34 *U. S. bankrupt act,* 1867.

VALIDITY OF INSOLVENT DEBTOR'S DISCHARGE.

1. The validity of a discharge under the two-third act cannot be questioned on an application to discharge the defendant on common bail, either on the ground of fraud or irregularity. Reed *v.* Gordon *et al.* 1 *Cowen,* 50.

VARIANCE.

1. Where it is not necessary to aver that the demand was due, if the proof shows that it was to become due, although the petition allege a debt due and payable, it is not a fatal variance. Linn *v.* Smith, (*Mich.*) 4. *N. B. R.* 12.

VENDOR.

1. A vendor of teas who retains them in his hands, a deposit in part payment being made, and the residue to be paid on a prompt day, is entitled to resell such portions as remain in his hands, and to prove against the estate of the former purchaser for the difference, if he has in the meantime become bankrupt. *Ex parte* Moffat, 4 *Jur.* 659; *Mont., D. & D.* 282. (Eng.)

2. Equitable right of. A vendor's equitable lien will be upheld by a court of bankruptcy *In re* Perdue, (*Ga.*) 2 *N. B. R.* 67.

3. Lien of. The lien of a vendor upon land for the purchase money thereof does not pass to the transferee of a note taken in part payment. *In re* Brooks, (*Ga.*) 2 *N. B. R.* 149; citing *in re* Perdue, 2 *N. B. R.* 67.

4. Of parol contract, when entitled to costs. Where there was a sufficient part performance to take a parol contract for sale out of the statute of frauds, and the purchaser became bankrupt, *held*, that the vendor, seeking to have effect given to his lien for unpaid purchase money, was entitled to have his costs out of the estate sold. *Ex parte* Cooper, 3 *Mont., D. & D.* 717. (Eng.)

5. Of real estate, when interest a provable claim. If, upon the sale of an estate, the vendor covenants that, on the payment of the purchase money, he will grant, sell and convey, and the vendee covenants to pay the purchase money on or before a day certain, or whenever a good title should be tendered to him; and it is agreed that the vendee, on or before the day named for payment, may require the purchase money to remain a charge upon the premises, so that, upon the completion of the conveyance by the vendor, the vendee should execute to him a proper mortgage, for securing the purchase money, with interest; but if the interest should be in arrear for thirty days, the vendee should be considered as a tenant to the vendor from the date thereof, at a yearly rent, with power to the vendor to distrain for rent reserved by lease, to the end that the interest and costs should be fully satisfied ; and the vendee requires the purchase money to remain a charge, and he is let into possession, and receives the rents; and the vendee becomes bankrupt, and, half a year's interest being in arrear for more than thirty days, the vendor distrains on the tenants, and the assignees satisfy the distress, and the vendee obtains his certificate, and the vendor brings an action against the bankrupt to recover interest accrued subsequently to the certificate ; the certificate is a bar, as the claim for interest was provable. Hope *v.* Booth, 1 *B. & Ad.* 498. (Eng.)

VERDICT.

1. And judgment after bankruptcy. If the verdict as well as the judgment, is after the bankruptcy, the costs are not provable. *Ex parte* Ponchier, 1 *Glyn & J.* 385. (Eng.)

2. Where a debt arises before bankruptcy but a verdict is obtained and costs taxed after, the costs are considered as part of the original debt, and the certificate extends to both, because both are provable. Lewis *v.* Piercy, 1 *H. Bl.* 29. (Eng.)

3. Where a defendant became bankrupt, between plea and verdict in an action on a bail bond, and obtained his certificate after final judgment. *Held*, that the debt should have been proved, and that the certificate was a discharge from both debt and costs. Dunsdale *v.* Eames, 4 *Moore*, 350; 2 *B. & B.* 8. (Eng.)

4. Before, and judgment after bankruptcy. A judgment for damages and costs in assumpsit, was a debt contracted within 46 Geo. 3, c. 135, s. 2, and provable though final judgment was not up until after the commission issued. *Ex parte* Birch, 7 *D. & R.* 436; 4 *B. & C.* 880. (Eng.)

5. Where a verdict is obtained before the act of bankruptcy, and final judgment signed afterwards, but before the issuing of a commission, the debt is provable. Robinson *v.* Vale, 4 *D. & R.* 430; 2 *B. & C.* 762. (Eng.)

6. In an action for damages on a tort a verdict was taken, subject to the award of an arbitrator, and the defendant became bankrupt between the verdict and the award. *Held*, that execution could not be issued on the judgment either for the damages or costs because the plaintiff might have proved the damages recovered under the commission by the production of the record. Beesbon *v.* White, 7 *Rice*, 209. (Eng.)

7. Where a cause and all matters in difference were referred at *nisi prius* to an arbitrator, and he found that a sum of money was due from the plaintiff to the defendant, and ordered that sum to be paid to the latter : and between the time of making the order of reference, and taxing costs and signing judgment, the plaintiff became bankrupt.

Held, that the amount of the taxed costs did not constitute a debt provable under the commission ; that he was not discharged as to that debt by his certificate. Haswell *v.* Thoragood, 7 *B. & C.* 705 ; see *ex parte* Harding, 5 *De G., Mac. & G.* 367, *contra.* (Eng.)

8. Where, in an action upon a contract, the verdict is before, and the judgment after the bankruptcy, the costs are provable. *Ex parte* Poucher, 1 *Glyn & J.* 385. (Eng.)

9. But not where, in an action of tort for words of the plaintiff in his trade, the defendant became bankrupt between verdict and judgment. Longfood *v.* Ellis, 1 *H. Bl.* 29, *n.* (Eng.)

10. A creditor who obtains a verdict before commission against a bankrupt, is entitled to prove for his costs as well as his debt under the commission, though judgment was not signed till after the commission issued. Aylett *v.* Harford, 2 *W. Bl.* 1317. (Eng.)

11. Setting aside. A defendant, who has become bankrupt and obtained his certificate after trial and verdict against him, has a right to set it aside for the want of a sufficient notice of trial, although his estate is insolvent, and his assignees are no parties to the application. Shepherd *v.* Thompson, 9 *M. & W.* 110 ; 1 *D., N. S.* 345. (Eng.)

VESSEL.

1. Claim against for damages. A vessel belonging to the bankrupt passed into the possession of the assignee as assets, and was attached there in a suit *in rem.* on a claim for damages occasioned by her collision with another vessel, prior to bankruptcy. The assignee applied for, and obtained an injunction to restrain the libellants in the premises. *In re* People's Mail Steamship Co. (*S. D. N. Y.*) 2 *N. B. R.* 170.

VOID IN PART, VOID IN TOTO.

1. A deed or judgment, void in part as being a fraud on creditors, is void in toto. Mackie *v.* Cairns, 5 *Cowen,* 547.

2. A contract, or judgment, illegal and void in part, as being against the provisions of a positive statute, is illegal and void in toto. *Id.*

VOIDABLE ASSIGNMENT.

1. An assignment by a debtor of all his estate in trust for distribution amongst his creditors, because it tends to defeat or delay all his creditors, if made within six months of the commencement of bankruptcy proceedings, being an act of bankruptcy, is not void against the creditors, in the absence of actual fraud, but voidable at the suit of the assignee in bankruptcy. Barnes *v.* Rettew, (*Pa.*) Unreported.

2. It seems to have been unquestioned that an assignment to a creditor, with notice of an act of bankruptcy already committed is as void under the English and our own bankrupt laws, and the title of the assignees in bankruptcy related back to the date of the act of bankruptcy. *In re* Grow, assignee, &c., 2 *N. B. R.* 69 ; s. c. 1 *L. T. B.* 111.

VOLUNTARY ASSIGNMENT.

1. A voluntary assignment made for the benefit of creditors, after the passage of the bankrupt law of the 19th August, 1841, and which gives a preference to one creditor over another, is a fraud upon that law, and the assignees in bankruptcy are entitled to recover the assets thus previously transferred. Cornwell's appeal, 7 *W. & S., Pa. R.* 305.

2. The execution of voluntary assignment by an insolvent is a bankrupt act, and he will be conclusively presumed to have intended, by the execution of the trust thereby created, to give the entire control of his property to the assignee of his own making, and thereby to hinder and delay his creditors. *In re* Smith, 3 *N. B. R.* 98.

3. Where a voluntary assignment for the benefit of creditors was made by debtors, and the deed of assignment placed in the hands of the assignee, who hesitated to accept for six hours, and then claimed the property, but before he concluded to accept the property was levied upon, by virtue of executions against the assignors, it was held, that the judgment creditors had obtained a lien upon the goods, and were entitled to have their debts satisfied in preference to the debts of the creditors provided for by the assignment. Crosby *v.* Hillyer, 24 *Wendell*, 280.

4. Must provide for a reassignment.

A decree annulling a voluntary assignment by a debtor of all his estate in trust for the equal benefit of all his creditors, made within six months before the commencement of proceedings under which he was adjudged a bankrupt, should contain a direction for a conveyance by the voluntary assignee, surrendering the estate to the assignee in bankruptcy. The accounting by the voluntary assignee should be under the decree, to the assignee in bankruptcy. There should be no subsequent account in a proceeding under state legislation in a court of the state, unless some extraordinary reason requires a distribution under the laws of the state for the benefit of the general body of the creditors. A mere general allowance in the decree of the reasonable charges and expenses of the voluntary assignee, should not be understood as including his expenses of a proposed account in a state court. Burkholder *et al. v.* Stump, (*Pa.*) 4 *N. B. R.* 191.

VOLUNTARY AND INVOLUNTARY BANKRUPTS.

1. An involuntary bankrupt who has complied with all the provisions of the bankrupt act, can apply for and receive a discharge the same as a voluntary bankrupt. The thirty-third section of the bankrupt act, as amended July 27, 1868, and July 14, 1870, is applicable to proceedings in involuntary bankruptcy. An insolvent, although having assets, and those assets having been duly surrendered to the assignee, but not amounting to the required fifty per cent. of the claims proven against his estate, is not entitled to a certificate of conformity, unless the bankrupt before, on, or at the time of hearing of the application for discharge, tender or file the assent in writing of a majority in number and value of his creditors, to whom he shall have become liable as

principal debtor, and who shall have proved their claims as required by section 33 of the bankrupt act as amended. In case any involuntary bankrupt does not tender or file the assent of his creditors, or show payment of his debts by the return of the assignee, or that his property and effects equal or will pay fifty per cent., so as to comply with the requirements of section 33 of the bankrupt act as amended, the certificate of conformity cannot be granted. *In re* Bunster, 5 *N. B. R.* 82.

VOLUNTARY CONVEYANCE.

1. Not always fraudulent. A voluntary conveyance is not *per se* fraudulent, even as against creditors to whom the grantor was indebted at the date of the deed. Fraser *v.* Western, 1 *Barb. C. & R.* 220 ; Sedgwick, assignee, *v.* Place *et al.* 5 *N. B. R.* 168.

2. When fraudulent to creditors. A debtor who conveys a portion of his property to his wife, does so fraudulently if he is owing debts, which, though paid at maturity, are paid by creating other indebtedness which he is unable to pay. Antroms, assignee, *v.* Kelly *et el.* (*Mo.*) 4 *N. B. R.* 189.

VOLUNTARY PETITIONS.

1. If any person residing within the jurisdiction of the United States owing debts provable under this act exceeding the amount of three hundred dollars, shall apply by petition addressed to the judge of the judicial district in which such debtor has resided or carried on business for the six months next immediately preceding the time of filing such petition, or for the longest period during such six months, setting forth *his place of residence, his inability to pay all his debts in full, his willingness to surrender all his estate and effects for the benefit of his creditors, and his desire to obtain the benefit of this act,* and shall annex to his petition a *schedule*, verified by oath before the court or before a register in bankruptcy, or before one of the commissioners of the circuit court of the U. S., containing a full and true statement of all his debts, and as far as possible to whom due, with the place of residence of each creditor, if known to the debtor, and if not known the fact to be stated, and the sum due to each creditor. Also the nature of each debt or demand, whether founded on written security, obligation, contract or otherwise. And also, the true cause and consideration of such indebtedness in each case, and the place where such indebtedness accrued, and a statement of any existing mortgage, pledge, lien, judgment or collateral or other security given for the payment of the same. And also, annex to his petition an accurate *inventory*, verified in like manner, of all his estate, both real and personal, assignable under this act, describing the same, and stating where it is situated, and whether there are any, and, if so, what incumbrances thereon. The filing of such petition shall be an act of bankruptcy, and such petitioner shall be adjudged a bankrupt. All citizens of the United States petitioning to be declared bankrupt, shall, on filing such petition, and before any proceedings thereon, take and subscribe an oath of allegiance and fidelity to the United States, which oath shall be filed and recorded with the proceedings in bankruptcy, and the judge of the distrct court; or if there be no opposing party, any register of said court to be designated by the judge, shall forthwith, if he be satisfied that the debts due from the petitioner exceed three hundred dollars, issue a *warrant*, to be signed by such judge or register, directed to the marshal of said district, authorizing him forthwith, as messenger, to publish notices in such newspapers as the warrant specifies, to serve written or printed notices by mail or personally, on all creditors upon the schedule filed with the debtor's petition, or whose names may be given him in addition by the debtor, and to give such personal or other to any person concerned as the warrant specifies, which notice shall state that a warrant in bankruptcy has been issued against the estate of the debtor. That the payment of any debts and the delivery of any property belonging to such debtor to him or for his use, and the transfer of any property, are forbidden by law, that a meeting of the creditors of the debtors, giving the names, residences, and amounts, so far as known, to prove their debts and choose one or more assignees of his estate, will be held

at a court of bankruptcy, to be holden at a time and place designated in the warrant, not less than ten nor more than ninety days after the issuing of the same. *Section* 11 *U. S. bankrupt act,* 1867.

VOLUNTARY SETTLEMENT.

1. Of property. If an individual being in debt shall make a voluntary conveyance of his entire property, it would be a clear case of fraud, but this would not apply if such conveyance be made by a person free from all embarrassments and without reference to future responsibilities. Between these extremes, however, numberless cases arise under facts and circumstances which must be minutely examined to ascertain their true character. To hold that a settlement of a small amount by an individual in independent circumstances, and which, if known to be public, would not affect his credit if fraudulent, would be a perversion of the statute (13 Elizabeth.) It did not intend thus to disturb the ordinary and safe transactions in society, made in good faith, and which at the time subjected the creditors to no hazard. If the debt of the creditor by whom the voluntary settlement is impeached, existed at the date of the settlement, and if it is shown that the remedy of the creditor is defeated or delayed by the existence of the settlement, it is immaterial whether the debtor was or was not solvent after making the settlement; but if a voluntary settlement or deed of gift be impeached by subsequent creditors whose debts had not been contracted at the date of the settlement, then it is necessary to show either that the settler made the settlement with express intent to delay, hinder or defraud creditors, or that after the settlement the settler had not sufficient means or reasonable expectations of being able to pay his then existing debts, that is to say, was reduced to a state of insolvency in which case the law infers that the settlement was made with intent to delay, hinder or defraud creditors, and therefore fraudulent and void. It is obvious that the fact of a voluntary settlement retaining money enough to pay the debts which he owed at the time of making the settlement, but not actually paying them, cannot give a different character to the settlement or take it out of the statute. It still remains a voluntary alienation or deed of gift whereby in the event the remedies of creditors are delayed, hindered, and defrauded, is void as against the plaintiff, seeking as a creditor to set such settlement aside. Sperett *v.* Willows, quoted in Freeman *v.* Pope, 9 *Eng. Law Rep.* 206, Sedgwick *v.* Place *et al.* 5 *N. B. R.* 168.

VOTE.

1. **Informal.** The U.S. bankrupt act of 1867, does not recognize such a thing as an informal vote of creditors; hence if at a meeting of creditors held for the purpose of choosing an assignee, none is chosen, through disagreement of creditors, the judge must make an appointment and not the register. *In re* Pearson, (*N. D. N. Y.*) 2 *N. B. R.* 151.

VOTING UPON DEBTS SOLD AFTER PROOF.

1. Debts proved and filed with the register may be postponed for investigation before the assignee, and not allowed to be voted upon for assignee. Efforts by bankrupt's friends to compromise and buy up his debts and stop proceedings in bankruptcy are no fraud upon the bankrupt act, and are no reason why the debts should be postponed and not voted upon for the election of an assignee. Debts proved before election and sold and assigned after proof must be voted upon by the actual owner and not by the original creditor, and the owner will be entitled to only one vote. *In re* Frank (*N. D. N. Y.*) 5 *N. B. R.* 194.

WAGES.

1. The guard of a stage coach, hired at weekly wages, is not a servant. *Ex parte* Skinner, 1 *Mont. & Bligh,* 417; 3 *D. & C.* 332. (Eng.)

2. It is not requisite to prove a hiring for a year certain, but it must be something more than a mere hiring by the week *Ex*

parte Collier, 4 *Deac. & Chit.* 520; 2 *Mont. & Ayr.* 29. (Eng.)

3. If a clerk and foreman was engaged at a weekly salary, and to have two suts of clothes per annum, it was a yearly hiring within s. 168, 12 and 13 Vict. c. 106. *Ex parte* Humphreys, 1 *Mont. & Bligh,* 413; 3 *Deac. & Chit.* 114. (Eng.)

4. Weekly laborers and workmen employed as excavators and bricklayers are not servants. *Ex parte* Crawfoot, 1 *Mont.* 270. (Eng.)

5. The workmen of a coachmaker, who worked by the piece, and received a specific sum for each job, under separate and distinct contracts, and where there was no hiring for a specific time, are not servants within the act. *Ex parte* Grellier, 1 *Mont.* 264. (Eng.)

6. A person engaged as a traveler at an annual salary is a servant or clerk within the act. *Ex parte* Neal, 1 *Mont. & Mac.* 194. (Eng.)

7. A clerk who had served more than six months is entitled to the allowance, although the bankrupt was not, in fact, a trader for more than two months out of the six. *Ex parte* Gough, 3 *Deac. & Chit.* 189. (Eng.)

8. Where clerks or servants claim to be paid in full, the court will include an allowance for notice according to the custom of the trade or profession. *Ex parte* Jennings, 7 *L. T., N. S.* 601. (Eng.)

9. A clerk voluntarily quitting the bankrupt's service nine months previously to the fiat through the approaching insolvency of the bankrupt and his decreasing business, the trade going on in the meantime, and he obtaining employment elsewhere, is not entitled to six months' wages in full, especially when he has allowed the first and final dividend to be declared before making his claim. *Ex parte* Gee, 3 *Deac.* 563; 1 *Mont. & Chit.* 99. (Eng.)

10. A clerk who voluntarily left an insolvent master, was not within 6 Geo. 4, c. 16, s. 48, as to wages. *Ex parte* Barnett, 3 *Mont. & Ayr.* 669. (Eng.)

11. The mate of a vessel, hired by the master, who was also one of the owners, was a servant within 6 Geo. 4. c. 16, s. 48. *Ex parte* Homborg, 2 *Mont.*, *D. & D.* 642; 6 *Jur.* 898. (Eng.)

12. A trader borrowed 550*l.* under an agreement, by which the lender was to become his clerk, at a salary of 220*l.* 10*s.* a year. The trader agreed to produce his accounts and balance sheet to the lender, who was to get in the debts, and alone to draw checks on the banking account. If the balance was in the trader's favor at any time, he might draw the amount of it. On payment of the loan, or on proceedings being taken to recover it, the agreement was to be at an and. The lender was to have the option of becoming a partner. On the trader becoming bankrupt, *held,* first, that the lender was a clerk entitled to three months' salary in full under 5 & 6 Vict. c. 122, s. 28. *Ex parte* Harris, *De Gex*, 165; 9 *Jur.* 497; 14 *L. J., Bank.* 26. (Eng.)

13. *Held,* secondly, that the circumstance of the clerk having been absent from business, owing to ill health, for the three months immediately preceding the bankruptcy with the bankrupt's sanction, did not take away his right. (Eng.)

14. In June, 1844, A. entered the service of B. as book-keeper and cashier, and so continued until December, 1848, without coming to any agreement as to the amount of his salary. It was stated by A. that in December, 1848, it was agreed between him and B., that the salary should be at the rate of 250*l.* a year, from June, 1844, and that the reason that such arrangement was not made before was, that B. was engaged in making experiments in a certain manufacture, from which he hoped to derive a considerable fortune, out of which A. expected to be paid. B. became bankrupt in February, 1849. *Held,* that A. was a clerk, and not a partner, and was entitled to prove for his salary. *Ex parte* Hickin, 3 *De G. & S.* 662; 14 *Jur.* 405; 19 *L. J., Bank.* 8. (Eng.)

15. Coal proprietors employed colliers to whom the work was let off at so much per score baskets, and each collier had a drawer attached to him, whom he brought

when he was himself hired. The colliers were not hired unless the managers approved of the drawers, or unless in case of disapproval, the colliers took drawers provided for them by the managers. The colliers paid the drawers out of their earnings according to an agreement between them (in which the coal proprietor took no part) and discharged the drawers as they thought fit, without interference on the part of the proprietor, except that the latter might discharge the collier if he unjustly discharged the drawer, and that both collier and drawer might be discharged for transgressing the rules of the mine. Upon the proprietor becoming bankrupt, and the colliers' wages being in arrear, *held,* that the drawers were not servants of the coal proprietors, so as to be entitled to payment in full of half a years' wages. *Ex parte* Ball, 3 *De G., Mac. & G.* 155; 17 *Jur.* 198; 22 *L. J., Bank.* 27. (Eng.)

16. The contracts of a trader with his clerks and his servants, are not dissolved by the issuing of commission of bankruptcy against him; therefore the clerk of a trader against whom a commission issues may, after the bankrupt has obtained his certificate, recover his salary for the whole year. Thomas *v.* Williams, 3 *N. & M.* 545; 1 *A. & E.* 685. (Eng.)

17. The clerk or servant must be paid by salary and not by commission. *Ex parte* Simmons, 30 *L. T.* 311; *ex parte* Hickin, 19 *L. J., Bank.* 8; 3 *De G. & S.* 662. (Eng.)

18. Payment of no objection to bankrupt's discharge. Servants' wages paid after the passage of the bankrupt act of 1867, as necessary family expenses, cannot be allowed as objection to the bankrupt's discharge as being a fraudulent preference. *In re* Rosenfeld, jr. (*N. J.*) 2 *N. B. R.* 49.

19. Where wages are due laborers, who had assigned a portion thereof, less than ten dollars each, for the purpose of obtaining advances thereon, it was held, that such advances will be allowed. *In re* Brown 3 *N. B. R.* 177.

20. Payments of necessary servants' wages by an insolvent, although exceeding

$50 to each, will not prevent a discharge. *In re* Rosenfeld, 2 *N. B. R.* 49; see *section 42 U. S. bankrupt act,* 1867.

21. To amount of $50. All creditors whose debts are duly proved and allowed, shall be entitled to share in the bankrupt's property and estate *pro rata*, without any priority or preference whatever, except that wages due from him to any operative, or clerk, or house servant, to an amount not exceeding fifty dollars, for labor performed within six months next preceding the adjudication of bankruptcy, shall be entitled to priority, and shall be first paid in full. *Section 27 U. S. bankrupt act,* 1867.

22. Wages to the amount of $50 each to several laborers, will be allowed for labor performed within six months next preceding the adjudication of bankruptcy. *In re* Brown, (*S. D. N. Y.*) 3 *N. B. R.* 177.

———

WAIVER.

1. By proof of debt. That no creditor proving his debt or claim shall be allowed to maintain any suit at law or in equity therefor against the bankrupt, but shall be deemed to have waived all right of action and suit against the bankrupt, and all proceedings already commenced, or unsatisfied judgments already obtained thereon, shall be deemed to be discharged and surrendered thereby. *Section* 21 *U. S. bankrupt act,* 1867.

2. Of privilege. Since the act of 16th June, 1836, exemption from arrest is a privilege, and submitting to it and giving bond, is a waiver of the privilege. Winder *v.* Smith, 6 *W. & S. Pa. Rep.* 424.

3. Of right of action. After an insolvent bond is forfeited, the issuing of an *als. ca. sa.* by the same plaintiff upon which the insolvent gave another bond, and was subsequently discharged by law, is not a waiver of his right of action upon the first bond. Heilner *v.* Bast *et al.,* 1. *P. & W. Pa. R.* 267.

———

WANT OF JURISDICTION.

1. A court of bankruptcy has no jurisdiction outside of its own judicial district. *In re* Little, (*S. D. N. Y.*) 2 *N. B. R.* 97.

2. In all summary proceedings under a statute, although enough is shown in the institution of them to give jurisdiction to the officer entrusted with the execution of the powers conferred, if, in the progress of the case, it is discovered that in fact the officer has not jurisdiction, it is his duty to stop and dismiss the proceedings. *In re* Wrigley, 8 *Wendell,* 134.

3. In granting discharge. It is not necessary, in support of an insolvent discharge, relied on as defence in an action, to show by proof *aliunde* the discharge, that the officer granting it had jurisdiction, if the facts set forth in it are sufficient for that purpose. So held in this case, when it was recited in the discharge that E. H., of the town, etc., of the county, etc., did present a petition in conjunction with so many of his creditors, etc., praying his discharge on making an assignment. It seems, however, that, notwithstanding the facts recited in the discharge, it is competent to a party opposing the discharge to show that the officer had not jurisdiction. Barber *v.* Winslow, 12 *Wendell,* 102.

4. Will result in dismissal of petition. A motion is made to dismiss a petition for want of jurisdiction, on the ground that a suit in equity or action at law would have been the proper mode to proceed, and not by petition, for the reason the parties would be precluded access to the circuit court as appellants or plaintiffs in error, and would have been deprived of the benefit from rules of evidence, forms and procedure to which parties to suits are accustomed, but would be, by this proceeding, subject to only the revisory power of the circuit judge at chambers or in open court. Petition dismissed, and injunction ancillory to the petition dissolved. Barstow *v.* Peckham *et al.* (*R. I.*) 5 *N. B. R.* 72.

———

WARRANT.

1. In insolvency, issuing of. It is no objection to issuing a warrant in insolvency against a debtor, that he has no creditor whose debts are not secured except the petitioner. O'Neil *v.* Glover, 5 *Grays'* (*Mass.*) 144.

2. Of insolvency, what allegation sufficient. A creditor's petition for a warrant in insolvency which alleges that the debtor within sixty days, and with intent to defraud the petitioner "has concealed his property or some part thereof to prevent its being attached or taken on legal process," is not so defective as to require the procedings in insolvency to be quashed, after the petitioning creditor, by order of the commissioner, has filed a specification of the particular acts of concealment relied on. O'Neil *v.* Glover, 5 *Grays'* (*Mass.*) 144.

3. Of possession, constitutionality of. The provision of the insolvent laws which authorizes the issuing of a warrant to take possession of all the estate of a debtor on the petition of a creditor, without a trial by jury on the facts alleged in the petition, is constitutional. O'Neil *v.* Glover, 5 *Grays'* (*Mass.*) 144.

4. Of seizure. Where a forfeiture for concealing soap was incurred by a soap-maker who became bankrupt, and a provisional assignment of his estate made after which the soap was condemned, and the bankrupt convicted, and thereupon a warrant issued to levy the penalty on his goods generally, such a warrant was bad, and could not justify a seizure of the soap in the hands of the assignees. Austin *v.* Whitehead, 6 *T. R.* 436. (Eng.)

5. Property held under, vesting in and not vesting in assignees. A. having sold a quantity of lac dye in warehouse to B. and being allowed to retain possession of the delivery warrant, pledged the same to C. for an advance of money, and shortly afterwards and before redeeming the warrant became bankrupt. It was held, that A. did not have possession, order and dispositiou of the goods at the time of his bankruptcy within 21 Jac. 1, c. 19, s. 11, and consequently property in the warrant did not vest in his assignees. Greening *v.* Clark, 6 *D. & R.* 735; 4 *B. & C.* 316. (Eng.)

6. According to the custom of the London docks the title to wine is not acknowledged, unless accompanied with the possession of dock warrants indorsed by the party to whom they were originally issued. Thus where A. received warrants from B. not indorsed by B., and indorsed and delivered them to C., who afterwards procured B.'s indorsement and A. became bankrupt, it was held, that for want of B.'s indorsement to A. and transfer his name into the company's books, A. never had the order and disposition of the wines, but that they passed to C., though the notice to the dock company of the transfer and of the indorsement by B. was subsequently to the bankruptcy. *Ex parte* Davenport, 1 *Deae. & Chit.* 397; 1 *Mont. & Bligh.* 165. (Eng.)

7. Return of. At the meeting held in pursuance of the notice, one of the registers of the court shall preside, and the messenger shall make return of the warrant and of his doings thereon, and if it appears that the notice to the creditors has not been given as required in the warrant, the meeting shall be forthwith adjourned, and a new notice given as required. If the debtor dies after the issuing of the warrant, the proceedings may be continued and concluded in like manner as if he had lived. *Sec.* 12 *U. S. bankrupt act*, 1867.

8. To marshal. The eleventh section of the United States bankrupt act of 1867, requires that the warrant to the marshal shall authorize him forthwith to publish notices in the newspapers specified, and to serve notice by mail, etc. Hence to make the proceedings regular, the publication must be completed before the commencement of the period of ten days immediately preceding the return day. *In re* Devlin *et al.* (*S. D. N. Y.*) *N. B. R. Sup.* viii.

9. To messenger. A warrant issued on the application of a partnership for the benefit of the insolvent laws, which directs the messenger to take possession of all the property of the said insolvent debtors, is sufficient. Hansen *v.* Paige, 3 *Gray*, (*Mass.*) 239.

10. The omission of the messenger to take possession of the separate property of the partners under a warrant in insolvency, duly issued upon the application of the partnership, is no ground for setting aside the proceedings after an assignment has been made by the commissioner of all the property of the partnership and of the individual partners. *Id.*

11. A messenger who has a warrant against a debtor, issued pursuant to the insolvent law, is justified in locking the debtor's store, though unoccupied, and taking the key into his own possession. Stevens *v.* Palmer, 12 *Met.* (*Mass.*) 464.

12. The messenger should copy the exact language contained in the warrant into the notices to creditors to be served and published, but the register may disregard all immaterial variance. *In re* Pulver, (*S. D. N. Y.*) *N. B. R. Sup.* xi.

___

WARRANT OF ATTORNEY.

1. A warrant of attorney given to a retiring member of a firm, at the same time the deed of dissolution is executed, to secure him the payment of the capital he had brought into the business. *Held*, that such warrant was not for an antecedent debt or demand within 12 & 13 Vict. c. 106, s. 135. Loader *v.* Hiscock, 1 *F. & F.* 132. (Eng.)

2. A warrant of attorney, which is not filed within the twenty-one days prescribed by 3 Geo. 4, c. 39, was void against the assignees in bankruptcy, although the petitioning creditor's debt, upon which the fiat was founded, did not exist at the time of the execution of the warrant of attorney, or within twenty-one days. Everett *v.* Wells, 2 *Scott, N. R.* 525; 9 *D. P. C.* 424; 2 *M. & G.* 269. (Eng.)

3. Attached to note. Where a creditor who has been carrying and renewing a note enters up judgment by virtue of a warrant of attorney attached, and issues execution, the debtor having three days previously absconded leaving his property and creditors unprotected, the business community and newspapers being in speculation as to his departure and means, and the creditor having come to the conclusion that "there was something wrong," and that his interests, as well as those of the surety on the note require that judgment should be entered, he obtains such a preference as is avoided by the 35th and 39th sections of the bankrupt

act of 1867. Golson *et al. v.* Neihoff *et al.* 5 *N. B. R.* 56.

4. Judgment under. A judgment on a warrant of attorney, duly entered up more than a year before the bankruptcy of the debtor, and registered before the bankruptcy, constitutes a lien under 1 & 2 Vict. c. 110, s. 13, upon real estate of the bankrupt debtor, within the meaning of the exception in the 12 & 13 Vict. c. 106, s. 184. *Ex parte* Boyle, 17 *Jur.* 979; 22 *L. J., Bank* 178. (Eng.)

5. Where a person had given a bond and warrant of attorney, and afterwards became insolvent, and obtained his discharge under the act, and judgment was afterwards entered upon the warrant of attorney, the court on motion, ordered the judgment to be set aside. Billings *v.* Skult, 1 *Johnston,* 106.

6. Where a judgment was signed, within twenty-one days, upon a warrant of attorney, given by a bankrupt, which had been filed within twenty-one days after its execution, but without any affidavit ever being filed, attesting that the warrant was filed within twenty-one days after its execution, it was held that the judgment and execution issued thereon were void as against the assignees. Acraman *v.* Hernamann, 16 *Q. B.* 998; 15 *Jur.* 1008; 20 *L. J., Q. B.* 355. (Eng.)

7. The fact that a judgment was entered upon a warrant of attorney, does not invalidate the lien if the creditor did not know of the failing circumstances of the debtor, and if said judgment was not entered upon contemplation of bankruptcy or insolvency. The lien of an execution is not impaired by a direction to the sheriff to hold the execution but not to levy for a few days, or until further order. *In re* Weeks, (*Ill.*) 4 *N. B. R.* 116.

8. Where goods are seized by an execution creditor *bona fide* on a judgment entered on a warrant of attorney, after a secret act of bankruptcy, but not sold until after the date and issuing of the fiat and notice, it was held, that the assignees of the bankrupt debtor were entitled to the goods. Skey *v.* Carter, 11 *M. & W.* 571; 2 *D. N. S.*

831; 5 *Scott, N. R.* 877, n.; 7 *Jur.* 427; 12 *L. J., Exch.* 511; *S. P.*, Whitmore *v.* Robinson, 1 *D. N. S.* 135; 8 *M. & W.* 463; 5 *Jur.* 1088; Lackington *v.* M'Lochlan, 5 *Scott, N. R.* 874. (Eng.)

9. Under 6 Geo. 4, c. 108, an execution on a judgment founded on a warrant of attorney to be good against a fiat must be so executed that the execution creditor has ceased to be a creditor of the bankrupt holding a security for his debt; the sale under the execution must therefore be complete before the fiat. Ward *v.* Dalton, 7 *C. B.* 643; 13 *Jur.* 734; 18 *L. J., C. P.* 236. (Eng.)

10. Where a sheriff seizes goods under a *fi. fa.* upon a judgment founded upon a warrant of attorney, such writ becomes void by the issuing of a fiat against the debtor before the sale. Graham *v.* Lynes, 1 *Q. B.* 491; 14 *L. J., Q. B.* 290; 9 *Jur.* 1104; *S. P.*, Goldschmidt *v.* Hamlet, 6 *M. & G.* 187; 6 *Scott, N. R.* 962; 1 *D. & L.* 801; Congreve *v.* Evetts, 10 *Exch.* 298. (Eng.)

11. A warrant of attorney was given to secure a debt in 1819, judgment was entered up, a *fi. fa.* issued and goods seized which were assigned over to the plaintiff in 1825, about a fortnight previously to the bankruptcy. It was held, that the assignees were not authorized by the 6 Geo. 4, c. 16, s. 108, in taking possession of the goods seized in execution. Wyner *v.* Kemble, 6 *B. & C.* 479; 9 *D. & R.* 511. (Eng.)

12. Judgment was entered up on a warrant of attorney given by two joint traders; and a *fi. fa.* issued returnable on the 2d May. On the first of that month the sheriff's officer received from the defendants the money directed to be levied. On the 2d May, one of them committed an act of bankruptcy, and the other on the 5th. On the 11th, a commission of bankruptcy issued, and on the 19th the sheriff paid over the money to the execution creditor. In an action by the assignees, it was held, that the creditor was entitled to retain it, not being a creditor having a security at the time of the bankruptcy. Morland *v.* Pellatt, 8 *B. & C.* 722; 2 *M. & R.* 411. (Eng.)

13. An execution founded on a warrant of attorney, and complete by sale prior to the fiat, was protected by 2 & 3 Vict. c. 29, notwithstanding the creditor before the sale had notice of an act of bankruptcy. Whitmore *v.* Green, 2 *D. & L.* 174; 14 *M. & W.* 104; 8 *Jur.* 697; 13 *L. J., Exch.* 311. (Eng.)

14. A creditor on a judgment founded upon a warrant of attorney, issued execution thereon, and seized and sold the goods of the debtor on a *fi. fa.*, without notice of any act of bankruptcy committed. On the day after the sale a fiat issued against the debtor. It was held, that the assignees were not entitled to recover from the creditor the proceeds of the sale, inasmuch as at the time of the fiat he was not a creditor of the bankrupt, within 6 Geo. 4, c. 16, s. 108. Ramsey *v.* Eaton, 10 *M. & W.* 22. (Eng.)

15. **To confess judgment.** D. being possessed of 299*l.* lent to W., whom she was about to marry. He, as security for the loan, gave to her and S. a warrant of attorney in 1837, to confess judgment of 600*l.* By the defeasance, which stated that the loan was made in contemplation of marriage, W. was to hold the money as long as D. and S. should please, paying interest to S. for her, and, on her request, S. might on a week's notice require payment of the principal, judgment was to be entered up forthwith, and execution was to issue on default of payment after notice. The marriage took place, judgment was issued up, and in 1845, S., at the wife's request, gave a week's notice, demanding payment, and as it was not paid, issued execution and levied on W.'s goods. W. in a few days afterwards became bankrupt, and his assignees applied to set aside the judgment and execution, on the grounds, first, that execution was irregular, the judgment not having been revived by *scire facias* and being more than a year old; and secondly, that the marriage between D. and W. had discharged the judgment. The court refused the application. Dolling *v.* White, 17 *Jur.* 505; 22 *L. J., Q. B.* 327; 1 *B. C. C.* 170. (Eng.)

16. **When a preference.** Where a firm was insolvent, and at the time of giving a note and a warrant of attorney to confess judgment had reason to believe that they could not pay their debts, in the ordinary course of business, the giving of such a note operated as a preference. Campbell *v.* Traders' National Bank, (*Ill.*) 3 *N. B. R.* 124.

17. When and when not valid. A debtor in embarrassed circumstances gave a favored creditor a warrant of attorney and shortly afterwards was declared insolvent; judgment was entered up on the warrant, and the debtor's goods seized in execution. It was held, that the warrant of attorney was voidable as against the assignees. Young *v.* Billiter, 7 *Jur., N. S.* 269; 30 *L. J., Q. B.* 153; 8 *H. L., Cas.* 682; *S. C.* in exchequer chamber, 6 *El. & Bl.* 1; 2 *Jur., N. S.* 438; 25 *L. J., Q. B.* 169. (Eng.)

18. A warrant of attorney, which was not filed within the twenty-one days prescribed by 3 Geo. 4, c. 39, was void against the assignees in bankruptcy, although judgment was signed and execution issued on it prior to the act of bankruptcy. Bittleson *v.* Cooper, 14 *M. & W.* 399. (Eng.)

19. Where a debtor's insolvency is not shown to have existed at the time of giving a warrant of attorney to confess judgment, he will not be presumed to have had knowledge of the fact of his insolvency, and a preference thus given several months previous to the fact of his insolvency becoming apparent, will be held valid. Armstrong *v.* Rickey Bros. (*Ohio,*) 2 *N. B. R.* 150; s. c. 3 *C. L. N.* 145; citing Buckingham *v.* McLean, 13 *How.* 169; Hall *v.* King, 4 *C. R.* 136; 3 *Met.* 245; 19 *N. H.* 109.

20. Where bankers made advances to one of their customers upon a guarantee and at the same time took from the principal debtor a warrant of attorney to cover the debt, and at the same time agreed with the guarantor that they would, at any time, at his request, enter up judgment and levy execution on the warrant of attorney; but by their neglect to file the warrant of attorney, or a true copy thereof, the warrant became void. It was held, that this neglect on the part of the bankers operated as a discharge of the surety. Watson *v.* Alcock, 4 *De G., Mac. & G.* 247; 17 *Jur.* 568; 22 *L. J., Chanc.* 858; see Parker *v.* Watson, 8 *Exch.* 404; 22 *L. J., Exch.* 167. (Eng.)

21. When in the order and distribution of bankrupt. C., to secure the payment of a debt, gave a warrant of attorney to A. The solicitor of C., as agent of A., deposited the warrant with B., as security for a debt due him by A. No express notice of this deposit was given to C., and A. afterwards became bankrupt. It was held, that the warrant of attorney was in the order and disposition of A. at the time of his bankruptcy, and that the circumstance of C.'s solicitor having notice did not amount to notice to C. of the deposit. *Ex parte* Price, 3 *Mont., D. & D.* 586; 13 *L. J., Bank.* 15. (Eng.)

WHEN TIME PRESUMED.

1. Where a trader has been proved to have traded in the usual course once, he will be presumed to have continued to carry on his business in the same manner until the time of his bankruptcy. Heamney *v.* Buch, 1 *Rose,* 356; 3 *Camp.* 233. (Eng.)

WIFE.

1. A husband in Mississippi gave promissory note to the trustee of his wife for alleged balance on account stated between them, growing out of the use of the separate personal and real property of the wife, and executed a deed of trust on certain land of the husband to secure payment of the note, and subsequently went into voluntary bankruptcy. The court decided, in an action brought by the assignee and a secured creditor, that the conveyance was fraudulent and void. *In re* Gillespie, (*Miss.*) 3 *N. B. R.* 117.

2. Where the wife of a bankrupt purchased the interest of a retiring member of an insurance firm, of which her husband was apparently an employee, it was held, under all the circumstances, that he was a partner, as the business of the firm mainly depended upon his exertions, and this purchase by the wife was an attempt to conceal his real interest in the concern. *In re* Rathbone, (*S. D. N. Y.*) 2 *N. B. R.* 89.

3. The wife of a bankrupt cannot hold property as against creditors, conveyed to her after her husband became aware of his insolvency. *In re* Adams, (*Mass.*) 3 *N. B. R.* 139.

4. When the wife of a bankrupt, duly summoned, failed to appear for examination before the register, and her counsel put in an affidavit explanatory of her non-attendance, but questioned the authority of the court to compel her to testify in the cause. The court decided that an order to show cause why an attachment should not issue against her, would be granted. *In re* Bellis & Milligan, (*S. D. N. Y.*) 3 *N. B. R.* 65.

5. A man in embarrassed circumstances cannot make use of his wife directly or indirectly, to cover up from his creditors any of his property, or any of his earnings, the fruit of his skill. *In re* Eldred, (*Ill.*) 3 *N. B. R.* 61.

6. As a creditor. A wife deposited money of her separate estate with her husband for safe keeping, and received from him portions thereof from time to time, but left a balance of $700 with him. The court decided that she was entitled, as a general creditor, to that amount; her husband having been declared a bankrupt. *In re* Bigelow, *et al.* (*S. D. N. Y.*) 2 *N. B. R.* 170.

7. Bankruptcy of previous to marriage. In an action against husband and wife to recover for goods sold to her before her marriage, where it appeared that the wife, while sole, on her petition duly filed, had been declared a bankrupt under the U. S. bankrupt act of 1841, and had presented a petition for her discharge and then intermarried with the other defendant, and subsequently to the marriage a certificate of discharge under a decree of the court was issued to her in her maiden name, it was holden, that such certificate was available to her and to her husband, as a defence to such suit. Chadwick *v.* Starrett, 27 *Maine Reports*, 138.

8. Cannot refuse to answer questions before register. Bankrupt's wife cannot refuse to answer questions before a register, because the matters inquired of are her own private business. *In re* Craig, (*S. D. N. Y.*) 4 *N. B. R.* 50.

9. Conveyance to. A conveyance settling property upon the wife and family of the grantor, will be considered fraudulent as to subsequent creditors, if the grantor be indebted at the time to such an extent that the settlement will embarrass him in the payment of his debts, although the debts then due may be paid subsequently by contracting other obligations. Antroms *v.* Kelly *et al.* 4 *N. B. R.* 189.

10. If the assignees in insolvency of a mortgagor by his request, and without objection from his creditors, convey to his wife an equity of redemption, without consideration and with notice, she, in seeking to redeem, will be subjected to the same equities as he would have been. Stone *v.* Lane, 10 *Allen,* (*Mass.*)

11. After a debtor's insolvency becomes known to him, he cannot convey real and personal property to his wife, without committing a fraud upon the U. S. bankrupt act of 1867, and thus depriving himself of the right to a discharge. *In re* Adams, (*Mass.*) 3 *N. B. R.* 139.

12. Entitled to witness fees. The wife of a bankrupt is entitled to witness fees for attendance and travel, as any other witness, where she appears before the register to be examined. *In re* Griffin, (*S. D. N. Y.*) 1 *N. B. R.* 83.

13. Examination of. The wife of a bankrupt may be examined when, on reasonable grounds, she is suspected of having, or of having had property in her possession, which should have been surrendered to the creditors, or to have participated actively in any other fraud upon the statute. *In re* Gilbert, (*Mass.*) 3 *N. B. R.* 37.

14. The wife of a bankrupt cannot be required to testify as witness against her husband, for the purpose of supplying evidence to set aside his discharge. Tenny & Gregory *v.* Collins, (*Mo.*) 4 *N. B. R.* 156.

15. A register issued order for the wife of a bankrupt to attend and be examined as a witness, and the order was served upon the husband, the wife failed to attend. The court held that the order was properly issued, and that the husband should prove to the satisfaction of the court, that he was unable to procure her attendance, otherwise the register is not warranted in certifying conformity to the requirements necessary to the granting of his discharge. *In re* Van Tuyl, (*S. D. N. Y.*) 2 *N. B. R.* 177.

16. A bankrupt's wife will not be examined except upon a *prima facie* case made out by affidavit. *In re* Gilbert, 3 *N. B. R.* 37.

17. Bankrupt's wife may be examined both before and after he has applied for his discharge. *In re* Seckindorf, 1 *N. B. R.* 185.

18. An application for an order to examine bankrupt's wife not made in good faith, or for the purpose of delaying the bankrupt obtaining his discharge, will be refused. *In re* Selig, *N. B. R. Sup.* xl.

19. Where order requiring wife of the bankrupt to attend and be examined as a witness, is properly granted, and bankrupt is duly apprised of the same, he will be refused a discharge if his wife fail to comply with the order, unless he can prove satisfactorily that he could not obtain her attendance. *In re* Van Tuyl, 3 *N. B. R.* 177.

20. Bankrupt's wife is not bound to appear and be examined, unless she is paid the usual and proper witness fees. *In re* Van Tuyl, 2 *N. B. R.* 25.

21. The order for bankrupt or his wife to attend and be examined, form No. 45, is in the nature of a summons, and may be furnished in blank to the registers, signed and sealed by the clerk. *In re* Bellamy, (*S. D. N. Y.*) *N. B. R. Sup.* xiv.

22. Under section 26 of the bankrupt act, bankrupt's wife may be summoned and compelled to attend and be examined as any other witness, and may be punished for contempt if she refuses to answer. *In re* Woolford, (*S. D. N. Y.*) 3 *N. B. R.* 113 ; *in re* Bellis & Milligan, 3 *N. B. R.* 65.

23. **Gift from, when presumed.** Where purchase is made of property by the husband, and the wife gives or lets him have money towards making payments, or such payments are made with her money and with her consent, it is to be presumed that the wife makes a gift to the husband of such money, especially in the absence of any express agreement, and the property must be subject to the husband's debts. Keating, assignee, *v.* Keefer, (*Mich.*) 5 *N. B. R.* 133.

24. **May be examined.** For good cause shown, the wife of any bankrupt may be required to attend before the court, to the end she may be examined as a witness ; and if such wife do not attend at the time and place specified in the order, the bankrupt shall not be entitled to a discharge unless he shall prove to the satisfaction of the court that he was unable to procure the attendance of his wife. *Sec.* 26 *U. S. bankrupt act*, 1867.

25. **May be petitioning creditor.** An adjudication of bankruptcy will be made against a trader or merchant where his own wife is the petitioning creditor, and claims in right of her separate estate. *In re* Overton, Northern District of New York. 5 *N. B. R.* 366.

26. **May prove security obtained from husband before marriage.** D. being possessed of 299*l.*, lent it to W., whom she was about to marry. He, as security for the loan, gave to her and S. a warrant of attorney in 1837, to confess judgment of 600*l.* By the defeasance, which stated that the loan was made in contemplation of marriage, W. was to hold the money as long as D. and S. should please, paying interest to S. for her, and on her request, S. might, on a week's notice, require payment of the principal. Judgment was to be entered up forthwith, and execution was to issue on default of payment after notice. The marriage took place, judgment was entered up, and in 1845, S., at the wife's request, gave a week's notice, demanding payment, and it was not paid, issued execution and levied on W.'s goods. W., in a few days afterwards, became bankrupt, and his assignees applied to set aside the judgment and execution, on the ground, first, that execution was irregular, the judgment not having been revived by *scire facias*, and being more than a year old ; and, secondly, that the marriage between D. and W. had discharged the judgment. The court refused the application. Dolling *v.* White, 17 *Jur.* 505 ; 22 *L. J., Q. B.* 327 ; 1 *B. C. C.* 170. (Eng.)

27. Must answer questions regarding her separate estate. The wife of a bankrupt is obliged to answer questions in regard to her own separate estate, and whether she was possessed of anything except what was given to her by her husband. *In re* Clark *et al.* (*S. D. N. Y.*) 4 *N. B. R.* 70.

28. Petition by to review decision of district court. The wife of a bankrupt petitioned the circuit court to review a decision of the district court, that she had valuable stock that belonged to her husband. The court decided that an assignee could not recover assets of third parties by summary proceedings, but must do so by bill in equity or suit at law. *In re* Bonesteel, (*S. D. N. Y.*) 3 *N. B. R.* 127.

29. Proof by. Bankrupt's wife admitted to prove. *Ex parte* Thring, 1 *Mont. & Chit.* 75. (Eng.)

30. Property of. Bankrupt may not always decline to answer questions concerning his wife's property, but shall testify under direction of the court. *In re* Craig, (*S. D. N. Y.*) 4 *N. B. R.* 50.

31. Where the husband's equitable interest in the estate or property of his wife, has been levied upon and sold under execution, he has no longer any interest or estate to be returned in his schedules. *In re* Hummitsh, (*Mo.*) 2 *N. B. R.* 3.

32. Property of, title in husband. Where a married woman saves her earnings, with which property is purchased, first in her husband's name, and subsequently conveyed to her or sold and other property purchased with the proceeds, which last property is deeded in the name of the wife. In the state of Michigan, this property is subject to the husband's debts. Keating, assignee, *v.* Keefer, (*Mich.*) 5 *N. B. R.* 133.

33. Property purchased in her name. When a man's wife purchases real estate which had been previously held on contract by the husband, but the deed is made out to the wife, although it was not recorded for a number of years, and it appears that the man himself was indebted at the time of the conveyance, the deed to the wife will be set aside, notwithstanding the wife has earned much of the money paid for the land by her own exertions. Such property will be declared, assets of the bankrupt and the wife will be directed to convey the property to the assignee. Keating, assignee, *v.* Keefer, (*Mich.*) 5 *N. B. R.* 133.

34. Right of dower. The wife of a bankrupt is not entitled to claim dower out of land owned by him when he filed his petition in bankruptcy, during his lifetime. Kelly *v.* Strange, (*N. C.*) 3 *N. B. R.* 2.

35. Right of dower of. The widow of a bankrupt, where petition in bankruptcy was filed after the act passed by the legislature of North Carolina, repealing the statutory provision and restoring the common law right of dower, the bankrupt dying after the issuing of the warrant in bankruptcy is entitled to dower in the land owned by the bankrupt at the time of the filing of his petition. The act referred to repealed the statutory provision in regard to dower—which in effect restored *eo instanti* the common law. The legislature by that act attempted to create additional exemptions to those theretofore allowed by law; those exemptions are void as to creditors whose debts are contracted previous to the passage of the act. The widow of a bankrupt is not entitled to the personal property exempted by the provisions of the 14th section of the act of 1867, nor is the assignee in bankruptcy. No title to exempt property passes to the assignee by the assignment, it remains in the bankrupt, at his death it passes to his legal representatives. *In re* Hester, (*N. C.*) 5 *N. B. R.* 285.

36. Right of to insurance on husband's life. An insurance on the debtor's life for the benefit of his wife, where the premiums have been paid after his insolvency, is to be set apart as exempt, where the appraised value does not exceed $300. *In re* Erben, (*Pa.*) 2 *N. B. R.* 66.

37. Separate estate of. A *femme sole* having contracted a debt and owning some shares of bank stock married. After marriage, the stock, with the consent of the husband, was transferred to a third person for the purpose of having it transferred back to her for her sole and separate use, which was accordingly done. She also held other shares of bank stock which had been transferred to her separate use by the executor of her father's estate. The creditor sued the husband and wife at law, and being met by a plea of the husband's bankruptcy, discontinued. He then filed a bill in equity for the purpose of reaching the bank stock. No fraud in the transfer to the wife's separate use being alleged, nor any act of the wife after marriage indicating an intention to charge this fund. *Held,* that the bill could not be sustained. The bankruptcy of the husband extinguishes the liabilty as to him; but it revives against the wife if she survives her husband. Vanderheyden v. Mallory, 1 *Comstock,* 1 (*N. Y.*) 452.

38. The bankruptcy of the husband, although it extinguishes the debt, as to him, and suspends the legal remedy as to her during the coverture, does not afford any ground for proceeding in equity to charge her separate estate. The creditor in such a case may prove his debt and share the distribution of the bankrupt's estate. *Id.*

39. Where C. was trustee for a married woman under a post nuptial agreement entered into between her and her husband, and was also one of the assignees of the husband in an assignment made for the benefit of his creditors, and property came to his hands in the latter character; *held*, that he was bound to apply the property as the law would apply it, rather than to the payment of a bond and warrant of attorney given by the husband in trust for his wife, and that even if he had notice of an ante-nuptial agreement between the husband and wife in respect to her separate estate, he was not concluded by such notice from contesting the legality of the agreement, nor from disregarding it so far as it conflicted with the rights of the husband's creditors. Borst v. Corey *et al.* 16 *Barb.* 136.

40. Voluntary conveyance to by husband. Where a person by the name of J. K. Place, in solvent circumstances, purchased a ground rent lease in 1865, and paid a portion of the purchase money down and took an assignment of the lease, which

was recorded during the same year, and commenced the erection of a house on the premises covered by the lease, and the building was completed during the following year, during which year two assignments of the lease were made and duly recorded—the first to a man by the name of Wallis, the second by Wallis to Susan A. Place, the wife of J. K. Place, which assignment to Mrs. Place was dated a few days after the assignment from J. K. Place to Wallis, and payments were made by J. K. Place (to the person from whom he had purchased the ground rent) during several subsequent years, the last of which was made November 20, 1867, and J. K. Place had also expended a large sum in improving the property, which premises were occupied by Mr. and Mrs. Place and their family. The copartnership of which Mr. Place was a member failed in November, 1867, although during the previous May there was reason to believe it to be insolvent. The investment of the lease cannot be regarded as an investment of the funds of the copartnership, although an account had been kept in the partnership books of the premises, to which account was debited several payments made therefor, which were in effect charged to J. K. Place. There being no evidence that J. K. Place intended to defraud his then existing creditors in making the investment, the plaintiff is not entitled to recover the property which was conveyed to Mrs. Place or to its proceeds. Sedgwick, assignee, v. Place *et al.* 5 *N. B. R.* 168.

WIDOW OF BANKRUPT.

1. The widow of a bankrupt, whose petition in bankruptcy was filed after the act passed by the legislature of North Carolina repealing the statutory provision and restoring the common law right of dower, the bankrupt dying after the issuing of the warrant in bankruptcy, is entitled to dower in the land owned by the bankrupt at the time of the filing of his petition. *In re* Hester, (*N. C.*) 5 *N. B. R.* 285.

2. The widow of a bankrupt is not entitled to the personal property exempted by the provisions of the 14th section of the act of 1867, nor is the assignee in bankruptcy.

No title to exempt property passes to the assignee by the assignment, it remains in the bankrupt; at his death it passes to his legal representatives. *Id.*

WITHDRAWAL.

1. Of papers. The original papers cannot be withdrawn from the files at the option of the bankrupt. The court may, however, order a withdrawal for good reason shown by party interested. *In re* McNair, (*N. C.*) 2 *N. B. R.* 109.

2. Specifications. Where a creditor opposes but subsequently withdraws his specifications, the bankrupt should take and subscribe the necessary oath after the withdrawal, although he has already taken it *In re* Machad, (*S. D. N. Y.*) 2 *N. B. R.* 113.

WITNESS.

1. A defendant is not made a competent witness by the fact of his having been discharged as a bankrupt after the suit was brought, especially if sued as an executor. Given *v.* Albert, 5 *W. & S. Pa. Rep.* 333.

2. Where, in assumpsit against several partners, one of them pleaded his discharge under the bankrupt act, and thereupon a *nolle prosequi* was entered as to him; *held*, that he was a competent witness for his co-partners, provided he released all interest in the surplus of his effects. Butcher *et al. v.* Forman *et al.* 6 *Hill*, 583.

3. Absence of material. When the debtor is brought up on the last day of term, the court will remand him until the next term, upon an affidavit by the creditor of the absence of material witness. Marscroft *v.* Butler, *Coleman & Caines' Cases*, 366.

4. Bankrupt as. It is no objection against a bankrupt being a witness, that the names of his assignees were not substituted in the action on his obtaining his certificate of conformity. Browne *v.* Insurance Company of Pennsylvania, 4 *Yates' Pa. Reports*, 119.

5. A bankrupt, after his discharge, is a competent witness for the plaintiffs, in an action brought by his sureties to avoid a note given by them and the bankrupt on the ground of usury. Morse *v.* Cloyes, 11 *Barb.* 100.

6. To exclude the bankrupt as a witness, in such a case, it must be shown that at least there may be a surplus of his estate to which he will be entitled. A surplus and a consequent interest in the witness will not be presumed. *Id.*

7. Compelling attendance. Where a person, summoned and neglecting to attend before the commissioner, was arrested under a warrant issued by the commissioner, it was held, in an action of false imprisonment against the solicitor to the fiat, who had applied for the warrant, that the warrant was a justification to him, though the commissioner stated, at the time of the application, that he was in doubt whether the warrant ought to issue, and that the parties applying must take it on their own responsibility. Cooper *v.* Harding, 7 *Q. B.* 928; 9 *Jur.* 777. (Eng.)

8. Where a party, who has been duly summoned to attend in order to be examined, and to produce a deed, fails to comply with the summons, a warrant by the commissioner, directing him to be arrested and brought before him to be examined and produce the document, is good, although the document was not in the party's possession, and over which he had no control. And if a witness finds the commissioners engaged in other business at the time appointed in the summons, he must wait till they are ready to examine him or dispense with his attendance. Wright *v.* Maude, 2 *D., N. S.* 517; 10 *M. & W.* 527; 6 *Jur.* 953; 12 *L. J., Exch.* 22. (Eng.)

9. The operation of a warrant to compel the attendance of a witness, as a legal cause of detainer, becomes expended, either by the party's being brought before the commissioner, or on his submitting; and that the commissioner had no jurisdiction to make a subsequent order for the detention of the party till costs were paid. Watson *v.* Bodell, 14 *M. & W.* 37; 9 *Jur.* 626; 14 *L. J., Exch.* 281. (Eng.)

10. A commissioner has power to compel parties to appear and give evidence before him, although there are no facts in dispute, and the difference on which he is called to adjudicate turns on a question of law. Watson v. Whitmore, 8 *Jur.* 964; 14 *L. J., Exch.* 41. (Eng.)

11. Competency of principal and guarantee. The liability of a principal to his guarantee, and who has not paid the money, is not discharged by the bankrupt law. The principal is therefore incompetent as a witness for the defendant in a suit brought by the creditor with guaranty. Coke v. Lewis, 8 *Penn. R.* 493.

12. Competency of purchaser as. In an action upon a promissory note, where the bankruptcy of the maker is alleged in his defence, and the certificate of discharge is attempted to be impeached, on the ground of a prior fraudulent sale of goods to a third person, which he did not include in his schedule of effects, the purchaser is a competent witness. Loud v. Pierce, 25 *Me. R.* 233.

13. Creditor of insolvent. A creditor is a competent witness to prove fraud in the petitioner who applies to be discharged under the insolvent laws. Green's case, 2 *Dallas' Penn. R.* 268.

14. Examination of. Witnesses may be examined after a bankrupt has filed his petition for a discharge. The time for filing objections to the discharge can be kept open by adjournments to any day which may be fixed for showing cause, until a reasonable time has elapsed for the examination of witnesses. *In re* Seckendorf, (*S. D. N. Y.*) 1 *N. B. R.* 185.

15. A lawyer, who is being examined as a witness touching a certain conveyance made to him by the bankrupt and wife, and a subsequent conveyance by him to the wife, cannot refuse to testify thereon as a matter within the privilege of confidential communications between attorney and client. *In re* Bellis & Milligan, (*S. D. N. Y.*) 3 *N. B. R.* 49.

16. A witness is not bound to answer a question that does not relate to any matter of fact in issue, or to any matter contained in his direct testimony, especially if a truthful answer to it will tend to degrade him *In re* Lewis, (*S. D. N. Y.*) 3 *N. B. R.* 153.

17. The 26th section of the U. S. bankrupt act of 1867, requires a witness to submit to an examination on oath upon all matters relating to the disposal or condition of the bankrupt's property, to his trade and dealings with others, and his accounts concerning the same, and to all other matters concerning his property and estate, and the due settlement thereof according to law. A witness submitting to an examination waives any objection he may have made, and in such case the register should refuse to certify any question for the decision of the judge. *In re* Fredenberg, (*S. D. N. Y.*) 1 *N. B. R.* 34.

18. Where a witness who purchased claims against a bankrupt's estate, refused by the advice of his counsel to answer questions (or loaded a direct answer thereto) relative to the money or consideration used in the purchase thereof from whom, and how he obtained the same otherwise than from the bankrupts, the witness testifying that he had not obtained the same from the bankrupts or either of them. The court decided that he must answer to the questions, and upon refusal, to be punished for contempt. *In re* Lathrop *et al.* (*S. D. N. Y.*) 4 *N. B. R.* 93.

19. A witness cannot refuse to answer questions concerning his dealing, &c. with the bankrupt, on the ground that his answer may furnish evidence against him in a civil case brought or to be brought on behalf of the assignee. *In re* Fay, (*Mass.*) 3 *N. B. R.* 163.

20. A witness cannot rightfully object to being sworn, or refuse to be examined upon any matters within the subjects mentioned in sec. 26 of the U. S. bankrupt act of 1867. *In re* Blake, 2 *N. B. R.* 2.

21. A witness must answer all proper questions relating to his trade and dealings with the bankrupt, prior to bankruptcy, and if necessary to the proper and complete answering of such questions, must produce any book containing the transactions with

the bankrupt. *In re* Earle, (*S. D. N. Y.*) 3 *N. B. R.* 81.

22. Husband and wife for each other. The supreme court of Pennsylvania held, that under the act of April, 1869, of that state, husband and wife are competent witnesses for each other in court proceedings. *In re* 28 *Pitts. L. J.* 285 ; s. c. 3 *C. L. N.* 292.

23. Petitioning creditor is a competent. In an action between other parties, the petitioning creditor is a competent witness to prove his own debt, upon which a commission of bankruptcy was awarded. Farrington *v.* Farrington, 4 *Mass.* 237.

24. Protection from arrest. A bankrupt attending commissioners in obedience to their summons, was arrested under an extent at the suit of the crown. It was held, that although the crown is not within the bankrupt statute, the bankrupt was entitled to his discharge, on the principle of the common law protecting witnesses attending for examination under regular process for that purpose. 1 *Rose,* 278 ; 19 *Ves.* 163 ; *S. P., ex parte* Temple, 2 *Ves.* 391 ; 2 *Rose,* 22. (Eng.)

25. Competency of debtor as. An insolvent debtor who has obtained his discharge, is a competent witness for his assignee, on releasing the latter from all claim against him as such. Greene *v.* Durfee, 6 *Cush.* (*Mass.*) 362.

26. Insolvent debtor may be. An insolvent debtor who has released all claims to a surplus is a competent witness for his assignees. Jaques *v.* Marquand, 6 *Cowen,* 497.

WOMEN (MARRIED).

1. A wife being a sole trader in London, is liable to a commission of bankruptcy, and her assignees will come in paramount to the assignees of the husband, though his was the prior bankruptcy. La Vie *v.* Philips, 1 *W. Bl.* 570 ; ₹ *Burr,* 1776. (Eng.)

2. The wife of a convict sentenced to transportation may be a trader and a bankrupt, although the husband is only on board the hulks, and she has occasional intercourse with him. *Ex parte* Franks, 7 *Bing.* 762 ; 1 *M. & Scott,* 1. (Eng.)

3. A commission having issued against a married woman, on a trading before marriage, it was suspended. *Ex parte* Mear, 2 *Bro. C. C.* 266. (Eng.)

4. After the issuing of a fiat, the petitioning creditor heard and believed that the party against whom it was issued was a married woman. The court would not, for this cause, on the petition of the petitioning creditor, order the fiat to be annulled, but merely suspended the prosecution of it. *Ex parte* Harland, 1 *Deac.* 75. (Eng.)

5. Execution against. A married woman, in execution with her husband, for a debt contracted by her before marriage, was not entitled to be discharged under 1 Geo. 4, c. 119, as she was not capable of executing a warrant of attorney, and complying with the other terms required by sec. 25. *Ex parte* Deacon, 5 *B. & A.* 759 ; see Chalk *v.* Deacon, 6 *Moore,* 128. (Eng.)

6. May carry on business on her own account. A married woman may carry on business on her own account, and, for her own interest, may employ all needed labor, workmen and agents, and she may also employ her own husband and pay him. Driggs *v.* Russell, (*Mich.*) 3 *N. B. R.* 39.

7. Note given to. A promissory note given to a married woman for a debt due her before her marriage, though not reduced to possession by her husband, passes by an assignment of his property under the United States bankrupt act of 1841 ; and a subsequent indorsement of the note by the husband and wife will not enable the indorsee, with notice of the circumstance, to maintain an action on the note without the consent of the assignee in bankruptcy. Smith *v.* Chandler, 3 *Grays'* (*Mass.*) 392.

8. Notes of. Under the act of 1862, a promissory note given by a married woman engaged in trade, and in the course of her business, might be enforced against her separate estate under the same allegations as if she were single; but if there is no intention expressed in the note which is the foundation of the petition in this case to bind her separate estate, and no allegation that it was given for the benefit of the separate estate, or in the course of her trading transactions, the petition must be dismissed, with permission to amend. *In re* Howland, (*N. D. N. Y.*) 2 *N. B. R.* 114.

9. Petition by. A married woman on her own petition, in which she stated herself to be a widow, was adjudicated a bankrupt, and she was afterwards indicted for concealment and embezzlement of her property, with intent to defraud her creditors, and two other persons were also indicted on account of aiding her. The examinations and answers of the three in bankruptcy were given in evidence in support of the prosecution. No caution was given to them by the commissioner on such examination, and they did not object to answer on the ground that their answers might criminate them. *Held*, although the wife was adjudicated a bankrupt the property belonged to her husband, and that the property was not proved as laid in the indictment. Reg. *v.* Robinson, 16 *L. T.*, *N. S.* 605; 15 *W. R.* 966; 10 *Cox*, *C. C.* 167; 1 *L. R.*, *C. C.* 80; 36 *L. J.*, *M. C.* 78. (Eng.)

10. Petitioning as legatee. A *femme covert* petitioning by her next friend, permitted to prove the value of a legacy of stock bequeathed to her separate use, but transferred into the use of her husband who sold it out, and become bankrupt, and a trustee appointed to receive the dividend. *Ex parte* Wills, 2 *Mont.*, *D. & D.* 504. (Eng.)

11. Security to. A married woman furnished money to her husband and took as security a note given by the firm of which he was a member. The court decided that the note was not an evidence of debt against the firm, but against the husband only, and that she might prove as against him and participate in the dividends of his individual estate, but not against the partnership estate. *In re* Frost *et al.* (*Mich.*) 3 *N. B. R.* 180.

WOMEN (SINGLE.)

A *femme sole* having contracted a debt in Rhode Island took the benefit of an insolvent act of that state passed after the debt was contracted, whereby her person was discharged from arrest, and then married in the same state, having no property. The creditor and the wife were inhabitants of Rhode Island at the time when the debt was contracted, when the insolvent act was passed, when the proceedings under it were had, and when the marriage took place. The husband was a citizen of Massachusetts, and after the marriage the wife came here and resided with him. The act provides that no man who shall intermarry with any woman who shall have had the benefit of the act shall be liable for any debt incurred by her before the benefit of the act was extended to her, for any greater amount than the value of the property which he acquired by the marriage. An action for debt having been brought here against the husband and wife, it was held that the husband was not liable and that the action could not be sustained. Pitkins *v.* Thompson, 13 *Pick.* (*Mass.*) 64.

———

WOOD.

1. Lien on. The owner of land who sells wood standing thereon, with authority to the vendee to cut it within a certain time, has no lien on the wood for the price, in case of the vendee's insolvency after the wood is cut, and before it is removed. Douglass *v.* Shumway, 33 *Grays'* (*Mass.*) 498.

———

WORKMAN.

1. Right of. The lien created by the statute of Wisconsin attaches from the time the work was commenced, or the materials furnished for the building upon which it was done or used. Any mechanic who had a lien at the filing of the publication in bankruptcy, would have a right to file a petition under section four of the act, so as to continue it, notwithstanding the commencement or pendency of bankruptcy proceedings. The bankrupt act provides for the protection of legal liens against the bankrupt's estate, instead of destroying them, and that where a party has a lien, when the petition in bankruptcy is filed ; but it is necessary, under the state law, to file a petition in the clerk's office, in order to continue it beyond a certain period ; that such party has the right to file such petition, and thereby continued the lien thereon. When a party has a lien or interest in the property, in the hands of an assignee in bankruptcy, he should apply to the U. S. court for relief, and it would grant the relief, or allow a suit to be brought in such court or state court, to determine the same ; but without such consent, parties have no right to sue, and are guilty of a contempt of the authority of the court if they do. Parties commencing suits in the state courts without such consent must give them up before they can be paid by order of the bankruptcy court. *In re* Cook & Gleason, 3 *C. L. N.* 410.

WRIT.

1. Appealed from, should not be prosecuted. If, pending an action in court, the defendant dies, and commissioners of insolvency on his estate are appointed by the judge of probate, and the claim in suit is, by the creditors, presented to them, and their adjudication upon it had, from which he appeals, he cannot prosecute his appeal by amending his writ in the action pending, but must commence a new suit, declaring for money had and received, as the statute provides. Nor is the case altered by the fact that the estate proves to be solvent. The adjudication and report of the commissioners having been accepted by the probate court, will bar the plaintiff from recovering in such pending suit, and the administrator will have costs from the time of his appearance to defend. Bates *v.* Ward, 49 *Maine Reports*, 87.

WRIT OF ENTRY.

1. If, after a grant of land, upon condition subsequent, the estate of the grantor is assigned under the insolvent laws of this commonwealth, the grantor cannot thereafter maintain a writ of entry, to receive possession of the granted premises for a breach of the condition. Stearns *v.* Harris, 8 *Allen,* (*Mass.*) 597.

2. Defence to action of. It is no defence to a writ of entry to recover land claimed by the demand and under a deed from an assignee in insolvency, that the clerk by whom all the proceedings in insolvency were recorded was appointed on the day of the filing of the creditor's petition on which the proceedings were founded, and months before the adjudication of insolvency and issuing of the warrant. Whitehead *v.* Mallory, 4 *Gray,* (*Mass.*) 180.

WRIT OF ERROR.

1. No questions of fact can be re-examined on a writ of error, hence a record sent up presenting nothing but facts to be reviewed in a writ of error, will be dismissed. Ruddick *v.* Billings, (*Iowa,*) 3 *N. B. R.* 14.

2. The assignee of an insolvent debtor may maintain a writ of error to reverse an erroneous judgment against the debtor, and cannot therefore avoid it by plea and proof. Johnson *v.* Thaxter, 7 *Grays'* (*Mass.*) 242.

3. In cases carried to the circuit court, by writ of error, the debt or damages claimed must amount to more than $500, and no question of fact can be re-examined upon such writ. Ruddick *v.* Billings, 3 *N. B. R.* 14.

WRITTEN MEMORANDUM.

1. Where a written memorandum does not specify the purpose for which deeds are deposited, the party will only be entitled to an order, as on a deposit, without any memorandum in writing. *Ex parte* Smith, 1 *Mont., D. & D.* 165 (Eng.)

COMPENDIUM

OF THE

UNITED STATES BANKRUPT ACT OF 1800.

COMPENDIUM

OF THE

UNITED STATES BANKRUPT ACT OF 1800.

SECTION 1. From and after 1st day of June, 1800, any merchant or other person residing in the United States, actually using the trade of merchandise by buying and selling, in gross and retail, or the banker, broker, factor, underwriter, or marine insurer, who shall, with intent to defraud his or her creditors, leave the state wherein he resides, or remain absent therefrom, or keep concealed, or keep house, so that he cannot be served with process; or willingly or fraudulently procure himself to be arrested, or his lands or other property to be attached, sequestered, or taken in execution; or shall secretly convey away or conceal his property to prevent levy thereon; or make or procure to be made any fraudulent conveyance of property; or make or admit of any fraudulent security or evidence of debt; or, being arrested for debt or having furnished.

SEC. 2. *Proceedings to Obtain a Commission of Bankruptcy.*—Judge of district court United States for district where debtor resided at the time of committing act of bankruptcy, on petition in writing against persons being bankrupt, to him to be exhibited by any one creditor, or by a greater number, being partners, whose single debt amounts to one thousand dollars, or by two creditors whose debts amount to one thousand five hundred dollars, shall have power, by commission under hand and seal, to appoint such good and substantial citizens of United States, and resident in such district, as such judge shall deem proper, not exceeding three, to be commissioners of bankruptcy, or, in case of vacancy or refusal to act, to appoint others, from time to time, as occasion may require.

Petitioning creditors to give bond to prove debt and bankruptcy of the party, and to proceed on the commission : *Provided always,* Before any commission shall issue, the creditor petitioning shall make oath of truth of debts, and give bond, to be taken by judge in name and for benefit of party charged as bankrupt, and in such penalty and with such surety as he shall require to be conditioned for proving of debts, as well before commissioners as upon trial at law, in case the due issuing forth of commission in manner herein prescribed, if such debt shall not be really due, or after such commission is taken out it cannot be proved that the party was bankrupt, then judge, upon petition of party aggrieved, in case there be occasion, deliver such bond to said party, who may sue thereon and recover such damages, under penalty of same as, upon trial at law, he shall make appear he has sustained by reason of any breach of condition thereof.

SEC. 3. Before the commissioners shall be capable of acting, shall respectfully take and subscribe following oath, administered by the judge issuing commission, or by any judge of superior court of United States, or any judge, justice, or chancellor of any state court, and filed in office of clerk of district court : I, A B., do swear, or affirm, that I will, faithfully and honestly, according to best of my skill and knowledge, execute the several processes and trusts reposed in me as a commissioner of bankruptcy against——, and that without favor, affection, prejudice, or malice ; and the commissioner shall then proceed, upon due examination and sufficient cause, to declare him bankrupt.

Before such examination be had, reasonable notice in writing shall be delivered to person charged as bankrupt ; or if he be not found at his usual place of abode, to some of the family above the age of twelve years; if no such person appear, it shall be fixed at front or other public door of house in which debtor usually resides. Commission to be superseded if not acted upon within thirty days, on application of party charged.

SEC. 4. Commissioners shall have power forthwith, after they have declared such person bankrupt to cause to be apprehended, by warrant under their hands and seals, the body of such bankrupt wheresoever to be found within the United States; *Provided,* They shall think there is reason to apprehend that said bankrupt intends to abscond or conceal himself; and in case it be necessary, in order to take body of said bankrupt, they shall have power to cause doors of dwelling-house to be broken, in which he or she shall be found.

SEC. 5. They shall take into their possession the bankrupt's property, papers and books. It shall also be duty of commissioners so appointed, forthwith to take into their possession all estate, real and personal, of every nature and description, and cause the same to be inventoried and appraised to the best value, necessary bed and wearing apparel excepted.

SEC. 6. Commissioners shall, forthwith, after they have declared such person a bankrupt, cause due notice to be given, and in such notice shall appoint some convenient time and place for creditors to meet, to choose assignee or assignees of estate and effects.

That in such choice no vote shall be given before or in behalf of any creditor whose debt shall not amount to $200.

SEC. 7. The commissioners as often as they shall see cause for the better preserving and securing bankrupt's estate, forthwith to appoint one or more assignees of estate and effects aforesaid.

SEC. 8. Such creditors of bankrupt as are authorized to vote in choice of assignees, may remove all or any of the assignees chosen, and may choose one or more in his or their place, and such assignee so removed shall deliver up all estate of bankrupt.

SEC. 9. Whenever new assignee is chosen, no suit at law or in equity shall be thereby abated; but it shall be lawful to allow name of such new assignee to be substituted in place of name of former assignee; and thereupon the suit shall be prosecuted in the name or names of new assignee, in the same manner as if they originally commenced suit in their own names.

SEC. 10. Assignment or assignments of commissioners of bankrupt's estate shall be good at law or in equity against bankrupt and all persons claiming under him, by any act done at the time, or after he shall have committed the act of bankruptcy upon which commission issued: *Provided,* in the case of a *bona fide* purchase made before issuing of commission from or under such bankrupt for valuable consideration, by any person having no knowledge or notice of any act of bankruptcy committed, such purchase shall not be invalidated or impeached.

SEC. 11. Said commissioners shall have power by deed, under their hands and seals, to assign and convey to assignee, to be appointed or chosen as aforesaid, any lands, tenements, hereditaments, which such bankrupt shall be seized of, or entitled to fee tail at law or in equity, in possession, remainder, or reversion, for the benefit of creditors. All such deeds being duly executed and recorded according to laws of the state in which such lands, tenements, or hereditaments may be situate, shall be good and effectual against all persons whom said bankrupt might or could bar of any estate, &c.

SEC. 12. If any bankrupt shall have conveyed or assured any property unto any person, upon condition of redemption by payment of money or otherwise, the commissioners may make tender of money or other performances, according to the nature of such condition.

SEC. 13. Commissioners shall have power to assign, for use aforesaid, all debts due to such bankrupt, or to any other person for his use or benefit, which assignment shall vest the property and right thereof in the assignee of such bankrupt, as fully as if bond, judgment, contract, or claim had originally belonged or been made to said assignee; except where a debtor shall have *bona fide* paid debt to bankrupt without notice of his bankruptcy.

SEC. 14. If complaint be made, or information given to commissioners, that any property or debts of bankrupt are in possession of any other person, or that any person is indebted to or for use of bankrupt, then commissioners to have power to summons such persons before them or the judge of the district court where such person resides, by such process or other measures as they may think convenient; and on their appearance may examine them touching their knowledge of property or debts of bankrupt; and when they are contumacious on such examination, they may be imprisoned and detained till they submit to examination, and they to forfeit double the value of all property or debts by them concealed.

SEC. 15. If any of said persons shall, after legal summons to appear before commissioners or judge to be examined, refuse to attend, or not attend, it shall be lawful for said commissioners or judge to direct their warrants for such person or persons, and on their refusal to come, they are to be imprisoned until they consent to be examined. Such witnesses as shall be sent for shall be allowed such compensation as commissioners or judge shall think fit, to be ratably borne by the creditors. Perjury to be punishable by fine not to exceed $4,000, and imprisoned not exceeding two years, and to be rendered incapable of being thereafter witness in any court of record.

SEC. 16. Any person who shall fraudulently or collusively claim any debts, or claim or detain any real or personal estate of bankrupt, such person shall forfeit double the value thereof, to and for use of creditors.

SEC. 17. Commissioners may assign property fraudulently conveyed away.

SEC. 18. If any person who shall become bankrupt within the intent and meaning of this Act, and against whom a commission of bankruptcy shall be duly issued, upon which commission such person shall be declared bankrupt, shall not within forty-two days after notice thereof in writing, to be left at the place of abode in case such persons be in prison, and notice given in some gazette that such commission has been issued, surrender himself and sign and subscribe such surrender, and submit to be examined, and fully to account for the disposal of property he has or is interested in any way, or may have or derive benefit from, except such part thereof as shall have been really and *bona fide* disposed of in a proper manner, and shall upon such examination, execute such deeds, &c., for the conveyance and delivery of all his property, as the commissioners shall direct, in trust for the payment of his debts, except his necessary wearing apparel and that of his wife and children, necessary beds and bedding; then he, upon wilful default or omission in any of the matters or things aforesaid, shall be adjudged a fraudulent bankrupt, and suffer imprisonment for not less than twelve months or more than ten years, and be deprived of benefits of the act. *Provided,* That if the bankrupt be in prison or custody at the time of commission, and is willing to surrender and to be examined under the Act, and can be brought against the commissioners for that purpose, the expense shall be paid from the bankrupt's effects; and in case he cannot be brought before the commissioners, then said some one of the commissioners shall attend the said bankrupt in prison or custody, and examine him as in other cases; and one of the assignees, or some one appointed by them, shall attend such bankrupt in prison or custody, and produce his books and papers, in order to enable him to prepare his proof, a copy whereof the assignees shall apply for and obtain from said bankrupt within a reasonable time after the same has been required.

SEC. 19. The commissioners shall appoint within the said forty-two days three several meetings for the purposes mentioned in section 18, the third meeting to be the last of the forty-two days, provided the district judge of the district within which commission issues shall have power to enlarge limited time aforesaid as he shall see fit, but not over fifty days.

SEC. 20. The commissioners or officers appointed by them to secure bankrupt's property may forcibly enter any place where the same may be.

SEC. 21. If bankrupt refuses to answer satisfactorily, or to subscribe to his examination, he may be imprisoned until he shall submit to the same; if convicted of perjury in statements he shall suffer imprisonment not less than two nor more ten years.

SEC. 22. Every bankrupt, after surrender, may at all reasonable times have access to his books and writings, to inspect and abstract from the same, within presence of the commissioners, and the bankrupt be free from arrest for the said forty-two days, or for a longer period, as shall be allowed for the finishing his examination. If arrested for debt or execution, on producing summons or notice of commissions, and giving officer a copy thereof, he shall be discharged. If the officer after this detain such bankrupt he shall forfeit ten dollars per diem for every day of such detention.

Sec. 23. Any person knowingly concealing a bankrupt, so that he shall fail to appear when summoned, shall suffer imprisonment not exceeding twelve months, or pay fine not exceeding $1,000.

Sec. 24. The commissioners shall have power to examine, on oath, the wife of any person lawfully declared bankrupt. If she refuse to obey summons, or to be examined, or to subscribe to the same, she is punishable, as by this act is provided against any other person in like cases.

Sec. 25. When any person is committed for any reason the warrant of commitment must specify the cause of commitment.

Sec. 26. After bankrupt has had his final examination, any person other than the bankrupt shall be entitled to five per cent. upon all property of the bankrupt's estate, unknown to the commissioner, which they may discover, the same to be paid out of the effects discovered. Any trustee having notice of the bankruptcy, who shall conceal any of bankrupt's property, for ten days after his final examination, shall forfeit double the value of the property concealed.

Sec. 27. If any person become bankrupt, and at such time, by consent of the owner, has in his possession and disposition any goods whereof he shall be reputed owner, and take upon himself the sale, alteration, or disposition thereof, as owner, the commissioner shall have power to assign the same for the benefit of the creditors as any other part of the estate of the bankrupt.

Sec. 28. If bankrupt, after issuing of commission of bankruptcy, shall pay the person suing out the same, or give such person goods or securities for his debt, whereby such person shall privately have a greater portion of his debt than the other creditors, such preference shall be a new act of bankruptcy, and, on proof thereof, such commission shall be superseded, and another commission may issue. The person so taking unlawful satisfaction shall forfeit the whole amount received or secured to the assignees, to be divided among the other creditors.

Sec. 29. Every assignee shall, after four months, and within twelve months after

commission has issued, give at least thirty days' notice of time and place of commissioners' meeting to make dividend of bankrupt's estate, at which creditors not before proving may prove their debts. Upon such meeting, the assignee shall render just and fair account of all his doings, under oath, if so required. In such accounts, he shall be allowed to retain all sums paid in issuing commission, and all other just allowances made as assignee, etc. And the commissioners shall order, in writing, a distribution of the bankrupt's estate among the various creditors who have proven their debts; and shall file the order, and deliver duplicates thereof to the assignee, [or, assignees.] The order to contain time and place of making same, sum of all debts proved against bankrupt's estate, and sum of all moneys remaining in hands of the assignee to be divided, and what the dividend. And the assignee, in pursuance of such order, shall proceed to distribute such dividend, etc.

Sec. 30. Within eighteen months a second dividend shall be declared, in case the whole property of bankrupt was not divided at first meeting, of which due notice shall be given, and similar proceedings had as at first meeting.

Sec. 31. In the distribution, creditors shall be paid *pro rata* their several claims proven, without regard to creditors security.

Sec. 32. The assignees shall at all reasonable times keep their books of account open to the creditors' inspection.

Sec. 33. Bankrupt, not being in prison or custody, is bound to attend the assignee when reasonably required by the same, and be allowed $3 per diem for such attendance.

Sec. 34. That any person becoming bankrupt who shall, within the time limited by this Act, surrender himself to the commissioners and conform strictly to this Act, shall be allowed five per cent. on the net proceeds of all the estate recovered, which shall be paid to him by the assignee, in case the net proceeds of the same, after such allowance is made, shall be sufficient to pay the creditors of said bankrupt, who shall have proved their debts under the commission, fifty per cent. on said debts respectively, and so as the said five per cent shall not exceed $500 dollars; and in case the net produce of said estate shall, in excess of allowance hereafter mentioned, be sufficient to pay said creditors seventy-five per cent. on the amount of their respective debts, that then bankrupt shall be allowed ten per cent. on the amount of such net produce, to be paid as aforesaid, so as such ten per cent. shall not in the whole exceed $800; and every such bankrupt shall be discharged from all debts owing by him at time he became bankrupt, which might have been proved. In case such bankrupt shall afterwards be arrested, prosecuted, or impleaded on account of any of said debts, he may appear without bail and plead general issue, and give this Act a special matter in evidence, and his discharge shall be *prima facie* evidence of his being a bankrupt within the purview of this Act, and verdict shall therefore be given to defendant unless plaintiff can sustain allegations of fraud or concealment. Discharge of bankrupt shall not release any partner.

Sec. 35. If bankrupt's estate does not pay his debts, he shall be allowed a sum, in option of commissioners, not to exceed $300 nor exceeding three per centum on his said estate.

Sec. 36. Before discharge can be granted under this act, commissioners shall certify to judge of district court that bankrupt and they and all concerned have conformed to all the requisitions of the Act. Any of creditors may be heard against certificate of discharge.

Sec. 37. If any creditor or pretended creditor shall exhibit to commissioners any fraudulent debt or demand, and bankrupt shall refuse to make discovery thereof, and suffer imposition upon his creditors, he shall lose all benefits under the Act; and the same if he lose at one time any amount not less that $50, or in the whole $300, after passing of the Act and within twelve months before he became a bankrupt, by gaming or wagering.

Sec. 38. Bankrupt may be discharged on *habeas corpus* if arrested upon debts owing before bankruptcy.

Sec. 39. Persons whose debts are due on a future day may prove the same, and becoming petitioning creditors. Obligees of following and respondentia bonds, and the assured in a policy of insurance, may claim under the commission.

Sec. 40. In case any person committed by commissioner's warrant shall obtain *habeas*

corpus, in order to be discharged, and there shall be any insufficiency in the form of warrant, the district judge before whom party is brought by *habeas corpus*, to commit such person to the same prison, there to remain until he shall conform, as aforesaid, unless it shall appear that he answered all questions put to him by the commissioners. In case such person was committed for not signing his examination, (unless it shall appear that he had good reason for not signing the same, or the commissioners had exceeded their authority in making such commitment,) and in case the jailor, to whom such person shall be committed, shall wilfully, or negligently allow his escape, such jailor shall be fined a sum not exceeding $3,000, for the use of creditors.

Sec. 41. The prisoner may be produced by jailor on demand of any creditor who has proved his debt. If jailor refuses, he is to be liable as for wilful escape.

Sec. 42. Offsets and mutual debts to be allowed.

Sec. 43. Assignees, with the consent of the commissioners and major part of creditors in value, who have proved their debts, may agree to arbitration and compromise.

Sec. 44. The bankrupt's estate may be disposed of at public auction without paying duty.

Sec. 45. If bankrupt die pending the proceedings, the commissioners shall nevertheless proceed to execute the commission as fully as if he were living.

Sec. 46. Commissioners may demand security for the expenses of the commission.

Sec. 47. District judges to fix compensation of commissioners.

Sec. 48. All penalties given by this Act for the benefit of creditors shall be recovered by action of debt, etc.

Sec. 49. In action brought against any commissioner or other authorized person under this Act for anything done by force of the same, defendant may plead general issue, and give Act in evidence.

Sec. 50. All property coming to bankrupt before he obtains certificate of discharge is to be vested in the commissioners.

Sec. 51. All proceedings of the commissioners are to be filed in the office of the clerk of the district, &c.

Sec. 52. It shall be lawful for creditors to attend and take part in any examination of bankrupt, and either party may apply for a jury to try questions in dispute.

SEC. 53. The commissioners may, during pendency of proceedings, grant bankrupt such allowance out of his estate as may be sufficient for necessary support of his family.

SEC. 54. A major part in value of the creditors of bankrupt may direct where moneys of the estate shall be deposited.

SEC. 55. In all matters, action of a majority of the commissioners shall be valid.

SEC. 56. In all cases of prosecution of debtor of bankrupt to obtain debt, &c., the commission, or a certified copy thereof, and the assignment of the commissioners of the bankrupt's estate shall be conclusive evidence of the issuing of the commission, &c.

SEC. 57. No person can be a second time discharged unless his estate shall pay 75 per centum of his debts.

SEC. 58. Claims of creditors may be tried by a jury upon his declaration of his unwillingness to submit same to the judgment of the commissioners.

SEC. 59. The lands and effects of a bankrupt may be sold on credit, on such security as major part in value of creditors may direct, providing the granting of bankrupt's certificate is not retarded thereby.

SEC. 60. The creditors of a bankrupt may relieve him from prison, and they may issue a new execution if he does not obtain a discharge.

SEC. 61. This act shall not repeal or annul the laws of any state which may be hereafter enacted, or are now in force, for relief of insolvents, except so far as the same may respect persons who are clearly within the purview of this act, and whose debts shall amount in cases specified in second section hereof to the sums therein mentioned, &c.

SEC. 62. Nothing in this law shall in any manner affect the right of preference to prior satisfaction of debts due to the United States as secured or provided by any law heretofore passed, nor shall be construed to lessen or impair any right to or security for moneys due to the United States or to any of the states.

SEC. 63. That nothing in this act shall invalidate or impair any lien existing at date of this act on lands or chattels of any person who may become a bankrupt.

SEC. 64. This act shall continue in force for five years, and thence to the end of the session of congress thereafter, and no longer : *Provided,* That the expiration of this act shall not prevent the complete execution of any commission which may have been previously thereto issued.

Approved April 4, 1800.

COMPENDIUM

OF THE

UNITED STATES BANKRUPT ACT OF 1841.

SECTION 1. All persons residing in any state, district, or territory may be bankrupts on their own petition, whose debts have not been created in consequence of defalcation as public officer; or as executor, administrator, guardian, or trustee, or while acting in any other fiduciary capacity.

Persons being merchants, or using the trade of merchandise, retailers of merchandise, bankers, factors, brokers, underwriters, or marine insurers, owing debts amounting to $2,000, may upon petition of one or more creditors, to whom they owe debts amounting to $500, be declared bankrupts.

Departing from the state, district, or territory, of which the bankrupt is an inhabitant, with intent to defraud his creditors; concealing himself to avoid being arrested; willingly or fraudulently procuring himself to be arrested, or his goods and chattels, lands, or tenements, attached, distrained, sequestered, or taken in execution; removing his goods, chattels, and effects, or concealing them to prevent their being levied upon, or taken in execution, or by other process; or making any fraudulent conveyance, &c., of real or personal estate.

Person declared bankrupt, at instance of creditor, may elect to try by jury validity of decree.

Bankrupt residing distance from court, judge may order trial by jury to be in county of bankrupt's residence.

All decrees of bankruptcy passed by court, and not re-examined, to be deemed final and conclusive.

SEC. 2. All future payments, securities, conveyances, or transfers of property, or agreements made or given by bankrupt, in contemplation of bankruptcy, or for the purpose of giving a preference, and all other payments, &c., to any person or persons whatever, not being a *bona fide* creditor or purchaser, for valuable consideration, without notice void, and assignee entitled to sue for same.

Bankrupt making such preferences, and payments, not entitled to discharge.

All dealings and transactions by and with bankrupt, *bona fide* made and entered into more than two months before petitioning, to be valid, provided there be no notice of prior act of bankruptcy, or intention of bankrupt to petition for decree.

If voluntary bankrupt have, since 1st January last, or at any time, in contemplation of the passing of the act, given preference to creditor, he is not to receive discharge unless the same be assented to by majority in interest of creditors not preferred.

Rights of married women, minors, or liens, mortgages, &c., not to be destroyed.

SEC. 3. On decree being made, all property and rights of property to be divested out of bankrupt by operation of law, from the time of such decree, and vested in such assignee as court may from time to time appoint.

Court may exercise power of appointment and removal of assignee at its discretion.

Power of assignee to sell, manage, and dispose of, sue for and defend same, under direction of court.

Assignee may prosecute and defend all suits in law or in equity, pending in which the bankrupt is a party.

Suits by or against assignee not to abate by his death or removal from office.

Goods of bankrupt exempt from operation of statute.

Assignee to designate and set apart same, having regard to circumstances of family.

Not to exceed in value $300, also Wearing apparel of bankrupt, wife, and children.

If exception be taken to determination of assignee in such cases, the court to decide.

Sec. 4. Bankrupt surrendering his property, and rights of property, and complying with requisitions of statute, shall (unless majority in number and value of creditors, who have proved their debts, file written dissent thereto) be entitled to discharge from debts, and, upon his petition for the purpose, be allowed certificate.

Discharge and certificate not to be granted until ninety days from decree in bankruptcy, nor until after seventy days' notice in some public newspaper, designated by court, to creditors who have proved debts, to show cause why same should not be granted.

Creditors, or other persons in interest, may appear and contest right of bankrupt thereto.

Where residence of creditor is known, service may be made on him personally, or by letter addressed to him at his known usual place of residence, as court may direct.

Bankrupt guilty of fraud or wilful concealment of property, or rights of property, or having preferred creditors, or having disobeyed orders, &c., or requisitions of Act, or having admitted a false or fictitious debt to be proved, not entitled to discharge or certificate.

Merchant, banker, factor, broker, underwriter, or marine insurer, not entitled to discharge or certificate, unless proper books have been kept after passing Act.

Nor any person who, after passing of the Act, shall apply trust funds to his own use.

Bankrupt's discharge not to release any surety or endorser, or person jointly liable with him.

Bankrupt may be examined, orally or on written interrogatories, before court, or a commissioner appointed by court therefor, on oath or affirmation, in all matters relating to his bankruptcy and touching his estate and effects.

Answering, swearing, or affirming falsely, perjury, and punishable accordingly.

Discharge and certificate of bankrupt to be deemed a discharge of all debts, contracts, etc., provable under decree, and may be pleaded accordingly.

And not to be impeached unless for fraud or wilful concealment of property, on prior reasonable notice, specifying in writing such fraud or concealment.

If discharge and certificate be withheld from bankrupt, he may demand trial by jury, upon an issue to be directed by court.

Or he may appeal within ten days from decision to circuit court next to be held for same district.

Manner of entering prayer for appeal.

Appeal must be tried at first term of circuit court after it be taken, unless continuance be granted.

And may be heard by said court summarily, or by a jury, at option of bankrupt.

Creditors may appear and object to decree and certificate of bankrupt.

But if court or jury be satisfied that bankrupt has complied with provisions of act, court to make decree of discharge and grant a certificate.

Sec. 5. Creditors proving debts under bankruptcy, to share in the bankrupt's estate and effects, without preference, such debts being *bona fide.*

Debts due by the bankrupt to the United States, and debts due to persons who, by the laws of the United States, have a preference, in consequence of having paid moneys as his sureties, to be first paid out of assets.

Persons who have performed labor, as an operative for bankrupt, entitled to full amount of wages, not exceeding $25.

Provided such labor was performed within six months prior to bankruptcy.

Creditors whose debts are payable at a future day, annuities, holders of bottomry and respondentia bonds, and of policies of insurance, sureties, indorsers, bail or persons having contingent demands against bankrupt, may prove such debts and may have them allowed when they become absolute. Annuitants and holders of debts payable in future may have the present value thereof ascertained, and allowed as debts in *presenti.*

Creditor proving his debt to waive all right of suit against bankrupt.

And all proceedings already commenced to be deemed surrendered.

Set-off to be allowed where there are mutual debts.

Debts to be proved before court or commissioner appointed for the purpose

Court may disallow proof of debt, founded in fraud, imposition, illegality or mistake.

Corporations to make proof of debts by president, cashier, treasurer or other officer who may be specially appointed.

Court to appoint commissioners to receive proof of debts, etc., such persons as have their residence in the county in which the bankrupt lives.

SEC. 6. District court in every district to have jurisdiction in matters and proceedings in bankruptcy arising under this and any other act to be hereafter passed in bankruptcy.

Jurisdiction to be exercised summarily, in the nature of summary proceedings in equity, and district court to be deemed always open.

District judge may adjourn any point or question arising in any case in bankruptcy into circuit court for district, in his discretion, to be there heard and determined, such court to be deemed always open.

Jurisdiction of district court to extend to all cases in bankruptcy.

Power of court to compel obedience to all orders and decrees, by process of contempt, similar to the circuit court in suits pending in equity.

District court in each district to prescribe rules and regulations in all matters in bankrutcy, subject to revision by circuit court of district.

Said courts to prescribe a tariff or table of fees and charges to be taxed by the officers of court or other persons for services rendered.

SEC. 7. Petitions by bankrupt, or by creditor against bankrupt, and all other proceedings in case to be had in district court in which bankrupt resides, or trades, except where otherwise provided by act.

Upon every petition notice to be published in one or more newspapers published in district, to be designated by court, at least twenty days before hearing.

And all persons interested may appear and oppose prayer of petition being granted.

Evidence by witnesses to be upon oath or affirmation, and may be oral or by deposition before the court or before commissioner, or before disinterested state judge in which the deposition is taken.

Proof of debts to be under oath or affirmation before court or commissioner appointed thereby, or before some disinterested state judge of the state where the creditors live.

Proof of debts may be contested.

Right of assignee or creditor to have an issue to try validity and amount of debts or claims.

The result (unless new trial be granted) to be evidence of validity and amount of debts or claims.

Answering, swearing or affirming falsely, perjury, and punishable accordingly.

SEC. 8. Circuit court where decree in bankruptcy passed to have concurrent jurisdiction with district court of same district of all suits at law and in equity brought by assignees against any person touching bankrupt's estate.

No suit at law or in equity to be maintained against assignee or persons claiming adverse interests in bankrupt's estate, unless brought within two years after decree in bankruptcy, or after cause of suit accrued.

SEC. 9. Sales, transfers and conveyances of bankrupt's estate to be made at such time and in such manner as court may appoint.

Assets to be paid into court by assignee within sixty days after receipt, subject to order of court as to its safe keeping and disposition; and court may require assignee to give bond for faithful discharge of his duties and compliance with orders of court.

Bond to be taken in name of United States, and on breach thereof may be suable, under court's direction.

SEC. 10. Court to order collection of assets at as early a period as practicable.

Dividend to be made of assets collected, among creditors who have proved debts once in six months from time of decree.

Notice of dividend to be given in newspaper in district, designated by court ten days before order therefor is passed.

Pendency of suit at law or in equity, by or against third persons, not to postpone dividend, except so far as assets may be necessary to satisfy same.

And all proceedings in bankruptcy to be brought to a close within two years from decree in bankruptcy (if practicable.)

Where creditor shall not have proved debt until dividend declared, he shall be entitled to payment *pro rata* out of remaining dividends, as other creditors have already received, before latter entitled to any portion thereof.

Sec. 11. Assignee, under order and direction of court, to have power to redeem mortgages, or other pledge, deposit, or lien upon bankrupt's real or personal estate, whether payable in *presenti* or *futuro*.

Also, under like direction, to compound debts, claims, or securities of bankrupt.

But no order so to do is to be made until notice of application be given in newspaper in district, to be designated by court, ten days before hearing, to enable creditors, &c., to oppose order being made.

Sec. 12. No person entitled under second decree in bankruptcy to discharge, unless his estate produce seventy-five per cent. on amount of debts.

Sec. 13. Proceedings in bankruptcy to be matters of record, but not necessary to be recorded at large, but filed, kept, and numbered in office of court, and a docket only, with number, to be kept with clerk of court.

Clerk in court to receive twenty-five cents for furnishing certified copy, and no more.

Officer of court, or commissioner, not to be allowed more than one dollar for taking proof of debts, but may be allowed his actual traveling expenses.

Sec. 14. Where two or more persons become insolvent, order may be made on petition of partners, or one of them, or on petition of creditors, whereupon the joint stock of partners and separate estate of each partner may be taken.

Joint creditors and separate creditors may prove debts.

Assignees to keep account of the joint and separate estates.

Proceeds of joint estate to be applied in payment of joint debts, and separate assets to pay separate debts.

If balance of separate estate after payment of separate debts, balance to be applied to payment of joint debts.

If balance of joint estate after payment of joint debts, balance to be applied to payment of separate debts.

Sum appropriated to separate estate of each partner to be applied to payment of separate debts.

Certificate of discharge to be granted or refused to each partner, as if separate decree had been made against him.

In other respects proceedings against partners to be conducted as if they were against one person.

Sec. 15. Conveyances of land sold by assignee to contain recital of decree in bankruptcy, and appointment of assignees.

Such recital, and a certified copy of order, to be evidence of bankruptcy and assignment to validate deed.

All deeds containing such recital and proofs shall pass title of bankrupt to lands.

Sec. 16. Jurisdiction of district court of United States vested in circuit court of United States for District of Columbia, and upon supreme or superior courts of any territory of the United States, in said District of Columbia, or in either of said territories.

Sec. 17. The Act to take effect from and after the 1st of February next, [1842.]

Approved August 19, 1841

NOTICE.

Since this volume was put through the press, Congress has passed the following amendments to the United States Bankruptcy Act, and therefore the first edition is thus supplemented, while in the bindery, and the plates are being so altered as to present the text complete in subsequent editions.
July 1, 1872.

AN ACT
Entitled an act to declare the true intent and meaning of section two of an act entitled " An Act to establish a uniform system of Bankruptcy throughout the United States," approved March second, eighteen hundred and sixty-seven.

Be it enacted by the Senate and House of Representatives of the United States of America in Congress assembled,

That the powers and jurisdiction granted to the several circuit courts of the United States, or any justice thereof, by section two of an act entitled " An Act to establish a uniform system of Bankruptcy throughout the United States," approved March second, eighteen hundred and sixty-seven, may be exercised in any district in which the powers or jurisdiction of a circuit court have been or may be conferred on the district court for such district, as if no such powers or jurisdiction had been conferred on such district court; it being the true intent and meaning of said act that the system of bankruptcy thereby established shall be uniform throughout the United States.
Approved June 10, 1872.

AN ACT
Entitled an act to amend " An Act to establish a uniform system of Bankruptcy throughout the United States."

Be it enacted by the Senate and House of Representatives of the United States of America in Congress assembled,

That the first proviso in section fourteen of an act approved March second, eighteen hundred and sixty-seven, entitled " An Act to establish a uniform system of Bankruptcy throughout the United States," be amended by striking out the words " eighteen hundred and sixty-four," and inserting in lieu thereof " eighteen hundred and seventy-one."
Approved June 10, 1872.

THE
UNITED STATES BANKRUPT ACT OF 1867.

SECTION 1. *Be it enacted by the Senate and House of Representatives of the United States of America in Congress assembled,* That the several district courts of the United States be, and they hereby are, constituted courts of bankruptcy, and they shall have original jurisdiction in their respective districts in all matters and proceedings in bankruptcy, and they are hereby authorized to hear and adjudicate upon the same according to the provisions of this act. The said courts shall be always open for the transaction of business under this act, and the powers and jurisdiction hereby granted and conferred shall be exercised as well in vacation as in term time ; and a judge sitting in chambers shall have the same powers and jurisdiction, including the power of keeping order and of punishing any contempt of his authority as when sitting in court. And the jurisdiction hereby conferred shall extend to all cases and controversies arising between the bankrupt and any creditor or creditors who shall claim any debt or demand under the bankruptcy ; to the collection of all the assets of the bankrupt; to the ascertainment and liquidation of the liens and other specific claims thereon ; to the adjustment of the various priorities and conflicting interests of all parties; and to the marshaling and disposition of the different funds and assets so as to secure the rights of all parties and due distribution of the assets among all the creditors ; and to all acts, matters, and things to be done under and in virtue of the bankruptcy, until the final distribution and settlement of the estate of the bankrupt, and the close of the proceedings in bankruptcy. The said courts shall have full authority to compel obedience to all orders and decrees passed by them in bankruptcy, by process of contempt and other remedial process, to the same extent that the circuit courts now have in any suit pending therein in equity. Said courts may sit for the transaction of business in bankruptcy at any place in the district, of which place, and the time of holding court, they shall have given notice, as well as at the places designated by law for holding such courts.

SEC. 2. *And be it further enacted,* That the several circuit courts of the United States within and for the districts where the proceedings in bankruptcy shall be pending shall have a general superintendence and jurisdiction of all cases and questions arising under this act; and, except when special provision is otherwise made, may, upon bill, petition, or other proper process of any party aggrieved, hear and determine the case as a court of equity. The powers and jurisdiction hereby granted may be exercised either by said court, or by any justice thereof, in term time or vacation. Said circuit courts shall also have concurrent jurisdiction with the district courts of the same district, of all suits at law or in equity, which may or shall be brought by the assignee in bankruptcy against any person claiming an adverse interest, or by such person against such assignee, touching any property or rights of property of said bankrupt transferable to or vested in such assignee ; but no suit at law or in equity shall in any case be maintainable by or against such assignee, or by or against any person claiming an adverse interest, touching the property and rights of property aforesaid, in any court whatsoever, unless the same shall be brought within in two years from the time the cause of action accrued, for or against such assignee : *provided,* that nothing herein contained shall revive a right of action barred at the time such assignee is appointed.

SEC. 3. *And be it further enacted,* That it shall be the duty of the judges of the *district* courts of the United States within and for the several districts to appoint in each congressional district in said districts, upon the nomination and recommendation of the chief justice of the supreme court of the United States, one or more registers in bankruptcy, to assist the judge of the district court in the performance of his duties under this act. No person shall be eligible to such appointment unless he be a counselor of said court, or of some one of the courts of record of the state in which he resides. Before entering upon the duties of his office, every person so appointed as register in bankruptcy shall give a bond to the United States, with condition that he will faithfully discharge the duties of his office, in a sum not less than one thousand dollars, to be fixed by said court, with sureties satisfactory to said court, or to either of the said justices thereof; and he shall, in open court, take and subscribe the oath prescribed in the act entitled "An act to prescribe an oath of office, and for other purposes," approved July second, eighteen hundred and sixty-two, and also that he will not, during his continuance in office, be, directly or indirectly, interested in or benefited by the fees or emoluments arising from any suit or matter pending in bankruptcy in either the district or circuit court in his district.

SEC. 4. *And be it further enacted,* That every register in bankruptcy, so appointed and qualified, shall have power, and it shall be his duty, to make adjudication of bankruptcy, to receive the surrender of any bankrupt, to administer oaths in all proceedings before him, to hold and preside at meetings of creditors, to take proof of debts, to make all computations of dividends, and all orders of distribution, and to furnish the assignee with a certified copy of such orders, and of the schedules of creditors and assets filed in each case, to audit and pass accounts of assignees, to grant protection, to pass the last examination of any bankrupt in cases whenever the assignee or a creditor do not oppose, and to sit in chambers and dispatch there such part of the administrative business of the court and such uncontested matters as shall be defined in general rules and orders, or as the district judge shall in any particular matter direct; and he shall also make short memoranda of his proceedings in each case in which he shall act, in a docket to be kept by him for that purpose, and he shall forthwith, as the proceedings are taken, for-

ward to the clerk of the district court a certified copy of said memoranda, which shall be entered by said clerk in the proper minute-book, to be kept in his office, and any register of the court may act for any other register thereof: *provided, however,* that nothing in this section contained shall empower a register to commit for contempt, or to hear a disputed adjudication, or any question of the allowance or suspension of an order of discharge; but in all matters where an issue of fact or of law is raised and contested by any party to the proceedings before him, it shall be his duty to cause the question or issue to be stated by the opposing parties in writing, and he shall adjourn the same into court for decision by the judge. No register shall be of counsel or attorney, either in or out of court, in any suit or matter pending in bankruptcy, in either the circuit or district court of his district, nor in an appeal therefrom; nor shall he be executor, administrator, guardian, commissioner, appraiser, divider, or assignee of or upon any estate within the jurisdiction of either of said courts of bankruptcy nor be interested in the fees or emoluments arising from either of said trusts. The fees of said registers, as established by this act, and by the general rules and orders required to be framed under it, shall be paid to them by the parties for whom the service may be rendered in the course of proceedings authorized by this act.

SEC. 5. *And be it further enacted,* That the judge of the district court may direct a register to attend at any place within the district, for the purpose of hearing such voluntary applications under this act as may not be opposed, of attending any meeting of creditors, or receiving any proof of debts, and, generally, for the prosecution of any bankruptcy or other proceedings under this act; and the traveling and incidental expenses of such register, and of any clerk or other officer attending him, incurred in so acting, shall be settled by the court *in accordance with the rules prescribed under the 10th section of this act,* and paid out of the assets of the estate in respect of which such register has so acted; or if there be no such assets, or if the assets shall be insufficient, then such expenses shall form a part of the costs in the case or cases in which the register shall have acted in such journey, to be apportioned by the judge; and such register, so acting, shall have and exercise all powers except the power of commitment, vested in the district court for the summoning and examination of persons or witnesses, and for requiring the production of books, papers, and documents : *provided, always,* that all depositions of persons and witnesses taken before said register, and all acts done by him, shall be reduced to writing and be signed by him, and shall be filed in the clerk's office as part of the proceedings. Such register shall be subjected to removal, by the judge of the district court, and all vacancies occurring by such removal, or by resignation, change of residence, death, or disability, shall be promptly filled by other fit persons, unless said court shall deem the continuance of the particular office unnecessary.

SEC. 6. *And be it further enacted,* That any party shall, during the proceedings before a register, be at liberty to take the opinion of the district judge upon any point or matter arising in the course of such proceedings, or upon the result of such proceedings which shall be stated by the register in the shape of a short certificate to the judge, who shall sign the same f he approve thereof; and such certificate, so signed, shall be binding on all the parties to the proceeding; but every such certificate may be discharged or varied by the judge at chambers or in open court. In any bankruptcy, or in any other proceedings within the jurisdiction of the court under this act, the parties concerned, on submitting to such jurisdiction, may at any stage of the proceedings, by consent, state any question or questions in a special case for the opinion of the court; and the judgment of the court shall be final, unless it be agreed and stated in such special case that either party may appeal, if, in such case, an appeal is allowed by this act. The parties may also, if they think fit, agree that, upon the question or questions raised by such special case being finally decided, a sum of money, fixed by the parties, or to be ascertained by the court, or in such manner as the court may direct, or any property, or the amount of any disputed debt or claim, shall be paid, delivered, or transferred by one of such parties to the other of them, either with or without costs.

SEC. 7. *And be it further enacted,* That parties and witnesses summoned be-

fore a register shall be bound to attend in pursuance of such summons at the place and time designated therein, and shall be entitled to protection, and be liable to process of contempt in like manner as parties and witnesses are now liable thereto in case of default in attendance under any writ of subpœna; and all persons wilfully and corruptly swearing or affirming falsely before a register, shall be liable to all the penalties, punishments, and consequences of perjury. If any person examined before a register shall refuse or decline to answer, or to swear to or sign his examination when taken, the register shall refer the matter to the judge, who shall have power to order the person so acting to pay the costs thereby occasioned, if such person be compellable by law to answer such question, or to sign such examination, and such person shall also be liable to be punished for contempt.

SEC. 8. *And be it further enacted,* That appeals may be taken from the district courts in all cases in equity, and writs of error may be allowed to said circuit courts from said district courts in cases at law under the jurisdiction created by this act when the debt or damages claimed amount to more than five hundred dollars; and any supposed creditor whose claim is wholly or in part rejected, or an assignee who is dissatisfied with the allowance of a claim, may appeal from the decision of the district court to the circuit court for the same district; but no appeal shall be allowed in any case from the district to the circuit court, unless it is claimed, and notice given thereof to the clerk of the district court, to be entered with the record of the proceedings, and also to the assignee or creditor, as the case may be, or to the defeated party in equity, within ten days after the entry of the decree or decision appealed from. The appeal shall be entered at the term of the circuit court, which shall be first held within and for the district next after the expiration of ten days from the time of claiming the same. But if the appellant in writing waives his appeal before any decision thereon, proceedings may be had in the district court as if no appeal had been taken, and no appeal shall be allowed, unless the appellant at the time of claiming the same shall give bond in manner now required by law in cases of such appeals. No·

writ of error shall be allowed, unless the party claiming it shall comply with the statutes regulating the granting of such writs.

SEC. 9. *And be it further enacted,* That in cases arising under this act, no appeal or writ of error shall be allowed in any case from the circuit courts to the supreme court of the United States, unless the matter in dispute in such case shall exceed two thousand dollars.

SEC. 10. *And be it further enacted,* That the justice of the supreme court of the United States to the provisions of this act shall frame general orders for the following purposes :

For regulating the practice and procedure of the district courts in bankruptcy, and the several forms of petitions, orders, and other proceedings to be used in said courts in all matters under this act ;

For regulating the duties of the various officers of said courts ;

For regulating the fees payable, and the charges and costs to be allowed, except such as are established by this act or by law, with respect to all proceedings in bankruptcy before said courts, not exceeding the rate of fees now allowed by law for similar services in other proceedings ;

For regulating the practice and procedure upon appeals ;

For regulating the filing, custody, and inspection of records ;

And generally for carrying the provisions of this act into effect.

After such general orders shall have been so framed, they, or any of them, may be rescinded or varied, and other general orders may be framed in manner aforesaid, and all such general orders so framed shall, from time to time, by the justices of the supreme court, be reported to congress, with such suggestions as said justices may think proper.

SEC. 11. *And be it further enacted,* That if any person residing within the jurisdiction of the United States, owing debts provable under this act exceeding the amount of three hundred dollars shall apply by petition, addressed to the judge of the judicial district in which such debtor has resided or carried on business for the six months next immediately preceding the time of filing such petition, or for the longest period during such six months, setting forth his place of residence, his inabilty to pay all his debts

in full, his willingness to surrender all his estate and effects for the benefit of his creditors, and his desire to obtain the benefit of this act, and shall annex to his petition a schedule, verified by oath before the court, or before a register in bankruptcy, or before one of the commissioners of the circuit court of the United States, containing a full and true statment of all his debts, and, as far as possible, to whom due, with the place of residence of each creditor, if known to the debtor, and, if not known, the fact to be so stated, and the sum due to each creditor ; also the nature of each debt or demand, whether founded on written security, obligation, contract, or otherwise, and also the true cause and consideration of such indebtedness in in each case, and the place where such indebtedness accrued, and a statement of any existing mortgage, pledge, lien, judgment, or collateral or other security given for the payment of the same ; and shall also annex to his petition an accurate inventory, verified in like manner, of all his estate, both real and personal, assignable under this act, describing the same and stating where it is situated and whether there are any, and if so, what encumbrances thereon, the filing of such petition shall be an act of bankruptcy, and such petitioner shall be adjudged a bankrupt ; *provided,* that all citizens of the United States petitioning to be declared bankrupt shall, in filing such petition, and before any proceedings thereon, take and subscribe an oath of allegiance and fidelity to the United States, which oath shall be filed and recorded with the proceedings in bankruptcy. And the judge of the district court, or, if there be no opposing party, any register of said court, to be designated by the judge, shall forthwith, if he be satisfied that the debts due from the petitioner exceed three hundred dollars, issue a warrant, to be signed by such judge or register, directed to the marshal of said district authorizing him forthwith, as messenger, to publish notices in such newspapers as the warrant specifies ; to serve written or printed notice, by mail or personally, on all creditors upon the schedule filed with the debtor's petition, or whose names may be given to him in addition by the debtor, and to give such personal or other notice to any persons concerned as the warrant specifies, which notice shall state ;

1st. That a warrant in bankruptcy has been issued against the estate of the debtor.

2d. That the payment of any debts and the delivery of any property belonging to such debtor to him or for his use, and the transfer of any property by him, are forbidden by law.

3d. That a meeting of the creditors of the debtor, giving the names, residences, and amounts, so far as known, to prove their debts and choose one or more assignees of his estate, will be held at a court of bankruptcy, to be holden at a time and place designated in the warrant, not less than ten nor more than ninety days after the issuing of the same.

SEC. 12. *And be it further enacted,* That at the meeting held in pursuance of the notice, one of the registers of the court shall preside, and the messenger shall make return of the warrant and of his doings thereon; and if it appears that the notice to the creditors has not been given as required in the warrant, the meeting shall forthwith be adjourned, and a new notice given as required. If the debtor dies after the issuing of the warrant, the proceedings may be continued and concluded in like manner as if he had lived.

SEC. 13. *And be it further enacted,* That the creditors shall, at the first meeting held after due notice from the messenger, in presence of a register designated by the court, choose one or more assignees of the estate of the debtor; the choice to be made by the greater part in value and in number of the creditors who have proved their debts. If no choice is made by the creditors at said meeting, the judge, or, if there be no opposing interest, the register, shall appoint one or more assignees. If an assignee, so chosen or appointed, fails within five days to express in writing his acceptance of the trust, the judge or register may fill the vacancy. All elections or appointments of assignees shall be subject to the approval of the judge; and when in his judgment it is for any cause needful or expedient, he may appoint additional assignees, or order a new election. The judge at any time may, and, upon the request in writing of any creditor who has proved his claim, shall require the assignee to give good and sufficient bond to the United States, with a condition for the faithful performance and discharge of his duties;

the bond shall be approved by the judge or register by his endorsement thereon, shall be filed with the record of the case, and inure to the benefit of all creditors proving their claims, and may be prosecuted in the name and for the benefit of any injured party. If the assignee fails to give the bond within such time as the judge orders, not exceeding ten days after notice to him of such order, the judge shall remove him and appoint another in his place.

SEC. 14. *And be it further enacted,* That as soon as said assignee is appointed and qualified, the judge, or, where there is no opposing interest, the register, shall, by an instrument under his hand, assign and convey to the assignee all the estate, real and personal, of the bankrupt, with all his deeds, books and papers relating thereto; and such assignment shall relate back to the commencement of said proceedings in bankruptcy, and thereupon, by operation of law, the title to all such property and estate, both real and personal, shall vest in said assignee, although the same is then attached on mesne process as the property of the debtor, and shall dissolve any such attachment made within four months next preceding the commencement of said proceedings : *provided, however,* that there shall be excepted from the operation of the provisions of this section the necessary household and kitchen furniture, and such other articles and necessaries of such bankrupt as the said assignee shall designate and set apart, having reference in the amount to the family, condition and circumstances of the bankrupt, but altogether not to exceed in value, in any case, the sum of five hundred dollars; and also the wearing apparel of such bankrupt, and that of his wife and children, and the uniform, arms and equipments of any person who is or has been a soldier in the militia or in the service of the United States, and such other property as now is, or hereafter shall be, exempted from attachment or seizure, or levy on execution, by the laws of the United States; and such other property not included in the foregoing exceptions as is exempted from levy and sale upon execution or other process, or order of any court, by the law of the state in which the bankrupt has his domicile at the time of the commencement of the proceedings in bankruptcy, to an amount not exceeding that allowed by such state exemption laws in force in the year eighteen hundred and sixty-four : *provided*, that the foregoing exception shall operate as a limitation upon the conveyance of the property of the bankrupt to his assignees, and in no case shall the property hereby excepted pass to the assignees, or the title of the bankrupt thereto be impaired or affected by any of the provisions of this act ; and the determination of the assignee in the matter shall, on exception taken, be subject to the final decision of the said court : *and provided further,* that no mortgage of any vessel, or of any other goods or chattels, made as security for any debt or debts, in good faith and for present considerations, and otherwise valid, and duly recorded, pursuant to any statute of the United States, or of any state, shall be invalidated or affected hereby ; and all the property conveyed by the bankrupt in fraud of his creditors ; all rights in equity, choses in action, patents, and patent-rights, and copy-rights ; all debts due him, or any person for his use, and all liens and securities therefor ; and all his rights of action for property or estate, real or personal, and for any cause of action which the bankrupt had against any person arising from contract, or from the unlawful taking or detention, or of injury to the property of the bankrupt ; and all his rights of redeeming such property or estate, with the like right, title, power, and authority to sell, manage, dispose of, sue for, and recover or defend the same, as the bankrupt might or could have had if no assignment had been made, shall, in virtue of the adjudication of bankruptcy and the appointment of his assignee, be at once vested in such assignee ; and he may sue for and recover the said estate, debts and effects, and may prosecute and defend all suits at law or in equity, pending at the time of the adjudication of bankruptcy, in which such bankrupt is a party in his own name, in the same manner and with the like effect as they might have been presented or defended by such bankrupt ; and a copy, duly certified by the clerk of the court under the seal thereof, of the assignment made by the judge or register, as the case may be, to him as assignee, shall be conclusive evidence of his title as such assignee to take, hold, sue for, and recover the property of the bankrupt, as herein before mentioned ; but no property held by the bankrupt in trust shall pass by such assignment. No person shall be entitled to maintain an action against an assignee in bankruptcy for anything done by him as such assignee, without previously giving him twenty days' notice of such action, specifying the cause thereof, to the end that such assignee may have an opportunity of tendering amends, should he see fit to do so. No person shall be entitled, as against the assignee, to withhold from him possession of any books of account of the bankrupt, or claim any lien thereon ; and no suit in which the assignee is a party shall be abated by his death or removal from office, but the same may be prosecuted and defended by his successors, or by the surviving or remaining assignee, as the case may be. The assignee shall have authority, under the order and direction of the court, to redeem or discharge any mortgage or conditional contract, or pledge or deposit, or lien upon any property, real or personal, whenever payable, and to tender due performance of the condition thereof, or to sell the same subject to such mortgage, lien, or other encumbrances. The debtor shall also, at the request of the assignee, and at the expense of the estate, make and execute any instruments, deeds, and writings which may be proper, to enable the assignee to possess himself fully of all the assets of the bankrupt. The assignee shall immediately give notice of his appointment by publication, at least once a week for three successive weeks, in such newspapers as shall for that purpose be designated by the court, due regard being had to their general circulation in the district, or in that portion of the district in which the bankrupt and his creditors shall reside, and shall, within six months, cause the assignment to him to be recorded in every registry of deeds or other office within the United States where a conveyance of any lands owned by the bankrupt ought by law to be recorded ; and the record of such assignment, or a duly certified copy thereof, shall be evidence thereof in all courts.

[And be it further enacted, *That said act shall be further amended as follows : The phrase "presented or defended," in the fourteenth section of said act, shall read "prosecuted or defended;" the phrase "nonresident debtors," in line five, section twenty-*

two of the act, as printed in the Statutes at Large, *shall read " non-resident creditors ;" that the word " or," in the next to the last line of the thirty-ninth section of the act, shall read " and; " and that the phrase " section thirteen," in the forty-second section of said act, shall read " section eleven ; " and the phrase " or spends any part thereof in gaming," in the forty-fourth section of said act, shall read, " or spend any part thereof in gaming ;" and that the words " with the senior register, or," and the phrase " to be delivered to the register," in the forty-seventh section of said act, be stricken out.*]

[And be it further enacted, *That the registers in bankruptcy shall have power to administer oath in all cases, and in relation to all matters in which oaths may be administered by commissioners of circuit courts of the United States, and such commissioners may take proof of debts in bankruptcy in all cases subject to revision of such proofs by registers or by court, according to the provisions of said act.*—AMENDMENT, APPROVED JULY 25, 1868.]

SEC. 15. *And be it further enacted,* That the assignee shall demand and receive from any and all persons holding the same, all the estate assigned, or to be assigned, under the provisions of this act; and he shall sell all unencumbered estate, real and personal, which comes to his hands, on such terms as he thinks most for the interest of the creditors; but upon petition of any person interested, and for cause shown, the court may make such order concerning the time, place, and manner of sale, as will, in its opinion, prove to the interest of the creditors; and the assignee shall keep a regular account of all money received by him as assignee, to which every creditor shall, at reasonable times, have free resort.

SEC. 16. *And be it further enacted,* That the assignee shall have the like remedy to recover all said estate, debts, and effects in his own name, as the debtor might have had if the decree in bankruptcy had not been rendered and no assignment had been made. If, at the time of the commencement of the proceedings in bankruptcy, an action is pending in the name of the debtor for the recovery of a debt or other thing which might or ought to pass to the assignee by the assign-

ment, the assignee shall if he requires it, be admitted to prosecute the action in his own name, in like manner and with like effect as if it had been originally commenced by him. No suit pending in the name of the assignee shall be abated by his death or removal; but upon the motion of the surviving, or remaining, or new assignee, as the case may be, he shall be admitted to prosecute the suit, in like manner and with like effect as if it had been originally commenced by him. In suits prosecuted by the assignee, a certified copy of the assignment made to him by the judge or register shall be conclusive evidence of his authority to sue.

SEC. 17. *And be it further enacted,* That the assignee shall, as soon as may be after receiving any money belonging to the estate, deposit the same in some bank in his name as assignee, or otherwise keep it distinct and apart from all other money in his possession; and shall, as far as practicable, keep all goods and effects belonging to the estate separate and apart from all other goods in his possession, or designated by appropriate marks, so that they may be easily and clearly distinguished, and may not be exposed or liable to be taken as his property or for the payment of his debts. When it appears that the distribution of the estate may be delayed by litigation or other cause, the court may direct the temporary investment of the money belonging to such estate in securities to be approved by the judge or a register of said court, or may authorize the same to be deposited in any convenient bank, upon such interest, not exceeding the legal rate, as the bank may contract with the assignee to pay thereon. He shall give written notice to all known creditors, by mail or otherwise, of all dividends, and such notice of meetings, after the first, as may be ordered by the court. He shall be allowed, and may retain, out of money in his hands, all the necessary disbursements made by him in the discharge of his duty, and a reasonable compensation for his services, in the discretion of the court. He may, under the direction of the court, submit any controversy arising in the settlement of demands against the estate, or of debts due to it, to the determination of arbitrators, to be chosen by him and the other party to the controversy, and may, under such direction, compound and settle any such .

controversy by agreement with the other party, as he thinks proper and most for the interest of the creditors.

SEC. 18. *And be it further enacted,* That the court, after due notice and hearing, may remove an assignee for any cause which, in the judgment of the court, renders such removal necessary or expedient. At a meeting called by order of the court in its diseretion for the purpose, or which shall be called upon the application of a majority of the creditors in number and value, the creditors may, with consent of the court, remove any assignee by such a vote as is hereinbefore provided for the choice of assignee. An assignee may, with the consent of the judge, resign his trust and be discharged therefrom. Vacancies caused by death or otherwise in the office of assignee may be filled by appointment of the court, or, at its discretion, by an election by the creditors, in the manner hereinbefore provided, at a regular meeting, or at a meeting called for the purpose, with such notice thereof in writing to all known creditors, and by such person as the court shall direct. The resignation or removal of an assignee shall in no way release him from performing all things requisite on his part for the proper closing up of his trust and the transmission thereof to his successors, nor shall it affect the liability of the principal or surety on the bond given by the assignee. When, by death or otherwise, the number of assignees is reduced, the estate of the debtor not lawfully disposed of shall vest in the remaining assignee or assignees, and the persons selected to fill vacancies, if any, with the same powers and duties relative thereto as if they were originally chosen. Any former assignee, his executors or administrators, upon request, and at the expense of the estate, shall make and execute to the new assignee all deeds, conveyances, and assurances, and do all other lawful acts requisite to enable him to recover and receive all the estate. And the court may make all orders which it may deem expedient to secure the proper fulfillment of the duties of any former assignee, and the rights and interests of all persons interested in the estate. No person who has received any preference contrary to the provisions of this act shall vote for or be eligible as assignee; but no title to property, real or personal, sold, trans-

ferred, or conveyed by an assignee, shall be affected or impaired by reason of his ineligibility. An assignee refusing or unreasonably neglecting to execute an instrument when lawfully required by the court, or disobeying a lawful order or decree of the court in the premises, may be punished as for a contempt of court.

SEC. 19. *And be it further enacted,* That all debts due and payable from the bankrupt at the time of the adjudication of bankruptcy, and all debts then existing but not payable until a future day, a rebate of interest being made when no interest is payable by the terms of the contract, may be proved against the estate of the bankrupt. All demands against the bankrupt for or on account of any goods or chattels wrongfully taken, converted, or withheld by him, may be proved and allowed as debts to the amount of the value of the property so taken or withheld, with interest. If the bankrupt shall be bound as drawer, indorser, surety, bail, or guarantor upon any bill, bond, note, or any other specialty or contract, or for any debt of another person, and his liability shall not have become absolute until after the adjudication of bankruptcy, the creditor may prove the same after such liability shall have become fixed, and before the final dividend shall have been declared. In all cases of contingent debts and contingent liabilities contracted by the bankrupt, and not herein otherwise provided for, the creditor may make claim therefor, and have his claim allowed, with the right to share in the dividends, if the contingency shall happen before the order for the final dividend; or he may at any time apply to the court to have the present value of the debt or liability ascertained and liquidated, which shall then be done in such manner as the court shall order, and he shall be allowed to prove for the amount so ascertained. Any person liable as bail, surety, guarantor, or otherwise for the bankrupt, who shall have paid the debt or any part thereof in discharge of the whole, shall be entitled to prove such debt, or to stand in the place of the creditor if he shall have proved the same, although such payments shall have been made after the proceedings in bankruptcy were commenced. And any person so liable for the bankrupt, and who has not paid the whole of said debt, but is still liable for the same or any part thereof, may, if the creditor shall fail or omit to prove such debt, prove the same, either in the name of the creditor or otherwise, as may be provided by the rules, and subject to such regulations and limitations as may be established by such rules. Where the bankrupt is liable to pay rent, or other debt falling due at fixed and stated periods, the creditor may prove for a proportionate part thereof up to the time of the bankruptcy, as if the same grew due from day to day, and not at such fixed and stated periods. If any bankrupt shall be liable for unliquidated damages arising out of any contract or promise, or on account of any goods or chattels wrongfully taken, converted or withheld, the court may cause such damages to be assessed in such mode as it may deem best, and the sum so assessed may be proved against the estate. No debts other than those above specified shall be proved or allowed against the estate.

SEC. 20. *And be it further enacted,* That in all cases of mutual debts or mutual credits between the parties, the account between them shall be stated, and one debt set off against the other, and the balance only shall be allowed or paid, but no set-off shall be allowed of a claim in its nature not provable against the estate: *provided,* that no set-off shall be allowed in favor of any debtor to the bankrupt of a claim purchased by or transferred to him after the filing of the petition. When a creditor has a mortgage or pledge of real or personal property of the bankrupt, or a lien thereon for securing the payment of a debt owing to him from the bankrupt, he shall be admitted as a creditor only for the balance of the debt after deducting the value of such property, to be ascertained by agreement between him and the assignee, or by a sale thereof, to be made in such manner as the court shall direct; or the creditor may release or convey his claim to the assignee upon such property, and be admitted to prove his whole debt. If the value of the property exceeds the sum for which it is so held as security, the assignee may release to the creditor the bankrupt's right of redemption therein on receiving such excess, or he may sell the property, subject to the claim of the creditor thereon; and in either case the assignee and creditor, respectively, shall execute all deeds and writings

necessary or proper to consummate the transaction. If the property is not so sold or released and delivered up, the creditor shall not be allowed to prove any part of his debt.

SEC. 21. *And be it further enacted,* That no creditor proving his debt or claim shall be allowed to maintain any suit at law or in equity therefor against the bankrupt, but shall be deemed to have waived all right of action and suit against the bankrupt, and all proceedings already commenced, or unsatisfied judgments already obtained thereon, shall be deemed to be discharged and surrendered thereby; and no creditor whose debt is provable under this act shall be allowed to prosecute to final judgment any suit at law or in equity therefor against the bankrupt, until the question of the debtor's discharge shall have been determined; and any such suit or proceedings shall, upon the application of the bankrupt, be stayed to await the determination of the court in bankruptcy on the question of the discharge, provided there be no unreasonable delay on the part of the bankrupt in endeavoring to obtain his discharge; and provided also, that if the amount due the creditor is in dispute, the suit, by leave of the court in bankruptcy, may proceed to judgment for the purpose of ascertaining the amount due, which amount may be proved in bankruptcy, but execution shall be stayed as aforesaid. If any bankrupt shall, at the time of adjudication, be liable upon any bill of exchange, promissory note, or other obligation in respect of distinct contracts as a member of two or more firms carrying on separate and distinct trades, and having distinct estates to be wound up in bankruptcy, or as a sole trader, and also as a member of a firm, the circumstance that such firms are in whole or in part composed of the same individuals, or that the sole contractor is also one of the joint contractors, shall not prevent proof and receipt of dividend in respect of such distinct contracts against the estates respectively liable upon such contracts.

SEC. 22. *And be it further enacted,* That all proofs of debts against the estate of the bankrupt, by or in behalf of creditors residing within the judicial district where proceedings in bankruptcy are pending, shall be made before one of the registers of the court in said district, and by or in behalf of non-resident debtors before any register in bankruptcy in the judicial districts where such creditors, or either of them, reside, or before any commissioner of the circuit court authorized to administer oaths in any district. To entitle a claimant against the estate of a bankrupt to have his demand allowed, it must be verified by a deposition in writing on oath, or solemn affirmation, before the proper register or commissioner, setting forth the demand, the consideration thereof, whether any and what securities are held therefor, and whether any and what payments have been made thereon; that the sum claimed is justly due from the bankrupt to the claimant; that the claimant has not, nor has any other person for his use, received any security or satisfaction whatever other than that by him set forth; that the claim was not procured for the purpose of influcueing the proceedings under this act, and that no bargain or agreement, express or implied, has been made or entered into, by or on behalf of such creditor, to sell, transfer, or dispose of the said claim, or any part thereof, against such bankrupt, or take or receive, directly or indirectly, any money, property, or consideration whatever, whereby the vote of such creditor or assignee, or any action on the part of such creditor or any other person in the proceedings under this act, is or shall be in any way affected, influenced, or controlled, and no claim shall be allowed unless all the statements set forth in such deposition shall appear to be true. Such oath, or solemn affirmation, shall be made by the claimant testifying of his own knowledge, unless he is absent from the United States, or prevented by some other good cause from testifying, in which cases the demand may be verified in like manner by the attorney or authorized agent of the claimant testifying to the best of his knowledge, information and belief, and setting forth his means of knowledge, or, if in a foreign country, the oath of the creditor may be taken before any minister, consul or vice-consul of the United States; and the court may, if it shall see fit, require or receive further pertinent evidence either for or against the admission of the claim. Corporations may verify their claims by the oath or solemn affirmation of their president, cashier or treasurer. If the proof is satisfactory to the register or commissioner, it shall be signed by the deponent and deliv-

ered or sent by mail to the assignee, who shall examine the same and compare it with the books and accounts of the bankrupt, and shall register in a book to be kept by him for that purpose, the names of creditors who have proved their claims, in the order in which such proof is received, stating the time of receipt of such proof, and the amount and nature of the debts, which books shall be open to the inspection of all the creditors. The court may, on the application of the assignee, or of the bankrupt, or without any application, examine upon oath the bankrupt, or any person tendering or who has made proof of claims, and may summon any person capable of giving evidence concerning such proof, or concerning the debt sought to be proved, and shall reject all claims not duly proved, or where the proof shows the claim to be founded in fraud, illegality or mistake.

SEC. 23. *And be it further enacted*, That when a claim is presented for proof before the election of the assignee, and the judge entertains doubts of its validity, or of the right of the creditor to prove it, and is of opinion that such validity or right ought to be investigated by the assignee, he may postpone the proof of the claim until the assignee is chosen. Any person, who, after the approval of this act, shall have accepted any preference, having reasonable cause to believe that the same was made or given by the debtor contrary to any provision of this act, shall not prove the debt or claim on account of which the preference was made or given, nor shall he receive any dividend therefrom until he shall first have surrendered to the assignee all property, money, benefit or advantage received by him under such preference. The court shall allow all debts duly proved, and shall cause a list thereof to be made and certified by one of the registers; and any creditor may act at all meetings by his duly constituted attorney the same as though personally present.

SEC. 24. *And be it further enacted*, That a supposed creditor who takes an appeal to the circuit court from the decision of the district court, rejecting his claim in whole or in part, shall, upon entering his appeal in the circuit court, file in the clerk's office a statement in writing of his claim, setting forth the same substantially, as in a declaration for the same cause of action at law, and the assignee shall plead or answer thereto in like manner, and like proceedings shall thereupon be had in the pleadings, trial and determination of the cause as in an action at law, commenced and prosecuted in the usual manner in the courts of the United States, except that no execution shall be awarded against the assignee for the amount of a debt found due to the creditor. The final judgment of the court shall be conclusive, and the list of debts shall, if necessary, be altered to conform thereto. The party prevailing in the suit shall be entitled to costs against the adverse party, to be taxed and recovered as in suits at law; if recovered against the assignee, they shall be allowed out of the estate. A bill of exchange, promissory note or other instrument, used in evidence upon the proof of a claim, and left in court or deposited in the clerk's office, may be delivered by the register or clerk having the custody thereof, to the person who used it, upon his filing a copy thereof, attested by the clerk of the court, who shall indorse upon it the name of the party against whose estate it has been proved, and the date and amount of any dividend declared thereon.

Sec. 25. *And be it further enacted*, That when it appears to the satisfaction of the court that the estate of the debtor, or any part thereof, is of a perishable nature, or liable to deteriorate in value, the court may order the same to be sold in such manner as may be deemed most expedient, under the discretion of the messenger or assignee, as the case may be, who shall hold the funds received in place of the estate disposed of; and whenever it appears to the satisfaction of the court that the title to any portion of an estate, real or personal, which has come into possession of the assignee, or which is claimed by him, is in dispute, the court may, upon the petition of the assignee, and after such notice to the claimant, his agent or attorney, as the court shall deem reasonable, order it to be sold, under the direction of the assignee, who shall hold the funds received in place of the estate disposed of; and the proceeds of the sale shall be considered the measure of the value of the property in any suit or controversy between the parties in any courts. But this provision shall not prevent the recovery of the property from the possession of the assignee by

any proper action commenced at any time before the court orders the sale.

Sec. 26. *And be it further enacted*, That the court may, on the application of the assignee in bankruptcy, or of any creditor, or without any application, at all times require the bankrupt, upon reasonable notice, to attend and submit to an examination on oath upon all matters relating to the disposal or condition of his property, to his trade and dealings with others, and his accounts concerning the same, to all debts due to or claimed from him, and to all other matters concerning his property and estate, and the due settlement thereof according to law, which examination shall be in writing, and shall be signed by the bankrupt, and be filed with the other proceedings; and the court may, in like manner, require the attendance of any other person as a witness, and if such person shall fail to attend, on being summoned thereto, the court may compel his attendance by warrant directed to the marshal, commanding him to arrest such person and bring him forthwith before the court, or before a register in bankruptcy, for examination as such witness. If the bankrupt is imprisoned, absent, or disabled from attendance, the court may order him to be produced by the jailor, or any officer in whose custody he may be, or may direct the examination to be had, taken and certified at such time and place and in such manner as the court may deem proper, and with like effect as if such examination had been in court. The bankrupt shall at all times, until his discharge, be subject to the order of the court, and shall, at the expense of the estate, execute all proper writings and instruments, and do and perform all acts required by the court touching the assigned property or estate, and to enable the assignee to demand, recover and receive all the property and estate assigned, wherever situated; and for neglect or refusal to obey any order of the court, such bankrupt may be committed and punished as for a contempt of court. If the bankrupt is without the district, and unable to return and personally attend at any of the times or do any of the acts which may be specified or required pursuant to this section, and if it appears that such absence was not caused by wilful default, and if, as soon as may be after the removal of such impediment, he offers to attend and submit to the order of the court in all respects, he shall be permitted to do so, with like effect as if he had not been in default. He shall also be at liberty, from time to time, upon oath to amend and correct his schedule of creditors and property, so that the same shall conform to the facts. For good cause shown, *the wife of any bankrupt* may be required to *attend* before the court, to the end that she may be examined as a witness; and if such wife do not attend at the time and place specified in the order, the bankrupt shall not be entitled to a discharge unless he shall prove to the satisfaction of the court that he was unable to procure the attendance of his wife. No bankrupt shall be liable to arrest during the pendency of the proceedings in bankruptcy in any civil action, unless the same is founded on some debt or claim from which his discharge or bankruptcy would not release him.

SEC. 27. *And be it further enacted,* That all creditors whose debts are duly proved and allowed shall be entitled to share in the bankrupt's property and estate *pro rata,* without any priority or preference whatever, except that wages due from him to any operative, or clerk, or house-servant, to an amount not exceeding fifty dollars, for labor performed within six months next preceding the adjudication of bankruptcy, shall be entitled to priority, and shall be first paid in full : *provided,* that any debt proved by any person liable as bail, surety, guarantor, or otherwise, for the bankrupt, shall not be paid to the person so proving the same until satisfactory evidence shall be produced of the payment of such debt by such person so liable, and the share to which such debt would be entitled may be paid into court, or otherwise held for the benefit of the party entitled thereto, as the court may direct. At the expiration of three months from the date of the adjudication of bankruptcy in any case, or as much earlier as the court may direct, the court, upon the request of the assignee, shall call a general meeting of the creditors, of which due notice shall be given, and the assignee shall then report, and exhibit to the court and to the creditors just and true accounts of all his receipts and payments, verified by his oath, and he shall produce and file vouchers for all payments for which vouch-

ers shall be required by any rule of the court ; he shall also submit the schedule of the bankrupt's creditors and property as amended, duly verified by the bankrupt, and a statement of the whole estate of the bankrupt as then ascertained, of the property recovered and of the property outstanding, specifying the cause of its being outstanding; also what debts or claims are yet undetermined, and stating what sum remains in his hands. At such meeting the majority in value of the creditors present shall determine whether any and what part of the net proceeds of the estate, after deducting and retaining a sum sufficient to provide for all undetermined claims, which by reason of the distant residence of the creditor, or for other sufficient reason, have not been proved, and for other expenses and contingencies, shall be divided among the creditors; but unless at least one half in value of the creditors shall attend such meeting either in person or by attorney, it shall be the duty of the assignee so to determine. In case a dividend is ordered, the register shall, within ten days after such meeting, prepare a list of creditors entitled to dividend, and shall calculate and set opposite to the name of each creditor who has proved his claim the dividend to which he is entitled out of the net proceeds of the estate set apart for dividend, and shall forward by mail to every creditor a statement of the dividend to which he is entitled, and such creditor shall be paid by the assignee in such manner as the court may direct.

SEC. 28. *And be it further enacted,* That the like proceedings shall be had at the expiration of the next three months, or earlier, if practicable, and a third meeting of creditors shall then be called by the court, and a final dividend then declared, unless any action at law or suit in equity be pending, or unless some other estate or effects of the debtor afterward come to the hands of the assignee, in which case the assignee shall, as soon as may be, convert such estate or effects into money ; and within two months after the same shall be so converted, the same shall be divided in manner aforesaid. Further dividends shall be made in like manner as often as occasion requires; and after the third meeting of creditors no further meeting shall be called, unless ordered by the court. If at any time there shall be in the hands of the assignee any outstanding debts or other property, due or belonging to the estate, which cannot be collected and received by the assignee without unreasonable or inconvenient delay or expense, the assignee may, under the direction of the court, sell and assign such debts or other property in such manner as the court shall order. No dividend already declared shall be disturbed by reason of debts being subsequently proved; but the creditors proving such debts shall be entitled to a dividend equal to those already received by the other creditors before any further payment is made to the latter. Preparatory to the final dividend, the assignee shall submit his account to the court and file the same, and give notice to the creditors of such filing, and shall also give notice that he will apply for a settlement of his account, and for a discharge from all liability as assignee, at a time to be specified in such notice, and at such time the court shall audit and pass the accounts of the assignee, and such assignee shall, if required by the court, be examined as to the truth of such account, and if found correct, he shall thereby be discharged from all liability as assignee to any creditor of the bankrupt. The court shall thereupon order a dividend of the estate and effects, or of such part thereof as it sees fit, among such of the creditors as have proved their claims, in proportion to the respective amount of their said debts. In addition to all expenses necessarily incurred by him in the execution of his trust, in any case, the assignee shall be entitled to an allowance for his services in such case, on all moneys received and paid out by him therein, for any sum not exceeding one thousand dollars, five per centum thereon; for any larger sum not exceeding five thousand dollars, two and a half per centum on the excess over one thousand dollars; and for any larger sum, one per centum on the excess over five thousand dollars; and if, at any time, there shall not be in his hands a sufficient amount of money to defray the necessary expenses required for the further execution of his trust, he shall not be obliged to proceed therein until the necessary funds are advanced or satisfactorily secured to him If by accident, mistake, or other cause, without fault of the assignee, either or both of the said second and third meetings should not be held within the times limited, the court may, upon motion of an interested party, order such meetings, with like effect as to the validity of the proceedings as if the meeting had been duly held. In the order for a dividend under this section, the following claims shall be entitled to priority or preference, and to be first paid in full in the following order :

1st. The fees, costs, and expenses of suits, and the several proceedings in bankruptcy under this act, and for the custody of property, as herein provided.

2d. All debts due to the United States, and all taxes and assessments under the laws thereof.

3d. All debts due to the state in which the proceedings in bankruptcy are pending, and all taxes and assessments made under the laws of such state.

4th. Wages due to any operative, clerk, or house-servant to an amount not exceeding fifty dollars, for labor performed within six months next preceding the first publication of the notice of proceedings in bankruptcy.

5th. All debts due to any persons who, by the laws of the United States, are or may be entitled to a priority or preference, in like manner as if this act had not been passed : *always provided*, that nothing contained in this act shall interfere with the assessment and collection of taxes by the authority of the United States or any state.

SEC. 29. *And be it further enacted,* That at any time after the expiration of six months from the adjudication of bankruptcy, or if no debts had been proved against the bankrupt, or if no assets have come to the hands of the assignee, at any time after the expiration of sixty days, and within one year from the adjudication of bankruptcy, the bankrupt may apply to the court for a discharge from his debts, and the court shall thereupon order notice to be given by mail to all the creditors who have proved their debts, and by publication at least once a week in such newspapers as the court shall designate, due regard being had to the general circulation of the same in the district, or in that portion of the district in which the bankrupt and his creditors shall reside, to appear on a day appointed for that purpose, and show cause why a discharge should not be granted to the bankrupt. No discharge shall be granted, or, if granted, be valid, if the bankrupt has wilfully sworn falsely in his affidavit annexed to his petition, schedule, or inventory, or upon any examination in the course of the proceedings in bankruptcy in relation to any material fact concerning his estate or his debts, or to any other material fact; or if he has concealed any part of his estate or his effects, or any books or writings relating thereto, or if he has been guilty of any fraud or negligence in the care, custody, or delivery to the assignee of the property belonging to him at the time of the presentation of his petition and inventory, excepting such property as he is permitted to retain under the provisions of this act, or if he has caused, permitted, or suffered any loss, waste, or destruction thereof; or if, within four months before the commencement of such proceedings, he has procured his lands, goods, money, or chattels to be attached, sequestered, or seized on execution; or if, since the passage of this act, he has destroyed, mutilated, altered, or falsified any of his books, documents, papers, writings, or securities, or has made or been privy to the making of any false or fraudulent entry in any book of account or other document, with intent to defraud his creditors; or has removed or caused to be removed any part of his property from the district, with intent to defraud his creditors; or if he has given any fraudulent preference contrary to the provisions of this act, or made any fraudulent payment, gift, transfer, conveyance, or assignment of any part of his property, or has lost any part thereof in gaming, or has admitted a false or fictitious debt against his estate; or if, having knowledge that any person has proved such false and fictitious debt, he has not disclosed the same to his assignee within one month after such knowledge; or if, being a merchant or tradesman he has not, subsequently to the passage of this act, kept proper books of account; or if he, or any person in his behalf, has procured the assent of any creditor to the discharge, or influenced the action of any creditor at any stage of the proceedings, by any pecuniary consideration or obligation; or if he has, in contemplation of becoming bankrupt, made any pledge, payment, transfer, assignment or conveyance of any part of his property, directly or indirectly, absolutely or condi-

tionally, for the purpose of preferring any creditor or person having a claim against him, or who is or may be under liability for him, or for the purpose of preventing the property from coming into the hands of the assignee, or of being distributed under this act in satisfaction of his debts; or if he has been convicted of any misdemeanor under this act, or has·been guilty of any fraud whatever contrary to the true intent of this act; and before any discharge is granted, the bankrupt shall take and subscribe an oath to the effect that he has not done, suffered, or been privy to any act, matter, or thing specified in this act as a ground for withholding such discharge, or as invalidating such discharge if granted.

Sec. 30. *And be it further enacted*, That no person who shall have been discharged under this act, and shall afterwards become bankrupt, on his own application shall be again entitled to a discharge whose estate is insufficient to pay seventy per centum of the debts proved against it, unless the assent in writing of three-fourths in value of his creditors who have proved their claims, is filed at or before the time of application for discharge; but a bankrupt who shall prove to the satisfaction of the court that he has paid all the debts owing by him at the time of any previous bankruptcy, or who has been voluntarily released therefrom by his creditors, shall be entitled to a discharge in the same manner and with the same effect as if he had not previously been bankrupt.

Sec. 31. *And be it further enacted*, That any creditor opposing the discharge of any bankrupt may file a specification in writing of the grounds of his opposition, and the court may, in its discretion, order any question of fact so presented to be tried at a stated session of the district court.

Sec. 32. *And be it further enacted*, That if it shall appear to the court that the bankrupt has in all things conformed to his duty under this act, and that he is entitled, under the provisions thereof to receive a discharge, the court shall grant him a discharge from all his debts except as hereinafter provided, and shall give him a certificate thereof under the seal of the court, in substance as follows:

District Court of the United States. District of   .   Whereas   has been duly adjudged a bankrupt under the act of congress establishing a uniform system of bankruptcy throughout the United States, and appears to have conformed to all the requirements of law in that behalf, . it is therefore ordered by the court that said be forever discharged from all debts and claims which by said act are made provable gainst his estate and which existed on the day of , on which day the petition for adjudication was filed by (or against him ; excepting such debts, if any as are by said act excepted from the operation of a discharge in bankruptcy. Given under my hand, and the seal of the court, at , in the said district, this day of A. D. .

(Seal.) , Judge.

SEC. 33. *And be it further enacted,* That no debt created by the fraud or embezzlement of the bankrupt, or by his defalcation as a public officer, or while acting in any fiduciary character, shall be discharged under this act; but the debt may be proved, and the dividend thereon shall be a payment on account of said debt; and no discharge granted under this act shall release, discharge, or affect any person liable for the same debt for or with the bankrupt, either as partner, joint contractor, indorser, surety, or otherwise. And in all proceedings in bankruptcy commenced after one year from the time this act shall go into operation, on discharge shall be granted to a debtor whose assets do not pay fifty per centum of the claims against his estate, unless the assent in writing of a majority in number and value of his creditors who have proved their claims is filed in the case at or before the time of application for discharge.

[Be it enacted by the Senate and House of Representatives in Congress assembled, *That the provisions of the second clause of the thirty-third section of said act shall not apply to cases of proceedings in bankruptcy commended prior to the first day of January, 1869, and the time during which the operation of the provision of said clause is postponed, shall be extended until the said first day of January, 1869 ; and said clause is amended so as to read as follows : In all proceedings in bankruptcy commenced after January, 1869, no discharge shall be granted to a debtor whose assets shall not be equal to or pay fifty per centum of the claims proved against his estate, upon which he shall be liable as the principal debtor, unless the assent*

in writing of a majority in number and value of his creditors to whom he shall have become liable as principal debtor and who shall have proved their claims be filed in the case at or before the time of the hearing of the application for discharge. AMENDMENT , APPROVED JULY 25, 1868:]

[Be it enacted by the Senate and House of Representatives of the United States of America in Congress assembled, *That the provisions of the second clause of the thirty-third section of said Act, as amended by the first section of an Act in amendment thereof, approved July twenty-seven, eighteen hundred and sixty-eight, shall not apply to those debts from which the bankrupt seeks a discharge which were contracted prior to the first day of January, eighteen hundred and sixty-nine.*—AMENDMENT, APPROVED, JULY 14, 1870.]

SEC. 34. *And be it further enacted,* That a discharge duly granted under this act shall, with the exceptions aforesaid, release the bankrupt from all debts, claims, liabilities, and demands which were or might have been proved against his estate in bankruptcy, and may be pleaded by a simple averment that on the day of its date such discharge was granted to him, setting the same forth in *hæc verba,* as a full and complete bar to all suits brought on any such debts, claims, liabilities, or demands, and the certificate shall be conclusive evidence in favor of such bankrupt of the fact and the regularity of such discharge : *always provided,* that any creditor or creditors of said bankrupt, whose debt was proved or provable against. the estate in bankruptcy, who shall see fit to contest the validity of said discharge on the ground that it was fraudulently obtained, may, at any time within two years after the date thereof, apply to the court which granted it to set aside and annul the same. Said application shall be in writing, shall specify which, in particular, of the several acts mentioned in section twenty-nine it is intended to give evidence of against the bankrupt, setting forth the grounds of avoidance, and no evidence shall be admitted as to any other of the said acts ; but said application shall be subject to amendment at the discretion of the court. The court shall cause reasonable notice of said application to be given to said bankrupt, and order him to appear and answer the same, within such time as to the court shall seem fit and proper. If, upon the hearing of said parties, the court shall find that the fraudulent acts, or any of them set forth as aforesaid by said creditor or creditors against the bankrupt, are proved, and that said creditor or creditors had no knowledge of the same until after the granting of said discharge, judgment shall be given in favor of said creditor or creditors, and the discharge of said bankrupt shall be set aside and annulled. But if said court shall find that said fraudulent acts, and all of them, set forth as aforesaid, are not proved, or that they were known to said creditor or creditors before the granting of said discharge, then judgment shall be rendered in favor of the bankrupt, and the validity of his discharge shall not be affected by said proceedings.

SEC. 35. *And be it further enacted*, That if any person, being insolvent, or in contemplation of insolvency, within four months before the filing of the petition by or against him, with a view to give a preference to any creditor or person having a claim against him, or who is under any liability for him, procures any part of his property to be attached, sequestered, or seized on execution, or makes any payment, pledge, assignment, transfer, or conveyance of any part of his property, either directly or indirectly, absolutely or conditionally, the person receiving such payment, pledge, assignment, transfer, or conveyance, or to be benefited thereby, or by such attachment, having reasonable cause to believe such person is insolvent, and that such attachment, payment, pledge, assignment, or conveyance, is made in fraud of the provisions of this act, the same shall be void, and the assignee may recover the property, or the value of it, from the person so receiving it, or so to be benefited; and if any person being insolvent, or in contemplation of insolvency or bankruptcy, within six months before the filing of the petition by or against him, makes any payment, sale, assignment, transfer, conveyance, or other disposition of any part of his property to any person who then has reasonable cause to believe him to be insolvent, or to be acting in contemplation of insolvency, and that such payment, sale, assignment, transfer, or other conveyance, is made with a view to prevent his property from coming to his assignee in bankruptcy, or to prevent the same from be-

ing distributed under this act, or to defeat the object of, or in any way impair, hinder, impede, or delay the operation and effect of, or to evade any of the provisions of this act, the sale, assignment, transfer, or conveyance shall be void, and the assignee may recover the property, or the value thereof, as assets of the bankrupt. And if such sale, assignment, transfer, or conveyance is not made in the usual and ordinary course of business of the debtor, the fact shall be *prima facie* evidence of fraud. Any contract, covenant, or security made or given by a bankrupt or other person with, or in trust for, any creditor, for securing the payment of any money as a consideration for or with intent to induce the creditor to forbear opposing the application for discharge of the bankrupt, shall be void; and if any creditor shall obtain any sum of money or other goods, chattels, or security from any person as an inducement for forbearing to oppose, or consenting to such application for discharge, every creditor so offending shall forfeit all right to any share or dividend in the estate of the bankrupt, and shall also forfeit double the value or amount of such money, goods, chattels, or security so obtained, to be recovered by the assignee for the benefit of the estate.

SEC. 36. *And be it further enacted*, That where two or more persons who are partners in trade shall be adjudged bankrupt, either on the petition of such partners, or any one of them, or on the petition of any creditor of the partners, a warrant shall issue in the manner provided by this act, upon which all the joint stock and property of the copartnership, and also all the separate estate of each of the partners, shall be taken, excepting such parts thereof as are hereinbefore excepted; and all the creditors of the company, and the separate creditors of each partner, shall be allowed to prove their respective debts; and the assignee shall be chosen by the creditors of the company, and shall also keep separate accounts of the joint stock and property of the copartnership, and of the separate estate of each member thereof; and after deducting out of the whole amount received by such assignee the whole of the expenses and disbursements, the net proceeds of the joint stock shall be appropriated to pay the creditors of the copartnership, and the net proceeds of the separate estate of each partner shall be appropriated to pay his separate creditors; and if there shall be any balance of the separate estate of any partner, after the payment of his separate debts, such balance shall be added to the joint stock for the payment of the joint creditors, and if there shall be any balance of the joint stock after payment of the joint debts, such balance shall be divided and appropriated to and among the separate estates of the several partners according to their respective right and interest therein, and as it would have been if the partnership had been dissolved without any bankruptcy; and the sum so appropriated to the separate estate of each partner shall be applied to the payment of his separate debts; and the certificate of discharge shall be granted or refused to each partner as the same would or ought to be if the proceedings had been against him alone under this act; and in all other respects the proceedings against partners shall be conducted in the like manner as if they had been commenced and prosecuted against one person alone. If such copartners reside in different districts, that court in which the petition is first filed shall retain exclusive jurisdiction over the case.

SEC. 37. *And be it further enacted*, That the provisions of this act shall apply to all moneyed, business, or commercial corporations and joint-stock companies, and that upon the petition of any officer of any such corporation or company duly authorized by a vote of a majority of the corporators present at any legal meeting called for the purpose, or upon the petition of any creditor or creditors of such corporation or company, made and presented in the manner hereinafter provided in respect to debtors, the like proceedings shall be had and taken as are hereinafter provided in the case of debtors; and all the provisions of this act which apply to the debtor, or set forth his duties in regard to furnishing schedules and inventories, executing papers, submitting to examinations, disclosing, making over, secreting, concealing, conveying, assigning, or paying away his money or property, shall in like manner, and with like force, effect, and penalties, apply to each and every officer of such corporation or company in relation to the same matters concerning the corporation or company, and the money and property there-

of. All payments, conveyances, and assignments declared fraudulent and void by this act when made by a debtor, shall in like manner, and to the like extent, and with like remedies, be fraudulent and void when made by a corporation or company. No allowance or discharge shall be granted to any corporation or joint-stock company, or to any person, or officer, or member thereof: *provided*, that whenever any corporation by proceedings under this act shall be declared bankrupt, all its property and assets shall be distributed to the creditors of such corporation, in the manner provided in this act in respect to natural persons.

SEC. 38. *And be it further enacted*, That the filing of a petition for adjudication in bankruptcy, either by a debtor in his own behalf, or by any creditor against a debtor, upon which an order may be issued by the court, or by a register in the manner provided in section 4, shall be deemed and taken to be the commencement of proceedings in bankruptcy under this act; the proceedings in all cases in bankruptcy shall be deemed matters of record, but the same shall not be required to be recorded at large, but shall be carefully filed, kept and numbered in the office of the clerk of the court, and a docket only, or short memorandum thereof, kept in books to be provided for that purpose, which shall be open to public inspection. Copies of such records, duly certified under seal of the court, shall in all cases be *prima facie* evidence of the facts therein stated. Evidence or examinations in any of the proceedings under this act may be taken before the court, or a register in bankruptcy, *viva voce*, or in writing, before a commissioner of the circuit court, or by affidavit, or on commission, and the court may direct a reference to a register in bankruptcy, or other suitable person, to take and certify such examination, and may compel the attendance of witnesses, the production of books and papers, and the giving of testimony in the same manner as in suits in equity in the circuit court.

SEC. 39. *And be it further enacted*, That any person residing and owing debts as aforesaid, who, after the passage of this act shall depart from the state, district or territory, of which he is an inhabitant, with intent to defraud his creditors, or, being absent, shall, with such intent, remain absent;

or shall conceal himself to avoid the service of legal process in any action for the recovery of a debt or demand provable under this act; or shall conceal or remove any of his property to avoid its being attached, taken, or sequestered on legal process; or shall make any assignment, gift, sale, conveyance or transfer of his estate, property, rights or credits, either within the United States or elsewhere, with intent to delay, defraud or hinder his creditors; or who has been arrested and held in custody under or by virtue of mesne process or execution, issued out of any court of any state, district or territory, within which such debtor resides or has property, founded upon a demand in its nature provable against a bankrupt's estate under this act, and for a sum exceeding one hundred dollars, and such process is remaining in force, and not discharged by payment, or in any other manner provided by the law of such state, district or territory applicable thereto, for a period of seven days; or has been actually imprisoned for more than seven days in a civil action, founded on contract, for the sum of one hundred dollars or upward; or who, being bankrupt or insolvent, or in contemplation of bankruptcy or insolvency, shall make any payment, gift, grant, sale, conveyance or transfer of money or other property, estate, rights or credits, or give any warrant to confess judgment, or procure or suffer his property to be taken on legal process, with intent to give a preference to one or more of his creditors, or to any person or persons who are or may be liable to him as indorsers, bail, sureties or otherwise, or with the intent, by such disposition of his property, to defeat or delay the operation of this act; or who being a banker, merchant or trader, has fraudulently stopped or suspended, and not resumed payment of his commercial paper, within a period of fourteen days, shall be deemed to have committed an act of bankruptcy, and, subject to the conditions hereinafter prescribed, shall be considered and adjudged a bankrupt, on the petition of one or more of his creditors, the aggregate of whose debts provable under this act amount to at least two hundred and fifty dollars, provided such petition is brought within six months after the act of bankruptcy shall have been committed. And if such person shall be ad-

judged a bankrupt, the assignee may recover back the money or other property so paid, conveyed, sold, assigned, or transferred contrary to this act, provided the person receiving such payment or conveyance had reasonable cause to believe that a fraud on this act was intended, or that the debtor was insolvent, and such creditor shall not be allowed to prove his debt in bankruptcy.

[And be it further enacted, *That the clause in the thirty-ninth section of said Act, which now reads "or who, being a banker, merchant, or trader, has fraudulently stopped or suspended and not resumed payment of his commercial paper within a period of fourteen days," shall be amended so as to read as follows: "or who, being a banker, broker, merchant, trader, manufacturer, or miner, has fraudulently stopped payment, or who has stopped or suspended and not resumed payment of his commercial paper within a period of fourteen days."—*AMENDMENT, APPROVED JULY 14, 1870.]

SEC. 40. *And be it further enacted,* That upon the filing of the petition authorized by the next preceding section, if it shall appear that sufficient grounds exist therefor, the court shall direct the entry of an order requiring the debtor to appear and show cause, at a court of bankruptcy to be holden at a time to be specified in the order, not less than five days from the service thereof, why the prayer of the petition should not be granted; and may also, by its injunction restrain the debtor, and any other person, in the meantime, from making any transfer or disposition of any of the debtor's property not excepted by this act from the operation thereof and from any interference therewith; and if it shall appear that there is probable cause for believing that the debtor is about to leave the district, or to remove or conceal his goods and chattels or his evidence of property, or make any fraudulent conveyance or disposition thereof, the court may issue a warrant to the marshal of the district, commanding him to arrest the alleged bankrupt and him safely keep, unless he shall give bail to the satisfaction of the court for his appearance from time to time, as required by the court, until the decision of the court upon the petition or the further order of the court, and forthwith to take possession provisionally of all the property and effects of the debtor, and safely keep the same until the further order of the court. A copy of the petition and of such order to show cause shall be served on such debtor by delivering the same to him personally, or leaving the same at his last or usual place of abode; or if such debtor cannot be found, or his place of residence ascertained, service shall be made by publication, in such manner as the judge may direct. No further proceedings, unless the debtor appear and consent thereto, shall be had until proof shall have been given to the satisfaction of the court, of such service or publication; and if such proof be not given on the return of such order, the proceedings shall be adjourned, and an order made that the notice be forthwith so served or published.

SEC. 41. *And be it further enacted*, That on such return day, or adjourned day, if the notice has been duly served or published, or shall be waived by the appearance and consent of the debtor, the court shall proceed summarily to hear the allegations of the petitioner and debtor, and may adjourn the proceedings from time to time on good cause shown, and shall, if the debtor on the same day so demand in writing, order a trial by jury at the first term of the court at which a jury shall be in attendance, to ascertain the facts of such alleged bankruptcy; and if, upon such hearing or trial, the debtor proves to the satisfaction of the court or the jury, as the case may be, that the facts set forth in the petition are not true, or that the debtor has paid and satisfied all liens upon his property in case the existence of such liens were the sole ground of the proceeding, the proceedings shall be dismissed, and the respondent shall recover his costs.

SEC. 42. *And be it further enacted*, That if the facts set forth in the petition are found to be true, or if default be made by the debtor to appear pursuant to the order, upon due proof of service thereof being made, the court shall adjudge the debtor to be a bankrupt, and, as such, subject to the provisions of this act, and shall forthwith issue a warrant to take possession of the estate of the debtor. The warrant shall be directed, and the property of the debtor shall be taken thereon, and shall be assigned and distributed in the same manner and with similar proceedings to those hereinbefore provided for the taking possession, assignment, and distribution of the property of the debtor

upon his own petition. The order of adjudication of bankruptcy shall require the bankrupt forthwith, or within such number of days, not exceeding five after the date of the order, or notice thereof, as shall by the order be prescribed, to make and deliver, or transmit by mail, post-paid, to the messenger, a schedule of the creditors and an inventory of his estate in the form and verified in the manner required of a petitioning debtor by section 13. If the debtor has failed to appear in person or by attorney, a certified copy of the adjudication shall be forthwith served on him by delivery or publication in the manner hereinbefore provided for the service of the order to show cause; and if the bankrupt is absent or cannot be found, such schedule and inventory shall be prepared by the messenger and the assignee from the best information they can obtain. If the petitioning creditor shall not appear and proceed on the return day, or adjourned day, the court may, upon the petition of any other creditor to the required amount, proceed to adjudicate on such petition, without requiring a new service or publication of notice to the debtor.

SEC. 43. *And be it further enacted*, That if, at the first meeting of creditors, or at any meeting of creditors to be specially called for that purpose, and of which previous notice shall have been given for such length of time and in such manner as the court may direct, three-fourths in value of the creditors whose claims have been proved shall determine and resolve that it is for the interest of the general body of the creditors that the estate of the bankrupt should be wound up and settled, and distribution made among the creditors by trustees, under the inspection and direction of a committee of the creditors, it shall be lawful for the creditors to certify and report such resolution to the court, and to nominate one or more trustees to take, and hold, and distribute the estate, under the direction of such committee. If it shall appear to the court, after hearing the bankrupt and such creditors as may desire to be heard, that the resolution was duly passed, and that the interests of the creditors will be promoted thereby, it shall confirm the same; and upon the execution and filing, by or on behalf of three-fourths in value of all the creditors whose claims have been proved, of a consent that the estate of the bankrupt be wound up and settled by said trustees, according to the terms of such resolution, the bankrupt, or his assignee in bankruptcy, if appointed, as the case may be, shall, under the direction of the court, and under oath, convey, transfer, and deliver all the property and estate of the bankrupt to the said trustee or trustees, who shall, upon such conveyance and transfer, have and hold the same in the same manner, and with the same powers and rights, in all respects, as the bankrupt would have had or held the same if no proceedings in bankruptcy had been taken, or as the assignee in bankruptcy would have done had such resolution not been passed; and such consent, and the proceedings thereunder, shall be as binding in all respects on any creditor whose debt is provable, who has not signed the same, as if he had signed it, and on any creditor whose debt, if provable, is not proved, as if he had proved it; and the court, by order, shall direct all acts and things needful to be done to carry into effect such resolution of the creditors; and the said trustees shall proceed to wind up and settle the estate under the direction and inspection of such committee of the creditors, for the equal benefit of all such creditors, and the winding up and settlement of any estate under the provisions of this section shall be deemed to be proceedings in bankruptcy under this act; and the said trustees shall have all the rights and powers of assignees in bankruptcy. The court, on the application of such trustees, shall have power to summon and examine, on oath or otherwise, the bankrupt, and any creditor, and any person indebted to the estate, or known or suspected of having any of the estate in his possession, or any other person whose examination may be material or necessary to aid the trustees in the execution of their trust, and to compel the attendance of such persons, and the production of books and papers, in the same manner as in other proceedings in bankruptcy under this act; and the bankrupt shall have the like right to apply for and obtain a discharge after the passage of such resolution and the appointment of such trustees as if such resolution had not been passed, and as if all the proceedings had continued in the manner provided in the preceding sections of this act. If the resolution shall not be duly reported, or the consent of the creditors shall not be

duly filed, or if, upon its filing, the court shall not think fit to approve thereof, the bankruptcy shall proceed as though no resolution had been passed, and the court may make all necessary orders for resuming the proceedings; and the period of time which shall have elapsed between the date of the resolution and the date of the order for resuming the proceedings shall not be reckoned in calculating periods of time prescribed by this act.

SEC. 44. *And be it further enacted,* That from and after the passage of this act, if any debtor or bankrupt shall, after the commencement of proceedings in bankruptcy, secrete or conceal any property belonging to his estate, or part with, conceal, or destroy, alter, mutilate, or falsify, or cause to be concealed, destroyed, altered, mutilated, or falsified, any book, deed, document, or writing relating thereto, or remove, or cause to be removed, the same or any part thereof, out of the district, or otherwise dispose of any part thereof, with intent to prevent it from coming into the possession of the assignee in bankruptcy, or to hinder, impede, or delay either of them in recovering or receiving the same, or make any payment, gift, sale, assignment, transfer, or conveyance of any property belonging to his estate with the like intent, or spends any part thereof in gaming; or shall, with intent to defraud, wilfully and fraudulently conceal from his assignees, or omit from his schedule any property or effects whatsoever; or if, in case of any person having, to his knowledge or belief, proved a false or fictitious debt against his estate, he shall fail to disclose the same to his assignee within one month after coming to the knowledge or belief thereof; or shall attempt to account for any of his property by fictitious losses or expenses; or shall, within three months before the commencement of proceedings in bankruptcy, under the false color and pretense of carrying on business and dealing in the ordinary course of trade, obtain on credit from any person any goods or chattels with intent to defraud; or shall, with intent to defraud his creditors, within three months next before the commencement of the proceedings in bankruptcy, pawn, pledge, or dispose of, otherwise than by *bona fide* transactions in the ordinary way of his trade, any of his goods or chattels which have been obtained on credit and remain unpaid for, he shall be deemed guilty of a misdemeanor, and, upon conviction thereof in any court of the United States, shall be punished by imprisonment, with or without hard labor, for a term not exceeding three years.

SEC. 45. *And be it further enacted*, That if any judge, register, clerk, marshal, messenger, assignee, or any other officer of the several courts of bankruptcy shall, for anything done or pretended to be done under this act, or under color of doing anything thereunder, wilfully demand or take, or appoint or allow any person whatever to take for him or on his account, or for or on account of any other person, or in trust for him or for any other person, any fee, emolument, gratuity, sum of money, or anything of value whatever, other than is allowed by this act, or which shall be allowed under the authority thereof, such person, when convicted thereof, shall forfeit and pay the sum of not less than three hundred dollars, and not exceeding five hundred dollars, and be imprisoned not exceeding three years.

SEC. 46. *And be it further enacted*, That if any person shall forge the signature of a judge, register, or other officer of the court, or shall forge or counterfeit the seal of the courts, or knowingly concur in using any such forged or counterfeit signature or seal for the purpose of authenticating any proceeding or document, or shall tender in evidence any such proceeding or document with a false or counterfeit signature of any such judge, register, or other officer, or a false or counterfeit seal of the court, subscribe or attached thereto, knowing such signature or seal to be false or counterfeit, any such person shall be guilty of felony, and upon conviction thereof, shall be liable to a fine of not less than five hundred dollars, and not more than five thousand dollars, and to be imprisoned not exceeding five years, at the discretion of the court.

SEC. 47. *And be it further enacted*, That in each case there shall be allowed and paid, in addition to the fees of the clerk of the court as now established by law, or as may be established by general order, under the provisions of this act, for fees in bankruptcy the following fees, which shall be applied to the payment for the services of the registers :

For issuing every warrant, two dollars.

For each day in which a meeting is held, three dollars.

For each order for a dividend, three dollars.

For every order substituting an arrangement by trust deed for bankruptcy, two dollars.

For every bond with sureties, two dollars.

For every application for any meeting in any matter under this act, one dollar.

For every day's service while actually employed under a special order of the court, a sum not exceeding five dollars, to be allowed by the court.

For taking depositions, the fees now allowed by law.

For every discharge when there is no opposition, two dollars.

Such fees shall have priority of payment over all other claims out of the estate, and before a warrant issues, the petitioner shall deposit with the senior register of the court, or with the clerk, to be delivered to the register, fifty dollars as security for the payment thereof ; and if there are not sufficient assets for the payment of the fees, the person upon whose petition the warrant is issued shall pay the same, and the court may issue an execution against him to compel payment to the register.

Before any dividend is ordered, the assignee shall pay out of the estate to the messenger the following fees, and no more :

1st. For service of warrant, two dollars.

2d. For all necessary travel, at the rate of five cents a mile, each way.

3d. For each written note to creditor named in the schedule, ten cents.

4th. For custody of property, publication of notices, and other services, his actual and necessary expenses upon returning the same in specific items, and making oath that they have been actually incurred and paid by him, and are just and reasonable, the same to be taxed or adjusted by the court, and the oath of the messenger shall not be conclusive as to the necessity of said expenses.

For cause shown, and upon hearing thereon, such further allowance may be made as the court, in its direction, may determine.

The enumeration of the foregoing fees shall not prevent the judges, who shall frame general rules and orders in accordance with the provisions of section 10, from prescribing a tariff of fees for all other services of the officers of courts of bankruptcy, or from reducing the fees prescribed in this section in classes of cases to be named in their rules and orders.

SEC. 48. *And be it further enacted,* That the word " assignee" and the word " creditor" shall include the plural also; and the word " messenger" shall include his assistant or assistants, except in the provision for the fees of that officer. The word "marshal" shall include the marshal's deputies; the word " person" shall also include " corporation;" and the word " oath" shall include " affirmation." And in all cases in which any particular number of days is prescribed by this act, or shall be mentioned in any rule or order of court, or general order which shall at any time be made under this act, for the doing of any act or for any other purpose, the same shall be reckoned, in the absence of any expression to the contrary, exclusive of the first and inclusive of the last day, unless the last day shall fall on a Sunday, Christmas day, or on any day appointed by the president of the United States as a day of public fast or thanksgiving, or on the Fourth of July, in which case the time shall be reckoned exclusive of that day also.

SEC. 49. *And be it further enacted,* That all the jurisdiction, power, and authority conferred upon and vested in the district court of the United States by this act in cases in bankruptcy, are hereby conferred upon and vested in the supreme court of the District of Columbia, and in and upon the supreme courts of the several territories of the United States, when the bankrupt resides in the said District of Columbia or in either of the said territories. And in those judicial districts which are not within any organized circuit of the United States, the power and jurisdiction of a circuit court in bankruptcy may be exercised by the district judge.

[Be it enacted by the Senate and House of Representatives of the United States of America in Congress assembled, *That the jurisdiction conferred upon the supreme courts of the territories by the act to which this is an amendment, may be exercised upon petitions regularly filed in that court, by either of the justices thereof while holding the district court in the district in which the petitioner or the alleged bankrupt resides, and said several supreme courts shall have the supervisory jurisdiction over all acts and decisions of each justice thereof as is conferred upon the circuit courts of the United States over proceedings in the district courts of the United States by the second section of said act.*

SEC. 2. And be it further enacted, *That in case of a vacancy in the office of district judge in any district, or in case any district judge shall, from sickness, absence or other disability, be unable to act, the circuit judge of the circuit in which such district is included may make, during such disability or vacancy, all necessary rules and orders preparatory to the final hearing of all cases in bankruptcy, and cause the same to be entered or issued, as the case may require by the clerk of the district court.*—AMENDMENT, APPROVED JUNE 30, 1870.]

SEC. 50. *And be it further enacted,* That this act shall commence and take effect as to the appointment of the officers created hereby, and the promulgation of rules and general orders, from and after the date of its approval : *provided,* that no petition or other. proceeding under this act shall be filed, received, or commenced before the first day of June, Anno Domini, eighteen hundred and sixty-seven.

Approved March 2d, 1867.

THE
ENGLISH BANKRUPTCY ACT OF 1869.

An Act to consolidate and amend the Law of Bankruptcy, 9th August, 1869.

WHEREAS it is expedient to consolidate and amend the law relating to bankruptcy:

Be it enacted by the Queen's most Excellent Majesty, by and with the advice and consent of the Lords Spiritual and Temporal, and Commons, in this present Parliament assembled, and by the authority of the same as follows:

PRELIMINARY.

1. This act may be cited as " The Bankruptcy Act, 1869."

2. This act shall not, except in so far as is expressly provided, apply to Scotland or Ireland.

3. This act shall not come into operation until the first day of January, one thousand eight hundred and seventy, which date is hereinafter referred to as the commencement of this act.

4. In this act, if not inconsistent with the context, the following terms have the meanings hereinafter respectively assigned to them; that is to say,

" The court " shall mean the court having jurisdiction in bankruptcy as by this act provided:

" The registrar " shall mean the registrar of " the court " as above defined:

" Prescribed " shall mean prescribed by rules of court to be made as in this act provided:

" Property " shall mean and include money, goods, things in action, land, and every description of property, whether real or personal; also, obligations, easements, and every description of estate, interest, and profit, present or future, vested or contingent, arising out of or incident to property as above defined:

" Debt provable in bankruptcy " shall include any debt or liability by this act made provable in bankruptcy:

" Person " shall include a body corporate:

" Trader " shall, for the purposes of this act, mean the several persons in that behalf mentioned in the first schedule to this act annexed.

5. A partnership association, or company, corporate, or registered under " The Companies Act, 1862," shall not be adjudged bankrupt under this act.

PART I.
ADJUDICATION AND VESTING OF PROPERTY.

ADJUDICATION.

6. A single creditor, or two or more creditors if the debt due to such single creditor, or the aggregate amount of debts due to such several creditors, from any debtor, amount to a sum of not less than fifty pounds, may present a petition to the court, praying that the debtor be adjudged a bankrupt, and alleging as the ground for such adjudication any one or more of the following acts or defaults, hereinafter deemed to be and included under the expression " acts of bankruptcy."

(1.) That the debtor has, in England or elsewhere, made a conveyance or assignment of his property to a trustee or trustees for the benefit of his creditors generally:

(2.) That the debtor has, in England or elsewhere, made a fraudulent conveyance, gift, delivery, or transfer of his property or of any part thereof:

(3.) That the debtor has, with intent to defeat or delay his creditors, done any of the following things, namely, departed out of England, or being out of England remained out of England; or being a trader departed from his dwelling house, or otherwise absented himself; or begun to keep house; or suffered himself to be outlawed:

(4.) That the debtor has filed in the prescribed manner in the court a declaration admitting his inability to pay his debts:

(5.) That execution issued against the debtor on any legal process for the purpose of obtaining payment of not less than fifty pounds has in the case of a trader been levied by seizure and sale of his goods:

(6.) That the creditor presenting the petition has served in the prescribed manner on the debtor a debtor's summons requiring the debtor to pay the sum due, of an amount of not less than fifty pounds, and the debtor being a trader has for the space of seven days, or not being a trader has for the space of three weeks, succeeding the service of such summons, neglected to pay such sum, or to secure or compound for the same.

But no person shall be adjudged a bankrupt on any of the above grounds, unless the act of bankruptcy on which the adjudication is grounded has occurred within six months before the presentation of the petition for adjudication; moreover, the debt of the petitioning creditor must be a liquidated sum due at law or in equity, and must not be a secured debt, unless the petitioner state in his petition that he will be ready to give up such security for the benefit of the creditors in the event of the debtor being adjudicated a bankrupt, or unless the petitioner is willing to give an estimate of the value of his security, in which latter case he may be admitted as a petitioning creditor to the extent of the balance of the debt due to him after deducting the value so estimated, but he shall, on an application being made by the trustee within the prescribed time after the date of the adjudication, give up his security to such trustee for the benefit of the creditors upon payment of such estimated value.

7. A debtor's summons may be granted by the court on a creditor proving to its satisfaction that a debt sufficient to support a petition in bankruptcy is due to him from the person against whom the summons is sought, and that the creditor has failed to obtain payment of his debt, after using reasonable efforts to do so. The summons shall be in the prescribed form, resembling, as nearly as circumstances admit, a writ issued by one of her majesty's superior courts. It shall state that, in the event of the debtor failing to pay the sum specified in the summons, or to compound for the same to the satisfaction of the creditor, a petition may be presented against him, praying that he may be adjudged a bankrupt. The summons shall have an endorsement thereon to the like effect, or such other prescribed endorsement as may be best calculated to indicate to the debtor the nature of the document served upon him, and the consequences of inattention to the requisitions therein made.

Any debtor served with a debtor's summons may apply to the court, in the prescribed manner and within the prescribed time, to dismiss such summons, on the ground that he is not indebted to the creditor serving such summons, or that he is not indebted to such amount as will justify such creditor in presenting a bankruptcy petition against him; and the court may dismiss the summons, with or without costs, if satisfied with the allegations made by the debtor, or it may be, upon such security (if any) being given as the court may require for payment to the creditor of the debt alleged by him to be due, and the costs of establishing such debt, stay all proceedings on the summons for such time as will be required for the trial of the question relating thereto: *Provided*, that when the summons shall have issued from the London court of bankruptcy, such trial shall be had either before such court or before any other court of competent jurisdiction, and when the summons shall have issued from a county court, before such court in all cases in which it has now jurisdiction, and in all other cases before some competent tribunal.

8. A petition praying that a debtor may be adjudged a bankrupt, in this act referred to as a bankruptcy petition, shall be served in the prescribed manner. At the hearing, the court shall require proof of the debt of the petitioning creditor, and of the trading, if necessary, and of the act of bankruptcy, or, if more than one act of bankruptcy is alleged in the petition, of some one of the alleged acts of bankruptcy, and, if satisfied with

such proof, shall adjudge the debtor to be bankrupt. The court may adjourn the petition, either conditionally or unconditionally, for the procurement of further evidence, or for any other just cause, or may dismiss the petition, with or without costs, as the court thinks just.

9. Where the debtor appears on the petition, and denies that he is indebted to the petitioner, or that he is indebted to such amount as would justify the petitioner in presenting a bankruptcy petition against him, the court, upon such security (if any) being given as the court may require, for payment to the petitioner of any debt which may be established against him in the due course of law, and of the costs of establishing such debt, may stay all proceedings on the petition for such time as may be required for trial of the question relating to such debt, and such trial shall be had in manner herein before provided with respect to disputed debts under debtor's summonses.

Where proceedings are stayed, the court may, if by reason of the delay caused by such stay of proceedings, or for any other cause it thinks just, adjudge the debtor a bankrupt, on the petition of some other creditor, and shall thereupon dismiss, upon such terms as it thinks just, the petition proceedings which have been stayed as aforesaid.

10. A copy of an order of the court adjudging the debtor to be bankrupt shall be published in the *London Gazette*, and be advertised locally in such manner (if any) as may be prescribed, and the date of such order shall be the date of the adjudication for the purposes of this act, and the production of a copy of the *Gazette* containing such order as aforesaid shall be conclusive evidence in all legal proceedings of the debtor having been duly adjudged a bankrupt, and of the date of the adjudication.

11. The bankruptcy of a debtor shall be deemed to have relation back to and to commence at the time of the act of bankruptcy being completed on which the order is made adjudging him to be a bankrupt; or if the bankrupt is proved to have committed more acts of bankruptcy than one, to have relation back to and to commence at the time of the first of the acts of bankruptcy that may be proved to have been committed by the bankrupt within twelve months next preceding the order of adjudication; but the bank-

ruptcy shall not relate to any prior act of bankruptcy, unless it be that at the time of committing such prior act the bankrupt was indebted to some creditor or creditors in a sum or sums sufficient to support a petition in bankruptcy, and unless such debt or debts are still remaining due at the time of the adjudication.

12. Where a debtor shall have been adjudicated a bankrupt, no creditor to whom the bankrupt is indebted in respect of any debt provable in the bankruptcy shall have any remedy against the property or person of the bankrupt in respect of such debt except in manner directed by this act. But this section shall not affect the power of any creditor holding a security upon the property of the bankrupt to realise or otherwise deal with such security in the same manner as he would have been entitled to realise or deal with the same if this section had not been passed.

13. The court may at any time after the presentation of a bankruptcy petition against the debtor, restrain further proceedings in any action, suit, execution or other legal process against the debtor in respect of any debt provable in bankruptcy, or it may allow such proceedings, whether in progress at the commencement of the bankruptcy or commenced during its continuance, to proceed upon such terms as the court may think just. The court may also, at any time after the prescutation of such petition, appoint a receiver or manager of the property or business of the debtor against whom the petition is presented, or of any part thereof, and may direct immediate possession to be taken of such property or business, or any part thereof.

APPOINTMENT OF TRUSTEES.

14. When an order has been made adjudging a debtor bankrupt, herein referred to as an order of adjudication, the property of the bankrupt shall become divisible amongst his creditors in proportion to the debts proved in the bankruptcy ; and for the purpose of effecting such division, the court shall, as soon as may be, summon a general meeting of his creditors, and the creditors assembled at such meeting shall and may do as follows :

1. They shall by resolution, appoint some fit person, whether a creditor or not, to fill the office of trustee of the property of the bankrupt, at such remuneration

as they may from time to time determine, if any; or they may resolve to leave his appointment to the committee of inspection hereinafter mentioned:

2. They shall, when they appoint a trustee by resolution declare what security is to be given, and to whom, by the person so appointed before he enters on the office of trustee.

3. They shall, by resolution, appoint some other fit persons, not exceeding five in number, and being creditors qualified to vote at such first meeting of creditors as is in this act mentioned, or authorized in the prescribed form by creditors so qualified to vote, to form a committee of inspection for the purpose of superintending the administration by the trustee of the bankrupt's property.

4. They may, by resolution, give direction as to the manner in which the property is to be administered by the trustee, and it shall be the duty of the trustee to conform to such directions, unless the court for some just cause otherwise orders.

15. The property of the bankrupt divisible amongst his creditors, and in this act referred to as the property of the bankrupt, shall not comprise the following particulars:

(1.) Property held by the bankrupt on trust for any other person:

(2.) The tools (if any) of his trade, and the necessary wearing apparel and bedding of himself, his wife and children, to a value, inclusive of tools and apparel and bedding, not exceeding twenty pounds in the whole:

But it shall comprise the following particulars:

(3.) All such property as may belong to or be vested in the bankrupt at the commencement of the bankruptcy, or may be acquired by or devolve on him during its continuance:

(4.) The capacity to exercise and to take proceedings for exercising all such powers in or over or in respect of property as might have been exercised by the bankrupt for his own benefit at the commencement of his bankruptcy or during its continuance, except the right of nomination to a vacant ecclesiastical benefice:

(5.) All goods and chattels being, at the commencement of the bankruptcy, in the possession, order, or disposition of the bankrupt, being a trader, by the consent and permission of the true owner of which goods and chattels the bankrupt is reputed owner, or of which he has taken upon himself the sale or disposition as owner ; provided that things in action, other than debts due to him in the course of his trade or business, shall not be deemed goods and chattels within the meaning of this clause.

16. The general meeting of creditors to be summoned as aforesaid by the court, and in this act referred to as the first meeting of creditors, shall be held in the prescribed manner and subject to the prescribed regulations as to the quorum, adjournment of meeting, and all other matters relating to the conduct of the meeting or the proceedings thereat.

Provided that,—

1. The meeting shall be presided over by the registrar, or, in the event of his being unable to attend through illness or any unavoidable cause, by such chairman as the meeting may elect:

2. A person shall not be entitled to vote as a creditor unless at or previously to the meeting he has in the prescribed manner proved a debt provable under the bankruptcy to be due to him:

3. A creditor shall not vote at the said meeting in respect of any unliquidated or contingent debt, or any debt the value of which is not ascertained:

4. A secured creditor shall, for the purpose of voting, be deemed to be a creditor only in respect of the balance (if any) due to him after deducting the value of his security; and the amount of such balance shall, until the security be realized, be determined in the prescribed manner. He may, however, at or previously to the meeting of creditors, give up the security to the trustee, and thereupon he shall rank as a creditor in respect of the whole sum due to him:

5. A "secured creditor" shall in this act mean any creditor holding any mortgage, charge, or lien on the bankrupt's estate, or any part thereof, as security for a debt due him:

6. Votes may be given either personally or by proxy:

7. An ordinary resolution shall be decided by a majority in value of the creditors present personally or by proxy at the meeting and voting on such resolution:

8. A special resolution shall be decided by a majority in number, and three-fourths in value, of the creditors present personally or by proxy at the meeting and voting on such resolution.

17. Until a trustee is appointed the registrar shall be the trustee for the purposes of this act, and immediately upon the order of adjudication being made the property of the bankrupt shall vest in the registrar. On the appointment of a trustee the property shall forthwith pass to and vest in the trustee appointed.

The expression "trustee," when used in this act, shall include the person for the time being filling the office of trustee, whether he be the registrar or not; but when the registrar holds the office of trustee he shall, unless the court otherwise orders, in the administration of the property of the bankrupt, apply to the court for directions as to the mode of administering such property, and shall not take possession thereof unless directed by the court.

18. The appointment of a trustee shall be reported to the court, and the court, upon being satisfied that the requisite security had been entered into by him, shall give a certificate delaring him to be trustee of the bankruptcy named in the certificate, and such certificate shall be conclusive evidence of the appointment of the trustee, and such appointment shall date from the date of the certificate. When the registrar holds the office of trustee, or when the trustee is changed, a like certificate of the court may be made declaring the person therein named to be trustee, and such certificate shall be conclusive evidence of the person therein named being trustee.

PART II.

ADMINISTRATION OF PROPERTY.

General Provisions affecting Administration of Property.

19. The bankrupt shall, to the utmost of his power, aid in the realization of his property, and the distribution of the proceeds amongst his creditors. He shall produce a statement of his affairs to the first meeting of creditors, and shall be publicly examined thereon on a day to be named by the court, and subject to such adjourned public examination as the court may direct. He shall give such inventory of his property, such list of his creditors and debtors, and of his debts due to and from them respectively, submit to such examination in respect of his property or his creditors, attend such meetings of his creditors, wait at such times on the trustee, execute such powers of attorney, conveyances, deeds, and instruments, and generally do all such acts and things in relation to his property and the distribution of the proceeds amongst his creditors, as may be reasonably required by the trustee, or may be prescribed by rules of court, or be directed by the court by any special order or orders made in reference to any particular bankruptcy, or made on the occasion of any special application by the trustee or any creditor.

If the bankrupt wilfully fail to perform the duties imposed on him by this section, or if he fail to deliver up possession to the trustee of any part of his property, which is divisible amongst his creditors under this act, and which may for the time being be in the possession or under the control of such bankrupt, he shall, in addition to any other punishment to which he may be subject, be guilty of a contempt of court, and may be punished accordingly.

20. The trustee shall, in the administration of the property of the bankrupt, and in the distribution thereof amongst his creditors, have regard to any directions that may be given by resolution of the creditors at any general meeting, or by the committee of inspection, and any directions so given by the creditors at any general meeting shall be deemed to override any directions given by the committee of inspection; the trustees shall call a meeting of the committee of inspection once at least every three months, when they shall audit his accounts, and determine whether any or what dividends to be paid; he may also call special meetings of the said committee as he thinks necessary.

Subject to the provisions of this act, and to such direction as aforesaid, the trustee shall exercise his own discretion in the management of the estate, and its distribution amongst the creditors. The trustee may from time to time summon general meetings of the creditors, for the purpose of ascertaining their wishes ; he may also apply to the court, in manner prescribed, for directions in relation to any particular matter arising under the bankruptcy.

The bankrupt, or any creditor, debtor, or other person aggrieved by any act of the trustee, may apply to the court, and the court may confirm, reverse, or modify the act complained of, and make such order in the premises as it thinks just. The court may from time to time, during the continuance of a bankruptcy, summon general meetings of the creditors for the purpose of ascertaining their wishes, and may, if the court thinks fit, direct the register to preside at such meetings.

The trustee shall, in relation to and for the purpose of acquiring or retaining possession of the property of the bankrupt, be in the same position in all respects as if he were a receiver of such property appointed by the court of chancery, and the court may ¬ his application, enforce such acquisition or retention of property accordingly .

21. The provisions of this act with respect to the first general meeting of creditors, shall apply to any subsequent meeting of creditors in a bankruptcy, with this exception, that the subsequent meetings of creditors may be summoned by the trustee, or by a member of the committee of inspection, and that such meetings may, unless otherwise directed by the court in the case of meetings summoned by the court, be presided over by any person chosen by the creditors assembled at such meeting, and that any creditor whose debt has been proved, or the value of whose debt has been ascertained at or subsequently to such first meeting, shall be allowed to be present and to vote thereat.

Dealings with Bankrupt's Property.

22. Where any portion of the property of the bankrupt consists of stock, shares in ships, shares, or any other property transferable in the books of any company, office, or person, the right to transfer such property shall be absolutely vested in the trustee to the same extent as the bankrupt might have exercised the same if he had not become bankrupt. Where any portion of such estate consists of copyhold or customary property, or any like property passing by surrender and admittance or in any similar manner, the trustee shall not be compellable to be admitted to such property, but may deal with the same in the same manner as if such property had been capable of being and had been duly surrendered or otherwise conveyed to such uses as the trustee may appoint; and any appointee of the trustee shall be admitted or otherwise invested with the property accordingly.

Where any portion of the property of the bankrupt consists of things in action, any action, suit, or other proceedings for the recovery of such things instituted by the trustee shall be instituted in his official name, as in this act provided ; and such thing shall, for the purpose of such action, suit, or other proceeding, be deemed to be assignable in law, and to have been duly assigned to the trustee in his official capacity.

The trustee shall, as soon as may be, take possession of the deeds, books, and documents of the bankrupt, and all other property capable of manual delivery, the trustee shall keep, in such manner as rules of court shall direct, proper books, in which he shall from time to time make or cause to be made entries or minutes of proceedings at meetings, and of such other matters as rules of court shall direct, and any creditor of the bankrupt may, subject to the control of the court, personally or by his agent inspect such books.

23. When any property of the bankrupt acquired by the trustee under this act consists of land of any tenure burdened with onerous covenants, or unmarketable share in companies, of unprofitable contracts, or of any other property that is unsaleable, or not readily saleable, by reason of its binding the possessor thereof to the performance of any onerous act, or to the payment of any sum of money, the trustee, notwithstanding he has endeavored to sell, or has taken possession of such property or exercised any act of ownership in relation thereto may by writing under his hand, disclaim such property, and upon the execution of such disclaimer the property disclaimed shall, if the same is a contract, be deemed to be determined from the date of the order of adjudication, and if the same is a lease be deemed to have been surrendered on the same date, and if the

same be shares in any company be deemed to be forfeited from that date, and if any other species of property it shall revert to the person entitled to the determination of the estate or interest of the bankrupt, but if there be no person in existence so entitled, then in no case shall any estate or interest therein remain in the bankrupt. Any person interested in any disclaimed property may apply to the court, and the court may, upon such application, order possession of the disclaimed property to be delivered up to him, or make such other order as to the possession thereof as may be just.

Any person injured by the operation of this section shall be deemed a creditor of the bankrupt to the extent of such injury, and may accordingly prove the same as a debt under the bankruptcy.

24. The trustees shall not be entitled to disclaim any property in pursuance of this act in cases where an application in writing has been made to him by any person interested in such property, requiring such trustee to decide whether he will disclaim or not, and the trustee has for a period of not less than twenty-eight days after the receipt of such application or such further time as may be allowed by the court declined or neglected to give notice whether he disclaims the same or not.

25. Subject to the provisions of this act, the trustee shall have power to do the following things:

(1.) To receive and decide upon proof of debts in the prescribed manner, and for such purpose to administer oaths:

(2.) To carry on the business of the bankrupt so far as may be necessary for the beneficial winding up of the same:

(3.) To bring or defend any action, suit or other legal proceeding relating to the property of the bankrupt:

(4.) To deal with any property, which the bankrupt is beneficially entitled as tenant in tail in the same manner as the bankrupt might have dealt with the same; and the sections fifty-six to seventy-three (both inclusive) of the act of the session of the third and fourth years of the reign of King William the Fourth (chapter seventy-four), "for the abolition of fines and recoveries, and for the substitution of more simple

modes of assurance," shall extend and apply to proceedings in bankruptcy under this act as if those sections were here re-enacted and made applicable in terms to such proceedings:

(5.) To exercise any powers the capacity to exercise which is vested in him under this act, and to execute all powers of attorney deeds and other instruments expedient or necessary for the purpose of carrying into effect the provisions of this act:

(6.) To sell all the property of the bankrupt (including the good will of the business, if any, and the book debts due or growing due to the bankrupt) by public auction or private contract, with power, if he thinks fit, to transfer the whole thereof to any person or company or to sell the same in parcels:

(7.) To give receipts for any money received by him, which receipt shall effectually discharge the person paying such moneys from all responsibility in respect of the application thereof:

(8.) To prove rank, claim and draw a dividend in the matter of the bankruptcy or sequestration of any debtor of the bankrupt:

26. The trustees may appoint the bankrupt himself to superintend the management of the property or of any part thereof, or to carry on the trade of the bankrupt (if any) for the benefit of the creditors, and in any other respect to aid in administering the property in such manner and on such terms as the creditors direct.

27. The trustee may, with the sanction of the committee of inspection, do all or any of the following things:

(1.) Mortgage or pledge any part of the property of the bankrupt for the purpose of raising money for the payment of his debts:

(2.) Refer any dispute to arbitration, compromise all debts, claims and liabilities, whether present or future, certain or contingent, liquidated or unliquidated, subsisting or supposed to subsist between the bankrupt and any debtor or person who may have incurred any liability to the bankrupt, upon the receipt of such sums, payable at such times and generally upon such terms as may be agreed upon:

(3.) Make such compromise or other arrangement as may be thought expedient with creditors, or persons claiming to be creditors in respect of any debts provable under the bankruptcy:

(4.) Make such compromise or other arrangement as may be thought expedient with respect to any claim arising out of or incidental to the property of the bankrupt, made or capable of being made on the trustee by any person or by the trustee on any person:

(5.) To divide in its existing form amongst the creditors, according to its estimated value, any property which from its peculiar nature or other special circumstances cannot advantageously be realized by sale.

The sanction given for the purpose of this section may be a general permission to to do all or any of the above-mentioned things, or a permission to do all or any of them in any specified case or cases.

28. The trustee may, with the sanction of a special resolution of the creditors assembled at any meeting of which notice has been given specifying the object of such meeting, accept any composition offered by the bankrupt, or assent to any general scheme of settlement of the affairs of the bankrupt upon such terms as may be thought expedient, and with or without a condition that the order of adjudication is to be annulled, subject nevertheless to the approval of the court, to be testified by the judge of the court signing the instrument containing the terms of such composition or scheme, or embodying such terms in an order of the court.

Where the annulling the order of adjudication is made a condition of any composition with the bankrupt or of any general scheme for the liquidation of his affairs, the court, if it approves of such composition or general scheme, shall annul the adjudicacation on an application made by or on behalf of any person interested, and the adjudication shall be annulled from and after the date of the order annulling the same.

The provisions of any composition or general scheme made in pursuance of this act may be enforced by the court on a motion made in a summary manner by any person interested, and any disobedience of the order of the court made on such motion shall be deemed to be a contempt of court. The approval of the court shall be conclusive as to the validity of any such composition or scheme, and it shall be binding on all the creditors so far as relates to any debts due to them and provable under the bankruptcy.

29. A trustee shall not, without the consent of the committee of inspection, employ a solicitor or other agent, but where the trustee is himself a solicitor he may contract to be paid a certain sum by way of percentage or otherwise as a remuneration for his services as trustee, including all professioual services, and any such contract shall, notwithstanding any law to the contrary, be lawful.

30. The trustee shall pay all sums from time to time received by him into such bank as the majority of the creditors in number and value at any general meeting shall appoint, and failing in such appointment into the bank of England; and if he at any time keep in his hands any sum exceeding fifty pounds for more than ten days he shall be subject to the following liabilities; that is to say,

(1.) He shall pay interest at the rate of twenty pounds per centum per annum on the excess of such sum above fifty pounds as he may retain in his hands.

(2.) Unless he can prove to the satisfaction of the court that his reason for retaining the money was sufficient, he shall, on the application of any creditor, be dismissed from his office by the court, and shall have no claim for remuneration, and be liable to any expenses to which the creditors may be put by or in consequence of his dismissal.

Payment of Debts and Distribution of Assets.

31. Demands in the nature of unliquidated damages arising otherwise than by reason of a contract or promise shall not be provable in bankruptcy, and no person having notice of any act of bankruptcy available for adjudication against the bankrupt shall prove for any debt or liability contracted by the bankrupt subsequently to the date of his so having notice.

Save as aforesaid, all debts and liabilities, present or future, certain or contingent, to which the bankrupt is subject at the date of the order of adjudication, or to which he may become subject during the continuance of the bankruptcy by reason of any obligation incurred previously to the date of the order of adjudication, shall be deemed to be debts provable in bankruptcy, and may be proved in the prescribed manner before the trustee in the bankruptcy.

An estimate shall be made according to the rules of the court for the time being in force, so far as the same may be applicable, and where they are not applicable at the discretion of the trustee, of the value of any debt or liability provable as aforesaid, which by reason of its being subject to any contingency or contingencies, or for any other reason, does not bear a certain value.

Any person aggrieved by any estimate made by the trustee as aforesaid may appeal to the court, and the court may, if it think the value of the debt or liability incapable of being fairly estimated, make an order to that effect, and upon such order being made such debt or liability shall for the purposes of this act, be deemed to be a debt not provable in bankruptcy, but if the court think that the value of the debt or liability is capable of being fairly estimated it may direct such value to be assessed with the consent of all the parties interested before the court itself without the intervention of a jury, or if such parties do not consent by a jury, either before the court itself or some other competent court, and may give all necessary directions for such purpose, and the amount of such value when assessed shall be provable as a debt under the bankruptcy.

"Liability" shall for the purposes of this act include any compensation for work or labor done, any obligation or possibility of an obligation to pay money or money's worth on the breach of any express or implied covenant, contract, agreement, or undertaking, whether such breach does or does not occur, or is or is not likely to occur or capable of occuring before the close of the bankruptcy, and generally it shall include any express or implied engagement, agreement, or undertaking, to pay, or capable of resulting in the payment of money or money's worth, whether such payment be as respects amount fixed or unliquidated ; as respects time present or future, certain or dependent on any one contingency or on two or more contin-

gencies ; or to mode of valuation capable of being ascertained by fixed rules, or assessable only by a jury, or as matter of opinion.

32. The debts hereinafter mentioned shall be paid in priority to all other debts. Between themselves such debts shall rank equally, and shall be paid in full, unless the property of the bankrupt is insufficient to meet them, in which case they shall abate in equal proportions between themselves ; that is to say.

(1.) All parochial or other local rates due from him at the date of the order of adjudication, and having become due and payable within twelve months next before such time, all assessed taxes, land tax, and property or income tax assessed on him up to the fifth day of April next before the date of the order of adjudication, and not exceeding in the whole one year's assessment ;

(2.) All wages or salary of any clerk or servant in the employment of the bankrupt at the date of the order of adjudication, not exceeding four months' wages or salary, and not exceeding fifty pounds ; all wages of any laborer or workman in the employment of the bankrupt at the date of the order of adjudication, and not exceeding two months wages ;

Save as aforesaid, all debts provable under the bankruptcy shall be paid *pari passu.*

33. Where at the time of the presentation of the petition for adjudication any person is apprenticed or is an articled clerk to the bankrupt, the order of adjudication shall, if either the bankrupt or apprentice or clerk give notice in writing to the trustee to that effect, be a complete discharge of the indenture of apprenticeship or articles of agreement ; and if any money has been paid by or on behalf of such apprentice or clerk to the bankrupt as a fee, the trustee may, on the application of the apprentice or clerk or of some person on his behalf, pay such sum as such trustee, subject to an appeal to the court, thinks reasonable, out of the bankrupt's property, to or for the use of the apprentice or clerk, regard being had to the amount paid by him or on his behalf, and to the time during which he served with the bankrupt under the indenture or articles before the commencement of the bankruptcy, and to the other circumstances of the case.

Where it appears expedient to a trustee,

he may, on the application of any apprentice or articled clerk to the bankrupt; or any person acting on behalf of such apprentice or articled clerk, instead of acting under the preceding provisions of this section, transfer the indenture of apprenticeship or articles of agreement to some other person.

34. The landlord or other person to whom any rent is due from the bankrupt may at any time, either before or after the commencement of the bankruptcy, distrain upon the goods or effects of the bankrupt for the rent due to him from the bankrupt, with this limitation, that if such distress for rent be levied after the commencement of the bankruptcy, it shall be available only for one year's rent accrued due prior to the date of the order of adjudication, but the landlord or other person to whom the rent may be due from the bankrupt may prove under the bankruptcy for the overplus due for which the distress may not have been available.

35. When any rent or other payment falls due at stated periods, and the order of adjudication is made at any time other than one of such periods, the person entitled to such rent or payment may prove for a proportionate part thereof up to the day of the adjudication as if such rent or payment grew due from day to day.

36. Interest on any debt provable in bankruptcy may be allowed by the trustee under the same circumstances in which interest would have been allowable by a jury if an action had been brought for such debt.

37. If any bankrupt is at the date of the order of adjudication liable in respect of distinct contracts as member of two or more distinct firms, or as a sole contractor, and also as member of a firm, the circumstance that such firms are in whole or in part composed of the same individuals, or that the sole contractor is also one of the joint contractors, shall not prevent proof in respect of such contracts against the properties respectively liable upon such contracts.

38. The trustee, with the consent of the creditors, testified by a resolution passed in general meeting, may from time time, during the continuance of the bankruptcy, make such allowance as may be approved by the creditors to the bankrupt out of his property for the support of the bankrupt and his family, or in consideration of his services if he is engaged in winding up his estate.

39. Where there have been mutual credits, mutual debts, or other mutual dealings between the bankrupt and any other person proving or claiming to prove a debt under his bankruptcy, an account shall be taken of what is due from the one party to the other in respect of such mutual dealings, and the sum due from the one party shall be set off against any sum due from the other party, and the balance of such account, and no more, shall be claimed or paid on either side respectively ; but a person shall not be entitled under this section to claim the benefit of any set-off against the property of a bankrupt in any case where he had, at the time of giving credit to the bankrupt, notice of an act of bankruptcy committed by such bankrupt and available against him for adjudication.

40. A creditor holding a specific security on the property of the bankrupt, or on any part thereof, may on giving up his security, prove for his whole debt.

He shall also be entitled to a dividend in respect of the balance due to him after realizing or giving credit for the value of his security, in manner and at the time prescribed.

A creditor holding such security as aforesaid and not complying with the foregoing conditions shall be excluded from all share in any dividend.

Dividends.

41. The trustee shall from time to time, when the committee of inspection determines, declare a dividend amongst the creditors who have proved to his satisfaction debts provable in bankruptcy, and shall distribute the same accordingly ; and in the event of his not declaring a dividend for the space of six months, he shall summon a meeting of the creditors, and explain to them his reasons for not declaring the same.

42. In the calculation and distribution of a dividend it shall be obligatory on the trustee to make provision for debts provable in bankruptcy appearing from the bankrupt's statements, or otherwise, to be due to persons resident in places so distant from the place where the trustee is acting that in the ordinary course of communication they have not had sufficient time to tender their proofs, or to establish them if disputed, and also for debts provable in bankruptcy, the subject of claims not yet determined.

43. Any creditor who has not proved his debt before the declaration of any dividend or dividends shall be entitled to be paid out of any monies for the time being in the hand of the trustee any dividend or dividends he may have failed to receive before such monies are made applicable to the payment of any future dividend or dividends, but he shall not be entitled to disturb the distribution of any dividend declared before his debt was proved by reason that he has not participated therein.

44. When the trustee has converted into money all the property of the bankrupt, or so much thereof as can, in the joint opinion of himself and of the committee of inspection, be realized without needlessly protracting the bankruptcy, he shall declare a final dividend, and give notice of the time at which it will be distributed.

45. The bankrupt shall be entitled to any surplus remaining after payment of his creditors, and of the costs, charges, and expenses of the bankruptcy.

46. No action or suit for dividend shall lie against the trustee, but if the trustee refuses to pay any dividend the court may, if it thinks fit, order the trustee to pay the same, and also to pay out of his own monies interest thereon for the time that it is withheld, and the costs of the application.

Close of Bankruptcy.

47. When the whole property of the bankrupt has been realized for the benefit of his creditors, or so much thereof as can, in the joint opinion of the trustee and committee of inspection, be realized without needlessly protracting the bankruptcy, or a composition or arrangement has been completed, the trustee shall make a report accordingly to the court, and the court, if satisfied that the whole of the property of the bankrupt has been realized for the benefit of his creditors, or so much thereof as can be realized without needlessly protracting the bankruptcy, or that a composition or arrangement has been completed, shall make an order that the bankruptcy has closed, and the bankruptcy shall be deemed to have closed at and after the date of such order.

A copy of the order closing the bankruptcy may be published in the *London Gazette*, and the production of a copy of such gazette containing a copy of the order shall be conclusive evidence of the order having been made and of the date and contents thereof.

Discharge of Bankruptcy.

48. When a bankruptcy is closed, or at any time during its continuance, with the assent of the creditors testified by a special resolution, the bankrupt may apply to the court for an order of discharge ; but such discharge shall not be granted unless it is proved to the court that one of the following conditions has been fulfilled, that is to say, either that a dividend of not less than ten shillings in the pound has been paid out of his property, or might have been paid except through the negligence or fraud of the trustee, or that a special resolution of his creditors has been passed to the effect that his bankruptcy or the failure to pay ten shillings in the pound has, in their opinion, arisen from circumstances for which the bankrupt cannot justly be held responsible, and that they desire that an order of discharge should be granted to him ; and that the court may suspend for such time as it deems to be just, or withhold altogether, the order of discharge in the circumstances following : namely, if it appears to the court on the representation of the creditors made by special resolution, of the truth of which representation the court is satisfied, or by other sufficient evidence, that the bankrupt has made default in giving up to his creditors the property which he is required by this act to give up; or that a prosecution has been commenced against him in pursuance of the provisions relating to the punishment of fraudulent debtors, contained in the "Debtors' Act of 1869," in respect of any offence alleged to have been committed by him against the said act.

49. An order of discharge shall not release the bankrupt from any debt or liability incurred by means of any fraud or breach of trust, nor from any debt or liability whereof he has obtained forbearance by any fraud, but it shall release the bankrupt from all other debts provable under the bankruptcy, with the exception of —
(1.) Debts due to the crown :
(2.) Debts with which the bankrupt stands charged at the suit of the crown or of any person for any offence against a statute relating to any branch of the

public revenue, or at the suit of the sheriff or other public officer on a bail bond entered into for the appearance of any person prosecuted for any such offence :

And he shall not be discharged from such excepted debts unless the commissioners of the treasury certify in writing their consent to his being discharged therefrom.

An order of discharge shall be sufficient evidence of the bankruptcy, and of the validity of the proceedings thereon, and in any proceedings that may be instituted against a bankrupt who has obtained an order of discharge in respect of any debt from which he is released by such order, the bankrupt may plead that the cause of action occurred before his discharge, and may give this act and the special matter in evidence.

50. The order of discharge shall not release any person who, at the date of the order of adjudication, was a partner with the bankrupt, or was jointly bound or had made any joint contract with him.

Release of Trustee.

51. When the bankruptcy is closed the trustee shall call a meeting of the creditors to consider an application to be made to the court for his release. At the meeting the trustee shall lay before the assembled creditors an account showing the manner in which the bankruptcy has been conducted, with a list of the unclaimed dividends if any, and of the property, if any, outstanding, and shall inform the· meeting that he proposes to apply to the court for release.

The creditors assembled at the meeting may express their opinion as to the conduct of the trustee, and they, or any of them, may appear before the court and oppose the release of the trustee.

The court, after hearing what, if anything, can be urged against the release of the trustee, shall grant or withhold the release accordingly, and if it withhold the release shall make such order as it thinks just, charging the trustee with the consequences of any act or default he may have done or made contrary to his duty, and shall suspend his release until such charging order has been complied with, and the court thinks just· to grant the release of the trustee.

52. Unclaimed dividends, and any other moneys arising from the property of the bankrupt, remaining under the control of the trustee at the close of the bankruptcy of any bankrupt, or accruing thereafter, shall be accounted and paid over to such account as may be directed by the rules of the court to be made with the sanction of the treasury ; and any parties entitled thereto may claim the same in manner directed by such rules. The trustee shall also deliver a list of any outstanding property of the bankrupt to the prescribed persons, and the same shall, when practicable, be got in and applied for the benefit of the creditors in the manner prescribed.

53. The order of the court releasing the trustee of a bankruptcy shall discharge him from all liability in respect of any act done or default made by him in the administration of the affairs of the bankrupt, or otherwise in relation to his conduct as trustee of such bankrupt; but such order may be revoked by the court on proof that it was obtained by fraud.

Status of Undischarged Bankrupt.

54. Where a person who has been made bankrupt who has not obtained his discharge, then, from and after the close of his bankruptcy, the following consequences shall ensue :

(1.) No portion of a debt provable under the bankruptcy shall be enforced against the property of the person so made bankrupt until the expiration of three years from the close of the bankruptcy : and during that time, if he pay to his creditors such additional sum as will, with the dividend paid out of his property during the bankruptcy, make up ten shillings in the pound, he shall be entitled to an order of discharge in the same manner as if a dividend of ten shillings in the pound had originally been paid out of his property ;

(2.) At the expiration of a period of three years from the close of the bankruptcy, if the debtor made bankrupt has not obtained an order of discharge, any balance remaining unpaid in respect of any debt proved in such bankruptcy (but without interest in the meantime) shall be deemed to be a subsisting debt in the nature of a judgment debt, and subject to the rights of any persons who have become creditors of the debtor since the close of his bankruptcy, may be enforced against any property of the debtor, with the sanction of the court which adjudicated such debtor a bankrupt, or of the court having jurisdiction in bankruptcy in the place where the property is situated, but to the extent only, and at the time and in manner directed by such court, and after giving such notice and doing such acts as may be prescribed in that behalf.

Audit.

55. The trustee having had his quarterly statements of accounts audited by the committee of inspection, shall, within the prescribed time, forward the certified statement in the prescribed form to an officer to be called the comptroller in bankruptcy, and if he fail to do so he shall be deemed guilty of a contempt of court to be punishable accordingly. The first and any subsequent comptroller shall be appointed by the lord chancellor, and hold office during his pleasure, and shall be paid such salary as the lord chancellor may, with the sanction of the treasury, direct. The comptroller shall be provided with such office in London, and with such officers, clerks and servants, as may be directed by the lord chancellor, with the approval of the treasury. The officers, clerks and servants in the office of the comptroller shall be appointed and dismissible by the comptroller, and there shall be allowed and paid to him such sum as the treasury may from time to time direct for the expenses of his office, and of such clerks and other persons as may be deemed necessary by the treasury.

56. Every trustee of a bankrupt shall from time to time, as may be prescribed, and not less than once in every year during the bankruptcy, transmit to the comptroller a statement showing the proceedings in such bankruptcy up to the date of the statement containing the prescribed particulars, and made out in the prescribed form; and any trustee failing to transmit accounts in compliance with this section shall be deemed guilty of a contempt of court, and be punishable accordingly.

57. The comptroller shall examine the statements transmitted to him, and shall call the trustee to account for any misfeasance, neglect, or omission which may appear on such statements, and may require the trustee to make good any loss the estate of the bankrupt may have sustained by such misfeasance, neglect, or omission. If the trustee fail to comply with such requisition of the comptroller, the comptroller may report the same to the court; and the court, after hearing the explanation, if any, of the trustee, shall make such order in the premises as it thinks just.

58. The comptroller may at any time require any trustee to answer any inquiry made by him in relation to any bankruptcy in which such trustee is engaged, and may, if he think fit, apply to the court to examine on oath such trustee or any other person concerning such bankruptcy; he may also direct a local investigation to be made of the books and vouchers of the trustees.

PART III.

CONSTITUTION AND POWERS OF COURT.

Description of Court.

59. From and after the commencement of this act the following provisions shall take effect with respect to the courts having jurisdiction in bankruptcy, and their officers; that is to say:

If the person sought to be adjudged a bankrupt reside or carry on business within the London bankruptcy district as hereinafter defined, or be not resident in England, then "the court" shall mean, for the purposes of this act, the court of bankruptcy in London as constituted by this act, and hereinafter referred to as the London bankruptcy court.

If the person sought to be adjudged a bankrupt, being resident in England, do not reside or carry on business within the London bankruptcy district, then "the court" shall, subject to the provisions hereinafter contained for removing the proceedings, mean the county court of the district in which such person resides or carries on business, hereinafter referred to as the local bankruptcy court.

60. The London bankruptcy district shall, for the purposes of this act, comprise the following places, that is to say, the city of London and the liberties thereof, and all

such parts of the metropolis and other places as are situated within the district of any county court described as a metropolitan county court in the list contained in the second schedule hereto.

61. The London bankruptcy court shall, from and after the commencement of this act, consist of a judge, to be called the chief judge in bankruptcy, and, subject to the provisions of this act with respect to the officers of the existing London bankruptcy court, of such number of registrars not exceeding four, clerks, ushers, and other subordinate officers, as may be determined by the chief judge with the sanction of the treasury.

Subject to the provisions of this act with respect to the appointment of the first chief judge, the office of chief judge in bankruptcy shall be filled by such one of the judges of her majesty's superior courts of common law of equity as may, with his assent, be assigned to hold such office by the lord chancellor; the judge so assigned shall hold the office of chief judge in bankruptcy in addition to the office of judge in the court to which he belongs. Any puisne judge or vice-chancellor appointed to any of the said courts after the passing of this act shall, when required by the lord chancellor, perform the duties of chief judge in bankruptcy.

62. Subject to the provisions in this act with respect to the officers of the existing London bankruptcy court, the registrars, clerks, ushers, and other subordinate officers thereof, shall be appointed by the chief judge for the time being, and may be removed by him and others appointed in their stead if the judge is of opinion that they are negligent, unskilful, untrustworthy in the performance of their duties, or ought in his opinion be removed for any other just cause.

63. Subject as aforesaid, there shall be paid, out of moneys provided by parliament, to the registrars, clerks, ushers, and other subordinate officers such salaries as the chief judge with the sanction of the treasury may determine.

64. Subject as aforesaid, the registrars, clerks, ushers, and other subordinate officers of the London bankruptcy court shall perform such duties as may from time to time be assigned to them by the chief judge with the assent of the lord chancellor.

65. The London court of bankruptcy shall continue to be a court of law and of equity and a principal court of record, and the chief judge in bankruptcy shall have all the powers, jurisdiction, and privileges possessed by any judge of her majesty's superior courts of common law at Westminster, or by any judge of her majesty's high court of chancery, and the orders of such judge shall be of the same force as if they were judgments in the superior courts of common law or decrees in the high court of chancery. The chief judge in bankruptcy may sit in chambers, and when in chambers shall have the same jurisdiction and exercise the same powers as if sitting in open court.

66. Every judge of a local court of bankruptcy shall, for the purpose of this act, in addition to his ordinary powers as a county court judge, have all the power and jurisdiction of a judge of her majesty's high court of chancery, and the orders of such judge may be enforced accordingly in manner prescribed.

67. The chief judge in bankruptcy and every judge of a local court of bankruptcy may, subject and in accordance with the rules of the court of the time being in force, delegate to the registrar or any other officer of his court such of the powers vested in him by this act as it may be expedient for the judge to delegate to him.

68. The lord chancellor shall, with the sanction of the treasury, from time to time prescribe a scale of fees to be charged for any business done by any court or officer thereof under this act; and the treasury shall direct whether the same shall be imposed by stamps or otherwise, and by whom and in what manner the same shall be collected, accounted for and appropriated, and whether any and what remuneration shall be allowed to any person performing any duties under this act.

69. No judge, registrar or officer having jurisdiction in bankruptcy, or attached to any court having jurisdiction in bankruptcy, shall, during his continuance in office, be capable of being elected or sitting as a member of the house of commons; and no registrar or officer of such court shall, during his continuance in office, either directly or indirectly, by himself or partner, act as an attorney or solicitor in any proceeding in any bankruptcy in any court of which he is registrar or officer, or in any appeal from

such court, or in any prosecution of a bankrupt by order of such court, under pain of dismissal by the judge; and such dismissal shall be in writing, stating the reasons for the same; and a copy thereof shall be sent to the chief judge in bankruptcy, who, if he shall see fit, may reinstate such registrar or officer.

70. Every attorney and solicitor of the superior courts shall be, and may practice as a solicitor of, and in the court of bankruptcy, and in matters before the chief judge or registrars, in the London court of bankruptcy, in court or in chambers, may appear and be heard without being required to employ counsel; and if any person not being such attorney or solicitor practices in the court of bankruptcy as attorney or solicitor, he shall be deemed guilty of a contempt of the court.

71. Every court having jurisdiction in bankruptcy under this act may review, rescind, or vary any order made by it in pursuance of this act. Any person aggrieved by any order of a local bankruptcy court in respect of a matter of fact or of law made in pursuance of this act may appeal to the chief judge in bankruptcy, and it shall be lawful for such judge to alter, reverse, or confirm such order as he thinks just. Any order made by the chief judge in bankruptcy, whether in respect of a matter brought before him on appeal or not, shall be subject to an appeal to the court of appeal in chancery (which court, for the purposes of this act, shall be and form a court of record, and shall have all the jurisdiction, powers, and authorities of the court of bankruptcy, to be exercisable either originally or on appeal, and shall have all the powers and authorities of the court of chancery relative to the trial of questions of fact, by jury, issue, or otherwise), and also, with the leave of the court of appeal, to the house of lords, but no appeal shall be entertained under this act except in conformity to such rules of court as may for the time being be in force in relation to such appeal.

72. Subject to the provisions of this act, every court having jurisdiction in bankruptcy under this act shall have full power to decide all questions of priorities, and all other questions whatsoever, whether of law or fact, arising in any case of bankruptcy coming within the cognizance of such court, or which the court may deem it expedient or necessary to decide for the purpose of doing complete justice or making a complete distribution of property in any such case; and no such court as aforesaid shall be subject to be restrained in the execution of its powers under this act by the order of any other court, nor shall any appeal lie from its decisions, except in manner directed by this act; and if in any proceedings in bankruptcy there arises any question of fact which the parties desire to be tried before a jury instead of by the court itself, or which the court thinks ought to be tried by a jury, the court may direct such trial to be had, and such trial may be had accordingly, in the London court of bankruptcy, in the same manner as if it were the trial of an issue in one of the superior courts of common law, and in the county court in the manner in which jury trials in ordinary cases are by law held in such court.

Orders and Warrants of Court.

73. Any order made by a court having jurisdiction in bankruptcy in England under this act shall be enforced in Scotland and Ireland in the courts having jurisdiction in bankruptcy in such countries respectively, in the same manner in all respects as if such order had been made by the courts which are hereby required to enforce the same; and in like manner any order made by the court in Scotland having jurisdiction in bankruptcy shall be enforced in England and Ireland, and any order made by the court having jurisdiction in bankruptcy in Ireland shall be enforced in England and Scotland by the courts respectively having jurisdiction in bankruptcy in the division of the United Kingdom where the orders made require to be enforced, and in the same manner in all respects as if such order had been made by the court required to enforce the same in a case of bankruptcy within its own jurisdiction.

74. The London bankruptcy court, the local bankruptcy court, the courts having jurisdiction in bankruptcy in Scotland and Ireland, and every British court elsewhere having jurisdiction in bankruptcy or insolvency, and the officers of such courts respectively, shall severally act in aid of and be auxiliary to each other in all matters of bankruptcy, and an order of the court seeking aid, together with a request to another

of the said courts, shall be deemed sufficient to enable the latter court to exercise, in regard to the matters directed by such order, the like jurisdiction which the court which made the request, as well as the court to which the request is made, could exercise in regard to similar matters within their respective jurisdictions.

75. Any court having jurisdiction in bankruptcy in England under this act may, if it think fit, order that a person named in the order, being in Scotland or in Ireland, shall be examined there.

76. Any warrant of a court having jurisdiction in bankruptcy in England under this act may be enforced in Scotland, Ireland, the Isle of Man, the Channel Islands, and elsewhere in her majesty's dominions, in the same manner and subject to the same privileges in and subject to which a warrant issued by any justice of the peace against a person for any indictable offence against the laws of England may be executed in such countries respectively, in pursuance of the acts of parliament in that behalf; and any search-warrant issued by a court having jurisdiction in bankruptcy under this act for the discovery of any property of a bankrupt may be executed in manner prescribed, or in the same manner and subject to the same privileges in and subject to which a search-warrant for property supposed to be stolen may be executed according to law.

77. Where any court having jurisdiction in bankruptcy under this act commits any person to prison, the commitment may be to such convenient prison as the court thinks expedient; and if the jailor of any prison refuses to receive any prisoner so committed, he shall be liable, for every such refusal, to a penalty not exceeding one hundred pounds.

General Rules.

78. The lord chancellor, with the advice of the chief judge in bankrupty, may, from time to time, make, and may, from time to time, revoke and alter, general rules, in this act described as rules of court, for the effectual execution of this act, and of the objects thereof, and the regulation of the practice and procedure of bankruptcy petitions, and the proceedings thereon.

Any general rules made as aforesaid may prescribe regulations as to the service of bankruptcy petitions, including provisions for substituted service; as to the valuing of any debts provable in bankruptcy; as to the valuation of securities held by creditors; as to the giving or withholding interest or discount on or in respect of debts or dividends; as to the funds out of which costs are to be paid, the order of payment, and the amount and taxation thereof; and as to any other matter or thing, whether similar or not to those above enumerated, in respect to which it may be expedient to make rules for carrying into effect the objects of this act; and any rules so made shall be deemed to be within the powers conferred by this act, and shall be of the same force as if they were enacted in the body of this act.

Any rules made in pursuance of the section shall be laid before parliament within three weeks after they are made, if parliament be then sitting; and if parliament be not then sitting, within three weeks after the beginning of the then next session of parliament, and any rules so made shall be judicially noticed.

Until rules have been made in pursuance of this act, and so far as such rules do not extend, the principles, practice, and rules on which courts having jurisdiction in bankruptcy have heretofore acted in dealing with bankruptcy proceedings shall be observed by any court having jurisdiction in bankruptcy cases under this act.

Change of Jurisdiction by Chancellor.

79. Notwithstanding anything in this act contained, the lord chancellor may, from time to time, by order under his hand, exclude any county court from having jurisdiction in bankruptcy, and, for the purposes of bankruptcy jurisdiction, may attach its district or any part thereof to any other county court or courts, and may from time to time revoke or alter any order so made.

PART IV.
SUPPLEMENTAL PROVISIONS.
As to Proceedings.

80. The following regulations shall be made with respect to proceedings in bankruptcy, namely:

(1.) Every bankruptcy petition shall be ac-companied by an affidavit of the peti-tioner in the prescribed form, verifying the statements contained in such peti-tion :

(2.) Where two or more bankruptcy peti-tions are presented against the same debtor or against debtors being mem-bers of the same partnership, the court may consolidate the proceedings, or any of them, upon such terms as the court thinks fit :

(3.) Where proceedings against the debtor are instituted in more courts than one, the London court of bankruptcy may, on the application of any creditor, di-rect the transfer of such proceedings to the London court of bankruptcy, or to any local bankruptcy court :

(4.) Where the petition does not proceed with due diligence on his petition the court may substitute as petitioner any other creditor to whom the debtor may be indebted in the amount required by this act in the case of a petitioning creditor :

(5.) Where the creditors resolve by a special resolution that it will be more conveni-ent that the proceedings in any local bankruptcy court should be transferred to the London court or to some other local court, or where the judge of a local court certifies that in his opinion the bankruptcy would be more advantage-ously conducted in the London court or in some other local court, and the cred-itors do not by resolution object to the transfer, the petition shall be transferred to and all subsequent proceedings there-on hand the London court or such other local court :

(6.) Subject to the provisions of this act, every court having original jurisdiction in bankruptcy shall be deemed to be the same court, and to have jurisdiction thoughout England ; and cases may be transferred from one court to another in such manner as may be prescribed :

(7.) A corporation may prove a debt, vote, and otherwise act in bankruptcy, by an agent duly authorized under the seal of the corporation :

(8.) A creditor may, in the prescribed man-ner by instrument in writing, appoint a person to represent him in all matters relating to any debtor or his affairs in which a creditor is concerned in pursu-ance of this act, and such representa-tive shall thereupon, for all the purposes of this act, stand in the same position as the creditor who appointed him :

(9.) When a debtor who has been adjudi-cated a bankrupt dies, the court may order that the proceedings in the matter be continued as if he were alive :

(10.) The court may, at any time, on proof to its satisfaction that proceedings in bankruptcy ought to be stayed, by rea-son that negotiations are pending for the liquidation of the affairs of the bank-rupt by arrangement or for the accept-ance of a composition by the creditors in pursuance of the provisions herein-after contained, or on proof to its sat-isfaction of any other sufficient reason for staying the same, make an order staying the same, either altogether or for a limited time, on such terms and subject to such conditions as the court may think just.

81. Whenever any adjudication in bank-ruptcy is annulled all sales and dispositions of property and payments duly made, and all acts theretofore done, by the trustee or any person acting under his authority, or by the court, shall be valid, but the property of the debtor who was adjudged a bankrupt shall in such case vest in such person as the court may appoint, or in default of any such ap-pointment revert to the bankrupt for all his estate or interest therein upon such terms and subject to such conditions, if any, as the court may declare by order. A copy of the order of the court annulling the adjudi-cation of a debtor as a bankrupt shall be forthwith published in the *London Gazette*, and advertised locally in the prescribed manner, and the production of a copy of the *Gazette* containing such order shall be con-clusive evidence of the fact of the adjudica-tion having been annulled, and of the terms of the order annulling the same.

62. No proceeding in bankruptcy shall be invalidated by any formal defect or by any irregularity, unless the court before which an objection is made to such proceeding is of opinion that substantial injustice has been caused by such defect or irregularity, and that such injustice cannot be remedied by any order of such court.

As to Trustees and Committee of Inspection.

83. The following regulations shall be made with respect to the trustee and committee of inspection:

(1.) The creditors may, if they think fit, appoint more persons than one to the office of trustee, and where more than one are appointed they shall declare whether any act required or authorised to be done by the trustee is to be done by all or any one or more of such persons, but all such persons are in this act included under the term "trustee," and shall be joint tenants of the property of the bankrupt. The creditors may also appoint persons to act as trustees in succession in the event of one or more of the persons first named declining to accept the office of trustee:

(2.) If any vacancy occur in the office of trustee by death, resignation, or otherwise, the creditors in general meeting shall fill up such vacancy, and a general meeting for the purpose of filling up such vacancy may be convened by the continuing trustee, if there be more than one or by the registrar on the requisition of any creditor:

(3.) If, through any cause whatever, there is no trustee acting during the continuance of a bankruptcy, the registrar of the court for the time being having jurisdiction in the bankruptcy shall act as such trustee:

(4.) The court may, upon cause shown, remove any trustee. The creditors may, by special resolution at a meeting specially called for that purpose, of which seven days' notice has been given, remove the trustee and appoint another person to fill his office, and the court shall give a certificate declaring him to be the trustee:

(5.) If a trustee be adjudged a bankrupt, he shall cease to be trustee, and the registrar shall, if there be no other trustee, call a meeting of creditors for the appointment of another trustee in his place:

(6.) The property of a bankrupt shall pass from trustee to trustee, including under that term the registrar when he fills the office of trustee, and shall vest in the trustee for the time being during his continuance in office, without any conveyance, assignment, or transfer whatever.

(7.) The trustee of a bankrupt may sue and be sued by the official name of "the trustee of the property of   , a bankrupt," inserting the name of the bankrupt, and by that name may hold property of every description, make contracts, sue and be sued, enter into any engagements binding upon himself and his successors in office, and do all other acts necessary or expedient to be done in the execution of his office:

(8.) The certificate of appointment of a trustee shall for all purposes of any law in force in the British dominions requiring registration, enrolment, or recording of conveyances or assignments of property be deemed to be a conveyance or assignment of property, and may be registered, enroled, and recorded accordingly:

(9.) All acts and things by this act authorised or required to be done by or to the registrar may be done within the district of each court having jurisdiction in bankruptcy by or to the registrar of that court:

(10.) Any member of the committee of inspection may resign his office by notice in writing signed by him, and delivered to the trustee:

(11.) The creditors may by resolution fix the quorum, required to be present at a meeting of the committee of inspection:

(12.) Any member of the committee of inspection may also be removed by a special resolution at any meeting of creditors of which the prescribed notice has been given, stating the object of the meeting:

(13.) On any vacancy occurring in the office of a member of the committee of inspection by removal, death, resignation, or otherwise, the trustee shall convene a meeting of creditors for the purpose of filling up such vacancy:

(14.) The continuing members of the committee of inspection may act, notwithstanding any vacancy in their body; and where the number of members of the committee of inspection is for the time being less than five, the creditors may increase that number so that it do not exceed five:

(15.) No defect or irregularity in the election of a trustee or of a member of the committee of inspection shall vitiate any act *bona fide* done by him; and no act or proceeding of the trustee or of the creditors shall be invalid by reason of any failure of the creditors to elect all or any members of the committee of inspection:

(16.) If a member of the committee of inspection becomes a bankrupt his office shall thereupon become vacant:

(17.) Where there is no committee of inspection, any act or thing or any direction or consent by this act authorized or required to be done or given by such committee may be done or given by the court on the application of the trustee:

84. The registrar may adjourn the first meeting of creditors from time to time and from place to place, subject to the directions of the court; but if, at such first meeting of creditors or at some adjournment thereof, no trustee is appointed by reason of the prescribed quorum not being present, or for any other reason whatever, the court may annul the adjudication, unless it deems it expedient to carry on the bankruptcy with the aid of the registrar as trustee. Moreover, if at any time during the bankruptcy no new trustee is appointed to fill a vacancy in that office, the court may either carry on the bankruptcy with the aid of the registrar as trustee or annul the order of adjudication, as it thinks just.

As to Power over Bankrupt.

85. The court upon the application of the trustee, may from time to time order that, for such time as the court thinks fit, not exceeding three months from the date of adjudication, post letters addressed to the bankrupt at any place or any of the places mentioned in the order, shall be re-directed, sent, or delivered by the postmaster general or the officers acting under him, to the trustee or otherwise as the court directs, and the same shall be done accordingly.

86. The court may, by warrant addressed to any constable or prescribed officer of the court, cause a debtor to be examined, and any books, paper, monies, goods and chattels in his possession to be seized, and him and them to be safely kept as prescribed

until such time as the court may order, under the following circumstances.

(1.) If, after a petition of bankruptcy is presented against such debtor, it appear to the court that there is probable reason for believing that he is about to go abroad or quit his place of residence with a view of avoiding service of the petition, or of avoiding appearing to the petition, or of avoiding examination in respect of his affairs, or otherwise delaying or embarrassing the proceedings in bankruptcy.

(2.) If, after a petition in bankruptcy has been presented against such debtor, it appear to the court that there is probable cause for believing that he is about to remove his goods or chattels with a view of preventing or delaying such goods or chattels being taken possession of by the trustee, or that there is probable ground for believing that he has concealed or is about to conceal or destroy any of his goods or chattels, or any books, documents, or writings which might be of use to his creditors in the course of his bankruptcy.

(3.) If, after the service of the petition on such debtor, or after an adjudication in bankruptcy against him, he remove any goods or chattels in his possession above the value of five pounds, without the leave of the trustee, or if, without good cause shown, he fails to attend any examination ordered by the court.

As to Property devolving on Trustee.

87. Where the goods of any trader have been taken in execution in respect of a judgment for a sum exceeding fifty pounds and sold, the sheriff, or in the case of a sale under the direction of the county court, the high bailiff or other officer of the county court, shall retain the proceeds of such sale in his hands for a period of fourteen days, and upon notice being served on him within that period of a bankruptcy, petition having been presented against such trader, shall hold the proceeds of such sale, after deducting expenses, on trust to pay the same to the trustee; but if no notice of such petition having been presented be served on him within such period of fourteen days, or if, such notice having been served, the trader

against whom the petition has been presented is not adjudged a bankrupt on such petition, or on any other petition of which the sheriff, high bailiff, or other officer has notice, he may deal with the proceeds of such sale in the same manner as he would have done had no notice of the presentation of a bankruptcy petition been served on him.

88. Where a bankrupt is a beneficed clergyman, the trustee may apply for a sequestration of the profits of the benefice, and the certificate of the appointment of the trustee shall be sufficient authority for the granting of sequestration without any writ or other proceeding, and the same shall accordingly be issued as on a writ of *levari facias* founded on a judgment against the bankrupt, and shall have priority over any sequestration issued after the commencement of the bankruptcy, except a sequestration issued before the date of the order of adjudication by or on behalf of a person who at the time of the issue thereof had not notice of an act of bankruptcy committed by the bankrupt, and available against him for adjudication : but the sequestrator shall allow out of the profits of the benefice to the bankrupt, while he performs the duties of the parish or place, such an annual sum, payable quarterly, as the bishop of the diocese in which the benefice is situate directs ; and the bishop may appoint to the bankrupt such or the like stipend as he might by law have appointed to a curate duly licensed to serve the benefice in case the bankrupt had been non-resident.

89. Where a bankrupt is or has been an officer of the army or navy, or an officer or clerk or otherwise employed or engaged in the civil service of the crown, or is in the enjoyment of any pension or compensation granted by the treasury, the trustee during the bankruptcy, and the register after the close of the bankruptcy, shall receive for distribution amongst the creditors so much of the bankrupt's pay, half pay, salary, emolument or pension, as the court, upon the application of the trustee, thinks just and reasonable, to be paid in such manner and at such times as the court, with the consent in writing of the chief officer of the department under which the pay, half pay, salary, emolument, pension, or compensation is enjoyed directs.

90. Where a bankrupt is in the receipt of a salary or income other than as aforesaid, the court upon the application of the trustee shall from time to time make such order as it thinks just for the payment of such salary or income, or of any part thereof, to the trustee during the bankruptcy, and to the registrar if necessary after the close of the bankruptcy, to be applied by him in such manner as the court may direct.

91. Any settlement of property made by a trader not being a settlement made before and in consideration of marriage, or made in favor of a purchaser or incumbrancer in good faith and for valuable consideration, or a settlement made on or for the wife or children of the settlor of property which has accrued to the settlor after marriage in right of his wife, shall, if the settlor becomes bankrupt within two years after the date of such settlement, be void as against the trustee of the bankrupt, appointed under this act, and shall, if the settlor becomes bankrupt at any subsequent time within ten years after the date of such settlement, unless the parties claiming under such settlement can prove that the settlor was at the time of making the settlement able to pay all his debts without the aid of the property comprised in such settlement, be void against such trustee. Any covenant or contract made by a trader, in consideration of marriage, for the future settlement upon or for his wife or children of any money or property wherein he had not at the date of his marriage any estate or interest, whether vested or contingent in possession or remainder, and not being money or property of or in right of his wife, shall upon his becoming bankrupt before such property or money has been actually transferred or paid pursuant to such contract or covenant, be void against his trustee appointed under this act. "Settlement" shall for the purposes of this section include any conveyance or transfer of property.

92. Every conveyance or transfer of property, or charge thereon made, every payment made, every obligation incurred, and every judicial proceeding taken or suffered by any person unable to pay his debts as they become due, from his own monies, in favor of any creditor, or any person in trust for any creditor, with a view of giving such creditor a preference over the other creditors, shall, if the person making, taking, paying or suffering the same become bankrupt

within three months after the date of making, taking, paying or suffering the same, be deemed fraudulent and void as against the trustee of the bankrupt appointed under this act ; but this section shall not affect the rights of a purchaser, payee or incumbrancer in good faith and for valuable consideration.

93. Any treasurer or other officer, or any banker, attorney, or agent of a bankrupt, shall pay and deliver to the trustee all monies and securities in his possession or power, as such officer or agent, if he be not by law entitled to retain as against the bankrupt or the trustee ; if he do not, he shall be guilty of a contempt of court, and may be punished accordingly on the application of the trustee.

94. Nothing in this act contained shall render invalid,—

(1.) Any payment made in good faith, and for value received, to any bankrupt before the date of the order of adjudication by a person not having at the time of such payment notice of any act of bankruptcy committed by the bankrupt, and available against him for adjudication :

(2.) Any payment or delivery of money or goods belonging to a bankrupt, made to such bankrupt by a depositary of such money or goods before the date of the order of adjudication, who had not, at the time of such payment or delivery, notice of any act of bankruptcy committed by the bankrupt, and available against him for adjudication :

(3.) Any contract or dealing with any bankrupt, made in good faith and for valuable consideration, before the date of the order of adjudication, by a person not having at the time of making such contract or dealing notice of any act of bankruptcy committed by the bankrupt, and available against him for adjudication.

95. Subject and without prejudice to the provisions of this act relating to the proceeds of the sale and seizure of goods of a trader, and to the provisions of this act avoiding certain settlements, and avoiding, on the ground of their constituting fraudulent preferences, certain conveyances, charges, payments, and judicial proceedings. the following transactions by and in relation to the property of a bankrupt shall be valid, notwithstanding any prior act of bankruptcy,—

(1.) Any disposition or contract with respect to the disposition of property by conveyance, transfer, charge, delivery of goods, payment of money, or otherwise howsoever made by any bankrupt in good faith and for valuable consideration, before the date of the order of adjudication, with any person not having, at the time of the making of such disposition of property, notice of any act of bankruptcy committed by the bankrupt, and available against him for adjudication :

(2.) Any execution or attachment against the land of the bankrupt, executed in good faith by seizure before the date of the order of adjudication, if the person on whose account such execution or attachment was issued had not, at the time of the same being so executed by seizure, notice of any act of bankruptcy committed by the bankrupt, and available against him for adjudication :

(3.) Any execution or attachment against the goods of any bankrupt, executed in good faith by seizure and sale before the date of the order of adjudication, if the person on whose account such execution or attachment was issued had not at the time of the same being executed by seizure and sale notice of any act of bankruptcy committed by the bankrupt, and available against him for jurisdiction.

As to Discovery of Bankrupt's Property.

96. The court may, on the application of the trustee, at any time after an order of adjudication has been made against a bankrupt, summon before it the bankrupt or his wife, or any person whatever known or suspected to have in his possession any of the estate or effects belonging to the bankrupt, or supposed to be indebted to the bankrupt, or any person whom the court may deem capable of giving information respecting the bankrupt, his trade dealings or property, and the court may require any such persons to produce any such persons to produce any documents in his custody or power relating to the bankrupt, his dealings or property ; and if any person so summoned, after having

been tendered a reasonable sum, refuses to come before the court at the time appointed, or refuses to produce such documents, having no lawful impediment made known to the court at the time of its sitting and allowed by it, the court may, by warrant addressed as aforesaid, cause such person to be apprehended and brought up for examination.

97. The court may examine upon oath, either by word of mouth, or by written interrogatories, any person so brought before it in manner aforesaid concerning the bankrupt, his dealings or property.

98. If any person on examination before the court admit he is indebted to the bankrupt, the court may, on the application of the trustee, order him to pay to the trustee, at such time and in such manner as to the court seems expedient, the amount admitted, or any part thereof, either in full discharge of the whole amount in question or not, as the court thinks fit, with or without costs of the examination.

99. Any person acting under warrant of the court may seize any property of the bankrupt divisible amongst his creditors under this act, and in the bankrupt's custody or possession, or in that of any other person, and with a view to such seizure may break open any house, building, or room of the bankrupt where the bankrupt is supposed to be, or any building or receptacle of the bankrupt where any of his property is supposed to be; and where the court is satisfied that there is reason to believe that property of the bankrupt is concealed in a house or place not belonging to him, the court may, if it thinks fit, grant a search warrant to any constable or prescribed officer of the court, who may execute the same according to the tenor thereof.

Joint and Separate Estates.

100. Any creditor whose debt is sufficient to entitle him to present a bankruptcy petition against all the partners of a firm may present such petition against any one or more partners of such firm without including the others.

101. Where there are more respondents than one to a petition, the court may dismiss the petition as to one or more of them, without prejudice to the effect of the petition as against the other or others of them.

102. Where one member of a partnership has been adjudicated a bankrupt, any other petition for adjudication against a member of the same partnership shall be filed in or transferred to the court in which the first mentioned petition is in course of prosecution, and unless the court otherwise directs, the property of such last mentioned member shall vest in the trustee appointed in respect of the property of the first mentioned member of the partnership, and the court may give such directions for amalgamating the proceedings in respect of the properties of the members of the same partnership as it thinks just.

103. If one partner of a firm is adjudged bankrupt, any creditor to whom the bankrupt is indebted jointly with the other partners of the firm or any of them, may prove his debt for the purpose of voting at any meeting of the creditors, and shall be entitled to vote thereat, but shall not receive any dividend out of the separate property of the bankrupt until all the separate creditors have received the full amount of their respective debts.

104. Where joint and separate properties are being administered, dividends of the joint and separate properties shall, subject to any order to the contrary that may be made by the court on the application of any person interested, be declared together; and the expenses of and incident to such dividends shall be fairly apportioned by the trustee between the joint and separate properties, regard being had to the work done for and the benefit received by each property.

105. Where a member of a partnership is adjudged a bankrupt, the court may authorise the trustee, with consent of the creditors, certified by a special resolution, to commence and prosecute any action or suit in the names of the trustee and of the bankrupt's partner; and any release by such partner of the debt or demand to which the action or suit relates shall be void; but notice of the application for authority to commence the action or suit shall be given to such partner, and he may show cause against it, and on his application the court may, if it think fit, direct that he shall receive his proper share of the proceeds of the action or suit, and if he does not claim any benefit therefrom he shall be indemnified against costs in respect thereof as the court directs

Evidence.

106. The registrar, or any other person presiding at a meeting of creditors under this act, shall cause minutes to be kept and duly entered in a book of all resolutions and proceedings of such meeting, and any such minute as aforesaid, if purporting to be signed by the chairman of the meeting at which such resolutions were passed or proceedings had, shall be received as evidence in all legal proceedings; and until the contrary is proved, every general meeting of the creditors in respect of the proceedings of which minutes have been so made shall be deemed to have been duly held and convened, and all resolutions passed thereat or proceedings had to have been duly passed and had.

107. Any petition or copy of a petition in bankruptcy, any order or copy of an order made by any court having jurisdiction in bankruptcy, any certificate or copy of a certificate made by any court having jurisdiction in bankruptcy, any deed or copy of a deed of arrangement in bankruptcy, and any other instrument or copy of an instrument, affidavit, or document made or used in the course of any bankruptcy proceedings, or other proceedings had under this act, may, if any such instrument as aforesaid or copy of an instrument appears to be sealed with the seal of any court having jurisdiction or purport to be signed by any judge having jurisdiction in bankruptcy under this act, be receivable in evidence in all legal proceedings whatever.

108. In case of the death of a bankrupt or his wife, or of a witness whose evidence has been received by any court in any proceeding under this act, the deposition of the person so deceased, purporting to be sealed with the seal of the court, or a copy thereof purporting to be sealed, shall be admitted as evidence of the matters therein deposed to.

109. Every court having jurisdiction in bankruptcy under this act shall have a seal describing such court in such manner as may be directed by order of the lord chancellor, and judicial notice shall be taken of such seal, and of the signature of the judge or registrar of any such court, in all legal proceedings.

Miscellaneous.

110. Where the registrar under the authority of this act attends at any place for the purpose of presiding at a meeting of creditors, or of receiving proofs, or of otherwise acting under this act, his traveling and incidental expenses incurred in so doing, and those of any clerk or officer attending him, shall, after being settled by the court, be paid out of the bankrupt's property, if sufficient, and otherwise shall be deemed part of the expenses of the court.

111. Any person to whom anything in action belonging to the bankrupt is assigned in pursuance of this act, may bring or defend any action or suit relating to such thing in action in his own name.

112. Where a bankrupt is a contractor in respect of any contract jointly with any other person or persons, such person or persons may sue and be sued in respect of such contract, with the joinder of the bankrupt.

113. Every deed, conveyance, assignment, surrender, admission, or other assurance relating solely to freehold, copyhold, or customary property, or to any mortgage, charge, or other incumbrance on, or any estate, right, or interest in any real or personal property which is part of the estate of any bankrupt, and which, after the execution of such deed, conveyance, assignment, surrender, admission, or other assurance, either at law or in equity, is or remains the estate of the bankrupt or the trustee under the bankruptcy, and every power of attorney, proxy, paper, writ, order, certificate, affidavit, bond or other instrument or writing relating solely to the property of any bankrupt, or to any proceeding under any bankruptcy, shall be exempt from stamp duty (except in respect of fees under this act.)

114. Where by this act any limited time from or after any date or event is appointed or allowed for the doing of any action or the taking of any proceeding, then in the computation of such limited time the same shall be taken as exclusive of the day of such date, or of the happening of such event, and as commencing at the beginning of the next following day; and the act or proceeding shall be done or taken at latest on the last day of such limited time according to such computation, unless such last day is a Sunday, Christmas day, Good Friday, or Monday or Tuesday in Easter week, or a day appointed for public fast, humiliation, or thanksgiving, or a day which, in pursu-

ance of a notification by the lord chancellor under this act, the court does not sit, in which case any act or proceeding shall be considered as done or taken in due time if it is done or taken on the next day afterwards, not being one of the days in this section specified.

Where by this act any act or proceeding is directed to be done or taken on a certain day, then if that day happens to be one of the days in this section specified, such act or proceeding shall be considered as done or taken in due time if it is done or taken on the next day afterwards, not being one of the days in this section specified.

115. The registrars and other officers of the courts acting in bankruptcy shall make to the comptroller in bankruptcy such returns of the business of their respective courts and offices, at such times and in such manner and form as may be prescribed by the rules of court, and from such returns the comptroller shall, in manner prescribed by the rules of court, frame books (which shall be, under the regulations of the rules of court, open for public information and searches,) and also a general annual report to the lord chancellor, judicial and financial respecting all matters within this act, which report shall be laid before both houses of parliament.

116. Where any dividends remain unclaimed for five years, then and in every such case the same shall be deemed vested in the crown, and shall be disposed of as the commissioners of Her Majesty's treasury direct; provided, that at any time after such vesting the lord chancellor or any court authorised by him may, by reason of the disability or absence beyond seas of the person entitled to the sum so vested, or for any other reason appearing to him sufficient, direct that the said sum shall be repaid out of money provided by parliament.

117. Where a bankrupt is a trustee within the trustee act, 1850, section thirty-two of that act shall have effect so as to authorise the court to appoint a new trustee in substitution for the bankrupt (whether voluntarily resigning or not), if it appears to the court expedient to do so, and all provisions of that act, and of any other act relative thereto, shall have effect accordingly.

118. No person, not being a trader, shall be adjudged a bankrupt in respect of a debt contracted before the date of the passing of the bankrupt act, 1861.

119. Where in any act of parliament, instrument or proceeding passed, executed, or taken before the commencement of this act mention is made of a commission of bankruptcy or fiat in bankruptcy, the same shall be construed, with reference to the proceedings under a petition for adjudication of bankruptcy, as if a commission of or a fiat in bankruptcy had been actually issued at the time of the presentation of such petition.

PART V.

PERSONS HAVING PRIVILEGE OF PARLIAMENT.

120. If a person having privilege of parliament commits an act of bankruptcy he may be dealt with under this act in like manner as if he had not such privilege.

121. If a person, being a member of the common house of parliament, is adjudged bankrupt, he shall be and remain during one year from the date of the order of adjudication incapable of sitting and voting in that house, unless within that time either the order is annulled or the creditors who prove debts under the bankruptcy are fully paid or satisfied.

Provided, that such debts (if any) as are disputed by the bankrupt shall be considered, for the purpose of this section, as paid or satisfied if within the time aforesaid he enters into a bond, in such sum and with such sureties as the court approve, to pay the amount to be recovered in any proceeding for the recovery of or concerning such debts, together with any costs to be given in such proceedings.

122. If within the time aforesaid the order of adjudication is not annulled, and the debts of the bankrupt are not fully paid or satisfied as aforesaid, then the court shall, immediately after the expiration of that time, certify the same to the speaker of the house of commons, and thereupon the seat of such member shall be vacant.

123. Where the seat of a member so becomes vacant the speaker during a recess of the house, whether by prorogation or by adjournment, shall forthwith, after receiving such certificate, cause notice thereof to be published in the *London Gazette;* and after

the expiration of six days after such publication shall (unless the house has met before that day, or will meet on the day of the issue) issue his warrant to the clerk of the crown to make out a new writ for electing another member in the room of the member whose seat has so become vacant.

124. The powers of the act of the twenty-fourth year of the reign of King George the Third, chapter twenty-six, "to repeal so much of two acts made in the tenth and fifteenth years of the reign of his present majesty as authorising the speaker of the house of commons to issue his warrant to the clerk of the crown for making out writs for the election of members to serve in parliament in the manner therein mentioned; and for substituting other provisions for the like purposes," so far as such powers enable the speaker to nominate and appoint other persons, being members of the house of commons, to issue warrants for the making out of new writs during the vacancy of the office of speaker, or during the absence out of the realm, shall extend to enable him to make the like nomination and appointment for issuing warrants, under the like circumstances and conditions, for the election of a member in the room of any bankrupt member whose seat becomes vacant under this act.

PART VI.

LIQUIDATION BY ARRANGEMENT.

Regulations.

125. The following regulations shall be made with respect to the liquidation by arrangement of the affairs of the debtor:

(1.) A debtor unable to pay his debts may summon a general meeting of his creditors, and such meeting may, by a special resolution as defined by this act, declare that the affairs of the debtor are to be liquidated by arrangement and not in bankruptcy, and may at that or some subsequent meeting, held at an interval of not more than a week, appoint a trustee, with or without a committee of inspection: ·

(2.) All the provisions of this act relating to a first meeting of creditors, and to subsequent meetings of creditors in the case of a bankruptcy, including the description of creditors entitled to vote at such meetings, and the debts in respect of which they are entitled to vote, shall apply respectively to the first meeting of creditors, and to subsequent meetings of creditors, for the purposes of this section, subject to the following modifications:

(a.) That every such meeting shall be presided over by such chairman as the meeting may elect; and

(b.) That no creditor shall be entitled to vote until he has proved by a statutory declaration a debt provable in bankruptcy to be due to him, and the amount of such debt, with any prescribed particulars; and any person wilfully making a false declaration in relation to such debt shall be guilty of a misdemeanor.

(3.) The debtor, unless prevented by sickness or other cause satisfactory to such meeting, shall be present at the meeting at which the special resolution is passed, and shall answer any inquiries made of him, and he, or if he is so prevented from being at such meeting some one on his behalf, shall produce to the meeting a statement showing the whole of his assets and debts, and the names and addresses of the creditors to whom his debts are due:

(4.) The special resolution, together with the statement of the assets and debts of the debtor, and the name of the trustee appointed, and of the members, if any, of the committee of inspection, shall be presented to the register, and it shall be his duty to enquire whether such resolution has been passed in manner directed by this section, but if satisfied that it was so passed, and that a trustee has been appointed with or without a committee of inspection, he shall forthwith register the resolution and the statement of the assets and debts of the debtor, and such resolution and statement shall be open for inspection on the prescribed conditions, and the liquidation by arrangement shall be deemed to have commenced as from the date of the appointment of the trustee:

(5.) All such property of the debtor as would, if he were made a bankrupt, be divisible amongst his creditors shall, from and after the date of the appointment of a trustee, vest in such trustee under a liquidation by arrangement, and be divisible amongst the creditors, and all such settlements, conveyances, transfers, charges, payments, obligations, and proceedings as would be void against the trustee in the case of a bankruptcy shall be void against the trustee in the case of liquidation by arrangement:

(6.) The certificate of the registrar in respect of the appointment of any trustee in the case of a liquidation by arrangement shall be of the same effect as a certificate of the court to the like effect in the case of a bankruptcy:

(7.) The trustee under a liquidation shall have the same powers, and perform the same duties, as a trustee under a bankruptcy, and the property of the debtor shall be distributed in the same manner as in a bankruptcy; and with the modi fication hereinafter mentioned all the provisions of this act shall, so far as the same are applicable, apply to the case or a liquidation by arrangement in the same manner as if the word "bankrupt" included a debtor whose affairs are under liquidation, and the word "bankruptcy" included liquidation by arrangement; and in constructing such provisions the appointment of a trustee under a liquidation shall, according to circumstances, be deemed to be equivalent to, and a substitute for the presentation of a petition in bankruptcy, or the service of such petition or an order of adjudication in bankruptcy:

(8.) The creditors at their first or any general meeting may prescribe the bank into which the trustee is to pay any moneys received by him, and the sum which he may retain in his hands.

(9.) The provisions of this act with respect to the close of the bankruptcy, discharge of a bankrupt, to the release of the trustee, and to the audit of accounts by the comptroller, shall not apply in the case of a debtor whose affairs are under liquidation by arrangement; but the close of the liquidation may be fixed, and the discharge of the debtor and the release of the trustee

may be granted by a special resolution of the creditors in general meeting, and the accounts may be audited in pursuance of such resolution, at such time and in such manner and upon such terms and conditions as the creditors think fit.

(10.) The trustee shall report to the registrar the discharge of the debtor, and a certificate of such discharge given by the registrar shall have the same effect as an order of discharge given to a bankrupt under this act.

(11.) Rules of court may be made in relation to proceedings on the occasion of liquidation by arrangement in the same manner and to the same extent and of the same authority as in respect of proceedings in bankruptcy.

(12.) If it appear to the court on satisfactory evidence that the liquidation by arrangement cannot, in consequence of legal difficulties, or of there being no trustee for the time being, or for any sufficient cause, proceed without injustice or undue delay to the creditors or to the debtor, the court may adjudge the debtor a bankrupt, and proceedings may be had accordingly:

(13.) Where no committee of inspection is appointed the trustee may act on his own discretion in cases where he would otherwise have been bound to refer to such committee:

(14.) In calculating a majority on a special resolution for the purposes of this section, creditors whose debts amount to sums not exceeding ten pounds shall be reckoned in the majority in value, but not in the majority in number:

PART VII.

COMPOSITION WITH CREDITORS.

Regulations.

126. The creditors of a debtor unable to pay his debts may, without any proceedings in bankruptcy, by an extraordinary resolution, resolve that a composition shall be accepted in satisfaction of the debts due to them from the debtor.

An extraordinary resolution of creditors shall be a resolution which has been passed by a majority in number and three-fourths in value of the creditors of the debtor, assembled at a general meeting to be held in manner prescribed, of which notice has been given in the prescribed manner, and has been confirmed by a majority in number and value of the creditors assembled at a subsequent general meeting, of which notice has been given in the prescribed manner, and held at an interval of not less than seven days nor more than fourteen days from the date of the meeting at which such resolution was first passed.

In calculating a majority for the purposes of a composition under this section, creditors whose debts amount to sums not exceeding ten pounds shall be reckoned in the majority in value, but not in the majority in number, and the value of the debts of secured creditors shall, as nearly as circumstances admit, be estimated in the same way, and the same description of creditors shall be entitled to vote at such general meetings as in bankruptcy.

The debtor, unless prevented by sickness or other cause satisfactory to such meetings, shall be present at both the meetings at which the extraordinary resolution is passed, and shall answer any inquiries made of him, and he, or if he is so prevented from being at such meetings, some one on his behalf, shall produce to the meetings a statement showing the whole of his assets and debts, and the names and addresses of the creditors to whom such debts respectively are due.

The extraordinary resolution, together with the statement of the debtor as to his assets and debts, shall be presented to the registrar, and it shall be his duty to inquire whether such resolution has been passed in manner directed by this section, and, if satisfied that it has been so passed, he shall forthwith register the resolution and statement of assets and debts, but until such registration has taken place, such resolution shall be of no validity : and any creditor of the debtor may inspect such statement at prescribed times, and on payment of such fee, if any, as may be prescribed.

The creditors may, by an extraordinary resolution, add to or vary the provisions of any composition previously accepted by them, without prejudice to any persons taking interests under such provisions who do not assent to such addition or variation; and any such extraordinary resolution shall be presented to the registrar in the same manner and with the same consequences as the extraordinary resolution by which the composition was accepted in the first instance.

The provisions of a composition accepted by an extraordinary resolution, in pursuance of this section, shall be binding on all the creditors whose names and addresses, and the amount of the debts due to whom, are shown in the statement of the debtor, produced to the meetings at which the resolution has passed, but shall not affect or prejudice the rights of any other creditors.

Where a debt arises on a bill of exchange or promissory note, if the debtor is ignorant of the holder of any such bill of exchange or promissory note, he shall be required to state the amount of such bill or note, the date on which it falls due, the name of the acceptor or person to whom it is payable, and any other particulars within his knowledge respecting the same, and the insertion of such particulars shall be deemed a sufficient description of the creditor of the debtor in respect of such debt, and any mistake made inadvertently by a debtor in the statement of his debts may be corrected after the prescribed notice has been given, with the consent of a general meeting of his creditors.

The provisions of any composition made in pursuance of this section may be enforced by the court on a motion made in a summary manner by any person interested, and any disobedience of the order of the court made on such motion shall be deemed to be a contempt of court.

Rules of court may be made in relation to proceedings on the occasion of the acceptance of a composition by an extraordinary resolution of creditors, in the same manner and to the same extent and of the same authority as in respect of proceedings in bankruptcy.

If it appear to the court, on satisfactory evidence, that a composition under this section cannot, in consequence of legal difficulties, or for any sufficient cause, proceed without injustice or undue delay to the creditors or to the debtor, the court may adjudge the debtor a bankrupt, and proceedings may be had accordingly.

127. The registration by the registrar of

a special resolution of the creditors, on the occasion of a liquidation by arrangement under part six of this act, or of an extraordinary resolution of the creditors on the occasion of a composition under the seventh part of this act, shall, in the absence of fraud, be conclusive evidence that such resolutions respectively were duly passed, and all the requisitions of this act in respect of such resolutions complied with.

PART VIII.

TEMPORARY PROVISIONS.

Bankruptcy Courts.

128. Such one of the present commissioners of the London bankruptcy court as may be chosen by her majesty shall be the first chief judge in the London bankruptcy court, as constituted under this act, and shall, as to tenure of office, salary, pension, and all other privileges except his title, continue in the same position in all respects as if his office had not been abolished by this act; but, save as aforesaid, from and after the commencement of this act the present commissioners of the London bankruptcy court shall cease to hold their offices.

129. The chief registrar, registrars, accountant in bankruptcy, taxing masters, official assignees, messengers, and all other officers holding offices or employed in the existing London bankruptcy court, herein called the Old London bankruptcy, at the commencement of this act, shall, unless the lord chancellor otherwise directs, be attached to the London bankruptcy court as constituted under this act, herein called the New London bankruptcy court. The officers so attached shall have the same relative rank, hold their offices by the same tenure and upon the same terms and conditions, and receive the same salaries as heretofore. The lord chancellor may, by order, make provision for winding up such portion of the business pending in the said old bankruptcy court as cannot conveniently be transferred to the new bankruptcy court, and for transferring to such last mentioned court any business capable of being conveniently transferred, and every officer attached to such last mentioned court shall conform to any order so made by the lord

chancellor. The lord chancellor may, by order, distribute the business to be performed in the said new bankruptcy court amongst the several officers attached thereto in such manner as he may think just, and such officers shall perform such duties in relation to such business as may be directed by the lord chancellor, with this qualification, that the duties required to be performed by them shall be the same or duties analogous to those which they have hitherto performed in the old bankruptcy court. The lord chancellor may, at any time, by order, release from the performance of any duties in the new bankruptcy court any officer of the old bankruptcy court whose services he may deem unnecessary, and the office held by any such person shall be deemed to be abolished unless it be an office required to be continued in pursuance of the provisions of this act relating to the constitution of the new bankruptcy court. Any person so released shall, whether his office be altogether abolished or not, be entitled to compensation in the same manner in all respects as if his office had been abolished.

130. From and after the commencement of this act, the country district courts of bankruptcy shall be abolished, and the commissioners, registrars, official assignees, messengers, ushers, clerks, and officers of the said courts respectively shall cease to hold their offices.

Such part of the business pending in any country district court of bankruptcy as the lord chancellor thinks fit shall be disposed of by the registrar of that court (who shall for that purpose continue to have and discharge all his powers and authorities, rights and duties), and the residue of that business shall be transferred to the London bankruptcy court, or to such county court or county courts as the lord chancellor, by order before or after its abolition, think fit to direct; but, subject as aforesaid, the office of any registrar in such country district court shall be abolished.

All books, papers, documents, and money in the custody or control of any such commissioners, registrars, official assignees, messengers, ushers, clerks, and officers, as such, shall be transferred to such courts or persons as the lord chancellor may direct. The lord chancellor shall also by order declare the person or persons in whom any property vested in any official assignee or other officer as such of any country district court hereby abolished is to vest, and such property shall vest accordingly.

131. The commissioners of Her Majesty's treasury may, on the petition of any person whose office or employment is abolished by or under this act, on the commencement of this act or on any other event, inquire whether any, and, if any, what compensation ought to be made to the petitioner, regard being had to the conditions on which his appointment was made, the nature of his office or employment, and the duration of his service; and if they think that his claim to compensation is established, may award to him, out of monies to be provided by parliament, such compensation, by annuity or otherwise, as under the circumstances of the case they think just and reasonable; provided that when any such person held his office during good behavior, or during good behavior subject only to removal by the lord chancellor by order, for some sufficient reason to be stated in such order, the lord chancellor may, with the approval of the commissioners of the treasury, award under special circumstances an amount equal to the salary of any such person; and in every other case the sum awarded shall not be less than two-thirds of the salary of such person.

132. Every person appointed to any office or employment created by this act shall in the first instance be selected from the persons whose office or employment is abolished by this act, unless, in the opinion of the lord chancellor, none of the last mentioned persons are fit for such office or employment.

133. When any subsequent vacancy occurs in any office or employment created by this act, and such vacancy is not filled up by the appointment of a person in the receipt of compensation under this act, no permanent appointment shall be made until notice of the vacancy has been given to the treasury, and until the lord chancellor has determined that no person in receipt of compensation under this act is fit for such office or employment.

134. The lord chancellor may nominate or appoint any commissioner whose office has been abolished under this act to some other judicial office of equal or greater salary for which he may be deemed fit by the lord chancellor, and to which he is entitled to nominate or appoint, and may nominate or appoint any other person whose office or employment has been abolished by this act, whom he may deem fit to fill a vacancy in any office or employment created by this act of equal or greater salary, to which he is entitled to nominate or appoint, provided that the person appointed be in the receipt of compensation or superanuation allowance equal to the amount of his salary at the time of the abolition of his office; and if the commissioner or other person so nominated or appointed declines to accept such office or employment, or neglects to execute the duties thereof satisfactorily, being in a competent state of health, he shall forfeit his right to compensation or superanuation allowance which may have been granted to him, or which he might otherwise be entitled to receive, unless he shall satisfy the lord chancellor that the office is one not suitable to his position, regard being had to his former office.

135. If any person to whom a compensation annuity is granted under this act accepts any public employment, he shall, during the continuance of that employment, receive only so much (if any) of that annuity as, with the remuneration of that employment, will amount to a sum not exceeding the salary or emoluments in respect of the loss whereof the annuity was awarded, and if the remuneration of that employment is equal to or greater than such salary or emoluments the annuity shall be suspended so long as he received that remuneration.

136. The registrars, clerks, and other persons holding their offices at the passing of this act who may be continued in their offices, shall, on their retirement therefrom, be allowed such superanuation as they would have been entitled to receive if this act had not been passed, and they had continued in their offices under the existing acts; and any other registrar, officer, or person appointed to any office under this act may be allowed superanuation in pursuance of the provisions of the Superanuation Act of 1859.

SCHEDULE I.

DESCRIPTION OF TRADERS

Alum makers, apothecaries, auctioneers,

bankers, bleachers, brokers, brickmakers, builders, calenderers, carpenters, carriers, cattle or sheep salesmen, coach proprietors, cowkeepers, dyers, fullers, keepers of inns, taverns, hotels, or coffee-houses, lime-burners, livery-stable keepers, market-gardeners, millers, packers, printers, sharebrokers, shipowners, shipwrights, stockbrokers, victuallers, stockjobbers, warehousemen, wharfingers, persons using the trade or profession of a scrivener, receiving other men's monies or estates into their trust or custody, persons insuring ships or their freight or other matters against perils of the sea, persons using the trade of merchandise by way of bargaining, exchange, bartering, commission, consignment, or otherwise, in gross or by retail, and persons who, either for themselves or as agents or factors for others, seek their living by buying and selling or buying and letting for hire goods or commodities, or by the workmanship or the conversion of goods or commodities; but a farmer, grazier, common laborer, or workman for hire shall not, nor shall a member of any partnership, association, or company which cannot be adjudged bankrupt under this act be deemed as such a trader for the purposes of this act.

THE CANADIAN INSOLVENT ACT OF 1869.

32 & 33 VIC. CAP XVI.

AN ACT RESPECTING INSOLVENCY.

PREAMBLE.

WHEREAS it is expedient that the Acts respecting Bankruptcy and Insolvency in the several Provinces of Ontario, Quebec, New Brunswick, and Nova Scotia, be amended and consolidated, and the Law on those subjects assimilated in the several Provinces of the Dominion : Therefore Her Majesty, by and with the advice and consent of the Senate and House of Commons of Canada, enacts as follows :

Application of Act.

1. This act shall apply to traders only.

OF VOLUNTARY ASSIGNMENTS.

Assignment to be made to Interim Assignee. Meeting of Creditors to be called.

2. Any debtor unable to meet his engagements, and desirous of making an assignment of his estate, and any debtor who is required to make an assignment, as hereinafter provided, shall make an assignment of his estate and effects to any official assignee resident within the county or place wherein the insolvent has his domicile ; or if there be no official assignee therein, then to an official assignee in the county or place nearest to the domicile of the insolvent, wherein an official assignee has been appointed, and the official assignee to whom such assignment is made shall be known as the interim assignee ; and forthwith upon the execution of the deed of assignment to him, a meeting of the creditors of the insolvent for the appointment of an assignee, shall be called by the interim assignee to be held at the place of business of the insolvent within a period not exceeding three weeks from the execution of the deed of assignment.

Calling of meeting and proceedings thereat. Schedule of liabilities and assets ; and what it must show. Insolvent to assist, and make a declaration on oath.

3. Such meeting shall be called by advertisement (Form A), and previous to such meeting the interim assignee shall prepare, and shall then exhibit, statements showing the position of the affairs of the insolvent ; and particularly a schedule (Form B), containing the names and residence of all his creditors, and the amount due to each, distinguishing between those amounts which are then actually overdue, or for which he is directly liable, and those for which he is only liable indirectly as indorser, surety, or otherwise, and which have not become due at the date of such meeting, the particulars of any negotiable paper bearing his name, the holders of which the interim assignee shall be unable to ascertain, the amount due to each creditor, and also any contingent liabilities, describing the same ; and a statement showing the amount and nature of all the assets of the insolvent, including an inventory of his estate and effects ; and the insolvent shall assist in the preparation of such statements and of the said schedule, and shall attend at such meeting for the purpose of being examined on oath touching the contents thereof, and touching his books of account and his estate and effects generally ; and at such meeting he shall file a declaration under oath stating whether or no such statements and schedule are correct, and if incorrect, in what particulars ; and the interim assignee shall also produce at such meeting, the insolvent's books of account, and all other documents and vouchers, if required so to do by any creditor.

Notice to each Creditor : what to contain.

4. At least ten days before the day fixed

for such meeting the interim assignee shall mail to each of the creditors of the insolvent, in so far as he shall then have been able to discover them, a notice of such meeting, with a list containing the names of all creditors holding direct claims, and also of all creditors holding indirect claims maturing before the meeting, amounting to one hundred dollars each, with the amount appearing to be due to each of them; and the aggregate amount of those under one hundred dollars.

Appointment of Assignee.
Irregularity not to vitiate it.

5. At such meeting, the creditors who have proved their claims in the manner hereinafter provided by the one hundred and twenty-second section, may appoint an assignee to the estate of the insolvent; and no neglect or irregularity in any of the proceedings antecedent to the appointment of an assignee shall vitiate such appointment, whether it be made under a voluntary assignment, or in compulsory liquidation.

In case no assignee is appointed, Interim Assignee to act, etc., otherwise to deliver estate to Assignee.

6. If no assignee be appointed at such meeting, or at any adjournment thereof; or if the assignee named refuses to act; or if no creditor attends at such meeting, the interim assignee shall be the assignee to the estate of the insolvent; but if any assignee be appointed thereat, he shall henceforth be the assignee of such estate; and the interim assignee shall immediately deliver over to him the whole of the estate of the insolvent, and all statements.

Form of Instrument of Assignment, and of Deed of Transfer by Interim Assignee.

7. The deed or instrument of assignment may be in the form O, and the deed of transfer by the interim assignee in the form D, or in any other forms equivalent thereto respectively, and if executed in any part of Canada other than the province of Quebec, they shall be in duplicate, and a copy of the list of creditors produced at the first meeting of creditors, shall be appended to the deed; and no particular description or detail of the property or effects assigned need be inserted in either of such deeds; and any number of counterparts of such deeds re-

quired by the assignee, and any further or other deeds or assurances required by the assignee, shall be executed by the insolvent, or by the interim assignee, as the case may be, at the request of the assignee, either at the time of the execution of such deed or instrument, or afterwards, to which counterparts no list of creditors need be appended.

If Interim Assignee fail to execute Deed of Transfer.

8. If the interim assignee shall fail or neglect to execute such deed of transfer within twenty-four hours after the nomination of an assignee at such meeting, he shall in the discretion of the judge be subject to imprisonment for a period not exceeding one month; and such imprisonment may be ordered by the judge upon the application of the person so nominated as assignee, or of any creditor, supported by affidavit to the satisfaction of the judge: and the interim assignee shall not be permitted to plead to or answer such application either as to its form or upon the merits in any manner or way whatever until after he shall have executed and delivered to the assignee such deed of transfer, and shall have also delivered over to him the whole of the estate and effects of the insolvent, with all books, instruments, vouchers and documents appertaining thereto.

Proceedings when Interim Assignee becomes the Assignee.
Deposit of the instrument: copies how certified.

9. If by election, or by failure of election, the interim assignee shall become assignee, his appointment shall be established, if by election, by an instrument, (form D D) declaring the fact, signed by the chairman and by one or more of the creditors present at the meeting appointing him, and authenticated by his own affidavit; and if by failure of election, by an instrument, declaring the fact, and signed and sworn to by himself before the judge, who shall have power to interrogate him specially upon the contents thereof, and shall not receive his oath if he has any reason to doubt the facts stated in such instrument; and the instrument of appointment shall be deposited in the office of the court with the deed of assignment; and a copy of such instrument certi-

fied by the clerk or prothonotary of the court wherein it is deposited under the seal of such court, shall serve all the purposes of the deed of transfer hereinbefore provided for, and for that purpose shall be annexed to the deed of assignment or in the province of Quebec to the copy thereof and registered therewith.

What the assignment shall be held to convey. Proviso : as to pledgee of the property of the Insolvent.

10. The assignment shall be held to convey and vest in the interim assignee in the first instance, the books of account of the insolvent, all vouchers, accounts, letters, and other papers and documents relating to his business, all monies and negotiable papers, stock, bonds, and other securities, as well as all the real estate of the insolvent, and all his interest therein, whether in fee or otherwise, and also all his personal estate, and movable property, debts, assets and effects, which he has or may become entitled to at any time before his discharge is effected under this act, excepting only such as are exempt from seizure and sale under execution, by virtue of the several statutes in such case made and provided ; and if an assignee be subsequently appointed, or if by the failure of election, the interim assignee becomes assignee, such assignee shall have the same rights in and to the whole of such estate and effects as were previously held under this act by the interim assignee : Provided always that no pledgee of any of the effects of the insolvent or any other party in possession thereof with a lien thereon, shall be deprived of the possession thereof, without payment of the amount legally chargeable as a preferential claim upon such effects ; except in the case hereinafter provided for of such pledgee or party in possession proving his claim against the estate and putting a value upon his security. But at any time before the maturity of any advance made upon the pledge of effects of the insolvent, or within fifteen days thereafter, the assignee shall have the right to sell such effects as he may sell the other effects of the insolvent ; and thereupon if the price is sufficient to cover such advance with interest and lawful charges, the pledgee shall carry out such sale and deliver the effects sold in conformity therewith, receiving the price thereof, but not otherwise.

11. Forthwith upon the execution of the deed of transfer, the assignee, if appointed in any part of Canada other than the province of Quebec, shall deposit one of the duplicates of the deed of assignment and of such deed of transfer, and if in the province of Quebec, authentic copies of each, in the office of the proper court ; and in either case the list of creditors shall accompany the instruments so deposited.

Registration of Deeds of Assignment and of Transfer.

12. If the insolvent possesses real estate, the deed of assignment with the deed of transfer annexed thereto, if any such deed of transfer be required and executed, or, if such real estate be in the province of Quebec, authentic copies thereof may be enregistered in the registry office for the registration division or county within which such real estate is situate ; and no subsequent registration of any deed or instrument of any kind executed by the insolvent, or which otherwise would have affected his real estate, shall have any force or effect thereon ; and if the real estate be in any part of Canada other than the province of Quebec, and deeds of assignment and of transfer be executed in the province of Quebec before notaries, copies of such deeds certified by the notary or other public officer in whose custody the originals remain, may be registered without other evidence of the execution thereof, and without any memorial ; and a certificate of such registration may be indorsed upon like copies, and if the property be in the province of Quebec and the deeds of assignment and transfer be executed elsewhere in the dominion, they may be enregistered at full length in the usual manner ; but it shall not be necessary to enregister or to refer on registration in any manner to, the list of creditors annexed to the deed of transfer.

COMPULSORY LIQUIDATION.

When a debtor's estate shall be subject to compulsory liquidation.

13. A debtor shall be deemed insolvent and his estate shall become subject to compulsory liquidation.

ABSCONDING.

a. If he absconds or is immediately about to abscond from any province in Canada with intent to defraud any creditor, or to defeat or delay the remedy of any creditor, or to avoid being arrested or served with legal process; or if being out of any such province in Canada he so remains with a like intent; or if he conceals himself within the limits of Canada with like intent;

SECRETION.

b. Or if he secretes or is immediately about to secrete any part of his estate and effects with intent to defraud his creditors, or to defeat or delay their demands or any of them;

FRAUDULENT ASSIGNMENT.

c. Or if he assigns, removes or disposes of, or is about or attempts to assign, remove or dispose of, any of his property with intent to defraud, defeat or delay his creditors, or any of them;

FRAUDULENTLY PROCURING EXECUTION.

d. Or if with such intent he has procured his money, goods, chattels, lands or property to be seized, levied on or taken under or by any process or execution, having operation where the debtor resides or has property, founded upon a demand in its nature provable under this act, and for a sum exceeding two hundred dollars, and if such process is in force and not discharged by payment or in any manner provided for by law;

IMPRISONED IN CIVIL ACTION.

e. Or if he has been actually imprisoned or upon the jail limits for more than thirty days in a civil action founded on contract for the sum of two hundred dollars or upwards, and still is so imprisoned or on the limits; or in case of such imprisonment he has escaped out of prison or from custody or from the limits;

NEGLECTING OR REFUSING TO APPEAR.

f. Or if he wilfully neglects or refuses to appear on any rule or order requiring his appearance, to be examined as to his debts under any statute or law in that behalf;

NEGLECTING OR REFUSING TO COMPLY.

g. Or if he wilfully refuses or neglects to obey or comply with any such rule or order made for payment of his debts or of any part of them;

NEGLECTING OR REFUSING TO OBEY ORDER IN CHANCERY.

h. Or if he wilfully neglects or refuses to obey or comply with the order or decree of the court of chancery or of any of the judges thereof, for payment of money;

ASSIGNMENT OTHER THAN BY THIS ACT.

i. Or if he has made any general conveyance or assignment of his property for the benefit of his creditors, otherwise than in the manner prescribed by this act, or if being unable to meet his liabilities in full, he makes any sale or conveyance of the whole or the main part of his stock in trade or of his assets, without the consent of his creditors, or without satisfying their claims;

PERMITS AN EXECUTION ON HIS PROPERTY.

j. Or if he permits any execution issued against him under which any of his chattels, land or property are seized, levied upon or taken in execution, to remain unsatisfied till within four days of the time fixed by the sheriff or officer for the sale thereof, or for fifteen days after such seizure; subject however to the privileged claim of the seizing creditor for the costs of such execution, and also to his claim for the costs of the judgment under which such execution has issued, which shall constitute a lien upon the effects seized, or shall not do so, according to the law as it existed previous to the passing of this act, in the province in which the execution shall issue.

If a debtor fails to meet his liabilities.

14. If a debtor ceases to meet his liabilities generally as they become due, any one or more claimants upon him for sums exceeding in the aggregate five hundred dollars, may make a demand upon him either

personally within the county or judicial district wherein such insolvent has his chief place of business, or at his domicile, upon some grown person of his family, or in his employ ; (Form E) requiring him to make an assignment of his estate and effects for the benefit of his creditors.

But if claims do not amount to $500, etc., Judge may make an order suspending proceedings.

15. If the debtor, on whom such demand is made, contends that the same was not made in conformity with this act, or that the claims of such creditor or creditors do not amount to five hundred dollars, or that they were procured in whole or in part for the purpose of enabling such creditor or creditors to take proceedings under this act, or that the stoppage of payment by such debtor was only temporary, and that it was not caused by any fraud or fraudulent intent, or by the insufficiency of the assets of such debtor to meet his liabilities, he may after notice to such claimant or claimants, but only within five days from such demand, present a petition to the judge praying that no further proceedings under this act may be taken upon such demand, and after hearing the parties and such evidence as may be adduced before him, the judge may grant the prayer of his petition, and thereafter such demand shall have no force or effect whatever ; and such petition may be granted with or without costs against either party ; but if it appears to the judge that such demand has been made without reasonable grounds, and merely as a means of enforcing payment under colour of proceedings under this act, he may condemn the creditors making it, to pay treble costs.

If the debtor be absent when the demand is made.

16. If at the time of such demand the debtor was absent from the province wherein such service was made, application may be made after due notice to the claimants, within the said period of five days, to the judge on his behalf, for an enlargement of the time for making an assignment; and thereupon if such debtor have not returned to such province the judge may make an order enlarging such period, and fixing the delay within which such assignment shall be made, but such enlargement of time may be refused by the judge if it be made to appear to his satisfaction that the same would be prejudicial to the interests of the creditors.

In certain cases such debtor's estate to become subject to compulsory liquidation.

17. If such petition be rejected, or if while such petition is pending, the debtor continues his trade, or proceeds with the realization of his assets, or if no such petition be presented within the aforesaid time, and the insolvent during the same time neglects to make an assignment of his estate and effects for the benefit of his creditors as provided by the second section of this act, his estate shall become subject to compulsory liquidation.

When act or omission shall not justify the placing of the estate in compulsory liquidation.

18. But no act or omission shall justify any proceeding to place the estate of an insolvent in compulsory liquidation, unless proceedings are taken under this act in respect of the same, within three months next after the act or omission relied upon as subjecting such estate thereto ; nor after a writ of attachment in compulsory liquidation has been issued while it remains in force, nor after a voluntary assignment has been made, or an assignee appointed under this act.

Affidavits in Province of Quebec, how made. Writ of Attachment founded thereon.

19. In the province of Quebec an affidavit may be made by a claimant for a sum of not less than two hundred dollars, or by the clerk or other duly authorized agent of such claimant, setting forth the particulars of his debt, the insolvency of the person indebted to him, and any fact or facts which under this act, subject the estate of such debtor to compulsory liquidation.—(Form F)—And upon such affidavit being filed with the prothonotary of the district within which the insolvent has his chief place of business, a writ of attachment (Form G) shall issue against the estate and effects of the insolvent, addressed to the sheriff of the district in which such writ issues, requiring such sheriff to seize and attach the estate and effects of the insolvent, and to summon him to appear before the court to answer the premises ;

and such writ shall be subject as nearly as can be to the rules of procedure of the court in ordinary suits, as to its issue, service, and return, and as to all proceedings subsequent thereto before any court or judge.

Affidavits in other Provinces, how made. Writ of Attachment.

20. In the province of Ontario, New Brunswick or Nova Scotia, in case any claimant by affidavit of himself or of any other individual (Form F), shows to the satisfaction of the judge that he is a creditor of the insolvent for a sum of not less than two hundred dollars, and also shows by the affidavits of two credible persons, such facts and circumstances as satisfy such judge that the debtor is insolvent within the meaning of this act, and that his estate has become subject to compulsory liquidation, such judge may order the issue of the writ of attachment (Form G), against the estate and effects of the insolvent, addressed to the sheriff of the county in which such writ issues, requiring such sheriff to seize and attach the estate and effects of the insolvent and to summon him to appear before the court to answer the premises, and such writ shall be subject as nearly as can be to the rules of procedure of the court in ordinary suits as to its issue and return, and as to all proceedings subsequent thereto before any court or judge.

Service of Writ, in case insolvent has no domicile or absconds.
Concurrent Writs.

21. If the defendant in any process for compulsory liquidation, has no domicile in any province of Canada, or absconds from the province in which he has his domicile, or remains without such province, or conceals himself within such province, service of the writ of attachment issued against him under this act, may be validly made upon him in any manner which the judge may order, upon application to him in that behalf; and in proceedings for compulsory liquidation, concurrent writs of attachment may be issued, if required by the plaintiff, addressed to the sheriffs of districts or counties in any part of Canada other than the district or county in which such proceedings are being carried on.

Return of Writs of Attachment.

22. Writs of attachment in proceedings for compulsory liquidation may be made returnable after the expiry of three days from the service thereof, when the defendant resides in Canada, and not more than fifteen miles from the place of return, or when the defendant has no domicile therein ; and of one additional day for every additional distance of fifteen miles between such residence, if in Canada, and such place of return ; and immediately upon the issue of a writ of attachment under this act, the sheriff shall give notice thereof by advertisement thereof (Form H.)

Sheriff to be Officer of Court issuing Writs. His duty in executing it.

23. For all the purposes of such writ of attachment and in respect of all his duties regarding it, the sheriff shall be an officer of the court issuing such writ, and subject to its summary jurisdiction as such; and under such writ he shall by himself or by such agent or messenger as he shall appoint for that purpose, whose authority shall be established by a copy of the writ addressed to him by name and description, and certified under the hand of the sheriff, seize and attach all the estate and effects of the insolvent within the limits of the county or district for which such sheriff is appointed, including his books of account, moneys and securities for money, and all his office or business papers, documents, and vouchers of every kind and description ; and shall return, with the writ, a report under oath stating in general terms his action thereon.

Sheriff may enter house and shop, etc., forcibly.

24. If the sheriff or officer charged with any writ of attachment is unable to obtain access to the interior of the house, shop, warehouse, or other premises of the defendant named in such writ, by reason of the same being locked, barred or fastened, such sheriff or officer shall have the right forcibly to open the same.

In whose custody Sheriff shall place estate : duty of such person.

25. If, in the county or district in which is situated the chief place of business of the

debtor, official assignees have been appointed for the purpose of this act, the sheriff shall place the estate and effects attached in the custody of one of such official assignees, who shall be guardian under such writ, but if not, he shall appoint as guardian such competent and responsible person as may be willing to assume such guardianship; and the person so placed in possession shall be bound to perform all the duties hereinbefore imposed upon the interim assignee, except the calling of a meeting of creditor for the appointment of an assignee.

When petition may be presented by Insolvent.
Hearing on Petition.
Proviso.

26. Except in cases wnere a petition has been presented as provided for by the fifteenth section of this act, the alleged insolvent may present a petition to the judge at any time within three days from the return day of the writ, but not afterwards; and may thereby pray for the setting aside of the attachment made under such writ, on the ground that his estate has not become subjected to compulsory liquidation; or if the writ of attachment has issued against a debtor by reason of his neglect to satisfy a writ of execution against him as hereinbefore provided, then on such ground, and also on the ground that such neglect was caused by a temporary embarrassment, and that it was not caused by any fraud or fraudulent intent, or by the insufficiency of the assets of such debtor to meet his liabilities; and such petition shall be heard and determined by the judge in a summary manner, and conformable to the evidence adduced before him thereon; but proceedings for compulsory liquidation shall not be contested either as to form or upon the merits, otherwise than by a summary petition, in the manner, upon the grounds, and within the delay, hereinbefore provided.

Meeting of creditors, how called.

27. Immediately upon the expiration of three days from the return day of the writ, if no petition to quash or to stay proceedings be filed, or upon the rendering of judgment on the petition to quash, if it be dismissed, or immediately upon such return with the consent of the insolvent, the judge, upon the application of the plaintiff, or of any creditor declaring in such application that he thereby intervenes for the prosecution ot the cause, shall order a meeting of the creditors to be held at a time and place named in such order, and after due notice thereof by advertisement, for the purpose of appointing an assignee; and the guardian shall perform the duties imposed upon the interim assignee by section four of this act.

Who will preside at meeting.
Appointment of Assignee.

28. At the time and place appointed, the judge or the prothonotary or clerk of the court in which the proceedings are carried on shall preside, and the creditors shall have the right to appoint an assignee to the estate and effects of the insolvent, and the presiding officer shall draw up and sign a record of the court, but if no creditor be present at such meeting, the presiding officer shall have power to adjourn such meeting.

Transfer of estate from guardian to Assignee.

29. Upon the appointment of the assignee, the guardian shall immediately deliver the estate and effects in his custody to such assignee: and by the effects of the insolvent, whether real or personal, movable or immovable, as existing at the date of the issue of the writ, and which may accrue to him by any title whatsoever, up to the time of his discharge under this act, and whether seized or not seized under the writ of attachment, shall vest in the said assignee in the same manner, to the same extent and with the same exceptions, as if he had been duly appointed assignee to such insolvent under a voluntary assignment of his estate and effects executed by the insolvent to an interim assignee, and such estate and effects had been duly transferred to him as hereinbefore provided.

Proof and registry of appointment.

30. An authentic copy or exemplification, under the hand of the court, of the record of appointment of an assignee, may be registered at full length in any registry office, without any proof of the signature of the officer and without any memorial; and such registration shall have the same effect as to the real estate of the

insolvent and in all other respects, as the registration under this act of a deed of assignment with deed of transfer annexed.

Appointment of Official Assignees by Board of Trade.
In places where there is no Board of Trade.
Security by and removal of Assignees.
Present Official Assignees continued.

31. The board of trade at any place, or the council thereof, shall within three months from the time at which this act shall come in force, and afterwards from time to time, within three months after any vacancy by the death, resignation or removal of any official assignee, name any number of persons within the county or district in which such board of trade exists, or within any county or district adjacent thereto in which there is no board of trade, to wit: at least one official assignee for each of such counties, and at least three official assignees in each district of the province of Quebec, to be official assignees for the purposes of this act, and at the time of such nomination shall declare what security for the due performance of his duties, shall be given by each of such official assignees before entering upon them; and a copy of the resolution naming such persons, certified by the secretary of the board, shall be transmitted to the prothonotary or clerk of the court in the district or county within which such assignees are resident respectively; and such copy shall be *prima facie* evidence of the appointment of an official assignee; but such nomination may be made by the judge in any district or county wherein or adjacent to which no board of trade exists, and also in such district or county wherein or adjacent to which a board of trade exists, but in which the board of trade shall have failed to make such nomination during the delay aforesaid, and in that case the judge shall certify such nomination under his hand, and shall file such certificate in the office of the court over which he presides; and such security as such judge shall declare in such nomination, shall be given by such official assignee; and the board or judge who has appointed an official assignee, or the judge having jurisdiction at the domicile of such official assignee, may remove him upon petition to that effect duly notified to such official assignee, and upon such no-

tice and for such causes as such board or judge may deem sufficient; but such removal shall not have the effect of removing such official assignee from the office of assignee to any estate to which he has previously been appointed; and all official assignees now holding that office shall continue to hold the same, but subject to all the provisions of this act with respect to official assignees.

To whom and for whose benefit the security shall be given.
Proviso: Creditors may require further security.
If more than one insolvent estate has claims on it.

32. Such security shall be taken in the name of office of the president of such board of trade or judge, for the benefit of the creditors of any person whose estate is or subsequently may be, in process of liquidation under this act; and in case of the default of any such official assignee in the performance of his duty, his security may be enforced and realized by the assignee of the estate which suffers by such default, then or subsequently appointed, who may sue in his own name as such assignee upon such security; *provided, always,* that the giving of such security shall not prevent the creditors of any insolvent from requiring security to be given for their benefit as hereinafter provided; but in that case the security taken in the name of the president of the board of trade or judge shall be regarded as supplementary to the security so required, and shall be enforceable only after discussion of such security; and upon the security so given coming to an end, the official assignee shall be incapable of being appointed interim assignee or guardian until new security be given instead thereof to the satisfaction of the official receiving the same; and if in case of such default it be found that more than one insolvent estate has claims upon such security, the total amount claimed, not exceeding the amount of such security, shall be payable to such of the assignees of such estates as shall be named by the president of such board of trade or judge by an instrument in writing, for that purpose, and may be claimed and recovered by such assignee after a copy of such nomination has been delivered to the surety, who shall be

discharged by such payment; and thereafter the assignee so named shall distribute the amount so received among the claimants thereof, including the estate represented by himself, in the next dividend sheet of such estate, subject to contestation like all other items in such sheet; and he shall receive in respect of the amount so received and distributed, a commission of one-half per centum thereon and no more.

Conservatory proceedings.

33. The interim assignee or guardian shall have the right in his own name, and in his capacity of interim assignee or guardian, as the case may be, to institute any conservatory process or any process or proceeding that may be necessary for the protection of the estate, provided that he shall first have obtained the authority of the judge for so doing.

Inspectors may be appointed by Creditors. Their duties, term of office, &c. Place for meetings to be fixed. Inspectors to represent the Creditors.

34. At the first meeting of creditors which shall be held for the appointment of an assignee either on a voluntary assignment or in compulsory liquidation, or at any subsequent meeting, the creditors may appoint one or more inspectors, either from among themselves, or otherwise, whose services may be gratuitous, or paid for, as the creditors shall decide at such meeting, and who shall superintend and direct the assignee in the performance of his duties under this act, until the next meeting of creditors; and if their appointment be not then or at some subsequent meeting revoked, they shall continue to hold the same till the final closing of the estate; and at such meeting and at subsequent meetings from time to time the creditors may fix, by resolution, the city, town, or other place in which meetings of creditors shall thereafter be held; and thereafter no meetings held elsewhere shall be valid; and whenever under this act the consent, authority or direction of the creditors is required, to enable the assignee to perform any act, or to adopt any course, the unanimous consent, sanction, authority or directions of the inspectors, if any there be, evidenced by a writing signed by them and deposited with the assignee, shall be held and taken to be the consent, sanction, authority or directions of the creditors in that behalf, save and except in the case of the proposed sale of the entire estate of the insolvent as hereinafter provided; subject always however to revision by the creditors at any meeting thereof held for the purpose.

If an offer of composition be made and accepted.

35. If at such meeting the insolvent shall make an offer of composition, and such offer be approved by the creditors, they may make such order as they may deem expedient, either for suspending the disposal of the estate and all or any proceedings tending thereto, for such time as may be fixed by such meeting, or for any other purpose

OF ASSIGNEES.

Notice by Assignee. Form.

36. Immediately upon his appointment the assignee shall give notice thereof by advertisement (Form I).

Calling meetings of Creditors.

37. The assignee shall call meetings of creditors, whenever required in writing so to do by the inspectors, or by five creditors stating in such writing the purpose of the intended meeting, and making themselves liable for the expense of calling the same; or whenever he is required so to do by the judge, on the application of any creditor, of which application he shall have notice; or whenever he shall himself require instructions from the creditors; and he shall state succinctly in the notice calling any meeting, the purposes of such meeting.

Assignee to obey instructions, and deposit moneys in a bank, etc. Interest thereon. Bank pass-book to be produced.

38. The assignee shall be subject to all rules, orders and directions, not contrary to law, or to the provisions of this act, which are made for his guidance by the creditors; and until he receives directions from the creditors in that behalf, if there be a bank or agency of a bank in the place or county in which the insolvent has his place of business, or within fifteen miles of such place, he shall deposit weekly, at interest, in the

name of the estate, all moneys received by him, in the bank or bank agency in or nearest to the place where the insolvent so carries on business; but he shall not deposit moneys belonging to the estate, in his own name in any bank, on pain of dismissal by the judge on the summary petition of any creditor; and the interest received upon deposits shall appertain to the estate, and shall be distributed in the same manner and subject to the same rights and privileges as the capital from which such interest accrued; and if in any account or dividend sheet made subsequent to any deposit in a bank, the assignee shall omit to account for or divide the interest then accrued thereon, he shall forfeit and pay to the estate to which such interest appertains, a sum equal to three times the amount of such interest; and he may be constrained so to do by the judge upon summary petition and by imprisonment as for a contempt of court; and at every meeting of inspectors or of creditors, the assignee shall produce a bank pass-book shewing the name in which the bank account of the estate is kept at such bank, and all the transactions with such bank connected with such account, of which production mention shall be made in the minutes of such meeting, or it shall be conclusively presumed not to have been produced thereat.

Further duties of Assignee, to keep minutes, etc.
To give further security, if required.
Form of bond, etc.

39. The interim assignee, assignee, or guardian, as the case may be, shall attend all meetings of creditors, and take and preserve minutes of such meetings, signed by himself, and signed and certified at the time by the chairman, or by three creditors present at the meeting; and the assignee shall also keep a correct register in duplicate of all his proceedings, and of the reception of all papers and documents served upon or delivered to him, and of all claims made to or before him, and shall enter therein in the first place the minutes of all meetings of creditors held before or at the time of his appointment, as delivered to him; one of which duplicates shall remain in the office of the prothonotary or clerk of the court, and shall be written up and completed by the assignee monthly from the duplicate in

his own possession; and also, if required, and independent of the security hereinbefore required to be given, the assignee, in any case, shall give such other security, and in such manner as shall be ordered by a resolution of the creditors, and shall conform himself to such directions in respect thereof, and in respect of any change or modification thereof or addition thereto, as are subsequently conveyed to him by similar resolutions; and in every such case, the bond or instrument of security shall be taken in favor of the creditors, by the name of the "Creditors of A. B., an Insolvent, under the Insolvent Act of 1869," and shall be deposited in the office of the court, and in case of default by the assignee on whose behalf it is given, may be sued upon by any assignee, who shall be subsequently appointed, to the same estate, in his own name as such assignee; and it shall be the duty of the assignee at the meeting by which he is appointed, if present thereat, or if not, then at the next meeting thereof, to bring before such meeting the question of the security to be given by him.

Powers of Insolvent vested in Assignee.
Exception.

40. All powers vested in any insolvent which he might have legally executed for his own benefit, shall vest in, and be executed by the assignee, in like manner and with like effect as they were vested in the insolvent, and might have been executed by him; put no power vested in the insolvent or property or effects held by him as trustee or otherwise for the benefit of others, shall vest in the assignee under this act.

Assignee to sell property of insolvent, and in what manner.
Proviso for sanction of Creditors.

41. The assignee shall wind up the affairs of the insolvent, by the sale, in a prudent manner, of all bank and other stocks, and of all movables belonging to him, and by the collection of all debts, but in all of such respects shall be guided by the direction of the creditors given as herein provided; but nothing in this act contained shall prevent the assignee from selling the entire estate and effects of the insolvent, real and personal, in one lot, either for a gross price, or at a dollar rate upon the liabilities of the in-

solvent, and upon such other terms and conditions as to the payment of the price, the payment or assumption and payment, by the purchaser of mortgages or hypothacary debts, and the payment of privileged debts, as may be considered advantageous, such conditions however, in the case of mortgages, hpyothecations, or privileged claims, not to diminish the security of the creditors holding the same nor to extend the term of payment agreed to by them, without their express consent : *Provided, always*, that such sale and all and every the terms and conditions thereof and connected therewith be first approved at a meeting of creditors ; and such meeting may be held at any time after the appointment of an assignee, provided notice by advertisement, as provided by this act has been given by the assignee, interim assignee or guardian, as the case may be.

Assignee to sue for debts due to insolvent. If the Insolvent sues for the same.

42. The assignee, in his own name as such, shall have the exclusive right to sue for the recovery of all debts due to or claimed by the insolvent, of every kind and nature whatsoever ; for rescinding agreements, deeds and instruments made in fraud of creditors and for the recovery back of moneys alleged to have been paid in fraud of creditors, and to take, both in the prosecution and defence of suits, all the proceedings that the insolvent might have taken for the benefit of the estate, or that any creditor might have taken for the benefit of the creditors generally ; and may intervene and represent the insolvent in all suits or proceedings by or against him, which are pending at the time of his appointment, and on his application may have his name inserted therein, in the place of that of the insolvent; and if after the appointment of an assignee, and before he has obtained his discharge under this act, the insolvent shall sue out any writ or institute or continue any proceedings of any kind or nature whatsoever, he shall give to the opposite party such security for costs as shall be ordered by the court before which such suit or proceeding is pending, before such party shall be bound to appear or plead to the same or take any further proceedings therein.

If a partner becomes insolvent, partnership thereby dissolved, etc.

43. If a partner in an unincorporated trading company or copartnership, becomes insolvent within the meaning of this act, and an assignee is appointed to the estate of such insolvent, such partnership shall thereby be held to be dissolved : and the assignee shall have all the rights of action and remedies against the other partners in such company or copartnership, which any partner could have or exercise by law or in equity against his copartners after the dissolution of the firm, and may avail himself of such rights of action and remedies, as if such copartnership or company had expired by afflux of time.

Sale of debts, the collection of which would be too onerous.

44. After having acted with due diligence in the collection of the debts, if the assignee finds there remain debts due, the attempt to collect which would be more onerous than beneficial to the estate, he may report the same to the creditors, and, with their sanction, he may obtain an order of the judge to sell the same by public auction, after such advertisement thereof as may be required by such order ; and, pending such advertisement, the assignee shall keep a list of the debts to be sold, open to inspection at his office, and shall also give free access to all documents and vouchers explanatory of such debts ; but all debts amounting to more than one hundred dollars shall be sold separately, except as herein otherwise provided.

A Creditor may obtain an order of a Judge authorizing him to take any special proceedings at his own risk.

45. If at any time any creditor of the insolvent shall desire to cause any proceeding to be taken which, in his opinion, would be for the benefit of the estate, and the assignee shall, under the authority of the creditors or of the inspectors, refuse or neglect to take such proceeding after being duly required so to do, such creditor shall have the right to obtain an order of the judge, authorizing him to take such proceeding in the name of the assignee, but at his own expense and risk, upon such terms and conditions as to indemnity to the assignee as the judge

may prescribe, and thereupon any benefit derived from such proceeding shall belong exclusively to the creditor instituting the same for his benefit, and that of any other creditors who have joined him in causing the institution of such proceeding; but if, before such order is granted, the assignee shall signify to the judge his readiness to institute such proceedings for the benefit of the creditors, the order shall be made prescribing the time within which he shall do so, and in that case the advantage derived from such proceeding shall appertain to the estate.

Rights of Purchasers of Insolvents' Debts.

46. The person who purchases a debt from the assignee may sue for it in his own name, as effectually as the insolvent might have done and as the assignee is hereby authorized to do; and a bill of sale (form K), signed and delivered to him by the assignee, shall be *prima facie* evidence of such purchase, without proof of the handwriting of the assignee; and no warranty, except as to the good faith of the assignee, shall be created by such sale and conveyance, not even that the debt is due.

Sale of Real Estate, on certain conditions.

47. The assignee may sell the real estate of the insolvent, but only after advertisement thereof, for a period of two months, and in the same manner as is required for the actual advertisement of sales of real estate by the sheriff in the district or place where such real estate is situate, and to such further extent as the assignee deems expedient; but the period of advertisement may be shortened to not less than one month by the creditors, with the approbation of the judge; but in the province of Quebec such abridgement shall not take place without the consent of the hypothecary creditors upon such real estate (if any there be), and if the price offered for any real estate at any public sale, duly advertised as aforesaid, is, in the opinion of the assignee, too small, he may withdraw such real estate, and sell it subsequently under such directions as he receives from the creditors.

Effect of Sales of Real Estate.
Form of Deed and Terms.

48. All sales of real estate so made by the assignee shall vest in the purchasers all the legal and equitable estate of the insolvent therein, and in all respects shall have the same effect as to mortgages, hypothecs, or privileges then existing thereon as if the same had been made by a sheriff in the province in which such real estate is situate, under a writ of execution issued in the ordinary course, but no other, greater, or less effect than such sheriff's sale; and the title conveyed by such sale shall have equal validity with a title credited by a sheriff's sale; and the deed of such sale which the assignee executes (form L) shall have the same effect as a sheriff's deed has in the province within which the real estate is situate; but he may grant such terms of credit as he may deem expedient, and as may be approved of by the creditors, for any part of the purchase money; except that no credit shall be given in the province of Quebec for any part of the purchase money coming to any hypothecary or privileged creditor without the consent of such creditor; and the assignee shall be entitled to reserve a special hypothec or mortgage by the deed of sale, as security for the payment of such part of the purchase money as shall be unpaid; and such deed may be executed before witnesses or before notaries, according to the exigency of the law of the place where the real estate sold is situate.

Sales in Quebec may be subject to certain charges.
Folle enchere.
Certificate of Registrar.
Code of Procedure to apply.
Order of distribution.

49. In the province of Quebec such sale may be made subject to all such charges and hypothecs as are permitted by the law of the said province to remain chargeable thereon, when sold by the sheriff, and also subject to such other charges and hypothecs thereon, as are not due at the time of sale, the time of payment whereof shall not however be extended by the conditions of such sale; and also subject to such other charges and hypothecs as may be consented to in writing by the holders or creditors thereof. And an order of re-sale for false bidding may be obtained from the judge by the assignee upon summary petition; and such re-sale may be proceeded with after the same notices and

advertisements, and with the same effect and consequences as to the false bidder, and all others, and by means of similar proceedings, as are provided in ordinary cases for such re-sales, in all essential particulars and as nearly as may be without being inconsistent with this act; and as soon as immovables are sold by the assignee, he shall procure from the registrar of the registration division in which each immovable is situate, a certificate of the hypothecs charged upon such immovable and registered up to the day of the issue of the writ of attachment, or of the execution of the deed of assignment by which the estate of the insolvent was brought within the purview of this act, as the case may be; and such certificate shall contain all the facts and circumstances required in the registrar's certificate obtained by the sheriff subsequent to the adjudication of an immovable in conformity with the provisions of the code of procedure and shall be made and charged for by the registrar in like manner; and the provisions of the code of procedure as to the collection of hypothecary, and privileged creditors, the necessity for and the filing of opposition for payment, and the costs thereon shall apply thereto under this act as nearly as the nature of the case will admit; and the collocation and distribution of the money arising from such sale shall be made in the dividend sheet in the same manner as to all the essential parts thereof, as the collocation and distribution of moneys arising from the sale of immovables are made in the appropriate court in ordinary cases, except in so far as the same may be inconsistent with any provision of this act.

Assignees, guardians, etc., to be subject to the orders of the Court, or Judge, etc.

50. Every interim assignee, guardian and assignee, shall be subject to the summary jurisdiction of the court or judge in the same manner and to the same extent as the ordinary officers of the court are subject to its jurisdiction, and the performance of their respective duties may be compelled, and all remedies sought or demanded for enforcing any claim for a debt, privilege, mortgage, hypothec, lien or right of property upon, in or to any effects or property in the hands, possession or custody of the assignee, may be obtained, by an order of the judge on summary petition in vacation, or of the court on a rule in term and not by any suit, attachment, opposition, seizure or other proceeding of any kind whatever; and obedience by the assignee to such order may be enforced by such judge or court under the penalty of imprisonment, as for contempt of court, or disobedience thereto, or he may be dismissed, in the discretion of the court or judge.

Assignee may be removed or resign.

51. Any assignee may be removed, either at the will of the creditors or upon his own resignation, by a resolution passed by the creditors present or represented at a meeting duly called for the purpose; and if the assignee dies or is removed they shall have the right of appointing another assignee, either at the meeting by which he is removed or at any other called for the purpose; but the assignee so removed shall, nevertheless, remain subject to the summary jurisdiction of the court and of any judge thereof, until he shall have fully accounted for his acts and conduct while he continued to be assignee.

Remuneration of Assignee, Interim Assignee and Guardian.

52. The remuneration of the interim assignee, guardian and assignee respectively, shall be fixed by the creditors at their first meeting or at any other meeting called for the purpose; but if not so fixed before a final dividend is declared, shall be put into the dividend sheet at a rate for the interim assignee or guardian, such as the assignee shall deem reasonable, and for the assignee not exceeding five per centum upon the cash receipts,—subject to contestation by any party interested as being insufficient or as exceeding the value of the services rendered, in the same manner as any other item of the dividend sheet; but no sum of money shall be inserted as a remuneration to the assignee unless the question of such remuneration shall have been previously brought before a meeting of creditors competent to decide it.

In case of death of Assignee, estate how vested.

53. Upon the death of an assignee the estate of the insolvent shall not descend to

the heirs or representatives of the assignee, but shall become vested in any assignee who shall be appointed by the creditors in his place and stead; and in case of the office of assignee becoming vacant from any cause, the estate shall be under the control of the judge until a new assignee is appointed.

Final account and discharge of Assignee.

54. After the declaration of a final dividend, or if after using due diligence the assignee has been unable to realize any assets to be divided, the assignee may prepare his final account, and may present a petition to the judge for his discharge from the office of assignee after giving notice of such petition to the insolvent and also to the inspectors if any have been appointed, or to the creditors by circular, if no inspector has been appointed; and shall produce and file with such petition a bank certificate of the deposit of any dividends remaining unclaimed, or of any balance in his hands, and a statement showing the nominal and estimated value of the assets of the insolvent, the amount of claims proved, dividing them into ordinary, privileged and hypothecary claims, the amount of dividends or composition paid to the ordinary creditors of the estate, and the entire expense of winding up the same, and thereupon the judge after causing the account to be audited by the inspectors or by some creditor or creditors named by him for the purpose, and after hearing the parties, may refuse or grant conditionally, or unconditionally the prayer of such petition.

OF DIVIDENDS.

Accounts and Statements by Assignee.

55. Upon the expiration of the period of one month from the first insertion of the advertisements giving notice of the appointment of an assignee, or as soon as may be after the expiration of such period, and afterwards from time to time at intervals of not more than three months, the assignee shall prepare and keep constantly accessible to the creditors, accounts and statements of his doings as such assignee, and of the position of the estate, and any similar intervals shall prepare dividends of the estate of the insolvent.

What claims shall rank on the estate.

56. All debts due and payable by the insolvent at the time of the execution of the deed of assignment, or at the time of the issue of a writ of attachment under this act, and all debts due but not then actually payable, subject to rebate of interest, shall have the right to rank upon the estate of the insolvent; and any person then being, as surety or otherwise, liable for any debt of the insolvent who subsequently pays such debt, shall thereafter stand in the place of the original creditor, if such creditor has proved his claim on such debt; or if he has not proved shall be entitled to prove against and rank upon the estate for such debt, to the same extent and with the same effect as such creditor might have done.

Case of Contingent Claims provided for.

57. If any creditor of the insolvent claims upon a contract dependent upon a condition or contingency, which does not happen previous to the declaration of the first dividend, a dividend shall be reserved upon the amount of such conditional or contingent claim until the condition or contingency is determined; but if it be made to appear to the judge that such reserve will probably retain the estate open for an undue length of time, he may, unless an estimate of the value thereof be agreed to between the claimant and the assignee, order the assignee to make an award upon the value of such contingent or conditional claim, and thereupon the assignee shall make an award after the same investigation, and in the same manner and subject to a similar appeal, as is hereinafter provided for the making of awards upon disputed claims and dividends, and for appeals from such awards; and in every such case the value so established or agreed to shall be ranked upon a debt payable absolutely.

Rank and privilege of Creditors: Proviso as to Creditors holding security.

58. In the preparation of the dividend sheet, due regard shall be had to the rank and privilege of every creditor, which rank and privilege, upon whatever they may legally be founded, shall not be disturbed by the provisions of this act, but no dividend shall be allotted or paid to any creditor holding security from the estate of the insol-

vent for his claim, until the amount for which he shall rank as creditor on the estate as to dividends therefrom, shall be established as hereinafter provided ; and such amount shall be the amount which he shall be held to represent in voting at meetings of creditors, and in computing the proportion of creditors, whenever under this act such proportion is required to be ascertained.

Seizure in execution after appointment of Assignee : its effect.

59. No lien or privilege upon either the personal or real estate of the insolvent shall be created for the amount of any judgment debt, or of the interest thereon, by the issue or delivery to the sheriff of any writ of execution, or by levying upon or seizing under such writ, the effects or estate of the insolvent, if before the payment over to the plaintiff of the moneys actually levied under such writ, the estate of the debtor shall have been assigned to an interim assignee, or shall have been placed in compulsory liquidation under this act ; but this provision shall not affect any lien or privilege acquired before the passing of this act, or any privilege for costs which the plaintiff possesses under the law of the province in which such writ shall have issued by reason of such issue, delivery, levy or seizure.

As to creditors holding security for their claim.
Their right to vote, etc.

60. If a creditor holds security from the insolvent or from his estate, or if there be more than one insolvent liable as partners, and the creditor holds security from or the liability of one of them, as security for a debt of the firm, he shall specify the nature and amount of such security or liability in his claim, and shall therein on his oath put a specified value thereon ; and the assignee, under the authority of the creditors, may either consent to the right to rank for such liability, or to the retention of the property or effects constituting such security or on which it attaches, by the creditor, at such specified value, or he may require from such creditor an assignment of such liability, or an assignment and delivery of such security, property or effects, at an advance of ten per centum upon such specified value, to be paid by him out of the estate so soon as he has realized

such security, in which he shall be bound to the exercise of ordinary diligence ; and in either of such cases the difference between the value at which the liability or security is retained or assumed, and the amount of the claim of such creditor, shall be the amount for which he shall rank and vote as aforesaid ; and if a creditor holds a claim based upon negotiable instruments upon which the insolvent is only indirectly or secondarily liable, and which is not mature or exigible, such creditor shall be considered to hold security within the meaning of this section, and shall put a value on the liability of the party primarily liable thereon, as being his security for the payment thereof ; but after the maturity of such liability and its nonpayment he shall be entitled to amend his claim and treat such liability as unsecured.

If the security is on realty or shipping.

61. But if the security consists of a mortgage upon real estate, or upon ships or shipping, the property mortgaged shall only be assigned and delivered to the creditor, subject to all previous mortgages, hypothecs and liens thereon, holding rank and priority before his claim, and upon his assuming and binding himself to pay all such previous mortgages, hypothecs and liens, and upon his securing such previous charges upon the property mortgaged, in the same manner and to the same extent as the same were previously secured thereon ; and thereafter the holders of such previous mortgages, hypothecs and liens shall have no further recourse or claim upon the estate of the insolvent ; and if there be mortgages, hypothecs or liens thereon subsequent to those of such creditor, he shall only obtain the property by consent of the subsequently secured creditors ; or upon their filing their claims specifying their security thereon as of no value, or upon paying them the value by them placed thereon ; or upon giving security to the assignee that the estate shall not be troubled by reason thereof.

Proceedings on the filing of a secured claim.

62. Upon a secured claim being filed, with a valuation of the security, it shall be the duty of the assignee to procure the authority of the inspectors or of the creditors at their first meeting thereafter, to consent to the retention of the security by the creditor,

or to require from him an assignment and delivery thereof; and if any meeting of inspectors or of creditors takes place without deciding upon the course to be adopted in respect of such security, the assignee shall act in the premises according to his discretion, and without delay.

Rank of several items of a creditor's claim. Supplementary oath of creditor may be required.

63. The amount due to a creditor upon each separate item of his claim at the time of the execution of a deed of assignment, or of the issue of a writ of attachment, as the case may be, and which shall remain due at the time of proving such claim, shall form part of the amount for which he shall rank upon the estate of the insolvent, until such item of claim be paid in full, except in cases of deduction of the proceeds or of the value of security, as herein before provided; but no claim or part of a claim shall be permitted to be ranked upon more than once, 'whether the claim so to rank be made by the same person or by different persons; and the assignee may at any time require from any creditor a supplementary oath, declaring what amount, if any, such creditor has received in payment of any item of the debt upon which his claim is founded, subsequent to the making of such claim, together with the particulars of such payment; and if any creditor refuses to produce or make such oath before the assignee within a reasonable time after he has been required so to do, he shall not be collocated in the dividend sheet.

Insolvent owing debts as members of copartnership.

64. If the insolvent owes debts both individually and as a member of a copartnership, or as a member of two different copartnerships, the claims against him shall rank first upon the estate by which the debts they represent were contracted, and shall only rank upon the other after all the creditors of that other have been paid in full.

Allowance to insolvent, how made, etc.

65. The creditors, or the same proportion of them that may grant a discharge to the debtor under this act, may allot to the insolvent, by way of allowance, any sum of money, or any property they may think proper; and the allowance so made shall be inserted in the dividend sheet, and shall be subject to contestation like any other item of collocation therein, but only on the ground of fraud or deceit in procuring it, or of the absence of consent by a sufficient proportion of the creditors.

As to costs in suits against Insolvent.

66. No costs incurred in suits against the insolvent after due notice of an assignment, or of the issue of a writ of attachment in compulsory liquidation has been given according to the provisions of this act, shall rank upon the estate of the insolvent; but all the taxable costs incurred in proceedings against him up to that time shall be added to the demand, for the recovery of which such proceedings were instituted; and shall rank upon the estate as if they formed part of the original debt.

Privilege of clerks, etc., for wages.

67. Clerks and other persons in the employ of the insolvent in and about his business or trade shall be collocated in the dividend sheet by special privilege for any arrears of salary or wages due and unpaid to them at the time of the execution of a deed of assignment or of the issue of a writ of attachment under this act, not exceeding four months of such arrears; but such privilege amount may be increased by order of the creditors.

Notice of dividend sheet and payment.

68. So soon as a dividend sheet is prepared, notice thereof (Form M) shall be given by advertisement, and after the expiry of one judicial day from the day of the last publication of such advertisement, all dividends which have not been objected to within that period shall be paid.

Debts of Insolvent for which claims are not filed.

69. If it appears to the assignee on his examination of the books of the insolvent, or otherwise, that the insolvent has creditors who have not taken the proceedings requisite to entitle them to be collocated, it shall be his duty to reserve dividends for such creditors according to the nature of the claims, and to notify them of such reserve, which

notification may be by letter through the post, addressed to such creditors' residence as nearly as the same can be ascertained by the assignee; and if such creditors do not file their claims and apply for such dividends previous to the declaration of the last dividend of the estate, the dividends reserved for them shall form part of such last dividend.

Claims objected to, how determined.

70. If any claim be objected to at any time, or if any dividend be objected to within the said period of one day, and any dispute arises between the creditors of the insolvent or between him and any creditor, as to the amount of the claim of any creditor, or as to the ranking or privilege of the claim of any creditor upon such dividend sheet, the assignee shall proceed thereon as hereinafter provided, shall hear and examine the parties and their witnesses under oath (which oath the assignee is hereby empowered to administer), shall take clear notes in writing of the parol evidence adduced before him, shall examine and verify the statements submitted to him, by the books and accounts of the insolvent, and by such evidence, vouchers and statements as may be furnished to him, and shall make an award in the premises, and as to the costs of such contestation, which award shall be deposited in the court, and shall be final, unless appealed from within three days from the date of its communication to the parties to the dispute.

Notice to be given of objections.
Award, how made.

71. The assignee shall not receive or notice any objection to any claim, dividend or collocation, unless such objection shall be filed before him in writing, stating distinctly the grounds of such objection, together with evidence of the previous service of a copy thereof on the claimant; and the claimant shall have three days thereafter to answer the same, which time, however, may be enlarged by the assignee, with a like delay to the contestant to reply; and upon the completion of an issue upon such objection the assignee shall fix a day for proceeding to take evidence thereon, and shall thereafter proceed therewith from day to day, unless he shall otherwise order, until the making of his award in the premises.

Inspectors may order Contestation of Claims.

72. It shall be the duty of the inspectors and of the assignee under their direction to examine the claims filed before the assignee, and to abtain information as to their correctness, and when they consider it expedient that any claim, dividend or collocation be contested, they may order the contestation thereof at the expense of the estate; and such contestation may be made in their names or in the names of any creditor consenting thereto.

As to Costs awarded by Assignee.

73. The award of the assignee as to costs may be made executory by execution in the same manner as an ordinary judgment of the court, by means of an order of the judge, obtained upon the application of the party to whom costs are awarded, made after notice to the opposite party; and the creditors may by resolution authorize and direct the costs of the contestation of any claim or any dividend to be paid out of the estate, and may make such order either before, pending or after such contestation.

If there be property under seizure at commencement of proceedings.

74. If at the time of the issue of a writ of attachment, or the execution of a deed of assignment, any immovable property or real estate of the insolvent be under seizure, or in process of sale, under any writ or execution or other order of any competent court, such sale shall be proceeded with by the officer charged with the same, unless stayed by order of the judge upon application by the guardian, interim assignee or assignee, upon special cases shown, and after notice to the plaintiff; reserving to the party prosecuting the sale his privileged claim on the proceeds of any subsequent sale, for such costs as he would have been entitled to be paid by privilege out of the proceeds of the sale of such property, if made under such writ or order; but if such sale be proceeded with, the moneys levied therefrom shall be paid over to the assignee for distribution, according to the rank or priority of the claimants thereon, and the officer charged with the execution shall make his return of such moneys to the assignee and pay them over to him, and his return to the court from

which the writ issued, declaring that he has done so, shall be a valid and sufficient return upon such writ in so far as regards the moneys so paid over:

Dividends unclaimed, how dealt with.

75. All dividends remaining unclaimed at the time of the discharge of the assignee shall be left in the bank where they are deposited, for three years, and if still unclaimed, shall then be paid over by such bank with the interest accrued thereon, to the government of Canada, and if afterwards duly claimed shall be paid over to the persons entitled thereto, with interest at the rate of four per centum from the time of the reception thereof by the government.

Balance payable to Insolvent.

76. If any balance remains of the estate of the insolvent or of the proceeds thereof, after the payment in full of all debts due by the insolvent, such balance shall be paid over to the insolvent upon his petition to that effect, duly notified to the creditors by advertisement and granted by the judge.

OF LEASES.

Lease more valuable than the rent to be sold : and subject to what conditions.

77. If the insolvent holds under a lease, property having a value above and beyond the amount of any rent payable under such lease, the assignee shall make a report thereon to the judge, containing his estimate of the value of the estate of the leased property in excess of the rent ; and thereupon the judge may order the rights of the insolvent in such leased premises to be sold, after such notice of such sale as he shall see fit to order ; and at the time and place appointed such lease shall be sold, upon such conditions as to the giving of security to the lessor, as the judge may order ; and such sale shall be so made subject to the payment of the rent and to all the covenants and conditions contained in the lease, and all such covenants and conditions shall be binding upon the lessor and upon the purchaser, as if the purchaser had been himself lessee and a party with the lessor to the lease.

Other cases of lease, how dealt with.

78. If the insolvent holds under a lease extending beyond the year current under its terms at the time of his insolvency, property which is not subject to the provisions of the last preceding section, or respecting which the judge does not make an order of sale, as therein provided, or which is not sold under such order, the creditors shall decide at any meeting which may be held more than one month before the determination of the yearly term of the lease current at the time of such meeting, whether the property so leased should be retained for the use of the estate, only up to the end of the then current yearly term, or, if the conditions of the lease permit of further extension, also up to the end of the next following yearly term thereof, and their decision shall be final.

If the lessor claims damages for receiving any property before the end of the lease.

79. From and after the time fixed for the retention of the leased property for the use of the estate, the lease shall be canceled and shall from thenceforth be inoperative and null ; and so soon as the resolution of the creditors as to such retention has been passed, such resolution shall be notified to the lessor, and if he contends that he will sustain any damage by the termination of the lease under such decision, he may make a claim for such damage, specifying the amount thereof under oath, in the same manner as in ordinary claims upon the estate, and the assignee shall proceed forthwith to make an award upon such claim, in the same manner, and after similar investigation and with the same right of appeal, as is herein provided for in case of claims or dividends objected to.

How such damage shall be estimated.

80. In making such claim, and in any award thereupon, the measure of damages shall be the difference between the value of the premises leased when the lease terminates under the resolution of the creditors, and the rent which the insolvent had agreed by the lease to pay during its continuance ; and the chance of leasing or not leasing the premises again, for a like rent, shall not enter into the computation of such

damages; and if damages are finally awarded to the lessor he shall rank for the amount upon the estate as an ordinary creditor.

Preferential claim of landlord limited.

81. The preferential lien of the landlord for rent in the provinces of Ontario, New Brunswick, or Nova Scotia is restricted to the arrears of rent due during the period of one year last previous to the execution of a deed of assignment, or the issue of a writ of attachment under this act, as the case may be, and from thence so long as the assignee shall retain the premises leased.

OF APPEAL.

Appeal to the Judge from award of Assignee, and proceedings consequent upon it.

82. There shall be an appeal to the judge from the award of an assignee made under this act, which appeal shall be by summary application, of which notice shall be given to the opposite party and to the assignee, within three days from the day on which the award is notified to the party complaining of it, and which shall be presented forthwith after the expiration of the delay required for notice of presentation ; and the assignee shall attend before the judge at the time and place indicated in such notice, and shall produce before him all evidence, notes of evidence, books, or proved extracts from books, documents, vouchers, and papers having reference to the matter in dispute ; and thereupon the judge may confirm such award, or modify it, or refer it back to the assignee for the taking of evidence, by such order as will satisfy the ends of justice ; and, pending any appeal, the assignee shall reserve a dividend equal to the amount of the dividend claimed.

Appeal from order of Judge.
Judge may refer it to the full Court.

83. If any of the parties to any appeal, contestation, matter or thing upon which a judge has made any final order or judgment, are dissatisfied with such order or judgment, they may in the province of Quebec move to revise the same or any appeal therefrom in like manner as from any final judgment of

the superior court, to the court of queen's bench on the appeal side thereof; in the province of Ontario they may appeal therefrom to either of the superior courts of common law or the court of chancery, or to any one of the judges of the said courts; in the province of New Brunswick to the supreme court of New Brunswick or to any one of the judges of the said court ; and in the province of Nova Scotia to the supreme court of Nova Scotia or to any one of the judges of said court; but any appeal to a single judge in the provinces of Ontario, New Brunswick or Nova Scotia may, in his discretion, be referred on a special case to be settled, to the full court, and on such terms in the meantime as he may think necessary and just.

Conditions of appeal.
Security.

84. Such appeal shall not be permitted, unless within five days from the day on which the order or judgment is rendered, or on which, in the province of Quebec, the delay for moving to revise the same expires, if no motion in revision be made, the party desiring to appeal causes to be served upon the opposite party and upon the assignee, an application in appeal, setting forth the proceeding before the judge, and his decision thereon, and praying for its revision, with a notice of the day on which such application is to be presented, and also within the said period of five days causes security to be given before the judge by two sufficient sureties, that he will duly prosecute such appeal, and pay all costs incurred by reason thereof by the respondent.

Costs on Appellant not proceeding according to his petition.

85. If the party appellant does not present his application on the day fixed for that purpose, the court or judge selected to be appealed to, as the case may be, shall order the record to be returned to the person or officer entitled to the custody thereof, and the party respondent may, on the following or any other day during the same term, produce before the court, or within six days thereafter before the judge, the copy of application served upon him, and obtain costs thereon against the appellant.

OF FRAUD AND FRAUDULENT PREFERENCES.

Gratuitous contracts made within three months of insolvency presumed fraudulent and void.

86. All gratuitous contracts or conveyances, or contracts or conveyance without consideration, or with a merely nominal consideration, respecting either real or personal estate made by a debtor afterwards becoming an insolvent with or to any person whomsoever, whether such person be his creditor or not, within three months next preceding the date of the assignment, or of the issue of the writ of attachment in compulsory liquidation, and all contracts by which creditors are injured obstructed or delayed, made by a debtor unable to meet his engagements, and afterwards becoming an insolvent, with a person knowing such inability or having probable cause for believing such inability to exist, or after such inability is public and notorious, whether such person be his creditor or not, are presumed to be made with intent to defraud his creditors.

Certain others voidable.

87. A contract or conveyance for consideration, respecting either real or personal estate, by which creditors are injured or obstructed, made by a debtor unable to meet his engagements with a person ignorant of such inability, whether such person be his creditor or not, and before such inability has become public and notorious, but within thirty days next before the execution of a deed of assignment or of the issue of a writ of attachment under this act, is voidable, and may be set aside by any court of competent jurisdiction, upon such terms as to the protection of such person from actual loss or liability by reason of such contract, as the court may order.

All contracts made with intent to impede or defraud Creditors, with the knowledge of party contracting, to be void.

88. All contracts, or conveyances made and acts done by a debtor, respecting either real or personal estate, with intent fraudulently to impede, obstruct or delay his creditors in their remedies against him, or with intent to defraud his creditors, or any of them, and so made, done and intended with the knowledge of the person contracting or acting with the debtor, whether such person be his creditor or not, and which have the effect of impeding, obstructing or delaying the creditors of their remedies, or of injuring them or any of them, are prohibited and are null and void, notwithstanding that such contracts, conveyances, or acts be in consideration or in contemplation of marriage.

Fraudulent Preferential Sales, etc., to be void.
And presumed fraudulent, if made within a certain time before assignment, etc.

89. If any sale, deposit, pledge, or transfer be made of any property real or personal by any person in contemplation of insolvency, by way of security for payment to any creditor, or if any property real or personal, movable or immovable, goods, effects, or valuable security, be given by way of payment by such person to any creditor, whereby such creditor obtains or will obtain an unjust preference over the other creditors, such sale, deposit, pledge, transfer, or payment shall be null and void, and the subject thereof may be recovered back for the benefit of the estate by the assignee, in any court of competent jurisdiction; and if the same be made within thirty days next before the execution of a deed of assignment, or the issue of a writ of attachment under this act, it shall be presumed to have been so made in contemplation of insolvency.

Payments made under certain circumstances by a debtor to be void.

90. Every payment made within thirty days next before the execution of a deed of assignment, or the issue of a writ of attachment under this act, by a debtor unable to meet his engagements in full, to a person knowing such inability, or having probable cause for believing the same to exist, is void, and the amount paid may be recovered back by suit in any competent court, for the benefit of the estate; *provided always*, that if any valuable security be given up in consideration of such payment, such security or the value thereof shall be restored to the creditor before the return of such payment can be demanded.

Transfers of debts of insolvent within thirty days of his insolvency to his debtors to enable them to set off, void.

91. Any transfer of a debt due by the insolvent, made within thirty days next previous to the execution of a deed of assignment or the issue of a writ of attachment under this act, or at any time afterwards, to a debtor knowing or having probable cause for believing the insolvent to be unable to meet his engagements, or in contemplation of his insolvency, for the purpose of enabling the debtor to set up by way of compensation or set-off the debt so transferred, is null and void as regards the estate of the insolvent; and the debt due to the estate of the insolvent shall not be compensated or affected in any manner by a claim so acquired ; but the purchaser thereof may rank on the estate in the place and stead of the original creditor.

Purchasing goods on credit, etc., by person knowing himself unable to pay, how punishable.
If by a firm.

92. Any person who purchases goods on credit or procures advances in money, knowing or believing himself to be unable to meet his engagements, and concealing the fact from the person thereby becoming his creditor, with the intent to defraud such person, or who by any false pretence obtains a term of credit for the payment of any advance or loan of money, or of the price or any part of the price of any goods, wares or merchandise, with intent to defraud the person thereby becoming his creditor, and who shall not afterwards have paid the debt or debts so incurred, shall be held to be guilty of a fraud, and shall be liable to imprisonment for such time as the court may order, not exceeding two years, unless the debt or costs be sooner paid ; and if such debt or debts be incurred by a partnership, then every member thereof who shall have known of the incurring, and of the intention to incur, such debt or debts, shall be similarly liable ; *provided always,* that in the suit or proceeding taken for the recovery of such debt or debts, the defendant be charged with such fraud, and be declared to be guilty of it by the judgment rendered in such suit or proceeding.

Fraud must be proved.
Award of imprisonment.

93. Whether the defendant in any such case appear and plead or make default, the plaintiff shall be bound to prove the fraud charged, and upon his proving it, if the trial be before a jury, the judge who tries the suit or proceeding shall immediately after the verdict rendered against the defendant for such fraud (if such verdict is given), or if not before a jury, then immediately upon his rendering his judgment in the premises, adjudge the term of imprisonment which the defendant shall undergo ; and he shall forthwith order and direct the defendant immediately to be taken into custody and imprisoned accordingly ; but such judgment shall not affect the ordinary remedies for the revision thereof or of any proceeding in the case.

OF COMPOSITION AND DISCHARGE.

Deed of composition, and executed by a certain proportion of creditors to bind all.

94. A deed of composition and discharge, executed by the majority in number of those of the creditors of an insolvent who are respectively creditors for sums of one hundred dollars and upwards, and who represent at least three-fourths in value of the liabilities of the insolvent subject to be computed in ascertaining such proportion, shall have the same effect with regard to the remainder of his creditors and be binding to the same extent upon him and upon them as if they were also parties to it ; and such a deed may be invoked, and acted upon under this act although made either before, pending or after proceedings upon an assignment, or for the compulsory liquidation of the estate of the insolvent ; the whole subject to the exceptions contained in section one hundred of this act.

Form and effect of such Deed.
If it be conditional on payment of the Composition.

95. Such deed of composition and discharge may be so made either in consideration of a composition payable in cash, or on terms of credit, or partially for cash and partially on credit ; and the payment of

such composition may be secured or not according to the pleasure of the creditors signing it; and the discharge therein contained may be absolute, or may be conditional upon the condition of the composition being paid; and such deed may contain instructions to the assignee as to the manner in which he is to proceed, and to deal with the estate and effects of the insolvent, subsequent to the deposit of such deed with him, which instructions shall be obeyed by the assignee; but if such discharge be conditional upon the composition being paid, and the deed of composition and discharge therein contained should cease to have effect, the assignee shall immediately resume possession of the entire estate and effects of the insolvent in the state and condition in which they shall then be; but the creditors holding claims which were provable before the execution of such deed shall not rank, vote or be computed as creditors concurrently with those who have acquired claims subsequent to the execution thereof for any greater sum than the balance of composition remaining unpaid; but after such subsequent creditors shall have received dividends to the amount of their claims, then such original creditors shall have the right to rank for the entire balance of their original claims then remaining unpaid, and shall be computed for all purposes for which the proportions of creditors require to be ascertained, as creditors for the full amount of such last mentioned balance.

Deed of Reconveyance by Assignee to Insolvent. Its effects.
If it be contested, and a payment of Compoposition during the contestation. Form and registration of Deeds.

96. The reconveyance by the assignee to the insolvent, or to any person for him of any part of his estate or effects, whether real or personal, if made in conformity with the terms of a deed of composition and discharge shall have the same effect (except as the same may be otherwise agreed by the conditions of such deed or reconveyance), as if such property had been sold by the assignee in the ordinary course, and after all the preliminary proceedings, notices and formalities herein required for such sale; and if such deed of composition and discharge be contested, and pending such con-

testation, any payment or instalment of the composition falls due under the terms of such deed, the payment thereof shall be postponed till after the expiration of ten days after final judgment upon such contestation; and if proceedings for revision or appeal be commenced, then until after the expiration of ten days after the judgment in revision or in appeal, as the case may be, and the deed of reconveyance need not contain any further or more special description of the effects and property reconveyed than is required to be inserted in the deed of assignment, and may be enregistered in like manner and with like effect.

Duty of Assignee receiving a Deed of Composition.

97. If the insolvent procures and deposits with the assignee a deed of composition and discharge, duly executed as aforesaid, the assignee shall immediately give notice of such deposit by advertisement; and if opposition to such composition and discharge be not made by a creditor, within three juridical days after the last publication of such notice, by filing with the assignee a declaration in writing, that he objects to such composition and discharge, the assignee shall act upon such deed of composition and discharge according to its terms; but if opposition be made thereto within the said period, or if made be not withdrawn, then he shall abstain from taking any action upon such deed until the same has been confirmed, as hereinafter provided.

Effect of consent of proper number of Creditors to a discharge.
As to holders of Negotiable Paper unknown to Insolvent.

98. The consent in writing of the said proportion of creditors to the discharge of a debtor absolutely frees and discharges him, after an assignment, or after his estate has been put in compulsory liquidation from all liabilities whatsoever (except such as are hereinafter specially excepted) existing against him and provable against his estate, which are mentioned or set forth in the statement of his affairs exhibited at the first meeting of his creditors, or which are shewn by any supplementary list of creditors furnished by the insolvent, previous to such discharge, and in time to permit of the cred

itors therein mentioned obtaining the same dividend as other creditors upon his estate, or which appear by any claim subsequently furnished to the assignee, whether such debts be exigible or not at the time of his insolvency, and whether the liability for them be direct or indirect; and if the holder of any negotiable paper is unknown to the insolvent, the insertion of the particulars of such paper in such statement of affairs or supplementary list, with the declaration that the holder thereof is unknown to him, shall bring the debt represented by such paper, and the holder thereof, within the operation of this section.

Discharge without composition not to affect secondary liabilities.

99. A discharge without composition under this act, whether consented to by any creditor or not, shall not operate any change in the liability of any person secondarily liable to such creditor for the debts of the insolvent, either as drawer or indorser of negotiable paper, or as guarantor, surety or otherwise, nor of any partner or other person liable jointly or severally with the insolvent to such creditor for any debt; nor shall it affect any mortgage, hypothec, lien or collateral security held by any such creditor as security for any debt thereby discharged.

Discharge under this Act not to apply to certain debts or liabilities.

100. A discharge under this act shall not apply, without the express consent of the creditor, to any debt for enforcing the payment of which the imprisonment of the debtor is permitted by this act, nor to any debt due as damages for assault of wilful injury to the person, seduction, libel, slander, or malicious arrest, nor for the maintenance of a parent, wife or child, or as a penalty for any offence of which the insolvent has been convicted, unless the creditor thereof shall file or claim therefor; nor shall any such discharge apply without such consent, to any debt due as a balance of account due by the insolvent as an assignee, tutor, curator, trustee, executor or administrator under a will, or under any order of court, or as a public officer; nor shall debts to which a discharge under this act does not apply, nor any privileged debts, nor the creditors thereof, be computed in ascertaining whether a suffi-

cient proportion of the creditors of the insolvent have voted upon, done or consented to any act, matter or thing under this act; but the creditor of any debt due as a balance of account by the insolvent as assignee, tutor, curator, trustee, executor, administrator or public officer may claim and accept a dividend thereon from the estate without being, by reason thereof, in any respect affected by any discharge obtained by the insolvent.

Confirmation of Discharge, and on what conditions it shall be granted.
Creditors or Assignee may oppose on certain grounds.
Proviso: as to non-keeping of certain books.
Further provision as to acts of fraud or preference, committed before certain periods.

101. An insolvent who has procured a consent to his discharge or the execution of a deed of composition and discharge, within the meaning of this act, may file in the office of the court the consent or deed of composition and discharge, and may then give notice (Form N) of the same being so filed, and of his intention to apply by petition to the court in the provinces of Quebec or Nova Scotia, or in the provinces of Ontario or New Brunswick to the judge, on a day named in such notice (which, however, shall not be before the day on which a dividend may be declared under this act), for a confirmation of the discharge effected thereby; and such notice shall be given by advertisement in the official *Gazette* for one month, and also for the same period, if the application is to be made in the province of Ontario, New Brunswick or Nova Scotia, in one newspaper, and if in the province of Quebec, in one newspaper published in French, and in one newspaper published in English, in or nearest the place of residence of the insolvent; and upon such application, any creditor of the insolvent or his assignee under the authority of the creditors, may appear and oppose such confirmation, either upon the ground of fraud or fraudulent preference within the meaning of this act, or of fraud or evil practice in procuring the consent of the creditors to the discharge, or their execution of the deed of composition and discharge, as the case may be, or of the insufficiency in number or value of the creditors consenting to or executing the same, or of the fraudulent retention and

concealment by the insolvent of some portion of his estate or effects, or of the evasion, prevarication or false swearing of the insolvent upon examination as to his estate and effects, or upon the ground that the insolvent has not kept an account book showing his receipts and disbursements of cash, and such other books of account as are suitable for his trade, or, that having at any time kept such book or books, he has refused to produce or deliver them to the assignee, or that he is wilfully in default to obey any provision of this act, or any order of the court or judge ; and if any of the said grounds be proved, the confirmation of his discharge shall be refused and such discharge set aside and annulled ; but in the provinces of Ontario and Quebec, the omission to keep such books before the coming into force of the insolvent act of 1864, and in the provinces of New Brunswick and Nova Scotia, such omission previous to the coming into force of this act, shall not be a sufficient ground for contesting the confirmation of the discharge of an insolvent ; and provided further that any act on the part of the insolvent, which might be held to be an act of fraud or fraudulent preference within the meaning of the insolvent act of 1864, or this act, but which would not amount to fraud if the said act or this act had not been passed, shall not be a ground for contesting the confirmation of the discharge of any insolvent, if such act was done by the insolvent, in the province of Ontario or Quebec, before the coming in force of the insolvent act of 1864, or in the province of Nova Scotia or New Brunswick, before the coming into force of this act.

If the insolvent does not file the Consent or Deed, for confirmation within a certain time, a creditor may notify him to do so, and apply for an order annulling the Deed.
Proviso : if the Deed be filed.

102. If the insolvent does not deposit such consent or such deed of composition and discharge, as the case may be, in the court, and give notice of his application for a confirmation of such discharge, within one month from the time at which the same has been effected under this act, and proceed therewith thereafter according to such notice, any creditor for a sum exceeding two hundred dollars, may cause to be served a notice in writing upon the insolvent, requiring him to file in the court the consent, or the deed of composition and discharge, as the case may be ; and may thereupon give one month's notice to the insolvent (Form O) of his intention to apply by petition to the court or judge who has authority under this act to confirm such discharge, on a day named in such notice, for the annulling of the discharge; and on the day so named may present a petition to the court or judge, in accordance with such notice, setting forth the reasons in support of such application, which may be any of the reasons upon which a confirmation of discharge may be opposed ; and upon such application, if the insolvent has not at least one week before the day fixed for the presentation thereof, filed in the office of the court the consent or deed under which the discharge is effected, the discharge shall be annulled without further inquiry except as to the service upon him of the notice to file the same ; but if such consent or deed be so filed, or if upon special application, leave be granted him to file the same at a subsequent time and he do then file the same, the court or judge, as the case may be, shall proceed thereon as upon an application for confirmation of such discharge.

Powers of Court or Judge on application for Confirmation of Discharge, etc.

103. The court or judge, as the case may be, upon hearing the application for confirmation of such discharge, the objections thereto, and any evidence adduced, shall have power to make an order, either confirming the discharge or annulling the same according to the effect of the evidence so adduced ; but if such evidence should be insufficient to sustain any of the grounds hereinbefore detailed as forming valid grounds for contesting such confirmation, but should nevertheless establish that the insolvent has been guilty of misconduct in the management of his business, by extravagance in his expenses, recklessness in indorsing or becoming surety for others, continuing his trade unduly after he believed himself to be insolvent, incurring debts without a reasonable expectation of paying them (of which reasonable expectation the proof shall lie on him, if such debt was contracted within thirty days of an assignment or the issue of a writ of attachment); or negligence in keep-

ing his books and accounts ; or if such facts be alleged by any contestation praying for the suspension of the discharge of the insolvent, or for its classification as second class, the court or judge may thereupon order the suspension of the operation of the discharge of the insolvent for a period not exceeding five years or may declare the discharge to be of the second class, or both, according to the discretion of the court or judge.

How the discharge shall be provable.

104. Until the court or judge, as the case may be, has confirmed such discharge, the burden of proof of the discharge being completely effected under the provisions of this act, shall be upon the insolvent; but the confirmation thereof, if not reversed in appeal, shall render the discharge thereby confirmed, final and conclusive ; and an authentic copy of the judgment confirming the same shall be sufficient evidence as well of such discharge as of the confirmation thereof.

Application to Court or Judge for discharge, if not obtained from Creditors.

105. If, after the expiration of one year from the date of an assignment made under this act, or from the date of the issue of a writ of attachment thereunder, as the case may be, the insolvent has not obtained from the required proportion of his creditors a consent to his discharge, or the execution of a deed of composition and discharge, he may apply by petition to the court or judge, having power hereunder to confirm his discharge, if consented to, to grant him his discharge, first giving notice of such application, (Form P) for one month in the manner hereinbefore provided for notice of application for confirmation of dicharge.

Proceedings on such application ; powers of the Court or Judge.

106. Upon such application, any creditor of the insolvent, or the assignee by authority of the creditors, may appear and oppose the granting of such discharge upon any ground upon which the confirmation of a discharge may be opposed under this act, or may claim the suspension or classification of the discharge or both; and whether such application be contested or not it shall be incumbent upon the insolvent to prove that he has in all respects conformed himself to the provisions of this act; and he shall submit himself to any order which the court or judge may make, upon or without an application to that effect, to the end that he be examined touching his estate and effects and his conduct and management of his af fairs and business generally, and touching each and every detail and particular thereof; and the court or judge may also require from the assignee a report in writing upon the conduct of the insolvent and the state of his books and affairs before and at the date of his insolvency ; and thereupon the court or judge, as the case may be, after hearing the insolvent, and the opposant, if any, and any evidence that may be adduced, may make an order either granting the discharge of the insolvent or refusing it ; or in like manner and under the like circumstances to those in and upon which the discharge could be suspended or classified as hereinbefore provided upon an application to confirm it, an order may be made suspending it for a like period, or declaring it to be of the second class, or both.

Suspension of Discharge, or its classification as second class, on application of Creditors.

107. At any time before judgment upon an application for obtaining a discharge, the creditors or the same proportion of them that may bind the remainder by a consent to a discharge, may file before the court, or judge before whom such application is pending, a declaration in writing, setting forth that it is their desire that the discharge of the insolvent should (if granted) be suspended for a period therein named not exceeding five years, or that it should be classed as second class, or both ; and thereupon if such court or judge should be of opinion that the insolvent is not shewn to have done or omitted anything, the doing or omission of which would deprive him of the right to his discharge under this act (but not otherwise) and shall therefore be of opinion to grant his discharge, such judge shall declare such opinion, and shall thereupon grant such discharge, but shall suspend the same as required by such declaration of the creditors.

Discharge obtained by fraud, to be void.

108. Every consent to a discharge or composition, and every discharge or confirmation, of any discharge or composition, which has been obtained by fraud or fraudulent preference, or by means of the consent of any creditor procured by the payment or promise of payment to such creditor, of any valuable consideration for such consent, or by any fraudulent contrivance or practice whatever tending to defeat the true intent and meaning of the provisions of this act in that behalf, shall be null and void.

EXAMINATION OF THE INSOLVENT AND OTHERS.

Examination of the insolvent, and how conducted and recorded.
How attested.

109. Immediately upon the expiry of the period of one month from the first insertion of the advertisement giving notice of the appointment of an assignee, a meeting of the creditors shall be held for the public examination of the insolvent, who shall be summoned to attend such meeting, the same being the first duly called by advertisement; and at such meeting the insolvent may be examined on oath, sworn before the assignee by or on behalf of any creditor present, in his turn; and the examination of the insolvent shall be reduced to writing by the assignee, and signed by the insolvent; and any question put to the insolvent at such meeting which he shall answer evasively or refuse to answer, shall also be written in such examination, with the replies made by the insolvent to such questions; and the insolvent shall sign such examination, or if he refuse to sign the same, his refusal shall be entered at the foot of the examination, with the reasons of such refusal, if any, as given by himself; and such examination shall be attested by the assignee and shall be filed in the office of the court.

Further Examination of Insolvent.

110. The insolvent may also from time to time examine as to his estate and effects upon oath, before the judge, by the assignee or by any creditor, upon an order from the judge obtained without notice to the insol-vent, upon petition, setting forth satisfactory reasons for such order,—and he may also be examined in like manner upon a *subpœna* issued as of course without such order, in any case in which a writ of attachment has been issued against his estate and effects; which *subpœna* may be procured by the plaintiff, or by any creditor intervening in the action for that purpose, or by the assignee, at any time after the return of the writ of attachment.

Subsequent Examination on Application for Discharge, etc.

111. The insolvent may also be examined on his application for a discharge or for confirmation of a discharge, or upon the application of any creditor for annulling a discharge; or upon any petition by him in the course of proceedings for the compulsory liquidation of his estate.

Other Persons may be Examined on Order of the Judge.

112. Any other person who is believed to possess information respecting the estate or effects of the insolvent, may also be from time to time examined before the judge upon oath, as to such estate or effects upon an order from the judge to that effect, which order the judge may grant upon petition setting forth satisfactory reasons for such order, without notice to the insolvent or to the person to be so examined.

Insolvent to Attend Meetings of Creditors.

113. The insolvent shall attend all meetings of his creditors, when summoned so to do by the assignee, and shall answer all questions that may be put to him at such meetings touching his business, and touching his estate and effects; and for every such attendance he shall be paid such sums as shall be ordered at such meeting, but not less than one dollar.

Examination of Wife or Husband of Insolvent.

114. If it be made known to the judge by the assignee by petition substantiated under oath, that any probable cause exists therefor, the judge may order the wife or husband of the insolvent, as the case may be, to be examined as to the reception, use, retention or concealment by or on behalf of

the insolvent, or by or on behalf of the person so examined, or any other person, of any of the estate or effects of the insolvent.

OF PROCEDURE GENERALLY.

Form of Deeds under this Act, and their effect in Provinces other than that in which they are executed.

115. All deeds of assignment, of transfer, of composition and of re-conveyance, shall be executed in the manner in which deeds are usually executed in the province wherein such deeds shall respectively bear date ; and if such deeds be executed in any part of Canada other than the province of Quebec, according to the form of execution of deeds prevailing there, they shall have the same force and effect in the province of Quebec as if they had been executed in that province before a notary ; and if such deeds be executed in that province before a notary, they shall have the same force and effect elsewhere in the Dominion as if they had been executed according to the law in force in such other province ; and copies of such deeds, certified as aforesaid, shall constitute before all courts and for all purposes, *prima facie* proof of the execution and of the contents of the originals of such deeds respectively, without production of the originals thereof

To what Assets certain sections shall apply. Proviso : as to certain Provinces ; and as to costs.

116. The operation of sections ten and twenty-nine of this act, shall extend to all the assets of the insolvent, of every kind and description, although they are actually under seizure under any ordinary writ of attachment, or under any writ of execution, so long as they are not actually sold by the sheriff or sheriff's officer under such writ ; but in the provinces of Nova Scotia and New Brunswick this section shall not apply to any writ of execution in the hands of the sheriff, at the time of the coming into force of this act ; and the rights, liens and privileges of the seizing or attaching creditor, for his costs upon any such writ, shall be the same as they were previous to the passing of this act, in the province in which such writ shall have issued.

Notices under this Act, how given.

117. Notices of meetings of creditors and all other notices herein required to be given by advertisement, without special designation of the nature of such notice, shall be so given by publication thereof for two weeks in the *Official Gazette*, also in the province of Quebec in every issue during two weeks of one newspaper in English and one in French, and in the provinces of Ontario, New Brunswick, and Nova Scotia, in one newspaper in English, published at or nearest to the place where the insolvent has his chief place of business ; and in any case, unless herein otherwise provided, the assignee or person giving such notice shall address notices thereof to all creditors and to all representatives of foreign creditors within Canada, and shall mail the same with the postage thereon paid, at the time of the insertion of the first advertisement.

How questions at meetings of Creditors shall be decided.

118. All questions discussed at meetings of creditors shall be decided by the majority in number of all creditors for sums of one hundred dollars and upwards, present or represented at such meeting, and representing also the majority in value of such creditors, unless herein otherwise specially provided ; but if the majority in number do not agree with the majority in value, the views of each section of the creditors shall be embodied in resolutions, and such resolutions with a statement of the vote taken thereon, shall be referred to the judge, who shall decide between them.

Questions as to number and value of creditors voting, how decided.

119. If for any purpose it becomes necessary to ascertain the proportion of the creditors of an insolvent who have voted at any meeting or concurred in any act or document, and if it be found that the whole of the creditors holding claims against an insolvent for sums of one hundred dollars and upwards, do not represent the proportion in value of the liabilities of the insolvent subject to be computed in that behalf and required to give validity to such vote, act or documents such proportion may be completed by the votes or concurrence of creditors

holding claims of less than one hundred dollars.

Notice pending delay.

120. Whenever a meeting of creditors cannot be held, or an application made, until the expiration of a delay named herein, notice of such meeting or application may be given pending such delay.

Certain things may be done at First Meeting, though not mentioned in Notice.

121. If the first meeting of creditors which takes place after the expiry of the period of one month from the advertisement of the appointment of an Assignee be called for the ordering of the affairs of the estate generally, and it be so stated in the notices calling such meeting, all the matters and things respecting which the creditors may vote, resolve or order, or which they may regulate under this act, may be voted, resolved or ordered upon and may be regulated at such meeting, without having been specially mentioned in the notices calling such meeting, notwithstanding anything to the contrary in this act contained, due regard being had, however, to the proportions of creditors required by this act for any such vote, resolution, order or regulation.

Form and Attestation of Claims, and before whom to be Attested.

122. The claims of creditors (Form Q) shall be furnished to the assignee or interim assignee as the case may be, in writing, and they shall be attested under oath, taken in Canada before the assignee or before any judge, commissioner for taking affidavits, or justice of the peace, and out of Canada before any judge of a court of record, any commissioner for taking affidavits appointed by any Canadian court, the chief municipal officer for any town or city, or any British consul or vice-consul, or before any person authorized by any statute of Canada or of any province therein to take affidavits to be used in any part of Canada.

Affidavits, before whom to be made.

123. Any affidavit requiring to be sworn in proceedings in insolvency, may be sworn before any commissioner for taking affidavits, appointed by any of the courts of law or of equity in any of the said provinces; or before any judge having civil jurisdiction in any of the said provinces; and such affidavit may be made by the party interested, or by his agent in that behalf having a personal knowledge of the matters therein stated.

Set-offs, how allowed.

124. The statutes of set-off shall apply to all claims in insolvency, and also to all suits instituted by an assignee for the recovery of debts due to the insolvent, in the same manner and to the same extent as if the insolvent were plaintiff or defendant, as the case may be, except in so far as any claim for set-off shall be affected by the provisions of this act respecting frauds or fraudulent preferences.

Services of Papers under this Act.

125. One clear day's notice of any petition motion, order or rule, shall be sufficient if the party notified resides within fifteen miles of the place where the proceeding is to be taken, and one extra day shall be sufficient allowance for each additional fifteen miles of distance between the place of service and the place of proceeding; and service of such notice shall be made in such manner as is now prescribed for similar services in the province in which the service is made.

Commissions for Examination of Witnesses.

126. The judge shall have the same power and authority in respect of the issuing and dealing with commissions for the examination of witnesses, as are possessed by the ordinary courts of record in the province in which the proceedings are being carried on, and may also on petition of either of the parties to a contestation before an assignee, order the issue of such a commission by the assignee.

Subpœnas to Witness.

127. In any proceeding or contestation in insolvency, the court or judge, or the assignee as the case may be, may order a writ of subpœna ad testificandum or of subpœna duces tecum to issue, commanding the attendance as a witness of any person within the limits of Canada.

Service of Process, etc.

128. All rules, writs of subpœna, orders and warrants, issued by any judge, court or

assignee in any matter or proceeding under this act, may be validly served in any part of Canada upon the party affected or to be affected thereby ; and the service of them, or any of them, may be validly made in such manner as is now prescribed for similar services in the province within which the service is made ; and the person charged with such service shall make his return thereof and on oath, or, if a sheriff or bailiff in the province of Quebec, may make such return under his oath of office.

Disobedience of Writs and Process, how punishable.
Proof of Default.

129. In case any person so served with a writ of *subpœna* or with an order to appear for examination, does not appear according to the exigency of such writ or process, the court or the-judge on whose order or within the limits of whose territorial jurisdiction the same is issued, may, upon proof made of the service thereof, and of such default, if the person served therewith has his domicile within the limits of the province within which such writ or process is issued, constrains such person to appear and testify, and punish him for non-appearance or for not testifying in the same manner as if such person had been summoned as a witness before such court or judge, in an ordinary suit ; and if the person so served and making default, has his domicile beyond the limits of the province within which such writ or process issued, such court or judge may transmit a certificate of such default to any of her majesty's superior courts of law or equity in that part of Canada in which the person so served may reside, and the court to which such certificate is sent, shall thereupon proceed against and punish such person so having made default, in like manner as it might have done if such person had neglected or refused to appear to a writ of subpœna or other similar process issued out of such last mentioned court ; and such certificate of default signed by the court, judge or assignee before whom default was made, and copies of such writ, process and of the return of service thereof, certified by the clerk of the court in which the order of transmission is made, shall be *prima facie* proof of such writ or process, service, return and of such default.

Expenses must be tendered to Person Summoned as a Witness, etc.

130. No such certificate of default shall be so transmitted, nor shall any person be punished for neglect or refusal to attend for examination in obedience to any such subpœna or other similar process, unless it be made to appear to the court or judge transmitting, and also to the court receiving such certificate, that a reasonable and sufficient sum of money, according to the rate *per diem*, and per mile allowed to witness by law and practice of the superior courts of law within the jurisdiction of which such person was found, to defray the expenses of coming and attending to give evidence, and of returning from giving evidence, had been tendered to such person at the time when the writ of subpœna, or other similar process, was served upon him.

Forms under the Act.
Construction of Statements.

131. The forms appended to this act, or other forms in equivalent terms shall be used in the proceedings for which such forms are provided ; and in every contestation of a claim, collocation or dividend, or of an application for a discharge, or for confirming or annulling a discharge, the facts upon which the contesting party relies, shall be set forth in detail, with particulars of time, place and circumstance, and no evidence shall be received upon any fact not so set forth ; but in every petition, application, motion, contestation, or other pleading under this act, the parties may state the facts upon which they rely, in plain and concise language, to the interpretation of which the rules of construction applicable to such language in the ordinary transactions of life shall apply.

Foreign discharges not to bar Debts contracted in Canada.

132. No plea or exception alleging or setting up any discharge or certificate of discharge granted under the bankrupt or insolvent law of any country whatsoever beyond the limits of Canada, shall be a valid defence or bar to any action instituted in any court of competent jurisdiction in Canada, for the recovery of any debt or obligation contracted within such limits.

As to amendments in proceedings under this act.

133. The rules of procedure as to the amendments of pleadings, which are in force at any place where any proceedings under this act are being carried on, shall apply to all proceedings under this act; and any court or judge, or assignee, before whom any of such proceedings are being carried on, shall have full power and authority to apply the appropriate rules as to amendments, to the proceedings so pending before him; and no pleading or proceeding shall be void by reason of any irregularity or default which can or may be amended under the rules and practice of the court.

Provision in case of Death of Insolvent. Representatives, how far liable.

134. The death of the insolvent, pending proceedings upon a voluntary assignment, or in compulsory liquidation, shall not affect such proceedings, or impede the winding up of his estate; and his heirs or other legal representatives may continue the proceedings on his behalf to the procuring of a discharge, or of the confirmation thereof, or of both; and the provisions of this act shall apply to the heirs, administrators or other legal representatives of any deceased person who, if living, would be subject to its provisions, but only in their capacity as such heirs, administrators or representatives, without their being held to be liable for the debts of the deceased, to any greater extent than they would have been if this act had not been passed.

Costs : on what property and in what order chargeable.

135. The costs of the proceedings in insolvency up to and inclusive of the notice of the appointment of the assignee, shall be paid by privilege as a first charge upon the assets of the insolvent; the disbursements necessary for winding up the estate shall be the next charge on the property chargeable with any mortgage, hypothec or lien, and upon the unincumbered assets of the estate respectively, in such proportions as may be justified by the nature of such disbursements, and their relation to the property as being incumbered or not, as the case may be; and the remuneration of the assignee and the costs of the judgment of confirmation of the discharge of the insolvent, or of the discharge if obtained direct from the court, and the costs of the discharge of the assignee being first taxed by the judge at the tariff, or if there be no tariff at the same rate as is usual for uncontested proceedings of a similar character, after notice to the inspectors, or to at least three creditors, shall also be paid therefrom as the last privileged charge thereon.

Provision as to Letters addressed to insolvent by Post.

136. The judge shall have the power, upon special cause being shewn before him under oath for so doing, to order the postmaster at the place of residence of the insolvent, to deliver letters addressed to him received at such post office to the assignee, and to authorize the assignee to open such letters in the presence of the prothonotary or clerk of the court of which such judge is a member; and if such letters be upon the business of the estate, the assignee shall retain them, giving communication of them however to the insolvent on request; and if they be not on the business of the estate they shall be resealed, endorsed as having been opened by the assignee, and returned to the post office; and a memorandum in writing of the doings of the assignee in respect of such letters, shall be made and signed by him and by the prothonotary or clerk, and deposited in the court.

Provision as to cases in which the Judge or Assignee has a claim on the Estate.

137. If the judge holds a claim against the estate of an insolvent, he shall be *ipso facto* disqualified from acting as a judge in any matter connected with such claim; and in such case the judge competent to act in matters of insolvency, in any of the counties adjoining that in which the insolvent has his chief place of business, and who is not disqualified under this section, shall be the judge who shall have jurisdiction in such matter, in the place and stead of the judge so disqualified; and if the assignee to any estate be a claimant thereon as a creditor, or be collocated for any charges, or remuneration, or be the agent, attorney, or representative of any claimant thereon, he shall not hear, award, or determine upon any contesta-

tion of his own claim or collocation, or of the claim of the person represented by him, or of any dividend thereon, or upon any contestation or issue raised by him, or by the person represented by him; but in such case contestation shall be decided by the judge, subject to appeal as hereinbefore provided; and upon a suggestion being filed before the judge, or the assignee, as the case may be, of his disqualification under this section, the judge or assignee shall be bound within twenty-four hours thereafter, to declare under his hand, by a writing filed with the assignee, whether such judge or assignee is so disqualified or not, and if he does not, he shall be conclusively held to be so disqualified; and the validity or correctness of such declaration may be contested, in the case of the judge, by summary petition before the judge who would be competent to act in the place or stead of the judge alleged to be disqualified, and in the case of the assignees, by the judge.

Rules of Practice and Tariff of Fees in the Province of Quebec; how to be made.
Present Rules, etc., to remain until altered.

138. In the province of Quebec, rules of practice for regulating the due conduct of proceedings under this act, before the court or judge, and tariffs of fees for the officers of the court, and for the advocates and attorneys practising in relation to such proceedings, shall be made forthwith after the passing of this act, and when necessary repealed or amended, and shall be promulgated, under or by the same authority and in the same manner as the rules of practice and tariff of fees of the superior court, and shall apply in the same manner and have the same effect in respect of the proceedings under this act, as the rules of practice and tariff of fees of the superior court apply to and affect the proceedings before that court; and bills of costs upon proceedings under this act may be taxed and proceeded upon in like manner, as bills of costs may now be taxed and proceeded upon in the said superior court; but until such rules of practice and tariff of fees have been made, the rules of practice and tariff of fees in insolvency, now in force in the said province, shall continue and remain in full force and effect.

And in the other Provinces.

139. In the province of Ontario the judges of the superior courts of common law, and of the court of chancery, or any five of them, of whom the chief justice of the province of Ontario, or the chancellor, or the chief justice of the common pleas, shall be one—in the province of New Brunswick, the judges of the supreme court of New Brunswick, or the majority of them—and in the province of Nova Scotia, the judges of the supreme court of Nova Scotia, or the majority of them—shall forthwith make, and frame and settle such forms, rules and regulations as shall be followed and observed in the said provinces respectively, in the proceedings in insolvency under this act, and shall fix and settle the costs, fees and charges which shall or may be had, taken or paid in all such cases by or to attorneys, solicitors, counsel, and officers of courts, whether for the officer or for the crown as a fee for the fee fund or otherwise, and by or to sheriffs, assignees or other persons whom it may be necessary to provide for.

Registration of Marriage Contracts of Traders in Quebec.
Consequence of Default.

140. In the province of Quebec every trader having a marriage contract with his wife, by which he gives or promises to give or pay or cause to be paid, any right, thing, or sum of money, shall enregister the same, if it be not already enregistered, within three months from the execution thereof; and every person not a trader, but hereafter becoming a trader, and having such a contract of marriage with his wife, shall cause such contract to be enregistered as aforesaid (if it be not previously there enregistered), within thirty days from becoming such trader; and in default of such registration the wife shall not be permitted to avail herself of its provisions in any claim upon the estate of such insolvent for any advantage conferred upon or promised to her by its terms; nor shall she be deprived by reason of its provisions of any advantage or right upon the estate of her husband, to which, in the absence of any such contract, she would have been entitled by law; but this

section shall be held to be only a continuance of the second paragraph of section twelve of the insolvent act of 1864, and shall not relieve any person from the consequences of any negligence in the observance of the provisions of the said paragraph.

Certain words in 29 Vic. c. 18, interpreted.

141. The words "any official assignee," used in the second section of the act twenty-ninth Victoria, chapter eighteen, are hereby declared to have meant, and to mean, any official assignee whatever, and shall be construed as if they were followed by the words "resident or appointed, in any part of the province of Canada." But this declaration shall not affect any contestation heretofore determined or now pending respecting the validity of any assignment heretofore made to an official assignee resident in a county or district different from that in which the domicile or place of business of the insolvent was situate at the time of such assignment.

Certain words in this Act interpreted.

142. The words "before notaries," or "before a notary," shall mean executed in notarial form, according to the laws of the province of Quebec; the words "the judge" shall, in the province of Quebec, signify a judge of the superior court of the province of Quebec, having jurisdiction at the domicile of the insolvent,—in the provinces of Ontario and New Brunswick a judge of the county court of the county or union of counties in which the proceedings are carried on,—and in the province of Nova Scotia a judge of probate,—except in cases proceeding in the city of Halifax, in which case they shall mean a judge of the supreme court of Nova Scotia; and the words "the court," shall, in the province of Quebec signify the said superior court, and in the provinces of Ontario and New Brunswick the county court, and in the province of Nova Scotia the superior court of Nova Scotia, unless it is otherwise expressed or unless the contex plainly requires a different construction.

Other words interpreted. "Day." "Official Gazette." "Creditor." "Collocated." Application to Companies and Partnerships. "Board of Trade."

143. The word "day" shall mean a juridical day; the words "Official Gazette" shall mean the Gazette which is used in any province as the official medium of communication between the lieutenant governor and the people; the word "creditor" shall be held to mean every person to whom the insolvent is liable, whether primarily or secondarily, and whether as principal or surety, and who shall have proved his claim against the estate of an insolvent in the manner provided by this act; but no proceeding, discharge, or composition had or consented to previous to the passing of this act, and not now the subject of dispute and in litigation on the ground that a creditor voting thereon or a party thereto had not proved his claim shall be held invalid by reason of any such creditor not having previously proved his claim as aforesaid, notwithstanding that such creditor or the claims he represents be requisite to complete the proportion necessary to give validity under this act to such proceeding, discharge or composition; the word "collocated" shall mean ranked or placed in the dividend sheet for some dividend or sum of money; and all the provisions of this act shall be held to apply equally to unincorporated trading companies and co-partnerships : and the chief office or chief place of business of such unincorporated trading companies and co-partnerships shall be their domicile or place of business as the case may be for the purposes of this act; and the words "board of trade" in the said act, are hereby declared to have meant and in this act shall mean any body of persons openly exercising the ordinary functions of a board of trade or chamber of commerce whether incorporate or not.

Limitation of Proceedings to set aside anything done under this act.

144. After the expiration of one year from the appointment of an assignee, no suit or proceeding shall be instituted or commenced for the setting aside of any act or proceeding preliminary to such appointment or of such appointment; nor shall any such appointment or the proceedings preliminary thereto be impeached, or the validity thereof put in issue by any pleading in any suit or proceeding; but after the expiration of the said period, as to all persons not previously contesting

the same and until set aside by the decision of a court of law or of equity, upon a previous contestation thereof, such appointment and the proceedings preliminary thereto, shall be conclusively presumed to be valid and sufficient.

OF IMPRISONMENT FOR DEBT.

Insolvent in Jail or on the limits may apply to Judge for discharge.
Proceedings thereon.

145. Any debtor confined in jail or on the limits in any civil suit who may have made the assignment provided for in the second section of this act ; or against whom process for compulsory liquidation under this act may have been issued, may at any time after the meeting of creditors provided for in the third section of this act, or the appointment of an asssignee under this act, make application to the judge of the county or district in which his domicile may be or in which the jail may be in which he is confined, for his discharge from imprisonment or confinement in such suit; and thereupon such judge may grant an order in writing directing the sheriff or jailor to bring the debtor before him for examination at such time and place in such county or district as may be thought fit ; and the said sheriff or jailer shall duly obey such order, and shall not be liable for any action for escape in consequence thereof, or for any action for the escape of the said debtor from his custody, unless the same shall have happened through his default or negligence :

Examination of Insolvent and Witness.
Judge may discharge him if the Examination be satisfactory.

2. In pursuance of such order the said confined debtor and any witnesses subpœnaed to attend and give evidence at such examination may be examined on oath at the time and place specified in such order before such judge, and if on such examination it shall appear to the satisfaction of the judge, that the said debtor has *bona fide* made an assignment as required by the tenth section of this act, and has not been guilty of any fraudulent disposal, concealment or reten-

tion of his estate or any part thereof or of his books and accounts or any material portion thereof, or otherwise in any way contravened the provisions of this act, such judge shall by his order in writing discharge the debtor from confinement or imprisonment, and on production of the order to the sheriff or jailer, the debtor shall be forthwith discharged without payment of any jail fees ; *provided always,* that no such order shall be made in any suit unless it be made to appear to the satisfaction of such judge that at least seven days' notice of the time and place of the said examination had been previously given to the plaintiff in such suit, or his attorney and to the assignee for the time being :

Minutes of Examination to be kept.
Postponement in certain cases.

3. The minutes of the examination herein mentioned shall be filed in the office of the clerk of the court out of which the process issued, and a copy thereof shall be delivered to the assignee, and if during the examination, or before any order be made the official assignee or the appointed assignee, or the creditor or any one of the creditors at whose suit or suits he shall be in custody, shall make affidavit that he has reason to believe that the debtor has not made a full disclosure in the matters under examination, the judge may grant a postponement of such examination for a period of not less than seven days nor more than fourteen days, unless the parties consent to an earlier day :

As to any subsequent arrest.

4. After such discharge, in case of any subsequent arrest in any civil suit as aforesaid for causes of action arising previous to the assignment or process for compulsory liquidation, the said debtor may, pending the further proceedings against him under this act, be forthwith discharged from confinement or imprisonment in such suit, on application to any judge on producing such previous discharge ; provided that nothing in this section contained shall interfere with the imprisonment of the said debtor, in pursuance of any of the provisions of this act.

OFFENCES AND PENALTIES.

Assignees, Guardians, and Interim Assignees, to be deemed Agents for certain purposes.

146. Every interim assignee to whom an assignment is made under this act, every guardian appointed under a writ of attachment in compulsory liquidation, and every assignee appointed under the provisions of this act, is an agent within the meaning of the seventy-sixth and following sections of the *act respecting larceny and other similar offences*, and every provision of this act, or resolution of the creditors, relating to the duties of an interim assignee, guardian or assignee, shall be held to be a direction in writing, within the meaning of the said seventy-sixth section; and in an indictment against an interim assignee, guardian or assignee under any of the said sections, the right of property in any moneys, security, matter or thing, may be laid in "the creditors of the insolvent (*naming him*), under the insolvent act of 1869," or in the name of any assignee subsequently appointed, in his quality of such assignee.

Certain acts by Insolvents to be Misdemeanors.

147. From and after the coming into force of this act, any insolvent who shall do any of the acts or things following with intent to defraud, or defeat the rights of his creditors, shall be guilty of a misdemeanor, and shall be liable, at the discretion of the court before which he shall be convicted, to punishment by imprisonment for not more than three years, or to any greater punishment attached to the offence by any existing statute.

Not fully Discovering or not Delivering Property, Books, Papers, etc.

If he shall not upon examination fully and truly discover to the best of his knowledge and belief, all his property, real and personal, inclusive of his rights and credits, and how and to whom, and for what consideration, and when he disposed of, assigned or transferred thereof or of any part thereof, except such part has been really and *bona fide* before sold or disposed of in the way of his trade or business if any, or laid out in the ordinary expenses of his family, or shall not deliver up to the assignee all such part thereof as is in his possession, custody or power, (except such portion thereof as is exempt from seizure as hereinbefore provided,) and also all books, papers and writings in his possession, custody or power relating to his property or affairs;

Removing Property.

If within thirty days prior to the execution of a deed of assignment, or the issue of a writ of attachment under this act, he shall, with intent to defraud his creditors, remove, conceal, or embezzle any part of his property, to the value of fifty dollars or upwards;

Not denouncing False Claims.

If in case of any person having to his knowledge or belief proves a false debt against his estate, he shall fail to disclose the same to his assignee within one month after coming to the knowledge or belief thereof;

False Schedule.

If he shall with intent to defraud, wilfully and fraudulently omit from his schedule any effects or property whatsoever;

Withholding Books, etc.

If he shall with intent to conceal the state of his affairs, or to defeat the object of this act or of any part thereof, conceal, or prevent or withhold the production of any book, deed, paper or writing relating to his property, dealings or affairs;

Falsifying Books, etc.

If he shall with intent to conceal the state of his affairs, or to defeat the object of the present act, or of any part thereof, part with, conceal, destroy, alter, mutilate or falsify, or cause to be concealed, destroyed, altered, mutilated or falsified, any book, paper, writing or security or document relating to his property, trade, dealings or affairs, or make or be privy to the making of any false or fraudulent entry or statement in or omission from any book, paper, document or writing relating thereto;

Stating Fictitious Losses.

If he shall, at his examination at any time, or at any meeting of his creditors held under this act, have attempted to account for any of his property by fictitious losses or expenses ;

Disposing of Goods not Paid for.

If within the three months next preceding the execution of a deed of assignment, or the issue of a writ of attachment in compulsory liquidation, he pawns, pledges or disposes of, otherwise than in the ordinary way of his trade, any property, goods or effects the price of which shall remain unpaid by him during such three months.

How Offences against this Act shall be tried.

148. All offences punishable under this act shall be tried as other offences of the same degree are triable in the province where such offence is committed, save that the jury empanelled to try the same shall be a special jury, to obtain which the prosecuting officer is required and authorized to take such proceedings as in a civil case are necessary to obtain such a jury.

Creditors taking consideration for granting Discharge, etc.

149. If any creditor of an insolvent, directly or indirectly, takes or receives from such insolvent any payment, gift, gratuity or preference, or any promise of payment, gift, gratuity or preference, as a consideration or inducement to consent to the discharge of such insolvent, or to execute a deed of composition and discharge with him, or if any creditor knowingly ranks upon the estate of the insolvent for a sum of money not due to him by the insolvent or by his estate, such creditor shall forfeit and pay a sum equal to treble the value of the payment, gift, gratuity or preference so taken, received or promised, or treble the amount improperly ranked for as the case may be, and the same shall be recoverable by the assignee for the benefit of the estate, by suit in any competent court, and when recovered, shall be distributed as part of the ordinary assets of the estate.

Punishment of Insolvent receiving Money, etc., and not handing the same to assignee.

150. If, after the issue of a writ of attachment in insolvency, or the execution of a deed of assignment, as the case may be, the insolvent retains or receives any portion of his estate or effects, or of his moneys, securities for money, business papers, documents, books of account or evidences of debt, or any sum or sums of money, belonging or due to him, and retains and withholds from his assignee, without lawful right, such portion of his estate or effects, or of his moneys, securities for money, business papers, documents, books of account, evidences of debt, sum or sums of money, the assignee may make application to the judge, by summary petition and after due notice to the insolvent, for an order for the delivery over to him of the effects, documents or moneys so retained ; and in default of such delivery in conformity with any order to be made by the judge upon such application, such insolvent may be imprisoned in the common gaol for such time, not exceeding one year, as such judge may order.

Certain Documents to be Evidence.

151. The deeds of assignment and of transfer, or in the province of Quebec, authentic copies thereof, or a duly authenticated copy of the record of appointment of an assignee, or a copy of the instrument of appointment of the interim assignee when he becomes assignee, certified by the clerk or prothonotary of the court in which such instrument is deposited, under the seal of such court, according to the mode in which the assignee is alleged to be appointed, shall be *prima facie* evidence in all courts, whether civil or criminal, of such appointment, and of the regularity of all proceedings at the time thereof and antecedent thereto.

Contributions to Building and Jury Fund in Quebec.

152. One per centum of all moneys proceeding from the sale by an assignee, under the provisions of this act, of any immovable property in the province of Quebec, shall be retained by the assignee out of such moneys, and shall, by such assignee, be paid over to the sheriff of the district, or of either of the counties of Gaspe or Bonaventure, as the case may be, within which the immovable property sold shall be situate, to form part of the building and jury fund of such district or county.

Governor in Council to have certain powers.

153. The governor in council shall have all the powers with respect to imposing a tax or duty upon proceedings under this act, which are conferred upon the governor in council by the thirty-second and thirty-third sections of the one hundred and ninth chapter of the consolidated statutes for Lower Canada, and by the Act entitled : *An Act to make provision for the erection or repair of court houses and gaols at certain places in Lower Canada*, (12 Vic., cap. 112.)

REPEAL OF ACTS.

Insolvent Act of 1864, and act amending it repealed : saving certain proceedings and matters.

Proviso : Procedure under this Act to apply and supersede that under Act of 1864.

154. The insolvent act of 1864, and the act to amend the same, passed by the parliament of the late province of Canada in the 29th year of her majesty's reign, are hereby repealed, except in so far as regards proceedings commenced and now pending thereunder, and as regards all contracts, acts, matters and things made and done before this act shall come into force, to which the said acts or any of the provisions thereof would have applied if not so repealed, and specially such as are contrary to the provisions of the said acts, having reference to fraud and fraudulent preferences, and to the enregistration of marriage contracts within the province of Quebec; and as to all such contracts, acts, matters and things, the provisions of the said acts shall remain in force, and shall be acted upon as if this act had never been passed; *provided, always,* that as respects matters of procedure merely, the provisions of this act shall for the future supersede those of the said acts even in cases commenced and now pending; and all securities given under the said acts shall remain valid, and may be enforced, in respect of all matters and things falling within their terms, whether before or after this act shall come into force and specially all securities heretofore given by official assignees shall serve and avail hereafter as if given under this act; and all other acts and parts of acts now in force in any of the said provinces which are inconsistent with the provisions hereof are also hereby repealed.

Short title, commencement and duration of Act.

155. This act shall be called and known as "The Insolvent Act of 1869," and shall come into force and take effect on and after the first day of September next, and shall cease to have effect at the end of four years thereafter, save as regards proceedings then in progress.

RULES

SUPREME COURT OF THE UNITED STATES

AND

RULES OF PRACTICE

FOR THE CIRCUIT AND DISTRICT COURTS OF THE UNITED STATES IN EQUITY
AND ADMIRALTY CASES ; ORDER IN REFERENCE TO APPEALS FROM
COURT OF CLAIMS AND GENERAL ORDERS IN BANKRUPTCY.

RULES OF THE SUPREME COURT OF THE UNITED STATES.

No. 1—*Clerk.*

The clerk of this court shall reside and keep the office at the seat of the National Government, and he shall not practice, either as an attorney or counselor, in this court, or any other court, while he shall continue to be clerk of this court.

The clerk shall not permit any original record or paper to be taken from the court-room, or from the office, without an order from the court.

No. 2—*Attorneys.*

It shall be requisite to the admission of attorneys or counselors, to practice in this court, that they shall have been such for three years past in the supreme courts of the states of which they respectively belong, and that their private and professional character shall appear to be fair.

They shall respectively take and subscribe the following oath or affirmation, viz :

I,   , do solemnly swear, (or affirm as the case may be,) that I will demean myself, as an attorney and counselor of this court, uprightly, and according to law, and that I will support the constitution of the United States.

No. 3—*Practice.*

This court consider the practice of the courts of king's bench, and of chancery, in England, as affording outlines for the practice of this court ; and they will, from time to time, make such alterations therein as circumstances may render necessary.

No. 4—*Bill of Exception.*

Hereafter the judges of the circuit and district courts shall not allow any bill of exceptions which shall contain the charge of the court at large to the jury in trials at common law, upon any general exception to the whole of such charge. But the party excepting shall be required to state distinctly the several matters of law in such charge to which he excepts ; and such matters of law, and those only, shall be inserted in the bill of exceptions, and allowed by the court.

No. 5—*Process.*

All processes of this court shall be in the name of the president of the United States.

When process at common law, or in equity, shall issue against a state, the same shall be served on the governor, or chief executive magistrate, and attorney-general of such state.

Process of subpœna, issuing out of this court, in any suit in equity, shall be served on the defendant sixty days before the return day of the said process; and if the defendant, on such service of the subpœna, shall not appear at the return day contained therein, the complainant shall be at liberty to proceed *ex parte*.

No. 6—*Motions*.

All motions hereafter made to the court shall be reduced to writing, and shall contain a brief statement of the facts and objects of the motion.

No motion to dismiss, except on special assignment by the court, shall be heard, unless previous notice has been given to the adverse party or the counsel or attorney of such party.

Motion Day.

The court will not hear arguments on Saturday, (unless for special cause it shall order to the contrary,) but will devote that day to the other business of the court; and on Friday in each week, during the sitting of the court motions in cases not required by the rules of the court to be put on the docket shall be entitled to preference, if such motions shall be made before the court shall have entered on the hearing of a cause upon the docket.

No. 7—*Law Library*.

1. During the session of the court, any gentleman or the bar having a cause on the docket, and wishing to use any book or books in the law library, shall be at liberty, upon application to the clerk of the court, to receive an order to take the same (not exceeding at any time three) from the library, he being thereby responsible for the due return of the same within a reasonable time, or when required by the clerk. And it shall be the duty of the clerk to keep, in a book for that purpose, a record of all books so delivered, which are to be charged against the party receiving the same. And in case the same shall not be so returned, the party receiving the same shall be responsible for and forfeit and pay twice the value thereof; as also one dollar per day for each day's detention beyond the limited time.

Conference Room.

2. The clerk shall take charge of the books of the court, together with such of the duplicate law books as congress may direct to be transferred to the court, and arrange them in the conference room, which he shall have fitted up in a proper manner; and he shall not permit such books to be taken therefrom by any one except the judges of the court.

No. 8—*Return to writ of error and return day*.

1. The clerk of the court to which any writ of error shall be directed may make return of the same, by transmitting a true copy of the record, and of all proceedings in the cause, under his hand and the seal of the court.

2. No cause will hereafter be heard until a complete record, containing in itself, without references *aliunde*, all the papers, exhibits, depositions, and other proceedings which are necessary to the hearing in this court shall be filed.

3. Whenever it shall be necessary or proper, in the opinion of the presiding judge in any circuit court, or district court exercising circuit court jurisdiction that original papers of any kind should be inspected in this court, upon appeal or writ of error, such presiding judge may make such rule or order for the safe-keeping, transporting, and return of such original papers as to him may seem proper; and this court will receive and consider such original papers in connection with the transcript of the proceedings.

Return Day.

4. In cases where final judgment is rendered more than thirty days before the first day of the next term of this court, the writ of error and citation, if taken before, must be returnable on the first day of said term, and be served before that day; but in cases where the judgment is rendered less than thirty days before the first day, the writ of error and citation may be made returnable on the third Monday of the said term, and be served before that day.

No. 9—*Docketing Cases*.

1. In all cases where a writ of error or

an appeal shall be brought to this court from any judgment or decree rendered thirty days before the commencement of the term, it shall be the duty of the plaintiff in error or appellant, as the case may be, to docket the cause and file the record thereof with the clerk of this court within the first six days of the term ; and if the writ of error or appeal shall be brought from a judgment or decree rendered less than thirty days before the commencement of the term, it shall be the duty of the plaintiff in error or appellant to docket the cause, and file the record thereof with the clerk of this court within the first thirty days of the term ; and if the plaintiff in error or appellant shall fail to comply with this rule, the defendant in error or appellee may have the case docketed and dismissed, upon producing a certificate from the clerk of the court wherein the judgment or decree was rendered, stating the cause, and certifying that such writ of error or appeal has been duly sued out and allowed. And in no case shall the plaintiff in error or appellant be entitled to docket the cause and file the record after the same shall have been docketed and dismissed under this rule, unless by order of the court.

2. But the defendant in error or appellee may, at his option, docket the cause, and file a copy of the record with the clerk of the court; and if the case is docketed, and a copy of the record filed with the clerk of this court by the plaintiff or appellant, within the periods of the time above limited and prescribed by this rule, or by the defendant in error or appellee at any time thereafter during the term, the case shall stand for argument at the term.

3. Upon the filing of the transcript of a record brought up by writ of error or appeal, the appearance of the counsel for the plaintiff in error or appellant shall be entered.

4. In all cases where the period of thirty days is mentioned in this rule, it shall be extended to sixty days in writs of error and appeals from California, Oregon, Washington, New Mexico, Utah, Nevada, Arizona, Montana, and Idaho.

No. 10—*Security for Costs.*

1. In all cases the clerk shall take of the party a bond, with competent surety, to se-cure his fees, in the penalty of two hundred dollars ; or a deposit of that amount to be placed in bank subject to his draft.

Printing Records.

2. In all cases, the clerk shall have fifteen copies of the records printed for the court, and the costs of printing shall be charged to the government in the expenses of the court.

3. The clerk shall furnish copies for the printer, shall supervise the printing, and shall take care of and distribute the printed copies to the judges, the reporter, and the parties, from time to time, as required.

4. In each case the clerk shall charge the parties the legal fees for but the one manuscript copy in that case.

5. In all cases the clerk shall deliver a copy of the printed record to each party ; and in cases of dismission, reversal, or affirmance with costs, the fees for the said manuscript copy of the record shall be taxed against the party against whom costs are given, and which charge includes the charge for the copy furnished him.

6. In cases of dismission for want of jurisdiction, each party shall be charged with one-half the legal fees for a copy.

Attachment for Costs.

7. Upon the clerk of this court producing satisfactory evidence, by affidavit, or the acknowledgment of the parties or their sureties, of having served a copy of the bill of fees due by them, respectively, in this court, on such parties or their sureties, an attachment shall issue against such parties or sureties, respectively, to compel payment of the said fees.

No. 11—*Translations.*

Whenever any record, transmitted to this court upon a writ of error or appeal, shall contain any document, paper, testimony, or other proceeding in a foreign language, and the record does not also contain a translation of such document, paper, testimony, or other proceeding, made under the authority of the inferior court, or admitted to be correct the record shall not be printed, but the case shall be reported to this court by the clerk, and the court will thereupon remand it to the inferior court, in order that a translation may be there supplied and inserted in the record.

No. 12—*Evidence.*

1. In all cases where further proof is ordered by the court, the depositions which shall be taken shall be by a commission to be issued from this court, or from any circuit court of the United States.

2. In all cases of admiralty and maritime jurisdiction, where new evidence shall be admissible in this court, the evidence by testimony of witnesses shall be taken under a commission to be issued from this court, or from any circuit court of the United States, under the direction of any judge thereof; and no such commission shall issue but upon interrogatories to be filed by the party applying for the commission, and notice to the opposite party or his agent or attorney, accompanied with a copy of the interrogatories so filed, to file cross-interrogatories within twenty days from the service of such notice : *Provided, however,* that nothing in this rule shall prevent any party from giving oral testimony in open court in cases where, by law, it is admissible.

No. 13—*Deeds, etc., not objected to, etc., admitted, etc.*

In all cases of equity and admiralty jurisdiction heard in this court, no objection shall hereafter be allowed to be taken to the admissibility of any deposition, deed, grant, or other exhibit found in the record as evidence, unless objection was taken thereto in the court below and entered of record ; but the same shall otherwise be deemed to have been admitted by consent.

No. 14—*Certiorari.*

No *certiorari* for diminution of the record shall be hereafter awarded in any cause, unless a motion therefor shall be made in writing, and the facts on which the same is founded shall, if not admitted by the other party, be verified by affidavit. And all motions for such *certiorari* shall be made at the first term of the entry of the cause ; otherwise the same shall not be granted unless upon special cause shown to the court accounting satisfactorily for the delay.

No. 15—*Death of a Party.*

1. Whenever, pending a writ of error or appeal in this court, either party shall die, the proper representatives in the personalty or realty of the deceased party, according to the nature of the case, may voluntarily come in and be admitted parties to the suit, and thereupon the cause shall be heard and determined as in other cases ; and if such representatives shall not voluntarily become parties, then the other party may suggest the death on the record, and thereupon, on motion, obtain an order, that unless such representatives shall become parties within the first ten days of the ensuing term, the party moving for such order, if defendant in error, shall be entitled to have the writ of error or appeal dismissed ; and if the party so moving shall be plaintiff in error, he shall be entitled to open the record, and on hearing have the same reversed if it be erroneous : *Provided, however,* That a copy of every such order shall be printed in some newspaper at the seat of government in which the laws of the United States shall be printed by authority, for three successive weeks, at least sixty days before the beginning of the term of the supreme court then next ensuing.

2. When the death of a party is suggested, and the representatives of the deceased do not appear by the tenth day of the second term next succeeding the suggestion, and no measures are taken by the opposite party within that time to compel their appearance, the case shall abate.

No. 16—*No Appearance of Plaintiff.*

Where there is no appearance for the plaintiff, when the case is called for trial, the defendant may have the plaintiff called and dismiss the writ of error, or may open the record and pray for an affirmance.

No. 17—*No Appearance of Defendant.*

Where the defendant fails to appear when the cause shall be called for trial, the court may proceed to hear an argument on the part of the plaintiff, and to give judgment according to the rights of the cause.

No. 18—*No Appearance of either party.*

When a case is reached in the regular call of the docket, and no appearance is entered for either party, the case shall be dismissed, at the costs of the plaintiff.

No. 19—*Neither party ready at Second Term.*

When a case is called for argument at two successive terms, and upon the call at the second term neither party is prepared to argue it, it shall be dismissed at the costs of the plaintiff, unless sufficient cause is shown for further postponement.

No. 20—*Printed Arguments.*

1. In all cases brought here on appeal, writ of error, or otherwise, the court will receive printed arguments without regard to number of the case on the docket, if the counsel on both sides shall choose so to submit the same within the first sixty days of the term; but twenty copies of the arguments, signed by attorneys or counselors of this court, must be first filed; ten of these copies for the court, two for the reporter, three to be retained by the clerk, and the residue for counsel.

2. When a case is reached in the regular call of the docket, and a printed argument shall be filed for one or both parties, the case shall stand on the same footing as if there was an appearance by counsel.

3. When a case is taken up for trial upon the regular call of the docket, and argued orally in behalf of only one of the parties, no printed argument will be received unless it is filed before the oral argument begins, and the court will proceed to consider and decide the case upon the *ex parte* argument.

No. 21—*Two Counsel.*

1. Only two counsel shall be permitted to argue for each party, plaintiff and defendant, in a cause.

Two Hours.

2. Two hours on each side shall be allowed in the argument of a cause, and no more, without special leave of the court granted before the argument begins. But the time thus allowed may be apportioned among counsel on the same side as they choose: *Provided, always*, a fair opening of the case shall be made by the party having the opening and closing argument.

Briefs.

3. Counsel will not be heard unless a printed brief or abstract of the case be first filed, together with the points made, and the authorities cited in support of them arranged under the respective points.

4. The brief filed on behalf of a plaintiff in error or an appellant shall also contain a statement of the errors relied upon, and in case of an appeal an abstract of the pleadings and proofs, exhibiting clearly and succinctly the issues presented.

5. Each error shall be separately alleged and particularly specified; otherwise it will be disregarded.

6. When the error alleged is to the charge of the court, the part of the charge referred to shall be quoted *totidem verbis* in the specification.

7. When the error alleged is to the admission or rejection of evidence, the specification shall quote the full substance of the evidence offered, or copy the offer as stated in the bill of exceptions. Any alleged error not in accordance with these rules will be disregarded.

8. Counsel will be confined to a discussion of the errors stated, but the court may, at its discretion, notice any other errors appearing in the record.

9. The same shall be signed by an attorney or counselor of this court.

10. If one of the parties omits to file such a statement, he cannot be heard, and the case will be heard *ex parte* upon the argument of the party by whom the statement is filed.

11. Twenty printed copies of the abstract, points, and authorities required by this rule shall be filed with the clerk by the plaintiff in error or appellant six days, and by the defendant in error or appellee three days, before the case is called for argument.

12. When no counsel appears for one of the parties, and no printed brief or argument is filed, only one counsel will he heard for the adverse party; but if a printed brief or argument is filed, the adverse party will be entitled to be heard by two counsel.

No. 22—*Order of argument.*

The plaintiff or appellant in this court shall be entitled to open and conclude the case. But when there are cross-appeals, they shall be argued together as one case, and the plaintiff in the court below shall be entitled to open and conclude the argument.

No. 23—*Interest.*

1. In cases where a writ of error is prosecuted to this court, and the judgment of the inferior court is affirmed, the interest shall be calculated and levied from the date of the judgment below, until the same is paid, at the same rate that similar judgments bear interest in the courts of the state where such judgment is rendered.

2. In all cases where a writ of error shall delay the proceedings on the judgment of the inferior court, and shall appear to have been sued out merely for delay, damages at the rate of *ten per cent.* in addition to interest, shall be awarded upon the amount of the judgment.

3. The same rule shall be applied to decrees for the payment of money in cases of chancery, unless otherwise ordered by this court.*

No. 24—*Costs.*

1. In all cases where any suit shall be dismissed in this court, except where the dismissal shall be for want of jurisdiction, costs shall be allowed to the defendant in error or appellee, as the case may be, unless otherwise agreed by the parties.

2. In all cases of affirmance of any judgment or decree in this court, costs shall be allowed to the defendant in error or appellee, as the case may be, unless otherwise ordered by the court.

3. In cases of reversal of any judgment or decree in this court, costs shall be allowed to the plaintiff in error or appellant, as the case may be, unless otherwise ordered by the court. The cost of the transcript of the record from the court below shall be a part of such costs and be taxable in that court as costs in the case.

4. Neither of the foregoing rules shall apply to cases where the United States are a party; but in such cases, no costs shall be allowed in this court for or against the United States.

5. In all cases of the dismissal of any suit in this court, it shall be the duty of the clerk to issue a mandate, or other proper process, in the nature of a *procedendo*, to the court below, for the purpose of informing

---

* Interest not allowed in admiralty, unless specially directed by the court. (20 How., p. 255)

such court of the proceedings in this court, so that further proceedings may be had in such court as to law and justice may appertain.

6. When costs are allowed in this court, it shall be the duty of the clerk to insert the amount thereof in the body of the mandate, or other proper process, sent to the court below, and annex to the same the bill of items taxed in detail.

No. 25—*Opinions of the Court.*

1. All opinions delivered by the court shall immediately, upon the delivery thereof, be delivered over to the clerk to be recorded. And it shall be the duty of the clerk to cause the same to be forthwith recorded and to deliver a copy to the reporter, as soon as the same shall be recorded.

2. The opinions of the court, as far as practicable, shall be recorded during the term, so that the publication of the reports may not be delayed thereby.

3. The original opinions of the court shall be filed with the clerk of this court for preservation.

No. 26—*Call of the Docket.*

1. The court on the second day in each term will commence calling the cases for argument in the order in which they stand on the docket, and proceed from day to day during the term, in the same order : (except as hereinafter provided,) and if the parties, or either of them, shall be ready when the case is called, the same will be heard ; and if neither party shall be ready to proceed in the argument, the cause shall go down to the foot of the docket, unless some good and satisfactory reason to the contrary shall be shown to the court.

2. Ten causes only shall be considered as liable to be called on each day during the term, including the one under argument.

3. Criminal cases may be advanced, by leave of the court, on motion of either party.

4. Revenue cases and cases in which the United States are concerned, which also involve or affect some matter of general public interest, may also, by leave of the court, be advanced on motion of the attorney-general.

5. No other cause shall be taken up out of the order on the docket, or be set down for any particular day, except under the spe-

cial and peculiar circumstances to be shown to the court. Every cause which shall have been called in its order, and passed, and put at the foot of the docket, shall, if not again reached during the term it was called, be continued to the next term of the court.

6. Two or more cases also involving the same question may, by the leave of the court, be heard together, but they must be argued as one case.

No. 27—*Adjournment.*

The court will, at every session, announce on what day it will adjourn at least ten days before the time which shall be fixed upon; and the court will take up no case for argument, nor receive any case upon printed briefs, within three days next before the day fixed upon for adjournment.

No. 28—*Dismissing Cases in Vacation.*

Whenever the plaintiff and defendant in a writ of error pending in this court, or the appellant and appellee in any appeal, shall at any time hereafter, in vacation and out of term time, by their respective attorneys, who are entered as such on the record, sign and file with the clerk an agreement in writing directing the case to be dismissed, and specifying the terms on which it is to be dismissed as to costs, and also paying to the clerk any fees that may be due to him, it shall be the duty of the clerk to enter the case dismissed, and to give to either party which may request it a copy of the agreement filed; but no mandate or other process is to issue without an order by the court.

No. 29—*Supersedeas.*

Supersedeas bonds in the circuit courts must be taken, with good and sufficient security, that the plaintiff in error or appellant shall prosecute his writ of appeal to effect and answer all damages and costs if he fail to make his plea good. Such indemnity, where the judgment or decree is for the recovery of money not otherwise secured, must be for the whole amount of the judgment or decree, including "just damages for delay," and costs and interest on the appeal; but in all suits where the property in controversy necessarily follows the event of the suit, as in real actions, replevin, and in suits on mortgages; or where the property is in the custody of the marshal, under admiralty process, as in case of capture or seizure; or where the proceeds thereof, or a bond for the value thereof, is in the custody or control of the court, indemnity in all such cases is only required in an amount sufficient to secure the sum recovered for the use and detention of the property and the costs of the suit and "just damages for delay," and costs and interest on the appeal.

ORDER IN REFERENCE TO

APPEALS FROM THE COURT OF CLAIMS;

REGULATIONS PRESCRIBED BY THE SUPREME COURT OF THE UNITED STATES UNDER WHICH APPEALS MAY BE TAKEN FROM THE COURT OF CLAIMS TO SAID SUPREME COURT.

Rule 1.

In all cases hereafter decided in the court of claims, in which, by the act of Congress, such appeals were allowable, they shall be heard in the supreme court upon the following record, and none other:

1. A transcript of the pleadings in the case, of the final judgment or decree of the court, and of such interlocutory orders, rulings, judgments and decrees, as may be necessary to a proper review of the case.

2. A finding of the facts in the case by said court of claims, and the conclusions of law on said facts on which the court founds its judgment or decree.

The finding of the facts and the conclusions of law to be stated separately and certified to this court as part of the record.

The facts so found are to be the ultimate facts or propositions which the evidence shall establish, in the nature of a special verdict, and not the evidence on which those ultimate facts are founded. (See Burr *vs.* Des Moines Co., 1 Wallace, 102.)

Rule 2.

In all cases in which the judgments or decrees have heretofore been rendered, where either party is by law entitled to an appeal, the party desiring it shall make application to the court of claims by petition for the allowance of such appeal. Said petition shall contain a distinct specification of the errors alleged to have been committed by said court in its rulings, judgment or decree in the case. The court shall, if the specification of alleged error be correctly and accurately stated, certify the same, or may certify such alterations and modifications of the points decided and alleged for error as, in the judgment of said court, shall distinctly, fully, and fairly present the points decided by the court. This, with the transcript mentioned in Rule 1, (except the statement of facts and law therein mentioned), shall constitute the record on which those cases shall be heard in the supreme court.

Rule 3

In all cases an order of allowance of appeal by the court of claims, or the chief justice thereof in vacation, is essential, and the limitation of time for granting such appeal shall cease to run from the time an application is made for the allowance of appeal.

Rule 4.

In all cases in which either party is entitled to appeal to the supreme court, the court of claims shall make and file their finding of facts, and the conclusions of law therein, in open court, before or at the time they enter their judgment in the case.

Rule 5.

In all such cases either party, on or before the hearing of the cause, may submit to the court a written request to find specifically as to the matter of fact which such party may deem material to the judgment in the case, and if the court fails or refuses to find in accordance with such prayer, then such prayer and refusal shall be made a part of the record, certified on the appeal, to this court.

RULES OF PRACTICE

FOR THE

COURTS OF EQUITY OF THE UNITED STATES.

PRELIMINARY REGULATIONS.

1. The circuit courts, as courts of equity, shall be deemed always open for the purposes of filing bills, answers, and other pleadings, for issuing and returning mesne and final process and commissions, and for making and directing all interlocutory motions, orders, rules, and other proceedings, preparatory to the hearing of all causes upon their merits.

2. The clerk's office shall be open and the clerk shall be in attendance therein on the first Monday of every month, for the purpose of receiving, entering, entertaining, and disposing of all motions, rules, orders, and other proceedings, which are grantable of course, and applied for or had by the parties or their solicitors, in all causes pending in equity, in pursuance of the rules hereby prescribed.

3. Any judge of the circuit court, as well in vacation as in term, may, at chambers, or on the rule days at the clerk's office, make and direct all such interlocutory orders, rules and other proceedings preparatory to the hearing of all causes upon their merits, in the same manner and with the same effect as the circuit court could make and direct the same in term, reasonable notice of the application therefor being first given to the adverse party, or his solicitor, to appear and show cause to the contrary at the next rule day thereafter, unless some other time is assigned by the judge for the hearing.

4. All motions, rules, orders, and other proceedings made and directed at chambers, or on rule days at the clerk's office, whether

special or of course, shall be entered by the clerk in an order book, to be kept at the clerk's office, on the day when they are made and directed; which book shall be open at all office hours to the free inspection of the parties in any suit in equity, and their solicitors. And, except in cases where personal or other notice is specially required or directed, such entry in the order book shall be deemed sufficient notice to the parties and their solicitors, without further service thereof, of all orders, rules, acts, notices, and other proceedings entered in such order book, touching any and all the matters in the suit to and in which they are parties and solicitors. And notice to the solicitors shall be deemed notice to the parties for whom they appear and whom they represent, in all cases where personal notice on the parties is not otherwise specially required. Where the solicitors for all the parties in a suit reside in or near the same town or city, the judges of the circuit court may, by rule, abridge the time for notice of rules, orders, or other proceedings not requiring personal service on the parties, in their discretion.

5. All motions and applications in the clerk's office for the issuing of mesne process and final process to enforce and execute decrees, for filing bills, answers, pleas, demurrers, and other pleadings; for making amendments to bills and answers; for taking bills *pro confesso:* for filing exceptions, and for other proceedings in the clerk's office which do not, by the rules hereinafter prescribed, require any allowance or order of the court, or of any judge thereof, shall be deemed motions and applications, grantable of course by the clerk of the court. But the same may be suspended, or altered, or rescinded by any judge of the court, upon special cause shown.

6. All motions for rules or orders and other proceedings, which are not grantable of course, or without notice, shall, unless a different time be assigned by a judge of the court, be made on a rule day, and entered in the order-book, and shall be heard at the rule day next after that on which the motion is made. And if the adverse party, or his solicitor, shall not then appear, or shall not show good cause against the same, the motion may be heard by any judge of the court *ex parte*, and granted, as if not objected to, or refused, in his discretion.

Process.

7. The process of subpœna shall constitute the proper mesne process in all suits in equity, in the first instance, to require the defendant to appear and answer the evigency of the bill; and, unless otherwise provided in these rules, or specially ordered by the circuit court, a writ of attachment, and, if the defendant cannot be found, a writ of sequestration, or a writ of assistance to enforce a delivery of possession, as the case may require, shall be the proper process to issue for the purpose of compelling obedience to any interlocutory or final order or decree of the court.

8. Final process to execute any decree may, if the decree be solely for the payment of money, be by a writ of execution, in the form used in the circuit court in suits at common law in actions of *assumpsit*. If the decree be for the performance of any specific act, as, for example, for the execution of a conveyance of land or the delivering up of deeds, or other documents, the decree shall, in all cases, prescribe the time within which the act shall be done, of which the defendant shall be bound without further service to take notice: and upon affidavit of the plaintiff, filed in the clerk's office, that the same has not been complied with within the prescribed time, the clerk shall issue a writ of attachment against the delinquent party, from which, if attached thereon, he shall not be discharged, unless upon a full compliance with the decree and the payment of all costs, or upon a special order of the court or of a judge thereof, upon motion and affidavit, enlarging the time for the performance thereof. If the delinquent party cannot be found, a writ of sequestration shall issue against his estate upon the return of *non est inventus*, to compel obedience to the decree.

9. When any decree or order is for the delivery of possession upon proof made by affidavit of a demand and refusal to obey the decree or order, the party prosecuting the same shall be entiled to a writ of assistance from the clerk of the court.

10. Every person, not being a party in any cause, who has obtained an order, or in whose favor an order shall have been made, shall be enabled to enforce obedience to such order by the same process as if he were a

party to the cause; and every person, not being a party in any cause, against whom obedience to any order of the court may be enforced, shall be liable to the same process for enforcing obedience to such order as if he were a party in the cause.

Service of Process.

11. No process of subpœna shall issue from the clerk's office in any suit in equity until the bill is filed in the office.

12. Whenever a bill is filed the clerk shall issue the process of subpœna thereon, as of course, upon the application of the plaintiff, which shall be .returnable into the clerk's office the next rule day, or the next rule day but one, at the election of the plaintiff, occurring after twenty days from the time of the issuing thereof. At the bottom of the subpœna shall be placed a memorandum, that the defendant is to enter his appearance in the suit in the clerk's office on or before the day at which the writ is returnable ; otherwise, the bill may be taken *pro confesso*. Where there are more than one defendant, a writ of subpœna may, at the election of the plaintiff, be sued out separately for each defendant, except in the case of husband and wife defendants, or a joint subpœna against all the defendants.

13. The service of all subpœnas shall be by a delivery of a copy thereof by the officer serving the same to the defendant personally, or, in case of husband and wife, to the husband personally, or by leaving a copy thereof at the dwelling-house or usual place of abode of each defendant, with some free white person who is a member or resident in the family.

14. Whenever any subpœna shall be returned not executed as to any defendant, the plaintiff shall be entitled to another subpœna, *toties quoties*, against such defendant, if he shall require it, until due service is made.

15. The service of all process, mesne and final, shall be by the marshal of the district, or his deputy, or by some other person specially appointed by the court for that purpose, and not otherwise. In the latter case, the person serving the process shall make affidavit thereof.

16. Upon the return of the snbpœna as served and executed upon any defendant,

the clerk shall enter the suit upon his docket as pending in the court, and shall state the time of the entry.

Appearance.

17. The appearance day of the defendant shall be the rule day to which the subpœna is made returnable, provided he has been served with the process twenty days before that day ; otherwise his appearance day shall be the next rule day succeeding the rule-day when the process is returnable.

The appearance of the defendant, either personally or by his solicitor, shall be entered in the order book on the day thereof by the clerk.

Bills taken pro confesso.

18. It shall be the duty of the defendant, unless the time shall be otherwise enlarged, for cause shown, by a judge of the court, upon motion for that purpose, to file his plea, demurrer, or answer to the bill, in the clerk's office, on the rule day next succeeding that of entering his appearance. In default thereof, the plaintiff may, at his election, enter an order (as of course) in the order book, that the bill be taken *pro confesso* ; and thereupon the cause shall be proceeded in *ex parte*, and the matter of the bill may be decreed by the court at the next ensuing term thereof accordingly, if the same can be done·without an answer, and is proper to be decreed ; or the plaintiff, if he requires any discovery or answer to enable him to obtain a proper decree, shall be entitled to process of attachment against the defendant, to compel an answer, and the defendant shall not, when arrested upon such process, be discharged therefrom, unless upon filing his answer, or otherwise complying with such order as the court or a judge thereof may direct, as to pleading to or fully answering the bill, within a period to be fixed by the court or judge, and undertaking to speed the cause.

19. When the bill is taken *pro confesso*, the court may proceed to a decree at the next ensuing term thereof, and such decree rendered shall be deemed absolute, unless the court shall, at the same term, set aside the same, or enlarge the time for filing the answer, upon cause shown upon motion and affidavit of the defendant. And no such

motion shall be granted, unless upon the payment of the costs of the plaintiff in the suit up to that time, or such part thereof as the court shall deem reasonable, and unless the defendant shall undertake to file his answer within such time as the court shall direct, and submit to such other terms as the court shall direct, for the purpose of speeding the cause.

Frame of bills.

20. Every bill, in the introductory part thereof, shall contain the names, places of abode, and citizenship of all the parties, plaintiffs and defendants, by and against whom the bill is brought. The form, in substance, shall be as follows : " To the judges of the circuit court of the United States for the district of —— : A. B., of ——, and a citizen of the state of ——, brings this his bill against C. D., of ——, and a citizen of the state of ——, and E. F., of ——, and a citizen of the state of ——. And thereupon your orator complains and says, that," &c.

21. The plaintiff, in his bill, shall be at liberty to omit, at his option, the part which is usually called the common confederacy clause of the bill, averring a confederacy between the defendants to injure or defraud the plaintiff; also what is commonly called the charging part of the bill, setting forth the matters or excuses which the defendant is supposed to intend to set up by way of defence to the bill; also what is commonly called the jurisdiction clause of the bill, that the acts complained of are contrary to equity, and that the defendant is without any remedy at law; and the bill shall not be demurrable therefor. And the plaintiff may, in the narrative or stating part of his bill, state and avoid, by counter-averments, at his option, any matter or thing which he supposes will be insisted upon by the defendant, by way of defence or excuse to the case made by the plaintiff for relief. , The prayer of the bill shall ask the special relief to which the plaintiff supposes himself entitled, and also shall contain a prayer for general relief; and if an injunction, or a writ of *ne exeat regno*, or any other special order pending the suit, is required, it shall also be specially asked for.

22. If any persons, other than those named as defendants in the bill, shall appear to be

necessary or proper parties thereto, the bill shall aver the reason why they are not made parties, by showing them to be without the jurisdiction of the court, or that they cannot be joined without ousting the jurisdiction of the court as to the other parties. And as to persons who are without the jurisdiction and may properly be made parties, the bill may pray that process may issue to make them parties to the bill if they should come within the jurisdiction.

23. The prayer for process of subpœna in the bill shall contain the names of all the defendants named in the introductory part of the bill, and if any of them are known to be infants under age, or otherwise under guardianship, shall state the fact, so that the court may take order thereon as justice may require, upon the return of the process. If an injunction, or a writ of *ne exeat regno*, or any other special order pending the suit, is asked for in the prayer for relief, that shall be sufficient without repeating the same in the prayer for process.

24. Every bill shall contain the signature of counsel annexed to it, which shall be considered as an affirmation on his part, that upon the instructions given to him and the case laid before him, there is good ground for the suit, in the manner in which it is framed.

25. In order to prevent unnecessary costs and expenses, and to promote brevity, succinctness, and directness in the allegations of bills and answers, the regular taxable costs for every bill and answer shall in no case exceed the sum which is allowed in the state court of chancery in the district, if any there be; but, if there be none, then it shall not exceed the sum of three dollars for every bill or answer.

Scandal and impertinence in bills.

26. Every bill shall be expressed in as brief and succinct terms as it reasonably can be, and shall contain no unnecessary recitals of deeds, documents, contracts, or other instruments, in *hæc verba*, or any other impertinent matter, or any scandalous matter not relevant to the suit. If it does, it may on exceptions be referred to a master by any judge of the court for impertinence or scandal; and if so found by him, the matter shall be expunged at the expense of the plaintiff, and he shall pay to the defendant

all his costs in the suit up to that time, unless the court or a judge thereof shall otherwise order. If the master shall report that the bill is not scandalous or impertinent, the plaintiff shall be entitled to all costs occasioned by the reference.

27. No order shall be made by any judge for referring any bill, answer or pleading, or other matter, or proceeding depending before the court for scandal or impertinence, unless exceptions are taken in writing and signed by counsel, describing the particular passages which are considered to be scandalous or impertinent; nor unless the exceptions shall be filed on or before the next rule day after the process on the bill shall be returnable, or after the answer or pleading is filed. And such order, when obtained, shall be considered as abandoned, unless the party obtaining the order shall, without any unnecessary delay, procure the master to examine and report for the same on or before the next succeeding rule day, or the master shall certify that further time is necessary for him to complete the examination.

Amendment of Bills.

28. The plaintiff shall be at liberty, as a matter of course, and without payment of costs, to amend his bill in any matters whatsoever, before any copy has been taken out of the clerk's office, and in any small matters afterward, such as filling blanks, correcting errors of dates, misnomer of parties, misdescription of premises, clerical errors, and generally in matters of form. But if he amend in a material point (as he may do of course), after a copy has been so taken, before any answer or plea, or demurrer to the bill, he shall pay to the defendant the costs occasioned thereby, and shall, without delay, furnish him a fair copy thereof, free of expense, with suitable references to the places where the same are to be inserted. And if the amendments are numerous, he shall furnish in like manner, to the defendant a copy of the whole bill as amended; and if there be more than one defendant, a copy shall be furnished to each defendant affected thereby.

29. After an answer, or plea, or demurrer is put in, and before replication, the plaintiff may, upon motion or petition, without notice, obtain an order from any judge of the court to amend his bill on or before the next succeeding rule day, upon payment of costs or without payment of costs, as the court or a judge thereof may in his discretion direct But after replication filed, the plaintiff shall not be permitted to withdraw it and to amend his bill, except upon a special order of a judge of the court, upon motion or petition, after due notice to the other party, and upon proof by affidavit that the same is not made for the purpose of vexation or delay, or that the matter of the preposed amendment is material, and could not with reasonable diligence have been sooner introduced into the bill, and upon the plaintiff's submitting to such other terms as may be imposed by the judge for speeding the cause.

30. If the plaintiff, so obtaining any order to amend his bill after answer, or plea, or demurrer, or after replication, shall not file his amendments or amended bill, as the case may require, in the clerk's office, on or before the next succeeding rule day, he shall be considered to have abandoned the same, and the cause shall proceed as if no application for any amendment had been made.

31—Demurrer and Pleas.

No demurrer or plea shall be allowed to be filed to any bill, unless upon a certificate of counsel, that in his opinion it is well founded in point of law, and supported by the affidavit of the defendant, that it is not interposed for delay; and if a plea that it is true in point of fact.

32. The defendant may, at any time before the bill is taken for confessed, or afterwards with the leave of the court, demur or plead to the whole bill, or to part of it, and he may demur to part, plead to part, and answer as to the residue; but in every case in which the bill specially charges fraud or combination, a plea to such part must be accompanied with an answer fortifying the plea, and explicitly denying the fraud and combination, and the facts on which the charge is founded.

33. The plaintiff may set down the demurrer or plea to be argued, or he may take issue on the plea. If, upon an issue, the facts stated in the plea be determined for the defendant, they shall avail him as far as in law and equity they ought to avail him.

34. If, upon the hearing, any demurrer or plea is overruled, the plaintiff shall be entitled to his costs in the cause up to that pe-

riod, unless the court shall be satisfied that the defendant has good ground in point of law or fact to interpose the same, and it was not interposed vexatiously or for delay. And upon the overruling of any plea or demurrer, the defendant shall be assigned to answer the bill, or so much thereof as is covered by the plea or demurrer, the next succeeding rule day, or at such other period as, consistently with justice and the rights of the defendant, the same can, in the judgment of the court, be reasonably done; in default whereof, the bill shall be taken against him, *pro confesso*, and the matter thereof proceeded in and decreed accordingly.

35. If, upon the hearing, any demurrer or plea shall be allowed, the defendant shall be entitled to his costs. But the court may, in its discretion, upon motion of the plaintiff, allow him to amend his bill upon such terms as it shall deem reasonable.

36. No demurrer or plea shall be held bad and overruled upon argument, only because such demurrer or plea shall not cover so much of the bill as it might by law have extended to.

37. No demurrer or plea shall be held bad and overruled upon argument, only because the answer of the defendant may extend to some part of the same matter, as may be covered by such demurrer or plea.

38. If the plaintiff shall not reply to any plea, or set down any plea or demurrer for argument, on the rule-day when the same is filed, or on the next succeeding rule day, he shall be deemed to admit the truth and sufficiency thereof, and his bill shall be dismissed as of course, unless a judge of the court shall allow him further time for the purpose.

Answers.

39. The rule, that if a defendant submits to answer he shall apply fully to all the matters of the bill, shall no longer apply in cases where he might by plea protect himself from such answer and discovery. And the defendant shall be entitled in all cases by answer to insist upon all matters of defense (not being matters of abatement, or to the character of the parties, or matters of form) in bar of or to the merits of the bill, of which he may be entitled to avail himself by a plea in bar; and in such answer he shall not be compellable to answer any other matters than he would be compellable to answer and discover upon filing a plea in bar, and an answer in support of such plea, touching the matters set forth in the bill, to avoid or repel the bar or defence. Thus, for example, a *bona fide* purchaser for a valuable consideration, without notice, may set up that defence by way of answer instead of plea, and shall be entitled to the same protection, and shall not be compellable to make any further answer or discovery of his title than he would be in any answer in support of such plea.

40. A defendant shall not be bound to answer any statement or charge in the bill, unless specially and particularly interrogated thereto; and a defendant shall not be bound to answer any interrogatory in the bill, except those interrogatories which such defendant is required to answer; and where a defendant shall answer any statement or charge in the bill, to which he is not interrogated, only by stating his ignorance of the matter so stated or charged, such answer shall be deemed impertinent.

DECEMBER TERM, 1850.

Ordered, That the fortieth rule heretofore adopted and promulgated by this court as one of the rules of practice in suits in equity in the circuit courts be, and the same is hereby, repealed and annulled. And it shall not hereafter be necessary to interrogate a defendant specially and particularly upon any statement in the bill, unless the complainant desires to do so, to obtain a discovery.

41. The interrogatories contained in the interrogating part of the bill shall be divided as conveniently as may be from each other, and numbered consecutively 1, 2, 3, &c.; and the interrogatories which each defendant is required to answer shall be specified in a note at the foot of the bill, in the form or to the effect following; that is to say—" The defendant (A. B.) is required to answer the interrogatories numbered respectively 1, 2, 3, &c.;" and the office copy of the bill taken by each defendant shall not contain any interrogatories except those which such defendant is so required to answer, unless such defendant shall require to be furnished with a copy of the whole bill.

42. The note at the foot of the bill, specifying the interrogatories which each defend

ant is required to answer, shall be considered and treated as part of the bill, and the addition of any such note to the bill, or any alteration in or addition to such note after the bill is filed, shall be considered and treated as an amendment of the bill.

43. Instead of the words of the bill now in use, preceding the interrogating part thereof, and beginning with the words "To the end, therefore," there shall hereafter be used words in the form or to the effect following : "To the end, therefore, that the said defendants may, if they can, show why your orator should not have the relief hereby prayed, and may, upon their several and respective corporal oaths, and according to the best and utmost of their several and respective knowledge, remembrance, information, and belief, full, true, direct, and perfeet answer make to such of the several interrogatories hereinafter numbered and set forth, as by the note hereunder written they are respectively required to answer; that is to say—

"1. Whether, &c.

"2. Whether, &c."

44. A defendant shall be at liberty, by answer, to decline answering any interrogatory, or part of an interrogatory, from answering which he might have protected himself by demurrer; and he shall be at liberty so to decline, notwithstanding he shall answer other parts of the bill from which he might have protected himself by demurrer.

45. No special replication to any answer shall be filed. But if any matter alleged in the answer shall make it necessary for the plaintiff to amend his bill, he may have leave to amend the same with or without the payment of costs, as the court, or a judge thereof, may in his discretion direct.

46. In every case where an amendment shall be made after answer filed, the defendant shall put in a new or supplemental answer, on or before the next succeeding rule day after that on which the amendment or amended bill is filed, unless the time is enlarged or otherwise ordered by a judge of the court ; and upon his default the like proceedings may be had as in cases of an omission to put in an answer.

Parties to Bills.

47. In all cases where it shall appear to the court that persons, who might otherwise be deemed necessary or proper parties to the suit, cannot be made parties by reason of their being out of the jurisdiction of the court, or incapable otherwise of being made parties, or because their joinder would oust the jurisdiction of the court as to the parties before the court, the court may in their discretion proceed in the cause without making such persons parties ; and in such cases the decree shall be without prejudice to the rights of the absent parties.

48. Where the parties on either side are very numerous, and cannot, without manifest inconvenience and oppressive delays in the suit, be all brought before it, the court in its discretion may dispense with making all of them parties, and may proceed in the suit, having sufficient parties before it to represent all the adverse interests of the plaintiffs and the defendants in the suit properly before it. But in such cases the decree shall be without prejudice to the rights and claims of all the absent parties.

49. In all suits concerning real estate which is vested in trustees by devise, and such trustees are competent to sell and give discharges for the proceeds of the sale, and for the rents and profits of the estate, such trustees shall represent the persons beneficially interested in the estate, or the proceeds, or the rents and profits, in the same manner and to the same extent, as the executors or administrators in suits concerning personal estate represent the persons beneficially interested in such personal estate; and in such cases it shall not be necessary to make the persons beneficially interested in such real estate, or rents and profits, parties to the suit; but the court may, upon consideration of the matter on the hearing, if it shall so think fit, order such persons to be made parties.

50. In suits to execute the trusts of a will, it shall not be necessary to make the heir-at law a party ; but the plaintiff shall be at liberty to make the heir-at-law a party where he desires to have the will established against him.

51. In all cases in which the plaintiff has a joint and several demand against several persons, either as principals or sureties, it shall not be necessary to bring before the court as parties to a suit concerning such de-

mand, all the persons liable thereto; but the plaintiff may proceed against one or more of the persons severally liable.

52. Where the defendant shall, by his answer, suggest that the bill is defective for want of parties, the plaintiff shall be at liberty, within fourteen days after answer filed, to set down the cause for argument upon that objection only; and the purpose for which the same is so set down shall be notified by an entry, to be made in the clerk's order book, in the form or to the effect following, (that is to say,) "Set down upon the defendant's objection for want of parties." And where the plaintiff shall not so set down his cause, but shall proceed therewith to a hearing, notwithstanding an objection for want of parties taken by the answer, he shall not, at the hearing of the cause, if the defendant's objection shall then be allowed, be entitled as of course to an order for liberty to amend his bill by adding parties. But the court, if it thinks fit, shall be at liberty to dismiss the bill.

53. If a defendant shall, at the hearing of a cause, object that a suit is defective for want of parties not having by plea or answer taken the objection, and therein specified by name or description the parties to whom the objection applies, the court (if it shall think fit) shall be at liberty to make a decree saving the rights of the absent parties.

Nominal Parties to Bills.

54. Where no account, payment, conveyance, or other direct relief is sought against a party to a suit, not being an infant, the party, upon service of the subpœna upon him, need not appear and answer the bill, unless the plaintiff specially requires him so to do by the prayer of his bill; but he may appear and answer at his option; and if he does not appear and answer he shall be bound by all the proceedings in the cause. If the plaintiff shall require him to appear and answer, he shall be entitled to the costs of all the proceedings against him, unless the court shall otherwise direct.

55. Whenever an injunction is asked for by the bill to stay proceedings at law, if the defendant do not enter his appearance and plead, demur or answer to the same within the time prescribed therefor by these rules, the plaintiff shall be entitled, as of course, upon motion without notice, to such injunction. But special injunctions shall be grantable only upon due notice to the other party by the court in term, or by a judge thereof in vacation, after a hearing, which may be ex parte, if the adverse party does not appear at the time and place ordered. In every case where an injunction, either the common injunction or a special injunction, is awarded in vacation, it shall, unless previously dissolved by the judge granting the same, continue until the next term of the court, or until it is dissolved by some other order of the court.

Bills of revivor and supplemental bills.

56. Whenever a suit in equity shall become abated by the death of either party, or by any other event, the same may be revived by a bill of revivor, or a bill in the nature of a bill of revivor, as the circumstances of the case may require, filed by the proper parties entitled to revive the same; which bill may be filed in the clerk's office at any time; and upon suggestion of the facts, the proper process of subpœna shall, as of course, be issued by the clerk, requiring the proper representatives of the other party to appear and show cause, if any they have, why the cause should not be revived. And if no cause shall be shown at the next rule day which shall occur after fourteen days from the time of the service of the same process, the suit shall stand revived, as of course.

57. Whenever any suit in equity shall become defective from any event happening after the filing of the bill, (as, for example, by change of interest in the parties,) or for any other reason a supplemental bill, or a bill in the nature of a supplemental bill, may be necessary to be filed in the cause, leave to file the same may be granted by any judge of the court on any rule day, upon proper cause shown, and due notice to the other party. And if leave is granted to file such supplemental bill, the defendant shall demur, plead, or answer thereto, on the next succeeding rule day after the supplemental bill is filed in the clerk's office, unless some other time shall be assigned by a judge of the court.

58. It shall not be necessary in any bill or revivor, or supplemental bill, to set forth

any of the statements in the original suit, unless the special circumstances of the case may require it.

Answers.

59. Every defendant may swear to his answer before any justice or judge of any court of the United States, or before any commissioner appointed by any circuit court to take testimony or depositions, or before any master in chancery appointed by any circuit court, or before any judge of any court of the state or territory.

Amendment of Answers.

60. After an answer is put in, it may be amended as of course, in any matter of form or by filling up a blank, or correcting a date, or reference to a document or other small matter, and be resworn, at any time before a replication is put in, or the cause is set down for a hearing upon bill and answer. But after replication, or such setting down for a hearing, it shall not be amended in any material matters, as by adding new facts or defences, or qualifying or altering the original statements, except by special leave of the court or of a judge thereof, upon motion and cause shown after due notice to the adverse party, supported, if required, by affidavit. And in every case where leave is so granted, the court or the judge granting the same may, in his discretion, require that the same be separately engrossed and added as a distinct amendment to the original answer, so as to be distinguishable therefrom.

Exceptions to Answers.

61. After an answer is filed on any rule day, the plaintiff shall be allowed until the next succeeding rule day to file in the clerk's office exceptions thereto for insufficiency, and no longer, unless a longer time shall be allowed for the purpose, upon cause shown to the court or a judge thereof; and if no exception shall be filed thereto within that period, the answer shall be deemed and taken to be sufficient.

62. When the same solicitor is employed for two or more defendants, and separate answers shall be filed, or other proceedings had by two or more of the defendants separately costs shall not be allowed for such separate answers or other proceedings, unless a master, upon reference to him, shall certify that such separate answers and other proceedings were necessary or proper, and ought not to have been joined together.

63. Where exceptions shall be filed to the answer for insufficiency within the period prescribed by these rules, if the defendant shall not submit to the same and file an amended answer on the next succeeding rule day, the plaintiff shall forthwith set them down for a hearing on the next succeeding rule day thereafter before a judge of the court, and shall enter, as of course, in the order-book, an order for that purpose. And if he shall not so set down the same for a hearing, the exceptions shall be deemed abandoned, and the answer shall be deemed sufficient : provided, however, that the court or any judge thereof, may, for good cause shown, enlarge the time for filing exceptions, or for answering the same in his discretion, upon such terms as he may deem reasonable.

64. If, at the hearing, the exceptions shall be allowed, the defendant shall be bound to put in a full and complete answer thereto on the next succeeding rule day ; otherwise the plaintiff shall, as of course, be entitled to take the bill, so far as the matter of such exceptions is concerned, as confessed, or, at his election, he may have a writ of attachment to compel the defendant to make a better answer to the matter of the exceptions ; and the defendant, when he is in custody upon such writ, shall not be discharged therefrom but by an order of the court, or of a judge thereof, upon his putting in such answer and complying with such terms as the court or judge may direct.

65. If, upon argument, the plaintiff's exceptions to the answer shall be overruled, or the answer shall be adjudged insufficient, the prevailing party shall be entitled to all the costs occasioned thereby, unless otherwise directed by the court, or the judge thereof, at the hearing upon the exceptions.

Replication and issue.

66. Whenever the answer of the defendant shall not be excepted to, or shall be adjudged or deemed sufficient, the plaintiff shall file the general replication thereto on or before the next succeeding rule day thereafter ; and in all cases where the general replication is filed, the cause shall be deemed to all intents and purposes at issue, without any rejoinder or other pleading on either

side. If the plaintiff shall omit or refuse to file such replication within the prescribed period, the defendant shall be entitled to an order, as of course, for a dismissal of the suit; and the suit shall thereupon stand dismissed, unless the court, or a judge thereof, shall, upon motion for cause shown, allow a replication to be filed *nunc pro tunc*, the plaintiff submitting to speed the cause, and to such other terms as may be directed.

Testimony—how taken.

67. After the cause is at issue, commissions to take testimony may be taken out in vacation as well as in term, jointly by both parties, or severally by either party, upon interrogatories filed by the party taking out the same in the clerk's office, ten days' notice thereof being given to the adverse party to file cross-interrogatories before the issuing of the commission; and if no cross-interrogatories are filed at the expiration of the time, the commission may issue *ex parte*. In all cases the commissioner or commissioners shall be named by the court, or by a judge thereof. If the parties shall so agree, the testimony may be taken upon oral interrogatories by the parties or their agents, without filing any written interrogatories.

DECEMBER TERM, 1854.

Ordered, That the sixty-seventh rule governing equity practice be so amended as to allow the presiding judge of any court exercising jurisdiction, either in term time or vacation, to vest in the clerk of said court general power to name commissioners to take testimony in like manner that the court or judge thereof can now do by the said sixty-seventh rule.

DECEMBER TERM, 1861.

Ordered, That the last paragraph in the sixty-seventh rule in equity be repealed, and the rule be amended as follows : Either party may give notice to the other that he desires the evidence to be adduced in the cause to be taken orally, and thereupon all the witnesses to be examined shall be examined before one of the examiners of the court, or before an examiner to be specially appointed by the court, the examiner to be furnished with a copy of the bill and answer,

if any; and such examination shall take place in the presence of the parties or their agents, by their counsel or solicitors, and the witnesses shall be subject to cross-examination and re-examination, and which shall be conducted as near as may be in the mode now used in common law courts. The depositions taken upon such oral examination shall be taken down in writing by the examiner in the form of narrative, unless he determines the examination shall be by question and answer, in special instances ; and, when completed, shall be read over to the witness and signed by him, in the presence of the parties or counsel, or such of them as may attend ; provided, if the witness shall refuse to sign the said deposition, then the examiner shall sign the same ; and the examiner may, upon all examinations, state any special matters to the court as he shall think fit; and any question or questions which may be objected to shall be noted by the examiner upon the deposition, but he shall not have power to decide on the competency, materiality, or relevancy of the questions ; and the court shall have power to deal with the costs of incompetent, immaterial, or irrelevant depositions, or parts of them, as may be just.

The compulsory attendance of witnesses. In case of refusal of witnesses to attend, or to answer any question put by the examiner, or by counsel or solicitor, the same practice shall be adopted as is now practiced with respect to witnesses to be produced on examination before an examiner of said court, on written interrogatories.

Notice shall be given by the respective counsel or solicitors, to the opposite counsel or solicitors or parties, of the time and place of the examination, for such reasonable time as the examiner may fix by order in each cause.

When the examination of witnesses before the examiner is concluded, the original deposition, authenticated by the signature of the examiner, shall be transmitted by him to the clerk of the court, to be there filed of record in the same mode as prescribed in the thirtieth section of act of congress, September 24, 1789.

Testimony may be taken on commission in the usual way, by written interrogatories and cross-interrogatories, on motion to the court in term time, or to a judge in vacation, for special reasons satisfactory to the court or judge.

DECEMBER TERM, 1869.

Amendment to 67th Rule.

Where the evidence to be adduced in a cause is to be taken orally, as provided in the order passed at the December term, 1861, amending the 67th general rule, the court may, on motion of either party, assign a time within which the complainant shall take his evidence in support of the bill, and a time thereafter within which the defendant shall take his evidence in defense, and a time thereafter within which the complainant shall take his evidence in reply; and no further evidence shall be taken in the cause unless by agreement of the parties, or by leave of court first obtained on motion for cause shown.

68. Testimony may also be taken in the cause, after it is at issue, by deposition, according to the acts of congress. But in such case, if no notice is given to the adverse party of the time and place of taking the deposition, he shall, upon motion and affidavit of the fact, be entitled to a cross-examination of the witness, either under a commission or by a new deposition taken under the acts of congress, if a court or a judge thereof shall, under all the circumstances, deem it reasonable.

69. Three months, and no more, shall be allowed for the taking of testimony after the cause is at issue, unless the court or judge thereof shall, upon special cause shown by either party, enlarge the time; and no testimony taken after such period shall be allowed to be read in evidence at the bearing. Immediately upon the return of the commissions and depositions containing the testimony into the clerk's office, publication thereof may be ordered in the clerk's office, by any judge of the court, upon due notice to the parties, or it may be enlarged, as he may deem reasonable under all the circumstances; but, by consent of the parties, publication of the testimony may at any time pass in the clerk's office, such consent being in writing, and a copy thereof entered in the order books, or indorsed upon the deposition or testimony.

Testimony de bene esse.

70. After any bill filed, and before the defendant hath answered the same, upon affidavit made that any of the plaintiff's witnesses are aged and infirm, or going out of the country, or that any one of them is a single witness to a material fact, the clerk of the court shall, as of course, upon the application of the plaintiff, issue a commission to such commissioner or commissioners as a judge of a court may direct, to take the examination of such witness or witnesses *de bene esse,* upon giving due notice to the adverse party of the time and place of taking his testimony.

Form of the Last Interrogatory.

71. The last interrogatory in the written interrogatories to take testimony now commonly in use shall in the future be altered, and stated in substance thus: " Do you know, or can you set forth, any other matter or thing which may be a benefit or advantage to the parties at issue in this cause, or either of them, or that may be material to the subject of this your examination, or the matters in question in this cause? If yea, set forth the same fully and at large in your answer.

Cross Bill.

72. Where a defendant in equity files a cross bill for discovery only against the plaintiff in the original bill, the defendant to the original bill shall first answer thereto before the original plaintiff shall be compellable to answer the cross bill. The answer of the original plaintiff to such cross bill may be read and used by the party filing the cross bill at the hearing, in the same manner and under the same restrictions as the answer praying relief may now be read and used.

Reference to and Proceedings before Masters.

73. Every decree for an account of the personal estate of a testator or intestate shall contain a direction to the master, to whom it is referred to take the same, to inquire and state to the court what parts, if any, of such personal estate are outstanding or undisposed of, unless the court shall otherwise direct.

74. Whenever any reference of any matter is made to a master to examine and report thereon, the party at whose instance or

for whose benefit the reference is made shall cause the same to be presented to the master for a hearing on or before the next rule day succeeding the time when the reference was made ; if he shall omit to do so, the adverse party shall be at liberty forthwith to cause proceedings to be had before the master, at the costs of the party procuring the reference.

75. Upon every such reference it shall be the duty of the master, as soon as he reasonably can after the same is brought before him, to assign a time and place for proceedings in the same, and to give due notice thereof to each of the parties, or their solicitors ; and if either party shall fail to appear at the time and place appointed, the master shall be at liberty to proceed *ex parte*, or, in his discretion, to adjourn the examination and proceedings to a future day, giving notice to the absent party or his solicitor of such adjournment ; and it shall be the duty of the master to proceed with all reasonable diligence in every such reference, and with the least practicable delay, and either party shall be at liberty to apply to the court, or a judge thereof, for an order to the master to speed the proceedings, and to make his report, and to certify to the court or judge the reasons for any delay.

76. In the reports made by the master to the court no part of any state of facts, charge, affidavit, deposition, examination, or answer brought in or used before them shall be stated or recited. But such state of facts, charge, affidavit, deposition, examination, or answer shall be identified, specified, and referred to, so as to inform the court what state of facts, charge, affidavit, deposition, examination, or answer were so brought in or used.

77. The master shall regulate all the proceedings in every hearing before him, upon every such reference ; and he shall have full authority to examine the parties in the cause, upon oath, touching all matters contained in the reference ; and also to require the production of all books, papers, writings, vouchers, and other documents applicable thereto ; and also to examine on oath, *viva voce*, all witnesses produced by the parties before him, and to order the examination of other witnesses to be taken, under a commission to be issued upon his certificate from the clerk's office, or by deposition, according to the acts of congress, or otherwise, as hereinafter provided ; and also to direct the mode in which the matters requiring evidence shall be proved before him ; and generally to do all other acts, and direct all other inquiries and proceedings in the matters before him, which he may deem necessary and proper to the justice and merits thereof and the rights of the parties.

78. Witnesses who live within the district may, upon due notice to the opposite party, be summoned to appear before the commissioner appointed to take testimony, or before a master or examiner appointed in any cause, by subpœna in the usual form, which may be issued by the clerk in blank, and filled up by the party praying the same, or by the commissioner, master, or examiner, requiring the attendance of the witnesses at the time and place specified, who shall be allowed for attendance the same compensation as for attendance in court ; and if any witness shall refuse to appear, or to give evidence, it shall be deemed a contempt of the court, which being certified to the clerk's office by the commissioner, master, or examiner, an attachment may issue thereupon by order of the court or of any judge thereof, in the same manner as if the contempt were for not attending, or for refusing to give testimony in the court. But nothing herein contained shall prevent the examination of witnesses *viva voce* when produced in open court, if the court shall, in its discretion deem it advisable.

79. All parties accounting before a master shall bring in their respective accounts in the form of debtor and creditor ; and any of the other parties who shall not be satisfied with the accounts so brought in shall be at liberty to examine the accounting party *viva voce*, or upon interrogatories in the master's office, or by deposition, as the master shall direct.

80. All affidavits, depositions, and documents which have been previously made, read, or used in the court, upon any proceeding in any cause or matter, may be used before the master

81. The master shall be at liberty to examine any creditor or other person coming in to claim before him, either upon written interrogatories or *viva voce*, or in both modes, as the nature of the case may appear to him to require. The evidence upon such exami-

nations shall be taken down by the master, or by some other person by his order and in his presence, if either party requires it, in order that the same may be used by the court, if necessary.

82. The circuit courts may appoint standing masters in chancery in their respective districts, both the judges concurring in the appointment; and they may also appoint a master *pro hac vice* in any particular case. The compensation to be allowed to every master in chancery for his services in any particular case shall be fixed by the circuit court in its discretion, having regard to all the circumstances thereof, and the compensation shall be charged upon and borne by such of the parties in the cause as the court shall direct. The master shall not retain his report as security for his compensation; but when the compensation is allowed by the court, he shall be entitled to an attachment for the amount against the party who is ordered to pay the same, if, upon notice thereof, he does not pay it within the time prescribed by the court.

Exceptions to Report of Master.

83. The master, as soon as his report is ready, shall return the same into the clerk's office, and the day of the return shall be entered by the clerk in the order book. The parties shall have one month from the time of filing the report to file exceptions thereto; and if no exceptions are within that period filed by either party, the report shall stand confirmed on the next rule day after the month is expired. If exceptions are filed, they shall stand for hearing before the court, if the court is then in session; or, if not, then at the next sitting of the court which shall be held thereafter by adjournment or otherwise.

84. And in order to prevent exceptions to reports from being filed for frivolous causes, or for mere delay, the party whose exceptions are overruled shall, for every exception overruled, pay costs to the other party, and for every exception allowed shall be entitled to costs—the costs to be fixed in each case by the court, by a standing rule of the circuit court.

Decrees.

85. Clerical mistakes in decrees, or decretal orders, or errors arising from any accidental slip or omission, may, at any time before an actual enrollment thereof, be corrected by order of the court or a judge thereof, upon petition, without the form or expense of a hearing.

86. In drawing up decrees and orders, neither the bill, nor answer, nor other pleadings, nor any part thereof, nor the report of any master, nor any other prior proceeding, shall be recited or stated in the decree or order; but the decree or order shall begin, in substance as follows : " This cause came on to be heard (or to be further heard as the case may be) at this term, and was argued by counsel; and thereupon, upon consideration thereof, it was ordered, adjudged, and decreed as follows, viz :" [Here insert the decree or order.]

Guardians and Prochein Amis.

87. Guardians *ad litem* to defend a suit may be appointed by the court, or by any judge thereof, for infants or other persons who are under guardianship, or otherwise incapable to sue tor themselves. All infants and other persons so incapable may sue by their guardians, if any, or by their *prochein ami;* subject, however, to such orders as the court may direct for the protection of infants and other persons.

88. Every petition for a rehearing shall contain the special matter or cause on which such rehearing is applied for, shall be signed by counsel, and the facts therein stated, if not apparent on the record, shall be verified by the oath of the party, or by some other person. No rehearing shall be granted after the term at which the final decree of the court shall have been entered and recorded, if an appeal lies to the supreme court. But if no appeal lies, the petition may be admitted at any time before the end of the next term of the court in the discretion of the court.

89. The circuit courts (both judges concurring therein) may make any other and further rules and regulations for the practice, proceedings, and process, mesne and final, in their respective districts, not inconsistent with the rules hereby prescribed in their discretion, and from time to time alter and amend the same.

90. In all cases where the rules prescribed by this court or by the circuit court do not

apply, the practice of the circuit court shall be regulated by the present practice of the high court of chancery in England, so far as the same may reasonably be applied consistently with the local circumstances and local convenience of the district where the court is held, not as positive rules, but as furnishing just analogies to regulate the practice.

91. Whenever, under these rules, an oath is or may be required to be taken, the party may, if conscientiously scrupulous of taking an oath, in lieu thereof, make solemn affirmation to the truth of the facts stated by him.

DECEMBER TERM, 1863.

92. *Ordered*, That in suits in equity for the foreclosure of mortgages in the circuit courts of the United States, or in any court of the territories having jurisdiction of the same, a decree may be rendered for any balance that may be found due to the complainant over and above the proceeds of the sale or sales, and execution may issue for the collection of the same, as is provided in the 8th rule of this court regulating the equity practice, where the decree is solely for the payment of money.

RULES OF PRACTICE

FOR

COURTS OF THE UNITED STATES

IN

ADMIRALTY AND MARITIME JURISDICTION, ON THE INSTANCE SIDE OF THE COURT, IN PURSUANCE OF THE ACT OF THE TWENTY-SECOND OF AUGUST, 1844, CHAP. 188.

1. No mesne process shall issue from the district courts in any civil cause of admiralty and maritime jurisdiction until the libel, or libel of information, shall be filed in the clerk's office from which such process is to issue. All process shall be served by the marshal, or by his deputy, or, where he or they are interested,. by some discreet and disinterested person appointed by the court.

2. In suits *in personam* the mesne process may be by a simple warrant of arrest of the person of the defendant in the nature of a capias, or by a warrant of arrest of the person of the defendant, with a clause therein that if he cannot be found, to attach his goods and chattels to the amount sued for; or if such property cannot be found, to attach his credits and effects to the amount sued for in the hands of the garnishees named therein; or by a simple monition, in the nature of a summons to appear and answer to the suit, as the libellant shall, in his libel or information pray for or elect.

3. In all suits *in personam* where a simple warrant of arrest issues and is executed, the marshal may take bail, with sufficient sureties, from the party arrested, by bond or stipulation, upon condition that he will appear in the suit and abide by all orders of the court, interlocutory or final, in the cause, and pay the money awarded by the final decree rendered therein in the court to which the process is returnable, or in any appellate court. And upon such bond or stipulation summary process of execution may and shall be issued against the principal and sureties by the court to which such process is returnable, to enforce the final decree so rendered, or upon appeal by the appellate court.

4. In all suits *in personam* where goods and chattels, or credits and effects are attached under such warrant authorizing the same, the attachment may be dissolved by order of the court to which the same warrant is returnable upon the defendant,

whose property is so attached, giving a bond or stipulation, with sufficient sureties, to abide by all orders, interlocutory or final, of the court, and pay amount awarded by the final decree rendered in the court to which the process is returnable, or in any appellate court; and upon such bond or stipulation summary process of execution shall and may be issued against the principal and sureties by the court to which such warrant is returnable, to enforce the final decree so rendered, or upon appeal by the appellate court.

5. Bonds or stipulations in admiralty suits, may be given and taken in open court, or at chambers, or before any commissioner of the court who is authorized by the court to take affidavits of bail and depositions in cases pending before the court.

6. In all suits *in personam* where bail is taken the court may, upon motion, for due cause shown, reduce the amount of the sum contained in the bond or stipulation therefor; and in all cases where a bond or stipulation is taken as bail, or upon dissolving an attachment of property, as aforesaid, if either of the sureties shall become insolvent pending the suit, new sureties may be required by the order of the court to be given, upon motion and due proof thereof.

7. In suits *in personam* no warrant of arrest, either of the person or property of the defendant, shall issue for a sum exceeding five hundred dollars, unless by the special order of the court upon affidavit or other proper proof showing the propriety thereof.

8. In all suits *in rem* against a ship, her tackle, sails, apparel, furniture, boats or other appurtenances, if such tackle, sails, apparel, furniture, boats or other appurtenances are in the possession or custody of any third person, the court may, after a due monition to such third person, and a hearing of the cause, if any, why the same should not be delivered over, award and decree that the same be delivered into the custody of the marshal or other proper officer, if upon the hearing, the same is required by law and justice.

9. In all cases of seizure, and in other suits and proceedings *in rem* the process, unless otherwise provided for by statute, shall be by a warrant of arrest of the ship, goods, or other thing to be arrested; and the marshal shall thereupon arrest and take the ship, goods or other thing into his possession for safe custody, and shall cause public notice thereof and of the time assigned for the return of such process and the hearing of the cause, to be given in such newspaper within the district as the district court shall order; and if there is no newspaper published therein, then in such other public places in the district as the court shall direct.

10. In all cases where any goods or other things are arrested, if the same are perishable, or are liable to deterioration, decay or injury by being detained in custody pending the suit, the court may, upon the application of either party, in its discretion, order the same or so much thereof to be sold as shall be perishable or liable to depreciation, decay or injury; and the proceeds, or so much thereof as shall be a full security to satisfy in decree, to be brought into court to abide the event of the suit; or the court may, upon the application of the claimant, order a delivery thereof to him, upon a due appraisement to be had under its direction, either upon the claimant's depositing in court so much money as the court shall order, or upon his giving a stipulation, with sureties in such sum as the court shall direct, to abide by and pay the money awarded by the final decree rendered by the court or the appellate court, if any appeal intervenes, as the one or the other course shall be ordered by the court.

11. In like manner, where any ship shall be arrested, the same may, upon the application of the claimant be delivered to him, upon a due appraisement to be had, under the direction of the court, upon the claimant's depositing in court so much money as the court shall order, or upon his giving a stipulation, with sureties as aforesaid; and if the claimant shall decline any such application, then the court may, in its discretion, upon the application of either party, upon due cause shown, order a sale of such ship, and the proceeds thereof to be brought into court, or otherwise disposed of, as it may deem most for the benefit of all concerned.

12. In all suits by material men for supplies or repairs, or other necessaries, for a foreign ship, or for a ship in a foreign port, the libellant may proceed against the ship and freight *in rem*, or against the master or owner alone *in personam*. And the like proceeding *in personam* but not *in rem* shall

apply to cases of domestic ships, for supplies, repairs, or other necessaries.

13. In all suits for mariner's wages the libellant may proceed against the ship, freight, and master, or against the ship and freight, or against the owner or the master alone *in personam*.

14. In all suits 'for pilotage the libellant may proceed against the ship and master, or against the ship alone, or against the owner alone, or the master alone, *in personam*.

15. In all suits for damage by collision the libellant may proceed against the ship and master, or against the ship alone, or against the master or the owner alone, *in personam*.

16. In all suits for an assault or beating on the high seas, or elsewhere within the admiralty and maritime jurisdiction, the suit shall be *in personam* only.

17. In all suits against the ship or freight founded upon a mere maritime hypothecation, either express or implied, of the master, for moneys taken up in a foreign port for supplies or repairs, or other necessaries for the voyage, without any claim of marine interest, the libellant may proceed either *in rem*, or against the master or the owner alone *in personam*.

18. In all suits on bottomry bonds, properly so called, the suit shall be *in rem* only against the property hypothecated, or the proceeds of the property, in whosesoever hands the same may be found, unless the master has, without authority, given the bottomry bond, or by his fraud or misconduct . has avoided the same, or has substracted the property, or unless the owner has, by his own misconduct or wrong, lost or subtracted the property, in which latter cases the suit may be *in personam* against the wrong-doer.

19. In all suits for salvage the suit may be *in rem* against the property saved, or the proceeds thereof, or *in personam* against the party at whose request and for whose benefit the salvage service has been performed.

20. In all petitory and possessory suits between part owners or adverse proprietors, or by the owners of a ship, or the majority thereof, against the master of a ship for the ascertainment of the title and delivery of the possession, or for the possession only, or by one or more part owners against the others to obtain security for the return of the ship from any voyage undertaken without their consent, or by one or more part owners against the others to obtain possession of the ship for any voyage, upon giving security for the safe return thereof, the process shall be by an arrest of the ship, and by a monition to the adverse party or parties to appear and make answer to the suit.

21. In all cases of a final decree for the payment of money the libellant shall have a writ of execution, in the nature of a *fieri facias*, commanding the marshal or his deputy to levy and collect the amount thereof out of the goods and chattels, lands and tenements, or other real estate of the defendant or stipulators.

22. All informations and libels of information upon seizures for any breach of the revenue, or navigation, or other laws of the United States, shall state the place of seizure, whether it be on land or on the high seas, or on navigable waters within the admiralty and maritime jurisdiction of the United States, and the district within which the property is brought, and where it then is. The information or libel of information shall also propound in distinct articles the matters relied on as grounds or causes of forfeiture, and aver the same to be contrary to the form of statute or statutes of the United States in such case provided, as the case may require, and shall conclude with a prayer of due process to enforce the forfeiture, and to give notice to all persons concerned in interest to appear and show cause at the return day of the process why the forfeiture should not be decreed.

23. All libels in instance causes, civil or maritime, shall state the nature of the cause; as, for example, that it is a cause, civil and maritime, of contract, or of tort or damage, or of salvage, or of possession, or otherwise, as the case may be; and if the libel be *in rem*, that the property is within the district; and if *in personam*, the names and occupations and places of residence of the parties. The libel shall also propound and articulate in distinct articles the various allegations of fact upon which the libellant relies in support of his suit, so that the defendant may be enabled to answer distinctly and separately the several matters contained in each article; and it shall conclude with a prayer of due process to enforce his rights *in rem*, or *in personam* (as the case may require),

and for such relief and redress as the court is competent to give in the premises. And the libellant may further require the defendant to answer on oath all interrogatories propounded by him touching all and singular the allegations in the libel at the close or conclusion thereof.

24. In all informations and libels, in causes of admirality and maritime jurisdiction, amendments, in matters of form, may be made at any time, on motion, to the court as of course. And new counts may be filed, and amendments, in matters of substance, may be made, upon motion, at any time before the final decree, upon such terms as the court shall impose. And where any defect of form is set down by the defendant upon special exceptions and is allowed, the court may, in granting leave to amend, impose terms upon the libellant.

25. In all cases of libels *in personam* the court may, in its discretion, upon the appearance of the defendant, where no bail has been taken and no attachment of property has been made to answer the exigency of the suit, require the defendant to give a stipulation, with sureties in such sum as the court shall direct, to pay all costs and expenses which shall be awarded against him in the suit, upon the final adjudication thereof, or by any interlocutory order, in the progress of the suit.

26. In suits *in rem* the party claiming the property shall verify his claim on oath or solemn affirmation, stating that the claimant by whom or on whose behalf the claim is made is the true and bona fide owner, and that no other person is the owner thereof. And where the claim is put in by an agent or consignee, he shall also make oath that he is duly authorized thereto by the owner; or if the property be, at the time of the arrest, in the possession of a master of a ship, that he is the lawful bailee thereof for the owner. And upon putting in such claim, the claimant shall file a stipulation, with sureties in such sum as the court shall direct, for the payment of all costs and expenses which shall be awarded against him by the final decree of the court, or, upon an appeal, by the appellate court.

27. In all libels in causes of civil and maritime jurisdiction, whether in *in rem* or *in personam*, the answer of the defendant to the allegations in the libel shall be on oath or solemn affirmation; and the answer shall be full and explicit and distinct to each separate article and separate allegation in libel, in the same order as numbered in the libel, and shall also answer in like manner each interrogatory propounded at the close of the libel.*

28. The libellant may except to the sufficiency, or fullness, or distinctness, or relevanoy of the answer to the articles and interrogatories in the libel; and if the court shall adjudge the same exceptions, or any of them, to be good and valid, the court shall order the defendant forthwith, within such time as the court shall direct, to answer the same, and may further order the defendant to pay such costs as the court shall adjudge reasonable.

29. If the defendant shall omit or refuse to make due answer to the libel upon the return-day of the process, or other day assigned by the court, the court shall pronounce him to be in contumacy and default; and thereupon the libel shall be adjudged to be taken *pro confesso* against him, and the court shall proceed to hear the cause *ex parte* and adjudge therein as to law and justice shall appertain. But the court may, in its discretion, set aside the default, and, upon the application of the defendant, admit him to make answer to the libel at any time before the final hearing and decree, upon his payment of all the costs of the suit up to the time of granting leave therefor.

30. In all cases where the defendant answers, but does not answer fully and explicitly and distinctly to all the matters in any article of the libel, and exception is taken thereto by the libellant, and the exception is allowed, the court may, by attachment, compel the defendant to make further answer thereto, or may direct the matter of the exception to be taken *pro confesso* against the defendant to the full purport and effect of the article to which it purports to answer, and as if no answer had been put in thereto.

31. The defendant may object, by his answer, to answer any allegation or interrogatory contained in the libel which will expose him to any prosecution or punishment

---

*Vide *post*, 49th Rule, p. 1032.

for a crime, or for any penalty or any forfeiture of his property for any penal offense.

32. The defendant shall have a right to require the personal answer of the libellant upon oath or solemn affirmation to any interrogatories which he may, at the close of his answer, propound to the libellant touching any matters charged in the libel, or touching any matter of defense set up in the answer, subject to the like exceptions as to matters which shall expose the libellant to any prosecution, or punishment, or forfeiture as is provided in the thirty-first rule. In default of due answer by the libellant to such interrogatories, the court may adjudge the libellant to be in default and dismiss the libel, or may compel his answer in the premises by attachment, or take the subject matter of the interrogatory *pro confesso* in favor of the defendant, as the court, in its discretion, shall deem most fit to promote public justice.

33. Where either the libellant or the defendant is out of the country, or unable, from sickness or other casualty, to make an answer to any interrogatory on oath or solemn affirmation at the proper time, the court may, in its discretion, in furtherance of the due administration of justice, dispense therewith, or may award a commission to take the answer of the defendant when and as soon as it may be practicable.

34. If any third person shall intervene in any cause of admiralty and maritime jurisdiction *in rem* for his own interest, and he is entitled, according to the course of admiralty proceedings, to be heard for his own interest therein, he shall propound the matter in suitable allegations, to which, if admitted by the court, the other party or parties in the suit may be required, by order of the court, to make due answer: and such further proceedings shall be had and decree rendered by the court therein as to law and justice shall appertain. But every such intervenor shall be required upon filing his allegations to give a stipulation, with sureties, to abide by the final decree rendered in the cause, and to pay all such costs and expenses and damages as shall be awarded by the court upon the final decree, whether it is rendered in the original or appellate court.

35. Stipulations in admiralty and maritime suits may be taken in open court, or by the proper judge at chambers, or, under his order, by any commissioner of the court who is a standing commissioner of the court, and is now by law authorized to take affidavits of bail, and also depositions in civil causes pending in the courts of the United States.

36. Exceptions may be taken to any libel, allegation, or answer, for surplusage, irrelevancy, impertinence, or scandal; and if, upon reference to a master, the exception shall be reported to be so objectionable, and allowed by the court, the matter shall be expunged, at the cost and expense of the party in whose libel or answer the same is found.

37. In cases of foreign attachment, the garnishee shall be required to answer on oath or solemn affirmation as to the debts, credits, or effects of the defendant in his hands, and to such interrogatories touching the same as may be propounded by the libellant; and if he shall refuse or neglect so to do, the court may award compulsory process *in personam* against him. If he admits any debts, credits, or effects, the same shall be held in his hands, liable to answer the exigency of the suit.

38. In cases of mariners' wages, or bottomry, or salvage, or other proceedings *in rem*, where freight or other proceeds of property are attached to or are bound by the suit, which are in the hands or possession of any person, the court may, upon due application, by petition of the party interested, require the party charged with the possession thereof to appear and show cause why the same should not be brought into court to answer the exigency of the suit; and if no sufficient cause be shown, the court may order the same to be brought into court to answer the exigency of the suit; and upon failure of the party to comply with the order, may award an attachment, or other compulsive process, to compel obedience thereto.

39. If, in any admiralty suit, the libellant shall not appear and prosecute his suit, according to the course and orders of the court, he shall be deemed in default and contumacy, and the court may, upon the application of the defendant, pronounce the suit to be deserted, and the same may be dismissed with costs.

40. The court may, in its discretion, upon the motion of the defendant and the payment of costs, rescind the decree in any suit

in which, on account of his contumacy and default, the matter of the libel shall have been decreed against him, and grant a rehearing thereof at any time within ten days after the decree has been entered, the defendant submitting to such further orders and terms in the premises as the court may direct.

41. All sales of property under any decree of admiralty shall be made by the marshal or his deputy, or other proper officer assigned by the court, where the marshal is a party in interest, in pursuance of the orders of the court; and the proceeds thereof, when sold, shall be forthwith paid into the registry of the court by the officer making the sale, to be disposed of by the court according to law.

42. All moneys paid into the registry of the court shall be deposited in some bank designated by the court, and shall be so deposited in the name of the court, and shall not be drawn out except by a check or checks, signed by a judge of the court, and countersigned by the clerk, stating on whose account and for whose use it is drawn, and in what suit and out of what fund in particular it is paid. The clerk shall keep a regular book, containing a memorandum and copy of all the checks so drawn and the date thereof.

43. Any person having an interest in any proceeds in the registry of the court shall have a right, by petition and summary proceeding, to intervene *pro interesse suo* for a delivery thereof to him; and upon due notice to the adverse parties, if any, the court shall and may proceed summarily to hear and decide thereon, and to decree therein according to law and justice. And if such petition or claim shall be deserted, or, upon a hearing, be dismissed, the court may in its discretion, award costs against the petitioner in favor of the adverse party.

44. In cases where the court shall deem it expedient or necessary for the purposes of justice, the court may refer any matters arising in the progress of the suit to one or more commissioners, to be appointed by the court to hear the parties and make report therein. And such commissioner or commissioners, shall have and possess all the powers in the premises which are usually given to or exercised by masters in chancery in references to them, including the power

to administer oaths to and to examine the parties and witnesses touching the premises.

45. All appeals from the district to the circuit court must be made while the court is sitting, or within such other period as shall be designated by the district court by its general rules, or by an order specially made in the particular suit.

46. In all cases not provided for by the foregoing rules the district and circuit courts are to regulate the practice of the said courts respectively, in such manner as they shall deem most expedient for the due administration of justice in suits in admiralty.

47. In all suits *in personam* where a simple warrant of arrest issues and is executed, bail shall be taken by the marshal and the court in those cases only in which it is required by the laws of the state where an arrest is made upon similar or analogous process issuing from the state courts. And imprisonment for debt, on process issuing out of the admiralty court, is abolished in all cases where, by the laws of the state in which the court is held, imprisonment for debt has been, or shall be hereafter, abolished, upon similar or analogous process issuing from a state court.

48. The twenty-seventh rule shall not apply to cases where the sum or value in dispute does not exceed fifty dollars, exclusive of costs, unless the district court shall be of opinion that the proceedings prescribed by that rule are necessary for the purposes of justice in the case before the court.

All rules and parts of rules heretofore adopted inconsistent with this order are hereby repealed and annulled.

49. Further proof taken in a circuit court upon an admiralty appeal shall be by deposition, taken before some commissioner appointed by a circuit court, pursuant to the acts of congress in that behalf, or before some officer authorized to take depositions by the thirtieth section of the act of congress of the 24th of September, 1789, upon an oral examination and cross-examination, unless the court in which such appeal shall be pending, or one of the judges thereof, shall, upon motion, allow a commission to issue to take such depositions upon written interrogatories and cross-interrogatories. When such deposition shall be taken by oral examination, a notification from the magistrate before whom it is to be taken, or

from the clerk of the court in which such appeal shall be pending, to the adverse party to be present at the taking of the same, and to put interrogatories, if he think fit, shall be served on the adverse party, or his attorney, allowing time for their attendance after being notified not less than twenty-four hours, and in addition thereto one day, Sundays exclusive, for every twenty miles travel: *Provided,* That the court in which such appeal may be pending, or either of the judges thereof, may, upon motion, increase or diminish the length of notice above required.

50. When oral evidence shall be taken down by the clerk of the district court, pursuant to the above mentioned section of the act of congress, and shall be transmitted to the circuit court, the same may be used in evidence on the appeal, saving to each party the right to take the depositions of the same witnesses, or either of them, if he should so elect.

51. When the defendant, in his answer, alleges new facts, these shall be considered as denied by the libellant, and no replication, general or special, shall be allowed. But within such time after the answer is filed as shall be fixed by the district court, either by general rule or by special order, the libellant may amend his libel so as to confess and avoid, or explain or add to the new matters set forth in the answer; and within such time as may be fixed, in like manner, the defendant shall answer such amendments.

52. The clerks of the district courts shall make up the records to be transmitted to the circuit courts on appeals, so that the same shall contain the following:

1. The style of the court.

2. The names of the parties setting forth the original parties, and those who have become parties before the appeal, if any change has taken place.

3. If bail was taken, or property was attached or arrested, the process of arrest or attachment and the service thereof, all bail and stipulations, and, if any sale has been made, the orders, warrants, and reports relating thereto.

4. The libel, with exhibits annexed thereto.

5. The pleadings of the defendant, with the exhibits annexed thereto.

6. The testimony on the part of the libellant, and any exhibits not annexed to the libel.

7. The testimony on the part of the defendant, and any exhibits not annexed to his pleadings.

8. Any order of the court to which exception was made.

9. Any report of an assessor or assessors, if excepted to, with the orders of the court respecting the same, and the exceptions to the report. If the report was not excepted to, only the fact that a reference was made, and so much of the report as shows what results were arrived at by the assessor, are to be stated.

10. The final decree.

11. The prayer for an appeal, and the action of the district court thereon; and no reasons of appeal shall be filed or inserted in the transcript.

The following shall be omitted:

1. The continuances.

2. All motions, rules, and orders not excepted to, which are merely preparatory for trial.

3. The commissions to take depositions, notices therefor, their captions, and certificates of their being sworn to, unless some exception to a deposition in the district court was founded on some one or more of these; in which case so much of either of them as may be involved in the exception shall be set out. In all other cases it shall be sufficient to give the name of the witness, and to copy the interrogatories and answers, and to state the names of the commissioner, and the place where and the date when the deposition was sworn to; and in the copying all depositions taken on interrogatories, the answers shall be inserted immediately following the question.

The clerk of the district court shall page the copy of the record thus made up, and shall make an index thereto, and he shall certify the entire document, at the end thereof, under the seal of the court, to be a transcript of the record of the district court in the cause named at the beginning of the copy made up pursuant to this rule; and no other certificate of the record shall be needful or inserted.

53. Whenever a cross libel is filed upon any counter-claim arising out of the same

cause of action for which the original libel was filed, the respondents in the cross libel shall give security, in the usual amount and form, to respond in damages as claimed in said cross libel, unless the court on cause shown shall otherwise direct; and all proceedings upon the original libel shall be stayed until such security shall be given.

GENERAL ORDERS IN BANKRUPTCY.

In pursuance of the tenth section of the act entitled " An act to establish a uniform system of bankruptcy throughout the United States," approved March 2, 1867, the justices of the supreme court of the United States have framed the following general orders, which shall constitute the rules of practice and procedure in bankruptcy in the district courts of the United States :

Duties of Clerks of District Courts.

The clerks of the several district courts shall enter upon each petition in bankruptcy the day, and the hour of the day, upon which the same shall be filed; and shall also make a similar note upon every subsequent paper filed with them; and the papers in each case shall be kept in a file by themselves. No paper shall be taken from the files for any purpose except by order of the court. Every paper shall have indorsed upon it a brief statement of its character. The clerks shall keep a docket, in which the cases shall be entered and numbered in the order in which they are commenced; and the number of each case shall be indorsed on every paper. The docket shall be so arranged that a brief memorandum of every proceeding in each case shall be entered therein, in a manner convenient for reference, and shall at all times be open for public inspection. The clerks shall also keep separate minute books for the record or proceedings in bankruptcy, in which shall be entered a minute of all the proceedings in each case, either of the court or of a register of the court, under their respective dates.

2—Process.

All process, summons, and subpœnas shall issue out of the court under the seal thereof, and be tested by the clerk; and blanks with the signature of the clerk and seal of the court may, upon application, be furnished to the registers.

3—Appearance.

Proceedings in bankruptcy may be conducted by the bankrupt in person in his own behalf, or by a petitioning or opposing creditor; but a creditor will only be allowed to manage before the court his individual interest. Either party may appear and conduct the proceedings by attorney, who shall be an attorney or counselor authorized to practice in the circuit or district court. The name of the attorney or counselor, with his place of residence and business, shall be entered upon the docket, with the date of the entry. All papers or proceedings offered by an attorney to be filed shall be indorsed as above required; and orders granted on motion shall contain the name of the party or attorney making the motion. Notices and orders which are not, by the act or by these rules, required to be served on the party personally, may be served upon his attorney.

4—Commencement of Proceedings.

Upon the filing of a petition in case of voluntary bankrnptcy, or as soon as any adjudication of bankruptcy is made upon a petition filed in case of involuntary bankruptcy, the petition shall be referred to one of the registers in such manner as the district court shall direct, and the petitioner shall furnish the register with a copy of the papers in the case, and thereafter all the proceedings required by the act shall be had before him, except such as are required by the act to be had in the district court, or by special order of the district judge, unless some other register is directed to act in the case.

The order designating the register to act upon any petition shall name a day upon which the bankrupt shall attend before the register, from which date he shall be subject to the orders of the court in all matters relating to his bankruptcy, and may receive from the register a protection against arrest, to continue until the final adjudication on his application for a discharge, unless suspended or vacated by order of the court.

A copy of the order shall forthwith be sent by mail to the register, or be delivered to him personally, by the clerk or other officer of the court.

5—Registers.

The time when and the place where the registers shall act upon the matters arising under the several cases referred to them, shall be fixed by special order of the district court, or by the register acting under the authority of a general order, in each case, made by the district court; and at such times and places the registers may perform the acts which they are empowered to do by the act, and conduct proceedings in relation to the following matters, when uncontested, viz: making adjudication of bankruptcy on petition of the debtor; directing, unless otherwise ordered by the court, the newspapers in which the notice shall be published by the messenger; administering oaths; receiving the surrender of a bankrupt; granting protection thereon; giving requisite direction for notices, advertisements, and other ministerial proceedings; taking proofs of claims; ordering payment of rates and taxes, and salary or wages of persons in the employment of the assignee; ordering amendments, or inspection, or copies, or extracts of any proceedings; taking accounts of proceeds of securities held by any creditor; taking evidence concerning expenses and charges against the bankrupt's estate; auditing and passing accounts of assignees; proceedings for the declaration and payment of dividends, and taxing costs in any of the proceedings, all of which shall be subject to the control of the court.

6—Dispatch of Business.

Every register, in performing the duties required of him under the act, and by these orders, or by orders of the district court, shall use all reasonable dispatch, and shall not adjourn the business but for good cause shown. Six hours' session shall constitute a days' sitting if the business requires; and when there is time to complete the proceedings in progress within the day, the party obtaining any adjournment or postponement thereof may be charged, if the court think proper, with all the costs incurred in consequence of the delay.

7—Examination and Filing of Papers.

It shall be the duty of the register to examine the bankrupt's petition and scedules filed therewith, and to certify whether the same are correct in form; or, if deficient, in what respect they are so; and the court may allow amendments to be made in the petition and schedules upon the application of the petitioner, upon proper cause shown at any time prior to the discharge of the bankrupt. At the close of the last examination of the bankrupt, the register having charge of the case shall file all the papers relating thereto in the office of the clerk of the district court, and these papers, together with those on file in the clerk's office, and the entries in the minute-book shall constitue the record in each case; and the clerk shall cause the papers in each case to be bound together.

8—Orders by the Register.

Whenever an order is made by a register in any proceeding in which notice is required to be given to either party before the order can be made, the fact that the notice was given, and the substance of the evidence of the manner in which it was given, shall be recited in the preamble to the order, and the fact also stated that no adverse iterest was represented at the time and place appointed for the hearing of the matter upon such notice; and whenever an order is made where adverse interests are represented before the register, the fact shall be stated that the opposing parties consented thereto, or that the adverse interest represented made no opposition to the granting of such order.

9—Notification of Assignee of his Appointment.

It shall be the duty of the register immediately upon the appointment of an assignee, as prescribed in sections twelve and thirteen of the act, (should he not be present at such meeting,) to notify him by personal or mail service, of his appointment; and in such notification the assignee so appointed shall be required to give notice forthwith to the court or register of his acceptance or rejection of the trust.

10—*Testimony, how taken.*

The examination of witnesses before a register in bankruptcy may be conducted by the party in person or by his counsel or attorney, and the witnesses shall be subject to examination and cross-examination, which shall be had in conformity with the mode now adopted in courts of law. The depositions upon such examination shall be taken down in writing by the register in the form of narrative, unless he determines that the examination shall be by question and answer in special instances, and when completed shall be read over to the witness and signed by him in the presence of the register. Any question or questions which may be objected to shall be noted by the register upon the deposition, but he shall not have power to decide on the competency, materiality or relevancy of the question; and the courts shall have power to deal with incompetent, immaterial or irrelevant depositions, or parts of them, as may be just. In case of refusal of a witness to attend, or to testify before a register, the same proceedings may be had as are now authorized with respect to witnesses to be produced on examination before an examiner of any of the courts of the United States on written interrogatories.

11—*Minutes before register, filing, etc.*

A memorandum made of each act performed by a register shall be in suitable form, to be entered upon the minute book of the court, and shall be forwarded to the clerk of the court not later than by mail the next day after the act has been performed. Whenever an issue is raised before the register in any proceedings, either of fact or law, he shall cause the same to be stated in writing in the manner required by the fourth and sixth sections of the act, and certify the same forthwith to the district judge for his decision. The pendency of the issue undecided before a judge shall not necessarily suspend or delay other proceedings before the register or court in the case.

12—*Accounts for services of register and marshal.*

Every register shall keep an accurate account of his traveling and incidental expenses, and those of any clerk or other officer attending him in the performance of his duties in any case or number of cases which may be referred to him; and shall make return of the same under oath, with proper vouchers, (when vouchers can be procured) on the first Tuesday in each month; and the marshal shall make his return, under oath, of his actual and necessary expenses in the service of every warrant addressed to him, and for custody of property, publication of notices and other services, and other actual and necessary expenses paid by him, with vouchers therefor whenever practicable, and also with a statement that the amounts charged by him are just and reasonable.

13—*Marshal as messenger.**

It shall be the duty of the marshal as messenger to take possession of the property of the bankrupt, and to prepare, within three days from the time of taking of such possession, a complete inventory of all the property, and to return it as soon as completed. The time for making the inventory and return may be enlarged, under proper circumstances, by special order of the district court. He shall also, in case the bankrupt is absent, or cannot be found, prepare a schedule of the names and residences of his creditors, and the amount due to each, from the books or other papers of the bankrupt that may be seized by him under his warrant, and from any other sources of information; but all statements upon which his return shall be made shall be in writing, and sworn to, by the parties making them, before one of the registers in bankruptcy of the court, or a commissioner of the courts of the United States. In cases of voluntary bankruptcy, the marshal may appoint special deputies to act, as he may designate, in one or more cases, as messengers, for the purpose of causing the notices to be published and served as required in the eleventh section of the act, and for no other purpose. In giving the notices required by the third subdivision of the eleventh section of the act, it shall be sufficient to give the names, residences, and the amount of the debts (in figures) due the several creditors, so far as known, and no more.

December Term, 1867.

It is ordered that rule thirteen be amended so as to read as follows:

---

* Vide amendment next following.

It shall be the duty of the marshal as messenger to take possession of the property of the bankrupt, and to prepare, within three days from the time of taking such possession, a complete inventory of all the property, and to return it as soon as completed. The time for making the inventory and return may be enlarged, under proper circumstances, by special order of the district court: [*Provided, however*, That if any goods or effects so taken into possession as the property of the bankrupt shall be claimed by or in behalf of any other person, the marshal shall forthwith notify the petitioning creditor of such claim, and may, within five days after so giving notice of such claim, deliver them to the claimant or his agent, unless the petitioning creditor or party at whose instance possession is taken shall, by bond with sufficient sureties, to be approved by the marshal, indemnify the marshal for the taking and detention of such goods and effects, and the expenses of defending against all claims thereto; and, in case of such indemnity, the marshal shall retain possession of such goods and effects, and proceed in relation thereto as if no such claim had been made: *And provided further*, That in case the petitioning creditor claims that any property not in the possession of the bankrupt belongs to him, and should be taken by the marshal, the marshal shall not be bound to take possession of the same, unless indemnified in like manner.] He shall also, in case the bankrupt is absent or cannot be found, prepare a schedule of the names and residences of his creditors, and the amount due to each, from the books or other papers of the bankrupt that may be seized by him under his warrant, and from any other sources of information; but all statements upon which his return shall be made shall be in writing, and sworn to by the parties making them, before one of the registers in bankruptcy of the court, or a commissioner of the courts of the United States. In cases of voluntary bankruptcy, the. marshal may appoint special deputies to act, as he may designate, in one or more cases, as messengers, for the purpose of causing the notices to be published and served as required in the eleventh section of the act, and for no other purpose. In giving the notices required by the third subdivision of the eleventh section of the act, it shall be sufficient to give the names, residences, and the amount of the debts (in figures) due the several creditors, so far as known, and no more.

14—*Petitions and Amendments.*

All petitions, and the schedules filed therewith, shall be printed or written out plainly, and without abbreviation or interlineation, except where such abbreviation and interlineation may be for the purpose of reference; and whenever any amendments are allowed, they shall be written and signed by the petitioner on a separate paper, in the same manner as the original schedules were signed and verified; and if the amendments are made to different schedules, the amendments to each schedule shall be made separately, with proper reference to the schedule proposed to be amended, and each amendment shall be verified by the oath of the petitioner in the same manner as the original schedules.

15—*Priority of Actions, (Involuntary Bankruptcy.)*

Whenever two or more petitions shall be filed by creditors against a common debtor, alleging separate acts of bankruptcy committed by said debtor on different days within six months prior to the filing of said petitions, and the debtor shall appear and show cause against an adjudication of bankruptcy against him on the petitions, that petition shall be first heard and tried which alleges the commission of the earliest act of bankruptcy; and in case the several acts of bankruptcy are alleged in the different petitions to have been committed on the same day, the court before which the same are pending may order them to be consolidated, and proceed to a hearing as upon one petition; and if an adjudication of bankruptcy be made upon either petition, or for the commission of a single act of bankruptcy, it shall not be necessary to proceed to a hearing upon the remaining petitions, unless proceedings be taken by the debtor for the purpose of causing such adjudication to be annulled or vacated.

16—*Filing Petitions in Different Districts.*

In case two or more petitions shall be filed against the same individul in different districts, the first hearing shall be had in the district in which the debtor has his domicile, and such petition may be amended by inserting an allegation of an act of bankruptcy committed at an earlier date than that first alleged, if such earlier act is charged in either of the other petitions ; and in case of two or more petitions against the same firm in different courts, each having jurisdiction over the case, the petition first filed shall be first heard, and may be amended by the insertion of an allegation of an earlier act of bankruptcy than that first alleged, if such earlier act is charged in either of the other petitions, and, in either case, the proceedings upon the other petitions may be stayed until an adjudication is made upon the petition first heard ; and the court which makes the first adjudication of bankruptcy shall retain jurisdiction over all proceedings therein until the same shall be closed. In case two or more petitions for adjudication of bankruptcy shall be filed in different districts by different members of the same copartnership for an adjudication of the bankruptcy of said copartnership, the court in which the petition is first filed having jurisdiction shall take and retain jurisdiction over all proceedings in such bankruptcy until the same shall be closed; and if such petitions shall be filed in the same district, action shall be first had upon the one first filed.

17—*Concerning Redemptions of Property and Compounding Claims.*

Whenever it may be deemed for the benefit of the estate of a bankrupt to redeem and discharge any mortgage or other pledge, or deposit, or lien upon any property, real or personal, or to relieve said property from any conditional contract, and to tender performance of the conditions thereof, or to compound any debts or other claims or securities due or belonging to the estate of the bankrupt, the assignee, or the bankrupt, or any creditor who has proved his debt, may file his petition therefor in the office of the clerk of the district court; and thereupon the court shall appoint a suitable time and place for the hearing thereof, notice of which shall be given in some newspaper, to be designated by the court, at least ten days before the hearing, so that all creditors and other persons interested may appear and show cause, if any they have, why an order should not be passed by the court upon the petition authorizing such act on the part of the assignee.

18—*Proceedings in case of Copartnerships.*

In case one or more members of a copartnership refuses to join in a petition to have the firm declared bankrupt, the parties refusing shall be entitled to resist the prayer of the petition in the same manner as if the petition had been filed by a creditor of the partnership, and notice of the filing of the petition shall be given to him in the same manner as provided by law and by these rules in the case of a debtor petitioned against; and he shall have the right to appear at the time fixed by the court for the hearing of the petition, and to make proof, if he can, that the copartnership is not insolvent, or has not committed an act of bankruptcy, and to take all other defenses which any debtor proceeded against is entitled to take by the provisions of the act; and in case an adjudication of bankruptcy is made upon the petition, such copartner shall be required to furnish to the marshal, as messenger, a schedule of his debts and an inventory of his property, in the same manner as is required by the act in cases of debtors against whom adjudication of bankruptcy shall be made.

16—*Duties of Assignees.*

The assignee shall, immediately on entering upon his duties, prepare a complete inventory of all the property of the bankrupt that comes into his possession ; and all sales of the same shall be by public auction, unless otherwise ordered by the court. Every assignee shall keep full, exact, and regular books of account of all receipts, payments, and expenditures of money by him, and shall make report to the court, within twenty days after receiving the deed of assignment, of the articles set off to the bankrupt by him, according to the provisions of the fourteenth section of the act, with the estimated value of each article, and any creditor may take exceptions to the determination of the assignee within twenty days after the filing of the report.

20—*Composition with Creditors, (Arbitration.)*

Whenever an assignee shall make application to the court for authorty to submit a controversy arising in the settlement of demands against the bankrupt's estate, or of debts due to it, to the determination of arbitrators, or for authority to compound and settle such controversy by agreement with the other party, the subject matter of the controversy and the reasons why the assignee thinks it proper and most for the interest of the creditors that it should be settled by arbitration or otherwise, shall be set forth clearly and distinctly in the application; and the court, upon examination of the same, may immediately proceed to take testimony and make an order thereon, or may direct the assignee to give notice of the application, either by publication or by mail, or both, to the creditors who have proved their claims to appear and show cause, on a day to be named in the order and notice why the application should not be granted, and may make such order thereon as may be just and proper.

21—Disposal of Property by Assignee.

In making sales of personal property the assignee shall give at least ten days' notice of the time and place of the sale, and of the articles to be sold, by advertisement in one or more newspaper, to be designated by the court or by a register, and by posted handbills or otherwise, as he may think best for the interest of the estate, or as the court may order, and he shall give like notice of the sale of any real estate at least twenty days before such sale. Upon his application to the court, and for good cause shown, the assignee may be authorized to sell any specified portion of the bankrupt's estate at private sale. The court by order in special cases, may dispense with newspaper and handbill advertisements. It making sale of the franchise of a corporation, it may be offered in fractional parts, or in certain number of shares, corresponding to the number of shares in the bankrupt corporation. And in making the sale of the real estate of a bankrupt, the assignee shall, unless otherwise ordered by the court, offer the same in lots or parcels, if it exists in separate parcels, in such manner as may be for the interest of the creditors of the estate.

22—Perishable Property.

In all cases where goods or other articles come into possession of the messenger or assignee which are perishable, or liable to deterioration in value, the court may, upon application, in its discretion, order the same to be sold, and the proceeds deposited in court.

23—Service of Notice.

The notice provided by the eighteenth section of the act shall be served by the marshal or his deputy, and notice to the creditors of the time and place of meeting provided by the section shall be given through the mail by letter, signed by the clerk of the court.

Every envelope containing a notice sent by the clerk or messenger shall have printed on it a direction to the postmaster at the place to which it is sent to return the same within ten days unless called for.

24—Opposition to Discharge.

A creditor opposing the application of a bankrupt for discharge shall enter his appearance in opposition thereto on the day when the creditors are required to show cause, and shall file his specification of the grounds of his opposition, in writing, within ten days thereafter, unless the time shall be enlarged by order of the district court in the case, and the court shall thereupon make an order as to the entry of said case for trial on the docket of the district court, and the time within which the same shall be heard and decided.

25—Second and Third Meeting of Creditors.

Whenever any bankrupt shall apply for his discharge, within three months from the date of his being adjudged a bankrupt, under the provisions of the twenty-ninth section of the act, the court may direct that the second and third meetings of creditors of said bankrupt required by the twenty-seventh and twenty-eighth sections of said act shall be had on the day which may be fixed in the order of notice for the creditors to appear and show cause why a discharge should not be granted such bankrupt; and the notices of such meeting shall be sufficient if it be added to the notice to show cause, that the second and third meetings of said creditors shall be had before the register upon the same day that cause may be shown against the discharge, or upon some previous days or day.

26—*Appeals.*

Appeals in equity from the district to the circuit court, and from the circuit to the supreme court of the United States, shall be regulated by the rules governing appeals in equity in the courts of the United States. Any supposed creditor who takes an appeal to the circuit court from the decision of the district court rejecting his claim, in whole or in part, according to the provisions of the eighth section of the act, shall give notice of his intention to enter the appeal within ten days from the entry of the final decision of the district court upon his claim ; and he shall file his appeal in the clerk's office of the circuit within ten days thereafter, setting forth a statement in writing of his claim in the manner prescribed by said section ; and the assignee shall plead or answer thereto in like manner within ten days after the statement shall be filed. Every issue thereon shall be made up in the court, and the cause placed upon the docket thereof, and shall be heard and decided in the same manner as other actions at law.

27—*Imprisoned Debtor.*

If at the time of preferring his petition the debtor shall be imprisoned, the court, upon his application, may order him to be produced upon *habeas corpus* by the jailor, or any officer in whose custody he may be, before the register, for the purpose of testifying in any matter relating to his bankruptcy ; and if committed after the filing of his petition upon process in any civil action founded upon a claim provable in bankruptcy, the court may, upon like application, discharge him from such imprisonment. If the petitioner, during the pendency of the proceedings in bankruptcy, be arrested or imprisoned upon process in any civil action, the district court, upon his application, may issue a writ of *habeas corpus* to bring him before the court, to ascertain whether such process has been issued for the collection of any claim provable in bankruptcy, and, if so provable, he shall be discharged ; if not, he shall be remanded to the custody in which he may lawfully be. Before granting the order for discharge, the court shall cause notice to be served upon the creditor, or his

attorney, so as to give him an opportunity of appearing and being heard before the granting of the order.

28—*Deposit and payment of moneys.*

The district court in each district shall designate certain national banks, if there are any within the judicial district, or, if there be none, then some other safe depository, in which all moneys received by assignees or paid into court in the course of any proceedings in bankruptcy shall be deposited ; and every assignee and the clerk of said court shall deposit all sums received by them, severally, on account of any bankrupt's estate, in one designated depository ; and every clerk and assignee shall make a report to the court of the funds received by him, and of deposits made by him, on the first Monday of every month. No moneys so deposited shall be drawn from such depository unless upon a check, or warrant, signed by the clerk of the court, or by an assignee, and countersigned by the judge of the court, or one of the registers designated for that purpose, stating the date, the sum, and the account for which it is drawn ; and the entry of the substance of such check or warrant, with the date thereof, the sum drawn for, and the account for which it is drawn, shall be forthwith made in a book kept for that purpose by the assignee or the clerk ; and all checks and drafts shall be entered in the order of time in which they are drawn, and shall be numbered in the case of each estate. A copy of this rule shall be furnished to the depository so designated, and also the name of any register authorized to countersign said checks.

29—*Prepayment or security of fees.*

The fees of the register, marshal, and clerk shall be paid or secured in all cases before they shall be compelled to perform the duties required of them by the parties requiring such service ; and, in the case of witnesses, their fees shall be tendered or paid at the time of the service of the summons or subpœna, and shall include their traveling expenses to and from the place at which they may be summoned to attend. The court may order the whole of such portion of the fees and costs in each case to be paid out of the fund in court in such case as shall seem just.

30—*As to fees and costs.*

To the clerk of the court.—For each notice required to be sent by mail, when signed by the clerk, ten cents; the postage to be prepaid by the party required to give such notice.

To the clerk and register.—For every copy of any paper in proceedings in bankruptcy, twenty-five cents for certifying the same, and, in addition thereto, ten cents for each folio of one hundred words.

To the register.—For every order made where notice is required to be given, and for certifying copy of the same to the clerk, one dollar.

For every certificate of question to be certified to the district judge, under the fourth and sixth sections of the act, one dollar.

For every proof of debt, twenty-five cents; and where testimony is taken, the fees prescribed by law may be added.

In cases where the debtor has no means, and makes proof, to the satisfaction of the court, that he is unable to pay the costs prescribed by the act and these orders, the judge, in his discretion, may direct that the fees and costs therein shall not exceed the sum required by the act to be deposited with the clerk.

31—*Costs in Contested Adjudications.*

In cases of involuntary bankruptcy, where the debtor resists an adjudication, and the court, after hearing, shall adjudge the debtor a bankrupt, the petitioning creditor shall recover, to be paid out of the fund, the same costs that are allowed by law to a party recovering in a suit in equity; and in case the petition shall be dismissed, the debtor may recover like costs from 'the petitioner.

32—*As to Forms and Schedules.*

The several forms specified in the schedules annexed to these orders for the several purposes therein stated shall be observed and used with such alterations as may be necessary to suit the circumstances of any particular case. In all cases where, by the provisions of the act, a special order is required to be made in any proceeding, or in any case instituted under the act in a district court of the United States, such order shall be framed by the court to suit the circumstances of the particular case; and the forms hereby prescribed shall be followed, as nearly as may be, and so far as the same are applicable to the circumstances requiring such special order. In proceedings in equity, instituted for the purpose of carrying into effect the provisions of the act, or for enforcing the rights and remedies given by it, the rules of equity practice established by the supreme court of the United States shall be followed as nearly as may be. In proceedings at law, instituted for the same purpose, the rules of the circuit court regulating the practice and procedure in cases at law shall be followed as nearly as may be.

DECEMBER TERM, 1867.

The thirty-second rule in bankruptcy is amended so as to read as follows:

The several forms specified in the schedules annexed to these orders for the several purposes therein stated shall be observed and used, with such alterations as may be necessary to suit the circumstances of any particular case. In all cases where, by the provisions of the act, a special order is required to be made in any proceeding, or in any case instituted under the act in a district court of the United States, such order shall be framed by the court to suit the circumstances of the particular case; and the forms hereby prescribed shall be followed as nearly as may be, and so far as the same are applicable to the circumstances requiring such special order. In proceedings in equity, instituted for the purpose of carrying into effect the provisions of the act, or for enforcing the rights and remedies given by it, the rules of equity practice established by the supreme court of the United States shall be followed as nearly as may be. In proceedings at law, instituted for the same purpose, the rules of the circuit court regulating the practice and procedure in cases at law shall be followed as nearly as may be. But the court, as the judge thereof, may, by special rule in any case, vary the time allowed for return of process, for appearance and pleading, and for taking testimony and publication, and may otherwise modify the rules for the preparation of any particular case so as to facilitate a speedy hearing.

33—*Omissions and Amendments.*

Whenever a debtor shall omit to state in the schedules annexed to his petition any of the facts required to be stated concerning his debts or his property, he shall state, either in its appropriate place in the schedules or in a separate affidavit to be filed with the petition, the reason for the omission, with such particularity as will enable the court to determine whether to admit the schedules as sufficient, or to require the debtor to make further efforts to complete the same according to the requirements of the law; and in making any application for amendment to the schedules the debtor shall state under oath the substance of the matters proposed to be included in the amendment, and the reasons why the same had not been incorporated in his schedules as originally filed, or as previously amended. In like manner, he may correct any statement made during the course of his examination.

RULES IN BANKRUPTCY

DISTRICT COURTS OF THE UNITED STATES.

ARKANSAS.—Eastern District.

Be it remembered, That a district court of the United States of America, in and for the eastern district of Arkansas, begun and holden on Monday, the seventh day of October, Anno Domini, one thousand eight hundred and sixty-seven : At the United States court room in the city of Little Rock, Arkansas, the Hon. Henry C. Caldwell, judge, presiding and holding said court; the following proceedings were had, to wit : On Saturday, January 4th A. D. 1868, as follows :

Ordered, That the following rules and orders be prescribed and adopted as rules and orders governing proceedings in bankruptcy, in the district court of the United States, for the eastern district of Arkansas, in addition to the general orders in bankruptcy and forms adopted by the justices of the supreme court of the United States.

RULE ONE.—*Reference of Petitions to Register.*

1. In voluntary bankruptcy, where the petition states that the debtor has resided or carried on business for the six months next immediately preceding the time of filing such petition, or for the longest period during such six months, in any one of the following named counties, to wit : Pulaski, Saline, Hot Spring, Jefferson, Dallas, Bradley, Drew, Desha, Chocot, Ashley, Calhoun, Union, Ouachita, Columbia, Hempstead, Lafayette, Pope, Yell, Perry, Montgomery, Clark, Pike, Conway, Prairie and Arkansas, such petition shall be referred to Albert W. Bishop, Esq., register in bankruptcy in the second congressional district.

2. Where the petitioning debtor resdes in any one of the following named counties, to wit : Green, Mississippi, Craighead, Randolph, Lawrence, Fulton, Izard, Searcy, Van Buren, Independence, Jackson, Poinsett, Crittenden, St. Francis, White, Monroe, Phillips, Woodruff, Cross, Marion and Newton ; the petition will be referred to Elisha Baxter, Esq., register in bankruptcy, in the first congressional district.

3. A petition may, for special reasons, be otherwise referred ; and in involuntary bankruptcy the register will be designated with reference to the special circumstances of each case.

RULE TWO.—*Registers' Certificate as to Correctness in form of Petition.*

The certificate of the register required by rule 7, of general orders in bankruptcy, as to the correctness in form of the petition and schedules, shall be indorsed on the petition or attached thereto, before the same is filed in the clerk's office ; and the register shall not grant said certificate, nor issue any warrant under form No. 6, unless the whole of the eleven sheets comprising schedule A and B, in form No. 1, make part of the schedules to the petition.

RULE THREE.—*Deposit of $50.*

The sum of fifty dollars mentioned in section 47 of the bankrupt act, shall be deposited in each case with the register, to whom the case is referred.

RULE FOUR.—*Clerk to furnish Blanks to Registers.*

1. The clerk shall furnish to each register blank forms process, summons and subpœnas with his signature and the seal of the court ;

and each of said blanks when used by register shall be countersigned by him.

2. Each register shall keep an account of said blanks used in each case, and return a copy of said account to the clerk in order that the fees of the latter may be properly taxed.

RULE FIVE.—*Appointment of Assignees.*

1. If no choice of an assignee is made by the creditors at the first meeting, or if an assignee chosen by the creditors fails within five days to express in writing his acceptance of the trust; or in case of a vacancy in the office of assignee caused by removal, resignation or otherwise, John Wassell, Esq., of the city of Little Rock, United States commissioner, will be appointed assignee where the judge is required to appoint.

And when the said John Wassell shall be appointed by any register, such appointment shall be entered "approved by the judge." In special cases, special orders for the appointment will be made.

3. Every election of assignee by the creditors when indorsed by the register having charge of the case as satisfactory, shall be entered by the clerk "approved;" unless otherwise ordered by the judge, subject, however, in all cases to the judge's order for a new election or removal.

RULE SIX.—*Assignee to give Bond in certain cases.*

In all cases when the estate of the bankrupt, in the opinion of the register will exceed the sum of five hundred dollars, the assignee before entering on his duties shall give bond to the United States, conditioned for the due and faithful discharge of his duties, in such sum and with such sureties, as shall be approved by the judge or register, by his indorsement thereon.

RULE SEVEN.—*Original Assignment to be Filed with Clerk.*

The original assignment of every estate in bankruptcy, shall be deposited with the clerk, and preserved among the files of the court pertaining to the case; and a certified copy under the seal of the court delivered to the assignee.

RULE EIGHT.—*Publication of Notices.*

1. All notices which under the bankrupt act required newspaper publication, shall be published in one or two newspapers, as the register may direct, to be selected by him, subject to the provisions and requirements of section seven of the act of congress of March 2d, 1867, U. S. statutes at large, pp. 466-7.

2. Notices of meetings of creditors, and of the bankrupt's application for discharge, must be published once a week for two consecutive weeks, the last publication, to be at least ten days before the meeting of creditors, or the time of hearing the application for discharge.

3. Notice of the appointment of assignees, must be published once a week for three successive weeks, and no other notice except of the sale of property by an assignee, or the marshal, shall be published more than once a week for two consecutive weeks, at the expense of the estate; unless a greater number of publications are required by law, or general orders.

4. The compensation allowed for publishing such notices, shall in no case exceed the rates allowed by the seventh section of the act of congress, of March 2d, 1867.

5. The marshal, clerk, and every register and assignee, when required to publish any notice, shall procure and return to the court to be filed with the papers in the case, a copy of such notice cut from each newspaper in which it is published, accompanied by the affidavit of the printer, or publisher of the paper, or other person having knowledge of the facts, showing that the required publications of such notice have been made; and no compensation shall be paid for the publication of any notice, until the printer or publisher furnishes the required proof of its due publication.

RULE NINE.—*Register to fix time and place of acting on cases referred to him.*

Each register shall fix the time when, and the place where he will act upon matters arising under the cases referred to him; unless the court by its order specifies a different time or place; and each register shall by writing filed with the clerk, state the time when, and the place at which he will attend for such action

RULE TEN.—*Issuing Certificate for Opinion of Court.*

All issues certified by a register for the

opinion of the court, shall briefly state the opinion of the register on the issue submitted.

RULE ELEVEN.—*Time of Holding Courts in Bankruptcy.*

A special court of bankruptcy will be holden on every Monday at 10 o'clock A. M., excepting such times as the judge may necessarily be absent from the city.

RULE TWELVE.—*Deposit of Moneys.*

1. In pursuance of rule 28, of the "general orders in bankruptcy," the "Merchants' National Bank of Little Rock, Arkansas," is designated as the bank in which all moneys received by assignee, or paid into court in the course of any proceedings in bankruptcy shall be deposited.

2. All moneys received by the clerk of the court on account of any bankrupt's estate, or paid into court in the course of any proceedings in bankruptcy, (except the sums deposited with the clerk under section 47 of the act,) shall be deposited in said bank.

3. The check or warrant for drawing moneys deposited by the clerk, shall be signed by the clerk and countersigned by Albert W. Bishop, Esq., register in bankruptcy, who is designated for that purpose.

4. And the check or warrant for drawing money deposited by an assignee, shall be signed by the assignee and said register in bankruptcy, Albert W. Bishop, Esq.

5. The clerk will furnish said bank a copy of this rule and also a copy of rule 28 of "general orders in bankruptcy."

A true copy from the record :

ATTEST :   *Clerk.*

CALIFORNIA.

RULE 1. In voluntary bankruptcy, the petition shall be referred to Form No. 4, as prescribed by the supreme court of the United States to the register of the congressional district in which the petition states that the debtor, whether an individual, a copartnership, corporation, or a joint stock company, has resided, or carried on business, for the six months next immediately preceding the time of filing the petition, or for the

longest period during such six months, unless otherwise ordered. A petition may be otherwise referred for special reasons, and in cases not herein provided for. In involuntary bankruptcy, the register will be designated with reference to the special circumstances of each case.

The order of reference, Form No. 4, in voluntary bankruptcy shall specify as the place where the register shall act upon the matters arising in the case, and warrant Form No. 59, in involuntary bankruptcy, shall specify as the place where the meeting of creditors will be held, the principal office of the register to whom the said matters shall be referred, to be by him designated by a writing filed with the clerk. But the court may, on the suggestion of the register, or on application of the parties, designate another place for said proceedings, when required by the special circumstances of the case.

All of the registers shall, by writing filed with the clerk, designate their principal office in their congressional district, and state the times when they will be in attendance at the same to discharge their duties.

2. The adjudication of bankruptcy, Form No. 58, shall contain a provision that the case be referred to one of the registers, naming him, to take such proceedings therein as are required by the act.

3. The register shall, under Rule No. 7 of the "general orders in bankruptcy," examine the duplicate copy of the petition and schedules specified in Form No. 4, and such duplicate copy shall either be a copy of such filed original, certified by the clerk under the seal of the court, or else a duplicate original, signed and verified in like manner with the original petition and schedules filed with the clerk, and shown by evidence satisfactory to the register to be such duplicate original; and the certificate of the register, required by said rule 7, as to correctness in form of the petition and schedules, shall be made in writing, and be signed by him, on the duplicate copy which he so examines, and he shall not issue any warrant under Form No. 6, until he shall have so made a certificate, after such examination, that the petition and schedules are correct in form. No such certificate shall be made unless the whole eleven pages composing schedules A and B, in Form No. 1, form part of the

schedules to the petition. (Amendment October 13, 1869.)

Provided, That if it shall appear to the register, in his discretion, that it is for the interest of the estate that the observance of the last clause of this rule be dispensed with, he shall be authorized to do so, and to issue the warrant forthwith.

4. The warrant issued under section 11 or section 42 of the act, according to Form No. 6 or 59, shall specify one of the newspapers published in the county stated in the petition, as the one in which the debtor, whether an individual, a copartnership, a corporation or a joint stock company, has resided or carried on business for the six months next immediately preceding the time of filing the petition, or for the longest period during such six months; in case a newspaper is published in such county, the selection of such newspaper to be made by the register to whom the petition or case is referred, but in case there is no paper published in said county, then the register is to designate a newspaper published nearest to the county seat of said county.

The notices to be published in pursuance of said warrant shall be published twice in the newspaper selected.

The warrant shall designate creditors on whom personal service is to be made, and notice shall be served by mail upon all creditors other than those so designated. No creditor resident out of this judicial district shall be designated for personal service.

The warrant Form No. 6 shall be regarded as " Process," under rule 2 of the " general orders in bankruptcy," and such warrant, before it is issued to the marshal, in addition to being signed by the clerk and sealed with the seal of the court, shall be signed by the judge or register at the foot thereof, in the following form, with the date :

" Issued by me, this   day of A. D. 187

District Judge, or
Register in Bankruptcy.

Whenever the order, Form No. 10, is used by a register, the conclusion of the form may be varied so that the order may be attested or signed by the register alone.

5. All proofs of debt which shall be made and verified prior to the election or appointment of an assignee, shall be delivered or sent to the register to whom the case is referred. If the register entertains doubts of the validity of any claim, or the right of a creditor to prove it, and is of opinion that such validity or right ought to be investigated by the assignee, he may postpone the proof of the claim.

6. Under rule 9, of the " general orders in bankruptcy," an assignee shall notify the register of his acceptance or rejection of the trust, and the register shall, immediately on receiving such notice, report it to the clerk of the court.

7. Every assignee shall immediately on receiving an assignment of an estate in bankruptcy, send or deliver such assignment to the clerk of the court, who shall make a true copy of it, and certify such copy under his hand and the seal of the court, and such certified copy shall then be placed and kept by him on file, and the original assignment shall be returned to the assignee.

8. Notice of the appointment of assignee shall be given by him by publication once a week for two successive weeks, in the same newspaper in which the notice of the issuing of the warrant in bankruptcy, has been previously published.

9. Notice of sale by an assignee under rule 21 of the "general orders in bankruptcy," shall be advertised in the same newspaper in which notice of the issuing of the warrant in bankruptcy, and of his appointment, has been previously published.

10. The notice to creditors of dividends or meetings, required by the 17th, 27th and 28th sections of the act, shall be such as is provided for by the order contained in Form No. 28, and the assignee shall publish the same in the same newspaper as he has published the notice of his appointment.

11. The list of debts provided for by section 23 of the act, shall be made and certified by the register to whom the petition or case is referred, and he shall place thereon all debts which are duly proved.

12. The assignee shall, under section 27 of the act, produce and file vouchers for all payments made by him, except as to items in regard to which the court shall, for reasonable cause, dispense with vouchers.

13. The notice by the assignee, under section 28 of the act, of the filing of his

account, and of his application for a settlement and discharge, shall be given by him by sending written or printed notices by mail, prepaid, of such filing, and of the time of such application, to all known creditors of the bankrupt.

14. All questions for trial on hearing under sections 31 and 34 of the act, shall be tried or heard at a stated session of the court, on four days' notice of the trial or hearing to be served by either party upon the other party, and upon the clerk, and a calendar of the same shall be made.

15. The application, under section 34 of the act, to set aside and annul a discharge, shall be verified by the oath or affirmation of the applicant, and the answer of the bankrupt to the application, shall answer specifically the allegations of the application and shall be verified in like manner.

16. The demand in writing for a trial by jury, under section 41 of the act, shall be signed by the debtor or his attorney.

17. All issues, questions, points and matters stated in writing, under rule 11, of the "general orders in bankruptcy," or under the 4th section or the 6th section of the act, or according to Form No. 70, and adjourned into court for decision, or stated in a special case for the opinion of the court, shall be certified to the judge by the register by a certificate, which shall also state, briefly, the opinion of the register on the issue, question, point or matter, and shall be delivered or sent to the clerk; and no oral or written argument shall be allowed on any issue or question, unless by special leave of court.

18. In case of the absence of the judge at the time and place noticed or appointed for any hearing or any proceeding before him in bankruptcy, or if the matter then fails to be called or acted on, the same shall be deemed continued, without other order, to the next sitting of the court thereafter, at which time the like proceedings may be had thereupon as if first noticed or appointed for such day.

19. If the marshal shall, under rule 13 of the "general orders in bankruptcy," appoint special deputies to act as messengers, he shall, as far as possible, designate one or more of such special deputies to be attached to the office of each register for the purpose of causing the notices to be published and served which are specified in the warrants issued in the cases referred to such register.

20. All notices served or sent by mail by the marshal, the clerk, or an assignee, shall be so written or printed and folded, that the direction, postage stamp and post mark shall be upon the notice itself, and not upon an envelope or other separate piece of paper.

21. Special cases not comprehended within the foregoing rules, or the "general orders in bankruptcy," or the forms, shall be submitted to the judge.

Adopted August 3, 1867:

22. In case no choice of an assignee is made by the creditors at their first meeting, or in case an assignee chosen by the creditors fails within five days to express in writing his acceptance of the trust; or in case of a vacancy in the office of an assignee caused by his removal, resignation, death or other cause, Henry C. Hyde, Esq., of San Francisco, counselor-at-law, will be appointed assignee. When the judge is required by the act to appoint the assignee, and also when the said Henry C. Hyde, Esq., shall be chosen assignee by the creditors of any bankrupt, or shall be appointed by any register as assignee, his appointment is hereby approved by the judge.

In special cases, vacancies in the office of assignee will be filled by an election by the creditors, or by the appointment of •an assignee other than the one above named.

Adopted March 5, 1868:

23. Orders to creditors to show cause why a discharge should not be granted, shall be made returnable at a special court, to be held at 11 o'clock A. M., on Tuesday of any week. In case there should be no session of the court on the day named in the order, the cause shall be deemed continued until the succeeding Tuesday at the same hour.

Adopted March 5, 1868:

24. The petition for discharge, Form No. 51, shall be presented to the register, who shall thereupon issue the order prescribed by the same form, returnable as above directed. Such order shall designate the paper or papers in which, and the time for which, the notices shall be published, the last publication to be at least ten days prior to the return day of the order. The register shall forthwith transmit to the clerk a list of all the creditors who have proved their debts, with their residences and post office address,

and the clerk shall thereupon mail the proper notices to such creditors, (Form No. 52) and certify to the register that he has so done.

Adopted March 5, 1868:

25. When the application for discharge shall be made within six months from the date of the adjudication, it shall be accompanied by a certificate from the assignee that no debts have been proved against the estate, or that no assets have come into his hands.

Amended March 24, 1869, by adding:

When the application shall be made after six months from the date of adjudication, it shall be accompanied by a certificate of the assignee, stating the names and residences of the creditors, the proof of whose debts have been received by him.

Adopted March 5, 1868:

26. The second and third meetings of the creditors under rule 25th of the "general orders in bankruptcy," shall be called by the register, except on the request of the assignee, accompanied by a similar certificate.

Adopted March 5, 1868:

27. On the return day of the order, the bankrupt shall present to the court a certificate of the register, certifying that the publications have been made, and the notices given pursuant to the order, that the proceedings before him have been regular, and that, so far as appears, the bankrupt has in all things conformed to his duty under the act.

Adopted March 5, 1868:

28. The bank of California is designated as the depository in bankruptcy under rule 28th of the supreme court. The requirements of this rule must be strictly observed by all parties.

Adopted March 5, 1868:

29. Separate accounts must be kept with the estate of each bankrupt, and all money must be deposited to the credit of the "district court of the United States for California, in bankruptcy: Estate of A—— B——, a bankrupt; C—— D——, assignee; E—— F——, register."

The name of the register designated to act in the ease, and of the assignee or assignees appointed, shall be furnished to the bank when the deposit is made. When more than one assignee has been appointed, the deposit shall be entered as made by all of them.

Adopted March 5, 1868:

30. All checks drawn against the fund so deposited shall be signed by all the assignees, and countersigned by the register designated to act in the case. In case the signature of any one or more of the assignees cannot, by reason of his or their absence, sickness, or from other cause, be obtained, the court may, by special order, permit the moneys to be drawn on the signature of the remaining assignee or assignees.

Adopted March 5, 1868:

31. The signature of the judge of the district court may be substituted in any case for that of the register.

Adopted March 5, 1868:

32. A copy of "general order 28," and of the five preceding rules, shall be served by the clerk on the Bank of California, together with the names of the registers for the district.

Adopted January 7, 1871:

33. All orders of sale, and orders of confirmation of sale in bankruptcy made by this court affecting real estate, shall be hereafter recorded in a book to be kept by the clerk of this court, which book shall be entitled "Orders of Sale and Confirmation in Bankruptcy, U. S. District Court," and shall constitute a part of the records of this court. Upon application to this court by any persons interested, and upon payment of the legal fees, the clerk shall record in said book any order of sale or order of confirmation of sale affecting real estate heretofore entered in any bankruptcy proceeding in this court.

Adopted March 6, 1871:

34. Except in those cases provided for by the 22d rule in bankruptcy of this court, no election or appointment of assignees will be recognized as valid until the same shall have been approved by the judge, as required in section 13 of the bankrupt act, and no assignment shall be made by any register to an assignee until the election or appointment of such assignee shall have been submitted to and approved by the judge.

CONNECTICUT.

HARTFORD, CONN. *Oct*, 26th, 1870.
AUDLEY W. GAZZAM, ESQ.

DEAR SIR,—I have to say in reply to your inquiry that I have never adopted a formal set of rules in bankruptcy for this district. I have had no difficulty in administering the law under the general orders.

Yours Respectfully,
WM. D. SHIPMAN.

GEORGIA.—Northern District.

INSTITUTION OF SUITS.

RULE 1. The mode of proceeding in this court in cases at common law, shall be by petition, as prescribed by the state judiciary act of 1799, which petition shall contain the substance of a declaration in stating the complaint, allegation or demand of the plaintiff.

2. In all suits in assumpsit on an account, a copy of the account shall be annexed to a copy of the petition and process, and served therewith on the defendant or defendants, according to the practice observed in the superior courts of this state.

3. Rules shall be held monthly, in the clerk's office, on the first Monday in every month, for the purpose of entering all proceedings and orders which may be entered at the rules, and not necessary to be taken or made in open court. The rules shall be held under the direction of the clerk; but the judge of the court may make or allow any special order in any cause not inconsistent with the regulations herein prescribed, which shall be entered in the rule book, and take effect accordingly.

4. When any person, plaintiff or defendant in any suit, shall be dead, it shall be lawful for the clerk at rules, upon application and suggestion of the death, to issue process to bring into court the executors or administrators of such deceased party; and he may also, on motion of the executors of a deceased party, permit them to enter themselves as parties, and to proceed in such suits.

5. The marshal shall be allowed time for serving process, at the rate of ten miles *per diem*, counting from Atlanta, and from the delivery to him or the date or entry in his office. A copy left at the defendant's usual place of residence shall be sufficient service.

6. When a writ shall be served twenty days or more, before any term, the defendant shall be held to plead at that term. If he file a dilatory plea, or demurrer, it shall be decided at that term; and if a plea to the merits, he shall be entitled to a continuance to the next term. Whatever rules or orders may be necessary to prepare the cause for trial at the second or any subsequent term, may be made at rules.

7. When pleadings are filed, or orders duly taken in term or at rules, the opposite party in the cause shall be bound to take notice thereof, without other service of rule, notice, or copy order. But when pleadings are filed, or other acts done before the clerk on any other day than a rule day, actual notice thereof will be required to be given to the opposite party, or to his attorney. When pleadings are filed in term or on a rule day, the opposite party shall have until the rule day next, after the expiration of twenty days, to reply, rejoin, &c.; and when filed on any other day, he shall have thirty days from the service of the rule, to plead; and in either case, if his place of residence shall exceed fifty miles from Atlanta, he shall be allowed time, at the rate of twenty miles *per diem*, for the excess of distance above fifty miles. And the same rule shall be applied, and the same time given, to both parties with regard to all pleadings subsequent to the declaration, except in the case provided for in the twenty-third rule.

8. Whenever a party fails to comply with the seventh rule, an order for judgment, or of *non pros.*, may be entered at the rules; but the same may be set aside at the next rules, on motion, payment of costs and pleading instanter, or for special cause shown, on motion made the first day of the next term; in which latter case the court will impose such other reasonable terms as the ends of justice may require.

9. A copy of every bond, deed, or other writing declared on, shall be filed in the clerk's office, and the defendant may have oyer of the original bond, deed, or other writing, before he shall be required to file his plea, provided notice of a demand of oyer be served on the plaintiff's attorney seven days before the day on which the defendant is bound to plead to the action.

10. If any frivolous or deceitful plea be filed, the adverse party shall not be obliged to demur to the same; but the clerk may give an order for judgment or *non pros.* at the rules; and the party against whom it is given shall be held to his motion to set aside

such order at the next term, as under the eighth rule.

11. No plea of *plene administravit* shall be received and filed unless accompanied with an office copy of the inventory and appraisement of the estate; and the defendant tendering such a plea shall be bound on ten days' notice in writing, to deposit with the clerk a full account of his administration, or the book or books containing the same.

12. Whenever any gentleman of the bar shall leave with the clerk instructions how to direct to him by mail, and a request to have the benefit of this rule, it shall be the duty of the clerk, within ten days after the rules, to forward to such gentleman an abstract of all the rules, orders, and entries made on each rule day, for which the clerk shall be entitled to demand one dollar for each month.

JUDGMENTS.

13. All judgments obtained at the same term, and entered up agreeably to the next rule, shall be of the same rank as to precedence. The same shall be regularly docketed in a book kept for the purpose, having successive columns, exhibiting at one view the date, the time, and nature of the executions sued out, the returns upon the same, and the date of satisfaction, with a column for miscellaneous occurrences.

14. Judgments, to retain their rank or precedence under the preceding rule, shall be entered up within five days after the party is entitled to the same; but may be entered at any time before the second term after, to take precedence from date. If not entered before the said second term, they shall not be entered without a motion at rules, or in open court, and then not until the rules next after such motion.

15. In all cases where judgment shall be signed for a penalty, satisfaction shall be entered on payment of principal, interest, and costs; and where the condition is for the performance of something other than the payment of money, the court will order a writ of enquiry upon the condition to determine the real amount due.

16. If a motion in arrest of judgment, or for a new trial, be intended to be made, the party shall give notice thereof, and of his grounds, within two days after verdict. No motion in arrest of judgment shall be heard after a new trial once had; but the motion in arrest of judgment and for a new trial may, in the first instance, be made simultaneously.

17. If judgment be taken by default, or judgment be given for plaintiff in demurrer, the court, on motion of plaintiff, will assess the damages, if the action be on single bill, promissory note, bill of exchange, or any written contract; or in all such cases the petit jury attending the court may assess the damages as in case of writ of inquiry at common law. The plaintiff in such case shall produce the writing on which the action is founded, but the execution shall be considered as established.

18. To prevent fraud in entering up judgment on warrant of attorney, no such judgment shall be signed unless accompanied with an affidavit of the debt specifying the amount actually due, and a legal verification of the letter of attorney. And if the warrant be of a date twelve months or more anterior, the affiaut shall further swear, to his belief, that the plaintiff is still living.

19. If a plaintiff take an order for judgment, the defendant may, notwithstanding, file his plea, and take the steps necessary to have an issue made up, if he means to move to set the order aside. The plaintiff in such case shall be bound to reply, and await the contingency of having the order of judgment set aside, in order that there may be no delay in the event of setting aside such order for judgment.

20. Whenever the existence of unsatisfied judgments or mortgages impedes the payment over of moneys levied and in the court, or in the hands of the marshal, it shall be sufficient to advertise in some one respectable Gazette for one month, a notice to the parties interested in such judgments to come forward and show to the court that such judgments are actually subsisting unsatisfied judgments. If the parties in interest fail to do this, the court may order the money to be paid over to the executions in the marshal's hands.

EXECUTIONS.

21. No execution shall issue until the rules next after the sitting of the court at which the judgment was obtained.

22. The marshal shall return every execution to the clerk, with a special note en-

dorsed, exhibiting what has been done under each execution, which executions and returns shall be filed and preserved in the record; and no new execution shall be signed until that previously issued has been duly returned, except by a special order of the judge.

DOCKETS.

23. No cause shall be docketed until the issue is made up, except where nothing is wanted but a similiter, or joinder in demurrer, in which cases the court will, on motion at any time during the term, order the necessary entry to be made by the clerk.

24. The docket shall be finally made up by the opening of the court on the second day of the term. Every cause called at four several terms, and not proceeded in, shall be omitted from the next docket, not to be restored but by order of court, no cause shown; provided the same has not been continued at defendant's motion.

25. Causes to which dilatory pleas or demurrers have been filed shall be placed on a separate docket, and shall have an early call.

26. Causes marked on the docket *settled*, *discontinued*, or otherwise terminated, shall not again be docketed without leave of court, or consent of both parties in writing.

27. The court will call over the docketed causes for trial, in their order, beginning with the issues, and will call the docket but once.

28. Either party may docket a cause entitled to be docketed, and the parties to every cause duly docketed may be compelled to trial without any further notice.

CONTINUANCES.

29. Motions for continuance on the ground of the absence of a witness, or the non-return of a commission, shall be accompanied with an affidavit stating what the party expects to prove by the witness or commission, and that he is not able to prove the same by any other means. The affidavit shall also show that due diligence has been used to procure such testimony, by stating the steps that have been taken, or the causes why the ordinary measures have not been pursued, to the end that the court may be satisfied that the party making such motion does not affect delay.

WRITS OF ENQUIRY.

30. A docket shall also be made of causes in which writs of enquiry are to be executed, and no writ of enquiry shall be executed in a cause not docketed.

31. If it be in any way known to the plaintiff's attorney, that the defendant has an attorney attending on his cause, no writ of enquiry shall be executed without reasonable notice given to such attorney.

JURIES.

32. The marshal shall obtain from the clerks of Fulton, Cobb, DeKalb, and Clayton counties, their respective lists of grand and petit jurors. The names of the grand and petit jurors shall be deposited in separate apartments in a box, to be provided by the marshal, from which box shall be drawn, in open court, or by the judge and clerk in vacation, twenty-three names to serve as grand jurors at the ensuing term, (whether regular or special) or the first term thereafter to which they may be summoned; and twenty-four names to serve, in like manner, as petit jurors. It shall be the duty of the clerk, within three days after receiving an order to that effect from the judge to deliver a *venire* for the jury or juries to the marshal, who shall thereupon serve a written or printed summons on each juror by delivering the same to him personally, or leaving it at his usual place of residence. Should there be a failure of the court, in consequence of the non-attendance of the judge, the jurors being summoned shall stand over to the next succeeding court.

33. The key of the jury box shall be kept by the clerk, and the box shall be kept by the marshal, or some person to whose care he commits it, at Atlanta.

Whenever it shall happen, from the non-attendance of the judge, that a court cannot be held, and no jury shall have been drawn for the next term, the clerk and marshal shall draw the juries for such term; and in the absence of the clerk and marshal, or either of them, their deputies, respectively, shall act in their behalf.

34. To all writs of *venire*, the marshal, or his deputy, shall make a return on oath to the clerk, exhibiting in three several columus those jurors on whom a summons has been served personally, those who have been

served by copies or notices left at their houses, and those who could not be found.

35. The clerk shall keep a book in which shall be entered the names of all persons who have been summoned as jurors, or bound in recognizance, and have made default; and shall enter opposite to the name of each defaulter, whether he be fined or excused, if fined, the amount of the fine, and if excused, by whom excused; which book shall be exhibited to the court at every sitting.

36. The marshal, in his summons to each juror, shall express the day, hour, place, and court at which he is to appear, and also whether he is to serve as petit or grand juror.

37. Within ten days after the adjournment of each court, the clerk shall publish in some one public print of the place where the court was held, the names of the defaulting jurors summoned to attend that term, with a notice that on the first day of the ensuing term they will be fined according to law, unless they make sufficient excuse on oath, which publication shall be continued for three weeks, and shall be a sufficient notice to such defaulters.

38. Lists and pannels of the persons summoned shall be kept and numbered, as in the law for regulating juries in the superior courts of this state.

39. When a jury shall not attend, of the persons so summoned, the court will summon a jury *de talibus circumstantibus*.

40. Jurors who have made default, may make oath to their excuse before any state magistrate, and file the same with the clerk on or before the first day of the ensuing term. If the excuse be deemed insufficient, the same penalties shall be inflicted as are inflicted by the state laws, or they may be moderated by the court according to circumstances. The mode of collecting fines so inflicted, shall be by attachment as for contempt.

41. Persons above sixty years of age shall be excused from serving on juries; other excuses must depend upon their particular merits.

EJECTMENTS.

42. No person shall be admitted as defendant in ejectment but on condition that on his appearance he shall confess the lease, entry, and ouster stated in the declaration, and such confession shall be entered on the docket.

MARSHAL'S SALES.

43. All sales of lands levied on under execution from this court, by the marshal thereof, shall be advertised for sale, and be sold only on the first Tuesday in every month, public notice thereof being published thirty days previously, in any one newspaper at Atlanta or Athens, as may be nearest to the place of such sale. When levies are made on lands that are situated within the counties of Rabun, Habersham, Hall, Jackson, Walton, Clarke, Oglethorpe, Greene, Taliaferro, Wilkes, Lincoln, Elbert, Madison, or Franklin, the sales shall be at Athens at the usual hours. And when situated in any other county, the same shall be sold at the court house in Atlanta, at the usual hours. All property shall be duly described, and the names of the parties, plaintiff and defendant, be inserted in the public notice given by the marshal.

44. Sales of all other articles levied on under execution, shall take place on the third Tuesday in every month at the court house in the county in which the levy is made, and after advertising three weeks in any public print of respectable circulation, nearest to the place of levy, or at any other place, by consent of parties.

The property to be sold shall be sufficiently described, and the parties, plaintiff and defendant, distinctly named. All property exempted from levy by the state laws, shall be exempted from levy under process of this court.

45. Whenever the marshal shall levy upon any animal property, the defendant, or in default of his doing so, the plaintiff shall have the right to replevy such property by giving satisfactory security for producing the same on any sale day, to be designated in conformity with the exigency of the process on which the levy is made, which bond, if given by the defendant, shall, upon forfeiture of the condition and request of the plaintiff, be assigned to the plaintiff for recovery.

SURVEYS.

46. Surveys of land in any quantity not exceeding two hundred acres, shall be laid

down by a scale of ten chains to an inch; if exceeding that quantity, by a scale of twenty chains to an inch.

47. No survey made under a rule of court, shall be received in evidence, unless it appear that at least fifteen days' notice of the time and place of commencing such survey was given to the opposite party, by or in behalf of the party who offers it in evidence.

48. Every surveyor shall represent on his plat, as nearly as he can, the different enclosures of the tenants, and the extent or boundaries within which each party has exercised acts of ownership by cultivation or otherwise; they are also required to deliver copies of surveys by them made, to each of the parties concerned, upon their application, and at their own proper costs, within ten days after such application is made; and the surveyor executing a survey and attending court to prove the same shall be allowed the *per diem* pay of a witness attending upon subpœna.

49. All objections to the regularity or admission of surveys, must be made before the jury is charged with the cause.

MOTION FOR NEW TRIAL, OR IN ARREST OF JUDGMENT.

50. In cases in which a party shall receive notice of a motion for a new trial, or in arrest of judgment, he shall have leave, notwithstanding to enter up his judgment and lodge his execution to bind property; but if the motion be sustained, the judgment and execution shall be wholly set aside. If either party shall die before a decision be had in the cause on such motion, his legal representative may enter himself party to the suit on motion, and be entitled to all the rights of the original party.

FINES AND FORFEITURES.

51. The clerk shall keep a regular debit and credit account of all fines and forfeitures imposed and money recovered on recognizauces, which amount shall be exhibited with his list of defaulters, and shall be annually attested.

COMMISSIONS TO EXAMINE WITNESSES.

52. Commissions for examining witnesses may be forwarded by mail, and when executed, may be returned in the same mode, provided that in the latter case, the commissioner who deposits it in the post office, certify the same on the envelope over the seal, and if deposited by a messenger, that the commissioner certify the delivery to the messenger, and the messenger certify the delivery to the office. And if it should pass through any number of hands successively, the same to be done by each, noting every stage of progress until delivered into the office.

53. The time to be allowed for the return of a commission from any part of the United States, if not exceeding one hundred miles distant, shall be one month; if at a greater distance, not exceeding five hundred miles, two months; if at a greater distance, not exceeding one thousand miles, three months; if from any part of the West India Islands, four months; if from any part of Europe, six months; if from any other place, it must be judged of specially by the court.

54. When a commission is returned it may be opened by leave of the clerk at rules, or at any time upon consent of both parties in writing, indorsed on the commission; and after the return of a commission, it shall be the property of both parties, and remain with the clerk to be used by either.

55. Either party to a cause at issue, or ordered for judgment, wishing to sue out a commission to examine witnesses, shall first file a copy of the interrogatories to be propounded to the witnesses, and shall give ten days' notice thereof, accompanied with a copy of such interrogatories to the opposite party or his attorney; and each party may name any number of commissioners not exceeding five, any two of whom shall be competent to examine the witnesses, or any one of them; and the cross interrogatories and commissioners in behalf of the opposite party shall be rendered within ten days after such notice. But on application to the judge, or on motion at rules, commission may be sued out by plaintiff, at any time after filing his declaration, or by the defendant at any time after filing his plea, though no issue be made up, and although the ten days' notice be not given, provided the same be necessary for the purposes of justice, and will expose the opposite party to no risk.

PLEAS.

56. The defendant may plead as many

several pleas to the merits as may be necessary to his defence.

57. The defendant shall not plead specially without the consent of the plaintiff, if by the rules of evidence the special matter can be given in evidence on the general issue.

58. If the plaintiff amend his declaration so as to substantially change his case, or the defence, the defendant shall have the same time to plead *de novo*, as is given by the seventh rule.

59. The defendant shall not plead two dilatory pleas, that is, a second after the first has been disposed of.

60. If the defendant shall plead *non est factum* in debt, or *non assumpsit* on a bill of exchange or promissory note, without an affidavit to the truth of his plea, the instrument declared on shall be produced by the plaintiff, but need not be proved. An executor or administrator in such cases may make affidavit to his belief.

61. A plaintiff may have leave to strike out an issue in fact for the purpose of filing a general demurrer, on payment of costs, and submission to such terms as will prevent delay.

62. Neither party shall, after pleading, demand the letter of attorney of the opposite party.

BAIL.

63. Bail may be required in any suit sounding in contract, provided an affidavit of the sum actually due be attached to the process, and an order indorsed thereon requiring bail to be taken. In all special cases, the order of a judge shall be obtained.

64. The obligation entered into by bail in a civil suit, shall be to surrender the principal, if in life, at any time before the bail shall become legally fixed, or made personally liable for the sum sued for in the original action.

65. Bail in civil suits shall become liable to pay the sum recovered in the original action, upon the return of *non est inventus* to a *ca. sa.* against the principal. And although bail has become fixed, he may have the privilege of surrendering his principal in discharge at any time before judgment against himself, on payment of costs and expenses.

66. A plaintiff shall not be at liberty to discontinue against the principal and proceed against the bail, but shall proceed to judgment and execution against the principal, and may have his election to bring an action on the bail bond, or issue a *scire facias* against the bail, upon the judgment against the principal, and obtain judgment thereon against the bail.

67. Bail to the marshal need not enter into a recognizance of special bail, but may of right surrender his principal to the marshal in office hours or in open court ; and he shall also be entitled to the aid of the marshal to retake the principal, upon a written demand to that effect, left at the marshal's office, and advancing a reasonable sum to defray all incidental expenses. He shall be entitled generally to all the privileges, rights and powers which may be acquired by entering into a recognizance or special bail.

68. It shall be in the power of a plaintiff, whenever he has a legal right to require bail, to direct the marshal to make such bail justify before the clerk, or a commissioner appointed by virtue of the act for the more convenient taking of affidavits and bail in civil causes depending in the courts of the United States, or before some state magistrate ; and the proceedings attending such justification shall be duly returned with the writ.

69. In all cases when defendants are imprisoned by virtue of any *capias adsatisfaciendum* issuing out of this court, the plaintiff in execution shall be bound to pay the jail fees of the prisoner monthly, or the prisoner, upon refusal so to do, may, upon such refusal, forthwith be discharged from confinement, under an order of this court, or either of the judges thereof.

AWARDS.

70. Upon the return of an award, or umpirage, under a rule of reference, a two day rule shall be served by either party upon the other, to show cause why it should not be confirmed by the court, and judgment entered thereon. If no sufficient cause be shown, the judgment shall be entered and execution had as in ordinary cases.

MISCELLANEOUS.

71. When the court is open and sitting, no rule or order shall be granted which can be obtained of course before the clerk, unless upon special cause shown.

72. On all rules to show cause, the party called on shall begin and end his cause; and on all special matters, either springing out of a cause at issue or otherwise, the actor or party submitting a point to the court shall in like manner begin and close, and the defendant who admits the plaintiff's case, and takes upon himself the burthen of the proof, shall have the like privilege.

73. No attorney of this court shall ever attempt to argue or explain a cause after having been fully heard, and the opinion of the court has been pronounced.

74. Every motion for a rule or order shall be submitted in writing, and shall be copied into the minutes from the writing submitted.

75. In actions of covenant, or on bonds for the performance of covenants, the plaintiff may assign as many breaches as he pleases.

76. The clerk shall issue subpœnas for all witnesses whose names are furnished him by the district attorney, or the defendant, to testify in criminal prosecutions.

77. Mutual existing debts in the same right or rights to recover money on contract, express or implied, may be set off against each other upon the defendant's filing with his plea a notice thereof, with a bill of particulars and copy of a written contract according to the nature of his discount. If the jury shall find a sum or balance due the defendant, he may file his declaration instanter, and take judgment for such balance.

78. In order to avoid bringing causes by management into the courts of the United States by creating nominal parties distinct from the parties in interest, whenever a suit is instituted to try the right to property, real or personal, and the defendant will make oath that he suspects and has cause to suspect, that the plaintiff has obtained or accepted a conveyance of the property from the real and actual owner, or from some public officer, for the sole purpose of bringing a suit in this court, when the title in fact exists in some other person, not entitled to sue in this court, the defendant shall not be required to plead to the action, until the facts so surmised, and stated in the defendant's affidavit, be denied on oath.

79. In the event of the death of the plaintiff to a suit, if no executor or administrator appear to enter himself party to the suit within twelve months after a suggestion of his death be entered of record, the suit shall finally abate. And in the event of a defendant's death, if the plaintiff sue out his summons to the executor or administrator to enter himself party, and he fail to do so within twelve months after service, the plaintiff may, by leave of court, on proof thereof, sign his judgment against the estate.

80. In no case shall the defendant be compelled to plead or answer until the plaintiff shall have given security for costs, if ten days' notice be given, to the plaintiff's attorney, that such security will be required; except where the party sues in *forma pauperis*.

81. Attorneys of unexceptionable character, who have been admitted into the supreme court, or any one of the circuit courts of the United States, shall be admitted, of course, to practice in this, and those who have been admitted in the state court, and practiced therein for three years, and are of unexceptionable character, shall be admitted to practice in this court.

82. Only two counsel on each side, shall be heard in any cause. One for the promovent shall be first heard, the two for respondent shall follow, and one for the promovent close in argument.

83. On points of law, gentlemen of the bar shall address themselves exclusively to the court.

84. After the argument of a cause, motion, or exception, upon matter of law submitted to the court, a statement of the points relied upon, and a note of the authorities cited, may be required of the counsel on both sides, by the court, before pronouncing its opinion thereon.

85. In all cases where payment or satisfaction shall be made on any judgment or execution, either in whole or in part, it shall be the duty of the attorney receiving the same forthwith to enter an acknowledgment thereof, and file the same of record in the office of the clerk of the court, who is required to record such acknowledgment among the other proceedings in the cause, and also to make a note thereof on the docket of judgments, opposite the place where such judgment is entered. And any attorney failing to comply with this rule, on or before the last day of the term next succeeding the making of such payment or satisfaction, shall be considered in contempt.

86. No attorney or other officer of the court shall be taken as bail in any suit or action depending or undetermined therein, or as security on any appeal or other proceeding.

87. No consent between attorneys or parties will be enforced by the court, unless it be in writing, and signed by the parties to the consent, or made in open court, and entered on the minutes.

88. All notices required to be given to any officer of court must be made in writing.

89. Witnesses shall first be examined by the party introducing them, then cross-examined by the adverse party ; further examination shall not be had but by leave of the court first obtained, and then only upon the declaration of the attorney or witness that a material fact has not been stated, to which fact so stated all further inquiries shall exclusively be directed; and in all cases in which more than one attorney is retained on either side, the examination and cross-examination shall be conducted by one of the council only ; and at the opening of the case both parties shall state to the court to which attorney the examination and cross-examination of witnesses is confided.

90. In all cases wherein no particular rules are herein set down, the practice of the court of king's bench at Westminister shall be pursued so far as the same be not repugnant to the above rules, or the laws of the United States.

SUITS BY THE UNITED STATES.

91. In suits by or in behalf of the United States, in which the plaintiffs are by the statute entitled to judgment at the return term of the writ, if the defendant pleads thereto, the district attorney may have the cause placed on the docket of the same term, and may bring the same to trial when called, unless at the instance of the defendant the court shall grant a continuance of the cause.

92. No plea shall be received in any suit instituted by the United States, or in their behalf, upon any bond for the payment of duties or other contract, or against persons accountable for public money, or any suit instituted upon a bail bond taken in consequence of such suit, unless such plea is accompanied by an affidavit of the truth of the matters in the said plea contained.

IN EQUITY.

93. Either party, plaintiff or defendant, may set down a cause for hearing on the equity docket, and no such cause shall be brought on at term unless the same has been set down for trial at least ten days before the first day of the term, but no party in default shall avail himself of this rule. If the cause shall not have been set down for hearing on a rule day, ten days' notice thereof shall be given to the opposite party.

94. A brief or abstract of the proceedings shall be furnished the judge at least six days before trial, or before argument had on the merits of the bill, answer, plea, demurrer or other important exception, by the solicitor desirous of obtaining the same, together with the points of law and fact intended to be presented by him and a note of the authorities expected to be relied on. And the solicitor for the opposite party shall, at or before the opening of such cause or argument, furnish the judge with a statement of the points intended to be made by him, together with a note of the authorities expected to be relied on.

GEORGIA.—Southern District.

RULE 1. A debtor's petition, unless there be special reasons for a different reference, in which case the judge will order as he may think expedient, will be referred by Form No. 4 to a register acting in that congressional district which embraces the place of residence, or of business that determines the jurisdiction.

A creditor's petition will be referred to a register designated by the judge in each case according to the special facts thereof; and the adjudication in bankruptcy, Form No. 59, will contain a provision making such reference, and naming the register.

2. The place for the register to act, to be specified in Form No. 4, or for the creditors to meet, to be specified in Form No. 59, shall be one of the offices of the register, as fixed by a general order of the court entered on the minutes. Generally, the office nearest the residence or place of business of the bankrupt will be the one designated. The day for the attendance of the bankrupt, or for the meeting of creditors, will be fixed al-

ways with due regard to the convenient and speedy progress of the case.

A register may, in any case referred to him, fix the time when he will act upon any matter touching the case not set down in orders or otherwise for some particular time.

3. The deposit of fifty dollars required by the 47th section of the act shall, in every case, be made with the clerk; who shall pay one-half thereof to the register at the time of furnishing him with a copy of the order of reference, the same to be applied to such fees of the register as are chargeable to the party who made the deposit. The other half shall, if necessary, be paid out by the clerk to the register in satisfaction as they accrue, of such further fees of the latter (so chargeable) as may arise after the first half shall have been exhausted. But the register must make to the court, on oath, returns of his fees, giving the several items specifically; and the clerk, in paying out the second half of the deposit, shall limit each payment to the amount appearing from such returns to be due and unpaid. If the whole of the deposit should be thus exhausted, any subsequent fees of the register, chargeable to the petitioner, shall be paid or secured as required by the "general orders."

The case of a debtor, whose costs are restricted by the judge under the "general orders" to the amount of the original deposit, will, of course, form an exception to all the regulations contained in this rule, except that requiring the deposit to be made with the clerk. In such a case the actual disbursements of the register and the marshal, shall, when properly returned, be paid by the clerk; but all other demands shall await the special order of the judge.

4. The copy of the petition and schedules to be furnished, according to the "general orders," to the register, may be either a copy certified by the clerk under the seal of the court, or a duplicate original, signed and verified throughout, in the same manner as the original filed with the clerk. The examination required by rule 7 of the general orders, shall be directed to the copy, or duplicate thus furnished; and upon it, if found to be correct in form, and all the particulars required by the act complied with, the certificate of correctness shall be entered and signed by the register. But this certificate

shall not be made unless the whole eleven sheets comprising schedules A and B, in *Form* No. 1, are present and arranged in their proper order; nor shall the register, in any case, issue a warrant without first having entered and signed such certificate. Moreover, in cases of involuntary bankruptcy, the original petition itself shall be submitted for examination to one of the registers, whose certificate, substantially in the following form shall be procured, as preliminary to presenting the petition to the court or judge: "I certify that I have carefully examined the annexed (or within) petition and the verification thereof, and that the same are in proper form and sufficient in substance to authorize an adjudication in bankruptcy, and the issuing of a warrant under the 42d section of the bankrupt act.

Given at   this   day of   18
                                             Register."

5. The register, or other officer of the court, before administering the proper oaths in verification of any writing whatever, shall see that the different pieces of paper of which it is composed, and those to which it refers as annexed, are properly fastened together in such manner as to give reasonable security against separation, loss or exchange of any part thereof. And all papers whatever, to be filed in proceedings in bankruptcy, shall be written in a fair and legible hand, or neatly printed, upon paper substantially of the length and width of "legal cap," securely fastened at the top, and folded to correspond in form and size with ordinary law papers.

6. All petitions shall be numbered consecutively; and the clerk shall enter the case under its proper title in his docket—giving to each at least one page thereof. He shall endorse its number on the petition, which shall thereafter be the designating number of the case until finally disposed of. Every other paper, proceeding or notice in the case shall be marked by the clerk, register, messenger, or other officer or party preparing it, with the designating number.

7. The clerk shall prepare envelopes of uniform size in which to keep, in their proper order, all the papers filed in each case. The designating number and the title of the case shall be plainly endorsed upon the envelope.

8. The marshal shall procure at the ex-

pense of the United States, and deliver to the clerk, blank forms of all necessary process; and the clerk will sign the same, and affix the seal of the court thereto, and furnish each register with the necessary number for his use; and the register, before issuing such process, shall sign or countersign the same, as may be proper in the case.

9. Letters to the registers, the clerk, or the marshal, requiring an answer, must be accompanied by envelopes, properly addressed, and with the proper postage stamps affixed, in which to inclose the reply, and whatever else may be required; and no register or other officer of the court will be required to answer any such letter unless this be done.

Whenever any receipt is desired from any officer of the court, it must be prepared and presented by the party desiring it.

10. The warrant, *Form* No. 6, shall be regarded as process under *Rule* 2 of the general orders; and such warrant shall, moreover, be signed by the judge or the register at the foot thereof in the following form, with the date: " Issued by me   186 .

District judge (or register in bankruptcy.")

11. Unless the warrant shall designate certain creditors to be served personally with notice, all may be served by mail. The deposit of notice in the post office where a creditor usually receives his letters and papers, duly addressed, and prepaid as a drop letter, will be good service by mail. No creditor residing out of the judicial district, in which the case is pending, will be designated for personal service. That in cases of voluntary bankruptcy, the petitioner shall have the option, by himself or attorney, of preparing the notices to his creditors, to be served under the warrant, provided the same are correctly prepared and furnished to the marshal, as messenger, in proper form and within such time as will enable him to mail the same, so as to give the requisite notice to the persons therein named. Notice of such option shall be given to the clerk before the issuing of the warrant, to be by him noted on the same.

The allowance to the marshal for preparation of such notice, when prepared by him, or the .examination thereof when prepared by the petitioner, shall be subject to the special order of the court in each case.

12. The warrant, whether under *Form* No. 6, or *Form* No 59, will specify two newspapers, in each of which the notices shall be published. And when this or any other publication appears in two or more newspapers, if correctly made in one, no accidental error in the others shall affect the sufficiency of the publication. And the marshal, clerk, and every register and assignee, when required to publish any notice or advertisement, shall return into court a copy, cut from each newspaper, of each notice or advertisement as published with a certificate showing that the required publi cation has been duly made.

13. In compliance with section seven of the act of congress, approved March 2d, 1867, requiring that such advertisements as may be ordered for publication in certain districts therein named, by any United States court or judge thereof, or by any officer of such courts, or by any executive officer of the United States, shall be published in some one or more newspapers in said district, to be selected by the clerk of the house of representatives. Therefore, all orders or notices required to be published during any proceedings in bankruptcy, shall be advertised in the " National Republican," of Augusta, or the " Savannah Republican," of Savannah—the two papers selected in Georgia by the clerk of the house of representatives.

14. Where no other form is prescribed, orders made by the register will accord with *Form* No. 10. They will, however, be signed by him alone; and the seal of the court need not be attached, nor referred to in the conclusion.

15. Proofs of debts, made prior to the election or appointment of an assignee, shall be handed or sent to the register to whom the case has been referred. If the register be doubtful of the validity of a claim, or of the creditor's right to prove it, and think that the same should be investigated by the assignee, he may postpone the proof of such claim until the assignee is chosen.

16. The acceptance or rejection by an assignee of the trust, shall be notified by him to the register, who shall report the same immediately to the clerk.

17. Every assignee shall, as soon as he receives an assignment, send or deliver it to the clerk, by whom it shall be copied, and

then return to the assignee. The copy shall be certified by the clerk under his hand and the seal of the court, and remain on file in his office.

18. The notice to creditors, of dividends or meetings, required by the 17th, 27th and 28th sections of the act, shall be such as provided by the order contained in *Form* No. 28, and the register shall select one newspaper in which the notice shall be published.

19. The list of debts provided for by section 23 of the act, shall be made and certified by the register to whom the case is referred; and he shall place thereon all debts which are duly proved.

21. Assignees will, as a general rule, be required to produce and file vouchers for all payments made by them, except payments of one dollar or less. In particular instances, for special cause shown, vouchers may be dispensed with by an order of the court.

21. The assignee of any creditor, after the adjudication in bankruptcy, may apply for an order for the examination of such bankrupt on oath or affirmation, which application shall state in brief terms, the grounds thereof, and shall be verified by oath, and presented to the register to whom the case stands referred, whereupon if it appear reasonable, the register may issue the proper order for the bankrupt's examination; and if he shall fail to obey, after due service, the court on application of the register, may compel the attendance by warrant directed to the marshal, commanding him to arrest such bankrupt, and bring him forthwith before the register for examination. Every bankrupt shall, at all times, be bound to attend the assignee upon the requirement of the register acting in his case, on reasonable notice in writing for that purpose, to be served personally, or left at his usual place of abode, in order to assist in making out the accounts of said bankrupt's estate and effects, and to give information as to his debts and property, for which he shall be entitled to receive from the assignee a reasonable compensation out of the estate.

22. All issues, questions, points and matters stated in writing, under *rule* 11 of the "general orders," or under the 4th or 6th sections of the act, or according to *Form* No. 50, and adjourned into court for decision, or stated in a special case for the opinion of the court, shall be briefly stated and certified to the judge, by the register, who shall also state briefly his opinion on the issue, question, point or matter, and it shall be delivered or sent to the clerk; and no oral or written argument shall be allowed on any such issue, question point or matter, unless by special leave of the court. Communications sent by a register, either to the judge or the clerk, shall have the name of the register indorsed thereon.

23. All questions for trial or hearing under sections 31 and 34 of the act, shall be tried or heard, at a stated session of the court, on four days' notice from either party to the other party and the clerk. And a calendar of those, and all other causes ready for hearing, shall be made by the clerk in duplicate—one for the bench, and one for the bar.

24. If any matter fails to be called or acted on by the court at the time and place appointed for any hearing or proceeding before it, or if the judge shall be absent, such matters shall, without other order, stand continued to the next sitting of the court.

25. The application under section 34 of the act, to set aside a discharge, shall be made on oath or affirmation, and the answer of the bankrupt thereto, shall respond specifically to each allegation, and be verified in like manner.

26. In cases not provided for by the act, the general orders, or these rules, the practice of this court shall be subject to the special order of the court, or the judge, and such orders will be made to conform as near as may be to the practice of this court in cases of similar or analogous character.

27. Except during the absence of the judge, the court will be open for the transaction of business, as a court of bankruptcy, at the United States court room, in the city of Savannah, on every Tuesday, at 10 o'clock A. M.

Ordered, That all moneys received by the clerk of the court, on account of any bankrupt's estate, or by an assignee, on account of any estate of which he is assignee, shall be deposited in the Merchants' National Bank, in the city of Savannah. The check or warrant for drawing moneys deposited by the clerk shall be signed by him, and countersigned by the judge. The check or warrant for drawing moneys deposited by the assignee, shall be signed by him, and countersigned by the register designated to act in the case of the estate on account of which such moneys were deposited.

ILLINOIS.—Southern District.

In addition to the general orders in bankruptcy prescribed by the supreme court of the United States, the following rules have been adopted by the district court of the United States for the southern district of Illinois.

1—*Deposit and Payment of Moneys.*

All moneys paid into the registry of the court, shall be deposited in the Ridgely National Bank, of Springfield, Illinois, and shall not be drawn from such depositary, unless upon a check signed by the clerk and countersigned by the judge. All moneys received by assignees in the course of any proceedings in bankruptcy, shall be paid into the registry of the court, and shall be forthwith deposited by the clerk in the designated depositary. But this rule shall not prevent the assignee from retaining out of the moneys in his hands, all his necessary disbursements, and the compensation allowed him by the court for his services.

2—*Opposition to Discharge.*

Opposition to a bankrupt's discharge may be filed with and heard before the register, who shall take testimony thereon, and report the same to the court with his opinion, on or before the day fixed for the hearing of the bankrupt's petition for discharge; and in case objections are made before the court, the same shall be referred to and heard before the register, who shall report the testimony, together with his opinion thereon, to the court. Upon filing the report and opinion of the register, the clerk shall notify the bankrupt and the opposing creditor of such filing, and if no exceptions are filed thereto within twenty days thereafter, the opinion of the register shall stand approved, and the discharge [shall be] granted or refused in accordance therewith.

3—*Homesteads.*

1. When a homestead is claimed by a bankrupt as exempt from the operation of the bankrupt law, and the property upon which the bankrupt resides and claims such homestead exemption is, in the opinion of the assignee, of greater value than $1,000, and such assignee is of opinion that the bankrupt is entitled to a homestead thereon, he shall notify the bankrupt to designate in writing some disinterested person, to act as one of three commissioners to appraise said property, and set off to said bankrupt his homestead thereon. The assignee shall also designate in writing, some disinterested person to act as one of said commissioners, and the two so designated shall in like manner select a third. The three commissioners so selected, shall, upon oath, to be administered to them by a register in bankruptcy or commissioner of a circuit court of the United States, and returned with their report, appraise said property; and if, in their opinion, the same is not of greater value than $1,000, the assignee shall, upon confirmation of their report, set off the same to said bankrupt under the provisions of section fourteen of the bankrupt law.

2. If, in the opinion of said commissioners, said property is of a greater value than $1,000, and can be divided without injury to the interests of said bankrupt's estate, they shall set off to said bankrupt so much thereof, including the dwelling house in which the bankrupt resides, as shall in their opinion be of the value of $1,000, and the residue of said premises shall be sold by the assignee, in such manner as the court, by general or special order may direct.

3. If, in the opinion of said commissioners, said property is of greater value than $1,000, and cannot be divided without injury, the bankrupt may, within twenty days after confirmation of their report, pay to the assignee the excess of the appraised value of said property over and above the sum of $1,000, and the assignee shall thereupon convey said property to said bankrupt. In default of such payment, the property shall be sold by the assignee, in such manner as the court, by general or special order may direct, and out of the proceeds thereof he shall pay to the bankrupt the sum of $1,000 in lieu of his homestead.

4. The commissioners shall, as soon as they have completed their duties, deliver their report, with [their] appointment and oath as such commissioners thereto attached, to the assignee, and shall receive as compensation for their services, the sum of five dollars each, for each day actually and necessarily employed in making the appraisement and setting off the homestead, together with their actual and necessary traveling expenses while so employed, to be paid by the assignee out of any moneys in his hands belonging to the estate of said bankrupt.

5. The assignee, as soon as he shall receive the report of the commissionrs, shall deliver a copy of the same to the bankrupt, and file the original in the clerk's office, and unless exceptions are filed to said report within twenty days after such filing, the same shall stand approved. If the bankrupt shall neglect or refuse to designate in writing a person to act as one of said commissioners, within twenty days after he shall have been notified by the assignee as provided in this rule, the assignee shall designate and appoint all of said commmissioners.

4—Sales of Unencumbered Property by Assignee.

1. Unless otherwise specially ordered by the court, the assignee shall, as soon as may be after the same shall come to his hands, sell all unencumbered estate of the bankrupt, both real and personal, not exempt from the operation of the bankrupt law, at public sale, to the highest and best bidder for cash, and shall give at least ten days' public notice in sales of personal property, and at least twenty days' public notice in sales of real estate, of the time, place and terms of sale, and of the articles or property to be sold, by advertisement in one or more newspapers, to be designated by the register in the particular case, and by posted handbills or otherwise, as the register may direct. All sales of real estate shall, unless specially ordered by the court, be made at such place, within the county where the same is situated, as in the opinion of the assignee will secure the most advantageous sale. Personal property may be sold in such lots and at such place as the assignee may think best for the interest of the estate. No sales shall be made by the assignee otherwise than as herein provided, unless by special order of the court, upon the petition of the assignee, or a creditor, or other person interested, and for good cause shown; but no special order shall be required for making public sales of real or personal estate in the manner provided for in this rule.

2. The assignee shall file in the clerk's office, without delay, a report of any sales of real estate made by him under any general or special order of the court, setting forth the time and place of sale, what notice of sale, if any, was given, the property sold, the purchase or purchasers, and the price paid for the same ; and if public notice of such sale was given, shall attach to his report a copy of the advertisement, with the certificate of the publisher or publishers of the newspapers in which the same was published that the same was published as required. If no exceptions are filed to such report within twenty days after the same is filed, the report shall stand approved, and the assignee shall execute and deliver to the purchasers all necessary deeds and conveyances of the property so sold.

RULE 5. In addition to the fees and expenses allowed to the messenger by the 47th section of the bankrupt act and such further allowance as may be made, for cause shown, in special cases, the following compensation shall be allowed and paid to the marshal as messenger for his services in bankrupt causes.

For service of any writ, or other process, order of court, or notice, where personal service is required, except summons of witnesses and notices to creditors under warrants, Forms 6 and 59, two dollars for each person upon whom such service may be made, and five dollars for each day actually and necessarily employed in making such service.

For making out notices to creditors under warrants. Forms 6 and 29, five cents for each folio of 100 words; and for making copies of writs or other papers where the same are required to be served by copy, ten cents for each folio of 100 words.

For serving summons of witness fifty cents for each person upon whom the same may be served.

For transporting persons arrested under

any warrant or order of court five cents per mile for each person, and five dollars per day and five cents per mile for each guard when necessary.

For each day actually and necessarily employed in taking possession of property under any warrant or order of court, making inventory, &c., five dollars.

Adopted April 11, 1870.

In addition to the general orders in bankruptcy prescribed by the supreme court of the United States, the following rules have been adopted by the district court of the United States for the southern district of Illinois :

RULE 1.—*Deposit and Payment of Moneys.*

All moneys paid into the registry of the court shall be deposited in the Ridgely National Bank, of Springfield, Illinois, and shall not be drawn from such depositary unless upon a check signed by the clerk and countersigned by the judge. All moneys received by the assignees in the course of any proceedings in bankruptcy, shall be paid into the registry of the court, and shall be forthwith deposited by the clerk in the designated depositary. But this rule shall not prevent the assignee from retaining out of the moneys in his hands, all his necessary disbursements, and the compensations allowed him by the court for his services.

RULE 2.—*Opposition to Discharge.*

Opposition to a bankrupt's discharge may be filed with and heard before the register, who shall take testimony thereon and report the same to the court, with his opinion, on or before the day fixed for the hearing of the bankrupt's petition for discharge; and in case objections are made before the court, the same shall be referred to and heard before the register, who shall report the testimony, together with his opinion thereon, to the court. Upon filing the report and opinion of the register, the clerk shall notify the bankrupt and the opposing creditor of such filing, and if no exceptions are filed thereto within twenty days thereafter, the opinion of the register shall stand approved, and the discharge shall be granted or refused in accordance therewith.

RULE 3.—*Homesteads.*

1. When a homestead is claimed by a bankrupt as exempt from the operation of the bankrupt law, and the property upon which the bankrupt resides and claims such homestead exemption is, in the opinion of the assignee, of greater value than $1,000, and such assignee is of opinion that the bankrupt is entitled to a homestead thereon, he shall notify the bankrupt to designate in writing some disinterested person, to act as one of three commissioners to appraise said property, and set off to the bankrupt his homestead thereon. The assignee shall also designate in writing some disinterested person to act as one of said commissioners, and the two so designated shall, in like manner, elect a third. The three commissioners so elected shall, upon oath, to be administered to them by a register in bankruptcy or commissioner of a circuit court of the United States, and returned with their report, appraise said property, and if, in their opinion, the same is not of greater value than $1,000, the assignee shall, upon confirmation of their report, set off the same to said bankrupt under the provisions of section 14 of the bankrupt law.

2. If, in the opinion of said commissioners, said property is of greater value than $1,000, and can be divided without injury to the interests of the bankrupt's estate, they shall set off to said bankrupt so much thereof, including the dwelling house in which the bankrupt resides, as shall, in their opinion, be of the value of $1,000, and the residue of said premises shall be sold by the assignee in such manner as the court, by general or special order, may direct.

3. If, in the opinion of said commissioners said property is of greater value than $1,000, and cannot be divided without injury, the bankrupt may, within twenty days after confirmation of their report, pay to the assignee the excess of the appraised value of said property over and above 'the sum of $1,000, and the assignee shall therefore convey said property to said bankrupt. In default of such payment, the property shall be sold by the assignee, in such manner as the court, by general or special order may direct, and out of the proceeds thereof, he shall pay to the bankrupt the sum of $1,000 in lieu of his homestead.

4. The commissioners shall, as soon as they have completed their duties, deliver their report, with [their] appointment and oath as such commissioners thereto attached, to the assignee, and shall receive as compensation for their services, the sum of $5 each for each day actually and necessarily employed in making the appraisement, and setting off the homestead, together with their actual and necessary traveling expenses while so employed, to be paid by the assignee out of any moneys in his hands belonging to the estate of said bankrupt.

5. The assignee, as soon as he shall receive the report of the commissioners, shall deliver a copy of the same to the bankrupt, and file the original in the clerk's office, and unless exceptions are filed to said report within twenty days after such filing, the same shall stand approved. If the bankrupt shall neglect or refuse to designate in writing a person to act as one of said commissioners, within twenty days after he shall have been notified by the assignee as provided in this rule, the assignee shall designate and appoint all of said commissioners.

RULE 4.—*Sale of Unencumbered Property by Assignee.*

1. Unless otherwise specially ordered by the court, the assignee shall, as soon as may be after the same shall come to his hands, sell all unencumbered estate of the bankrupt both real and personal, not exempt from the operation of the bankrupt law, at public sale, to the highest and best bidder for cash, and shall give at least ten days' public notice on sales of personal property, and at least twenty days' public notice in sales of real estate, of the time, place and terms of sale, and of the article or property to be sold, by advertisement in one or more newspapers, to be designated by the register in the particular case, and by posted handbills or otherwise, as the register may direct. All sales of real estate, shall unless specially ordered by the court, be made at such place within the county where such is situated, as in the opinion of the assignee will secure the most advantageous sale. Personal property may be sold in such lots, and at such place as the assignee may think best for the interest of the estate. No sales shall be made by the assignee otherwise than as herein provided, unless by special order of

the court, upon the petition of the assignee, or a creditor, or other person interested, and for good cause shown; but no special order shall be required for making public sales of real or personal estate in the manner provided for in this rule.

2. The assignee shall file in the clerk's office, without delay, a report of any sale of real estate made by him under any general or special order of the court, setting forth the time and place of sale, what notice of sale, if any was given, the property sold, the purchaser or purchasers, and the price paid for the same; and if public notice of such sale was given, shall attach to his report a copy of the advertisement, with the certificate of the publisher or publishers of the newspapers in which the same was published that the same was published as required. If no exceptions are filed to such report within twenty days after the same is filed, the report shall stand approved, and the assignee shall execute and deliver to the purchasers, all necessary deed and conveyances of the property so sold.

SPRINGFIELD, ILL., *April 17th*, 1871.
A. W. GAZZAM, ESQ., 95 Liberty street, N. Y.

SIR: I respond to your request of March 20, addressed to Judge Treat. I inclose herewith a copy of the only rule in bankruptcy adopted by this court since April 1, 1870.

Your letter was handed to me by Judge Treat some time ago, and the copy of the rule prepared, but, by some oversight, it was not sent. Please pardon the neglect.
Respectfully,
GEO. P. BOWEN, *Clerk.*

INDIANA.

It is ordered by the district court of the United States for the district of Indiana, that, in addition to the rules and regulations prescribed by the act of congress, to establish a uniform system of bankruptcy throughout the United States, approved March 2, 1867, and to the rules, orders, and regulations in bankruptcy lately promulgated by the supreme court of the United States, and subordinate thereto, the following rules of practice in bankruptcy be adopted for the government of proceedings in bankruptcy in the said district court:

Stated Sessions.

RULE 1. A stated session of the district court shall be held at the United States court-house, in Indianapolis, on the first Tuesday in every month, at which session all questions of law and of fact arising under the provisions of the fourth, sixth and thirty-first sections of the bankrupt act, and also all cases for trial under the 24th rule of the general orders promulgated by the supreme court of the United States, shall stand for hearing and decision. And said stated session shall be continued so long as business may require. All persons concerned must take notice of the pendency of such questions and cases in manner aforesaid, without any special notification thereof, except so far as said act and general orders require it.

Evidence.

2. In all cases to be tried by the court arising under the foregoing rule, the register before whom such cases and questions may arise shall, before the trial thereof in the district court, and pursuant to the tenth of said general orders, take down in writing all the evidence offered on both sides; and he shall, along with the questions arising in such cases, and all documentary evidence filed with him, certify the same to the district court. And said court will decide all such questions and cases on the matters so certified alone, unless, for good cause shown, the court shall allow the other evidence to be offered.

Notices.

3. The newspaper notices contemplated in No. 6 of the forms of proceeding, lately promulgated by the supreme court, shall be published twice in the Indianapolis *Journal* or Indianapolis *Herald*, and twice in a newspaper of general circulation nearest the residence of each bankrupt in the proceeding, all to be designated by the register to whom the case shall have been referred. But if the bankrupt shall reside in Marion county, Indiana, then such notices shall be published twice both in said *Journal* and *Herald*, and not elsewhere.

4. The notices to creditors contemplated in No. 6 of the forms of proceeding in bankruptcy, promulgated by the supreme court, shall, in all cases, be sent through the mail,

unless specially otherwise ordered by the court. No other mode of notifying a creditor residing out of the state of Indiana will in any case be allowed. *Provided, however,* that the written acknowledgment by any creditor, under his signature, of due notice in such case shall be equivalent to service of such notice by the marshal.

5. The notices contemplated by the fourteenth section of said act, to be given by assignees in bankruptcy, shall be published for three weeks successively in like manner as is provided in the preceding third rule.

6. The newspaper notices contemplated by rule No. 21 of the general orders, promulgated by the supreme court relating to bankruptcy, shall be published in a newspaper of general circulation nearest the place of the sale mentioned in the notice.

7. All notices to creditors contemplated by the 17th, 27th and 28th sections of said bankrupt act shall be given by letters through the mail.

8. Notices by any assignee in bankruptcy of the filing of his account, and of his application for a settlement and discharge, as contemplated by the 28th section of said bankrupt act, shall be given through the mail to all known creditors.

Reference to Register.

9. In all cases of voluntary bankruptcy, if the petitioner shall, at any time before reference, file with his petition a written request that the matters shall be referred to a designated register, the same shall, as of course, be so referred, unless the court shall, for good cause, otherwise order. But if no such request be made, the court will, as of course, order the reference to the register of the congressional district in which the bankrupt resides, unless, for good cause, the court deems it proper to refer it to some other register.

10. In cases of involuntary bankruptcy, the court will, in view to the interest and convenience of all parties and the furtherance of justice, refer the matter to such register as may, under all the circumstances be deemed most advisable.

Order of Reference.

11. Every adjudication in bankruptcy, under No. 58 of said forms of proceeding in bankruptcy, promulgated by the supreme

court, shall contain an order referring the case to the register, as provided in the 9th and 10th of these rules.

Surrender.

12. In every case of voluntary bankruptcy the register to whom the petition is referred shall receive from the bankrupt a surrender substantially in the form following:

I, the undersigned, a bankrupt, surrender to a register in bankruptcy, all my property in possession and in action.
Witness my hand, the   day of 186 .   (Signed.)

Form.

13. Whenever the Form No. 10 of said forms of proceeding in bankruptcy is used by the register, the conclusion of the same may be so varied as to be attested and signed by him.

Assignee's Notice of Acceptance.

14. Under rule No. 9 of said general orders in bankruptcy, the notice of the acceptance of his appointment by every assignee in bankruptcy, as given in No. 16 of said forms of proceedings in bankruptcy, he shall immediately forward to the proper register, and, on the receipt thereof, such register shall report it to the clerk.

Assignment.

15. Every assignee, on receiving the assignment of an estate in bankruptcy, shall, as soon as may be, deliver the same to the clerk, who shall make a copy thereof, certified under the seal of the court, and file such copy in his office, and thereupon redeliver the original to the said assignee.

Vouchers.

16. Under the provisions of the 27th section of said bankrupt act, every assignee shall produce and file vouchers for all payments claimed to have been made by him, except in cases in which he shall be, for good cause, excused therefrom by the court.

List of Debts Proved.

17. The list of debts contemplated by the 23rd section of said bankrupt act, shall be made and certified by the register to whom the case shall have been referred; and it shall contain a statement of all the debts which, up to the time of the making of such list and certificate, shall have been duly proved.

Affidavits.

18. All motions founded on alleged matter of fact not of record, and all applications made under the *proviso* to the 34th section of said bankrupt act, shall be in writing and sworn to by the party making such motion or application, or by his agent or attorney.

Register's Certificate.

19. The examination and certificate of the register touching the correctness of the form of the petition and schedules filed therewith, as contemplated by the 7th rule of the general orders in bankruptcy, promulgated by the supreme court, may be made by any register before the filing of such petition and schedules, and if not so made before that time, the register to whom such matter is referred, shall make such examination and certificate before he does any other official act in relation to the proceedings

Such certificate may be substantially as follows:

U. S. District Court, Indiana Dist.

In the matter of	
by whom a petition for adjudication in bankruptcy was filed on the day of , 18 .	In bankruptcy, No.

I, the undersigned, register in bankruptcy for the   congressional district of Indiana, certify that I have examined the petition and schedules in the above entitled case touching their correctness in form; and that the same are [correct in form or deficient in form in this, to wit: stating the deficiency, as the case may be.]
Witness my hand, the   day of   , 18 .   A. B., *Register.*

Decisions and Entries.

20. All decisions made at the stated sessions of the court, as provided in the first of these rules, shall be entered in the order book; and in every case in which any register must do any official act under any such decision, the clerk shall forthwith certify from the order book a copy of such deci-

sion under the seal of the court to such register.

All questions for the decision of the judge, certified to him by registers and not embraced in the foregoing provisions of this rule, nor in said first rule, will be answered by the judge in writing, indorsed by him on the paper containing such questions at such times as the judge may choose; and the judge will thereupon transmit such papers and answer to the register who certified such question, by mail or other safe mode of transmission, and on receipt of the same the register shall enter such question and and answer on his docket.

Fees.

21. The clerk shall file no petition in bankruptcy unless the same be accompanied by a deposit with him of fifty dollars pursuant to the 57th section of said bankrupt act. The clerk shall forward said sums of money along with the order of reference to the proper register. When the register has performed all his duties in each case respectively, and has satisfied his legal fees therein, if there be any surplus left of said fifty dollars, he shall forthwith deliver such surplus to the clerk; and the same shall be applied, first, to the payment of any fees due to any other officer of the court in the case, and, secondly, to the use of the creditors.

The fees of officers other than registers must be paid as the services are rendered. In lieu thereof, however, the clerk may accept a written undertaking with surety to his satisfaction, for the payment of such fees; in which case for all fees remaining sixty days unpaid, *scire facias* may isssue against the principal and surety on such undertaking.

Marshal's Fees.

22. Under No 6 of the forms of proceeding in bankruptcy promulgated by the supreme court, providing for a notice to each creditor, containing the "names of the several creditors of the bankrupt, with their places of residence and amount of their debts respectively," to be made and given by the marshal, he shall be allowed, in addition to the fees by law prescribed for such notices and for the service thereof, the sum of ten cents for every one hundred words and figures contained in so much of said notice as

describes the names of the several creditors of the bankrupt, with their place of residence and the amount of their debts, respectively, to be allowed and paid to him as other legal fees are allowed and paid.

Bank of Deposit.

23. The Indianapolis National Bank and such other national banks as shall hereafter be designated by the court, shall be banks of deposit under rule 24th of the general orders in bankruptcy promulgated by the supreme court.

OTTUMWA, IOWA, *Oct.* 15*th,* 1870.
A. W. GAZZAM, ESQ., UTICA, N. Y.
SIR : We have no published rules in bankruptcy in this state. I am, therefore, not able to furnish you with a copy.
Very respectfully,
J. M. LOVE.

TOPEKA, KANSAS, *Oct.* 17*th,* 1870.
AUDLEY W. GAZZAM, ESQ., UTICA, N. Y.
We have no printed rules in bankruptcy.
Respectfully yours,
MARKEO DELAKAY.

KENTUCKY.

Present—Hon. Bland Ballard, judge.
The court adopted rules regulating proceedings in bankruptcy, as follows, viz. :

Filing of Petitions.

RULE 1. The petitioner may file his petition with the clerk at any place in his district where the court may be held by law.

Reference of Petitions.

2. In voluntary bankruptcy, the petition shall be referred, of course, to the register of the congressional district in which the petitioner resides or carries on business, but a petition may be otherwise refused by the court for special reasons. The register to whom the petition is referred shall receive a surrender from the bankrupt, substantially, in the following form :
"I, A. B., bankrupt, by these presents surrender all my property and effects as required by the act of congress. A. B."

And he shall, at the request of the bankrupt, issue to him a "grant of protection," substantially, in the following form :

"A. B. having filed his petition in bankruptcy, and the same having been referred to me, I do, by authority of the fourth and twenty-eighth sections of the bankrupt act, grant him protection against arrest during the pendency of the proceedings in bankruptcy, in any civil action, unless the same is founded on some debt or claim, from which his discharge in bankruptcy would not release him. *Register.*

In involuntary bankruptcy the register will be designated with reference to the special circumstances of each case.

The order, Form No. 4, shall specify the place where the register shall act in the case, and the warrant, Form No. 59, shall specify the place where the meeting of the creditors will be held, and, in either case, the place so specified shall be one of the places designated by the register as the locality of his office.

Each register may have as many offices in his district as he may deem proper, and he shall designate the locality of each by a writing filed with the several clerks of the district court in this district. The day named in the order, Form No. 4, for the attendance of the bankrupt before the register, and the day named in warrant, Form No. 59, for the meeting of the creditors, will be fixed with reference to the convenience and speedy progress of the case.

Every register may, in any case referred to him, fix the times when he will act upon the several matters arising in such cases other than the attendance of the bankrupt as fixed by order, Form No. 4, and the meeting of the creditors, as fixed by the warrant, Form 59; but the register shall not, without leave of the court, change the place named in the order, Form No. 4, or the place specified in warrant, Form No. 59.

Adjudication of Bankruptcy.

3. The adjudication of bankruptcy, Form No. 58, shall contain a provision that the case be referred to one of the registers, naming him, to take such proceedings thereon as are required by the act.

Fees of Register.

4. Whenever a petition is referred to a register, the clerk at the time he delivers to the register a copy of the order of reference, shall deliver to him the fifty dollars, deposited with the clerk, under section forty-seven of the act, the same, whether delivered to him by the petitioner or the clerk, to be applied to the payment of such fees of the register, clerk, and marshal, as are chargeable to the petitioner making the deposit. If the fees exceed fifty dollars, those chargeable to the petitioner shall be paid, or secured in like manner with the other fees provided for by rule 29 of the "general orders in bankruptcy."

Where, however, under rule 30 of the "general orders in bankruptcy," the judge shall direct that the fees and costs in the cose shall not exceed the sum required by the act to be deposited, and the fees and costs properly chargeable, but for said order, exceed such sum, the disbursements paid out by the register and marshal for the purposes specified in rule 12 of the "general orders in bankruptcy," and returned by them as chargeable to the petitioner, shall be refunded to them severally out of such sum, and the remainder shall be applied *pro rata* to the payment of the fees of the clerk, marshal, and register, who shall in such case perform the duties required of them, without first requiring security or payment for their fees.

The marshal, clerk, and register, in such last named cases, shall report to the court their fees and charges on the first Monday in April, July, October and January.

Certificate of Register to Form of Petition.

5. The register shall, under rule 7 of the "general orders in bankruptcy," examine a duplicate copy of the petition and schedules specified in Form No. 4—and such duplicate copy shall either be a *copy* of such *original*, certified by the clerk, under the seal of the court, or a *duplicate original*, signed and verified in a like manner, with original petition and schedules, filed with the clerk, and shown by evidence satisfactory to the register to be such duplicate original, and the certificate of the register required by rule 7, as to correctness in form of the petition and schedules, shall be made and signed by him on the duplicate, which he so examines; and he shall not issue any warrant under Form No. 6, until he shall have so made a certificate, after such examination. No such certificate shall be

made unless the whole eleven sheets composing schedules A and B, in Form No. 1, form part of the schedule to the petition.

Publication of notice.

6. The warrant issued under section 11 or section 42 of the act, according to Form 6 or Form 59, shall specify one newspaper in or nearest the county in which the debtor has resided or carried on business, and one published daily in Louisville, in which notices shall be published. The election of such papers to be made by the register to whom the petition in the case is referred, and such notice shall be published twice in each newspaper elected.

The notices to creditors, under Forms 6 and 42, shall be by mail, unless otherwise ordered, for good cause specified in the warrant.

No creditor, resident out of this district, shall be designated for personal service.

The warrant, Form No. 6, shall be regarded as process under rule 2 of the general orders in bankruptcy, and such warrant shall, before it is issued to the marshal, in addition to being signed by the clerk, and sealed with the seal of the court, be countersigned by the register at the foot thereof in the following form, with the date, viz:

"Issued by me,   , 18   .
,
Register in Bankruptcy.

Whenever Form No. 10 is used by the register, the conclusions thereof may be varied, so that it may be attested or signed by the register alone.

Proofs of Debts Prior to Election of Assignee.

7. All proofs of debts which shall be made and verified prior to the election or appointment of an assignee, shall be delivered or sent to the register to whom the case is referred. If the register entertains doubts of the validity of any claim, or of the right of the creditor to prove it, and is of opinion that such validity or right ought to be investigated by the assignee, he may postpone the proof of the claim until the assignee is chosen.

Assignee.

8. In case no choice of assignee is made by the creditors at their first meeting, or in case an assignee, chosen by the creditors, fails, within five days, to express in writing his acceptance of the trust, or in case of a vacancy in the office of assignee, caused by removal, death, or otherwise, Richard M. Moseby, Esq., of the city of Louisville, or Stephen E. Jones, Esq., of the same city, will be appointed assignee, when the judge is required by the act to appoint the assignee; and when either of them shall be appointed by any register, such appointment is hereby approved by the judge. In special cases, a vacancy in the office of assignee will be filled by an election by the creditors, or by the appointment of an assignee other than above named.

Notice of Acceptance by Assignee.

9. Under rule 9 of the "general orders in bankruptcy," the assignee shall notify the register of his acceptance or rejection of the trust, and the register shall, immediately on receiving such notice, report it to the clerk of the court.

Copy of Assignment by Clerk.

10. Every assignee shall, immediately on receiving an assignment of an estate in bankruptcy send or deliver such assignment to the clerk of the court, who shall make a true copy of it, and certify such copy under his hand and the seal of the court, and such certified copy shall be placed and kept by him on file, and the original returned to the assignee.

Notice of appointment of Assignee.

11. Notice of the appointment of an assignee shall be given by publication in the same newspapers as the notices to creditors were given, once a week for three successive weeks.

Assignee's Notice of Sales.

12. Notices of sale by an assignee, under rule 21 of the "general orders in bankruptcy," shall be published in the same newspaper as the notices to creditors are published.

Notice of Dividends or Meetings.

13. The notice to creditors of dividends or meetings required by the 17th, 27th and 28th sections of the act, shall be such as is provided for by the order contained in Form No. 28, and the assignee shall select one of the newspapers (in which the previous notices were published), in which this notice shall be published.

Debts Certified by Register.

14. The list of debts provided for by section 23 of the act shall be made and certified by the register, to whom the petition is referred, and he shall place thereon all debts which are duly proven.

Vouchers of Assignee.

15. The assignee shall, under section 27 of the act, produce and file vouchers for all payments made by him, except as to items, in regard to which the court shall, for reasonable excuse, dispense with vouchers.

Notice to Creditors.

16. The notice by the assignee under section 28 of the act of the filing of his account, and of his application for a settlement and discharge shall be given by him by sending written or printed notices by mail, prepaid, of such filing, and of the time of such application to all known creditors of the bankrupt.

Trial of Objections to Discharge.

17. The questions of fact specified in writing, under section 31 of the act, by a creditor opposing the discharge of a bankrupt, shall be tried at a stated session of the court, on ten days' notice of trial, to be served by either party upon the other party, and upon the clerk, and a balance of the same shall be kept.

Verifications of Applications.

18. The application under section 34 of the act, to set aside and annul a discharge, shall be verified by the oath or affirmation of the applicant, and answer of the bankrupt to the application shall answer specially the allegations of the application, and shall be verified in like manner.

Jury Trial.

19. The demand in writing for a trial by jury under section 41 of the act, shall be signed by the debtor or his attorney.

Issues of Law and Fact.

20. When any issue of fact or law is raised and contested by any party to the proceedings before a register, and is stated and adjourned into court for decision, as provided in section 4 of the act, the writing stating such issue shall be sent to the clerk, in whose office the petition under which the question arises was filed. And the issue so stated and adjourned will be disposed of by the court only when the judge is present at such place; but points and matters certified to the judge under section 6 will be disposed of by him at any time when the certificate is delivered or sent to him, and is accompanied with postage stamps sufficient to satisfy the postage on the answer, if any is required to be sent by mail.

On all points and matters so certified, the register shall briefly state his own opinion, either in the certificate or in a writing attached thereto.

All decisions by the judge, of the points and matters certified, shall be entered by the register in his docket, and he shall forward a certified copy of the same to the clerk, at the time, and in the manner that he is required to forward other proceedings.

Banks of Deposit.

21. In pursuance of rule 28 of the "general orders in bankruptcy," the following banks in this district are designated as those in which all moneys received by assignees or paid into court in the course of any proceedings in bankruptcy shall be deposited, viz: " First National Bank of Paducah; Henderson National Bank; First National Bank of Louisville; First National Bank of Covington; Lexington City National Bank; First National Bank of Lexington; and Clark County National Bank of Winchester; Farmer's National Bank of Richmond; Central National Bank of Danville."

All moneys received by the clerk of the court on account of any bankrupt estate, or paid into court in the course of any proceedings in bankruptcy, (except the sums deposited with the clerk, under section 47 of the act,) shall be deposited in one of said banks, and all sums received by an assignee on account of any estate of which he is assignee shall be deposited in such one of said banks as he shall select, by a writing signed by him and filed with the clerk.

The check or warrant for drawing moneys deposited by the clerk shall be signed by the clerk and countersigned by the judge. The check or warrant for drawing moneys deposited by an assignee, shall be signed by him and countersigned by the register designated to act in the case of the estate on account of which such moneys are deposited.

Publication of Notices.

22. The marshal and the clerk, and every register or assignee, when required to publish any notice or advertisement, shall preserve and return to the court a copy cut from each newspaper in which it is published, of each notice and advertisement as published, with a certificate as to the particulars of the publishing, showing that the required publication has been made.

Continuance.

23. In case of the absence of the judge at the time and place noticed or appointed for any hearing or proceeding before him in bankruptcy, or if the matter then fails to be called or acted on, the same shall be deemed continued, without other order, to the next sitting of the court thereafter, at which time the like proceedings may be had thereupon as if first noticed or appointed for such day.

Notices by Mail.

24. All notices served or sent by mail shall be so written, or printed and folded, that the directions, postage stamp, and post mark shall be upon the notice itself, and not upon an envelope or other separate piece of paper, and when returned as not called for, shall be delivered to the clerk or register, to be filed with the papers of the case.

Special Cases.

25. Special cases not comprehended within the foregoing rules, or the "General Orders in Bankruptcy," or the forms, shall be submitted to the judge.

Form and Shape of Papers.

26. The petition, schedules, and all other proceedings in bankruptcy, shall be written or printed upon "flat cap paper," with a blank space at the top, convenient for binding.

27. Whenever a paper is required to be sent or delivered to the clerk, it shall be sent or delivered to that clerk in whose office the original petition to which the paper relates was filed.

Clerk District Court.

CLERK's OFFICE, UNITED STATES COURTS, KENTUCKY DISTRICT, LOUISVILLE, KY., *April 15th*, 1871.

A. W. GAZZAM, ESQ.,
New York City:

DEAR SIR:—In answer to yours of 20th March, 1871, addressed to his honor, the judge, I send you first, a certificate of discharge used in our court here previous to the enactment of amendments to the bankrupt law, marked 1. Numbers 2, 3 and 4 are certificates of discharge which we now use and have since the amendments made to the bankrupt law. I also send you rules in equity and common law cases in bankruptcy recently adopted by this court.

Very respectfully, &c.,
W. H. MERIWETHER, Clerk.
By ERNEST TROLL, D. C.

DISTRICT COURT OF THE UNITED STATES.

District of Kentucky, (at   ) Sct.

Whereas,   has been duly adjudged bankrupt, under the act of congress establishing a uniform system of bankruptcy throughout the United States, and appears to have conformed to all the requirements of law in that behalf, it is therefore ordered by the court, that said   be forever discharged from all debts and claims which by said act are made provable against   estate, and which existed on the   day of   eighteen hundred and sixty   , on which day the petition for adjudication was filed by   excepting such debts, if any, as are by said act excepted from the operation of a discharge in bankruptcy.

Given under my hand and the seal of the court at   in the said district, this   day of   , A. D. eighteen hundred and sixty

, *Judge.*

District of Kentucky, (at Louisville,) Sct.

Whereas,   has been duly adjudged a bankrupt, under the act of congress establishing a uniform system of bankruptcy throughout the United States, and appears to have conformed to all the requirements of law in that behalf,

It is therefore ordered by the court, that said   be forever discharged from all debts and claims which by said act are made provable against his estate, and which existed on the   day of   eighteen hundred and seventy   on which day the petition for adjudication was filed by   excepting such debts, as were contracted on or after the 1st day of January, 1869, and such, if any, as are by said act excepted from the operation of a discharge in bankruptcy.

Given under my hand and the seal of the court at Louisville, in said district, this   day of   A. D. eighteen hundred and seventy   .

    , *Judge.*

District of Kentucky, (at Louisville,) Sct.

Whereas,   has been duly adjudged a bankrupt, under the act of congress establishing a uniform system of bankruptcy throughout the United States, and it appearing that his assets are equal to fifty per centum of the claims proved against his estate, upon which he is liable as principal debtor, and appears to have otherwise conformed to all the requirements of law in that behalf,

It is therefore ordered by the court, that said   be forever discharged from all debts and claims which by said act are made provable against his estate, and which existed on the   day of   eighteen hundred and seventy   on which day the petition for adjudication was filed by   excepting such debts, if any, as are by said act excepted from the operation of a discharge in bankruptcy.

Given under my hand and the seal of the court at Louisville, in said district, this   day of   A. D. eighteen hundred and seventy   .

    , *Judge.*

District of Kentucky, (at Louisville,) Sct.

Whereas,   has been duly adjudged a bankrupt, under the act of congress establishing a uniform system of bankruptcy throughout the United States, and has filed the assent in writing of a majority in number and value of his creditors, to whom he is liable as principal debtor, who have proved their claims, and appears to have otherwise conformed to all the requirements of law in that behalf, *It is therefore ordered by the court,* that said   be forever discharged from all debts and claims which by said act are made provable against his estate, and which existed on the   day of   , eighteen hundred and seventy   , on which day the petition for adjudication was filed by   , excepting such debts, if any, as are by said act excepted from the operation of a discharge in bankruptcy.

Given under my hand and the seal of the court, at Louisville, in said district, this   day of   A. D., eighteen hundred and seventy

    Judge.

LOUISIANA.

Adopted by the Hon. Edward H. Durell, judge of the district court of the United States for the district of Louisiana, July 15, 1867.

RULE 1. In voluntary bankruptcy, where the petition states that the debtor, whether an individual, a copartnership, a corporation or a joint stock company, has resided or carried on business for the six months next immediately preceding the time of filing the petition, or for the longest period during such six months, in the district of Louisiana, the petitions shall be referred, according to Form No. 4, to the register of the congressioual district within which the bankrupt resides. A petition may be otherwise referred for special reasons, or in cases not herein provided for. In involuntary bankruptcy, the register may be designated with reference to the special circumstances of each case. But in case no designation is made, cases will be referred as in voluntary bankruptcy. The order, Form No. 4, designating the register to act upon the petition in voluntary bankruptcy shall specify as the place where the register shall act upon the matters arising under the case, and the warrant, Form No. 59, in involuntary bankruptcy, shall, in a like case, specify as the place where the meeting of the creditors will be held, the office of the register, as designated by him by a writing filed with the clerk. The day named in the order, Form No. 4, for the attendance of the bankrupt before the register, in voluntary bankruptcy, and the day named in the warrant Form No. 59, for the meeting of creditors in involuntary bankruptcy, will be fixed with reference to the speedy and convenient progress of the case.

Every register may, in any case referred to him, fix the times when he will act upon the several matters arising under such case, other than the attendance of the bankrupt, as fixed by the order, Form No. 4, and the meeting of creditors as fixed by the warrant, Form No. 59; but the register shall not, without leave of the court, be at liberty to change the place specified in the order, Form No. 4, or to act upon the matters arising under a case in involuntary bankruptcy at any other place than the one specified in the warrant, Form No. 59, as the place for the meeting of creditors.

2. The adjudication of bankruptcy, Form No. 58, shall contain a provision that the case be referred to one of the registers, as provided by rule No. 1, naming him to take such proceedings thereon as are required by the act.

3. Whenever a petition is referred to a register in a voluntary case, and whenever, in an involuntary case, an order is made on an adjudication of bankruptcy, referring the case to a register, the clerk, at the time he sends or delivers to the register a copy of the order of reference, shall pay to him the sum of twenty-five dollars out of the fifty dollars deposited with the clerk under section 47 of the act, the same to be applied to the payment of such fees of the register as are chargeable to the petitioner making the deposit. Whenever, by a return made to the court by the register, of the fees so chargeable for services rendered by him, it shall appear that the aggregate amount of such fees exceeds the aggregate payments made thereon to the register out of the fifty dollars, the clerk shall, if requested by the register, make further payments to him thereon to the amount of such fees, until the fifty dollars shall all of it be paid out, and thereafter the fees of the register which are chargeable to such petitioner shall be paid or secured in like manner with the other fees provided for by rule 29 of the "general orders in bankruptcy."

The foregoing provisions of this rule shall not apply to a case at voluntary bankruptcy, where, under rule 30 of the "general orders in bankruptcy," the judge shall direct that the fees and costs in the case shall not exceed the sum required by the act to be deposited with the clerk; but in every such case such of the disbursements paid out by the register and marshal for the purposes specified in rule 12 of the "general orders in bankruptcy," and returned by them under oath, under said rule 12 as one chargeable to the petitioning debtor, shall be refunded to them severally by the clerk out of such sum; and the clerk, marshal, and register shall perform the duties required of them by such petitioning debtors without first requiring payment or security for their fees, subject to the application by the court to the payment of such fees. of so much of such sum as shall remain after refunding such disbursements.

4. The register shall under rule 7 of the "general orders in bankruptcy," examine the duplicate copy of the petition and schedules specified in Form No. 4, and such duplicate copy shall either be a copy of such filed original, certified by the clerk under the seal of the court, or else a duplicate original, signed and verified in like manner with the original petition and schedules filed with the clerk, and shown by evidence satisfactory to the register to be such duplicate original; and the certificate of the register required by said rule 7 as to the correctness in form of the petition and schedules shall be made in writing, and be signed by him, on the duplicate copy which he so examines, and he shall not issue any warrant under Form No. 6 until he shall have so made a certificate, after such examination, that the petition and schedules are correct in form. No such certificate shall be made unless the whole eleven of the sheets composing schedules A and B, in Form No. 1, constitute part of the schedules to the petition.

5. The warrant issued under section 11 or 42 of the act, according to Form No. 6 or Form No. 59, shall specify two of the newspapers named in rule 20 of these rules. The notices to be published in pursuance of the warrant shall be published twice in each newspaper selected. The warrant shall designate the creditors on whom personal service is to be made, and notice shall be

served by mail upon all creditors other than those so designated. No creditor resident, out of this district shall be designated for personal service. The warrant Form No. 6 shall be regarded as process under rule 2 of the "general orders in bankruptcy," and such warrant shall, before it is issued to the marshal, in addition to being signed by the clerk and sealed with the seal of the court, be signed by the judge or the register at the foot thereof, in the following form, with the date :

"Issued by me , 18

"*District Judge, or* "*Register in Bankruptcy.*"

6. All proofs of debts which shall be made, and verified prior to the election or appointment of an assignee shall be delivered or sent to the register to whom the case is referred. If the register entertain doubts of the validity of any claim, or of the right of a creditor to prove it, and is of opinion that such validity or right ought to be investigated by the assignee, he may postpone the proof of the claim until the assignee is chosen.

7. Under rule 9 of the " general orders in bankruptcy," an assignee shall notify the register of his acceptance or rejection of the trust, and the register shall immediately, on receiving such notice, report it to the clerk of the court.

8. Every assignee shall, immediately on receiving an assignment of an estate in bankruptcy, send or deliver such assignment to the clerk of the court, who shall make a true copy of it, and certify such copy under his hand and the seal of the court, and such certified copy shall then be placed and kept by him on file, and the original assignment shall be returned to the assignee.

9. Notice of the appointment of an assignee shall be given by publication once a week for three successive weeks in two of the newspapers named in rule 20, one of which shall be a newspaper published in the city of New Orleans, and the other to be selected by the register with due regard to the requirements of section 14 of the act, and in accordance with rule 20 of these rules.

10. Notices of sale by an assignee under rule 21 of the "general orders in bank-

ruptcy," shall be advertised in two of the newspapers named in rule 20, one of which shall be a newspaper published in the city of New Orleans, and the other to be selected by the register with due regard to the requirements of section 14 of the act, and in accordance with rule 20 of these rules.

11. The notice to creditors of dividends or meetings, required by the 17th, 27th and 28th sections of the act, shall be such as is provided for, by the order contained in Form No. 28, and shall be published in the newspapers designated in rule 20, and according to the provisions of said rule.

12. The list of debts provided for by section 23 of the act shall be made and certified by the register to whom the petition or case is referred, and he shall place thereon all debts which are duly proved.

13. The assignee shall, under section 27 of the act, produce and file vouchers for all payments made by him, except as to items in regard to which the court shall, for reasonable cause, dispense with.

14. The notice by the assignee, under section 28 of the act, of the filing of his accounts, and of his application for a settlement and discharge, shall be given by him by sending written or printed notices by mail, prepaid, of such filing, and of the time of such application, to all known creditors of the bankrupt.

15. All questions for trial or hearing, under sections 31 and 34 of the act, shall be tried or heard at a stated session of the court, on four days' notice of trial or hearing, to be served by either party upon the other party, or his attorney, and upon the clerk, and a calendar of the same shall be made.

16. The application, under section 34 of the act, to set aside and annul a discharge, shall be verified by the oath or affirmation of the applicant, and the answer of the bankrupt to the application shall answer specifically the allegations of the application, and shall be verified in like manner.

17. The demand in writing for a trial by jury, under section 41 of the act, shall be signed by the debtor or his attorney.

18. All issues, questions, points, and matters stated in writing, under rule 11 of the "general orders in bankruptcy," under the 4th section or the 6th section of the

act, or according to Form No. 50, and adjourned into court for decision, or stated in a special case for the opinion of the court, shall be certified to the judge by the register by a certificate which shall also state briefly the opinion of the register on the issue, question, point, or matter, and shall be delivered or sent to the clerk; and no oral or written argument shall be allowed on any such issue or question, unless by special lease of the court.

19. In pursuance of rule 28 of the "general orders in bankruptcy," the Louisiana National Bank in this district is designated as that in which all moneys received by assignees or paid into court in the course of any proceeding in bankruptcy shall be deposited. All moneys received by the clerk of the court on account of any bankrupt estate, or paid into court in the course of any proceeding in bankruptcy (except the sums deposited with the clerk under section 47 of the act), shall be deposited in said bank, and all sums received by an assignee on account of any estate of which he is assignee shall be deposited in the said bank; the check or warrant for drawing moneys deposited by the clerk shall be signed by the clerk and countersigned by the register designated to act in the case of the estate on account of which such moneys were deposited.

20. The laws of the United States having made it the duty of the house of representatives to select three papers in the state of Louisiana in which "all such advertisements as may he ordered for publication in said district, by an United States court, or judge thereof, or by any officer of such courts, or by any executive officer of the United States, shall be published," and the said clerk having, in compliance with the law, designated the New Orleans Republican, the New Orleans Tribune, and the Homer Iliad as such newspapers, they are hereby designated as those in which all publications required by the act, or the "general orders in bankruptcy," or these rules, may be made, namely: every advertisement in proceedings in bankruptcy, required to be published, shall be inserted in the New Orleans Republican; in cases where a notice is required to be inserted in more than one newspaper, it shall also be published in either the New Orleans Tribune or the Homer Iliad, "due regard being had to the general circulation in the district, or in that portion of the district in which said bankrupt and his creditors reside." The marshal and the clerk and every register or assignee, when required to publish any notice or advertisement, shall preserve and return to the court a copy, cut from such newspaper in which it is published, of each notice and advertisement as published, with a certificate as to the particulars of the publishing, showing that the required publication has been made.

21. In case of the absence of the judge at the time and place noticed or appointed for any hearing or proceeding before him in bankruptcy, or if the matter then fails to be called or acted on, the same shall be deemed continued, without other order, to the next sitting of the court thereafter, at which time the like proceedings may be had thereupon as if first noticed or appointed for such day.

22. If the marshal shall, under rule 13 of the "general orders in bankruptcy," appoint special deputies to act as messengers, he shall, as far as possible, designate one or more of such special deputies to be attached to the office of each register, for the purpose of causing the notices to be published and served, which are specified in the warrants issued in the cases referred to such register.

23. All notices, served or sent by mail by the marshal, the clerk, or an assignee, shall be so written or printed and folded, that the direction, postage stamp, and post mark, shall be upon the notice itself, and not upon an envelope or other separate piece of paper.

24. Special cases not comprehended within the foregoing rules, or the "general orders in bankruptcy," or the forms, shall be submitted to the judge.

CONGRESSIONAL DISTRICTS.

An Act to divide the state of Louisiana in five Congressional Districts.

SECTION 1. *Be it enacted by the senate and house of representatives of the state of Louisiana, in general assembly convened,* That until otherwise directed by law, the state shall be divided into five congressional districts, as follows, and the qualified electors of each district shall chose one representative:

The First Congressional District

shall comprise the parishes of St. Bernard and Plaquemines, the right bank of the parish of Orleans, the ninth, eighth, seventh, sixth and fifth representative districts of the parish of Orleans, and that portion of the fourth representative district of the parish of Orleans which is included between St. Louis, Rampart and Canal streets, and the lake Pontchartrain.

The Second Congressional District

shall comprise that portion of the fourth representative district of the parish of Orleans which is included between St. Louis, Rampart and Canal streets, and the Mississippi river, third, second and first representative districts of the parish of Orleans, and that portion of the tenth representative district of the parish of Orleans which is known and designated by existing statutes as the tenth ward of the city of New Orleans.

The Third Congressional District

shall comprise that part of the tenth representative district of the parish of Orleans which is known and designated as the eleventh ward of the city of New Orleans, and the parishes of Jefferson, Washington, St. Tammany, St. Helena, Livingstone, St. Charles, St. John the Baptist, St. James, Ascension, East Baton Rouge, East Feliciana, West Feliciana, Terribonne and Lafourche.

The Fourth Congressional District

shall comprise the parishes of Natchitoches, Sabine, Rapides, Calcasien, St. Landry, Vermillion, Aroyelles, Point Coupee, Lafayette, St. Martin, West Baton Rouge, Iberville, Assumption and St. Mary.

The Fifth Congressional District

shall comprise the parishes of Bossier, Claiborne, Union, Morehouse, Carroll, Rienville, Jackson, Ouachita, . Caldwell, Franklin, Madison, Teusas, Concordia, Calahoula, Winn, Caddo and De Soto.

Approved, April 4, 1865.

Adopted November 26, 1869:

25. Immediately upon the adjudication of bankruptcy by the court or a register in bankruptcy, the bankrupt or the marshal (as the case may be), in every case shall make a surrrender of the assets and estate embraced in schedule B, and all the property not therein embraced, to an assignee to be appointed by the court, of whose appointment and qualification due notice will be given by the clerk of this court.

Order Concerning Examination of Bankrupts before Discharge, made November 17, 1869.

Ordered, That before the discharge of any bankrupt is granted, that the assignee in person or by his attorney, shall examine the bankrupt under section 26 of the act, before the register of this court in that case. That notice of the day for examination shall be given in the order for the creditors to show cause why the discharge should not be granted, which day shall be prior to the day for the hearing upon the question of discharge.

CLERK'S OFFICE, U. S. DIST. CT. LA.

I certify the foregoing to be true copies from the minutes of said court.

December 25th, 1870.

NOVEMBER TERM, A. D. 1869.

For New Orleans, Wednesday, the 12th day of February, 1870.

Rule in Bankruptcy.

Whereas, it appears that petitions for adjudication of bankruptcy are sometimes filed by or against supposed bankrupts with no intention on the part of the petitioner to proceed with the cause at once, and whereas, delay in such cases may work great injustice and inconvenience to persons dealing with such supposed bankrupts in ignorance of such petitions and to creditors and others.

It is ordered, that all bankrupts petitioning for the benefit of the act shall prosecute the proceedings with due diligence, and if any such petitioners shall fail to procure an adjudication and warrant, and to give the warrant to the marshal for service within twenty-one days from the day of his petition, the petition shall be dismissed on motion, unless there be good cause for the delay, or unless some one or more of his creditors shall undertake to carry on the proceedings. And if any creditor petitioning for proceedings against a supposed bankrupt shall, unless for good cause, fail to apply for an order of notice to the debtor, within five days after filing his petition, it shall be dismissed, unless some other creditors shall have undertaken to prosecute the petition.

FEBRUARY TERM, A. D. 1870.

New Orleans, Friday the 29th day of April, 1870.

Rule in Bankruptcy.

Ordered, That that part of the order of the court adopted January 31st, 1868, ordering the clerk of this court to assign bankrupt cases in rotation to the registers, be revoked and set aside. *And it is further ordered,* that rule first, adopted by this court on the 15th day of July, 1869, be so amended as to allow petitioners in a voluntary bankruptcy and petitioning creditors in an involuntary bankruptcy case, to have his or their case referred to the register of his or their choice.

MAINE.

1. *Ordered* : That the following rules and orders be prescribed and adopted as rules and orders, governing proceedings in bankruptcy and forms adopted by the justices of the supreme court of the United States.

Rules in Bankruptcy.

RULE 1. It being necessary that there should be a uniformity in the blanks used in bankruptcy proceedings, *it is ordered,* that the clerk procure all the necessary blanks, and furnish the same at reasonable rates to parties requiring them, and that no other blanks than those so furnished by the clerk be received by the registers, or used in any proceeding in bankruptcy, or allowed to become a part of the files of the court.

2. In voluntary bankruptcy, the petition shall be referred to the register in the congressional district in which the petition states the debtor has resided or carried on his business for the six months next immediately preceding the time of filing his petition, or for the longest period during said six months. A petition may for special reasons be otherwise referred, and in involuntary bankruptcy, the register will be designated with reference to the special circumstances of each case.

3. The certificate of the register required by rule 7 of the general orders in bankruptcy, as to the correctness in form of the petition and schedules, shall be made in writing and be signed by him on the copy furnished him, and he shall not issue any warrant under Form No. 6, until he shall have made a certificate after such examination, that the petition and schedules are correct in form. No such certificate shall be made, unless all of the sheet composing schedules A and B, Form No. 1, make part of the schedules to the petition.

4. Each register will hold monthly sessions in each county in his district, the time and place of such sessions to be designated by him, by a notice filed with the clerk and approved by the judge. The places so designated shall constitute the office of the register in such county, where the meeting of the creditors shall be held, and the register shall act upon the other matters arising in the case unless otherwise directed. Every register may in any case referred to him, fix the time when he will act upon the several matters arising in the case, unless otherwise ordered by the judge.

5. The register shall select a newspaper published in the county stated in the petition as the one in which the debtor has resided or carried on his business, in which newspaper all notices required in the cause shall be published. The newspaper making the lowest proposals for such advertising shall be entered, due regard being had as to its conclusion. Notices of meetings of creditors must be published once a week for two successive weeks, the first publication to be at least ten days before the meeting; the same notice must be given of the bankrupt's application for discharge. When notice is published in a daily paper, it must also be published once at least in the weekly issue, if any of the same paper. Notice of appointments of assignees, must be published at least once a week for three successive weeks.

The marshal, clerk, and every register or assignee, when required to publish any notice or advertisement, shall preserve and return to the court a copy cut from each newspaper in which it is published of each notice and advertisement as published, with a certificate as to the particulars of the publishing, showing that the required publications have been made.

6. All process issued in blank by the clerk to the register shall bear the certificate of the register of the date when the same is issued by him.

7. In all cases where the estate of the bankrupt in the opinion of the register will exceed one thousand dollars, the assignee, before entering on his duties, shall give bond to the United States with a condition for the faithful discharge of his duties, in such sum and with such sureties as shall be approved by the judge or one of the registers by his endorsement thereon.

8. Either party desiring to be heard on any matters certified to the judge by a register for decision, must forthwith notify the clerk, and the same will be set down for a hearing at as early a day as is practicable. If either party is not ready on the day assigned, unless for good cause, the question will be disposed of without argument from the party in default. The register will in all cases certified to the judge, inform the parties of this rule, and will also advise the judge of his opinions on matter so certified.

9. The following banks are designated as depositaries in bankruptcy, viz: Canal National Bank of Portland, First National Bank of Auburn, Freeman's National Bank of Augusta, Rockland National Bank of Richland, Merchant's National Bank of Bangor. All moneys received by assignees or paid into court in the course of any proceeding in bankruptcy, must be deposited in one of said banks under the 28th rule established by the supreme court for proceedings in bankruptcy, and a strict compliance with the requirements of said rule must be observed in all cases by all parties. Separate accounts must be kept with the estate of each bankrupt, and all moneys must be deposited to the credit of the district court of the United States. In bankruptcy Estate of A. B., bankrupts   C. D., assignee.   E. F., *Register*.

All checks drawn on Canal National Bank, by the assignee, must be countersigned by J. D. Fessenden, assignee.

All checks drawn on First National Bank, Auburn, by an assignee, must be countersigned by Seth May, register.

All checks drawn on Freeman's National

Bank, Augusta, by an assignee, must be countersigned by S. S. Marble, register.

All checks drawn by an assignee on the Rockland National Bank, must be countersigned by Peter Shacher, register.

All checks drawn on Merchant's National Bank, Bangor, by an assignee, must be countersigned by Charles Hamlin, register.

The signature of the judge of the district court may be substituted for that of any register.

10. The evidence in all cases to be heard by the judge must be taken before a register or commissioner, and oral testimony on any disputed matter will not be received at the hearing.

11. A special court of bankruptcy will be holden on first Monday of each month at ten o'clock A. M., excepting during the month of August, and such other times as the judge may necessarily be absent from the city.

12. In addition to the fifty dollars required by the 47th section of the act, there shall be deposited with the clerk, upon the filing of the petition, not less than ten dollars to meet the clerk's fees, and not less than ten dollars to meet the marshal's fees in each case.

13. Whenever a debtor shall desire to be discharged from his liabilities as a member of his copartnership, as well as from his individual indebtment, Form No. 1, as prescribed by the rules and orders of the supreme court, shall be altered by setting forth therein a description of such firm, with the name and places of residence of the copartners, and shall pray for the discharge of the petitioner from his liabilities as a member of such firm.

Ordered, That the following additional rules in bankruptcy be adopted:

14. Whenever a petition is referred to a register in a voluntary case, and whenever in an involuntary case, an order is made on an adjudication of bankruptcy, referring the case to a register, the clerk, at the time he delivers to the register a copy of the order of reference, shall pay to him fifteen dollars out of the fifty dollars deposited with the clerk under section 47 of the act, to be applied to the payment of such fees of the register as are chargeable to the petitioner.

15. Applications for discharge in bankruptcy must be published three weeks suc-

cessively in two papers, to be designated by the register, the last publication to be thirty days at least prior to the day assigned for the hearing of the application.

16. That notice to creditors to appear and show cause why a discharge should not be granted the bankrupt, must be returnable at a special court, holden under rule 11 of this court. The second and third meetings of creditors under the 29th section of the act, may be holden previously on the same day.

17. Registers may issue the order prescribed by Form No. 51, and they shall transmit to the clerk a list of all the proofs of debt, in the case which have been furnished to the register or assignee, containing the names, residences, and post-office addresses the creditors, with sufficient particularity to enable the notices, Form No. 52, to be served properly by the clerk, who shall, as soon as practicable, mail the proper notices to such creditors.

18. The registers in each case referred to them, shall, on or before the return day specified in order Form No. 51, examine and certify to the court, as to the regularity of the proceedings in the cause, with a view to the petitioner's discharge.

19. All assignments shall have the seal of the court, and every assignee shall immediately, on receiving an assignment of an estate in bankruptcy, send or deliver such assignment to the clerk of the court, who shall make a true copy of it, and certify the same under his hand and the seal of the court, which copy shall be kept on file and the original assignment shall be returned to the assignee.

20. The register to whom the cause is referred, in all cases where there is no opposing interests, may pass all necessary orders respecting the disposal of the property of the bankrupt, under rules 21 and 22 of general orders, such orders of the register to be under the seal of the court, and attested by the clerk.

21. The register in charge of the cause, may designate the day of hearing by the judge, on the application of the bankrupt for his discharge, and issue an order of notice thereon, per Form No. 51. The original application and order of notice shall forthwith be filed with the clerk, who shall notify the creditors. Form No. 52, as now required by rule 17 of this court. If the second and third meeting of creditors have not been called, either under the provisions of the act or of rule 24 of general rules and orders, the register shall order such meeting to be called by the assignee, to be held a reasonable time previous to the time appointed for hearing of applications for discharge.

22. *Ordered,* That rule 10 in bankruptcy of this court, " that the evidence in all cases to be heard by the judgment, be taken before a register or commissioner, and oral testimony on any disputed matter will not be received at the hearing," be, and the same is hereby revoked and the following is substituted therefor : " The evidence in all cases to be heard by the judge may be taken, orally at the hearing, or by deposition according to law."

23. *Ordered,* That hereafter, in cases of order to show cause made according to Form No. 51 on petition of bankrupts for discharges from their debt, no meetings of the creditors except the first shall be ordered or held, unless some assets have come to the hands of the assignee, and all forms, rules and orders requiring second and third meetings in such cases are revoked.

24. The certificate of the register as to regularity of proceedings shall hereafter set forth the date of adjudication of bankruptcy, and whether as copartner in any firm, disclosing such firm.

The meeting of creditors, if held, and when, and that notice was duly given of each meeting.

The date of filing of petition for discharge, and when returnable, and style of copartnership if the petition prays for discharge from copartnership debts.

The notice ordered on petition for discharge, and whether the same was duly given, reciting dates of papers in which published.

Number of creditors who have proved their claims, and whether notice was given to all of time of hearing on petition for discharge.

The amount of assets returned by assignee, if any, if none to be so stated.

Date of final examination of bankrupt.

Date of oath of bankrupt required by 29th section.

Return of all papers to court by register.

Registers will hereafter be held responsible for the entire accuracy of all papers issued or received by them in course of any proceedings in bankruptcy; they will, therefore make a careful examination of papers when presented by other persons, and will not receive them if defective or inaccurate; the expense attending correcting such inaccuracies will be borne by the register in charge of the cause.

25. A decree of bankruptcy will not be superseded upon the bankrupt's petition in any case after filing his petition for discharge.

Prior to filing such petition the bankruptcy may be superseded upon petition of the bankrupt and the written assent of the assignee and all the creditors who have proved their claims, and upon notice for three weeks in the paper designated by the register for publication of the usual notices in the cause, and special notice by mail to all creditors named in schedules annexed to petition in bankruptcy.

The certificate of the register of a compliance with this rule must be produced on the return day of the notice of the petition.

26. A creditor desiring an examination of a bankrupt must apply to the register for an order, according to Form No. 45; by petition duly verified, showing good cause for granting of the order; the examination must be completed and filed with the clerk, on or before the return day of the petition for discharge, unless the time shall be extended by the judge; the examination will not be ordered after such return day excepting on application to the judge, and for special causes verified by affidavit.

27. Specifications of grounds of opposition to a discharge of the bankrupt must be filed within ten days of the appearance of the objecting creditor, and will be disposed of at the next succeeding return day, unless the time shall be extended for cause supported by affidavit; if the creditor is in default the objection will be overruled; if the bankrupt is in default, a hearing will be had *ex parte*, on the objections filed.

MARYLAND.

At a district court of the United States of America, for the district of Maryland, held at the city of Baltimore, in and for said district, on the 26th day of October, in the year of our Lord one thousand eight hundred and sixty-seven:

Ordered, That the following rules, orders and regulations be prescribed as rules governing proceedings in bankruptcy in the district court of the United States for the district of Maryland, under the act entitled "An act to establish a uniform system of bankruptcy throughout the United States," approved March 2d 1867, in addition and with reference to the "general orders in bankruptcy," and the forms specified in the schedules thereto annexed, framed by the justices of the supreme court of the United States, in pursuance of the tenth section of said act, and adopted by said court, and promulgated May 16, 1867.

RULE 1. In voluntary bankruptcy the petitious will be referred by Form No. 4 to the register of the congressional district in which the debtor resides, (or if a copartnership, a corporation or joint stock company,) has resided or carried on business. In involuntary bankruptcy, the register will be designated with reference to the special circumstances of each case. Every register may, in any case referred to him, fix the times when he will act upon the several matters arising under such case other than the attendance of the bankrupt, as fixed by the order, Form No. 4, and the meeting of creditors as fixed by the warrant, Form No. 59, but the register shall not, without leave of the court, be at liberty to change the place specified in the order, Form No. 4, or to act upon the matters arising under case of involuntary bankruptcy at any other place than the one specified in the warrant, Form No 59, as the place for the meeting of the creditors.

2. The adjudication of bankruptcy, Form No. 58, shall contain a provision that the case be referred to one of the registers, naming him, to take such proceedings thereon as are required by the act.

3. Whenever a petition is referred to a register in a voluntary case, and whenever, in an involuntary case, an order is made on an adjudication of bankruptcy, referring the case to a register, the clerk, at the time he sends or delivers to the register a copy of the order of reference, shall pay to him the fifty dollars deposited with the clerk under section 47 of the act, to be applied to the payment of such fees of the register as are chargeable to the petitioner making the de-

posit, an account of which fee shall be certified by the register unto court; and if said fee shall not amount to the said sum of fifty dollars, the balance shall be returned by the register to the clerk, to be applied under the order of the court to any other expense in the case, but whenever, under rule 30 of the "general orders in bankruptcy," the judge shall direct that the fees and costs in the case shall not exceed the sum required by the act, to be deposited with the clerk, such of the disbursements paid out by the register and marshal for the purposes specified in rule 12 of the "general orders in bankruptcy," and returned by them under oath, under rule 12, as are chargeable to the petitioning debtor, shall be refunded to them severally by the clerk, out of such sum; and the clerk, marshal, and register shall perform the duties required of them by such petitioning debtor without first requiring payment or security for their fees, subject to the application by the court to such fees of so much of such sum as shall remain after refunding such disbursements.

But before the court will pass any order directing that the fees and costs shall not exceed the sum required by the bankrupt act to be deposited with the clerk, it will require the debtor to be orally examined before it, except where he resides at a distance from the city of Baltimore, in such cases the court will require the deposition or depositions of third parties as to the inability of the petitioner to pay the fees.

4. The register shall, under rule 7 of the "general orders in bankruptcy," examine the duplicate copy of the petition and schedules specified in Form No. 4, and such duplicate copy shall either be a copy of such filed original, certified by the clerk under the seal of the court, or else a duplicate original, signed and verified in like manner with the original petition and schedules filed with the clerk, and shown by evidence satisfactory to the register to be such duplicate original, and the certificate of the register required by said rule 7 as to the correctness in form of the petition and schedules shall be made in writing and be signed by him, on the duplicate copy which he so examines; and he shall not issue any warrant under Form No. 6 until he shall have so made a certificate, after such examination that the petition

and schedules are correct in form. No such certificate shall be made unless the whole eleven of the sheets composing schedules A and B, in Form No. 1, form part of the schedules to the petition.

5. The warrant issued under section 11 or 42 of the act, according to Form No. 6, or Form 59, shall specify two, if there be two, and if not, then one of the newspapers named in rule 21, published in the county stated in the petition as the one in which the debtor, whether an individual, a copartnership, a corporation or a joint stock company, has resided or carried on business for the six months next immediately preceding the time of filing the petition, or for the largest period during such six months, the selection of such newspapers to be made by the register to whom the petition or case is referred. The notices to be published in pursuance of the warrant, shall be published twice in each newspaper selected.

The warrant shall designate the creditors on whom personal service is to be made, and notice shall be served by mail upon all creditors other than those so designated. No creditor resident out of this district shall be designated for personal service.

The warrant, Form No. 6, shall be regarded as process under rule 2 of the "general orders in bankruptcy," and such warrant shall, before it is issued to the marshal, in addition to being signed by the clerk and sealed with the seal of the court, be countersigned by the judge, or register, at the foot thereof. Whenever the order, Form No. 10, is used by a register the conclusion of said form may be varied so that the order may be attested or signed by the register alone.

6. All proof of debts which shall be made and verified prior to the election or appointment of an assignee, shall be delivered or sent to the register to whom the case is referred. If the register entertains doubts of the validity of any claim, or of the right of a creditor to prove it, and is of opinion that such validity or right ought to be investigated by the assignee, he may postpone the proof of the claim until the assignee is chosen.

7. In case no choice of an assignee is made by the creditors at their first meet-

ing, the court will appoint the person receiving the greatest number of votes and representing the largest amount of debts, voting at said meeting. In special cases where an assignee, chosen by the creditors, fails within five days to express in writing his acceptance of the trust, or in case of a vacancy in the office of an assignee, caused by removal, resignation, death or other cause, the same will be filled by the court, or in its discretion by an election by the creditors, in the manner provided for in the 13th and 18th sections of the act.

8. Under rule 9 of the "general orders in bankruptcy" an assignee shall notify the register of his acceptance or rejection of the trust, and the register shall immediately, on receiving such notice, report it to the clerk of the court.

9. Every assignee shall, immediately on receiving an assignment of an estate in bankruptcy, send or deliver a duplicate thereof to the clerk of the court, which shall be placed and kept with the papers in the case.

10. Notice of the appointment of an assignee shall be given by publication once a week for three successive weeks in two of the newspapers named in rule 21, at least one of which shall be a newspaper published in the city of Baltimore.

11. Notices of sale by an assignee under rule 21 of the "general orders in bankruptcy," shall be advertised in two, if there be two, and if not, then in one of the newspapers named in rule 21, published in the county where the sale is to take place.

12. The notice to creditors of dividends or meetings, required by the 17th, 27th and 28th sections of the act, shall be such as is provided for by the order contained in Form No. 28, and the register shall select one newspaper, in which the notice shall be published, from among the newspapers specified in rule 21.

13. The list of debts provided for by section 23 of the act, shall be made and certified by the register to whom the petition shall be referred, and he shall place thereon all debts which are duly proved.

14. The assignee shall, under section 27 of the act, produce and file vouchers for all payments made by him, except as to items in regard to which the court shall, for reasonable cause, dispense with vouchers.

15. The notice by the assignee, under section 28, of the act, of the filing of his account, and of his application for a settlement and discharge, shall be given by him by sending written or printed notices by mail, prepaid, of such filing, and of the time of such application, to all known creditors of the bankrupt.

16. All questions for trial or hearing, under sections 31 and 34, of the act, shall be tried or heard at a stated session of the court, on four days' notice of trial or hearing, to be served by either party upon the other party, *and upon the clerk, and a calendar of the same shall be made.*

17. The application under section 34, of the act to set aside and annul a discharge, shall be verified by the oath or affirmation of the applicant; and the answer of the bankrupt to the application, shall answer specifically the allegations of the application, and shall be verified in like manner.

18. The demand in writing for a jury, under section 41 of the act, shall be signed by the debtor or his attorney.

19. All issues, questions, points and matters stated in writing, under rule 11, of the "general orders in bankruptcy," or under the 4th section or the 6th section of the act, or according to Form No. 50, and adjourned unto court for decision, or stated in a special case for the opinion of the court, shall be certified to the judge by the register by a certificate, which shall also state briefly the opinion of the register on the issue, question, point or matter, and shall be delivered or sent to the clerk; and no oral or written argument shall be allowed on any such issue or question, unless by special leave of the court.

20. In pursuance of rule 28 of the "general orders in bankruptcy," the following national banks in this district are designated as those in which all moneys received by assignees or paid into court in the course of any proceedings in bankruptcy, shall be deposited, namely:

National Bank of Baltimore.
National Bank of Easton, Maryland.
National Farmers' Bank, Annapolis.
First National Bank of Hagerstown.

All moneys received by the clerk of the court on account of any bankrupt estate, or paid into court in the course of any proceedings in bankruptcy, except the sums deposited with the clerk, under section 47 of the act, shall be deposited in said bank, in the city of Baltimore; and all sums received by an assignee, on account of any estate of which he is assignee, shall be deposited in such one of said banks, as he shall select by a writing to be signed by him, and filed with the clerk.

21. The following newspapers are designated as those in which all publications required by the act, or the "general orders in bankruptcy," or these rules may be made, namely:

In Baltimore city, the Daily Gazette and American.
In Allegany County, Alleganian.
In Anne Arundel County, Republican.
In Baltimore County, Maryland Journal.
In Cecil County, Democrat.
In Carroll County, Westminster Advocate.
In Caroline County, Denton Journal.
In Calvert County, Calvert Journal.
In Charles County, Port Tobacco Times.
In Dorchester County, Democrat.
In Frederick County, Frederick Examiner.
In Harford County, the Belair Ægis.
In Howard County, Howard County Record.
In Kent County, Kent News.
In Montgomery County, Rockville Sentinel.
In Prince George County, the Marlboro Gazette.
In Queen Anne County, Centreville Observer.
In Somerset county, Herald.
In St. Mary county, St. Mary Beacon.
In Talbot county, The Easton Star.
In Worcester county, The Shield.
In Washington county, The Maryland Free Press.

The marshal and the clerk, and every register or assignee, when required to publish any notice or advertisement, shall preserve and return to the court, a copy cut from each newspaper in which it is published, of each notice and advertisement as published, with a certificate as to the particulars of the publishing, showing that the required publication had been made.

22. In case of the absence of the judge, at the time and place noticed or appointed for any hearing or proceeding before him in bankruptcy, or if the matter then fails to be called or acted on, the same shall be deemed continued, without other order, to the next sitting of the court thereafter, at which time the like proceedings may be had thereupon, as if first noticed or appointed for such day.

23. If the marshal shall, under rule 13, of the "general orders in bankruptcy," appoint special deputies to act as messengers, he shall as far as possible, designate one or more of such special deputies to be attached to the office of each register, for the purpose of causing the notices to be published and served, which are specified in the warrants issued, in the cases referred to such register.

24. All notices served or sent by mail by the marshal, the clerk or an assignee, shall be so written or printed and folded, that the direction, postage stamp and post mark, shall be upon the notice itself; and not upon an envelope or other separate piece of paper.

25. Upon application by the petitioning debtor to the register for leave to amend his petition and schedules, where such amendments are not contested, the register may allow such amendments to be made, observing the provisions of rules 14 and 33, of the "general orders in bankruptcy." The register shall file with the clerk the original amendments permitted to be made. When they are so filed, the register will act upon them, in conformity with rule 7 of said "general orders in bankruptcy," and rule 4 of this court in bankruptcy.

26. Special cases not comprehended within the foregoing rules, or "general orders in bankruptcy," or the forms, shall be submitted to the judge.

DECEMBER 31, 1867.

27. That in all future applications for a discharge by a bankrupt under the 29th section of the act, the bankrupt will file his petition with the clerk, who will thereupon send a copy of the same with the court's order thereon to the register who has the case in charge, and all proceedings under said petition shall be held before said register, who will certify the same to the court, together with the oath required to be taken by the bankrupt, and upon his certificate that the bankrupt has complied with all the requirements of the said act, the court will sign his certificate of discharge, if there be no creditors opposing the same.

JANUARY 8, 1868.

28. In all cases where there is property or assets returned hy a bankrupt, the assignee or assignees will be required to give a bond as required by the 13th section of the bankrupt act, in double the amount of the value of such property or assets, within ten days after the acceptance of the trust, which amount shall be ascertained by the register, and the bond approved by him.

MARCH 25, 1868.

29. *Ordered*, That hereafter in cases of order to show cause, made according to Form No. 51, on petitions of bankrupts for discharge from their debts, no meeting of creditors except the first shall be ordered or had unless some assets have come to the hands of the assignee ; but where in any such case any assets have come to the hands of the assignee, then the order to show cause shall contain a permission under general order No. 25, for the holding of the second and third meeting of the creditors, and for notices therefor.

MASSACHUSETTS.

Ordered, That the following rules and orders are hereby prescribed, governing proceeding in bankruptcy in this district :

RULE 1. The following national banks are designated as depositaries in bankruptcy, under rule 28 of the general order, promulgated by the superior court, viz: For deposits by the clerk, The Revere National Bank of Boston. For deposits by register and assignees. :

Dist.

1. The National Bank of Commerce of New Bedford.
2. Neponset National Bank of Canton.
3. The Globe National Bank of Boston.
4. The Union National Bank of Boston.
5. Salem National Bank, Salem.
6. The National Pemberton Bank of Lawrence.
7. The old Lowell National Bank.
8. Mechanics' National Bank, Worcester.
9. The First National Bank of Amherst.
10. Pittsfield National Bank.

2. Every assignee shall, immediately upon receiving an assignment of an estate in bankruptcy, send or deliver the same to the clerk of the court, who shall make and certify a true copy thereof under his hand and the seal of the court, and such copy shall then be placed and kept by him on file, and the original assignment shall be returned to the assignee.

3. Registers shall call the attention of all assignees in their respective districts, to the tenor of rule 28 of the general orders, and of the above rule of this court, shall notify them that a strict compliance with those rules is expected.

4. Whenever a debtor shall desire to be discharged from his liabilities as a member of a copartnership, (the firm not being in bankruptcy,) as well as from his individual liabilities, Form No. 1, as prescribed by the supreme court, shall be altered by setting forth therein a description of such firm, with the names and places of residence of the partners, and shall pray for the discharge of the petitioner from his liabilities as a member of such firm.

5. The deposit of $50 shall be made with the clerk before the order of reference to the register shall be issued.

6. For custody of deposits, keeping accounts thereof, and drawing orders and checks, the clerk shall be paid a fee of one dollar in each case.

7. In each case in bankruptcy in which the first meeting of creditors shall have been held, the clerk shall deliver to the register, to whom the said case shall have been referred, the sum of twenty-five dollars from the deposit of fifty dollars made in said case.

8. The three preceding rules may be modified by the court whenever the circumstances of any case may require it. Such additional fees as are allowed by law to the register, shall be paid by the parties liable by law to pay the same.

9. Before a debtor makes application to the court to order that the fees and costs in his case shall not exceed the sum required to be deposited, he shall give the clerk, the marshal and the register, to whom the case has been or is to be referred, at least five days' notice in writing of his intention to make such application ; such application shall be in writing, and sworn or affirmed to by the debtor, and he shall be present when

said application is presented to the judge, and may be examined on his oath or affirmation in respect to his means and his ability to pay the fees and costs prescribed by said act.

10. The order of notice upon bankrupt's petition for discharge, shall be published in two newspapers once a week for three weeks. Tuesday and Friday of each week shall be the days for hearings, designated in the orders on bankrupt's petition for discharge.

11. Entry of appearance to oppose a bankrupt's discharge, will in all cases be presumed to be waived, unless the specification of the grounds of opposition be filed, or further time be applied for within the ten days allowed by general order No. 24 of supreme court rules.

12. Whenever at any meeting of the creditors of a bankrupt the allowance of any debt or claim offered for proof shall be objected to in whole or in part, the register may, if he deem it expedient, require the objection to be fully stated, and the evidence on both sides to be forthwith produced before him, and shall report the evidence and his views of the case to the court as soon as may be. And whenever it shall appear that frivolous objections are made to the proof of debts, the court will make such order concerning costs as may be just and expedient.

13. For cause shown in any special case leave may be granted to any creditor to examine the bankrupts before the appointment of the assignee. After the assignee is appointed any creditors who may obtain an order for the examination of the bankrupt shall notify the assignee thereof, and the assignee shall attend the examination and take care that it is as thorough and complete as may be necessary. The assignee and any creditor may carry on and continue any such examination as fully and effectually as the creditor at whose petition it is obtained, subject to all proper regulations concerning the costs and expenses thereof, and to such other regulations as to the time and manner of the examination as the register may find convenient. No second order for a general examination of any bankrupt will be granted as of course, but an order therefor may be refused, or so restricted and modified in the matter of inquiry, or otherwise, as the justice of any case may require. Nor will any order for

examination be granted as of course unless applied for within five months after adjudication of bankruptcy, and in those cases in which the bankrupt has a right to ask for his discharge, before the expiration of five months, the order for examination shall be applied for before the return day upon the bankrupt's application for discharge upon good cause shown for the delay, the order may be issued after those periods.

14. Contested motions and hearings in bankruptcy of which the party desiring to be heard shall have given four days' written notice to the adverse party, will be taken up on Saturday mornings at ten o'clock, or as soon after that hour as motions in criminal cases shall have been disposed of; the clerk shall keep a list of such hearings for each Saturday in the order in which he shall have been notified thereof by either party, and the cases will be called by the court in that order.

15. Whenever an order for a meeting of creditors is issued by a register he shall forthwith send in a notice thereof to the clerk of the court for his information and that of the court in the premises.

16. No order to show cause shall be issued on any petition for a bankrupt's discharge until the second and third meetings of the creditors of said bankrupt shall have been ordered, and the return day of any such order shall be at least two days after the time appointed for such third meetings.

17. WHEREAS, It appears that petitions for adjudication of bankruptcy are sometimes filed, by or against supposed bankrupts with no intention on the part of the petitioner to proceed with the cause at once; and whereas delay in such cases may work great injustice and inconvenience to persons dealing with such supposed bankrupts in ignorance of such petitions and to creditors and others, it is *ordered*, that all bankrupts petitioning for the benefit of the act, shall prosecute the proceedings with due diligence, and if any such petitioner shall fail to procure an adjudication and warrant and to give the warrant to the marshal for service within 21 days from the day of filing his petition, the petition shall be dismissed on motion, unless there be good cause for the delay, or unless some one or more of his creditors shall undertake to carry on the proceedings. And if any creditor petitioning

for proceedings against a supposed bankrupt, shall, unless for good cause, fail to apply for an order of notice to the debtor within five days after filing his petition, it shall be dismissed unless some other creditor shall have undertaken to prosecute the petition.

18. Excepting as hereinafter provided, hearings on questions of the discharge of bankrupts will be had before the court in their order on the docket at some convenient time in each term. Either party may set down the case for hearing by notice to the clerk and to the adverse party, on or before the first day of any term. When both parties agree thereto an order will issue to a register or commissioner to take all the evidence and report the same to the court.

When either party desires a trial by jury, he shall move for issues to be framed therefor on some motion day on due notice, and in season to allow the trial, if one should be ordered to be had before the jury which may be in session at or first after the time of filing the specifications unless cause be shown for the delay. Trials by the court will be upon the competent evidence whether oral or written which may be then offered by either party, or upon the evidence taken by the register as the case may be.

December 8th, 1868.

19. Whenever an order for a meeting of creditors is issued by a register, he shall forthwith send in a notice thereof to the clerk of the court, for his information, and that of the court in the premises.

November 25th, 1868.

20. Cases in bankruptcy will be referred to the register in whose district the bankrupt, or if copartners, the major part of them reside. Cases of partners whose residences are equally divided between different districts will be regulated by reference in rotation to the several registers, so as to secure equality in the numbers of references as nearly as may be. To effect this purpose within the city of Boston, the ward of the city in which each bankrupt resides shall be stated in the petition or in an affidavit to be filed before the cause is referred.

This order is directory merely and will be carefully observed, but is not to affect the jurisdiction of any register in any cause, or under any circumstances.

March 2d, 1869.

21. It is ordered, that at each general meeting of creditors of bankrupts, after the first and at each adjournment thereof, it shall be the duty of the assignee or assignees in each case to exhibit and deliver to the register all proofs of debts received by them from any register, other than the one holding such meetings, unless he shall have already done so. And at each meeting the register shall exhibit to the creditors present a list of all debts proved since the last preceding meeting, and any person interested may at any such meeting take objection to the proof of any debt so exhibited, as fully as he might or could have done had said debt been then first offered for proof, subject always to such terms and conditions concerning notice to the proving creditor as may fully secure his right to be heard therein.

22. Objections to the approval of any assignee who shall be duly elected, must be made in writing, specifying fully the reasons of objection, and be filed with the register at the meeting at which the election is had, and the register shall proceed at once or as soon thereafter as may be practicable and consistant with a due hearing, to take all evidence that may be offered pertinent to such objections, and whether for or against the appointment, and shall report the same to the court. Further evidence or argument will not be heard by the court unless in special cases and for satisfactory reasons.

Sept. 9th, 1869.

23. At or before any bankrupt takes the oath prescribed by section 28 of the statute, it shall be the duty of the register to require the bankrupt to answer under oath whether he has ever before been discharged under the bankrupt act of March 2nd, 1867, and to make return to court of his answer thereto.

24. In all cases of involuntary bankruptcy in which the bankrupt is absent or cannot be found, it shall be the duty of the petitioning creditor to furnish to the marshal on oath within five days after the day of the adjudication, a schedule giving the names and places of residence of all the creditors of said bankrupt, according to the best information of said petitioning creditor. If the debtor is found and served with notice to furnish a schedule of his creditors and fails to do so, the petitioning creditor may apply for an

attachment against the debtor, and in default of such application shall furnish such schedule as aforesaid.

25. The registers may authorize assignees to make sales of assets not being lands or other real estate and of which the value is found to be less than $800, at private sale, upon good cause shown and when there is no opposition. To be binding and conclusive as between creditors and the assignee, such sales should be made after notice to them.

26. It shall be the duty of the register to see that the cash expenses in each case which by section 28 of the statute are a first charge upon the assets, are paid by the assignee before his accounts are allowed.

MICHIGAN.—Western District.

RULE 1. When the "general superintendence and jurisdiction" authorized to be exercised by the second section of the "act to establish a uniform system of bankruptcy throughout the United States," approved March 2, 1867, is intended to be invoked, the party so intending shall file in the office of the clerk of circuit court a petition verified by affidavit setting forth briefly the facts of the case and the relief sought, and he shall at the same time deposit such sum of money as the clerk shall deem necessary to cover the costs, or in lieu thereof the clerk may in his discretion take an undertaking which he shall deem sufficient for that purpose.

The clerk shall thereupon in a book to be kept for such proceedings, docket the case and enter in order, that the adverse party, within time, to be fixed by the order, file an answer verified by affidavit if he desires to answer, and a copy of such order, with a caption, stating the style of the case and that it is bankruptcy, shall thereupon be served by the marshal upon such adverse party. The marshal's return of service shall be in the following form :

A. B. v. C. D., Cri. Ct., U. S. West. Dist. Mich., in bankruptcy. I served the order in this case dated   day of   , A. D. 18 , by (state the manner of service). E. F., marshal. Fees, .

Upon filing of the answer the petitioner may reply under oath within a time to be fixed by the clerk upon his application. ·

2. The counsel of the petitioner at the time of filing shall file also a brief, setting forth the points and authorities intended to be relied upon. If the counsel for the adverse party desires to submit a brief he shall file it within the time fixed for the filing of the answer. The counsel for the petitioner may submit a closing brief within a time to be fixed by the clerk. The time fixed by the clerk as aforesaid may be enlarged by the written argument of the parties, or their counsel, filed with the clerk.

3. When the case is ready to be submitted the clerk shall transmit the papers to the circuit judge.

4. If either party shall desire to be heard in oral argument he shall notify the other party and the circuit judge as early as may be, and thereupon the judge will fix a time and place for such argument.

5. When the decision of the judge is made the clerk shall enter it in the proper book and transmit a certified copy to the district court.

6. The petition mentioned in the foregoing rule No. 1 shall be filed within ten days from the filing of the order complained, unless the time shall be extended by the district judge, by an order filed with clerk within the said ten days.

A failure to file the petition in the time shall be held to be a waive of the right to file the same, and none shall be filed thereafter.

August 5th, 1867.

IN THE DISTRICT COURT, }
WESTERN DISTRICT OF MICHIGAN. }

Ordered, Petitions in bankruptcy requested by general order 4 to be referred to one of the registers, shall, unless otherwise specially ordered, be referred to the register appointed in the congressional district within which the petitioner resides, except when the petitioner resides in the county of Eaton, the reference shall be to the register of the fourth congressional district. In involuntary bankruptcy the register shall be designated with reference to the special circumstances of each case.

Ordered, All notices of proceedings in bankruptcy required to be published, shall, when the petitioner resides in the second congressional district, be published in the Kalamazoo Telegraph and Kalamazoo Gazette. When the petitioner resides in the fourth congressional district, be published in the Grand Rapids Eagle, and the Grand Rapids Democrat, unless otherwise specially ordered. Notice to be published in pursuance of warrant according to Form No. 6, or Form No. 59, shall be published twice in each newspaper designated in the warrant.

Ordered, The First National Bank of Grand Rapids, and the Michigan National Bank of Kalamazoo, are hereby designated as deposit banks under general order 28.

November 23d, 1870.

UNITED STATES DIST. COURT,
WESTERN DISTRICT OF MICHIGAN.

Ordered, That no petition shall be filed by a non-resident petitioning creditor to obtain an adjudication of bankruptcy against his debtor, unless the petition shall first be indorsed by the name of an attorney or councellor authorized to practice in the circuit or district courts, upon whom papers in the case in any subsequent stays of the proceedings may be served. This rule will not deprive a non-resident party from appearing in person to conduct the proceedings under general order 3. And in case of a resident petitioning creditor, the petition shall be indorsed either by the name of an attorney or counselor by the name of the petitioner, or prosecuting in person.

MISSISSIPPI.

Preparation of Papers.

RULE 1. No paper shall be received or filed of less size than a full size leaf of foolscap. The different form, composing Schedules A and B respectively, shall be fastened together in some convenient form, and if the same is not so done when filed, the clerk shall arrange and fasten such schedules, for which he shall be allowed a fee of fifty cents.

2. The petition and affidavits thereto, shall compose one document, schedule A one document, and schedule B one document. The certificate by the clerk, of the day and hour upon which the same were filed, shall only ne necessrry to be endorsed on the back of each document as aforesaid.

Order of Reference.

3. Unless otherwise specially ordered, each petition and schedules accompanying the same, shall be referred to the register of the district in which the petitioner, a bankrupt, shall reside, according to Form No. 4, at the place stated in the order heretofore made, provided that references heretofore made at Lupelo and Aberdeen shall be made at Okolowa, but may be adjourned by the register, to such other place as he may believe will convenience himself and the parties interested.

Duplicate Petitions and Schedules.

4. The duplicate copies of the petition and schedules required to be filed with the register shall be either a copy certified by the clerk to be such, or shall be verified by the affidavit of the petitioner or his attorney, that he has composed the same with the petition and schedules filed with the clerk, and that it is a true copy thereof; which copy so attested shall be by the petitioner or his attorney, filed with the register at the time and place designated in the order of reference, but the register may pass the adjudication at such time and place as he may appoint after the papers are filed with him and may then make any preliminary order necessary therein.

Publication of Notices.

5. Unless otherwise specially ordered, the register to whom the cause is referred shall designate one newspaser in which all publications of notices required to be made in the cause shall be made, which shall be one of the newspapers approved by the clerk of the House of Representatives of the Congress of the United States, unless the act of Congress, in relation thereto, shall be repealed, and shall be such one of said newspapers as said register shall believe will give notice to the greatest number of the parties interested therein. Provided, that no notice of the first meeting of creditors shall be within less than ten days of the time of meeting and shall not exceed two insertions, and if two, they shall be in different weeks, and but one insertion in notice of final discharge, unless specially ordered, which shall be ten days previous to such meeting.

Assignees and their Duties in relation to Exempt Property.

6. Assignees shall, as soon as they have received the deed of assignment, deliver the same to the clerk who shall take a copy thereof and certify the same under the seal of the court, to be filed by him with the papers in the cause, and return the original to the assignee. The assignee shall, so soon as he receives the schedules from the register, or within as short a time as he well can proceed to the residence of the bankrupts and take possession of the estate, of every description, and shall immediately allot and set off to the bankrupt, to be thereafter excepted from further proceedings in bankruptcy, unless otherwise ordered by the court for good cause shown, (1.) All his wearing apparel and that of his wife and children. If the bankrupt is or has been a soldier in the military service of the United States, his uniform, arms and equipments. (2.) All the property exempt by the laws of the state of Mississippi from seizure by execution or of administration in the year 1864; which consists of the following articles, or so much thereof as the bankrupt may have surrendered. The tools of a mechanic necessary for his trade; the tools of a laborer necessary for his employment; the agricultural implements necessary for two male laborers. The school books of a family, or a student, and the books, maps and globes used by teachers in schools, academies and colleges; the libraries of attorneys at law, physicians and ministers of the gospel, not exceeding two hundred and fifty dollars in value. The arms and accoutrements of the enrolled militia of the state. If the head of a family, or housekeeper, the following: one work horse or mule, four cows and calves, twenty head of stock hogs, one hundred and fifty bushels of corn, twenty bushels of wheat or rice, eight hundred pounds of pork or bacon, one yoke of oxen, one cart or wagon, and if a householder with a family, the land and buildings occupied as a residence, not, however, to exceed one hundred and sixty acres in quantity, or fifteen hundred dollars in value. Should the value of the buildings, or so much thereof, with the grounds as may be necessary for a homestead, exceed the value of fifteen hundred dollars, and the same cannot be separated

from the other real estate connected therewith, without manifestly impairing its value, the assignee shall report the same to the register at his next regular sitting at the place to which said cause stands referred, of which he shall give five days' notice to the bankrupt, when the register shall take in writing any proof that be offered by either party, and shall make such order in relation thereto as he may deem proper and just, which order shall be subject to exemptions by either party, or by any creditor who may have proved his debt, when the exceptions and proof shall be forwarded to the judge for his decision and direction. (3.) The assignee shall allot and set off in like manner such other articles of family necessity as he may deem reasonable, having due regard to the number and condition of the family, provided the same does not exceed in value the sum of five hundred dollars. These articles must be articles of *real family necessity* at the time, not such as may only become so in the future, or are only articles of convenience or luxury. The assignee shall report his proceedings in the following form :

IN THE DISTRICT COURT OF THE UNITED STATES
FOR THE NORTHERN DISTRICT
OF MISSISSIPPI.

In the matter of

Bankrupt.

To the judge of said court:

The undersigned, assignee of said bankrupt, on the day of   18 , proceeded to the residence of said

and after having examined the property surrendered by him in pursuance of the act of congress, and rules of the court, designated and set apart to said bankrupt, to be retained by him as his own, the property,

a particular description of which will be found in the accompanying schedule.

Sworn to and subscribed before me, this   day of   , 18 .

Assignee, etc.

Register.

The schedule will be made out according to Form No. 20, of general rules, and if unexcepted to, will be signed by the register, and a certified copy furnished to the bankrupt, he paying the fee for the same. The report so made out shall be filed with the register at the next regular sitting, at the place to which said cause stands referred, or is adjourned, and remain subject to exceptions by any party interested therein for twenty days, and if unexcepted to, will stand approved, without further order, but if excepted to, the register shall proceed to take proof thereon, offered by either party, and shall render his opinion on the same with such orders as he may deem proper, subject to exceptions by either party, when such report, proof and order shall be forwarded to the judge for his decision and direction. The allotting and setting apart the exempt property, must in all cases be done by the assignee himself, and cannot be by him delegated to another.

Sales and Compromises.

7. Assignees will, as soon as they conveniently can, sell the unincumbered property surrendered to them, for cash; if in the opinion of the assignee, the property will sell for as good or better price at public sale, he wi'l, if personal property, give ten days' notice, and if real estate twenty days' notice of the time and place of sale with a sufficient description of the property to be sold, which notice shall be (unless otherwise specially ordered by the register) by written advertisements or printed handbills, by the latter mode if the property is of greater value than one thousand dollars; and if in any case the supposed value of the property exceeds one thousand dollars, and the assignee is of the opinion that it will enhance the value thereof, he may advertise for not exceeding two weekly insertions, in the newspaper that will give the greatest publicity to those desiring to purchase; in addition to the other modes, the notice by written advertisements shall be by posting at not less than four public places, and if by printed posters, at a sufficient number of public places so as to give notice to the greatest number of probable bidders. When the assignee shall be satisfied that a more advantageous sale can be made privately than publicly, he shall receive such bids or offers as shall be made, in writing, signed by the person proposing to purchase, and shall report the same with the affidavits of two respectable witnesses, stating that they have examined the property, and believe the price offered a fair and reasonable one, or as much as could be obtained at public sale, to the register at the next regular setting at the place to which the cause stands referred; and unless exceptions shall be filed thereto within three days, or the register shall from his own knowledge, believe the sale should not be made, the same will stand approved without further order, but should exceptions be filed, the register will take such proof as may be offered by either party and render his decision thereon, subject to exceptions by any party in interest, when all the proceedings in relation thereto shall be certified and sent to the judge for his decision and direction, provided the assignee may sell at private sale, without first reporting the same as above, any articles not exceeding fifty dollars in value, if in his opinion, the price is as much as could be obtained at public sale, after deducting the expenses of a public sale. Public sales made under the first provision of this rule, will be reported to the register at his next regular sitting at the place to which the cause stands referred, to be subject to exceptions by any party in interest, for one day, and if unexcepted to, will stand approved without further order, but if excepted to, the like proceedings will be had as above provided in case of exception to private sales.

Incumbered Property and Secured Debts

When property is incumbered either by mortgage, vendor's lien, judgment lien, or otherwise, the assignee will take immediate steps to inform himself of the amount of the incumbrance, the value of the property incumbered, and all other facts connected therewith, which he will report to the register for such action as may be necessary for the disposition of all questions connected therewith. Upon such report being made, the register will proceed to make such orders as he may deem proper, first giving five days' notice to the party holding such lien or incumbrance of the time and place when and where said cause will be considered, unless the same shall be waived by such party, such order, when made, to be subject to exceptions as in other cases; when the register will proceed to take proof, and certify the questions and proof to the court for decision and direction.

Parties holding such incumbrance, a lien will be required to establish the same according to Form No. 21, adopted by the justices of the supreme court of the United States. In all cases in which property is sold for the satisfaction of secured debts, or in which proceedings are had in which the general creditors are not interested the costs of such sale or proceedings will be paid out of the fund realized thereby, or by the party for whose benefit they are had.

Of Debts and Choses in Action.

The assignee will, as soon as he can, proceed to collect all debts and claims due to the estate, and surrendered to him, and all other claims and right of action whether surrendered or not, which may have come to his knowledge, and when the same cannot otherwise be collected, will bring suit therefor, in the court of the district in which the debtor resides, *provided,* that when in his opinion the costs, expenses, and delay of such proceeding will, together with the uncertainty of realizing anything therefrom, not justify the same, he will make report thereof to the register to whom the cause is referred, together with any propositions of compromise which may have been offered, when the register will direct the compromise to be made, or a sale thereof, either by public or private sale, as he may deem most to the interest of the creditors of said estate; which will be conducted in all respects as sales of personal property. *Provided,* however, that the assignee may sell or compromise any debt or claim, the value of which does not exceed fifty dollars, without such report and order.

Of Perishable Property.

In all cases in which property surrendered by the bankrupt in his schedule is of a perishable nature, the marshal, as messenger, before the appointment of the assignee, or the assignee afterward, shall immediately apply to the register by petition, setting forth the property and its character, when, if in the opinion of the register it should be sold, he will so order, and prescribe the terms of sale.

Of Property to which the Title is in Dispute.

In all cases in which property has come into the possession of the assignee, the title to which is in dispute, the assignee shall report the same to the register to whom the cause stands referred, when the register will fix a time and place for hearing the same, and will cause the adverse claimant to be summoned, at least five days prior thereto, to appear and show cause, if any he has, why said property should not be sold, and the proceeds paid into court to abide such order as the court may make in reference thereto. If opposition is made, the register will take in writing such proof as may be offered thereon, and as he may deem right and proper, and upon the application of either party, will certify the same with the proof to the judge for his decision and direction thereon, and if the register or judge, as the case may be, shall order a sale of such property, the assignee will make and report such sale, subject to exceptions as in other cases, and after retaining the costs and expenses of such sale, will pay to the clerk of the court the remainder to be deposited and subject to the further order of the court in relation thereto.

Duties of Bankrupt in Relation to His Estate Before Delivering to the Assignee.

8. The petitioner shall take all reasonable and necessary care of the estate of every description, until it shall be delivered to the assignee, and if necessary will apply to the register or judge for such orders, and process as may be necessary to protect and secure the same.

Graining Crops and the Disposition to be made of the same.

9. Graining crops owned by the bankrupt at the time of filing his petition, will be scheduled as personal property, with a general description of the same. The assignee and bankrupt may agree themselves as to the value of the same, at the time of filing the petition, or may submit the same to references mutually chosen by them, which, soon as ascertained, will be a lien on such crop until the same is paid, and if not paid within a reasonable time after the maturity of the crop, will be taken possession of by the assignee, and so much of the same sold as may be necessary to pay the amount so due, and deliver the remainder

to the bankrupt, or if the bankrupt declines taking the crop upon those terms, the assignee will proceed to sell the interest so assigned to him, at public or private sale as he may deem best, to be made, reported and subject to exceptions as in the sales of personal property.

Reports and Settlements of Assignees.

10. Should no assets have been received by the assignee within sixty days from the date of adjudication, other than an amount sufficient to pay his costs, or that no debts have been proven against the estate of the bankrupt, he shall, upon application of the bankrupt, grant his certificate thereof, in the following form:

UNITED STATES   District,
       of Mississippi.

In the matter of
       Bankrupt.

I,   assignee of the estate of said bankrupt, do hereby certify that no assets thereof have been received by me, or that no debts have been proven against the same.
This   day of   , 18

              , *Assignee.*

Should assets more than sufficient to pay costs be received by the assignee, he will file with the register, within ninety days from the date of the adjudication, a report of the same, verified by affidavit, and will, on or before the day fixed for the second and third meeting of creditors, file with the register his final settlement, or, if not then prepared to make his final settlement, will file his report showing the condition of said estate, and his reasons for asking further time for making his final settlement; and the notice for the second and third meeting of creditors shall be deemed notice to all parties entitled to except thereto, to appear and file the same. Should the register be of the opinion that the reasons given for an extension of time in which to make final settlement are sufficient, he will fix a time and place when and where the same shall be made, which order shall be deemed sufficient notice to all parties entitled to except thereto, to appear and file the same. The register, when he deems it necessary, will examine the assignee on oath as to his administration of said estate. The assignee, unless otherwise specially ordered, will pay over to the clerk of the court, to be kept on deposit, any balance in his hands upon his first report, or final account to be subject to the further order of the court, and will not pay out any more except costs, without the order of the register or judge. The register shall examine the final account of the assignees and the vouchers submitted therewith. Each item of credit claimed (except for his own costs, or where the sum does not exceed five dollars) must be sustained by a voucher, and in no case in which the fees and compensation fixed by the act of congress, rules adopted by the justices of the supreme court, or by this court, shall a greater compensation be allowed, and the compensation for other services shall be only such as is reasonable. The assignee will, on or before the day fixed for the hearing of his final account, satisfy the register of his own affidavit or otherwise, that he has given notice of his appointment, as required by law.

Examination of bankrupts or other witness.

11. Whenever any creditor who may have before or then may prove his claim, and desires to examine the bankrupt, his wife, or other witnesses, in relation to matters stated in section 26 of the bankrupt act, he shall present to the register or judge a petition setting forth and specifying the acts, charges and matters upon which he desires such examination to be had, verified by his affidavit, when, if deemed sufficient by the register or judge, a certified copy of the same will be delivered to the bankrupt five days before the time fixed for such examination. The order for such examination, and all other proceedings therein, will be conducted according to Forms No. 45, 46, 48, and 49 of general rules. The same course will be pursued when the examination is had upon the part of the asssignee. The register will also proceed to examine the bankrupt, his wife, or other witnesses without application, whenever in his opinion it is necessary for the proper settlement of the estate and attainment of justice. Unless otherwise ordered by the court, no other examination than those above mentioned will be made.

Proceedings for final Discharge.

12. Petitions for final discharge, unless otherwise specially ordered, will be according to Form No. 51, general rules, and will be filed with the register, to whom the cause stands referred, who will thereupon enter the order of the court thereon, and for the second and third meeting of creditors according to Form No. 51, except that the meeting will be before the register as above, and will immediately forward a copy of the same, with a list of the creditors and their residences, to the clerk, who will give the notice by publication and by mail, according to Form No. 52, general rules, adding thereto, that the second and third meeting of the creditors will be had at the same time and place, and that the assignee's final account will be submitted for examination and allowance, or that no assets have come to the hands of the assignees, as the case may be.

At the time fixed to show cause, the register shall permit any person who may, before that time, have proved his debt, or who may then prove the same, and from which it shall appear that his interest will be expected by such dischrrge, to enter opposition thereto, which the register will enter on his docket and allow such opposing creditor ten days in which to file his specifications. Should the specifications only relate to irregularity in the proceedings, the register will cause the necessary amendments to be made, but should they embrace any of the causes stated in section 29 of the act, the register will examine the proceedings, and if in all other respects they have been regular, he will certify the same, together with all the papers to the cause, and transmit them to the clerk of the court for further proceedings; should no opposition be made on the day and hour fixed to show cause, the register will examine the proceedings, and if found in conformity to the act of congress, rules and orders made therein, will certify the same, and transmit the papers in the cause to the clerk. Should any material amendments be proved necessary, he will cause the same to be made, and certify the case for final discharge, as if no amendments had been necessary. When opposition is made and specifications are filed, either party may proceed to take testimony thereon, before the register or a commissioner of any United States court, by giving to the other party, or his attorney, five days' notice of the time and place of taking the same, if within the district, and if out of the district, and not over one hundred miles, ten days' notice, or if over one hundred miles, twenty days' notice of the time and place of taking such depositions.

Fees, Costs and Expenses of the Marshal

13. The marshal shall make out and verify his costs and expenses for executing the warrant No. 6, according to the form annexed thereto; when the warrant is not returned at the place where executed, the expense incurred making return will be added as part of the costs, but mileage will not be charged for the execution of this process. In the execution of all other processes under the bankrupt law, the marshal will be allowed five cents per mile for travel in going to and returning, to be paid by the party at whose instance the service is had, and to be taxed as part of the costs in the case; the marshal will not be required to execute such process without the payment of his fees; he will indorse on the back of the process the fees paid or due for such service; he will in all cases indorse the amount of fees received and by whom paid, and will pay over to the clerk any balance of funds paid him as fees, after the payment of such as may be due him, which sum will be subject to the payment of other fees due in the cause.

Of the Register.

The register will make out and forward with the papers sent to the clerk for final discharge, his fee bill, in which he will state the items of service with the fees charged for each, with the aggregate amount, the amount received, and from whom received, the balance due him, or the amount overpaid him. The register's fees fixed by the act of congress are as follows:

For issuing each warrant $2 00
For each day in which a meeting is held 3 00
For each order of a dividend 3 00
For each order substituting an arrangement by trust deed................ 2 00
For every bond with sureties......... 2 00

For every application for a meeting in any matter under this act.......... $1 00

For every days' service while actually employed under a special order of the court, to be allowed by the court, a sum not exceeding.............. 5 00

For taking depositions, the fees now allowed by law, for each folio of 100 words............................ 20

Under the general rules adopted by the justices of the supreme court, the following :

For each certificate of copy of proceedings in bankruptcy .... $ 25

For each folio of 100 words......... 10

For every order made when notice is required to be given, and for certifying copy of the same to the clerk... 1 00

For every certificate of question to be certified to the district judge, under the 4th and 5th sections of the act.. 1 00

For every proof of debt by the creditor or his attorney................. 1 25

Where testimony of the parties is taken, the fees prescribed by law. In addition to the above the register will be allowed the following fees for specific services rendered under these rules :

For examining papers, passing adjudication and certificate.............. $2 00

Order appointing assignee and deed of assignment...... 90

Auditing final account of assignee, and order of discharge................. 2 00

Each order of sale.................. 1 00

Each written opinion upon exceptions, filed for making out and certifying his fee bill 75

All postage and express fees :

For each day in which a meeting of creditors is held................... 3 00

The second and third meeting of creditors. when held on the same day, is but one meeting, or a meeting in which but one fee can be charged.

For one days' service upon the order to show cause against the discharge, including examination of papers and certificate........................ $5 00

Traveling expenses 2 00

Final discharge.................... 2 00

Making up minutes................. 1 00

Making pro rata distribution......... 2 00

For every other service not mentioned above, such fees as may be deemed reasonable by the court.

In all cases in which exceptions are filed before the register to reports, applications for the examination of witnesses, opposition to final discharge and all other cases in which an issue is made with the bankrupt or assignee, the party taking the same will, if required by the officer called upon to perform such service, pay the fees therefor before they shall be required to perform the service, or may deposit with the register a sufficient sum to pay the cost of such proceedings, which will be taxed and paid by the register, to be refunded by the opposite party, or paid out of the estate, if the question shall be decided in favor of the party instituting such proceedings.

Of the Assignee.

Assignees will, in their accounts, state such item of service for which compensation is claimed, and will be allowed under the bankrupt act the following fees and commissions :

For all sums of money received and paid out by him therein, for any sum not exceeding one thousand dollars, five per centum ; for all sums over one thousand dollars, and not exceeding five thousand dollars, two and one-half per centum ; and for all sums over five thousand dollars, one per centum.

The following fees are allowed for specific services under these rules :

For setting off exempt property, and reporting the same................ $5 00

For travel in going to and returning from the residence of bankrupt, for each mile so traveled............. 5

For making out and mailing notice to the newspaper, and all services connected therewith.................. 50

For advertising sale.... .... 2 00

When sale is made at any other place than the county site of the county in which the assignee resides, for each mile of the distance going to and returning from the county site to place of sale. 50

When the bankrupt resides in a different county from the county in which the assignee resides, then five cents per mile from the county site of the county of the bankrupt to the place of sale, and in compensation for travel in going to and returning from the residence of the bankrupt, in setting off exemptions, where the bankrupt and assignee reside in different counties, mileage will only be allowed from the county site of the bankrupt to his residence.

For reporting each sale.............. $1 00

Where notice of sales are made by printed handbills, or newspaper advertisements, the cost of the same in addition to the paying, and for all necessary expenses in taking care of property, and the services not above mentioned, such sum as the register may deem reasonable.

Of the Printer.

The number of publications of notice by the marshal, as messenger, will not exceed two, for which, in each publication, the fee is $3 00

The notice for appointment given by assignee, will be three publications, the fee for each of which is........   1 00

Or, for the whole 3 00

Notice to show cause against final discharge will be but one publication, to be made ten days before the time appointed to show cause, and of meeting of creditors; the fee for which is,   3 00

A copy of the notice, cut out of the paper attached to the receipt for the payment of such publication, shall be by the printer forwarded to the party making the publication, with dates and number of publication, and shall be sufficient evidence of publication.

The proof of notice in case of final discharge, shall be made to the register by the certificate of the clerk, stating that the notice has been made, as required by the order.

Of the Clerk.

The clerk is allowed the fees prescribed by the act of congress, approved February 26th, 1853, for similar services in the circuit and district courts. Those most usually arising under proceedings in bankruptcy, are:

For receiving and filing original papers, with certificate of the day and hour of filing, for each document........ $0 25

For making dockets and indexes, and taking costs..................... 2 00

For copy of any paper, per folio of one hundred words 10

If certificate and seal is made to the same, the fee is.................... 35

For warrant, with seal of the court... 1 20

For each notice given.............. $0 10

For all postage and express fees :

For receiving, entering and filing each document or paper filed in the cause   10

For each process, other than summons for witness, with seal of court...... 1 20

For each subpœna for witness 25

For receiving and paying out money, one per cent on the amount received, kept and paid out.

For arranging and binding papers as final record...................... $0 50

For entering any return, rule, order, continuance, judgment, decree or recognizance, drawing any bond or making any record, certificate, return or report, for each folio.... 15

This fee embraces all orders and proceedings had, either by the judges, registers or the court, and which may be required to be entered on the minutes of the court.

By general rules of the justices of the supreme court, ten cents are allowed for each notice sent to a creditor, under proceedings for final discharge, in addition to the postage to be prepaid. The fees allowed for issuing process, copy, entries, certificate, seal, etc., furnish a rule for the taxation of these costs; the great difference in the amount of service to be performed in the numerous cases, necessarily varies the amount in the different sums due in each.

All balances of fees remaining in the hands of any officer after payment of his fees will be deposited by him with the other funds belonging to the cause, and subject to the order of the court thereon.

15. All rules and orders heretofore made, in either the northern or southern district courts of Mississippi, in conflict with these rules, orders and regulations, are hereby rescinded.

Adopted this *October 29th*, 1868.

In the District Court of the United States,
For Northern District of Mississippi,
Sitting in Bankruptcy.

It is hereby ordered that George R. Hill be appointed a commissioner of the district court of the United States, for the southern district of Mississippi, and that he also be appointed a special commissioner to whom applications for final discharge shall be referred, without further order; that he examine and report what fees are due each officer, and the amount due to, and from such officer, also what amount of funds are due secured creditors, and upon what fund the same is a lien; and what funds, if any, are subject to general creditors; and that he proceed to state an account, showing the amount due preferred creditors; the amount due secured creditors, each, and the pro rata amount due each general creditor who has proved his claim, according to the forms adopted by the justices of the supreme court of the United States. It is ordered that when a pro rata distribution is made by said commissioner, he shall be allowed a fee of three dollars; and when there is no fund for distribution to creditors, a fee of one dollar, in each case, to be paid as the other costs in the case.

(Signed,)

MISSOURI.—Eastern District.

RULE 1. The Missouri Democrat and the Missouri Republican, printed in St. Louis county, and designated as the newspapers in which all required publications in bankruptcy for the eastern district are to be made, unless otherwise specially ordered. If not otherwise required by law or general order, said publications shall be only twice—once in the daily and once in the weekly editions of said newspapers.

2. The National Bank of the state of Missouri in St. Louis, is the designated depository for the eastern district, of moneys received by the clerk or assignee under the bankrupt act; and all checks signed by an assignee, as such under said act or general orders, shall, before payment, be countersigned by the register who has charge of the specified case.

3. If no choice of an assignee is made by the creditors at their first meeting, or, if an assignee chosen by the creditors fails within five days to express in writing his acceptance of the trust, or in case of a vacancy in the office of assignee, caused by removal, resignation, or otherwise, George J. Davis, of the city of St. Louis, United States commissioner, will be appointed assignee when the judge is required to appoint; and when the said George J. Davis shall be appointed by any register, such appointment shall be entered, "approved by the judge."

In special cases, special orders for the appointment will be made. Every election for one assignee by the creditors, when indorsed by the register having charge of the case as satisfactory, shall be entered by the clerk "approved," unless otherwise ordered by the judge; subject however, in all cases, to the judge's order for a new election or removal.

4. The following shall hereafter be the taxed costs for the publication of notices in newspapers, under the bankrupt act:

As marshal's notice as messenger under warrant, two times, as ordered....	$5 00
Notice by assignee of his appointment, two times...........................	
Notice by assignee of meeting of creditors, to show cause, two times.....	4 00
Notice by assignee of dividend meeting	3 00
Advertisement of sales by messenger or assignee, per square of eight lines, one time.................................	1 00
And for each subsequent insertion, per square.............................	50
United notice of meeting of creditors to show cause, &c., two times........	5 00

5. *Ordered*, That the fifty dollars required by law to be paid to the clerk as security for costs in each case in bankruptcy for the benefit of the register, be paid by the clerk to the registers respectively to whom the cases are referred, and receipts therefor be taken accordingly. Also, that each register in certifying to the court that a bankrupt is entitled to his discharge, or that opposition thereto is made, certify what fees are still due to the register.

UNITED STATES OF AMERICA, \
  EASTERN DISTRICT OF MISSOURI. } ss.

I, Benjamin J. Hickman, clerk of the district court of the United States in and for the eastern district of Missouri, do hereby certify the writing hereto annexed to be a true copy in special rules in bankruptcy for said district court, as fully as the same remain of record in said case in my office. In witness whereof, I hereto subscribe my name, and affix the seal of said court at office in the city of St. Louis, in said district, the eighth day of November, in the year of our Lord, eighteen hundred and seventy.

L. S.   *Clerk of said Court.*

MISSOURI.—Western District.

Ordered, That the following rules, orders and regulations be prescribed as rules governing proceedings in bankruptcy in the district court of the United States for the western district of Missouri, under an act entitled "An act to establish a uniform system of bankruptcy through the United States," approved March 2d, A. D. 1867, in addition, and with reference to the general orders in bankruptcy, and the forms and schedules thereto annexed, framed by the justices of the supreme court of the United States, in pursuance of the tenth section of said act, and adopted by said court, and promulgated May 16th, 1867:

RULE 1. The entries in the minute books of orders and minutes in each case in bankruptcy shall be consecutive, and under the respective dates thereof, and separate from those in all other cases; so that all entries pertaining to each case may be under the head of that case, and in regular succession.

2. No paper prepared for filing shall be received unless it is legibly written or printed in roll form on paper of the size called "legal cap," with a margin of at least one and a half inches wide on the upper end of each sheet, and with a margin of one inch on the left of each page. The heading of schedules, when they cannot be at the top of the page, shall be immediately under the left margin thereof, and in appropriate columns. No such paper shall be less than a half sheet, and the last page thereof shall be in blank, and exclusively for the indorsement thereon by the clerk, register, or other officer of the court. Each petition, motion in writing, schedules, &c., shall be on a page or sheet of paper separate from all other petitions, motions in writing, schedules, &c., in order that the proper indorsements may be made thereon.

3. All notices shall be served by mail, unless the law, warrant, or a special order requires personal service.

4. The sum of fifty dollars mentioned in section 47 of the bankrupt act, shall be deposited in each case with the register, to whom the case is referred; and each register shall pay over to the clerk of the court ten dollars out of the amount so deposited, to be accounted for by him.

5. Each register shall fix the time when, and place where, he will act upon matters arising under the cases referred to him, unless the court, by its order, specifies a different time or place; and each register shall, by writing filed with the clerk, state the time when, and place at which he will attend.

6 The clerk shall furnish to each register blank forms of process, summons and subpœnas, with his signature and the seal of the court, and each of said blanks when used by a register shall be countersigned by him. Each register shall keep an account of said blanks so used, and return a copy of said account to the clerk, in order that the fees of the latter may be properly taxed. The time and place designated in the warrant by the register for the first general meeting of creditors, together with the fact that said warrant has been delivered to the marshal, shall be certified in each case forthwith to the clerk for entry upon the minute books.

7. Every election of an assignee, when indorsed as satisfactory by the register having charge of the case, and every appointment of an assignee by him shall be entered by the clerk, "approved," unless the judge orders otherwise; subject, however, in all cases to the judge's order for a new election or removal.

8. All proofs of debt which shall have been made and verified prior to the election or appointment of an assignee, shall be delivered or sent to the register to whom the case is referred. If the register entertains doubts of the validity of any claim, or of the right of the creditor to prove it, and is of the opinion that such validity or right ought to be investigated by the assignee, he may postpone the hearing of the claim until the assignee is chosen.

9. All officers shall produce and file with the clerk, vouchers for all payments made by them which they shall claim as costs.

10. All issues certified by a register for the opinion of the court shall briefly state the opinion of the register on the issue submitted.

11. All notices which, under the bankrupt act, require newspaper publication, shall be published once in the daily, if there is a daily issue of the paper designated, and in two consecutive numbers of the weekly edition of said paper, and only twice in any weekly newspaper, unless otherwise specially ordered. And the publication of all

notices shall be verified immediately thereafter by the affidavit of the printer or publisher, which shall be sent to the register ; and a copy of all newspapers used or employed for publication under said act shall be regularly sent to the clerk of the court, who is required to file the same.

12. In case of the absence of the judge at the time and place appointed for any hearing or proceeding in bankruptcy before him, or if the matter then fails to be called or acted on, the same shall be deemed continued to the next sitting thereafter of the court.

13. All notices sent by mail by the marshal, clerk or assignee shall be so written or printed and folded, that the superscription, postage stamp, and postmark shall be upon the notice itself, and not upon an envelope or other separate piece of paper.

14. Unless otherwise ordered by the judge, the several registers in bankruptcy in this district will cause all notices pertaining to a case in bankruptcy to be published in the newspaper wherein the first notice in the case shall have been ordered to be published.

15. No item of any fee bill or account presented by the clerk, register, assignee, or messenger for fees, charges, or expenses will be allowed by the register or court in any case, unless such fee bill or account shall be sufficiently explicit as to the item of fees charged, the services rendered or expenses incurred, to enable the court or register to pass upon the legality or reasonableness of the same, from the face of such fee bill or account.

16. All examinations of bankrupts or witnesses in reference to the estate of the bankrupt, under the 26th section of the bankrupt act, shall be before the register to whom the case was referred.

No witnesses shall be subpœnaed unless the register shall have cause to suppose that such witness will testify to facts tending to recover property withheld from the assignee. If the assignee or a creditor shall desire the examination of witnesses, the applicant shall, in an affidavit, state the facts which he supposes can be shown by the witness, and thereupon the register shall either grant or refuse the application. Witnesses shall be subpœnaed in the usual way. The bankrupt, or wife, shall attend

upon written or printed notice, transmitted through the mail by the register. Examination shall be reduced to writing and signed by the party testifying, and otherwise conform to law and the orders of court.

17. The general meeting of creditors, provided for by the 27th section of the bankrupt act shall be had before the register to whom the case was originally referred, and the request of the assignee for the second meeting shall be addressed to and filed with such register, who, as well as the assignee is to act upon all matters to be done and transacted at such meeting, that is to say : The register, such duties as properly belong to him, and the assignee such as he may do or are imposed by law on him ; and the creditors such as they have a right to determine. The notice provided for in the section aforesaid shall be given by the assignee upon the order of the register.

18. All assignees in bankruptcy shall, upon the request of the bankrupt, receipt for any property delivered to them by such bankrupt, specifying in said receipts the property so delivered, and for which a receipt is demanded; and the several registers shall, on the examination before them, exhibit to the said bankrupt, the inventory filed by the assignee, and require him to answer whether said inventory is correct, and if incorrect, in what particular.

And the several assignees are hereby required to file with the register to whom the case has been or may hereafter be referred, an inventory of the estate of the bankrupt in all cases now pending, or which may hereafter be filed.

19. In all cases now pending and such as may hereafter be brought, if a continuance becomes necessary and is granted on account of the neglect of any officer in discharging his duty, the cost incurred on account of each continuance will be charged against the delinquent and the amount thereof deducted from his fee bill when it is finally passed upon.

In all cases in which a continuance is granted without a good and sufficient cause appearing in the minutes of the register, the cost will be deducted from register's fees.

20. Henceforth, until otherwise ordered, each case in bankruptcy will be referred to a

register by the special order of the court, the rule heretofore governing, of referring cases in accordance with the territorial subdivisions of the district being hereby suspended. And so much of rule seven of this court as authorizes the clerk, without further action by the court, to enter the appointment, by a register, of an assignee as "approved," is suspended, and hereafter the appointment of assignee in each case, will be submitted to the judge, and no further action will be taken therein, until such appointment has been by him approved.

NEW YORK.—Northern District.

RULE 1. The act of congress, entitled, "An act to establish a uniform system of bankruptcy throughout the United States," approved March 2d, 1867, the general orders in bankruptcy adopted by the justices of the supreme court, and the following rules, shall, until otherwise ordered, be rules of practice in bankruptcy in this court, in respect to all matters and proceedings therein provided for.

In cases not provided for, either by said bankrupt act, general orders or rules, the practice of this court shall be subject to the special order of the district court or judge, and will be made to conform, as near as may be, to the practice of the district court in other cases of similar character, or to the practice established by the rules in bankruptcy adopted in the southern district of New York.

Whenever any special order hereafter made by the district court, in any particular case, shall conflict with these rules, the direction of such special order shall be followed in such case.

2. Except during the absence or inability of the district judge, the district court will be open for the transaction of business as a court of bankruptcy, at the United States court room in the city of Buffalo, on every Tuesday and Friday, from 10 o'clock A. M., until 1 o'clock P. M., unless the business before it shall sooner be disposed of. Except at the stated sessions of the court, no case or matter in bankruptcy will, under ordinary circumstances, be taken up on Mondays, Wednesdays, Thursdays or Saturdays, or on other days after the hour last named, or after the judge shall have disposed of all the business before him and left the court room for the day. At such stated sessions, all other business will have preference, except during the first half hour after the opening of the court in the morning of each day, and except, also, that trials by jury in bankruptcy cases, may be moved in their order with other trials by jury in civil cases.

3. All papers used in court or filed in proceedings in bankruptcy, whether prepared by parties to the proceedings or their attorneys, or by any register in bankruptcy, or other officer of the court, or by any assignee in bankruptcy, shall be written in a fair and legible hand, or else properly printed, upon paper substantially the size and width of that called legal cap or foolscap, and folded in the form and size in which law papers written on foolscap paper are usually folded.

Every such paper containing more than three folios, shall have the folios therein duly marked and numbered; and the folios of all copies thereof shall be marked and numbered in the same manner, so as to admit of easy reference.

Papers not requiring full sheets of foolscap, may be written or printed on half or quarter sheets; and notices not requiring to be filed may be on smaller portions thereof.

All papers to be filed shall be prepared with a white margin of at least one inch wide along the head of each and every half or quarter sheet thereof, in order that they may be properly and securely fastened together at such head, to constitute the final record in the case, and also with a white margin at least one inch wide on the left hand side thereof.

No paper not prepared in compliance with this rule, and also in compliance with the general orders in bankruptcy, shall be filed by the clerk without the special order of the court or judge; and no attorney not admitted in the district court shall be allowed to practice therein in cases of bankruptcy.

4. Every register in bankruptcy, or other officer of the court before administering the proper oaths in verification of any peti-

tion, schedule, inventory, deposition, affidavit or other paper, shall see that the different sheets or pieces of paper of which it is composed, and those to which it refers as annexed, are properly fastened together in such manner as to give reasonable security against the separation, loss or change of any part thereof.

Before any petition under the 11th section of the bankrupt act shall be presented to the court or judge, or be filed with the clerk, the petitioner shall obtain from a register in bankruptcy a certificate substantially in the form following, to wit :

"I do hereby certify that I have carefully examined the annexed or within petition, and the schedule and inventory thereto annexed, and also the verification thereof, and that the same are proper in form, and sufficient in substance to authorize an adjudication in bankruptcy, and the issuing of a warrant under the 11th section of the bankrupt act.

"Given at   this   day of   186 .
                                "A. B.
        "*Register in Bankruptcy.*"

Which certificate shall be endorsed on or annexed to such petition by the register. Before making such certificate, the register will carefully examine every part of the petition, schedule and inventory, to ascertain whether the petitioner has fully complied with every requirement of the bankrupt act, and of the general orders and rules of court applicable thereto; and particularly that they are substantially in the form prescribed by such general orders; that all the blanks of both such schedule and inventory are properly filled, and filled by using the word "none" where that is proper; that both the real and personal property of the petitioner, and the place where each part of the same is situated, are set forth in detail and sufficiently described, and that the incumbrances thereon are stated; or that it is stated that there is no incumbrance thereon. He will also ascertain that the petitioner has fully set forth in his schedule, in respect to every debt stated therein, all the particulars required by the 11th section of the bankrupt act.

And the registers are specially enjoined to refuse such certificate, and to decline making any order of adjudication in bankruptcy upon any petition, until every requisite of the bankrupt act and of the general orders are fully and strictly complied with.

6. Before any petition under the 39th section of the bankrupt act shall be presented to the court or judge, the petitioner shall procure the certificate of a register in bankruptcy, to be endorsed on or annexed to such petition, substantially in the following form, viz :

"I certify that I have carefully examined the annexed or within petition, and the verification thereof and also the proof of the debts, and of the act of bankruptcy, annexed, and that the same are in proper form, and sufficient in substance to authorize an adjudication in bankruptcy, and the issuing of a warrant under the 39th section of the bankrupt act.

"Given at   this   day of   18 ."

7. All petitions filed under the 11th or 39th sections of the bankrupt act shall be numbered consecutively, and the clerk shall enter the case under its proper title in his docket, giving to such case a full page thereof. He shall place its number at the head of the outside filing of said petition, which number shall thereafter be the designating number of such case until finally disposed of. Every other paper, proceeding or notice, in such case or matter, shall be marked by the clerk register, messenger, or other officer or party preparing it, with such designating number at the head of the outside filing, or, if there be no outside filing, on or near the upper left hand corner.

8. In case of the absence of the district judge from the city of Buffalo, or whenever he shall be unable to attend to business by reason of sickness or other cause, petitions in cases of voluntary bankruptcy may be filed with the clerk, and the usual order for reference thereof to a register designated in the order, may be entered upon the direction of Joseph L. Fairchild, Esq , one of the registers in bankruptcy, who is hereby designated and authorized to sit in chambers at Buffalo for that purpose. And in case of the like absence of the judge at the time appointed for showing cause, or for any hearing or proceeding in any matter of bankruptcy, or if any such matter, for want of time or other cause, shall not be acted on at the time appointed therefor, the same shall be continued, without special order for that purpose, to the next sitting of the court thereafter, at

which time the like proceedings may be had thereon as if the day of such subsequent sitting had been originally appointed for such proceedings.

9. The clerk shall prepare and number envelopes of uniform size, as nearly as practicable, in which to keep separately the papers filed in each case, while the same is in progress. The designating number and the title of the case shall be endorsed upon the envelope.

10. A copy of every other order of the court made at the time of making an order referring the petition of a debtor to a register in bankruptcy, and which contains any directions in regard to the contents of the warrant to be issued thereon, publication or service of notice, or in regard to the action of the register on such petition, shall be attached by the clerk to the certified copy of such order of reference furnished to the register.

11. In cases of voluntary bankruptcy, the register to whom the debtor's petition, under the 11th section of the bankrupt act shall be referred, shall proceed to consider such petition at the time and place fixed in the order of reference for his first action thereon, and shall then act on such petition and shall make the order of adjudication of bankruptcy, or other proper order thereon, on the same day, or on some day to which the hearing on such petition may then be adjourned. On such hearing any creditor of the petitioner who has proved his debt, or who shall prove the same on such hearing, may oppose the prayer of said petition for adjudication of bankruptcy, by filing with the register an answer or objections thereto as hereinafter provided.

12. The warrant issued to the marshal, as messenger, under the 11th section of the bankrupt act, shall designate the creditors (if any) on whom personal service is to be made; and notice shall be served by mail upon all creditors not so designated. No creditor shall be designated as one on whom personal service is to be made, except for special reasons of an imperative or very important character.

13. The 11th section of the bankrupt act expressly requiring that the warrant to be issued under that section, shall be issued and signed by the judge or register authorized to grant the same, there will be added to the form of said warrant as prescribed by the general orders in bankruptcy, immediately under the signature and official designation of the clerk of the district court and as a part of such warrant, when granted and issued by a register, the following words, or the substance thereof: " Given under the hand and seal of the undersigned, a register in bankruptcy for the said judicial district, by whom this warrant is granted, signed and issued, in pursuance of the 11th section of the act of congress above referred to, on the day last above mentioned." Whenever such warrant shall be issued by the judge of the district court, the same addition shall be made, except that the words " district judge of the United States," shall be substituted for the words "a register in bank ruptcy."

14. When the proceeding is instituted by or on behalf of the bankrupt, a duplicate copy of his petition, schedule and inventory, as required by the 11th section of the bankrupt act, shall be left with the register to whom his petition is referred, at or before the time fixed in the order of reference for the first attendance of the petitioner before such register.

Such copy shall be certified by the clerk or register in bankruptcy to be a true copy, or shall be verified as such by the affidavit of the petitioner or of his attorney duly sworn or affirmed to before a register in bankruptcy, a commissioner appointed by the circuit court, or a notary public. In either case the petitioner must, at his peril, ascertain that such copy is strictly correct.

15. A party appearing to show cause against or oppose the prayer of a petition under the 11th or 39th sections of the bankrupt act, shall file a brief statement in writing, of the grounds of his opposition or objections thereto, if such objections relate solely to questions of law or practice in respect to the regularity or sufficiency of the petition. If his opposition to such petition is founded upon a denial of any statement of fact contained in such petition. or upon the alleged existence of other facts not stated therein, he shall, by an answer to such petition, set forth in writing, in distinct and separate articles, and according to his best knowledge, information and belief, his denial of each material allegation so denied by him, and each allegation of new matter, so

that distinct and separate issues may be readily framed thereon; and he shall annex thereto his affidavit that he has read said answer so signed by him, or heard the same read, and knows the contents thereof, and that the same is true of his own knowledge, except as to the matters therein stated on information and belief, and that to those matters he believes it to be true.

16. The court, at its own instance, or on motion of either party will refer to a register, commissioner, or referee, designated or appointed for the purpose, for examination and report, such matters arising in proceedings in bankruptcy, as under the provisions of the bankrupt act, may properly be so referred.

17. Exceptions may be filed to the report of a register, referee or commissioner, upon any matter referred to him, within eight days after the filing of such report; and exceptions to the admission or rejection of evidence may be filed within four days after the return of proofs is filed, and either party may then apply for an order fixing a time for the hearing upon such exceptions.

18. When a trial by jury is to be had, no formal pleadings shall be necessary to present the issue, but the order for such trial shall contain the issues made by the petition, answer, and other papers presenting the issues to be tried.

19. Causes cannot be noticed for proof, nor witnesses be called and sworn, in open court, (except in trials before a jury) without the previous special allowance of the court, on adequate cause shown.

20. When proofs are to be made out of court, and the case is ready therefore, either party may apply for an order to take the same; and the name and residence of the register, or other officer or person before whom such proofs are to be taken, shall be stated in the order.

21. A copy of the order shall be delivered to the person before whom the testimony is to be taken by the party for whom it is entered, and all parties interested shall thereafter for themselves ascertain and take notice of the time and place of taking the same, which time and place shall be fixed by the person before whom it is to be taken, in such manner that such parties may have a reasonable time to prepare therefor.

22. All returns and reports from registers in bankruptcy or other officers of the court, or referees, shall be directed to the clerk of the court at Buffalo, N. Y., and shall be sent free of postage or other charges; and in case of unreasonable delay on the part of the register or other officer or referee in making a return or report in any case, an order will be granted requiring him to make such return or report, or to show cause on a day specified why he has not done so.

23. Letters to the register, clerk or marshal requiring an answer, should be accompanied by envelopes, properly addressed, and with the proper postage stamps affixed, in which to enclose the reply and whatever else may be required, and no register or officer of the court will be required to answer any such letter unless this be done, and his fees in addition are enclosed. Whenever any receipt is desired for any such officer, it must be prepared and presented by the party desiring it and with the proper revenue stamp thereon.

24. In every certificate made by a register stating any case, point, or matter for the opinion of the district judge under the 4th or 6th section of the bankrupt act, according to Form 50, established by the general orders in bankruptcy, the facts agreed upon by the parties to the controversy shall be clearly and fully stated with reasonable certainty of time and place; and this shall be followed by a brief statement of the claim made, or position assumed, by each of the parties to the controversy. The register shall then add thereto such proposed order, adjudication or decision, as in his judgment ought to be made, and which shall be in such form that the district judge may signify his approval thereof by his signature. The register shall then afford to each of the opposing parties or their attorneys a reasonable opportunity to consent, in writing, to the register's decision thereon. The court will, on the approval and confirmation of such decision of the register, make such order for costs, against any party declining to assent thereto, as may be deemed proper. In case all parties to such controversy shall assent to such adjudication or decision of the register, he shall file the same and proceed with the case upon the basis thereof, as though such controversy had not arisen.

25. It shall be the duty of the assignee, as soon as practicable after his appointment

shall be complete, to take into his possession all the estate, real and personal, of every name and nature, of the bankrupt, with the exceptions mentioned in the bankrupt act ; and also all the deeds and books of account, papers and writings of the bankrupt pertaining thereto ; and for this purpose the assignee shall make diligent inquiry into the affairs and transactions of the bankrupt.

Every assignee shall, under section 27 of the bankrupt act, produce and file with his account, proper vouchers for all payments made by him, except payments of one dollar or less, and except items in regard to which the court shall for reasonable cause, and by special order dispense with vouchers. The items so excepted may be allowed to a reasonable extent, upon the positive oath of assignee, that the amounts charged therein were actually and necessarily paid.

In cases of voluntary bankruptcy when the assignee or any creditor shall, after the adjudication of bankruptcy, have good reason to suspect that the bankrupt has property or any right of property which he has not set forth in his inventory, or that he has made any fraudulent or void disposition of his property, or any part thereof, or that he has not given and has not used due diligence to ascertain and give the full names and the residences of his creditors, or the amount of his debts, as required by the bankrupt act ; or that he has not given a full and accurate inventory of his estate, real and personal, describing the same and where it is situated as required by the said act ; or that he has done, suffered or omitted any other act or thing which may bar his right to a discharge, such assignee or creditor, upon application to the court, or the register acting in the case, stating briefly and under oath the grounds of his suspicion, may, on due cause shown by affidavit, apply for an order for the examination of the bankrupt on oath or affirmation. And if, upon due service on the bankrupt of a copy of any such order and notice of the time and place appointed for such examination, the bankrupt shall fail to appear and fully to submit himself to such examination, and to subscribe his disposition, application may forthwith be made to the court, upon an affidavit stating the facts of the case, for compulsory process against

such bankrupt. On any such examination the bankrupt may be examined upon oath in respect to all the matters above mentioned, and also in respect to all due to him or to any person for his use ; all rights of property, chosen in action, rights in equity, interests in patents, patent rights or copy rights ; and all rights in action for any property or estate, real or personal, or the unlawful taking, detention, or injury thereof, or arising upon contract.

27. In cases of involuntary bankruptcy, it shall be the duty of the assignee, as soon as practicable after he shall be appointed and qualified, to apply to the bankrupt for a full and true account of all his property and rights of property, and of all the deeds and books of account, papers and writings of the bankrupt pertaining thereto, as required by the bankrupt act ; and if the bankrupt shall refuse to give such account, or if the assignee or any creditor of the bankrupt shall have good reason to suspect that he has practiced any concealment in giving such account, such assignee or creditor may, on application to the court, and due cause shown by affidavit, have an order for the examination of such bankrupt, and, if necessary, for compulsory process against him, as provided in the last preceding rule.

28. Every bankrupt shall at all times be bound to attend the assignee upon the requirement of the register acting in his case, and on reasonable notice in writing for that purpose, to be served personally or left at his usual place of abode, in order to assist in making out the accounts of the said bankrupt's estate and effects, and to attend any court to be examined in any suit or proceeding respecting the same, for which he shall be entitled to receive from the assignee a reasonable compensation out of the estate.

29. If, in any case, the assignee or any creditor of the bankrupt shall have good reason to believe that any of the property, interests, rights, credits, or equities of the bankrupt, or any assurance or evidence thereof, and of which he has not given a satisfactory account, is in the possession, under the control, or within the knowledge of any other person, or that any other person is indebted to said bankrupt in a sum not stated, or larger than that stated in the inventory of the bankrupt, such assignee or creditor, upon application to the court, and

due cause shown by affidavit, may have an order for the examination of any such person, and, if necessary, for compulsory process against him, as provided in the preceding rules.

When an order for the examination of any bankrupt or other person shall be made, any creditor, or the bankrupt himself, at the time and place appointed for such examination, or at any other time to which such examination may be continued or adjourned, may, at his own expense, produce witnesses touching the subject matter of such examination, and shall be entitled to the ordinary process of subpœna, to be issued by the clerk or register, requiring the attendance of such witnesses, which subpœna the witnesses shall be bound to obey, provided their legal fees are paid or tendered on the service of such subpœna.

30. All motions and applications of which notices shall be required, shall, unless otherwise provided for by law, the general orders, or these rules, or by special order, be noticed for some Tuesday or Friday, at 10 o'clock, A. M., and the notice shall be accompanied by a copy of the affidavits or other papers on which the motion or application is to be made, except in cases where a reference to such papers and a statement that the same will be used on making a special motion, is sufficient under the general practice of the court. All rules, notices and orders, when not otherwise provided for, shall be rules, orders or notices of eight days when served personally, and one-half that time in addition when served by mail.

When the object is to bring a party into contempt for disobeying any process, or any rule or order of the court or of a register, the service shall be personal, unless otherwise ordered by the court.

31. Affidavits of the publication of notices in a newspaper, shall show that the same were published in the regular edition and issue of such newspaper, and shall state the day or days on which the same were published. Such affidavits must be sworn or affirmed before a register in bankruptcy, the clerk of the court, a commissioner appointed by the circuit court of the United States, or a notary public, and shall be substantially in the following form :

NORTHERN DISTRICT OF NEW YORK, } ss.
    County of }

A. B. *of*   *in said county, being duly sworn, doth depose and say that he is* (the printer, the publisher, or foreman in the office, as the case may be), *of the a public newspaper published in said county, and that the notice of which the annexed is a printed copy cut from said newspaper, was printed and published in the regular edition and issue of said newspaper on the following days, viz*: On the   *and*   *days of*   186 : (or *on the*   *and days of*   *and on the days of*   186 .)

Subscribed and sworn before me, this day of   186 .

32. The notice of the appointment of the assignee of a bankrupt, required to be given by him under the provisions of the 14th section of the bankrupt act, shall be published once a week for three successive weeks, in each of the newspapers in which the notice of the first meeting of the creditors of such bankrupt was directed to be published. And notices to creditors to appear and show cause why a discharge should not be granted to a bankrupt, shall be published twice a week for three successive weeks, in the same newspapers, unless the district court shall otherwise direct.

Notices to creditors of dividends, notice that an assignee will apply for a settlement of his accounts and for a discharge from all his liability as assignee, and notices of meetings, required by the 17th, 27th and 28th sections of the bankrupt act, and notices of sale by an assignee, required to be given under the 21st general order, shall be published twice in the same newspaper ; the last publication of such notices of sale to be made at least the number of days before the sale required by such general order.

33. All notices served or sent by mail by the marshal or messenger, the clerk, or an assignee in bankruptcy, shall, when practicable, be so prepared, directed and folded, that the direction, postage stamp and postmark shall be upon the notice itself, and not on an envelope or other piece of paper. Whenever any notice sent by mail by the marshal, or a messenger, in pursuance of a warrant issued under section 11 or section 42 of the bankrupt act, shall be returned to

him by reason of its-non-delivery, he shall preserve the same in his office in separate bundles, so arranged that they may be referred to by parties interested in their examination. Whenever any notice sent by the clerk, by mail, under any of the provisions of said act, or the general orders in bankruptcy, shall be so returned, the same shall be filed by the clerk with the papers in the cause.

34. The list of debts provided for by section 23 of the bankrupt act, shall be made and certified by the register to whom the original petition in the case was referred, unless another register shall have been specially designated for that duty by the district court. The register shall place thereon all debts which have been duly proved and which have not been disallowed by the court, unless it shall be otherwise specially ordered by the district court.

35. Applications, under section 34 of the bankrupt act, to set aside and annul the discharge granted to any bankrupt, shall clearly set forth in separate and distinct articles, and with reasonable certainty of time and place according to the best knowledge, information and belief of the applicant, all the material facts and allegations on which the application is based.

The bankrupt shall admit or deny, or otherwise answer the several allegations of such application, in distinct articles, in like manner; and such application and answer shall severally be verified by affidavit substantially in the form prescribed by rule 15.

36. The fifty dollars required to be deposited as security for registers' fees, shall, until otherwise ordered, be deposited with the clerk according to general order No. 30. The provisional disposition and ultimate disbursement of the same will be regulated by rules hereafter to be promulgated, or by special order.

37. In pursuance of the 28th general order in bankruptcy, the following national banks are hereby designated as those in which all moneys received by assignees in bankruptcy, or paid into court in the course of any proceedings in bankruptcy shall be deposited, viz:

1. The Albany City National Bank at Albany; in all cases in which the bankrupt at the time of the filing of the first petition therein resided in either of the counties of Albany, Rensselaer, Washington, Warren, Essex, Clinton, St. Lawrence, Franklin, Fulton, Hamilton, Montgomery, Saratoga, Schenectady, Schoharie, Delaware, Otsego and Chenango.

2. The First National Bank of Utica, at Utica; in all cases in which the bankrupt at the time of the filing of the first petition therein resided in either of the counties of Oneida, Jefferson, Madison, Lewis and Herkimer.

3. The Syracuse National Bank, at Syracuse; in all cases in which the bankrupt at the time of the filing of the first petition therein resided in either of the counties of Onondaga, Oswego, Cortland, Cayuga, Wayne and Seneca.

4. The Flour City National Bank, at Rochester; in all cases in which the bankrupt at the time of the filing of the first petition therein resided in either of the counties of Monroe, Orleans, Ontario, Livingston and Yates.

5. The Chemung Canal National Bank of Elmira, at Elmira; in all cases in which the bankrupt at the time of the filing of the first petition therein resided in either of the counties of Chemung, Steuben, Allegany, Tioga, Tompkins, Broome and Schuyler.

6. The First National Bank of Buffalo, at Buffalo; in all cases in which the bankrupt at the time of the filing of the first petition therein resided in either of the counties of Erie, Chautauqua, Niagara, Cattaraugus, Genesee and Wyoming.

Deposits made in said banks by any assignee in bankruptcy under said 28th general order, shall be made to his credit *as such assignee in the particular case in which such moneys have been received ;* and a separate account shall be kept in each case according to its proper designating number and title. Checks drawn by assignees in bankruptcy for moneys deposited by them in such deposit banks, shall contain the number and title of the case in which they are drawn; shall be signed by the assignee as such; and shall state "the date, the sum and account for which it is drawn," and shall be countersigned by the register in bankruptcy having charge of or acting as such in the case in which said checks are drawn. When such checks are drawn for the payment of dividends declared, they shall be made payable to the order of the persons entitled to such dividends, unless the register acting in the case shall, by reason of the small amount of separate dividends, authorize the drawing of a check payable to the order of the assignee for the aggregate of several of such dividends, or shall for some other reason authorize the making of such check payable to the order of some other person, or to bearer.

The designation of banks of deposit hereby made, is upon the condition that the said First National Bank of Buffalo and the Flour City National Bank severally agree to allow and credit to the assignee, in each account, separately, whenever such account is about to be closed, interest at the rate of *five* per cent. per annum on the daily balance of such account, and shall file with the clerk of this court, whenever required, a satisfactory bond, executed by one or more persons, as a further security for the safe keeping and proper repayment of such deposit—such bond to be approved by the judge of this court; and that each of the other banks designated shall credit in like manner *four and a half* per cent. interest on such daily balances, and file a similar bond whenever such bond shall be required.

The clerk will certify a copy of this rule, and transmit the same, by mail or otherwise, to each of said banks, and will also certify to each bank the name of the register in bankruptcy appointed for the district to which each of the counties named in designating such bank belongs; and whenever the register of any other district shall be designated to act in any case where the bankrupt at the time of the filing of the first petition therein resided in either of the said counties, the clerk will, on the application of the assignee appointed in such case, certify to the proper deposit bank the name of the register authorized under the rule to countersign checks in such case.

38. Is amended so as to read as follows: The following newspapers are hereby designated as those in which notices required to be published in cases of bankruptcy are to be inserted, except in cases where, for special reasons, other directions shall be given by the district court, viz:

When the alleged bankrupt resides in the county of Albany, Albany Evening Journal, and the Albany Argus; Allegany, Angelica Reporter, and the Cuba True Patriot; Broome, Binghamton Daily Republican, and the Binghamton Democrat; Cayuga, Auburn Daily Advertiser, and the Northern Christian Advocate; Cattaraugus, Cat-

taraugus, Republican, and the Cattaraugus Union; Chautauqua, Jamestown Journal, and the Mayville Sentinel; Chenango, Telegraph and Chronicle, and the Chenango Union; Chemung, Elmira Daily Advertiser, and the Elmira Daily Gazette; Clinton, Plattsburgh Sentinel, and the Plattsburgh Republican; Cortland, Gazette and Banner, and the Cortland County Democrat; Delaware, Delaware Republican, and the Delaware Gazette; Erie, Buffalo Commercial Advertiser, and the Buffalo Daily Courier; Essex, Essex County Republican, and the Elizabethtown Post; Franklin, Malone Palladium, and the Franklin Gazette; Fulton and Hamilton, Johnstown Independent, and the Fulton County Democrat; Genesee, Batavia Advocate, and the Spirit of the Times; Herkimer, Journal and Courier, and the Herkimer County Democrat; Jefferson, Northern New York Journal, and the Watertown Re-Union; Lewis, Journal and Republican, and the Lewis County Democrat; Livingston, Western New York Advertiser, and the Union and the Constitution; Madison, Republican, and the Oneida Observer; Monroe, Rochester Daily Union and Advertiser, and the Rochester Daily Democrat; Montgomery, Montgomery County Republican, and the Montgomery Democrat; Niagara, Lockport Union, and the Lockport Journal; Ontario, Ontario Repository and Messenger, and the Geneva Courier; Oneida, Utica Morning Herald, and the Utica Daily Observer; Oswego, Commercial Advertiser & Times, and the Oswego Palladium; Onondaga, Syracuse Daily Standard, and the Syracuse Daily Courier and Union; Otsego, Otsego Republican, and the Freemen's Journal; Orleans, Orleans American, and the Orleans Republican; Rensselaer, Troy Daily Times, and the Troy Daily Press; Schoharie, Schoharie Republican, and the Schoharie Union; Schenectady, Schenectady Daily Union, and the Evening Star; Saratoga, Saratogian, and the Saratoga Sentinel; St. Lawrence, Courier and Freeman, and the Ogdensburgh Advance; Seneca, Seneca County Courier, and the Seneca Observer; Steuben, Canisteo Valley Times, and the Steuben Farmers' Advocate; Schuyler, Havana Journal, and the Watkins Independent, or in the Schuyler County Democrat; Tioga, Oswego

Times, and the Oswego Gazette; Tompkins, Ithaca Journal, and the Ithaca Democrat; Washington, Salem Press, and the Sandy Hill Herald; Warren, Glen's Falls Messenger, and the Glen's Falls Republican; Wayne, Lyons Weekly Republican, and the Wayne Democratic Press; Wyoming, New Yorker, and the Democrat; Yates, Penn Yan Express, and the Penn Yan Democrat.

The warrants issued by registers directing notices of the first meeting of creditors shall direct the publication of such notices in the two designated papers of the county in which the bankrupt so resides, unless the register shall, for special reasons relating to the residence of the bankrupt or his creditors, deem it more suitable, in lieu thereof, to publish the same in the newspapers designated in an adjoining county, in which case the register may direct such publication in such adjoining county. Such warrants shall, unless otherwise specially ordered, direct that such notices shall be published *twice* in each of the two selected papers.

In any case, where the circumstances require it, such publication may be made in other papers by the special order of the court or judge.

Due proof of the publication of such notices shall be furnished to the marshal, officer or party directing and paying for such publication, and such proof shall be filed with the papers or proceedings to which they particularly relate.

The fees of printers for making such publication and furnishing the proof thereof, are those prescribed by the act of congress of the 26th of February, 1853, viz: forty cents per folio for the first insertion, and twenty cents per folio for each subsequent insertion; but as these rates are not considered remunerative, and publishers have declined to publish bankrupt notices at such rates, messengers and assignees are authorized, in cases where publishers decline to publish such notices for the fees prescribed by the act of congress, to allow and pay, if necessary, the fees allowed by the laws of the state for the like publication of similar notices in legal proceedings under the laws of the state.

Notwithstanding the provisions of this rule, the court, in cases where, by accident or inadvertence, and without intention to disregard the rule or omit the prescribed notices, a different but substantially equivalent publication has been made, will exercise its discretion in waiving any technical irregularity, and acting upon a notice published in good faith, and giving proper information to all parties interested, although not published in strict conformity to this rule.

The following additional rules have been adopted:

39. Whenever a petition, under section 11 of the bankrupt act, shall be referred to a register in bankruptcy, and whenever, in a case of involuntary bankruptcy, an order shall be made upon an adjudication in bankruptcy referring such case to a register, the clerk shall advance to such register, on account of his fees, chargeable to the petitioner, the sum of twenty-five dollars out of the fifty dollars deposited with the clerk under section 47 of the bankrupt act. Whenever a detailed statement of his fees so chargeable shall be made and filed by the register, showing that the aggregate amount of the same exceeds the aggregate of the advances made on account thereof, the clerk, if requested by the register, shall make further reasonable advances to him on account of such fees, until the amount so deposited and all interest received by the clerk thereon shall be exhausted; and whenever the aggregate of the fees of the register, chargeable to such petitioner, shall equal or exceed the said sum of fifty dollars, all such fees in excess thereof, and all subsequent fees of such register, so chargeable to such petitioner, shall be paid or secured as provided for by general order No. 29.

Within forty days after the proceedings in a case referred to a register, as aforesaid, shall be finally closed, such register shall make, under oath, and file ₍with₎ the clerk, a detailed statement of his fees charged or chargeable to or against the petitioner in such case, and of the sums advanced or paid to him by the clerk, or by or on behalf of the petitioner, on account thereof; and he shall within ten days thereafter pay over to the clerk, so much of the moneys so advanced as is not required for the payment thereof. Such statement shall be made in and relate to such case only, and shall be so prepared, as a separate paper, that it may be made a part of the record in such case; and it is recommended to registers to make and file, within the first ten days of every calendar month, the statements above required, in all cases closed during the preceding month.

Whenever it shall satisfactorily appear from any such statement that there is a balance due to said register for fees so chargeable as aforesaid, the clerk shall, on demand, pay such balance, or so much thereof as the residue of the fifty dollars so deposited by the petitioner, and the interest received by the clerk thereon, will pay of the same.

40. When in a case of voluntary bankruptcy the petitioner owes debts as a partner, and desires to obtain a discharge, which shall, in form, be a discharge from his debts as such partner, as well as in his individual capacity. he shall, in his petition, and in the proper schedule thereto annexed, or in proper amendments thereto, state the name or names of his partner or partners, and also the firm name of such copartnership, and whether the copartnership still subsists; and shall designate the debts owing by him as a member of such copartnership as partnership debts. He shall also in like manner set forth in his inventory, the joint property, rights, credits and estate (if any) of such copartnership, and the location, sitnation, &c., thereof, as required by the bankrupt act.

41. In order to save unnecessary expense and labor, the registers will, when practicable, include in a single certificate copies of the momoranda of all their proceedings in the some case, upon the same day, which are required to be forwarded to the clerk, under the provisions of the bankrupt act and of the general orders; and they will send no certified copy of memorandum, or of docket entry, other than those required by the said act or orders.

42. There shall be added to the adjudication of bankruptcy, in an involuntary bankruptcy case, as in Form No. 58, an order referring the case to one of the registers in bankruptcy, to take such proceedings therein as may be necessary.

43. The notice in writing of the acceptance of the trust, which is required to be given by an assignee in bankruptcy, may be given to the register having charge of the case, who will transmit the same to the clerk of the court, with the other papers in the case, as required by the 7th general order.

44. Every assignee in bankruptcy, if required by the register having the case in charge, shall give a bond, with a surety or sureties, as provided for in the 13th section of the bankrupt act; the form and penalty of such bond, and the sufficiency of the surety or sureties therein, to be approved by such register. It shall be the duty of the registers to require such bond, upon the request in writing of any creditor who has proved his claim, or whenever it shall otherwise appear to be proper to do so.

45. In order to guard against the loss or destruction of the evidence of an assignment, every assignee, on receiving an assignment of an estate in bankruptcy, in which the assets are sufficient to justify the expenditure, shall send or deliver such assignment to the clerk of the court, who shall make a true copy thereof, and certify the same under his hand and the seal of the court, and send or deliver said certified copy to such assignee; and the original assignment shall then be placed and kept on file with the other papers in the case.

46. Whenever it shall appear by the inventory of the bankrupt or otherwise, that he has real or personal property, or choses or rights in action, or any other legal or equitable interests, beyond the limits of the United States, or debts due to him from any person residing abroad, the register having his case in charge may, and, on the request of the assignee shall, require the bankrupt to execute and acknowledge in due and proper form, a full assignment thereof, and of all his other property, real and personal, equitable interests, choses in action, and rights of action of every name, nature and kind whatsoever, and wherever the same may be situated. And if the bankrupt shall neglect or refuse to execute such assignment, he may, on due application to the court, be compelled to do so by process of attachment or other proper proceeding.

47. It shall be the duty of every assignee within fifteen days after receiving an assignment of the estate of any bankrupt, to set apart from the property of such bankrupt such part thereof as is specially excepted by section 14 of the bankrupt act; and also such other articles and necessaries as shall be designated by such assignee (having reference to the family condition and circumstan-

ces of the bankrupt), as being proper to be set apart for the use of the bankrupt, as provided for by said 14th section. And such assignee, within five days thereafter, shall file with the clerk of the court a full report of his decisions and doings in this respect, and of the articles set off to the bankrupt by him, with the estimated value of each article, as required by the 19th general order; and in which he shall also state whether there remains any property or other assets, or valuable things for the benefit of the creditors of the bankrupt. The bankrupt, or any creditor who has proved his debts, may except to the said report or any part thereof, by stating each of his objections thereto in proper form, and in a separate article, and filing the same with the clerk of the court within twenty days after the filing of such report; and if not so excepted to, the report shall stand confirmed. If so excepted to the effect thereof, and of the designation and the setting apart aforesaid, shall be suspended until the order of the court upon such exception shall modify or confirm the said report.

For his miscellaneous services, for which no other fee is provided, and for designating and setting apart such property, and making and filing his report thereof, within the time and in the manner above prescribed, the assignee shall be entitled to a fee of five dollars; and for travel (when absolutely necessary for the purpose of designating and setting apart such property) six cents per mile for each mile going and returning; he shall also be allowed ten cents per folio for each folio of one hundred words contained in such report. Such fees shall be paid by the bankrupt unless assets sufficient to pay the same remain in the hands of the assignee.

48. Whenever, by reason of the sickness, necessary absence or other *disability* of the register in bankruptcy having any case or matter in charge, he shall be unable to hear the same, or to proceed therein at the time and place appointed therefor, the same may be adjourned by him by a written notice and order stating such adjournment, and the time and place to which it is made, and posting the same on the outer office or room in which such hearing or proceeding was intended to be had.

49. The oath required by the 29th section of the bankrupt act to be taken and subscribed by a bankrupt before his discharge can be granted, shall follow the language of such section as near as may be, and shall be substantially in the following form, viz:

No.

IN THE DISTRICT COURT OF THE UNITED STATES FOR THE NORTHERN DISTRICT OF NEW YORK.

In the matter of A. B.

A Bankrupt. } *In bankruptcy.*

NORTHERN DISTRICT OF NEW YORK, *ss*.

A. B., the petitioner above named being duly sworn, deposes and says, that he has not wilfully sworn falsely in his affidavit annexed to his petition, schedule or inventory, filed in this case or upon any examination in the course of the proceedings in bankruptcy, in relation to any material fact concerning his estate or his debts, or in any other material fact; that he has not concealed any part of his estate or effects, or any books or writings relating thereto; that he has not been guilty of any fraud or negligence in the care, custody or delivery to the assignee of the property belonging to him at the time of the presentation of his petition and inventory, excepting such property as he is permitted to retain under the provisions of the bankrupt act passed by congress, approved March 2, 1867, and entitled "An act to establish a uniform system of bankruptcy throughout the United States;" that he has not caused, permitted or suffered any loss, waste or destruction thereof; that he did not within four months before the commencement of such proceedings, procure his lands, goods, money or chattels, or any part thereof, to be attached, sequestered or seized on execution; that since the passage of the said act he has not destroyed, mutilated, altered or falsified any of his books, documents, papers, writings or securities; that he has not made or been privy to the making of any false or fraudulent entry in any book of account or other document, with intent to defraud his creditors; that he has not removed or caused to be removed any part of his property from this district with intent to defraud his creditors; that he has not given any fraudulent preference contrary to the provisions of the said act, or made any fraudulent payment, gift, transfer, conveyance or assignment of any part of his property, or lost any part thereof in gaming; that he has not admitted a false or fictitious debt against his estate; that he has not had knowledge that any person has proved a false or fictitious debt against his estate, without having disclosed the same to his assignee within one month after such knowledge; that he has not, whilst being a merchant or tradesman, failed, subsequectly to the passage of this act, to keep proper books of account; that he has not, nor has any person in his behalf procured the assent of any creditor to the discharge, or influenced the action of any creditor, at any stage of the proceedings, by any pecuniary consideration or obligation; that he has not, in contemplation of becoming bankrupt, made any pledge, payment, transfer, assignment or conveyance of any part of his property, directly or indirectly, absolutely or conditionally, for the purpose of preferring any creditor or person having a claim against him, or who was or might be under liability for him, or for the purpose of preventing the property coming into the hands of the assignee, or of being distributed under said bankrupt act in satisfaction of his debts; that he has not been convicted of any misdemeanor under said act, or been guilty of any fraud whatever, contrary to the true intent thereof; and that he has not done, suffered, or been privy to any act, matter or thing, specified in the said bankrupt act, as a ground for withholding a discharge, or as invalidating a discharge if granted.

A. B.

Subscribed and sworn before me by }
the above named A. B. at   in }
the State of   this day of   18 . }

50. A creditor opposing the discharge of a bankrupt, shall set forth, succinctly and clearly, in separate articles, as his specification of the grounds of his opposition, each of his objections to such discharge, with the grounds thereof, if such objections raise only questions of law or practice, in respect to the substance, form, sufficiency, regularity or effect of the petition, schedule or inventory of the bankrupt, or of the proceedings had thereon. If his opposition to a discharge is founded upon a denial of any statement contained in such petition, schedule or inventory, or upon the alleged existence of any fact not stated therein, or not

conclusively appearing upon the records of the court, he shall set forth in writing, in distinct and separate articles, each of such objections, and the facts on which it is based, according to his best knowledge, information and belief, and with requisite certainty of time and place; and shall also set forth in like manner, and in clear and express terms, his denial of each material statement controverted by him, so that distinct and separate issues may be readily framed thereon; and such allegations and denials shall be verified by affidavit as provided for in rule 15.

The bankrupt, if he desires to deny any of such new allegations, or to avoid the effect thereof by the allegation of new matter, shall make and verify his denials and allegations in the manner above provided; and such new allegations may in like manner be denied, or avoided by the opposing creditor.

51. Whenever it shall become necessary to adjourn the first meeting of creditors under the 12th section of the bankrupt act, and to give a new notice, as provided for in that section, it shall not be necessary to serve such new notice upon creditors who were duly and properly served with the notice of meeting required by the warrant issued under the 11th or the 42d sections of the act, or to publish notices of the adjourned meeting, if the notices directed by such warrant were duly published as required by such warrant. It shall be sufficient, in case such notices were not so published, to publish such new notices twice in each of the newspapers designated in such warrant. If proper notices were not served upon any creditor, it shall be sufficient to serve the new notice personally or by mail, as may be directed by the register, on such creditors as were not properly served with the notices directed by the warrant. The said new notices so to be published and served shall severally contain substantially the same statements as were contained in the notices directed by the warrant, except that they shall state the meeting to be held to be "an adjourned meeting," and that it will be held in pursuance of the 12th section of the bankrupt act. This may be done by inserting in place of the "a" before the word "meeting" in said notices, the words "in pursuance of the 12th section of the bank-

rupt act, an adjourned." Such new notices must be served and such publication of new notices completed at least twelve days before the day fixed for the holding of such adjourned meeting.

52. Witnesses or persons subpœnaed or summoned to attend before the court, or before a register, shall be paid or tendered their fees for their necessary travel and for one day's attendance, at the rate allowed by act of Congress, or no proceedings to compel obedience to such subpœna, or summons can be taken against them.

53. Every assignee shall be allowed fifty cents for drawing a notice of dividend, or a notice of the meetings of creditors required to be given or published under the 17th section of the bankrupt act, or a notice of his application for a settlement of his accounts and for a discharge of his liability as assignee, and the like sum for a copy thereof for publication and attending to the publication thereof, in each of the newspapers in which he is required to publish the same. He shall also be allowed the same sum for a single copy of such written notice of a dividend which he shall post in his office or place of business. And he shall not be required to give any other written notice of a dividend under said 17th section ;—the register being required by the 27th section of the act, to "forward by mail to every creditor a statement of the dividend to which he is entitled." The notice of dividends to be posted as aforesaid, shall be adressed substantially as follows :—To each and every creditor of A.—— B————, a bankrupt."

54. Nothing in these rules contained shall require any register, marshal, messenger, clerk or assignee to render any service or make any disbursements, unless the fees therefor or the amount of such disbursements shall have been previously advanced or secured to him.

55. All applications for the calling of a second or a third meeting of creditors, made after the expiration of three months from date of adjudication in bankruptcy in the case in which such application shall be made, shall be made to the register in bankruptcy to whom such case shall stand referred, and by the assignee in bankruptcy as required by the 27th and 28th sections of the bankrupt act ; and hereafter no order for the second and third meetings of creditors shall be made

by the district court unless the application for the discharge of the bankrupt shall be made within three months from the time the applicant was adjudged a bankrupt. Such order, when made by a register, shall be signed by the register making the same, and the signature and the seal of the clerk shall not be required to be affixed thereto.

56. Whenever the fees of the register in bankruptcy, to whom any case has been referred, shall have been duly taxed by the clerk, after service of eight days' notice of such taxation, with a copy of the bill of such fees, upon the attorney of the bankrupt, or upon the bankrupt himself if he conduct the proceedings in person, and on the assignee of such bankrupt, and no proof of the service of a proper notice of a motion for a retaxation, or of an appeal from such taxation shall have been filed with the clerk within six days after the filing of such taxed bill ; or, whenever a detailed bill or account of such fees shall be filed with the clerk accompanied by an agreement in writing thereto annexed, signed by such bankrupt, or his attorney, the assignee of such bankrupt, and the register presenting such bill, by which the amount of such register's fees shall be fixed and agreed upon, the clerk shall be and he hereby is authorized and directed without any special or further order, to pay such register the amount due him for such fees (after deducting the advances and payments already made on account thereof), or so much thereof as can be paid by the moneys deposited with the clerk as security for such fees and the interest that has accrued thereon on being furnished by such register with his proper receipt or voucher therefor, as a payment or part payment of such fees. Provided, nevertheless, that no moneys shall be paid in any case, under the provisions of this rule, unless the register entitled to the same shall have filed in the clerk's office the papers in such case, which he is required to file with the clerk by the 7th general order in bankruptcy ; and provided, further, that no moneys shall be so paid without the taxation of the register's bill of fees in any case, when any creditor who has proved his debt shall have filed with the clerk a notice that he requires the fees of such register to be duly taxed.

57. It shall be the duty of the register in bankruptcy, to whom any cases in bank-

ruptcy shall have been referred, to require proper security from the assignee or assignees therein, whenever the amount of assets likely to come to the hands of the assignees or any other cause may render such requirement necessary or proper; to exercise a general supervision over the acts and doings of such assignees in order to secure a proper execution of their duties, and the prompt and proper deposit or disposition of all moneys or other assets which may come to their hands as such assignees; to ascertain by suitable inquiries from time to time, whether security or additional security should be required of any assignee, or any deposit bank, and the amount thereof, and to report the same whenever necessary, to the district judge for his action; to require all assignees to take proper measures for the declaration and payment of proper dividends to creditors, and for the passing and final settlement of their accounts before such registers in due time and form; to see that all suitable and proper action is had and returns made and filed, by the different officers of the court and assignees in such cases; and, generally, to take all such action in each case referred to them as may be within their power, and shall appear to be necessary to promote the interests and secure the just rights of creditors, or to secure the filing, at the proper time, of all the process, papers, and proceedings in such case, which ought to be placed upon the files of the court.

58. Every creditor appearing to show cause against the discharge of a bankrupt, shall furnish to the clerk a notice or statement in writing, signed by him or by his attorney, that he appears in opposition to such discharge, and desires that his appearance for that purpose may be entered; and the filing of such notice or statement at the time fixed for showing cause, shall be a sufficient entry of such appearance.

59. The First National Bank of the city of Buffalo is, in pursuance of general order No. 28, in bankruptcy, designated as a depository in which all moneys which have been, or shall hereafter be paid into court in the course of any proceedings in bankruptcy, shall be deposited; the clerk of this court shall so deposit any such moneys which have been, or shall hereafter be received by him. But this rule shall not ap-

ply to the case of moneys deposited by assignees under existing rules.

60. Upon the hearing of an application for a final discharge, in a case where the proceedings were commenced after the first day of January, 1869, it will be referred to a register to take the necessary proofs, and to ascertain and report to the court, with all convenient speed, whether the assets of the bankrupt were or were not equal to fifty per cent. of the claims against the estate of such bankrupt upon which he was liable as the principal debtor, which had been proved prior to the making of such order; and whether the assent in writing of a majority in number and value of such creditors who had so proved such claims, had been filed in the case, at or before the time of such hearing of the application for such discharge; and also, whether such bankrupt has in all things conformed to his duty under the bankruptcy act, and the amendments thereof, and is entitled to a discharge. And such order of reference will provide that the assignee, or any creditor of such bankrupt, as well as the said bankrupt, may appear and produce proofs, and examine and cross-examine witnesses upon the reference; and that the proceedings and report of the register shall stand confirmed and be conclusive, unless the same shall be excepted to within the time and in the manner required by the rules and practice of this court.

61. Upon the filing of the petition, schedule and inventory of a debtor, in conformity to the provisions of the 11th section of the bankruptcy act, and of the general orders in bankruptcy, together with the certificate of a register annexed thereto, as provided by rule 5, the clerk may enter, as of course, the usual order of reference thereof to the register of the congressional district in which such petitioner is stated in such petition to reside, in the form prescribed for such orders of reference by the general orders in bankruptcy, and specifying the office of such register as the place where the register shall act upon the matters arising in the case in which such petition is filed.

62. Upon the filing of the petition of a creditor or creditors of any debtor, and due proof of the debt and of the acts of bankruptcy therein alleged, in conformity to the 39th section of the bankruptcy act and the

general orders in bankruptcy, and the forms thereby prescribed, together with the certificate of a register, as required by the 6th general rule in bankruptcy, then in force, the clerk may enter, as of course, and without special authority from the district judge, the usual order, according to form No. 57 annexed to the general orders in bankruptcy, for the debtor or debtors named in such petition to show cause before the court, at the United States court rooms at Buffalo, at ten o'clock in the forenoon of such Tuesday or Friday, not less than six nor more than thirty days distant, as to said clerk shall appear expedient, and may include in such order the usual injunction clause, as authorized by the 40th section of the bankruptcy act.

63. It is hereby ordered that the 56 general rule in bankruptcy heretofore adopted by this court, shall be and the same hereby is amended by inserting at the end thereof as following, viz : If the register in charge of any case shall file his separate certificate therein, that to the best of his knowledge, information and belief all the proceedings and business in the case required or expected to be had therein before the register have been had and concluded ; and that all the papers relating to such case which have been filed or used before, or deposited with him as such register, and which are required to be filed by the 7th general order in bankruptcy, have been sent free of postage or other charges to the clerk of the dictrict court of this district, to be filed in his office; and if the clerk on an examination of the papers in the case shall be of the opinion that all such papers have reached his office and been filed, the clerk shall consider the same as sufficient proof of the filing of the papers referred to in said 7th general order and this rule.

64. It appearing by the annexed letter from register Hackley, that the Northern New York Journal has been discontinued by a sale to "The New York Reformer," It is hereby ordered that the 38th general rule in bankruptcy be, and the same is hereby amended by striking out the words "The Northern New York Journal," and inserting in lieu thereof the words, "The New York Reformer."

And it is further ordered that publications of notices heretofore directed to be made in the said Northern New York Journal, may in lieu thereof be made or continued in the said New York Reformer, and that the clerk transmit a certified copy of this order to the register Hackley.

65. In order that the judge of this court may have some means of determining whether assignees in bankruptcy deposit the money received by them as such assignees, as they are required to do by the 38th general order in bankruptcy, and the 37th general rule in bankruptcy, adopted by this court, and in order that the court may also be informed whether such assignees duly make report on the first Monday in each month of the funds received and deposits made by them during the preceding month, as required by said general order, the several deposit banks designated by general rule in bankruptcy No. 37, heretofore adopted by this court, are hereby specially requested to transmit to the clerk of this court, on or before the fifteenth day of October next, a statement of the aggregate amount theretofore deposited in such banks in each case in which such deposits have been made prior to the first day of September, 1871, giving in each case the number of such case, the name of the bankrupt or bankrupts, and the name of the assignee or assignees, and also the aggregate of such moneys which have been withdrawn, and also to transmit to the clerk of this court on or before the twentieth day of the months of January, April, July and October, in each year after 1871, a like report of the aggregate of all sums remaining in deposit on the first day of each of said months, in each case, and the aggregate amount of all deposits made between the first day of the month in which the previous report was required to be made, and the first day of the month in which such report for the three succeeding months is required to be made, giving in each case the number of the case and the name of the assignee or assignees therein; and every register in bankruptcy is hereby requested to make a report to the clerk of this court, within thirty days from the date hereof, of the name of every assignee who has failed to deposit funds received by him as required by such general order, or who has failed to make the monthly return required by such general order ; or who has failed, after due request

by the register, to close his trust or to pass his accounts as assignee within a reasonable time after his appointment or election as such assignee, and such registers are also directed to file with the clerk, (after proper note thereof in their registers, and at their earliest convenience,) any return or report of any assignee in bankruptcy under said general order and also all accounts of assignees which have been or shall be passed and allowed by such registers.

And the clerk of this court is hereby directed to transmit a certified copy of this order to each of the deposit banks designated in the bankruptcy rules of this court, and to each of the registers in bankruptcy in this district.

November 10th, 1871. It is ordered that the following additional rules in bankruptcy be, and the same hereby are, adopted and added to the general rules of bankruptcy, heretofore adopted by this court, viz.

RULE 66. As petitions for adjudication bankruptcy are sometimes filed by or against a supposed bankrupt without any intention, on the part of the petitioner, to proceed thereon with due diligence, for the benefit of all the creditors of said supposed bankrupt, but with the intention of forcing a compromise for the benefit of the debtor or obtaining a fraudulent preference or other unlawful advantage over his general creditors, by means whereof gross injustice or great inconvenience may result to creditors of such supposed bankrupt or debtor, or to persons dealing with him in ignorance of such petition, all such petitioners are to be required to proceed with due diligence; and if, in any case, a petitioner shall fail to procure an adjudication, and to place the proper warrant in the hands of the marshal for execution within thirty days from the filing of his petition, such petition may be dismissed on motion of any person interested, or by the court without special motion unless good cause shall be shown for the delay, or unless some creditor of the bankrupt shall appear to prosecute such petition or carry on the proceedings.

And if any creditor, who shall have filed a petition against any supposed bankrupt, shall fail to obtain an order to show cause against an adjudication within five days after the filing of such petition, or if any debtor, who shall have filed his voluntary petition for a discharge from his debts shall fail to procure an order referring the same to a register for further proceedings within five days after the filing of such petition, such petition shall stand dismissed without motion or special order, unless the court or the judge thereof shall, before the expiration of said five days, have otherwise ordered, and the clerk will report to the judge whenever any petitioner shall fail to prosecute his petition with due and proper diligence.

And whenever a petitioner in bankruptcy shall fail to prosecute the proceedings upon his petition with proper diligence before the register, it shall be the duty of the register to require such petitioner to exercise such diligence and prosecute such proceedings without unreasonable delay, and in case of neglect to comply with such requirement, the register shall report the fact to the court for its action.

67. Any person who may be liable as bail, surety, guarantor or otherwise, for any debt of a bankrupt, and who has not paid the whole of said debt, but is still liable for the same or any part thereof, may, if the creditor shall omit or fail to prove said debt, prove the same in the name of such creditor, after ten days' previous notice of his intention to prove said debt in case such creditor shall fail to make due proof thereof. Such notice shall be in writing, and shall be served personally or by leaving at the residence of such creditor with some person of suitable age and discretion, if the parties reside in the same city, town, or village; and if not so residing, the same shall be served by mail, with the postage thereon fully paid, to the proper address of such creditor. Such notice shall also contain a brief description of the debt, and of any instrument in writing by which it may be evidenced, together with a brief statement of the character of the liability therefor of the person giving such notice, and a notification that in case such creditor shall fail or omit to prove said debt within ten days after the service of such notice, the person giving such notice will prove the same in the name of such creditor.

The proof of such debt shall contain, in addition to the matters now required, the statement that it is made by the person or persons making the same as being liable for the bankrupt as surety, bail, guarantor, or otherwise, and it shall also state, in general terms, the obligation, or the facts and circumstances out of which such liability arose; the amount, if any, such person or persons has or have paid on account thereof, and the amount he or they is or are still liable to pay; and in case he or they shall have secured the payment thereof, the manner in which it is secured, and also the fact that the notice hereinbefore prescribed has been given, and stating to whom and what manner. Such proof shall be verified by the oath of the person making the same or by the oath of some other person or persons who has or have knowledge of the facts stated therein.

In case the person proving such debt shall produce to, and deposit with the assignee of the bankrupt, a consent in writing (duly acknowledged or proved) of the creditor in whose name such proof shall be made, that the proper dividends from the estate of the bankrupt, on account of such debt, be paid to the person proving the same, as a payment and dividend upon the said debt so proved, all such dividends properly payable thereon shall be paid to the person making such proof.

In case such consent shall not be produced, the assignee shall pay the dividends to such creditor, and in case he shall refuse or neglect to apply for the payment of any dividend for thirty days after notice that the same has been declared and is payable, such dividend shall be paid into court subject to its order.

68. Whenever at any meeting of the creditors of a bankrupt, the allowance of any debt or claim offered for proof, or which have been before proved, shall be objected to in whole or in part, the register, if he deemed it just and expedient, may require the objections to be fully stated, and, if the person offering or who made such proof, is present or represented, may require the evidence on both sides to be produced forthwith, or as soon after as practicable, before him, and he shall take the evidence offered and shall report the evidence and his views of the case to the court as soon thereafter as may be. And whenever it shall appear that frivolous objections are made to the proof of debts, or that unfounded claims have been made, the court will make such order concerning costs as may be just and expedient.

69. At each second or subsequent general meeting of the creditors of a bankrupt, and at each adjournment thereof, it shall be the duty of the assignee or assignees of such bankrupt to exhibit to the register, and under his direction to the creditors of such bankrupt, all proofs of debts or demands against said bankrupt's estate, together with his accounts of receipts, disbursements and payments, and any person interested may, at any such meeting, take objection to the proof of any debt so exhibited for the first time, as fully as he might or could have done had said debt been then first offered for proof; subject always to such terms and conditions concerning notice to the proving creditor as may fully secure his right to be heard in all proceedings in respect thereto.

70. Upon special cause therefore being shown to the register in charge, he may grant leave to any creditor to examine a bankrupt before the appointment of his assignment. After the appointment of an assignee of any bankrupt, any creditor who may obtain an order from the court over a register for the examination of such bankrupt, shall notify the assignee thereof, and it shall be the duty of such assignee to attend the examination and take care that it

is as thorough and complete as may be necessary whenever a thorough examination of said bankrupt is deemed important to the interest of his general creditors. The assignee and any creditor may carry on and continue any such examination as fully and effectually as the creditor at whose instance the order therefore was obtained, subject to all proper regulations concerning the costs and expenses thereof: and to such other regulations as to the time and manner of examination as the register may find convenient. No second order for a general examination of any bankrupt will be granted as of course, but an order therefor may be granted whenever there are special reasons therefor, and may be so restricted and guarded in respect to the extent and matters of the inquiry, or otherwise, as the justice of the case may require. Nor will any examination be granted as of course, unless applied for within five months after the adjudication of bankruptcy in the case. Upon good cause shown for the delay the order may be granted after the expiration of such period of five months.

71. No order to show cause shall hereafter be granted on any petition for a bankrupt's discharge in any case in which the original petition was filed after the first day of January, 1871, until the second and third meetings of the creditors of said bankrupt have been ordered; and the return day of any such order to show cause shall be at least fifteen days after the time appointed for such third meeting.

72. Objections to the approval of any assignee who shall be duly elected must be made in writing, specifying fully the reasons of objection, and must be filed with the register at the meeting at which the election is had; and the register shall proceed at once or as soon thereafter as may be practicable and consistent with a due hearing, to take all evidence that may be offered pertinent to such objections, and whether for or against the appointment, and shall report the same to the court with his opinion thereon. Further evidence or argument will not be heard by the court except in special cases, and when satisfactory reasons therefor shall be shown by affidavit or by the register's report.

The 59th general rule in bankruptcy having been abrogated by the provisions of the act of congress relating to the deposit of moneys paid into court, it is hereby ordered that the following be and the same hereby is adopted and substituted in place and in stead of said rule 59, and that it be placed and numbered as rule 59 of the general rules in bankruptcy of this court, viz.:

59. The several deposit banks designated by general rule in bankruptcy No. 37 heretofore adopted by this court, are

specially requested to transmit to the clerk of this court, on or before the twentieth day of the months of January and July, in each year, a report of the aggregate of all sums remaining in deposit on the first day of each of said months in each case, and the aggrogate amount of .all deposits made between the first day of the month in which the previous report was required to be made, and the first day of the month in which such report, for the six preceding months is required to be made, giving in each case the number of the case and the name of the assignee or assignees therein, and every register in bankruptcy is hereby requested to make a report to the clerk of this court within thirty days after the first days of January and July in each year of the name of every assignee who has failed to deposit funds received by him as required by general order No. 28, and said general rule No. 37; or who has failed to make the monthly returns required by such general order; or who has failed after due request by the register, to close his trust and pass his accounts as assignee within a reasonable time after his appointment or election as such assignee. And such registers are also directed to file with the clerk (after proper note thereof in their registers and at their earliest convenience) any return or report of any assignee in bankruptcy under said goneral order, and also to file with the clerk as soon as it can be properly done, all final or other accounts of assignees which have been or shall be passed and allowed by such registers.

NEW YORK—Southern District.

[The rules numbered from 1 to 25, both inclusive, were adopted originally June 23d, 1867, and are here printed as subsequently amended. The rules subsequently adopted are added, with the dates of their adoption.]

RULE 1. In voluntary bankruptcy, where the petition states that the debtor whether an individual, a copartnership, a corporation, or a joint stock company, has resided or carried on business for the six months next immediately preceding the time of filing the petition, or for the longest period during such six months, in the city and county of New York, the petitions shall be referred in rotation, by Form No. 4, to the several registers appointed in the six congressional districts therein, commencing with the fourth and ending with the ninth, in the order of the times of filing such petitions; and where in any other county, the petition shall be referred, by Form No. 4, to the register appointed in the congressional district in which such county is embraced. A petition may be otherwise referred for special reasons, or in cases not herein provided for. In involuntary bankruptcy, the register

will be designated with reference to the special circumstances of each case.

The order, Form No. 4, designating the register to act upon the petition, in voluntary bankruptcy, shall, in the case of a register in any district in the city and county of New York, specify as the place where the register shall act upon the matter arising under the case, and the warrant, Form No. 59, in involuntary bankruptcy, shall in a like case, specify as the place where the meeting of the creditors will be held, the office of the register as designated by him, by a writing filed with the clerk. In the case of a register in any district other than one in the city and county of New York, the order, Form No. 4, in voluntary bankruptcy, shall specify as the place where the register shall act upon the matters arising under the case, an office of the register as designated by him in like manner, in the county in which is the place of residence of the petitioner, or the place of business of the copartnership, corporation or joint stock company, as set forth in the petition, having due regard always to the proximity and convenience of such office to such place of residence or place of business; and in a like case, in the warrant, Form No. 59, in involuntary bankruptcy, the place will be designated with reference to the special circumstances of the case.

The day named in the order, Form No. 4, for the attendance of the bankrupt before the register, in voluntary bankruptcy, and the day named in the warrant, Form No. 59, for the meeting of creditors, in involuntary bankruptcy, will be fixed with reference to the convenient and speedy progress of the case.

Every register in the district other than the city and county of New York, shall by a writing filed with the clerk, designate the days on which he will attend at a place or places within each county in his district.

Every register may in any case referred to him, fix the time when he will act upon the several matters arising under such case, other than the attendance of the bankrupt, as fixed by the order, Form No. 4, and the meeting of creditors as fixed by the warrant, Form No. 59; but the register shall not, without leave of the court, be at liberty to change the place specified in the order, Form No. 4, or to act upon the matters arising under a case in involuntary bankruptcy at any other place than one specified in the warrant, Form No. 59, as the place for the meeting of creditors.

2. The adjudication of bankruptcy, Form No. 58, shall contain a provision that the case be referred to one of the registers, naming him, to take such proceedings thereon as are required by the act.

3. Whenever a petition is referred to a

register in a voluntary case, and whenever, in an involuntary cuse, an order is made, on an adjudication of bankruptcy, referring the case to a register, the clerk, at the time he sends or delivers to the register a copy of the order of reference, shall pay to him the sum of twenty-five dollars out of the fifty dollars deposited with the clerk under section 47 of the act, the same to be applied to the payment of such fees of the register as are chargeable to the petitioner making the deposit. Whenever, by a return made to the court, by the register, of the fees so chargeable for services rendered by him, it shall appear that the aggregate amount of such fees exceeds the aggregate payments made thereon to the register out of the fifty dollars, the clerk shall, if requested by the register, make further payments to him thereon to the amount of such fees, until the fifty dollars shall all of it be paid out, and thereafter the fees of the register which are chargeable to such petitioner shall be paid or secured in like manner with the other fees provided for by rule 29 of the "general orders in bankruptcy."

The foregoing provisions of this rule shall not apply to a case of voluntary bankruptcy, where, under rule 30 of the "general orders in bankruptcy," the judge shall direct that the fees and costs in the case shall not exceed the sum required by the act to be deposited with the clerk; but, in every such case, such of the disbursements paid out by the register and marshal for the purposes specified in rule 12 of the "general orders in bankruptcy," and returned by them under oath, under said rule 12, as are chargeable to the petitioning debtor, shall be refunded to them severally by the clerk out of such sum; and the clerk, marshal, and register shall perform the duties required of them by such petitioning debtor without first requiring payment or security for their fees, subject to the application by the court to such fees, of so much of such sum as shall remain after refunding such disbursements.

4. The register shall, under rule 7 of the "general orders in bankruptcy," examine the duplicate copy of the petition and schedules specified in Form No. 4, and such duplicate copy shall either be a copy of such filed original, certified by the clerk under the seal of the court, or else a duplicate

original, signed and verified in like manner with the original petition and schedules filed with the clerk, and shown by evidence satisfactory to the register to be such duplicate original; and the certificate of the register, required by said rule 7, as to the correctness in form of the petition and schedules, shall be made in writing, and be signed by him, on the duplicate copy which he so examines; and he shall not issue any warrant under Form No. 6, until he shall have so made a certificate, after such examination, that the petition and schedules are correct in form. No such certificate shall be made unless the whole eleven of the sheets composing schedules A and B, in Form No. 1, form part of the schedules to the petition.

5. The warrant issued under section 11 or section 42 of the act, according to Form No. 6 or Form No. 59, shall specify two, if there be two, and if not, then one, of the newspapers named in rule 21, published in the county stated in the petition as the one in which the debtor, whether an individual, a copartnership, a corporation, or a joint stock company, has resided or carried on business for the six months next immediately preceding the time of filing the petition, or for the longest period during such six months, the selection of such newspapers to be made by the register to whom the petition or case is referred. The notices to be published in pursuance of the warrant shall be published twice in each newspaper selected.

The warrant shall designate the creditors on whom personal service is to be made, and notice shall be served by mail upon all creditors other than those so designated. No creditor resident out of this district shall be designated for personal service.

Whenever a debtor shall furnish, at his own expense, to the marshal, printed copies of the notices required to be served by the warrant, no fee shall be allowed to the marshal for copying into the notices the names and places of residence of the creditors and the amounts of their debts.

The warrant, Form No. 6, shall be regarded as process under rule 2 of the "general orders in bankruptcy," and such warrant shall, before it is issued to the marshal, in addition to being signed by the clerk and sealed with the seal of the court, be signed by the judge or the register at the foot thereof, in the following form, with the date: "Issued by me, 18 ,

District Judge [*or Register in Bankruptcy.*"]

Whenever the order, Form No. 10, is used by a register, the conclusion of said form be varied so that the order may be attested or signed by the register alone.

6. All proofs of debt which shall be made and verified prior to the election or appointment of an assignee, shall be delivered or sent to the register to whom the case is referred. If the register entertains doubts of the validity of any claim, or of the right of a creditor to prove it, and is of opinion that such validity or right ought to be investigated by the assignee, he may postpone the proof of the claim until the assignee is chosen.

7. In case no choice of an assignee is made by the creditors at their first meeting, or in case an assignee chosen by the creditors fails, within five days, to express in writing his acceptance of the trust, or in case of a vacancy in the office of an assignee caused by his removal, resignation, death, or other cause, John Sedgwick, esquire, of the city of New York, counselor-at-law, will be appointed assignee where the judge is required by the act to appoint the assignee, and where the said John Sedgwick shall be appointed by any register, such appointment is hereby approved by the judge. In special cases, vacancies in the office of assignee will be filled by an election by the creditors, or by the appointment of an assignee other than the one above named.

8. Under rule 9 of the "general orders in bankruptcy," an assignee shall notify the register of his acceptance or rejection of the trust, and the register shall immediately on receiving such notice report it to the clerk of the court.

9. Every assignee shall, immediately on receiving an assignment of an estate in bankruptcy, send or deliver such assignment to the clerk of the court, who shall make a true copy of it, and certify such copy under his hand and the seal of the court, and such certified copy shall then be placed and kept by him on file, and the original assignment shall be returned to the assignee.

10. Notice of the appointment of an assignee shall be given by publication once a week for three successive weeks in two of the newspapers named in rule 21, at least one of which shall be a newspaper published in the city and county of New York, such newspapers to be selected by the register with due regard to the requirements of section 14 of the act.

11. Notices of sale by an assignee under rule 21 of the "general orders in bankruptcy" shall be advertised in two, if there be two, and, if not, then in one, of the newspapers named in rule 21, published in the county where the sale is to take place, the selection of such newspapers to be made by the register.

12. The notice to creditors of dividends or meetings, required by the 17th, 27th and 28th sections of the act, shall be such as is provided for by the order contained in Form No. 28, and the register shall select one newspaper, in which the notice shall be published, from among the newspapers specified in rule 21.

13. The list of debts provided for by section 23 of the act, shall be made and certified by the register to whom the petition or case is referred, and he shall place thereon all debts which are duly proved.

14. The assignee shall, under section 27 of the act, produce and file vouchers for all payments made by him, except as to items in regard to which the court shall, for reasonable cause, dispense with vouchers.

15. The notice by the assignee, under section 28 of the act, of the filing of his account, and of his application for a settlement and discharge, shall be given by him by sending written or printed notices by mail, prepaid, of such filing, and of the time of such application, to all known creditors of the bankrupt.

16. All questions for trial or hearing, under sections 31 and 34 of the act, and all questions under section 41 of the act, which are not ordered to be tried by a jury, shall be brought on upon testimony taken before a register, a commissioner or a referee, and shall be tried or heard by the court, and will be so tried or heard on any Saturday in term, at a stated session of the court, on four days' notice of trial or hearing, to be served by either party upon the other party, and upon the clerk, and a

separate calendar of the same shall be made by the clerk for every Saturday in term, on which the cases shall be arranged in the order in which the same are numbered, according to general order No. 1.

17. The application, under section 34 of the act, to set aside and annul a discharge, shall be verified by the oath or affirmation of the applicant, and the answer of the bankrupt to the application shall answer specifically the allegations of the application, and shall be verified in like manner.

18. The demand in writing for a trial by jury, under section 41 of the act, shall be signed by the debtor or his attorney.

19. All issues, questions, points, and matters stated in writing, under rule 11 of the "general orders in bankruptcy," or under the 4th section or the 6th section of the act, or according to Form No. 50, and adjourned into court for decision, or stated in a special case for the opinion of the court, shall be certified to the judge by the register by a certificate, which shall also state briefly the opinion of the register on the issue, question, point or matter, and shall be delivered or sent to the clerk ; and no oral or written argument shall be allowed on any such issue or question, unless by special leave of the court.

20. In pursuance of rule 28 of the "general orders in bankruptcy," the following national banks in this district are designated as those in which all moneys received by assignees or paid into court in the course of any proceedings in bankruptcy shall be deposited, namely :

In the city and county of New York— Bank of New York, National Banking Association.

In Westchester County — Westchester County National Bank, at Peekskill ; and First National Bank, at Sing Sing.

In Putnam County—Putnam County National Bank, at Carmel.

In Rockland County—Rockland County National Bank, at Nyack.

In Orange County—Highland National Bank, at Newburgh ; Goshen National Bank, at Goshen and Walkill National Bank, at Middletown.

In Sullivan County—National Union Bank at Monticello.

In Dutchess County—Farmers' and Manufacturers' National Bank, at Poughkeepsie.

In Columbia County—Farmers' National Bank, at Hudson.

In Ulster County—National Ulster County Bank, at Kingston.

In Greene County—Tanners' National Bank, at Catskill.

All moneys received by the clerk of the court on account of any bankrupt estate, or paid into court in the course of any proceedings in bankruptcy (except the sums deposited with the clerk under section 47 of the act), shall be deposited in said bank in the city and county of New York ; and all sums received by an assignee on account of any estate of which he is assignee, shall be deposited in such one of said banks as he shall select by a writing to be signed by him and filed with the clerk. The check, or warrant, for drawing moneys deposited by the clerk, shall be signed by the clerk and countersigned by the judge. The check, or warrant, for drawing moneys deposited by an assignee, shall be signed by him and countersigned by the register designated to act in the case of the estate on account of which such moneys were deposited.

21. The following newspapers are designated as those in which all publications required by the act, or the "general orders in bankruptcy," or these rules, may be made, namely :

In the City and County of New York— Daily morning paper—Times. Daily evening paper—Commercial Advertiser.

In Westchester County—Statesman, at Yonkers ; and Republican, at Sing Sing.

In Putnam County—Putnam Free Press, at Carmel ; and Cold Spring Recorder, at Cold Spring.

In Rockland County—Rockland County Journal, at Nyack ; and Rockland County Messenger, at Haverstraw.

In Orange County—Daily Journal, at Newburgh ; Goshen Democrat, at Goshen ; Middletown Press, at Middletown ; and Tri States' Union, at Port Jervis.

In Sullivan County—Monticello Republican, at Monticello.

In Dutchess County—Poughkeepsie Eagle at Poughkeepsie ; and Poughkeepsie Telegraph, at Poughkeepsie.

In Columbia County—Columbia Republican, at Hudson ; and Hudson Gazette, at Hudson.

In Ulster County—Kingston Journal, at

Kingston; and Kingston Argus, at Kingston.

In Greene County—Examiner, at Catskill; and Windham Journal, at Windham.

The marshal and the clerk, and every register or assignee, when required to publish any notice or advertisement, shall preserve and return to the court a copy, cut from each newspaper in which it is published, of each notice and advertisement as published, with a certificate as to the particulars of the publishing, showing that the required publication has been made.

22. In case of the absence of the judge at the time and place noticed or appointed for any hearing or proceeding before him in bankruptcy, or if the matter then fails to be called or acted on, the same shall be deemed continued, without other order, to the next sitting of the court thereafter, at which time the like proceedings may be had thereupon as if first noticed or appointed for such day.

23. If the marshal shall, under rule 13 of the "general orders in bankruptcy," appoint special deputies to act as messengers, he shall, as far as possible, designate one or more of such special deputies to be attached to the office of each register, for the purpose of causing the notices to be published and served, which are specified in the warrants issued in the cases referred to such register.

24. All notices served or sent by mail by the marshal, clerk, or assignee, shall be so written or printed and folded that the direction, postage stamp and postmark shall be upon the notice itself, and not upon an envelope or other separate piece of paper.

25. Special cases not comprehended within the foregoing rules. or the "general orders in bankruptcy," or the forms shall be submitted to the judge

NEW RULES.

September 9th, 1867.

The register to whom a case is referred shall have power to make the order in Form No. 51. under section 29 of the act.

September 25th, 1867.

In every case where a petition for discharge is filed hereafter, the clerk will enter a special order referring it to the register in charge of the case, to make an order to show cause therein, and to sit in cham-

bers on the return thereof and pass the last examination of the bankrupt, if there be no opposition, and certify to the court whether the bankrupt has in all things conformed to his duty under the act, and has conformed to all the requirements of the act.

October 11th, 1867.

Every register shall, immediately on directing an order to show cause, Form No. 51, to issue, transmit to the clerk a list of all the proofs of debt in the case which have been furnished to the register or the assignee, containing the names, residences, and postoffice addresses of the creditors, with sufficient particularity to enable the notices, Form No. 52, to be served properly.

October 12th, 1867.

Every assignee shall, forthwith transmit to the clerk of the court a memorandum showing the names of the creditors, and their places of residence and postoffice addresses, when stated, and the amounts of their debts, in all cases in which proofs of debt have heretofore been furnished to the assignee; and hereafter every assignee shall transmit to the clerk a like memorandum in every case in which a proof of debt shall be furnished to the assignee, as soon as it shall be received by the assignee.

December 9th, 1867.

The following prices, and no more, shall be paid for publishing in the newspapers designated by rule 21 for the city and county of New York, the following notices: In the New York Daily Times, for the publication, two times, of the notice by the marshal, as messenger, under a warrant, five dollars; for the publication, three times, of the notice by an assignee or trustee, of his appointment, five dollars; for the publication three times, of the notice by the clerk to show cause against the granting of a discharge, seven dollars; for the publication of other notices, an average of the above rates. In the New York Commercial Advertiser: for the publication, two times, of the notice by the marshal, as messenger, under a warrant, four dollars and twenty-five cents; for the publication, three times, of the notice by an assignee or trustee, of his appointment, four dollars and twenty-five cents; for the publication, three times, of the notice by the clerk, to show cause against the granting of a discharge, six dollars ; for the publication of other notices, an average of the above rates.

January 23d, 1868.

Hereafter, in cases of orders to show cause, made according to Form No. 51, on petitions of bankrupts for discharges from their debts, no meeting of creditors except the first shall be ordered or had, unless some assets have come to the hands of the assignee ; but where, in any such case, any assets have come to the hands of the assignee, then the order to show cause shall contain a provision, under general order No. 25, for the holding of the second and third meetings of creditors and for notices thereof.

November 10th, 1868.

In taking testimony, all registers, referees and commissioners shall, where testimony is written down by question and answer, number the questions put to each witness continuously, from the commencement of his direct examination to the final close of his examination, direct and cross.

See Errata No. 1, additional rules, p. 1158.

OHIO.—Northern District.

At a court in bankruptcy held in and for the northern district of Ohio, at the United States court room in the city of Cleveland, on the 18th day of July, 1867 :

Present, the Hon. Charles T. Sherman, *District Judge.*

Ordered, That the following rules be and they are hereby adopted and prescribed for the regulation and government of the proceedings in bankruptcy, in the district court of the United States for the northern district of Ohio, pursuant to the act entitled, " An act to establish a uniform system of bankruptcy throughout the United States," approved March 2, 1867.

RULE 1. The act of congress entitled, "An act to establish a uniform system of bankruptcy throughout the United States," approved March 2d, 1867 ; the general orders in bankruptcy adopted by the justices of the supreme court, and the following rules, shall, until otherwise ordered, be rules of practice in bankruptcy in this court, in respect to all matters and proceedings therein provided for.

In cases not provided for, either by said bankrupt act, general orders, or rules, the practice of this court shall be subject to the special order of the district court or judge, and will be made to conform as near as may be to the practice of the district court in other cases of similar character.

Whenever any special order hereafter made by the district court in any particular case shall conflict with these rules, the direction of such special order shall be followed in such case.

2. Except during the absence of the district judge, the district court will be open for the transaction of business, as a court of bankruptcy, at the United States court room, in the city of Cleveland, on every Tuesday, Wednesday and Thursday, from 10 o'clock A. M., until 1 o'clock P. M., unless the business before it shall sooner be disposed of.

3. All papers used in court, or filed in proceedings in bankruptcy, whether prepared by parties to the proceedings or their attorneys, or by any register in bankruptcy or other officer of the court, or by any assignee in bankruptcy, shall be written in a fair and legible hand, or properly printed, upon paper substantially of the size and width of that known as legal cap, and folded in the form and size in which law papers are usually folded.

All papers to be filed shall be prepared with a white margin of at least one and one-half inches wide along the head of each and every sheet thereof, in order that they may be properly and securely fastened together at such head, to constitute the final record in the case ; and also with a white margin at least one inch wide at the left hand side thereof.

No paper not prepared in compliance with this rule, and also in compliance with the general orders in bankruptcy, shall be filed by the clerk without the special order of the court or judge ; and no attorney not admitted in the circuit or district court shall be allowed to practice therein in cases of bankruptcy.

4. Every register in bankruptcy, or other officer of the court, before administering the proper oaths in verification of any petition, schedule, inventory, deposition, affidavits, or other papers, shall see that the different sheets, or pieces of paper of

which is composed, and those to which it refers as annexed, are properly fastened together in such a manner as to give reasonable security against the separation, loss or exchange of any part thereof.

5. Upon the filing of a petition in a case of voluntary bankruptcy, the same shall be referred, of course to the register of the congressional district in which the petitioner resides; or it may be referred to such other register as may be specially designated by the judge, which reference shall be noted on the back of the petition by the clerk; and the clerk shall forthwith make for the petitioner, to furnish to the proper register, a certified copy of the petition and the other papers and schedules filed therewith. He shall also make and transmit to the register the order of reference, as in Form No. 4, prescribed by the supreme court, designating therein a day whereon the petitioner shall be required to attend before him at his office, or such other place as he may designate, not more than five days after the day on which the register shall probably receive the said order, and shall also when necessary send to such petitioner, by mail, notice of the time and place as designated in said order, for his attendance; and upon receiving notice of the adjudication in bankruptcy in the case, the clerk shall forthwith issue to the marshal, as messenger, the warrant prescribed in Form No. 6.

6. Every register, before he makes an order of adjudication of bankruptcy, shall carefully examine and certify in the order of adjudication that the petition and schedules thereto annexed are correct in form. Before making such certificate the register will carefully examine every part of the petition, schedule and inventory, to ascertain whether the petitioner has fully complied with every requirement of the bankrupt act, and of the general orders and rules of court applicable thereto; and particularly that they are substantially in the form prescribed by such general orders; that all the blanks of both such schedule and inventory are properly filled, using the word "none," where that is proper; that both the real and personal property of the petitioner, and the place where each part of the same is situated, are set forth in detail and sufficiently described; and that the incumbrances thereon are

stated; or that it is stated that there is no incumbrance thereon. He will also ascertain that the petitioner has fully set forth in his schedule, in respect to every debt stated therein, all the particulars required by the 11th section of the bankrupt act.

And the registers are specially enjoined to refuse such certificate, and to decline making any order of adjudication in bankruptcy upon any petition, until every requisite of the bankrupt act and of the general orders are fully and strictly complied with.

7. Before any petition under the 39th section of the bankrupt act shall be presented to the court, or judge, the petitioner shall procure the certificate of a register in bankruptcy, to be indorsed on or annexed to such petition, substantially in the following form, viz:

" I certify that I have carefully examined the annexed (or within) petition and the verification thereof, and that the same are in proper form and sufficient in substance to authorize an adjudication in bankruptcy, and the issuing of a warrant under the 42d section of the bankrupt act

" Given at   this   day of   18 ."

8. All petitions filed under the bankrupt act shall be numbered consecutively; and the clerk shall enter the case under its proper title in his docket, giving to each case two pages thereof. He shall place its number at the head of the outside filing of said petition, which number shall thereafter be the designating number of such case until finally disposed of. Every other paper, proceeding or notice, in such case or matter, shall be marked by the clerk, register, messenger, or other officer or party preparing it, with such designating number at the head of the outside filing, on or near the upper left hand corner.

9. The clerk shall prepare and number envelopes of uniform size, as nearly as practicable, in which to keep separately the papers filed in each case, while the same is in progress. The designating number and the title of the case shall be indorsed upon the envelope.

10. A copy of every other order of the court made at the time of making an order referring the petition of a debtor to a register in bankruptcy, which contains any directions in regard to the action of the register on such petition, shall be attached by the

clerk to the certified copy of such order of reference furnished to the register.

11. In cases of voluntary bankruptcy, the register to whom the debtor's petition shall be referred, shall proceed to consider such petition at the time and place fixed in the order of reference for his first action thereon; and he shall then act on such petition, and shall make the order of adjudication of bankruptcy, or other proper order thereon, on the same day, or on some day to which the hearing on such petition may then be adjourned. On such hearing any creditor of the petitioner who has proved his debt, or who shall prove the same on such hearing, may oppose the prayer of such petition, by filing with the register an answer or objections thereto as hereinafter provided.

12. The warrant issued to the marshal, as messenger, under the 11th section of the bankrupt act, shall designate the creditors (if any) on whom personal service is to be made; and notice shall be served by mail upon all creditors not so designated. No creditor shall be designated as one on whom personal service is to be made, except for special reasons of an imperative or very important character.

13. The marshal shall, under rule 13 of the general orders, appoint special deputies to act as messengers, and shall designate one or more to attend at the office of each register, when required, for the purpose of serving notices and subpoenas, and performing such other official duties as may be necessary.

14. Whenever a petition is referred to a register in a voluntary case, and whenever, in an involuntary case, an order is made on an adjudication of bankruptcy, referring the case to a register, the clerk, at the time he sends or delivers to the register a copy of the order of reference, shall transmit therewith to him the sum of twenty dollars out of the fifty dollars deposited with the clerk under section 47 of the act; the same to be applied to the payment of such fees of the register as are chargeable in the petitioner making the deposit. Whenever, by a return made to the court, under oath by the register, of the fees so chargeable for services rendered by him, it shall appear that the aggregate amount of such fees exceeds the amount so transmitted, the clerk shall, if requested by the register, make further pay-

ment to him thereon to the amount of such fees, until the fifty dollars shall be exhausted; and thereafter the fees of the register which are chargeable to such petitioners, shall be paid or secured in like manner as the other fees provided for by rule 29 of the "general orders in bankruptcy." The foregoing provisions of this rule shall not apply to a case of voluntary bankruptcy, where under rule 30 of the "general orders in bankruptcy," the judge shall direct that the fees and costs in the case shall not exceed the sum required by the act to be deposited with the clerk; but in every such case, such of the disbursements made by the register and marshal for the purposes specified in rule 12 of the "general orders in bankruptcy," and returned by them under oath, under said rule 12, as are chargeable to the petitioning debtor, shall be refunded to them severally by the clerk out of such sum; and the clerk, marshal and register, shall perform the duties required of them by such petitioning debtor, without first requiring payment or security for their fees; subject to the application by the court, to such fees, of so much as shall remain after refunding such disbursements.

15. A party appearing to show cause against or oppose the prayer of a petition under the 11th or 39th sections of the bankrupt act, shall file a brief statement, in writing, of the grounds of his opposition or objections thereto, if such objections relate solely to questions of law or practice in respect to the regularity or sufficiency of the petition. If his opposition to such petition is founded upon a denial of any statement of facts contained in such petition or upon the alleged existence of other facts not stated therein, he shall, by answer to such petition, set forth in writing, in distinct and separate articles, and according to his best knowledge, information and belief, his denial of each material allegation so denied by him, and each allegation of new matter, so that distinct and separate issues may be readily framed thereon; and he shall annex thereto his affidavit that he has read said answer so signed by him, or heard the same read, and knows the contents thereof, and that the same is true of his own knowledge, except as to the matters therein stated on information and belief, and that as to those believes it to be true.

16. The court, at its own instance, or on motion of either party, will refer to a register, commissioner or referee, designated or appointed for the purpose, for examination and report, such matters arising in proceedings in bankruptcy, as, under the provisions of the bankrupt act may properly be so referred.

17. Exceptions may be filed to the report of a register, referee or commissioner, upon any matter referred to him (except the adjudication of bankruptcy), within eight days after the filing of such report; and exceptions to the admission or rejection of evidence may be filed within four days after the return of proofs so filed; and either party may then apply for an order fixing a time for hearing upon such exceptions.

When a trial by jury is to be had, no formal pleading shall be necesary to present the issue, but the same shall be tried upon the issues made by the petition, answer and other papers.

19. All returns and reports from registers in bankruptcy or other officers of the court, referees, shall be directed to the clerk of the court at Cleveland, Ohio, and shall be sent free of postage or other charge.

20. Letters to the register clerk or marshal requiring an answer, should be accompanied by envelopes, properly addressed, and with the proper postage stamps affixed, in which to inclose the reply and whatever else may be required; and no register or other officer of the court will be required to answer any such letter unless this be done. Whenever any receipt is desired from any such officer, it must be prepared and presented by the party desiring it.

21. In every certificate made by a register stating any case point, or matter for the opinion of the district judge under the 4th or 6th sections of the bankrupt act, according to form No. 50 established by the general orders in bankruptcy, the facts agreed upon by the parties to the controversy shall be clearly and fully stated with reasonable certainty of time and place; and this shall be followed by a brief statement of the claim made, or position assumed, by each of the parties in the controversy. The register shall add thereto such proposed order, adjudication or decision, as in his judgment ought to be made, which shall be in such form that the district judge may signify his approval thereof by his signature. The register shall then afford to each of the opposing parties, or their attorneys, a reasonable opportunity to consent, in writing, to the register's decision thereon. The court will, on the approval and confirmation of such decision of the register, make such order for costs, against any party declining to assent thereto, as may be deemed proper. In case all parties to such controversy shall assent to such adjudication or decision of the register, he shall file the same and proceed with the case upon the basis thereof, as though such controversy had not arisen.

22. If, after the order of adjudication of bankruptcy, and before the appointment of an assignee any property of the bankrupt, in the opinion of the court or register, requires to be taken possession of, the court or register may issue an order to the marshal as messenger to take possession thereof, and adopt such measures relative thereto as may be deemed proper, and account to the assignee for the same or its proceeds.

23. It shall be the duty of the assignee, as soon as practicable after his appointment shall be complete, to take into his possession all the estate of the bankrupt real and personal, of every name and nature, with the exceptions mentioned in the bankrupt act; and also all the deeds and books of account, papers and writings of the bankrupt pertaining thereto; and for this purpose the assignee shall make diligent inquiry into the affairs and transactions of the bankrupt; and he shall be provided, on application to the clerk, with a certified copy of such bankrupt's petition and schedules therewith filed, the expense whereof shall be taxed in the bill of costs in the case. Every assignee shall, under section 27 of the bankrupt act, produce and file with his account, proper vouchers for all payments made by him, except payments of one dollar or less, and except items in regard to which the court shall for reasonable cause, and by special order, dispense with vouchers. The items so excepted may be allowed to a reasonable extent, upon the oath of the assignee, that the amounts charged therein were actually and necessarily paid.

24. In cases of voluntary bankruptcy wherein the assignee or any creditor, after the adjudication of bankruptcy, has reason

to suspect that the petitioner has property or rights therein not disclosed, or which he conceals, such assignee or creditor may apply for an order for the examination of such petitioner on oath or affirmation, which application shall state the grounds of such suspicion in brief terms and shall be verified by oath, and presented to the court or the register to whom the cases stand referred. Whereupon if it appear reasonable the court or register, (as the case may be,) may issue the proper order for such bankrupt's examination; and if he shall fail to obey such order, after due service, the court may compel his attendance by warrant directed to the marshal, commanding him to arrest such bankrupt and bring him forthwith before the court, or register, for such examination.

25. In cases of involuntary bankruptcy, it shall be the duty of the assignee, as soon as practicable after he shall be appointed and qualified, to apply to the bankrupt for a full and true account of all his property and rights of property, and of all the deeds and books of account, papers and writings of the bankrupt pertaining thereto, as required by the bankrupt act; and if the bankrupt shall refuse to give such account, or if the assignee, or any creditor of the bankrupt, shall have good reason to suspect that he has practiced any concealment, or fraud, in giving such account, such assignee or creditor may, on application to the court, and due cause shown by affidavit, have an order for the examination of such bankrupt; and, if necessary, for compulsory process against him, as provided in the last preceding rule.

26. Under rule 9 of the "general orders in bankruptcy," an assignee shall notify the register of his acceptance or rejection of the trust, and the register shall immediately, on receiving such notice, report it to the clerk of the court. Every assignee shall, immediately on receiving an assignment of an estate in bankruptcy, send or deliver such assignment to the clerk of the court, who shall make a true copy of it, and certify such copy under his hand and the seal of the court; and such certified copy shall then be placed and kept by him on file, and the original assignment shall be returned to the assignee.

27. Every bankrupt shall at all times be bound to attend the assignee upon the requirement of the register acting in his case, on reasonable notice in writing for that purpose, to be served personally or left at his usual place of abode, in order to assist in making out the accounts of said bankrupt's estate and effects, and to give information as to his debts and property; and also to attend any court to be examined in any suit or proceeding respecting the same, for which he shall be entitled to receive from the assignee a reasonable compensation out of the estate.

28. When an order for the examination of any bankrupt or other person shall be made, any creditor, or the bankrupt himself, at the time and place appointed for such examination, or at any other time to which such examination may be continued or adjourned, may, at his own expense, produce witnesses touching the subject matter of such examination, and shall be entitled to the ordinary process of subpœna, to be issued by the clerk or register, requiring the attendance of such witnesses, which subpœna the witnesses shall be bound to obey, provided their legal fees are paid or tendered on the service of such subpœna.

29. Application, under section 34 of the bankrupt act, to set aside and annul the discharge granted to any bankrupt, shall clearly set forth, in separate and distinct articles, and with reasonable certainty of time and place, according to the best knowledge, information and belief of the applicant, all the material facts and allegations on which the application is based; the bankrupt shall admit or deny, or otherwise answer the several allegations of such application, in distinct articles, in like manner; and such application and answer shall severally be verified by affidavit, substantially in the form prescribed by rule 15.

30. That for securing the payment of the disbursements, expenses and charges of the clerk, marshal, and other officers of the court, in cases in bankruptcy, the petitioner be, and he is hereby required to deposit with the clerk, on the filing of his petition, (or at any subsequent time prior to the application for final discharge, when thereto required), in addition to the $50 required by law to be deposited for the register, the further sum of fifty dollars in money, or

that he give security to the satisfaction of the clerk, for the payment of such disbursements, expenses and charges.

31. In pursuance of rule No. 28 of the "general orders in bankruptcy," the following banks in this district are designated as those in which all moneys received by assignees or paid into court in the course of any proceedings in bankruptcy, shall be deposited, to wit:

In the 4th congressional district—Rutan, Riddle & Co., bankers, Bellefontaine.

In the 5th congressional district—First National Bank of Findlay, at Findlay.

In the 8th congressional district—First National Bank of Mansfield, at Mansfield.

In the 9th congressional district—First National Bank of Norwalk, at Norwalk.

In the 10th congressional district—Toledo National Bank, at Toledo.

In the 13th congressional district—Knox County National Bank, at Mt. Vernon.

In the 14th congressional district—First National Bank of Elyria, at Elyria.

In the 17th congressional district—Farmers' National Bank of Salem, at Salem.

In the 18th congressional district—First National Bank of Cleveland, at Cleveland.

In the 19th congressional district—First National Bank of Warren, at Warren.

All moneys received by the clerk of the court on account of any bankrupt's estate, shall be deposited in said First National Bank in the city of Cleveland; and all sums received by an assignee on account of any estate of which he is assignee, shall be deposited in such one of said banks as he shall select by a writing to be signed by him and filed with the clerk. The check, or warrant, for drawing monies deposited by the clerk, shall be signed by the clerk and countersigned by the judge. The check, or warrant, for drawing monies deposited by an assignee, shall be signed by him and countersigned by the register designated to act in the case of the estate on account of which such monies were deposited.

32. The warrant issued under sections 11 and 42 of the act, according to Forms No. 6 and No. 59 shall specify that the notice to creditors shall be published at least once in the Daily Cleveland Herald and also at least once in some other newspaper printed or of general circulation in the county wherein the petitioner shall reside, to be named by the petitioner or his attorney, or in default thereof by the register or officer issuing such warrant. All other notices required by law, or by the "general orders in bankruptcy" or by these rules to be published in a newspaper, excepting notices of the sale of property, shall be published at least once in one of the newspapers in which the notice of the first meeting of creditors was directed by the warrant to be published. The marshal, the clerk, and every assignee, shall preserve and return to the court, or register, as the case may be, a copy cut from each newspaper of such notice or advertisement as may be published by them respectively, with a proper certificate of the publication thereof.

33. Ordered that the marshal shall procure, at the expense of the United States, and deliver to the clerk, blank forms of all the necessary process; and the clerk having signed the same and affixed the seal of the court thereto, shall furnish each register with the necessary number thereof for his use; and the register before issuing such process shall sign or countersign the same, as may be proper in the case.

The usual and all legal fees of the clerk for preparing and issuing such process to the register, and for making copies of petitions and other papers, shall be taxed as costs in the case, to be paid as other costs are required to be paid.

34. That, in cases of voluntary bankruptcy, the petitioner shall have the option, by himself or attorney, of preparing the notice to his creditors to be served under the warrant, provided the same are correctly prepared and furnished to the marshal as messenger, in proper form and within such time as will enable him to mail the same so as to give the requisite notice to the persons therein named. Notice of such option shall be given to the clerk before the issuing of the warrant, to be by him noted on the same.

The allowance to the marshal for preparation of such notices, when prepared by him, or the examination thereof when prepared by the petitioner, shall be subject to the special order of the court in each case.

DISTRICT COURT OF THE UNITED STATES, }
NORTHERN DISTRICT OF OHIO, }

CLEVELAND, *March* 31, 1871.

A. W. GAZZAM, ESQ.

DEAR SIR: In answer to your letter, I can

state that I have adopted no new rules in bankruptcy since November 4, 1870.

Very respectfully,

C. T. SHERMAN.

OHIO.—Southern District.

ADDITIONAL RULES, UNITED STATES CIRCUIT AND DISTRICT COURTS.

Ordered: That the clerk make a careful compilation of the rules adopted by the circuit and district courts since the publication of the rules in the year 1860, and now in force, stating the date of the adoption of such rules, and the court in which it was adopted, and that he caused the same to be printed for the use of the court and the bar.

CIRCUIT COURT.

January 12th, 1860.

RULE : Exceptions to the form and manner of taking and returning depositions, including the proof of the official character of the person taking them, shall be filed in the clerk's office, at least one day, before the case is called for trial, and unless so filed, shall be held to be waived.

April 18th, 1862.

Ordered by the court: That hereafter no person be permitted to occupy either of the rooms in the third story of this building, except the members of the court, the clerk and his deputies, the district attorney and his assistants, the marshal and his deputies, and the grand and petit juries of this court.

May 10th, 1862.

Ordered by the court: That the marshal be and he is hereby authorized to employ not more than four bailiffs to attend upon each general term of the circuit and district courts ; and not more than three at each special term of said courts ; this order to take effect from the first day of this term.

August 4th, 1862.

Ordered by the court: That instead of personal security for costs, the plaintiff may deposit with the clerk of the court such sum as the clerk may deem sufficient, and the amount may be increased from time to time as the court or either of the judges thereof may direct.

October 23d, 1862.

Ordered : That any person lawfully summoned to attend as a grand juror of this court, shall fail to be present at the opening thereof, at the term for which he is summoned, a writ of attachment shall be issued against said juror, returnable forthwith, in order that he be properly dealt with as for a contempt of court.

October 23d, 1862.

Ordered: That the marshal upon receiving moneys on execution decrees, or orders of sale, pay the same except his own costs, into the court to the clerk thereof ; the clerk shall thereupon deposit such moneys, except his own costs, as may be directed by the district judge, causing the depository to specify the case in which the same was received, and the same shall be drawn upon the check of the clerk, countersigned by the district or circuit judge, and not otherwise.

Ordered : That when a cause in chancery is settled by the parties, or dismissed without prejudice by consent of parties, and a decree for costs only is entered, the parties may waive the making of a complete record, by filing with the clerk a written agreement to that effect, signed by the parties or their counsel.

Ordered further : That, when an action at law is discontinued, or the plaintiff in such action becomes nonsuited, no complete record shall be made unless specially directed by the court or one of the judges thereof.

October 26th, 1862.

Ordered by the court : That so much of the present rule as requires a special and adjourned term of this court, on the third Tuesday of December and the third Tuesday of February, be rescinded, and, instead of said terms, there shall be a special and adjourned term on the third Tuesday of January in each year.

November 6th, 1862.

Ordered by the court : That no attorney or counselor-at-law, or any clerk of this court, or marshal or his deputies, shall be received as bail or security in any cause or matter in this court, and that no attorney or counselor-at-law be summoned to serve on any grand or petit jury.

November 18th, 1862.

Ordered : That in issuing the writ in any case marked " collection case," the clerk shall endorse the time at which the plaintiff shall be entitled to a judgment, if no cause for a continuance be shown, a copy of which endorsement shall, with the writ, be served on the defendant by the marshal.

Ordered : That executions on judgments entered as aforesaid shall be returnable on the first day of the next term of the court, if thirty days shall intervene before the return day; otherwise such execution shall be returnable on the first day of the next succeeding term.

October 24th, 1863.

Ordered : That all orders or rules appointing special or adjourned terms of this court, except that authorized to be had on the third Tuesday of June in each year, be rescinded.

October 26th, 1863.

Ordered : That accounts of commissioners of this court against the United States, for their fees for " per diems," and on subpoenas and other writs in criminal cases, will not be certified to by either of the judges of this court, unless it shall have been previously certified by the district attorney of the United States for this district, that the case was a proper one for inquiry by the commission, and shall signify his assent that process issue, and that witnesses shall be subpoenaed.

October 30th, 1863.

Ordered : That all appointments of masters and examiners in chancery heretofore made by this court, excepting those made in special cases, and for special purposes, be and the same are hereby revoked.

Ordered : That Aaron F. Perry, John L. Miner, Charles P. James, and Alexander Todd, Esquires, be and they are hereby appointed masters and examiners in chancery in all cases on the equity side of this court not included in the exception stated in the foregoing rule.

January 6th, 1864.

Ordered : That hereafter all gentlemen of the bar practicing either in the circuit or district courts shall subscribe their names to a roll of this bar to be provided by the clerk, and that no person shall be permitted to subscribe said roll unless he shall have complied with the rule of this court respecting the admission of attorneys and counselors. It is further ordered that a fee of five dollars be paid to the clerk by each counselor subscribing said roll.

October 3d, 1865.

Ordered : That so much of the eighth rule as declares a party to a suit incompetent as a witness be rescinded, and that so much of the statute of Ohio as provides that a party to a suit shall be competent as a witness in said cases, be and the same is adopted as a rule of this court.

November 23d, 1865.

Ordered : That all witnesses in attendance at this court shall claim their certificates for mileage and per diem at the time of their discharge from such attendance, or within ten days thereafter, or, in default thereof, they shall forfeit such claim, unless in special cases to be adjudged by the court.

October 29, 1866.

Ordered : That the clerk issue the necessary certificates to all witnesses subpoenaed on behalf of the United States in all causes, civil as well as criminal, and when such witnesses shall produce such certificates to the marshal, the said marshal is hereby ordered to pay the same.

March 19th, 1867.

Ordered : That if any person summoned as a grand or petit juror in this court shall fail to attend according to the command of the process, unless excused before the commencement of the term at which he is required to attend, for a reason satisfactory to the judge, a rule shall be entered and served, requiring him, within ten days, to show cause why he should not be fined or otherwise dealt with, as for contempt of court.

Ordered : That if, on the call of the cases assigned for a particular day of the term, counsel shall fail to appear and answer in any case, it shall be continued, or, if liable to be dimissed under any rule of court, the dismissal shall be entered; and such continuance or dismissal shall be set aside only for cause shown.

April 2d, 1867.

Ordered : That the special term of this court set for the first Tuesday of June annually, be and the same is hereby abolished.

CIRCUIT COURT.

October 20th, 1868.

RULE 1. When the "general superintendence and jurisdiction" authorized to be exercised by the second section of the "Act to establish a uniform system of bankruptcy throughout the United States," approved March 2d, 1867, is intended to be invoked, the party so intending shall file in the office of the clerk of the circuit court a petition verified by affidavit, setting forth briefly the facts of the case and the relief sought, and he shall, at the same time, deposit such sum of money as the clerk shall deem necessary to cover the costs, or, in lieu thereof, the clerk may, in his discretion, take an undertaking which he shall deem sufficient for that purpose. The clerk shall thereupon docket the case, and enter an order that the adverse party, within a time to be fixed by the order, shall file an answer verified by affidavit, if he desire to answer; and a copy of such order, with a caption stating the style of the case, and that it is in bankruptcy, shall thereupon be served by the marshal upon such adverse party.

The marshal's return of service shall be in the following form: A. B. vs. C. D., Cir. Ct. U. S., S. Dist. O., in bankruptcy. I served the order in this, dated day of , A. D. 1868. [State the manner of service.] E. F., *Marshal.* Fees.

Upon the filing of the answer, the petitioner may reply under oath within a time to be fixed by the clerk upon his application.

2. The counsel for the petitioner at the time of filing the petition shall file also a brief, setting forth the points, and authorities intended to be relied upon.

If the counsel for the adverse party desire to submit a brief, he shall file it within the time fixed for the filing of the answer.

The counsel for the petitioner may submit a closing brief within a time to be fixed by the clerk.

The times fixed by the clerk as aforesaid, may be enlarged by the written agreement of the parties or their counsel filed with the clerk.

3. When the case is ready to be submitted, the clerk shall transmit the paper to the circuit judge.

4. If either party shall desire to be heard in oral argument, he shall notify the other party, and the circuit judge, as early as may be, and thereupon the judge shall fix a time and place for such argument.

5. The clerk and marshal shall be allowed the same fees, as are allowed by law for like services in proceedings in bankruptcy in the district court. When the decision of the judge is made, the clerk shall enter it in the proper book and transmit a certified copy to the district court.

6. The petition mentioned in the foregoing rule No. 1 shall be filed within ten days from the entry of the order complained of, unless the time shall be extended by the district judge, by an order filed with the clerk within said ten days; a failure to file the petition in time shall be held to be a waiver of the right to file the same and none shall be filed thereafter.

NOTE.—These rules are not intended to affect the right as given by the section referred to, to file a bill in equity, when that course shall be preferred. In such cases, these rules will apply as far as applicable, and such special orders in addition will be made, in each case, as may be deemed proper.

December 22d, 1868.

Ordered: That hereafter when any party to a suit in this court, or any claimant, in any case under the internal revenue laws, shall demand a special jury, the cost of summoning such jury and the compensation of the jurors, shall be paid by the party or claimant making such demand.

January 22d, 1869.

Ordered by the court: That the rule prescribing the oath for admission to the bar of this court, be rescinded, and hereafter the following shall be the form: You do solemnly swear, that you will support and defend the constitution of the United States, and that you will bear true faith and allegiance to the same, and that you will well and faithfully discharge your duties as an attorney and counselor at law, solicitor in chancery, and proctor and advocate in admiralty, to this court and your clients, according to the best of your skill and understanding, and this you do as you shall answer to God.

February 3d, 1869.

Ordered: That counsel filing precipes for subpœnas or other process, shall when practicable state the residence of the parties to be served or where they may be found or if the process be for the seizure of property, the place where the same may be, shall be stated. And it shall be the duty of the clerk, in issuing the process, to set forth therein, the information as above required in the precipe.

October 11th, 1869.

Ordered : That hereafter in all applications for a continuance, by either party, on the grounds of the absence of a material witness, or witnesses, the party making such application, shall state, not only the materiality of the testimony of the witness or witnesses, but also the facts he expects to prove by such absent witness or witnesses.

DISTRICT COURT.

May 31st, 1861.

Ordered by the court : That so much of rule IV of the admiralty rules of this court, as requires the publication of notices in admiralty causes, in the Daily Gazette or the Daily Enquirer of Cincinnati, at the option of the proctor for the party for whom, or at whose instance the notice shall be published, is hereby rescinded ; and hereafter such notice may be published in any daily paper in Cincinnati of general circulation in the city, which may be designated by such proctor ; or if no designation be made, then in such daily paper as the marshal shall select for that purpose.

March 19th, 1869.

Ordered : That if any person summoned as a grand or petit juror in this court shall fail to attend according to the command of the process, unless excused before the commencement of the term, at which he is required to attend, for a reason satisfactory to the judge, a rule shall be entered and served requiring him within ten days, to show cause why he should not be fined, or otherwise dealt with as for a contempt of court.

April 2d, 1867.

Ordered by the Court : That the special term of this court set for the first Tuesday of June, annually, be and the same is hereby abolished.

March 10th, 1868.

Ordered : That in all causes after a decree of forfeiture of a still of a less value than one thousand dollars fit for use in the production of distilled spirits, that the marshal shall destroy such still so as to prevent its use for the purpose of distillation, and shall sell said property as other property forfeited.

March 12th, 1868.

Ordered : That in all cases where the marshal takes possession of a distillery by virtue of a process, issued from this court for a violation of the internal revenue laws,

he shall in all cases, where he shall hereafter take such possession, immediately cause the head of the still to be taken off, or the machinery to be disconnected in such manner as to render it imposible for distillation to be carried on; the expenses arising out of compliance with this order, shall be returned by the marshal as a part of his disbursements in the cause. It is further ordered, that whenever any premises are held in custody by the marshal, under such process issued as aforesaid, admission to such premises shall, at all times, upon the written order of the marshal, be permitted, for any internal revenue officer who would be entitled to admission, were the same not in custody of the marshal.

July 3d, 1868.

Ordered : That in case of seizure under the internal revenue laws, where a claimant applies for a delivery of the property seized in the absence of the judge, the clerk of this court, by the consent and approval of the district attorney, is hereby authorized to take the bond of the claimant in accordance with the statute.

February 3d, 1869.

Ordered : That counsel filing receipts for subpoenas or other process, shall when practicable, state the residences of the parties to be served, or where they may be found, or if the process be for the seizure of property, the place where the same may be found, shall be stated, and it shall be the duty of the clerk in issuing the process, to set forth therein, the information as above required in the precipe.

November 26th, 1869.

Ordered : That the following rules be adopted as standing rules of this court in all proceedings in rem, under the internal revenue laws until further ordered.

1. In all suits in rem, under and by virtue of the internal revenue laws of the United States, the party claiming the property shall verify his claim on oath or solemn affirmation, stating that the claimant by whom or on whose behalf the claim is made, is the true and *bona fide* owner, and that no other person is the owner thereof And when the claim is put in by an agent, he shall also make oath, that he is duly authorized to make such claim by the owner or owners of the property, and upon entering or putting in such claim,

the claimant shall file a stipulation with sureties in such sum as the court shall direct, for not less than two hundred and fifty dollars, for the payment of all costs and expenses, which shall be awarded against him by the final decree of the court, or upon an appeal by the appellate court.

2. No order to appraise and bond out property proceeded against under, and by virtue of the internal revenue law, will be granted to the claimant, unless a written notice is served upon the district attorney, at least twenty-four hours before such application is made to the court, stating the number of the case and the property which is desired to be released to the claimant, and the name or names of the proposed sureties upon such bond shall be given to the district attorney to enable him to examine the sufficiency of such sureties not less than twenty-four hours before presenting them for appeal to the court.

DISTRICT COURT.

1. *Ordered:* That upon filing a petition in a case of voluntary bankruptcy, the petition or a duplicate thereof, together with other papers filed therewith shall be indorsed by the clerk, "filed," and the same shall be referred of course to the register of the congressional district in which the petitioner shall reside, which reference shall be noted on the back of the petition by the clerk; and the clerk shall forthwith issue to such register the order pescribed by Form No. 4, designating therein a day not more than five days fiom the day on which the register shall receive such order, when the bankrupt shall attend before him, at his office, or such other place as he may designate, and thereupon the case shall be proceeded in as required by law, and the rules prescribed by the supreme court.

2. *Ordered:* That the clerk shall procure blank forms of all necessary process; and having signed the same, and affixed the seal of the court thereto, shall furnish each register with the necessary number thereof for his use, and the register before issuing such process shall countersign the same. The usual and legal fees of the court for preparing and issuing such process to the register, shall be taxed as costs in the case, to be paid as other costs are required to be paid.

3. *Ordered:* That for the present and until other depositories are designated, all moneys received by assignee or paid into court in cases in bankruptcy, shall be deposited in the Central National Bank at Cincinnati.

4. *Ordered:* That all notices required by law, or the rules in bankruptcy, to be published in a newspaper, shall be published at least once in such daily paper printed at Cincinnati, and at least once in some local paper printed at the seat of justice of the county in which the bankrupt may reside, as shall be designated by the register.

5. *Ordered:* That the First National Bank at Dayton, the First National Bank at Circleville, the First National Bank at St. Clairsville, the Muskingum National Bank at Janesville, the Franklin National Bank at Columbus, the First National Bank at Marrietta, the First National Bank at Portsmouth, the Chillicothe National Bank at Chillicothe, the Citizens' National Bank at Urbana, be and they are hereby designated as additional depositories within and for the southern district of Ohio, in which moneys received by assignees, or paid into court in any proceeding in bankruptcy, shall be deposited.

6. *Ordered:* That the clerk and marshal may demand of each applicant or petitioner in bankrupt cases before they perform any service or duties required of them, their fees, or they may require a deposit of such sum or sums in money as they—the clerk and marshal—may deem necessary.

7. *Ordered:* That the order entered June 17th, 1867, in reference to petitions in voluntary bankruptcy be so modified as applicable to the first and second congressional districts, as to permit the reference of any petition, either to the register of the district in which the petioner resides, or to the register of the district in which the petitioner has his place of business, as may be requested by his attorney.

8. *Ordered:* That whenever a debtor shall furnish at his own expense, to the marshal, printed copies of the notices required to be served by the warrant, no fee shall be allowed to the marshal for copying into the notices, the names and places of residences of the creditors, and the amounts of their debts, and, that whenever a debtor shall furnish at his own expense, to the marshal, copies of the notices required to be

served by the warrant, addressed to the creditors, and duly stamped in accordance with the United States postage laws, the fees to be secured to the marshal, shall be those prescribed, viz : 1. For service of warrant, $2.00. 2. For necessary travel at five cents per mile. 3. For each note to creditors named in schedule, 10 cents. 4. Actual and necessary expenses of publication of notices in cases where the law has not fixed the fee.

9. *Ordered:* That the First National Bank at Gallipolis, be, and the same is hereby designated as a depository in all cases and proceedings in bankruptcy within the eleventh congressional district.

10. *Ordered:* That all issues, questions points and matters stated in writing in rule 11, of the "general orders in bankruptcy," or under the 4th section, or the 6th section of the act, or according to Form No. 50, and adjourned into court for decision, or stated in a special case for the opinion of the court, shall be certified to the judge by the register, by a certificate which shall also state briefly the opinion of the register on the issue, question, point or matter, and shall be delivered or sent to the clerk ; and no oral or written argument shall be allowed on any such issue or question, unless by special leave of the court.

11. *Ordered:* That in all cases where services are necessarily performed in proceedings in bankruptcy, by the marshal or other officer, for which no compensation is allowed or prescribed by the statute, or the 1uies and orders in bankruptcy, there shall be allowed and paid by the person properly chargeable therewith, such compensation as shall be fair and reasonable in the judgment of the court upon the facts presented. And in cases where a copy of any paper or document in such proceedings is necessary, the officer making the copy shall be entitled to ten cents for every hundred words ; but this shall not apply to cases where printed notices are used.

12. *Ordered:* That the rule adopted June 17th, 1867, directing the mode of the publication of notices required by law, be so changed except as to the notice of the adjudication in bankruptcy, as to authorize the register to publish the required notices in such paper or papers, as in his judgment will reach the largest number of the creditors in the case.

February 9th, 1870.

Ordered: That objections to the discharge of a bankrupt shall be referred to the register, without any special order for that purpose, before whom the proceedings are pending, who shall summon such witnesses as may be required by the objecting creditor or creditors, or the bankrupt, and order the production of such books and papers, as may be necessary at the hearing, giving due notice of the time and place of such hearing before him.

Ordered: That at least one day before the time fixed for hearing objections to a discharge, the counsel for the opposing creditor or creditors, shall make known to the register in writing the exceptions on which he intends to rely ; and no evidence shall be admitted by the register, except as to the exceptions so relied on.

Ordered: That the register within ten days after the examination is closed, shall file with the clerk an abstract of the evidence before him, together with his opinion or conclusion thereon.

Ordered: That the register may require the opposing creditor or creditors, to deposit funds, or enter into a stipulation, for the payment of the costs and expenses which may accrue from the investigation or hearing as above provided for.

OREGON.

DISTRICT COURT.

[The following nine rules are applicable to all actions, suits or proceedings in this court, unless otherwise specially provided.]

RULE 1. Any person may be admitted to the bar of this court as an attorney at law, or proctor in admiralty upon the certificate of two attorneys of this court, to the effect that such person is of good moral character, and when it further appears that such person has been admitted to the bar of the supreme court of this state; the applicant upon his admission shall take and file with the clerk the oath of allegiance required by the act of congress, and further swear to maintain the respect due to the courts of justice and judicial officers and to demean himself as an officer of this court faithfully and uprightly, and sign the roll of attorneys.

2. The clerk shall not file any paper containing interlineations or erasure, nor unless the contents thereof can be read by a person of ordinary skill; nor unless the name of the court, the title of the cause and the paper and the names of the parties and the attorney or proctor, if there be one, is intelligibly indorsed on it.

3. The banking house of Ladd and Tilton in the city of Portland is hereby designated as the place of deposit for moneys paid into court, except as otherwise provided in the bankrupt act.

4. A copy of the complaint, or libel, certified by the attorney or proctor of the plaintiff, or libellant, as the case may be, must be served on one of the defendants with the summons or other mesne process; a copy of the libel in a suit *in rem* need not be so served, but a claimant or intervenor in such suit may take a copy thereof from the clerk and the cost of such copy may be taxed in his favor as a disbursement, if he be otherwise entitled to recover costs therein.

5. A party filing a pleading, other than those mentioned in rule 4, must within the time required or allowed to file the same, serve upon the attorney or proctor of the adverse party, a certified copy thereof.

6. A party filing a paper other than those mentioned in rules 4 and 5, need not serve a copy thereof, but the adverse party may take a copy thereof from the clerk, and the cost of such copy may be taxed in his favor as a disbursement, if he be otherwise entitled to recover costs therein.

7. All motions which are not motions of course can only be heard after ten days' notice to the adverse party, his attorney or proctor, but upon good cause shown a shorter time may be prescribed. No affidavit or other paper, not a public record, can be read in the support of a motion, unless the same or a copy thereof was served with the notice or filed by the time of such service.

8. A party shall not be allowed to tax as costs or disbursements the expenses of a witness not examined or a deposition not read in a case, except upon the special order of the court or judge upon sufficient cause shown therefor.

9. Whenever a civil cause is at issue upon the question of fact or law ten days before the first day of a term, the clerk must place the same upon the docket for trial or other disposition, and whenever an issue is formed in such a cause during a term or less than ten days before the first day thereof, it may be put upon the docket for trial or other disposition upon the motion of either party, four days' notice thereof being given to the adverse party.

[The following 2 rules are applicable only to civil and criminal actions and proceedings at law.]

10. In all actions and proceedings at common law, whether civil or criminal, the practice of this court, except so far as the same is otherwise provided for by the laws of congress or the rules of this court, shall be the same as that prescribed to the circuit courts of the state of Oregon, by the act entitled "An act to provide a code of civil procedure," approved October 11th, 1862, and the act amendatory thereof, approved October 20th, 1864, excepting sections 6 and 7 of the last mentioned act, amendatory of sections 194 and 228 of the first mentioned act; and the act entitled "An act to provide a code of criminal procedure, and to define crimes and their punishment," approved October 19th, 1864. The term "practice" as used in this rule shall be construed to include the formation of grand and trial juries, and the enforcement of judgments.

11. Grand and trial jurors shall be selected and summoned by the marshal of the district, or his deputy, from the body of the district, or some portion thereof, upon the order of the court or judge thereof, as the business of the court, or the public interest may require; but no person otherwise qualified is exempt from serving as such juror, because he has served as a member of any fire company.

[The following 12 rules are applicable to suits and proceedings in admiralty.]

12. All process shall bear test of the day on which it is sealed, and shall be made returnable on the first Monday of the month following; provided, that in case said Monday is less than twenty days from the day of the sealing of said process, then the said process shall be returnable on the first Monday of the next month thereafter.

13. In suits *in rem*, the mesne process shall be served, and the required notice given at least fourteen days before the return day

of the process, unless a shorter time shall be prescribed by special order, founded on the exigencies of the particular case ; all process and all notices for publication in a newspaper, in pursuance of rule 9 of the rules of practice in admiralty and maritime causes, prescribed by the supreme court, shall be drawn up by the clerk, and no process except subpœna shall be issued by him in blank.

14. The notice mentioned in the last preceding rule shall contain the title of the suit, a summary statement of the cause of suit, the amount of the demand, and the day and place fixed for the return of the process, and shall have affixed, at the close thereof, the name of the proctor of the libellant, and that of the marshal, or his deputy intrusted with the execution of the process.

15. The notice prescribed by rule 9 of the supreme court may be published in any daily paper, published in the city of Portland, at the option of the marshal, or the deputy intrusted with the process.

16. Exceptions taken to any libel, allegation or answer, in pursuance of rule 28 of the supreme court, must be filed on the return day of the process, on the part of the defendant, and by the libellant within four days from the filing of the answer or allegation to which he excepts ; whereupon the party filing the libel, allegation or answer excepted to, shall, in four days thereafter, either give notice to the party excepting, of his submitting to the exceptions, or set the same down for hearing on the first Monday of the month following ; in default whereof, the like order may be entered, of course, as if the exception had been allowed by the court. If a party submit to exceptions for insufficiency, he shall answer further within four days after notice of his submitting.

17. Every pleading in instance causes, civil or maritime, must be subscribed by the party or his proctor, and except a demurrer, must also be verified by the oath or affirmation of the party, to the effect that he believes it to be true. If the party pleading is not within the district, the verification may be made on his behalf by his agent or attorney, in which case the verification must state the reason why the same is not made by the party, and the grounds or reasons of his belief, unless the same be made upon the personal knowledge of such agent or attorney.

18. At the time of commencing a suit, the libellant must give a stipulation, with one or more sufficient sureties, to be taken and approved by the clerk, in the sum of not less than two hundred dollars, to the effect that he will pay all costs and disbursements that may be adjudged against him, by the final decree of this court, or of any appellate court ; but this rule shall not apply to suits for seamen's wages or suits for salvage, when the salvors have come into port in possession of the property libelled.

19. A claimant or person intervening for his interest in a suit *in rem*, must at the time of making such claim or so intervening, give a stipulation for costs and disbursements in like manner and to the like effect as the libellant is required by rule 18.

20. A stipulation for costs and disbursements shall be accompanied by the affidavit of each surety therein, to the effect that he is worth the sum named in the stipulation over and above all just debts and liabilities; and that he is a resident freeholder or householder within the district.

21. Instead of giving a stipulation as required in rule 18 and 19 the party, at his option, may in lieu thereof, deposit with the clerk of the court the sum of two hundred dollars in money.

22. When interrogatories are propounded by the defendant at the close of his answer, touching any matter charged in the libel, or touching any matter of defence set up in the answer, according to rule 32 of the supreme court, the libellant shall answer the same within ten days, unless for sufficient cause shown, he shall, by special order, be allowed a longer period, and the court may, in its discretion, require such interrogatories to be answered in a shorter time or immediately.

23. When interrogatories are propounded to a garnishee, according to rule 37 of the supreme court, a copy thereof shall be served upon the garnishee personally, or in case of his absence from his dwelling house, or usual place of abode, by leaving such copy with some person over fourteen years of age, who is a member or resident of the family ; and the garnishee shall be required to answer the interrogatories within ten days from such service, unless a longer period

shall, by special order, be allowed for that purpose; and the court may, in its discretion, require such interrogatories to be answered within a shorter time or immediately.

[The following 35 Rules are applicable to petitions and proceedings in bankruptcy.]

24. In cases of voluntary bankruptcy the petition shall be referred to the register by the clerk by Form No. 4 of the "general orders and forms in bankruptcy," without any special application to the judge.

25. The register shall under rule No. 7 of the "general orders in bankruptcy," examine the duplicate copy of the petition and schedules specified in Form No. 4 and such duplicate copy shall either be a copy of such filed original, certified by the clerk under the seal of the court, or else a duplicate original, signed and verified in like manner with the original petition and schedules filed with the clerk, and shown by evidence satisfactory to the register to be such duplicate original; and the certificate of the register, required by said rule No. 7, as to the correctness in form of the petition and schedules, shall be made in writing, and signed by him, on the duplicate copy which he so examines; and he shall not issue any warrant under Form No. 6, until he shall have so made a certificate after such examination, that the petition and schedules are correct in form. No such certificate shall be made unless the whole eleven pages composing schedules A and B, in Form No. 1, form part of the schedules to the petition.

26. Every assignee shall, immediately on receiving an assignment of an estate in bankruptcy, send or deliver such assignment to the clerk of the court, who shall make a true copy of it, and certify such copy under his hand and the seal of the court, and such certified copy shall then be placed and kept by him on file, and the original assignment shall be returned to the assignee.

27. Notice of the appointment of an assignee shall be given by him by publication once a week for three successive weeks, in the same newspaper in which the notice of the issuing of the warrant in bankruptcy has been previously published.

28. Notice of sale by an assignee under rule 21, of the "general orders in bank-

ruptcy" shall be advertised in the same newspaper in which notice of the issuing of the warrant has been previously published.

29. The notice to creditors of dividends or meetings, required by sections 17, 27, and 28 of the act, shall be such as is provided for by the order contained in Form No. 28, and the assignee shall publish the same in the newspaper in which he published the notice of his appointment.

30. Notice of application for final discharge, and of the second and third meeting of creditors under rule 25 of the "general orders in bankruptcy" shall be given by publication once a week for three successive weeks, in the same newspaper in which the notice of the issuing of the warrant in bankruptcy has been previously published.

31. The list of debts provided for by section 23 of the act, shall be made and certified by the register, and he shall place thereon all debts which are duly proved.

32. The assignee shall under section 27 of the act, produce and file vouchers for all payments made by him, except as to items in regard to which the court shall for reasonable cause, dispense with vouchers.

33. The assignee shall give the notice required by section 28, by sending a written or printed notice to each of the creditors.

34. All questions for trial or hearing under sections 31 and 34 of the act, shall be tried or heard at a stated session of the court, on four days' notice of the trial or hearing, to be served by either party upon the other, and upon the clerk, and thereupon the same shall be placed upon the docket of the court.

35. The demand in writing for a trial by jury under section 41 of the act, shall be signed by the debtor or his attorney.

36. All pleadings or allegations of fact shall be special and be verified in the manner prescribed by the general rules of this court in actions at law, unless otherwise specially provided by the act.

37. All issues, questions, points, and matters stated in writing under rule 11 of the "general orders in bankruptcy," or under sections 4 or 6 of the act, or according to Form No. 50, and adjourned into court for decision, or state in a special case for the opinion of the court, shall be certified to the judge by the register by a certificate, which

shall also state briefly the opinion of the register on the issue, question, point, or matter, and shall be delivered or sent to the clerk, and no oral or written argument shall be allowed on any such issue or question, unless by special leave of the court.

38. In case of the absence of the judge at the time and place noticed or appointed for any hearing or proceeding before him in bankruptcy, or if the matter then fails to be called or acted on, the same shall be deemed continued without other order, to the next setting of the court thereafter, at which time the like proceedings may be had thereupon as if first noticed or appointed for such day.

39. All notices, served or sent by mail by the marshal, clerk or assignee, shall be so written or printed and folded that the dircetion, postage stamp and post mark, shall be upon the notice itself, and not upon an envelope or other separate piece of paper.

40. In all cases when the creditors of the bankrupt fail to elect an assignee as allowed by the act, John Catlin, Esq., is hereby appointed, and the register is required to make the order in all such cases for the appointment of said John Catlin, Esq., as assignee, and in no case shall the attorney of the bankrupt be appointed assignee of his estate.

41. The warrant, Form No. 6, shall be regarded as process under rule 2 of the "general orders in bankruptcy," and such warrant shall, before it is issued to the marshal, in addition to being signed by the clerk and sealed by the seal of the court, be signed by the judge or register at the foot thereof, in the following form, with the date : " Issued by me, 18 , district judge (r register in bankruptcy.")

42. Whenever the order, Form No. 10, is used by a register, the conclusion of said form may be varied so that the order may be attested or signed by the register alone.

43. All proofs of debt which shall be made and verified prior to the election or appointment of an assignee, shall be delivered or sent to the register; if the register entertain doubts of the validity of any claim, or of the right of a creditor to prove it, and is of opinion that such validity or right ought to be investigated by the assignee, he may postpone the proof of the claim until the assignee is chosen.

44. Under rule 9 of the "general orders in bankruptcy," the assignee must notify the register of his acceptance or rejection of the trust, and the register must immediately, on receiving such notice, report the fact to the clerk of the court.

45. Upon the filing of a creditor's petition to have a debtor adjudged a bankrupt, unless otherwise ordered, the clerk must make a special order referring the same to the register, who shall thereupon have power to make the order, contained in Form No. 57; and if upon the return of such order before the register, no opposition is made thereto, such register may and shall have power to make the order contained in Form No. 58, and also to issue the warrants thereon, contained in Form No. 59.

46. Upon making the special order in pursuance of rule 45, the clerk must forthwith transmit to such register a copy of such special order and the creditor's petition and proofs in support thereof, and the register must not make the order contained in Form No. 58, as authorized by said rule 45, unless the creditor first deliver to him the certificate of the clerk, to the effect that no appearance has been entered in his office by or on behalf of the debtor.

47. Upon the filing of a bankrupt's petition for final discharge, the clerk must make a special order referring the same to the register, who shall thereupon have power to make the order contained in Form No. 51, and to sit in chambers on the return thereof and pass the last examination of the bankrupt, and if there be no opposition to such petition, and it shall appear that the bankrupt has in all things conformed to the requirements of the bankrupt act, the register shall make an order for the final discharge of the bankrupt, and file the same with the papers relating to the case as prescribed in rule 7 of the "general orders in bankruptcy."

48. Upon making the order contained in Form No. 51, the register must forthwith transmit to the clerk a complete list of the proofs of the debt in the case, containing the name, residence, and post office address of each creditor with sufficient particularity to enable the clerk to properly prepare the notices in Form No. 52.

49. Upon receiving a proof of debt the assignee must forthwith transmit to the regis-

ter a memorandum of such proof, which shall contain the particulars specified in rule 48, together with the amount of such debt.

50 Upon the making of an order to show cause upon a creditor's petition as provided in rule 45, the register may and shall have power, upon petition and sufficient cause shown therefor, to make an order, directing the clerk to issue a writ of injunction to restrain the debtor and any other person, as provided in section 40 of the act, and also directing the clerk to issue a warrant for the arrest of the alleged bankrupt and to take possession of his property and effects as provided in said section, upon such undertaking being given to the adverse party and filed with the clerk for the payment of the damages he may sustain, in case the issurance and execution of said writ or warrant is wrongful, as the register shall deem sufficient and proper.

51. In all cases of voluntary bankruptcy, when there are no assets, a certificate of final discharge shall not be granted until all fees and expenses including the publication of notices, are fully paid and receipts therefor filed with the clerk.

52. Whenever an assignee has good reason to believe that a claim is founded in fraud, illegality or mistake, or that the person holding the same ought not to be allowed under the act, to prove it in bankruptcy, it shall be the duty of such assignee to file with the clerk his objections thereto ; and such clerk must then transmit to the register a certified copy of such objections and of the proof of such debt, who shall thereupon have power at the convenience of the parties or at such time as he may appoint, to hear and determine the controversy and reject or allow such claim in whole or in part.

53. No person but the assignee shall be permitted to object to the allowance of a claim against the bankrupt's estate or the right of a person holding the same to make proof thereof; but whenever it appears probable that a claim is founded in fraud, illegality, or mistake, or that the person holding the same is not entitled to make proof thereof, and that the assignee neglects or refuses to contest the allowance of such claim or the right to make such proof, the bankrupt or any creditor upon application to the court or judge may have a rule upon the assignee requiring him to make such contest

or to permit such bankrupt or creditor to do so in the name of such assignee :—*Provided*, it further appears that the allowance to such claim by the assignee might be unjust or injurious to the rights of such bankrupt or creditor.

54. The register may of his own motion postpone the proof of a claim before the election of an assignee under the circumstances mentioned in section 23 of the act, and may in like manner, at any stage of the proceeding, reject a claim when it appears from the proof that the same is founded in fraud, illegality, or mistake.

55. When a claim is contested by the assignee, or in his name, the prevailing party shall be entitled to the costs and expenses of such contest, including the per diem of the register, to be taxed and certified to the court by the register. If such claim be rejected, upon filing such certificate with the clerk, an order must be entered that the assignee recovered such costs and expenses from the adverse party, which may be enforced by execution as an ordinary judgment for money, but if such claim is allowed an order shall be entered by the clerk, that the assignee pay to the adverse party his costs and expenses as expenses incurred in the execution of his trust.

56. When a claim is contested as mentioned in rule 55, the register may in his discretion demand and, if required by the assignee, shall demand of the party, whose claim is contested as aforesaid, an undertaking or deposit not exceeding $100 as a security for the costs and expenses of such contest, and unless such undertaking or deposit is given or made within a reasonable time after such demand, to be prescribed by the register, he shall reject such claim for want thereof.

57. When a claim contested by the assignee is allowed in part and rejected in part, the register shall apportion the costs and expenses of such contest to be allowed the creditor as he may deem just and equitable.

58. The register shall act upon the matters referred to or before him by virtue of any provision of the bankrupt act, or rule 5 of the " general orders in bankruptcy," or of these rules, unless otherwise specially ordered, at his office in the city of Portland, or in the United States district court room therein, at such time or times as he may appoint and

prescribe ; and to the end that bankrupt's estates may be settled up without unnecessary delay or expense, the register shall determine and dispose of all matters that may be referred to or come before him as aforesaid with all convenient dispatch, and shall take special care that no party be allowed to procrastinate or unnecessarily delay the proceedings before him, and that any party causing delay or unnecessary expense in such proceedings be charged with the consequences thereof.

59. " The First National Bank of Portland" is hereby designated in pursuance of rule 28 of the " general orders," as the depository of all money received by any assignee or paid into court in the course of any proceedings in bankruptcy.

CIRCUIT COURT.

RULE 1. In all actions and proceedings at common law, whether civil or criminal, the practice of this court, except so far as the same is otherwise provided for by the laws of congress or the rules of this court, shall be the same as that prescribed for the circuit courts of the state of Oregon, by the act, entitled " An act to provide a code of civil procedure," approved October 11th, 1862, and the act amendatory thereof, approved October 20th, 1864, excepting sections 6 and 7 of the last mentioned act, amendatory of sections 194 and 228 of the first mentioned act ; and the act entitled " An act to provide a code of criminal procedure, and to define crimes and their punishment," approved October 19th, 1864. The term " practice " as used in this rule shall be construed to include the formation of grand and trial juries, and the enforcement of judgments.

2. Grand and trial jurors shall be selected and summoned by the marshal of the district, or his deputy, from the body of the district, or some portion thereof, as the business of the court or public interest may require, upon the order of the court or a judge thereof; but no person otherwise qualified is exempt from serving as such juror because he has served as a member of any fire company.

3. Any person may be admitted to the bar of this court, as an attorney at law, solicitor in chancery, and proctor in admiralty, upon the certificate of two attorneys of this court, that such person is of good moral character, and when it further appears that such person has been admitted to the bar of the supreme court of this state, or the district court of the United States for the district of Oregon. The applicant, upon his admission, shall take and file with the clerk the oath of allegiance, required by the act of congress, and further swear, to maintain the respect due to the courts of justice and judicial officers, and to demean himself as an officer of this court faithfully and uprightly ; and sign the roll of attorneys.

4. That the clerk of this court, while holding said office, is authorized and empowered to take affidavits and bail in civil cases, depending in the courts of the United States, and to execute all the powers and perform all the duties conferred, required or authorized by any act of congress now existing, or hereafter to be passed, having relation to such commissioners, their power or duties.

5. The clerk of the district court, when a writ of error is directed thereto, must make returns of the same, by transmitting a true copy of the record and proceedings in the cause, under his hand and the seal of the court.

6. Upon a writ of error to the judgment of the district court, the plaintiff in error must, by the first day of the term of this court next succeeding the date of such writ, file with the clerk of this court the record of this cause, and if the plaintiff in error shall fail to comply with this rule, the defendant in error may have the writ of error dismissed, upon the certificate of the clerk of the district court showing that such writ of error has been allowed and served.

7. Every appeal to this court in a cause of admiralty and maritime jurisdiction, shall be in writing, signed by the party or his proctor, and delivered to the clerk of the district court, from the decree of which the appeal is taken ; and it shall be returned to the clerk of this court, with the necessary documents and proceedings within twenty days thereafter, unless further time be allowed by the court or one of the judges thereof.

8. The appeal shall briefly state the allegations or prayers of the parties to the suit in the district court in the proceedings in that court, and the decree, with the time of rendering the same. It shall also state,

whether it is intended on the appeal to make new allegations, to pray different relief, or to ask a new decision on the facts; and the appellants shall be concluded in this behalf by the appeal filed.

9. A copy of the appeal shall at the same time be served on the proctor of the appellees in the court below and an affidavit or admission of the due service of such a copy shall be filed with the appeal, and no process or order shall be necessary to bring the appellees into this court.

10. The appellee may move this court to have the decree in the district court carried into effect, subject to the judgment of this court, or of the supreme court, on giving his own stipulation to abide and perform the decree of such court, and this court will make such order, unless the appellant shall give security, by the stipulation of himself and sufficient sureties, for payment of all damages and costs on the appeal in this court and in the supreme court, in such sums as the court shall direct.

11. In all cases, in causes of admiralty and maritime jurisdiction not expressly provided for by the rules of this court, or the supreme court of the United States, the rules of the district court of the United States for the district of Oregon are to be deemed the rules of this court.

12. Rules 2, 3, 4, 5, 6, 7, 8 and 9 of the district court of the United States for the district of Oregon, shall be held and deemed to be rules of this court, and applicable to like proceedings and matters therein.

PENNSYLVANIA.
Western District.

At a court of bankruptcy held in and for the western district of Pennsylvania, at the United States court room, in the city of Pittsburgh, on the 9th day of July, in the year of our Lord one thousand eight hundred and sixty-seven.

Present, Hon. Wilson McCandless,
U. S. District Judge.

Ordered, That the following rules be and they are hereby adopted and prescribed for the regulation and government of the proceedings in bankruptcy, in the district court of the United States, for the western district of Pennsylvania, pursuant to the act entitled, "An act to es-

tablish a uniform system of bankruptcy throughout the United States," approved March 2d, 1867.

RULE 1. The act of congress entitled, "An act to establish a uniform system of bankruptcy throughout the United States," approved March 2d, 1867, the general orders in bankruptcy adopted by the justices of the supreme court, and the following rules shall, until otherwise ordered, be rules of practice in bankruptcy in this court, in respect to all matters and proceedings therein provided for. In cases not provided for, either by said bankrupt act, general orders or rules, the practice of this court shall be subject to the special order of the district court, or judge, and will be made to conform, as near as may be, to the practice of the district court in other cases of similar character. Whenever any special order hereafter made by the district court, in any particular case, shall conflict with these rules, the direction of any special order shall be followed in such case.

2. Except during the absence of the district judge, the district court will be opened for the transaction of business as a court of bankruptcy at the United States court room, in the city of Pittsburgh, on each juridical day of the week, between the hours of 11 A. M. and 1 P. M., unless the business shall sooner be disposed of. But the business in bankruptcy will not be permitted to interfere with the regular course of jury trials, and all the records in bankruptcy from the respective registers shall be returnable to the clerk's office, at Pittsburgh, where the same shall be kept.

RULE 3.

SEC. 1. All papers used in court, or filed in proceedings in bankruptcy, whether prepared by parties to the proceedings, or their attorneys, or by any register in bankruptcy, or other officer of the court, or by any assignee in bankruptcy, shall be written in a fair and legible hand, or else properly printed, upon paper substantially of the size and width of that called full cap, and folded in the form and size in which law papers, written on full cap paper, are usually folded.

SEC. 2. Every such paper containing more than two folios, shall have the folios therein duly marked and numbered, and the folios of all copies thereof, shall be marked and numbered in the same manner, so as to admit of easy reference.

SEC. 3. Papers not requiring full sheets, of full cap, may be written or printed on half sheets, and notices not requiring to be filed, may be on smaller portions thereof.

SEC. 4. All papers to be filed, shall be prepared with a white margin, of at least one inch wide along the head of each and every half sheet thereof, in order that they may be properly and securely fastened together at such head, to constitute the final record in the case, and also with a white margin, at-least one inch wide, at the left hand side thereof.

SEC. 5. No paper not prepared in compliance with this rule, and in compliance also with the general orders in bankruptcy, shall be filed by the clerk without the special orders of the court or judge; and no attorney, not admitted in the district court, shall be allowed to practice therein in cases of bankruptcy.

4. Every register in bankruptcy, or other officer of the court, before administering the proper oaths in verification of any petition, schedule, inventory, deposition, affidavit or other paper, shall see that the different sheets or pieces of paper of which it is composed, and those to which it refers as annexed, are properly fastened together in such manner as to give reasonable security against the separation, loss or change of any part thereof.

5. Before any petition, under the 11th section of the bankrupt act, shall be presented to the court or judge, or be filed with the clerk, the petitioner shall obtain from the register in bankruptcy of the congressional district in which the said petitioner resides, a certificate substantially in the form following, to wit:

"I do hereby certify that I have carefully examined the annexed or within petition, and the schedule and inventory thereto. annexed, and also the verifications thereof, and that the same are proper in form, and sufficient in substance, to authorize an adjudication in bankruptcy, and the issuing of a warrant under the 11th section of the bankrupt act, and I do further certify that I have received the $50.00

required by the act to be deposited for register's fees."

Given at   this   day of   186

A. B.
Register in Bankruptcy.

Which certificate shall be endorsed on or annexed to such petition by the register. Before making such certificate, the register shall carefully examine every part of the petition, schedule and inventory, to ascertain whether the petitioner has fully complied with every requirement of the bankrupt act, and of the general orders and rules of court applicable thereto, and particularly that they are substantially in the form prescribed by such general orders, that all the blanks of both such schedule and inventory are properly filled, and filled by using the word "none" where that is proper; that both the real and personal property of the petitioner, and the place where each part of the same is situated, are set forth in detail and sufficiently described, and that the incumbrances thereon are stated, or that it is stated that there is no incumbrance thereon. He will also ascertain that the petitioner has fully set forth in his schedule, in respect to every debt stated therein, all the particulars required by the 11th section of the bankrupt act. And the registers are specially enjoined to refuse such certificate and to decline making any order of adjudication in bankruptcy upon any petition, until every requisite of the bankrupt act, and of the general orders, is fully and strictly complied with.

6. Before any petition, under the 39th section of the bankrupt act, shall be presented to the court or judge, the petitioner shall procure the certificate of the register in bankruptcy of the congressional district in which the debtor resides, to be endorsed on or annexed to such petition substantially in the following form, viz:

"I certify that I have carefully examined the annexed or within petition, and the verification thereof, and that the same are in proper form, and sufficient in substance to authorize an adjudication in bankruptcy and the issuing of a warrant, under the 39th section of the bankrupt act."

Given at   this   day of   186

7. All petitions filed under the 11th or 39th sections of the bankrupt act, shall be numbered consecutively, and the clerk shall enter the case, under its proper title in his docket, giving to such case a full page thereof. He shall place its number at the head of the outside filing of said petition, which number shall thereafter be the designating number of such case until finally disposed of; every other paper, proceeding or notice in such case or matter shall be marked by the clerk, register, messenger or other officer or party preparing it, with such designating number at the head of the outside filing, on or near the upper left hand corner.

8. In case of the absence of the district judge from the city of Pittsburgh, or whenever he shall be unable to attend to business by reason of sickness or other cause, petitions in cases of voluntary bankruptcy may be filed with the clerk, and the usual order for the reference thereof to a register designated in the order, may be entered upon the direction of Samuel Harper, Esq., one of the registers in bankruptcy, who is hereby designated and authorized to sit in the United States court room, at Pittsburgh, for that purpose. And in case of the like absence of the judge, at the time appointed for showing cause, or for any hearing or proceeding in any matter in bankruptcy; or if any such matter, for want of time or other cause, shall not be acted on at the time appointed therefor, the same shall be continued, without special order for that purpose, to the next sitting of the court thereafter, at which time the like proceedings may be had thereon as if the day of such subsequent sitting had been originally appointed for such proceedings.

9. In all cases of involuntary bankruptcy duplicate petitions must be filed with the clerk.

10. In cases of voluntary bankruptcy, the register to whom the debtor's petition, under the 11th section of the bankrupt act, shall be referred, shall proceed to consider such petition at the time and place fixed in the order of reference for his first action thereon, and shall then act on such petition and shall make the order of adjudication of bankruptcy, or other proper order thereon on the same day, or on some day to which the hearing on such petition

may then be adjourned. On such hearing any creditor of the petitioner who has proved his debt, or who shall prove the same on such hearing, may oppose the prayer of said petitioner by filing with the register an answer or objection thereto, as hereinafter provided.

11. The warrant issued to the marshal, as messenger, under the 11th section of the bankrupt act, shall designate the creditors (if any) on whom personal service is to be made; and notice shall be served by mail upon all creditors not so designated.

12. When the proceeding is instituted by or on behalf of the bankrupt, a duplicate copy of this petition, schedule and inventory, as required by the 11th section of the bankrupt act, shall be left with the register to whom his petition is referred, at or before the time fixed in the order of reference, for the first attendance of the petitioner before such register. Such copy shall be certified by the clerk, or a register in bankruptcy, to be a true copy, or shall be verified as such, by the affidavit of the petitioner, or of his attorney, duly sworn or affirmed to before a register in bankruptcy, or a commissioner appointed by the circuit court. In either case the petitioner must, at his peril, ascertain that such copy is strictly correct.

13. A party appearing to show cause against or to oppose the prayer of a petitioner under the 11th or 39th sections of the bankrupt act, shall file a brief statement, in writing, of the grounds of his opposition or objections thereto, if such objections relate solely to questions of law or practice in respect to regularity or sufficiency of the petition. If his opposition to such petition is founded upon a denial of any statement of fact contained in such petition, he shall set forth in writing, in distinct and separate articles, and according to his best knowledge, information and belief, his denial of each material allegation so denied by him, and each allegation of new matter, so that distinct and separate issues may be readily framed thereon; and he shall annex thereto his affidavit, that he has read said answer, so signed by him, or heard the same read, and knows the contents thereof, and that the same is true of his own knowledge, except as to matters therein stated on information and belief,

and that, as to those matters, he believes it to be true.

14. The court, at its own instance, or on motion of either party, will refer to a register, commissioner or referee, designated or appointed for the purpose of examination and report such matters arising in proceedings in bankruptcy, as under the provisions of the bankrupt act, may properly be so referred.

15. Exceptions may be filed to the report of a register, referee or commissioner, upon any matter referred to him, within eight days after the filing of such report.

16. When a trial by jury is to be had, no formal pleadings shall be necessary to present the issue, but the order for such trial shall contain the issues made by the petition, answer and other papers presenting the issues to be tried.

17. All returns and reports from registers in bankruptcy, or other officers of the court, or referees, shall be directed to the clerk of the court, Pittsburgh, Penn., and shall be sent, postage and other charges paid; and in case of unreasonable delay on the part of the register, or other officer or referee, in making a return or report in any case, an order will be granted, requiring him to make such return, or report, or show cause, on a day specified, why he has not done so.

18. Letters to the register, clerk or marshal, requiring an answer, shall be accompanied by envelopes properly addressed, and with proper postage stamps affixed, in which to inclose the reply, and whatever else may be required, and no register or officer of the court, will be required to answer any such letter, unless this be done, and his fees, in addition, are inclosed. Whenever any receipt is desired from any such officer, it must be prepared, and presented by the party desiring it, and with the proper revenue stamp thereon.

19. In every certificate made by a register, stating any case, point or matter for the opinion of the district judge, under the 4th or 6th sections of the bankrupt act, according to Form No. 50, established by the general orders in bankruptcy, the facts agreed upon by the parties to the controversy shall be clearly and fully stated, with reasonable certainty of time and place, and this shall be followed by a brief statement of the claim made, or position assumed, by each of the parties to the controversy. The register shall then add thereto such proposed order, adjudication or decision, as in his judgment ought to be made, and which shall be in such form that the district judge may signify his approval thereof by his signature. The register shall then afford to each of the opposing parties, or their attorneys, a reasonable opportunity to consent, in writing, to the register's decision thereon. The court will, on the approval and confirmation of such decision of the register, make such orders for costs, against any party declining to assent thereto, as may be deemed proper. In case all parties to such controversy shall assent to such adjudication or decision of the register, he shall file the same, and proceed with the case upon the basis thereof, as though such controversy had not arisen.

Rule 20.

Sec. 1. It shall be the duty of the assignee, as soon as practicable after his appointment shall be complete, to take into his possession all the estate, real and personal, of every name and nature, of the bankrupt, with the exceptions mentioned in the bankrupt act; and also all the deeds and books of accounts, papers and writings of the bankrupt pertaining thereto, and for this purpose the assignee shall make diligent inquiry into the affairs and transactions of the bankrupt.

Sec. 2. Every assignee shall, under section 27th of the bankrupt act, produce and file with his account, proper vouchers for all payments made by him, except payments of one dollar or less, and except items in regard to which the court shall, for reasonable cause and by special order, dispense with vouchers. The items so excepted may be allowed to a reasonable extent, upon the positive oath of the assignee, that the amounts charged therein were actually and necessarily paid.

21. In cases of voluntary bankruptcy, when the assignee or any creditor shall, after the adjudication of bankruptcy, have good reason to suspect that the bankrupt has property, or any right of property which he has not set forth in his inventory, such assignee or creditor

upon application to the court or the register acting in the case, stating briefly, and under oath, the grounds of his suspicion may, on due cause, shown by affidavit, apply for an order for the examination of the bankrupt, on oath or affirmation. And if, upon due service on the bankrupt of a copy of any such order and notice of the time and place appointed for such examination, the bankrupt shall fail to appear, and fully to submit himself to such examination, and to subscribe his deposition, application may forthwith be made to the court, upon an affidavit stating the facts of the case, for compulsory process against such bankrupt.

22 In cases of involuntary bankruptcy, it shall be the duty of the assignee, as soon as practicable after he shall be appointed and qualified, to apply to the bankrupt for a full and true account of all his property and rights of property, and of all the deeds and books of account, papers and writings of the bankrupt pertaining thereto, as required by the bankrupt act ; and if the bankrupt shall refuse to give such account, or if the assignee, or any creditor of the bankrupt, shall have good reason to suspect that he has practiced any concealment in giving such account, such assignee or creditor may, on application to the court, and due cause shown by affidavit, have an order for the examination of such bankrupt, and if necessary, compulsory process against him, as provided in the last preceding rule.

23. Every bankrupt shall, at all times, be bound to attend the assignee, upon the requirement of the register acting in his case, and on reasonable notice, in writing, for that purpose, to be served personally, or left at his usual place of abode, in order to assist in making out the accounts of the said bankrupt's estate and effects, and to at tend any court to be examined in any suit or proceeding respecting the same, for which he shall be entitled to receive from the assignee a reasonable compensation out of the estate.

24. When an order for the examination of any bankrupt or other person, shall be made, any creditor, or the bankrupt himself, at the time and place appointed for such examination, or at any other time to which such examination may be continued or adjourned, may, at his own expense, produce witnesses touching the subject matter of such examination, and shall be entitled to the ordinary process of subpœna, to be issued by the clerk or register, requiring the attendance of such witnesses, which sub pœna the witnesses shall be bound to obey, provided their legal fees are paid or tendered on the service of such subpœna.

25. When the object is to bring a party into contempt for disobeying any process, or any rule or order of the court or of a register, the service shall be personal, unless otherwise ordered by the court.

26. Affidavits of the publication of notices in a newspaper, shall show that the same were published in the regular edition and issue of such newspaper and shall state the day or days on which the same were published. Such affidavits must be sworn or affirmed to before a register in bankruptcy, the clerk of the court, a commissioner appointed by the circuit court of the United States, or a notary public, and shall be substantially in the following form :

Western District of Pennsylvania, ⎱
  County of   , ⎰ ss.

A. B. of   , in said county, being duly sworn, doth depose and say, that he is (the printer, the publisher or the foreman, in the office, as the case may be,) of the   , public newspaper published in said county, and the notice of which the annexed is a copy cut from said newspaper, was printed and published in the regular edition and issue of said newspaper on the following days, viz: On the   and   days of   186   : (or on the   and   days of 186   .)

Subscribed and sworn before me, this   day of   186   .

RULE 27.

SEC. 1. The notice of the appointment of the assignee of a bankrupt, required to be given by him, under the provisions of the 11th section of the bankrupt act, shall be published once a week, for three successive weeks, in each of the newspapers in which the notice of the first meeting of the creditors of such bankrupt was directed to be published.

SEC. 2. Notices to creditors of dividends, and notices of meetings, required by the 17th, 27th and 28th sections of the bankrupt act, and notices of sale by an assignee, required to be given under the 21st general order, shall be published twice in the same newspapers; the last publication of such notices of sale to be made at least the number of days before the sale required by such general order.

28. The notices required by the bankrupt act, by general orders, and by these rules, in all cases, in the 22d district, shall be published in three newspapers in the city of Pittsburgh, to be selected by the register, one of which shall be of opposite political sentiments to the other two. And the said register may alternate in his selection, so that from time to time the notices will appear in the different papers of the city. The registers in all the other congressional districts in the western judicial district of Pennsylvania, shall select two newspapers, one of each political party in the county, where the case in bankruptcy originates, in which shall be published the notices required by the bankrupt law, general orders and these rules, and the notices shall be published four times in each newspaper.

29. All notices served or sent by mail, by the marshal, clerk or assignee, shall, when practicable, be so prepared, directed and folded, that the direction, postage stamp and post mark shall be upon the notice itself and not on an envelope or other piece of paper, and shall have printed thereon a direction to the postmaster at the place to which it is sent, to return the same within ten days, unless called for.

30. The list of debts provided for by section 23 of the bankrupt act, shall be made and certified by the register to whom the original petition in the case was referred, unless another register shall have been specially designated for that duty by the district court. The register shall place thereon all debts which have been duly proved, and which have not been disallowed by the court, unless it shall be otherwise specially ordered by the district court.

RULE 31.

SEC. 1. Applications under section 34 of the bankrupt act, to set aside and annul the discharge granted to any bankrupt, shall clearly set forth in separate and distinct articles, and with reasonable certainty of time and place, according to the best knowledge, information and belief of the applicant, all the material facts and allegations on which the application is based.

SEC. 2. The bankrupt shall admit or deny or otherwise answer the several allegations of such application, in distinct articles, in like manner; and such application and answer shall severally be verified by affidavit substantially in the form prescribed by rule 15.

32. The fifty dollars required to be deposited for register's fees, shall, until otherwise ordered, in cases of voluntary petitions, be deposited with the registers, and in cases of involuntary petitions with the clerk, at the time of the filing of the same, according to the 47th section of the act, and in case of an adjudication of bankruptcy, to be deposited by him with the register. The provisional disposition, and ultimate disbursement of the same, will be regulated by rules which may hereafter be promulgated, or by special order.

33. Deposits made in a national bank, selected as a depository, under the 28th general order, shall be made by the assignee to his credit, as assignee in the particular case in which such moneys have been received, and a separate account shall be kept in each case, according to its proper number and title. Samuel Harper, Esq., one of the registers of this court, is hereby designated for the purpose of countersigning all checks drawn on any such deposit bank at Pittsburgh. A certified copy of this rule shall be furnished by the clerk to such deposit bank.

34. The Iron City National Bank of Pittsburgh, and the Merchants' and Manufacturers' National Bank of Pittsburgh, are hereby designated as deposit banks, in all cases in bankruptcy, arising in the 22d congressional district. And the deposit banks, in all the other congressional districts in this judicial district, will be selected and designated hereafter, by special order, upon the recommendation of the registers of the respective districts.

35. In case no choice of an assignee is made by the creditors at their first meeting, or in case an assignee, chosen by the creditors, fails, within five days, to express in writing his acceptance of the trust, or in case of a vacancy in the office of an assignee, caused by his removal, resignation,

death, or other cause, John H. Bailey, Esq., of the city of Pittsburgh, counselor-at-law, will be appointed assignee where the judge is required by the act to appoint the assignee, and also where the assignee is appointable by the register, subject to the approval of the judge.

36. The registers in the respective congressional districts, may fix certain days on which they will be present at the "county seat," or other place, of their several counties, for the purpose of attending to cases in bankruptcy, of which due notice shall be given in the newspapers of the county elected by them to publish notices in bankruptcy.

RHODE ISLAND.

At a special district court of the United States for the district of Rhode Island, held at the city of Providence, in said district, on the first day of July, A. D. 1867.

Present—J. Russell Bullock,

District Judge.

Ordered, That the following rules govern proceedings in bankruptcy in this district, in addition to (and with) reference to the general orders and forms prescribed by the justices of the supreme court of the United States:

RULE 1. In voluntary bankruptcy, the petitions in the order of the time of filing, shall be referred in rotation by Form 4 to the registers appointed in the two congressional districts, commencing with the eastern or first district. A petition may be otherwise referred, upon application, for special reasons satisfactory to the court. In involuntary bankruptcy, the register will be designated with reference to the special circumstances of each case.

The order, Form 4, designating the register to act upon the petition in voluntary bankruptcy, shall specify as the place where the register shall act upon the matters arising under the case, and the warrant, Form 59, in involuntary bankruptcy, shall in a like case specify as the place where the meeting of the creditors will be held, the office of the register as designated by him, by a writing filed with the clerk.

The day named in the order, Form 4, for the attendance of the bankrupt before the register in voluntary bankruptcy, and the day named in the warrant, Form 59, for the meeting of creditors in involuntary bankruptcy, will be fixed with reference to the speedy progress of the case.

Each register shall, by a writing filed with the clerk, designate the day, or days, if any, on which he will attend at a place or places, other than his regular office.

Each register may, in any case referred to him, fix the times when he will act upon the several matters arising under such case, other than the attendance of the bankrupt as fixed by the order, Form 4, and the meeting of creditors as fixed by the warrant Form 59; but the register shall not, without leave of the court, be at liberty to change the place specified in the order, Form 4, or to act upon the matters arising under a case of involuntary bankruptcy, at any other place than the one specified in the warrant, Form 59, as the place for the meeting of creditors.

2. The adjudication of bankruptcy, Form 58, shall contain a provision that the case be referred to one of the registers, naming him, to take such proceedings thereon as are required by the act.

3. Whenever a petition is referred to a register in a voluntary case, and whenever in an involuntary case, an order is made on an adjudication of bankruptcy, referring the case to a register, the clerk, at the time he delivers to the register a copy of the order of reference, shall pay to him fifteen dollars, out of the *fifty* dollars deposited with the clerk under section 47 of the act, to be applied to the payment of such fees of the register as are chargeable to the petitioner.

Whenever by any monthly return made to the court by the register, under general rule 12, it appears that the fees of the register up to that time exceed in amount the sum already received by him out of said fifty dollars, the clerk shall, if requested by the register, make further payment to him theron, to the amount of such fees, until the fifty dollars shall have been all paid out; and thereafter the fees of the register which are chargeable to such petitioner shall be paid or secured, as provided by rule 29 "general orders," &c.

The foregoing provisions of this rule shall not apply to a case of voluntary bankruptcy where, under rule 30 of "general orders," the judge shall direct that the fees and costs in the case shall not exceed the sum required by the act to be deposited with the clerk; but in every such case, such of the disbursements paid out by the register and marshal for the purposes specified in rule 12 of "general orders," and returned by them under oath under said rule, as are chargeable to the petitioner debtor, shall be refunded to them severally by the clerk out of such sum; and the clerk, marshal, and register shall perform the duties required of them by such petitioning debtor without first requiring payment or security for their fees, subject to the application by the court to such fees, of so much of said sum as shall remain after refunding such disbursements.

4. The register shall, under rule 7 of "general orders," examine the duplicate copy of the petition and schedule specified in Form 4, and such duplicate copy shall be a copy of such filed original, certified by the clerk, under the seal of the court, as duly verified by the petitioner. For certifying the same, the clerk shall be allowed the fee prescribed in paragraph 2, general rule 30; and when the clerk, at the request of the petitioner or his solicitor, furnishes such duplicate copy, he shall be allowed the fees fixed by the same paragraph of the same general rule 30.

And the certificate required of the register by general rule 7 shall be in writing, and endorsed on such duplicate copy; nor shall he issue any warrant under Form 6 until after such examination and certificate as to the correctness in form of the petition and of all of the schedules, A and B, in Form 1, accompanying. And all petitions and schedules filed after this date shall be upon paper of a uniform size; and all petitions and schedules and other papers in each case shall have an *ample* margin, to allow of their being bound together, as required by general rule 7.

5. The warrant issued under section 11 or section 42 of the act, according to Form 6 or 59, as the case may be, shall specify two newspapers, one of which shall be a daily, published in the city of Providence, and one published in the county in which the debtor or debtors has or have resided, or carried on business, for six months next immediately preceding the time of filing the petition; the selection of such newspapers

to be made by the register; the notices to be published at least twice in each newspaper selected.

The warrant shall designate the creditors on whom personal service is to be made, and notice shall be served by mail on all creditors not so designated. Personal service need not be made on any creditor resident out of the district.

When a debtor shall seasonably furnish at his own expense, to the marshal, printed copies of the notices required, no fee shall be allowed the marshal for copying into the notices the names and residence of the creditors and the amount of their debts.

The warrant, Form 6, shall be regarded as process under rule 2 of "general orders," and shall, before issued to the marshal, be signed and sealed by the clerk, and when issued by the register shall be signed thus: "Issued by me , 18 . A B , register in bankruptcy."

When the order, Form 10, is issued by a register, the conclusion of it may be so varied and attested by him accordingly.

6. All proof of debts made before the appointment of an assignee shall be delivered to the proper register. If he entertains doubts of the validity of the claim, he may postpone the proof thereof until the assignee is chosen and qualified.

7. In case no choice of an assignee is made by the creditors at their first meeting, or in case an assignee chosen by them fails within five days to express in writing his acceptance, or, in case of a vacancy in the office from death or other cause, Samuel W. Peckham, of Providence, will be appointed to the office, where the judge is required to appoint. Where the said Samuel W. Peckham shall be appointed by any register, such appointment is hereby approved by the judge. In special cases vacancies in the office of the assignee must be filled by the election of creditors, or by the appointment of an assignee other than the one above named

8. Under rule 9 of the "general orders," an assignee shall notify the register of his acceptance or rejection of the trust, and the register shall at once report it to the clerk.

9. Every assignee shall, on receiving an assignment, deliver the same to the clerk, who shall make a certified copy thereof, which copy shall be placed on file, and the origininal returned to the assignee.

10. The assignee shall give notice of his appointment by publication once a week, for three successive weeks, in two of the newspapers named in rule 21, one of which shall be a daily newspaper published in the city of Providence; such newspapers to be selected by the register with due regard to the requirements of section 14 of the act.

11. Notices of sale by an assignee under rule 21 of "general orders," shall be advertised in a daily newspaper published in the city of Providence, and in one of the newspapers named in rule 21, published in the county where the sale is to take place, when the sale takes place out of the city of Providence; the selection of the newspapers in the city of Providence to be made by the register.

12. The notice to creditors of dividends or meetings, required by the 17th, 27th and 28th sections of the act, shall be such as is provided for by the order contained in Form 28, and the register shall select from among the newspapers specified in rule 21, in which the notice shall be published, that one having the largest circulation in the locality of the residence of the creditors of the debtor.

13. The list of debts provided for by section 23 of the act shall be certified by the register to whom the case is referred, and he shall place thereon all debts duly proved.

14. The assignee shall, under section 27 of the act, produce and file vouchers for all payments made by him.

15. The notice by the assignee, under section 28 of the act, of the filing of his account, and of his application for a settlement and discharge, shall be given by him by sending notices by mail, prepaid, of such filing, and of the time of such application, to all known creditors of the bankrupt, directed to the respective places of residence of such creditors, or to their usual post office address.

16. All questions for trial or hearing, under sections 31 and 34 of the act, shall be heard or tried at a session of the court to be holden at Providence on the first Wednesday in every month, or at any stated session of the court holden at that place, on six days' notice of trial and hearing, to be served by either party upon the other, and upon the clerk, and a calendar of the same shall be made.

17. The demand in writing for a jury trial, under section 41 of the act, shall be signed by the debtor or his attorney, and filed the same day with the clerk, who shall endorse thereon the day of such filing.

18. The application under section 34 of the act, to set aside and annul a discharge, shall be verified by the oath or affirmation of the applicant, and the answer of the bankrupt to the application shall answer specifically the allegations of the application, and shall be verified in like manner.

19. All issues, questions, points and matters stated in writing under rule 11 of the "general orders in bankruptcy," or under the 4th section or the 6th section of the act, or according to Form 50, and adjourned into court for decision, or stated in a special case for the opinion of the court, shall be certified to the judge by the register, with his own opinion on the question, and delivered to the clerk; and no argument on such issue or question will be allowed unless requested by the court.

20. In pursuance of rule 28 of "general orders," and until further ordered, the Second National Bank of Providence is designated as that in which all moneys received by assignees or paid into court in the course of any proceedings in bankruptcy, shall be deposited. All moneys received by the clerk on account of any bankrupt estate, or paid into court in the course of any proceedings in bankruptcy, (except sums deposited with the clerk under section 47,) shall be deposited in said bank; and all sums received by an assignee on account of any estate of which he is assignee, shall be deposited in said bank.

The check or warrant for drawing moneys deposited by the clerk, shall be signed by him and countersigned by the judge.

The check or warrant for drawing moneys deposited by an assignee, shall be signed by him and countersigned by the proper register.

21. The following newspapers are designated as those in which all publications required by the act, by the "general orders" or these rules, may be made, viz:

County of Providence—Providence Daily Journal, Providence Morning Herald, Providence Daily Press, and Woonsocket Patriot.

County of Newport—Newport Daily News.

County of Bristol—Bristol Phenix.

County of Kent—East Greenwich Pendulum.

County of Washington—Narragansett Times.

The marshal, clerk, register or assignee shall return to the court a newspaper copy of each notice or advertisement required to be published by them, with a certificate showing that the required publication has been made.

22. In case of the absence of the judge at the time and place appointed for any hearing or proceeding before him in bankruptcy, or if the matter then fails to be called or acted on, the same shall be deemed continued without other order to the next sitting of the court thereafter, when like proceedings may be had as if such continuance had not occurred.

23. All notices served or sent by mail by the marshal, clerk, or an assignee, shall be so written or printed and folded that the direction and postage stamp and post mark shall be upon the notice itself, and not upon an envelope.

24. Special cases not embraced in these rules, or in the general orders, or forms, shall be submitted to the judge.

Adopted in open court, July 1st, 1867.

AMENDMENTS TO RULES.

At a special term of the district court of the United States of America for the district of Rhode Island, held at the city of Providence, in and for said district, on the thirteenth day of July, in the year of our Lord eighteen hundred and sixty-seven—

Present—J. RUSSELL BULLOCK,
District Judge.

Ordered, That rule 5 of said rules, orders, and regulations be amended by striking out the words " by the petitioner, or in default thereof."

Ordered, That rule 7 of said rules, orders, and regulations be amended by striking out the words " also where the register appoints subject to the approval of the judge," and inserting instead the following : " Where the said Samuel W. Peckham shall be appointed by any register, such appointment is hereby approved by the judge ;" and also by striking out the last sentence and inserting instead the following: " In special cases vacancies in the office of assignee will be filled by an election by the creditors, or by the appointment of an assignee other than the one above named."

Ordered, That rule 10 of said rules, orders, and regulations be amended by striking out the word "assignee" where it last occurs, and inserting instead the word "register."

Ordered, That rule 11 of said rules, orders, and regulations be amended by striking out the word " assignee" where it last occurs, and inserting instead the word " register."

Ordered, That rule 12 of said rules, orders, and regulations be amended by striking out the word "assignee," and inserting instead the word " register."

25. A creditor desiring the examination of a bankrupt must apply to the register for an order according to Form No. 45, by petition duly verified, showing good cause for granting the same.

The examination must be completed and filed with the clerk on or before the return day for the petition for discharge unless the time should be extended by the judge. An examination will not be ordered after such return day excepting on application to the judge and for special cause verified by affidavit.

Adopted December 1st, 1869.

NEW YORK, *March* 20, 1871.

HON. J. P. KNOWLES, *Judge of the U. S. District Court for the Southern District of New York :*

DEAR SIR—If you have adopted any further rules in bankruptcy since December 1, 1869, copies of the same would be a great favor. Yours truly,
A. W. GAZZAM.

In response to above (was it intended for me ?) I enclose a copy of the only rule adopted by me since December, 1869. It is a transcript of a rule of Judge Fox, of Maine. Yours respectfully,
JOHN P. KNOWLES,
Dist. Judge.

PROVIDENCE, *April* 6, 1871.

VERMONT.

At a term of the district court of the United States of America for the district of Vermont, held at the city of Burlington, in and for said district, on the 5th day of July, A. D. 1867.

Present, The Hon. DAVID A. SMALLEY,
District Judge.

Ordered, That the following rules, orders and regulations be prescribed as rules governing proceedings in bankruptcy in the district court of the United States for the district of Vermont, under the act entitled " An act to establish a uniform system of bankruptcy throughout the United States," approved March 2d, 1867, in addition to and with reference to the " general orders in bankruptcy," and the forms specified in the schedules thereto annexed, framed by the justices of the supreme court of the United States, in pursuance of the tenth section of said act, and adopted by said court, and promulgated May 16th, 1867.

Clerk.

RULE 1. In cases not provided for either by the bankrupt act or the general orders in bankruptcy or these rules, the practice of this court shall be subject to the special order of the district court or the judge, and will be made to conform, as near as may be, to the practice of the district court in cases of a similar character in this district.

Whenever any special order hereafter made by the district court in any particular case shall conflict with these rules, the direction of such special order shall be followed in such case.

2. Except during the absence of the district judge, the district court will be open for the transaction of business as a court of bankruptcy, at the United States court room, in the city of Burlington, on Tuesday and Wednesday of every week, from 10 A. M. to 3 P. M.

3. All papers used in court or filed in proceedings in bankruptcy, by whomsoever prepared, shall be written in a fair and legible hand, or else properly printed.

No paper not prepared in compliance with this rule, and also in compliance with the "general orders in bankruptcy," shall be filed by the clerk without the special order of the court or judge ; and no attorney not admitted to the district court shall be allowed to practice therein in cases in bankruptcy.

4. The adjudication of bankruptcy, Form No. 58, shall contain a provision that the case be referred to one of the registers, naming him, to take such proceedings thereon as are required by the act.

5. The fifty dollars required to be deposited as security for the register's fees, under section 47 of the act, shall, until otherwise ordered, be deposited with the clerk. Whenever a petition is referred to a register in a case of voluntary bankruptcy, and whenever, in case of involuntary bankruptcy, an order is made on an adjudication of bankruptcy, referring the case to a register, the clerk, at the time he sends or delivers to the register a copy of the order of reference, shall pay him the sum of twenty dollars out of the fifty dollars so deposited, the same to be applied to the payment of such fees of the register as are chargeable to the petitioner making the deposit. Whenever, by a return made to the court, under oath, by the register, of the fees so chargeable for services rendered by him, it shall appear that the aggregate amount of such fees exceed the aggregate payments made thereon to the register out of the fifty dollars, the clerk shall, if requested by the register, make further payments to him thereon to the amount of such fees, until the fifty dollars shall all of it be paid out, and thereafter the fees of the register which are chargeable to such petitioner shall be paid or secured in like manner with the other fees provided for by rule 29 of the "general orders in bankruptcy."

The foregoing provisions of this rule shall not apply to a case of voluntary bankruptcy where, under rule 30 of the "general orders in bankruptcy," the judge shall direct that the fees and costs in the case shall not exceed the sum required by the act to be deposited with the clerk ; but, in every such case, such of the disbursements paid out by the register and marshal for the purposes specified in rule 12 of the "general orders in bankruptcy," and returned by them under oath, under said rule 12, as are chargeable to the petitioning debtor, shall be refunded to them severally by the clerk out of such sum ; and the clerk, marshal, and register shall perform the duties required of them by such petitioning debtor without first requiring payment or security for their fees, subject to the application by the court to such fees of so much of such sum as shall remain after refunding such disbursements.

6. The register shall, under rule 7 of the "general orders in bankruptcy," examine the duplicate copy of the petition and schedules specified in Form 4, and such duplicate copy shall be a copy of such filed original, certified by the clerk under the

seal of the court and the certificate of the register, required by said rule 7, as to the correctness in form of the petition and schedules, shall be made in writing, and be signed by him on the duplicate copy which he so examines; and he shall not issue any warrant under Form No. 6, until he shall have so made a certificate, after such examination, that the petitions and schedules are correct in form.

No such certificate shall be made unless the whole eleven of the sheets composing schedules A and B, in Form No. 1, form part of the schedules to the petition.

7. The warrant issued under section 11 or section 42 of the act, according to Form No. 6 or Form No. 59, shall specify the two newspapers named in rule 8, in which notice shall be published. The notices to be published in pursuance of the warrant, to be published twice in each newspaper selected. The warrant shall designate the creditors on whom personal service is to be made, and notice shall be served by mail upon all persons other than those designated. No creditor out of this district shall be designated for personal service. The warrant, Form No. 6, shall be regarded as process under rule 2 of the "general orders in bankruptcy," and such warrant shall, before it is issued to the marshal, be signed by the clerk, and sealed with the seal of the court.

8. The following newspapers are designated as those in which all publications required by the act, or the "general orders in bankruptcy," or these rules shall be made.

In all cases where the bankrupt resides in the county of Bennington, they shall be published in the Manchester Journal, at Manchester, and the Burlington Sentinel, published at Burlington; and where the bankrupt resides in the county of Rutland, they shall be published in the Rutland Herald, at Rutland, and in the said Burlington Sentinel; and where the bankrupt resides in the county of Addison, they shall be published in the Middlebury Register, at Middlebury, and the said Burlington Sentinel; and where the bankrupt resides in the counties of Chittenden or Grand Isle, they shall be published in the Burlington Times, at Burlington, and the said Burlington Sentinel; and where the bankrupt resides in the county of Franklin, they shall be published in the St. Alban's Messenger and the said Burlington Sentinel; and where the bankrupt resides in the county of Washington, they shall be published in the Montpelier Freeman, at Montpelier, and the said Burlington Sentinel; and where the bankrupt resides in the county of Lamoille, it shall be published in the Newsdealer, at Hyde Park, and the said Burlington Sentinel; and where the bankrupt resides in the county of Orleans, they shall be published in the Newport Express, at Newport, and the said Burlington Sentinel; and where the bankrupt reside in the counties of Caledonia or Essex, they shall be published in the North Star, at Danville, and the said Burlington Sentinel; and where the bankrupt resides in the county of Windsor, they shall be published in the Vermont Journal, at Windsor, and the said Burlington Sentinel; and where the bankrupt resides in the county of Orange, they shall be published in the Orange County Eagle, at Randolph, and the said Burlington Sentinel; and where the bankrupt resides in the county of Windham, they shall be published in the Times, at Bellows Falls, and the said Burlington Sentinel.

9. In pursuance to rule 28 of "general orders in bankruptcy," the following National Banks in this district are designated as those in which all monies received by assignees or paid into court, or to the clerk in proceedings in bankruptcy, shall be deposited; when the bankrupt resides in the county of Bennington, in the First National Bank of Bennington; where the bankrupt resides in the county of Rutland, in the National Bank of Rutland; where the bankrubt resides in the counties of Addison, Chittenden, Grand Isle, Franklin, and Lamoille, in the Merchant's National Bank of Burlington; where the bankrupt resides in the county of Washington, in the Montpelier National Bank at Montpelier; where the bankrupt resides in the counties of Orleans, Essex or Caledonia, in the First National Bank at St. Johnsbury; where the bankrupt resides in the counties of Orange, Windsor, or Windham, in the National Bank of Bellows Falls, at Bellows Falls.

All monies received by the clerk of the court on account of any bankrupt estate, or paid into court in any proceeding in bankruptcy, (except sums deposited with the clerk under section 47 of the act) shall be deposited in the Merchant's National Bank of Burlington.

The check or warrant for drawing monies deposited by the clerk, shall be signed by the clerk and countersigned by the judge.

For drawing monies deposited by an assignee in the counties of Addison, Chittenden, Grand Isle, Franklin and Lamoille, shall be signed by him and countersigned by the clerk of the court, and money deposited by an assignee in any other bank shall be signed by him and countersigned by the register having charge of the case.

10. In case no choice of an assignee is made by the creditors at their first meeting, or in case an assignee chosen by the creditors shall fail within the course of five days to express in writing his acceptance of the trust, or in case of a vacancy in the office of assignee, caused by his removal, resignation, death or other cause, within the counties of Bennington and Rutland, Jacob Edgerton, Esq., of Rutland, will be appointed assignee, where the judge is required by the act to appoint the assignee, and when the said Edgerton shall be appointed by the register within those counties, such appointment is hereby confirmed.

In any such case arising in the counties of Addison, Chittenden, Franklin, or Grand Isle, Wm. H. Hoyt, Esq., of Burlington, will be appointed or approved as above.

In any such case arising in the counties of Orleans, Caledonia, or Essex, Lucius Robinson, Esq., of Newport, will be appointed or approved as above.

In any such case arising in the county of Lamoille, W. H. H. Bingham, Esq., of Stowe, will be appointed or approved as above.

In any such case arising in the county of Washington, Chas. Reed, Esq., of Montpelier, will be appointed or approved as above.

In any such case arising in the counties of Windham, Windsor, or Orange, Geo. Slate, Esq., of Bellows Falls, will be appointed or approved as above.

11. Under rule 9, of the "general orders in bankruptcy," an assignee shall immediately notify the register of his acceptance or rejection of the trust, and the register shall immediately, on receiving such notice, report it to the clerk of the court.

12. Every assignee shall, immediately on receiving an assignment of an estate in bankruptcy, send or deliver such assignment to the clerk of the court, who shall make a true copy of it, and certify such copy under his hand and the seal of the court, and such certified copy shall then be placed and kept by him on file, and the original assignment shall be returned to the assignee.

13. Notice of the appointment of an assignee shall be given by publication once a week, for three successive weeks, in two newspapers, as provided in rule 8.

14. Notices of a sale by an assignee, under rule 21 of the "general orders in bankruptcy," shall be advertised for two weeks, as provided in rule 8.

15. The notices to creditors of dividend, or meetings as required by sections 17, 27 and 28 of the act, shall be such as is provided for in Form No. 28, and published three weeks successively as provided in rule 8.

16. All proofs of debt which shall be made and verified prior to the election or appointment of an assignee, shall be delivered or sent to the register, to whom the case is referred. If the register entertains doubts of the validity of any claims, or of the right of a creditor to prove it, and is of opinion that such validity or right ought to be investigated by the assignee, he may postpone the proof of the claim until the assignee is chosen.

17. The list of debts provided for by section 23 of the act, shall be made and certified by the register, to whom the petition or case is referred, and he shall place thereon all debts which are duly proved.

18. The assignee shall, under section 27 of the act, produce and file with the clerk, vouchers for all payments made by him, except as to items, in regard to which the court shall, for reasonable cause, dispense with vouchers.

19. The notice of the assignee, under section 28 of the act, of the filing of his account, and of his application for a settlement and discharge, shall be given by him by sending written or printed notices by mail, pre-paid, of such filing, and of the time of such application, to all known creditors of the bankrupt, and it shall be published three weeks successively, as provided in rule 8.

20. The marshal and the clerk, and every

register or assignee, when required to publish any notice or advertisement, shall preserve and return to the court a copy of each newspaper in which it is published, with a certificate, showing that the required publication has been made.

21. In case of the absence of the judge at the time and place noticed or appointed for any hearing or proceeding before him in bankruptcy, or if the matter then fails to be called or acted on, the same shall be deemed continued, without other order, to the next sitting of the court thereof, at which time the like proceedings may be had thereupon as if first noticed or appointed for such day.

22. All notices served or sent by mail by the marshal, the clerk, or an assignee, shall be so written or printed and folded that the direction, postage stamp and postmark shall be upon the notice itself, and not upon an envelope or other separate piece of paper.

23. The court, at its own instance, or on motion of either party, will refer to a register, commissioner, or referee, designated or appointed for the purpose, for examination and report, such matters arising in proceedings in bankruptcy as, under the provisions of the bankrupt act, may properly be so referred.

24. Exceptions may be filed to the report of register, referee or commissioner, upon any matter referred to him, within eight days after the filing of such report; and exceptions to the admission or rejection of evidence may be filed within four days after the return of proofs is filed, and either party may then apply for an order fixing a time for the hearing upon such exceptions.

25. All returns and reports from registers of bankruptcy, or other officers of the court, or referees, shall be directed to the clerk of the court at Burlington, Vermont, and shall be sent free of postage or other charges; and in case of unreasonable delay on the part of the register, or other officer, or referee in making a return or report in any case, an order will be granted requiring him to make such return or report, or show cause on a day specified why he has not done so.

26. It shall be the duty of the assignee, as soon as practicable after his appointment shall be complete, to take into his possession all the estate, real and personal, of every name and nature of the bankruptcy, with the exceptions mentioned in the bankrupt act; and also all the deeds and books of account, papers and writings of the bankrupt, pertaining thereto; and for this purpose the assignee shall make diligent inquiry into the affairs and transactions of the bankrupt.

27. In cases of involuntary bankruptcy, it shall be the duty of the assignee, as soon as practicable after he shall be appointed and qualified, to apply to the bankrupt for a full and true account of all his property and rights of property, and of all the deeds and books of accounts, papers and writings of the bankrupt pertaining thereto, as required by the bankrupt act; and if the bankrupt shall refuse to give such account, or if the assignee or any creditor of the bankrupt shall have good reason to suspect that he has practiced any concealment in giving such account, such assignee or creditor may on application to the court, and due cause shown by affidavit, have an order for the examination of such bankrupt, and, if necessary, for compulsory process against him, as provided in the last preceding rule.

VIRGINIA.

"At an adjourned term of the district court of the United States of America, for the district of Virginia, held at the city of Richmond in and for said district, on the 21st day of September, in the year of our Lord, one thousand eight hundred and sixty-nine—

"*Present*, The honorable JOHN C. UNDERWOOD, *District Judge.*

"*Ordered:* That the following rules, orders and regulations, be substituted in the place of the rules adopted December 31, 1867, governing proceedings in bankruptcy in the district court of the United States for the district of Virginia, under the act entitled " an act to establish a uniform system of bankruptcy throughout the United States," approved March 2d, 1867, (in addition to, and with reference to the 'general orders in bankruptcy,' and the forms specified in the schedules thereto annexed, framed by the justices of the supreme court of the United States,) in pursuance of the tenth section of said act, and adopted by said court, and promulgated September 21, 1869."

Extract from the minutes.

District Clerk.

RULE 1. In voluntary bankruptcy, when

the petition states that the debtor, whether an individual, a copartnership, a corporation or a joint stock company, has resided or carried on business for the six months next immediately preceding the time of filing the petition, or for the longest period during such six months, in the district of Virginia, the petitions shall be referred by Form No. 4, "general orders in bankruptcy," to the register of the congressional district in which the petitioner resides, unless the petitioner, or his attorney, shall desire a different reference for convenience.

A petition may be otherwise referred for special reasons or in cases not herein provided for.

In involuntary bankruptcy the register will be designated with reference to the special circumstances of the case.

The order, Form No. 4, designating the register to act upon the petition in cases of voluntary bankruptcy, shall specify the place where the register shall act upon the matters arising under the case, and the warrant, Form No. 59, in involuntary bankruptcy, shall in a like case specify the place where the meeting of the creditors will be held. The day named in the order, Form No. 4, for the attendance of the bankrupt before the register in voluntary bankruptcy, and the day named in the warrant, Form No. 59, for the meeting of creditors, will be fixed with reference to the convenient and speedy progress of the case.

Every register in a district, other than the 3rd congressional district, shall, by writing filed with the clerk, designate the day on which he will attend at a place or places within the district.

Every register may, in any cases referred to him, fix the times when he will act upon the several matters arising under such case, other than the attendance of the bankrupt, as fixed by the order, Form No. 4, and meeting of creditors as fixed by the warrant, Form No. 59; but the register shall not, without leave of the court, be at liberty to change the place specified in the order, Form No. 4, or to act upon the matters arising under a case in involuntary bankruptcy at any other place than the one specified in the warrant, Form No. 59, as the place for the meeting of creditors. R. 1. S. D. N. Y.

2. The adjudication of bankruptcy, Form No. 58, shall contain a provision that the case be referred to one of the registers, naming him, to take such proceedings thereon as are required by the act. R. 2, S. D. N. Y.

3. Whenever a petition is referred to a register in a voluntary case, and whenever in an involuntary case an order is made, on an adjudication of bankruptcy, referring a case to a register, the clerk at the time he sends or delivers to the register a copy of the order of reference, shall pay to him the sum of twenty-five dollars out of the fifty dollars deposited with the clerk, under section 47 of the act, the same to be applied to the payment of such fees of the register as are chargeable to the petitioner making the deposit, and thereafter the other fees of the register which are chargeable to such petitioner, shall be paid or secured in like manner with the other fees, provided for by rule 29 of the "general orders in bankruptcy." R. 3, S. D. N. Y.

4. The register shall, under rule 6 of the "general orders in bankruptcy," examine the duplicate copy of the petition, and schedules specified in Form No. 4, and such duplicate copy shall be either a copy of such filed original, certified by the clerk under seal of the court, or else a duplicate original signed and verified in like manner with the original petition and schedules filed with the clerk, and shown by evidence satisfactory to the register to be such duplicate original, and the certificate of the register required by said rule 7 as to the correctness in form of the petition and schedules shall be made in writing, and be signed by him on the duplicate copy which he so examines, and he shall not issue any warrant under Form No. 6, until he shall have so made a certificate, after such examination, that the petition and schedules are correct in form. R. 4, S. D. N. Y.

5. The warrant issued under section 11, or section 42, of the act, according to Form No. 6, or Form No. 59, shall specify one of the newspapers named in rule 19, the selection of such newspaper to be made by the register to whom the case is referred. The notices to be published in pursuance of the warrant, shall be published twice in the newspaper selected.

The warrant shall designate the creditors upon whom personal service is to be made, and notice shall be served by mail upon all creditors other than those so designated. No creditor resident out of this district shall be designated for personal service. R. 5, S. D. N. Y.

6. All proof of debt which shall be made and verified prior to the selection or appointment of an assignee, shall be delivered or sent to the register to whom the case is referred. If the register entertains doubts of the validity of any claim, or of the right of a creditor to prove it, and is of opinion that such validity or right ought to be investigated by the assignee, he may postpone the proof of the claim until the assignee is chosen. R. 6, S. D. N. Y.

7. Under rule 9, of the "general orders in bankruptcy," an assignee shall notify the register of the acceptance or rejection of the trust, and the register shall immediately on receiving such notice, report it to the clerk of the court. R. 8, S. D. N. Y.

8. Every assignee shall immediately on receiving an assignment of an estate in bankruptcy, send or deliver such assignment to the clerk of the court, who shall make a true copy of it, and certify such copy under his hand and the seal of the court, and such certified copy shall be placed and kept by him on file, and the original assignment shall be returned to the assignee. R. 9 S. D. N. Y.

9. Notice of an appointment of an assignee shall be given by publication once a week for three successive weeks in one of the newspapers named in rule 19, such newspaper to be selected by the register. R. 10, S. D. N. Y.

10. Notices of sale by an assignee, under rule 21 of the "general orders in bankruptcy," shall be advertised in one of the newspapers named in rule 19, the selection of such newspaper to be named by the register. R. 11, S. D. N. Y.

11. The notice to creditors of dividends or meetings required by the 17th, 27th, and 28th sections of the act, shall be such as is provided for by the order contained in Form No. 28, and the register shall select one newspaper in which the notice shall be published from those specified in rule 19. R. 12. S. D. N. Y.

12. The list of debts provided by section 23 of the act, shall be made and certified by the register to whom the petition or case is referred, and he shall place thereon all debts which are duly proved. R. 13, S. D. N. Y.

13. The assignee shall, under section 27 of the act, produce and file vouchers for all payments made by him, except as to items, in regard to which the court shall for reasonable cause dispense with vouchers. R. 14, S. D. N. Y.

14. The notice by the assignee under section 28 of the act, of the filing of his account, and of his application for a settlement and discharge, shall be given by him, by sending written or printed notices, by mail prepaid, of such application to all known creditors of the bankrupt. R. 15, S. D. N. Y.

15. All questions for trial or hearing, under section 31 and 34 of the act, shall be tried or heard at a stated session of the court on four days' notice of trial or hearing, to be served by either party upon the other party, and upon the clerk, and a calendar of the same shall be made, or as the court may direct in special cases. R. 16, S. D. N. Y.

16. The application under section 34 of the act, to set aside and annul a discharge, shall be verified by the oath or affirmation of the applicant, and the answer of the bankrupt to the application shall answer specifically the allegations of the application, and shall be verified in like manner. R. 17, S. D. N. Y.

17. The demand for a trial by jury under section 41 of the act, shall be in writing and shall be signed by the debtor or his attorney. R. 18, S. D. N. Y.

18. All issues, questions, points and matters stated in writing, under rule 11 of the "general orders in bankruptcy," or under the 4th section or the 6th section of the act, or according to Form No. 50, and adjourned into court for decision, or stated in a special case for the opinion of the court, shall be certified to the judge by the register by a certificate, which shall also state briefly the opinion of the register on the issue, question, point or matter, and shall be delivered or sent to the clerk; and no oral or written argument shall be allowed on any such issue or question, unless by special leave of the court, R. 19, S. D. N. Y.

19. The following newspapers are designated as those in which all publications required by the act, or the "general orders in bankruptcy," or these rules, may be made,

until others are appointed according to law, namely. In the city of Richmond, The Virginia State Journal. In the city of Lynchburg, The Evening Press. The marshal and the clerk, and every register and assignee, when required to publish any notice or advertisement, shall preserve and return to the court a copy, cut from each newspaper in which it is published, of each notice and advertisement, as published, with a certificate and affidavit of the publisher as to the particulars of the publishing, showing that the required publication has been made. R. 21, S. D. N. Y.

20. In all cases of voluntary bankruptcy where no assets are returned, the deposit of fifty dollars shall cover all costs except the publication under petition for final discharge, and certificate of discharge, and shall be distributed in the following proportion:

To the register, twenty-five dollars.

To the clerk, ten dollars.

To the marshal, seven dollars.

To the printer, eight dollars.

21. In addition to the fifty dollars deposited on filing a petition in every case of voluntary bankruptcy, where no assets are returned, the sum of eight dollars is to be paid to the bankrupt for printers' fees for the publication of the last notice, and one dollar for a certified copy of the discharge. Also, in cases, where there are no assets to go into the assignee's hands, one dollar for the assignee's report setting off exempted property. No other fees are to be allowed in cases where there are no assets, and no opposition to the bankrupt's discharge. § 47. G. O. 29.

22. On the bankrupt or his attorney's filing with the register a petition for final discharge, the register will issue an order to show cause why the prayer of the petitioner should not be granted, and shall serve personally, or send by mail, prepaid, to all the creditors of the bankrupt who have proved their claims, printed or written notice of the bankrupt's application for final discharge, and the time fixed for the meeting of said creditors, and by publication at least once a week in a newspaper designated in rule 19, and after the meeting of said creditors, the register will examine the proceedings in the case, and if he finds them in all respects to have been in conformity with the act, he will make

and file his certificate therefor, together with all the papers in the case, and an abstract of the case with the clerk, and also certify that there is no opposition to the bankrupt's discharge, whereupon the bankrupt or his attorney may apply to the court for the final discharge of the bankrupt. § 29.

23. In case of the absence of the judge at the time or place noticed or appointed for any hearing or proceeding before him in bankruptcy, or if the matter then fails to be called or acted on, the same shall be deemed continued, without other order, to the next sitting of the court thereafter, at which time the like proceedings may be had thereupon as if first noticed or appointed for such day. R. 22, S. D. N. Y.

24. If the marshal, under rule 13, of the "general orders in bankruptcy," appoint special deputies to act as messengers, he shall, as far as possible, designate one or more of such special deputies to be attached to the office of each register, for the purpose of causing the notices to be published and served which are specified in the warrants issued in the cases referred to such register. R. 23, S. D. N. Y.

25. In all cases where monies come into the hands of assignees from sales of realty or personalty, the said assignees shall first settle the costs and expenses of the register, marshal, clerk and publisher, that have accrued, before any further disposition is made of the fund. § 28.

26. In all cases where monies have come into the hands of officers of this court, they shall forthwith deposit the same in the nearest national depository not to the credit of themselves as individuals, but as said officers of the court, unless by order of the court in special cases. § 17.

27. The register to whom a case is referred shall have power to make the order in Form No. 51 under section 29 of the act. § 4. 29.

28. Every assignee shall forthwith transmit to the clerk of the court a memorandum showing the names of the creditors and their places of residence, and, when stated, their postoffice address, and the amounts of their debts in all cases in which proofs of debts have been previously furnished the assignee; and hereafter, every assignee shall transmit to the clerk

of the court a like memorandum in every case in which proof of debt shall be furnished to the assignee, as soon as it shall be received. R. S. D. N. Y.

29. Hereafter in all cases to show cause, made according to Form 51, on petitions of bankrupts for discharge from their debts, no meeting of creditors, except the first, shall be ordered or had unless some assets have come to the hands of the assignee. R. S. D. N. Y.

30. In taking testimony, where the same is written down by question and answer, the questions put to each witness shall be numbered continuing from the commencement to the final close of his direct and cross examination. R. S. D. N. Y.

. 31. Upon the examination of the bankrupt or witnesses before any register, every objection made by either party to any question or answer shall be passed upon by said register, and either party shall be allowed to take formal exceptions to such decision, which exceptions shall be certified to the court, and upon the coming in of the court's decision thereon, the register shall strike out or allow any question or answer accordingly. R. S. D. N. Y.

32. When a petition in involuntary bankruptcy is contested, no trial by jury shall be allowed unless on the return day of the order to show cause a demand in writing for such trial be filed, and in case no such demand be made, the case shall be referred to one of the registers of the court, who shall summarily proceed to hear the allegations and proofs of the petitioner and debtor, and shall reduce the same to writing and forthwith report the same to the court, together with his opinions on the same. If counsel wish to argue the case before the court, they shall file a notification to that effect in writing with the register upon the closing of the testimony in the case, otherwise the court will decide without further hearing.

When the debtor does not appear on the return day, and the order to show cause appears to have been properly served, the clerk shall forthwith enter an adjudication of bankruptcy, and refer the case to a register, who shall proceed regularly therein as in a case of voluntary bankruptcy. § 4. 41.

33. The register shall designate the papers in which all sales to be made by assignees in cases referred to him shall be advertised, and no other allowance for printing shall be made unless specially authorized by said register or by the court.

34. In all cases when the assignee does not notify the register of his acceptance of his appointment in five days after he receives notice thereof, he shall be considered to have declined, and the register shall appoint an assignee in his place. § 13.

Every assignee hereafter appointed, when the schedules of the bankrupt show assets, shall file his bond in each case with the register, in the penalty and with security to be approved by him conditioned for the faithful performance of his duty.

All such bonds shall be filed by the register with the papers in the case, and the same may be inspected at any time by any creditor or his attorney under the supervision of the register.

All notices to assignees of their appointment shall contain a clause notifying them that unless they accept the same within five days after the receipt of the notice, such neglect to accept will be considered a declination, and further notifying them that they will be required to file their bond with the register within ten days after receipt of the notice in penalty and with security to be approved by the registers, and such notice shall likewise state the penalty of the bond to be required.

All assignees heretofore appointed shall file his bond in each case in which assets are reported or are returned in schedules, in a penalty and with security to be approved by the register within ten days after notification to that effect by the register. § 13.

36. Whenever any assignee shall fail to file bond as required by rule 35, within ten days after the receipt of notice to file the same, he shall be considered as removed, and the court shall appoint a new assignee upon the report of the register, of such failure.

Any assignee shall have the right to appeal to the court from any decision of the register as to the penalty or security in his bond, and such appeal shall stay proceedings as to his removal until decided: *Provided*, that no appeal shall be allowed any assignee unless it shall appear that the penalty of the bond required by the register is in excess of the amount of the property reported, or surrendered by the bankrupt in his schedules of assets : *Provided also*, that no appeal shall be taken because of the register's refusal to accept sureties who cannot justify in the sum required in real estate ; and all appeals taken from the decision of the register shall be in writing, setting forth the grounds of the appeal, and be forwarded forthwith to the court by the register, with such reasons as he may have to offer in support of his action. § 13.

27. The register shall fix the time and place of sale of all sales by the assignees, in cases referred to him, unless otherwise fixed by the court. It shall be his duty to examine the assignee at any time to see that he has complied with the law and general orders in bankruptcy, and the rules and orders of this court, and to ascertain generally whether he has faithfully performed his duty. He shall at all times have free access to the books and accounts of any assignee, and may require the same to be exhibited to any creditor who desires it.

38. Petitions by assignees or creditors to sell real estate free from incumbrance, and to transfer the liens from the realty to the fund in court, may be filed before the court or a register, and an order to show cause issue as of course, notifying all creditors claiming liens on said real estate to appear on some day in such order named, providing that a copy of such order be served on each creditor at least ten days before the day of appearance, or notice given by publication to be ordered by the court or register, instead of personal notice.

If on the day of appearance no cause is shown, an order to issue to sell the real estate in the petition described free and discharged from all incumbrance, and the lien thereon shall be transferred to the fund in court produced by the sale.

If cause is shown, the register shall forthwith proceed to take such testimony as may be produced for or against said application, and shall forward petition, order, cause shown, and proofs to sustain either, with all proceeding under them, to the court.

In re Barrow 1. B. R. 123—In re Loeb 1. B. R. 123—In re Salmon 2. B. R. 19.—Ex parte Christie, 3 How. 292—Houston vs. City Bank, 6 How. 486. § 20.

39. All sales of real estate sold free and discharged from liens and incumbrances, shall be reported in writing to the court or register that ordered the same, as together with the proof of the advertisement and of the expense as per rule 9, and as soon as such sale shall have been made.

No sale shall be final until ratified by the said court. All such reports shall lie in the office of the clerk or register in which the same shall be filed for ten days, and if not excepted to, in writing, in the office where the same is filed within that time, the sale shall be considered ratified as of course.

40. When such sale shall be excepted to, if before a register, he shall at once proceed to take all testimony which may be produced by any party in interest before him, and reduce the same to writing, and shall then return all the proceedings to the court. If the exception is filed to a sale reported to the court, the clerk will enter an order of reference to any register the parties may agree upon, or if they fail to agree, then to the register having charge of the case, and such register shall reduce to writing such evidence as may be produced before him, and shall return the whole proceedings and evidence to the court. § 4.

41. In all petitions filed in any cause before a court or register, in the nature of proceedings in equity, praying for any relief, and where any parties are made respondents thereto, the clerk or register will issue an order as of course directed to said parties respondent, requiring them to show cause why the petitioner should not have the relief prayed, and providing that a copy of said order be served on each respondent at least ten days before the day set for hearing said cause, which day shall be specified in the order. If no cause is shown on the day set, the party shall be entitled to the relief prayed to that effect, and a decree shall be entered as of course.

If cause is shown and either party desire it, an order shall be made by the clerk or register referring the petition and answer to such register as the parties may agree upon, or if they fail to agree then to the register having charge of the cause who shall take such testimony as they may produce, and report the same to the court. Upon such report coming in, any party may call up the case for a hearing on five days' notice to the others or to their solicitors in court.

42. The clerk shall keep a docket to be

called the notice docket, and no motion *ex parte* will be heard nor any such order made by the court in any cause unless notice of such motion or the substance of the order which is asked be entered upon the notice docket at least twenty-four hours before it is made in court. Each notice entered on the notice docket shall be equivalent to personal notice to all parties to all proceedings in the cause and their solicitors. The entry in the docket shall specify the time and place of making the motion or application for the order. R. 4. Rules of equity practice in C. C. U. S.

43. In all cases where testimony is being taken thirty days and no more, shall be allowed for taking the same, and no testimony shall be taken after that time unless allowed by the court or register for special cause shown, and all references to take testimony shall be returned into court in ten days after the time for taking the testimony has expired.

44. It shall be the duty of the clerk of this court to tax all costs in matters in bankruptcy.

45· All assignees are prohibited from disposing of any property belonging to the estates of bankrupts, until they shall have complied with the terms of rule No. 35.

46. In proceedings by an assignee to recover assets of a bankrupt, he shall file a petition or complaint, briefly and clearly stating his cause of action. The clerk shall then issue an order, directing the defendant to show cause, by a day named in said order, why judgment should not be entered as asked.

A copy of this petition and order shall be served on the defendant at least thirty days before the day named therein for showing cause. If no cause be shown under oath on the day named, judgment shall be entered as prayed, and execution issued forthwith. All petitions to recover on open accounts, shall be accompanied by a copy of such account, which copy shall also be served with the petition and order. § 1.

47. All judgments and decrees of this court may be enforced by any writs or other process used by the circuit courts of the state of Virginia as courts of law, or the courts of the United States as courts of equity.

48. All service of writs, process or notice,

may be as provided by the code of Virginia, or the general orders in bankruptcy.

49. The report of assignees, required by rule No. 28 of the general orders in bankruptcy, to be made on the first Monday of every month, shall specify in which national depository the assets in his hands in that case are placed under rule 25, or in what manner they are disposed of.

50. In all cases where suits are instituted by this court by assignees or others, except proceedings in involuntary bankruptcy, the party instituting said suit shall deposit ten dollars with the clerk towards his costs when he brings the suit.

51. Special cases not comprehended within the foregoing rules or the "general orders in bankruptcy," or the forms, shall be submitted to the court. R. 25. S. D. N. Y.

ABBREVIATIONS.

R. S. D. N. Y—Rules in bankruptcy southern dist. N. Y. § Sections of act of congress to establish a uniform system of bankruptcy. B. R. Bankrupt Register. R. Equity Practice C. C. U. S. Rules of practice for the courts of equity of the United States.

United States District Court, ⎰
District of Virginia. ⎱

Ordered, That no register of this court in bankruptcy hold any dividend meeting, nor any assignee pay out, or retain for his own use any moneys received from the settlement of the estate of any bankrupt, until he shall have first paid the taxed bill of costs of the marshal, register, printer and clerk, and every assignee is forbidden to pay any bills of the officers of this court, until they are examined and taxed by the proper officer. All bills shall be taxed by the clerk of the court.

It is ordered, That the clerk of this court shall tax and approve all fee bills against bankrupts, according to legal fees allowed in bankruptcy proceedings, and that the said clerk shall, when so requested by any of the said officers, as well for them as himself, issue executions for the same, to be levied for out of any property belonging to the said bankrupt; *provided,* his exemption set aside in bankruptcy, exceed the amount of the state exemption allowed in the year 1864, but in no case shall any part of state exemption be taken.

November 15th, 1870.

An extract from the minutes.

ED. J. UNDERWOOD,
District Clerk.

ERRATA.

THE FOLLOWING RULES WERE OVERLOOKED OR HAVE BEEN ADOPTED SINCE THIS VOLUME WAS STEREOTYPED.

ADDITIONAL RULES.

ADDITIONAL STANDING RULE.

At a stated term of the District Court of the United States of America, for the Southern District of New-York, held at the United States Court Rooms, in the City of New-York, on Saturday the thirteenth day of November, in the year of our Lord one thousand eight hundred and sixty-nine :

Ordered, It shall be the duty of every Register, from time to time, to call the attention of assignees chosen or appointed, in cases referred to him, to the provision of General Order, No. 28, requiring every assignee to make a report to the Court, on the first Monday of every month, of the funds received by him, and of deposits made by him; and to bring to the notice of the Court all cases of failure by assignees to comply with such provision, after being notified to do so by the Register.

Witness, the Honorable SAMUEL BLATCH-
FORD, Judge of the said Court, and the
[L. S.] seal thereof, at the city of New-York, in said District, this 13th day of November, A. D. 1869.

GEORGE F. BETTS, *Clerk.*

December 30th, 1871.

Rule 7 of the Rules in Bankruptcy of this Court, is hereby amended so as to read as follows :

In case no choice of an assignee is made by the creditors at their first meeting, or in case an assignee chosen by the creditors fails within five days to express in writing his acceptance of the trust, or in case of a vacancy in the office of an assignee, caused by his removal, resignation, death, or other cause, John H. Platt, Esq., of the city of New-York, counsellor at law, will be appointed assignee, where the appointment is made by the Judge; and where the said John H. Platt shall be appointed by any Register, such appointment is hereby approved by the Judge. In special cases, vacancies in the office of assignee will be filled by an election by the creditors, or by the appointment of an assignee other than the one above named.

No. 1.

UNITED STATES DISTRICT COURT.

RULE 30.— ADDITIONAL STANDING RULE.

At a stated term of the District Court of the United States of America, for the Southern District of New York, held at the United States Court Rooms, in the city of New York, on Tuesday, the 20th day of February, in the year of our Lord one thousand eight hundred and seventy-two :

Ordered, Hereafter, in all cases of Voluntary Bankruptcy, where the schedules filed by the petitioner shall give the address of a creditor as "New York City," they shall in addition state the street and number; and the same provision shall apply to schedules and lists of creditors furnished by the bankrupt or by creditors, in proceedings in involuntary bankruptcy. In all proofs of debt, where the address of the creditor is given as "New York City" the street and number shall be added. All notices mailed by the Marshal or the Clerk to creditors residing in the City of New York, shall be directed to the street address of the creditor; and the Marshal, in making return of the execution of a warrant, and the Clerk in making return of the mailing of notices to creditors, under an order to show cause why a bankrupt's discharge should not be granted, shall, in addition, certify to the Register a list of those creditors whose notices have been returned from the post-office.

Witness, the Honorable SAMUEL BLATCH-
FORD, Judge of said Court, and the seal
[L. S.] thereof, at the City of New York, in the said district, this 20th day of February, A. D. 1872.

GEO. F. BETTS, *Clerk.*

FORMS IN BANKRUPTCY.

FORMS IN BANKRUPTCY.

Form No. 1.

PETITION BY DEBTOR.

To the Honorable   , Judge of the District Court of the United States, for the   District of   :—

THE PETITION of   , of the   of   , in the County of   , and State of   , and District aforesaid, Respectfully Represents :—That he has   for   months next immediately preceding the filing of this petition, at   , within said Judicial District; that he owes debts exceeding the amount of three hundred dollars, and is unable to pay all of the same in full; that he is willing to surrender all his estate and effect for the benefit of his Creditors, and desires to obtain the benefit of the Act entitled "An Act to Establish a Uniform System of Bankruptcy throughout the United States," approved March 2, 1867 :

That the Schedule hereto annexed, marked A, and verified by Your Petitioner's oath, contains a full and true statement of all his debts, and (so far as it is possible to ascertain) the names and places of residence of his creditors, and such further statements concerning said debts as are required by the provisions of said Act :

That the Schedule hereto annexed, marked B, and verified by Your Petitioner's oath, contains an accurate inventory of all his estate, both real and personal, assignable under the provisions of said Act :

WHEREFORE, YOUR PETITIONER PRAYS, that he may be adjudged by the Court to be a Bankrupt, within the purview of said Act; and that he may be Decreed to have a Certificate of Discharge from all his debts provable under the same.

——————— ———————, *Solicitor,* [or, *Attorney,*] &c.

Oath to foregoing Petition.

[N. B.—If Petitioner is not a citizen, the last clause of this oath should be omitted.]

UNITED STATES OF AMERICA.
                District of   , *ss :*

I,   , the Petitioning Debtor mentioned and described in the foregoing Petition, do hereby make solemn oath [*or,* affirmation] that the statements contained therein are true according to the best of my knowledge, information and belief; and I do further make oath [*or,* affirmation] that I am a citizen of the United States of America, and that I will bear true faith and allegiance to the same.

——————— ———————, *Petitioner.*

Subscribed and sworn [*or* affirmed] to, before me, this   day of   , A. D. 18   .

——— ———————,
U. S. District Judge, [*Register in Bankruptcy,* or, *U. S. Commissioner.*]

[Petition by Debtor.] SCHEDULE A. (1.)

Statement of all Creditors who are to be Paid in Full, or to whom Priority is secured, according to the provisions of the 28th Section of said Act.

Order of Payment; Preferred Claims.	Reference to Ledger or Voucher.	Names of Creditors.	Residences and Occupations.	Amount.	Where and when contracted.	Nature and Consideration of the Debt, and whether contracted as copartner or joint contractor; and if so, with whom.
				$ c.		
1. Debts due to the United States, and taxes and assessments under the laws thereof.						
2. Debts due to the State of , and taxes and assessments under the laws of said State.						
3. Wages due clerk, servant, &c., to an amount not exceeding, $50 for Labor performed within Six Months.						
4. Other debts Preferred by said Act.						

———— *Petitioner.*

[Petition by Debtor.]

SCHEDULE A. (2.)

Creditors holding Securities.

[N. B.—Particulars of Securities held, with dates of same, and when given, to be stated under the names of the several creditors, and also Particulars concerning each Debt, as required by the 11th Section of the Act, and whether contracted as copartner or joint contractor with any other person; and if so, with whom.]

Reference to Ledger or Voucher.	Names of Creditors.	Residences and Description.	When and Where Contracted.	Value of Securities.	Amount of Debts.
				$ c.	£ c.
Ledger [A.] page.... [150.]	[John Brown]..........	Residing at Lien, by Judgment of Court, in the State of [Pennsylvania,] upon my Real Estate, situate in township of , in said State, (describing it.)		$	£
Ledger [B.] page .... [75.]	[Samuel Johnson].......	Residing at Pledge of 150 shares, Stock of [Cumberland Coal Company] a Company incorporated under the laws of the State of Maryland,] and doing business at Certificate of said Stock transferred to said [Johnson.]			
Ledger [C.] page .... [96.]	[William Peters]........	Residing at Mortgages upon my real Estate in , made to secure his Liability as Endorser on certain Promissory Notes made by me, and described as follows: Or for Liability as Surety. Or for Liability as Bail. Or for any other Liability for which Mortgages may be given.			
Ledger [D.] page .... [146.]	[John Jones]...........	Residing at Note of A B, dated , at four months for $. Note of C D, dated , at six months for $. Note of E F, dated , at nine months for $. Delivered to said Jones, as Collateral Security for his Debt, on the day of , 18 .			
Ledger [E.] page .... [200.]	[George Smith]........	Residing at Six bales of Cotton weighing pounds, valued at ; five bales of Wool weighing pounds, valued at ; six barrels Whisky, valued at . Delivered to said [Smith,] in pledge for his Debt, on the day of , 186 .			

[N. B.—The above examples will serve as a proper guide.]

_____ , Petitioner.

[Petition by Debtor.]

(3.)

SCHEDULE A.

Creditors whose Claims are Unsecured.

[N. B.—When the Name and Residence (or either) of any Drawer, Maker, Endorser or Holder of any Bill or Note, &c., are unknown, the fact must be stated, and also the Name, Residence, and Occupation of the last holder known to the Petitioner. The debt due to each creditor must be stated in full, and any claim by way of Set-off stated in the schedule of property. The Nature of each debt and demand, whether founded on Written Security, Obligation, Contract, or Otherwise, and also the True Cause and Consideration of such Indebtedness in each case and the Place where such Indebtedness accrued.]

Reference to Ledger or Voucher.	Names of Creditors.	Residences and Occupations.	Amount.	When and Where Contracted.	Nature and Consideration of the Debt, and whether any Judgment, Bond, Bill of Exchange, Promissory Note, &c., and whether contracted as copartner or joint contractor, with any other person; and, if so, with whom.
			c.		

—————————, *Petitioner.*

[Petition by Debtor.]

SCHEDULE A. — — — — (4.)

Liabilities on Notes or Bills Discounted which ought to be paid by the Drawers, Makers, or Acceptors.

[N. B.—The Dates of the Notes or Bills, and when Due, with the Names, Residences, and the Business, or Occupation of the Drawers, Makers, or Acceptors thereof, are to be set forth under the Names of the Holders. If the Names of the Holders are not known, the name of the last holder known to the petitioner should be stated, and his Business and place of Residence. The same particulars as to Notes or Bills on which the petitioner is liable as Endorser.]

Reference to Ledger or Voucher.	Names of Holders as far as known.	Place of Residence and Occupation.	Place where Contracted.	Amount.	Nature of Liability, whether same was contracted as copartner or joint contractor, or with any other person; and, if so, with whom.
				£	

—————, Petitioner.

[Petition by Debtor.]   (5.)

SCHEDULE A.

Accommodation Paper.

[N. B.—The Dates of the Notes or Bills, and when Due, with the Names, Residences, and Business or Occupation of the Drawers. Makers, and Acceptors thereof, are to be set forth under the Names of the Holders ; if the Bankrupt be liable as Drawer, Maker, Acceptor, or Endorser thereof, it is to be stated accordingly. If the names of the Holders are not known, the name of the last Holder known to the petitioner should be stated, with his Business and Place of Residence. Same particulars as to other commercial paper.]

Reference to Ledger or Voucher.	Names of Holders.	Residences of Holders and Particul'rs of Notes or Bills.	Place where Contracted.	Amount.		Whether liability was contracted as co-partner or joint contractor; or with any other Person ; and, if so, with whom.
				$	c.	

———————, Petitioner.

[N. B.—Here will follow oath to Schedule A, hereinafter prescribed.]

[Petition by Debtor.]

SCHEDULE B. (1.)

Statement of all Real and Personal Estate and Effects Whatever, which are now in the Possession, Enjoyment, or under the Control of the Petitioner, or which are held by any other person, In Trust, for his use, or to the Possession or Enjoyment of which he is entitled at the date of filing Petition.

[INTEREST IN LANDS.]

Particular Description of all Real Estate owned by Petitioner, or held by him, and whether under Contract or Lease.	Encumbrances thereon, if any, and Dates thereof.	Statement of all Particulars relating thereto.	Estimated Value.

——————, Petitioner.

[Petition by Debtor.]   SCHEDULE B.   (2.)

Personal Property.

	Dollars.	Cts.
a.—Cash on hand		
b.—Bills of Exchange, Promissory Notes, or Securities of any description, (each to be set out separately).		
c. Stock in Trade, in my business of , at , of the value of		
d.—Household Goods and Furniture, Household Stores, Wearing Apparel and Ornaments of the Person....		
e.—Books, Prints, and Pictures....		
f.—Horses, Cows, Sheep, and other Animals....		
g.—Carriages, and other Vehicles		
h.—Farming Stock, and Implements of Husbandry.		
i.—Shipping, and Shares in Vessels....		
k.—Machinery, Fixtures, and Apparatus used in Business; with the place where each is situated		
l.—Goods or Personal Property of any other Description, with the place where each is situated....		

—————— ——————————, *Petitioner.*

[Petition by Debtor.]   SCHEDULE B.   (3.)

Choses in Action.

	Dollars.	Cts.
a.—Debts due Petitioner on open Account....		
b –Stocks in Incorporated Companies, and Interest in Joint-stock Companies.		
c.—Policies of Insurance....		
d.—Unliquidated Claims of every nature, with their Estimated Value......		

—————— ————, *Petitioner.*

147

[Petition of Debtor.]   SCHEDULE B.   (4.)

Property in Reversion, Remainder, or Expectancy, including Property held in Trust for the Petitioner, or subject to any Power or Right to Dispose of, or to Charge.

[N B.—A Particular Description of each Interest must be Entered. If all or any of the debtor's Property has been Conveyed by Deed of Assignment, or otherwise, for the benefit of Creditors, the date of such Deed should be stated, the Name and Address of the Person to whom the Property was Conveyed, the Amount realized from the Proceeds thereof, and the Disposal of the Same, as far as known to the Petitioner.]

General Interest.	Particular Description.	Supposed Value of my Interest.
		Dolls. Cts.
Interest in Land........	Real Estate and Leasehold Property, with Locality, Names and Descriptions of Parties now Enjoying the Same, and the Value thereof ; also the Nature of my Interest therein, and from Whom, and in what Manner it is derived............	
Personal Property.......	Personal Property, with Locality, Names and Descriptions of Persons now Enjoying the Same; also the Nature of my Interest therein, and from Whom and in what Manner it is derived............	
Prope'y in Money, Stock, Shares, Bonds, Annuities, etc., etc.	Annuities, Money in Public or other Funds, Shares in Railroad and other Companies, showing in whose names the same are standing. with Names and Descriptions of persons now Enjoying the Same; also the Nature of my Interest therein, and from Whom. and in what Manner it is derived............	
Rights and Powers.....	Rights and Powers wherein I, or any other Person or Persons in Trust for me or for my benefit, have any power to Dispose of, Charge, or Exercise....	
		Amn't realized from proceeds of property conveyed.
Property heretofore conveyed for benefit of Creditors.		Dolls. Cts.
What portion of Debtor's Property has been Conveyed by Deed of Assignment, or otherwise, for Benefit of Creditors; Date of such Deed, Name and Address of Party to whom Conveyed; Amount realized therefrom and Disposal of same, so far as known to Petitioner.	Description of Property of Debtor heretofore conveyed for benefit of Creditor by deed of assignment, or otherwise ; date of such deed or instrument of conveyance, wtih name and address of party to whom made; amount realized from same, and the disposal of such property, so far as known to Petitioner.	

——————— ————————, *Petitioner.*

[Petition of Debtor.] SCHEDULE B (4.)

*A Particular Statement of the property claimed as Excepted from the
Operation of said Act, by the provisions of the 14th Section thereof,
giving Each Item of Property and its Valuation ; and, if any portion
of it is Real Estate, its Location, Description, and Present Use.*

[N. B.—The property claimed to be Exempt under the Laws of any State is to be described
separately from the rest, and reference given to the Statute of said State creating the
Exception.

		Valuation.	
		Dolls.	Cts.
Property claimed to be Excepted from the operations of said Act, and which may be set apart by the Assignee, under the 14th Section			
Property claimed to be Exempt by State laws ; its Valuation; whether Real or Personal Estate ; its Description and Present Use, and under what State law exemption is claimed.			

_____, *Petitioner.*

[Petition of Debtor.]　　　　SCHEDULE B.　　　　　　(6.)

The following is a True List of all Books, Papers, Deeds, and Writings relating to my Trade, Business, Dealings, Estate, and effects, or any Part thereof, which, at the date of this Petition, are in my Possession or under my Custody, and Control, or which are in the Possession or Custody of any Person in Trust for me, or for my Use, Benefit, or Advantage; and also of All others which have been heretofore, at any time, in my Possession, or under my Custody or Control, and which are now held by the Parties whose names are hereinafter set forth, with the reason for their Custody of the same :—

BOOKS ....

DEEDS ....

PAPERS, ETC..... ....

———————　————————, *Petitioner.*

[N. B.—Here follows oath to Schedule B as hereinafter prescribed.]

OATHS TO SCHEDULES A AND B.

[N. B.—The following forms of oaths to Schedules A and B of the Petition by Debtor are prescribed, and they are to be annexed to the same, respectfully.]

Oath to Schedule A.

UNITED STATES OF AMERICA.

District of , ss:

On this day of , A. D. 18 , before me personally came the person mentioned in and who subscribed to the foregoing Petition and Schedule, marked A, respectfully, and who being by me first duly sworn [or affirmed], did declare the said Schedule to be a statement of all his debts, &c., in accordance with the Act of Congress entitled " An Act to Establish a Uniform System of Bankruptcy throughout the United States," approved March 2, 1867.

District Judge, [or, Register; or, U. S. Commissioner.]

Oath to Schedule B.

UNITED STATES OF AMERICA.

District of ss:

On this day of , A. D. 18 , before me pesonally came the person mentioned in and who subscribed to the foregoing Petition and Schedule, marked B, respectively, and who being by me first duly sworn [or, affirmed], did declare the said Schedule to be a statement of all his estate, both real and personal, in accordance with the Act of Congress entitled " An Act to Establish a Uniform System of Bankruptcy throughout the United States," approved March 2, 1867.

District Judge, [or, Register ; or, U. S. Commissioner.]

Form No. 2.

COPARTNERSHIP PETITION.

[In case of a copartnership, the form will be as follows :]

To the Honorable Judge of the District Court of the United States for the District of .

THE PETITION of , and , of , in the County of , and State of , and District aforesaid, respectfully represents : That the said , and , copartners transacting business at , in the County of , and State of , and in said district, have for the months.

[Or,

THAT the said and members of a copartnership composed of themselves, and one of of , in the County of , and State of , have for the months :— next immediately preceding the filing of this Petition at within said Judicial District; that the members of said copartnership owe debts exceeding the amount of *three hundred dollars,* and are unable to pay all their debts in full ; that they are willing to surrender all their estate and effects for the benefit of their creditors, and desire to obtain the benefit of the Act entitled " An Act to Establish a Uniform System of Bankruptcy throughout the United States," approved March 2, 1867.

That the Schedule hereto annexed, marked A, and verified by their oaths, contains a

Full and True Statement of all the debts of said Copartnership, and, as far as possible, the Names and Places of Residence of their Creditors, and the further statements concerning such debts required by the provisions of said Act.

That the Schedule hereto annexed, marked B, verified by their oaths, contains an accurate Inventory of all the estate of said Copartnership as required by the provisions of said Act.

And said   further states, that the Schedule hereto annexed, marked C, verified by his oath, contains a Full and True Statement of all his Individual debts; and, as far as possible, the names and Places of Residence of his Creditors; and the further Statements concerning such debts required by the provisions of said Act; and that the Schedule hereto annexed, marked D, verified by his oath, contains an accurate Inventory of all his Individual Estate as required by the provisions of said Act.

And said   further states, that the Schedule hereto annexed, marked E, verified by his oath, contains a Full and True Statement of all his Individual debts, and, as far as possible, the Names and Places of Residence of his Creditors, and the further Statements concerning such debts required by the provisions of said Act; and that the Schedule hereto annexed, marked F, verified by his oath, contains an accurate Inventory of all his Individual Estate as required by the provisions of said Act.

[N. B.—Similar clauses to be added for Individual Schedules of each Copartner joining in the Petition.]

WHEREFORE YOUR PETITIONERS PRAY, that after due proceedings had, they may be adjudged by a Decree of the Court to the Bankrupts within the purview of said Act; and upon their compliance with all the requirements of the said Act; and all the orders and directions of the Court made in pursuance thereof, they may be severally decreed to have a CERTIFICATE OF DISCHARGE FROM ALL THEIR DEBTS provable under said Act, and otherwise entitled to all the benefits thereof.

—————— ——————,
—————— ——————,
Petitioners.

[N. B.—The Form of the Oath to the Petition is to be modified by employing the plural for the singular number, and by the addition of clauses to cover the Schedules of each Copartner.]

————

Form No. 3.

CORPORATION PETITION.

[N. B.—If a petition in Bankruptcy is filed by a Corporation, an authenticated copy of a Vote or other action of the Stockholders, (or, party or parties entitled to act in behalf of such Corporation,) authorizing such proceedings should be filed with the Petition, and which, in substance, should be as follows:)

Statement to accompany Petition of Corporation, (In Bankruptcy.)

AT A MEETING OF THE STOCKHOLDERS, [or, of the Board of Directors, or, Trustees, as the Case may be,] of the   Company, [or, Association, or, Bank, or, Society,] a Corporation created by   , of the State of   , held at   , in the county of   , and State of   , on this   day of   , A. D. 18   , the Condition of the Affairs of said Corporation having been inquired into, and it being ascertained to the Satisfaction of said meeting that the said Corporation was Insolvent, and that its Affairs ought to be wound up, it was Voted, [or Resolved] by a Majority of the Corporators [or, Stockholders, or, Directors, or, Trustees] present at such Meeting, (which was duly called and notified for the purpose of taking action upon the subject aforesaid;) that   be, and   thereby—Authorized,

Empowered, and Required to file a Petition in the District Court of the United States for the   District of   , within which said Corporation has carried on its business, for the purpose of having the same adjudged Bankrupt; and that such proceedings be had thereon as are provided by the Act of Congress entitled " An Act to Establish a Uniform System of Bankruptcy throughout the United States, " approved March 2, 1867.

IN WITNESS WHEREOF, I have hereunto subscribed my name as President [or, other officer or agent] of said Corportion, and affixed the Seal of the same

{ Seal } { of Corporation. } this   day of   A. D. 18 .

———————— ————————,

President, [or, *other officer*] *of said Corporation.*

[N. B.—In case of a Corporation, the following changes are to be made in the form of Petition already described, viz: The substitution of the Name of the Corporation for that of the Individual Petitioner, and the omission of the Prayer for a Discharge and the following passage substituted : " *And that like proceedings may be had in the premises as in said act are provided in respect to natural persons.*" The language of the Oath to the Corporation Petition may be changed to correspond with the form of the Petition.]

———————

Form No. 4.

ORDER OF REFERENCE TO REGISTER.

In the District Court of the United States,
For the   District of

In the Matter of	
	⎫
	⎬ IN BANKRUPTCY.
A Petitioner for Adjudication in Bankruptcy of himself.	⎭

District of   , *ss :*
WHEREAS   , of the County of   , State of
and District aforesaid, has, on this   day of   , A. D. 18 , at
o'clock   m., filed in the office of the Clerk of said Court a Petition for Adjudication in Bankruptcy against himself, according to the provisions of the Act of Congress entitled " An Act to Establish a Uniform System of Bankruptcy throughout the United States," approved March 2, 1867,

It is thereupon *Ordered*, That said Petition be referred to   , one of the Registers in Bankruptcy of this Court, to make Adjudication thereon, and take such other proceedings therein as are required by said Act; and *further*, That the said   shall, on or before the   day of   , at   o'clock   m., file with said Register a duplicate copy of said Petition and the Schedules thereto annexed, and that he attend before said Register on said day, and thenceforth as said Register may direct, to submit to such orders as may be made by said Register, or by this Court relating to his said Bankruptcy.

And further, that until otherwise ordered by the Court, the said Register shall act upon the matters arising in this case at his office, at   , at such times as he shall fix for that purpose.

Witness the Honorable   , Judge of the said Court, and

seal thereof, at　　　　　, in said District, on　　　　the　　　day of　　　　　　　,
A. D. 18　　.

{ Seal of }
{ the Court. }

―――――――――　――――――――　,
Clerk of District Court, for said District.

―――――

Form No. 5.

ADJUDICATION OF BANKRUPTCY UPON DEBTOR'S PETITION.

In the District Court of the United States,
For the　　　　　　District of　　　　　　.

· 　In the Matter of
By whom a Petition for Adjudication of Bank- ruptcy was filed on the　　　　　day of 　　　　, A. D. 18　　, in said Court.

} IN BANKRUPTCY.

　　　　　　　　　　At　　　　　　　　, in said District,
　　　　　　　　　　on the　　　day of　　　, A. D. 18　.
　　　　　　　　　　Before　　　　, one of the Registers, of
　　　　　　　　　　said Court in Bankruptcy.

I, THE UNDERSIGNED, a Register of said Court in Bankruptcy, upon good proof before me　　　　　　　　, taken, do find, that the said　　　　　　　　has become a bankrupt within the true intent and meaning of the Act of Congress entitled "An act to Establish a Uniform System of Bankruptcy throughout the United States," approved March 2, 1867 ; and I do hereby declare and adjudge him a Bankrupt accordingly.

―――――――　――――――――　,
Register in Bankruptcy.

[N. B.—When a Debtor is declared a Bankrupt upon a Creditor's Petition, the Order should be made by the Court and entered as an Order of the Court in substantially the form above prescribed.]

―――――

Form No. 6.

WARRANT TO MESSENGER.

(Voluntary Bankruptcy.)

In the District Court of the United States,
For the　　　　Dristrict of

In the Matter of
By whom a Petition for Adjudication of Bank- ruptcy was filed on the　　　　　day of 　　　　, A.D. 18　, in said Court.

} IN BANKRUPTCY.

　　　　　　District of　　　　　, ss :
To the Marshal of the　　　　District of　　　　:—

GREETING:—Whereas, a Petition for Adjudication of Bankruptcy and for Relief, under the Act of Congress entitled "An act to Establish a Uniform System of Bankruptcy throughout the United States," approved March 2, 1867, was, on the day of   , 18 , filed by   , of   , in said District, upon which he hath been found and adjudged a Bankrupt, there being no opposing party thereto:—YOU ARE, THEREFORE, HEREBY DIRECTED, AS MESSENGER, to publish   times in the—[*Here name the newspapers in which the notice is to be published,*] (the first publication to be made forthwith,) the following notice, to wit:—

THIS IS TO GIVE NOTICE: That on the   day of   , A. D. 18 , a Warrant in Bankruptcy was issued against the Estate of   , of   , in the county of   , and State of   , who has been adjudged a Bankrupt, on his own Petition; that the Payment of any Debts and Delivery of any Property belonging to such Bankrupt, to him, or for his use, and the Transfer of any Property by him are forbidden by Law; that a Meeting of the Creditors of the said Bankrupt, to Prove their Debts, and to Choose one or more assignees of his Estate, will be held at a Court of Bankruptcy, to be holden [*Here designate the Place, and Building, Room, or Office where the Court is to be held,*] before   , Register, on the   day of   , A.D. 18 , at   o'clock   M.

AND YOU ARE FURTHER DIRECTED to Serve Written or Printed Notice, *forthwith,* either by Mail or Personally, [*Those upon whom personal Service is to be made should be designated by the Court, or Register,*] on all Creditors upon the Schedule filed with said Bankrupt's Petition, [*or,* where names may be given you in addition thereto by the Debtor,] at least ten days before the appointed meeting of said Court, in the following form, to wit:—

To Mr.   , of   , County of   , and State of   , Creditor of   ,
Bankrupt.

You are hereby notified that a Warrant in Bankruptcy has been issued out of the District Court of the United States, for the   District of   , against the estate of   , adjudged a Bankrupt, upon his own Petition:—That the Payment of any Debts, and the Delivery of any Property belonging to said Bankrupt, to him, or for his use, and the transfer of any Property by him are Forbidden by Law:—That a Meeting of the Creditors of said Bankrupt, to wit: [Here insert names of the Several Creditors of Bankrupt, with their places of residence and amount of their debts, respectively, in the following form, e. g.:—

A. B.   , | Boston, Mass.................. | $500

to Prove their Debts and Choose one or more Assignees of his Estate, will be held at a Court of Bankruptcy, to be holden on the   day of   , A.D. 18 , at o'clock,   M., at [*Here insert the Place, Building, Room, or Office where the Court will be held,*] before   , Register.

And have you then there this Warrant, with your doings thereon.

Witness the Honorable   , Judge of the said Court, and the

{ Seal of } seal thereof, at   , in said District, on the day of   ,
{ the Court. } A.D. 18 .

————————————————————,
Clerk of District Court, for said District.

Form No. 7.

RETURN OF MESSENGER TO ACCOMPANY WARRANT.

[N. B.—This Return may be Endorsed on the Warrant, or follow the signature of the Clerk.]

District of   , *ss:*

At   , on the   day of   , A. D. 18 .—By virtue of the within Warrant, I have caused the notice therein ordered to be published, by advertisement,   times, in the Newspapers within mentioned; the first publication of which was on the   . day of   , A.D. 18 , in [*Here mention Newspapers in which*

148

first publication was had]:—And I also, on the　　　day of　　　, A.D. 18　, sent by mail or served personally upon the creditors and others named in said Warrant a copy of the notice required thereby to be sent to, or served on them:—And all of the said notices were according to the directions set out in said Warrant.

FEES.

1. For service of warrant...	$2	00
2. For necessary travel　　　miles, at 5 cents per mile, each way...		
3. For each written note to Creditor named in the Schedule, 10 cents.		
4. For actual and necessary expenses in publication of notices......		
[N.B.—*If there are any other necessary expenses, the same may be inserted in specific terms, numbering the same consecutively.*]		

————— —————,
U. S. Marshal, as Messenger,
District of

District of　　　　　　　, *ss:*
　　　　　　, A. D. 18　. Then personally appeared the　　　　　，
and made oath that the above Expenses returned by him, in addition to his fees, were actually and necessarily incurred and paid by him, and that the same are just and reasonable.

　　　　Before me,　　　　　　　　　————— —————,

District Judge,
[or, *Register in Bankruptcy.*]

————

Form No. 8.

REGISTER'S OATH OF OFFICE.

UNITED STATES OF AMERICA,
　　　　　　District of　　　　　　, *ss:*
　　I,　　　, having been duly nominated and recommended by the Chief Justice of the Supreme Court of the United States, and appointed by the District Judge of the United States for the　　　district of　　　, as a Register in Bankruptcy under the act entitled "An Act to Establish a Uniform System of Bankruptcy throughout the United States," approved March 2, 1867, do solemnly swear that I have never voluntarily borne arms against the United States since I have been a citizen thereof; that I have voluntarily given no aid, countenance, counsel, or encouragement to persons engaged in armed hostility thereto; that I have neither sought nor accepted, nor attempted to exercise the functions of any office whatever under any authority or pretended authority in hostility to the United States; that I have not yielded a voluntary support to any pretended government, authority, power, or constitution within the United States hostile or inimical thereto. And I do further swear, that to the best of my knowledge and ability, I will support and defend the Constitution of the United States against all enemies, foreign and domestic; that I will bear true faith and allegiance to the same; that I take this obligation freely, without any mental reservation or purpose of evasion; and that I will well and faithfully discharge the duties of the office on which I am about to enter; and also, that I will not, during my continuance in office, be directly or indirectly interested in, or benefited by the fees or emoluments

arising from any suit or matter pending in bankruptcy in either the District or Circuit Court in this District. So help me God.

Subscribed and   to, before me this   day of   , A. D. 18 .

_____ _____,

District Judge.

———

Form No. 9.

OFFICIAL BOND OF REGISTER.

In the District Court of the United States,
For the   District of

IN BANKRUPTCY.

KNOW ALL MEN BY THESE PRESENTS : That we [*Insert names and residences in full of Bondsmen*] are held and firmly bound to the United States of America in the sum of
       dollars, lawful money of the United States, to be paid to the said United States, for the payment of which, well and truly to be made, we bind ourselves and each of us, our and each of our heirs, executors, and administrators, jointly and severally, firmly by these presents.

Sealed with our seals, and dated this   day of   , Anno Domini one thousand eight hundred and

Whereas the said   , having been on the   day of
A.D. 18 , appointed by the Honorable   , Judge of the District Court of the United States for the   District of   ,
a Register in Bankruptcy, in and for said District, this Bond is executed pursuant to the Third Section of the Act of Congress entitled "An Act to Establish a Uniform System of Bankruptcy throughout the United States," approved March 2, 1867, and is conditioned for the faithful discharge of the duties pertaining to said office of Register in Bankruptcy.

In witness whereof we have hereunto set our hands and seals this   day of   ,
A.D. one thousand eight hundred and   .

_____ _____, [L. S.]
_____ _____, [L. S.]

Signed, sealed, and filed in office of the Clerk of said District Court.

Attest: ,

Clerk   *District of*

[N. B.—The above bond to be endorsed with the approval of the Judge of the District Court thus: "I HEREBY APPROVE THE WITHIN BOND, AND DECLARE THE SURETIES THEREON TO BE SATISFACTORY ;" and the usual certificate of the Clerk of the District, as to the exact time and date of filing.]

Form No. 10.

COMMON ORDER.

In the District Court of the United States,
For the   District of

In the matter of

                    Bankrupt .

⎫
⎬ IN BANKRUPTCY.
⎭

At   , in said district,
     on the   day of   , A. D. 18   .
Before Mr.   , one of the Registers
     of said District Court, in Bankruptcy.

District of   , *ss :*
Upon the application   , of   , in the County of   , and
State of   , there being no opposing interest, [*or,* the party, or parties, appearing
assenting thereto.] IT IS ORDERED : [*Here insert the order.*]
     Witness the Honorable   , Judge of the said Court, and the seal
          thereof, at   , in said District, on the
{ Seal of the Court. }   day of   , A. D. 18   .

———————— ————————,
Clerk of District Court, for said District.

————

Form No. 11.

CERTIFIED MEMORANDUM OF FIRST MEETING OF CREDITORS.

In the District Court of the United States,
     For the   District of

In the Matter of

                    Bankrupt .

⎫
⎬ IN BANKRUPTCY.
⎭

At   , in said District,
     on the   day of   , A. D. 18   .
Before Mr.

Register in Bankruptcy.

District of   , *ss :*
MEMORANDUM.—This being the day appointed by the Court for the First Meeting of
Creditors under the said Bankruptcy, whereof the notice required in that behalf has
been duly given, I, the undersigned, Register of the said Court in Bankruptcy, set at the
time and place above mentioned, pursuant to such notice, to take the proof of debts and
for the choice of assignee under the said Bankruptcy ; and I do hereby certify that the
greater part in number and in value of the creditors who have proved their debts were
present, or duly represented, and made choice of   , of   , in the
County of   , and State of   , as the Assignee of the said Bankrupt's estate.

[*Or*,

Failed to make choice of an Assignee of said Bankrupt's estate, and there being no op posing interest, I appointed   , of   , in the County of   , and State of   , as Assignee of the same.

[*Or*,

Failed to make choice of an Assignee of said Bankrupt's estate, and there being no opposing interest, I further certify to the Court the failure to make such choice of Assignee, in order that the Court may take action in the premises.

Register in Bankruptcy.

[N. B.—When the matter of appointment is referred to the Court, the Register may, if requested, certify the names of the persons proposed at the Creditor's meeting and the voice given for each.]

Form No. 12.

ABSTRACTS OF PROCEEDINGS UNDER SECTION FOUR—FORM OF MEMO RANDUM TO BE RETURNED TO CLERK BY REGISTER, OR HIS ACTION IN EACH CASE.

In the District Court of the United States,
For the   District of   .

In the Matter of

           Bankrupt.

} In Bankruptcy.

At   , in said District, on the   day of   , A. D. 18 .
Before Mr.   ,

Register in Bankruptcy.

District of   *ss :*

Memorandum.—This day attended the first meeting of Creditors of the Bankrupt aforesaid, at said   , where choice was made of assignee as appears by the papers herewith returned. [*Here insert particular statement of all that was done before the Register.*]

Register in Bankruptcy.

N. B.—A memorandum of what is done in each case respectively must be returned on separate sheets of paper.]

Form No. 13.

CREDITORS WHO HAVE PROVED THEIR DEBTS AT FIRST MEETING.

In the District Court of the United States,
For the　　　　　　District of　　　　　　．

In the Matter of

　　　　　Bankrupt.

} IN BANKRUPTCY.

At　　　　　　　　, in said District, on
the　　day of　　, A. D. 18　,
Before Mr.　　　　　　,
Register in Bankruptcy.

District of　　　　　, *ss:*
The following is a list of Creditors who have this day proved their debts:

Names of Creditors.	Residence.	Debts Proved.	
		Dolls.	Cts.

　　　　　　　　　　　　　　　　　　　　—————— ——————,
Register of Bankruptcy.

Form No. 14.

FORM OF SPECIAL LETTER OF ATTORNEY.

In the Matter of

　　　　　Bankrupt.

} IN BANKRUPTCY.

To ——————　——————

SIR: [*or,* Messrs., *or,* Gentlemen,] I, [*or,* we,]
hereby authorize you, or any one of you, to attend the meeting of Creditors in this matter, advertised or directed to be holden at　　　　　　, on the　　　　day of
　　　　, before　　　　　, or on the day advertised in the [*Name the Newspapers,*] or any adjournment thereof, and then and there　　　　for　　　　, and in
　　　　　name to vote for or against any proposal or resolution that may be lawfully
made or passed at such meeting or adjourned meeting; and in the choice of an Assignee,

or Assignees of the Estate of the said Bankrupt, and for , or ,
to accept such appointment of Assignee.
  Dated this   day of   , A. D. 18 .
  Witness to the signature of   ,

---- ----.

  Exhibited to me this   day of   , A. D. 18 .

Register in Bankruptcy.

Form No. 15.

CHOICE OF ASSIGNEES.

(First Meeting of Creditors.)

In the District Court of the United States,
For the   District of   .

In the Matter of

          Bankrupt.

} IN BANKRUPTCY.

At   , in said District,
  on the   day of   A. D. 18 ,
Before Mr.   ,

Register in Bankruptcy.

    District of   , *ss :*

MEMORANDUM.—This being the day appointed by the Court for the First Meeting of Creditors in the above Bankruptcy, and of which due notice has been given in the [*Here insert the name of the Newspapers in which notice was published,*] and by special notice served personally, or through the mail. We, whose names are hereunder written, being the greater part in number and in value, of the Creditors of the said   ,
Bankrupt aforesaid, present at this Meeting, and who have proved our Debts, have chosen, and do hereby nominate and choose [*Here insert the name or names of Assignees, with their places of residence, respectively*] to be the assignee of the said Bankrupt's Estate and Effects, and we do desire that he [*or,* they] may be appointed such assignee, accordingly :

Names of Creditors above mentioned.	Residences of the same.	Am't of Debt.	
		Dolls.	Cts.
			.

I [*or,* we] do hereby accept the said Trust, [*or,* Appointment.]

---- ----;
---- ----;

Assignee .

I,   , a Register of the said Court in Bankruptcy, do hereby approve of, and confirm the said choice of Assignee .

            —————— —————— ,
             Register in Bankruptcy.

        hereby appoint Mr.   , of   , to act as Solicitor, and Attorney in the above Bankruptcy.

            —————— —————— .
            Register [or, *Assignee.*]

—————— —————— ,
   District Judge.

*N. B.—If no attorney be appointed, strike the latter form out, and when the appointment is made file an appointment as above, signed by the Assignee.

The District Judge will endorse hereon, in case of approval of the above, thus :—" Approved."

——————

Form No. 16.

NOTIFICATION OF APPOINTMENT OF ASSIGNEE.

In the District Court of the United States,
For the   District of   .

In the Matter of

         IN BANKRUPTCY.

    Bankrupt.

—————— ——————
   District of   , *ss* :
  To   , of   , in the County of   .
   and State of   :—

I DO HEREBY CERTIFY to you, that you were duly chosen [or, appointed] assignee [or one of the assignees] of the Estate and effects of the above named Bankrupt, at the First Meeting of the Creditors, on the   day of   , A. D. 18 , and I do hereby approve and confirm said election [or, appointment ;] and I do further certify, that the greater part in value and in number of the Creditors of said Bankrupt who had proved their claims were present, or were duly represented at said meeting.

  Dated at   , the   day of   , A. D. 18 .

          —————— —————— ,
    Judge of said District, [or, *Register in Bankruptcy.*]

[N. B.—If the appointment is made by the Judge, the last clause should be omitted.]

      Acceptance of Assignee.
   [N. B.—To be endorsed on notification, or to follow it.]

TO WHOM IT MAY CONCERN : Be it known, that I hereby signify my acceptance of the Trust of Assignee of the Estate of the above [or, within] named Bankrupt this day of   , A. D. 18 .

—————— ——————

Form No. 17.

BOND OF ASSIGNEE.

In the District Court of the United States,
For the   District of   .

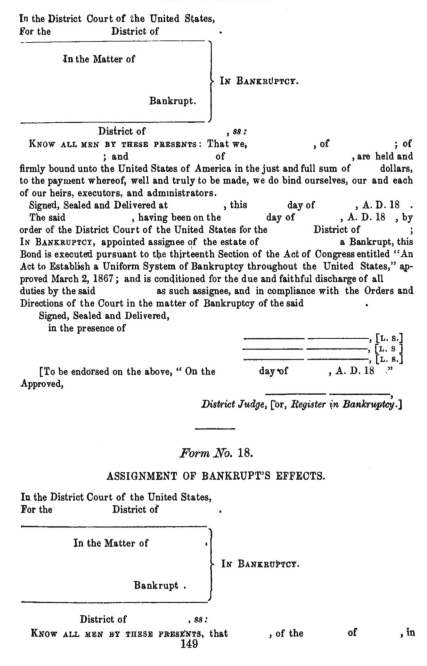

In the Matter of

Bankrupt.

In Bankruptcy.

District of   , *ss :*

KNOW ALL MEN BY THESE PRESENTS : That we,   , of   ; of
; and   of   , are held and
firmly bound unto the United States of America in the just and full sum of   dollars,
to the payment whereof, well and truly to be made, we do bind ourselves, our and each
of our heirs, executors, and administrators.

Signed, Sealed and Delivered at   , this   day of   , A. D. 18 .
The said   , having been on the   day of   , A. D. 18 , by
order of the District Court of the United States for the   District of   ;
IN BANKRUPTCY, appointed assignee of the estate of   a Bankrupt, this
Bond is executed pursuant to the thirteenth Section of the Act of Congress entitled "An
Act to Establish a Uniform System of Bankruptcy throughout the United States," ap-
proved March 2, 1867 ; and is conditioned for the due and faithful discharge of all
duties by the said   as such assignee, and in compliance with the Orders and
Directions of the Court in the matter of Bankruptcy of the said   .

Signed, Sealed and Delivered,
    in the presence of

————— —————————, [L. S.]
————— —————————, [L. S]
————— —————————, [L. S.]

[To be endorsed on the above, " On the   day of   , A. D. 18 ."
Approved,

————— —————,

District Judge, [or, *Register in Bankruptcy.*]

———

Form No. 18.

ASSIGNMENT OF BANKRUPT'S EFFECTS.

In the District Court of the United States,
For the   District of   .

In the Matter of

Bankrupt .

In Bankruptcy.

District of   , *ss :*

KNOW ALL MEN BY THESE PRESENTS, that   , of the   of   , in the County of   , and State of   , in said District have been duly appointed assignee [*If more than one assignee is appointed, insert accordingly*] in said matter. Now, THEREFORE, I,   , Judge of said District Court, [*or*, Register in Bankruptcy of said District,] by virtue of the authority vested in me by the 14th Section of an Act of Congress entitled "An Act to Establish a Uniform System of Bankruptcy throughout the United States," approved March 2, 1867, do hereby convey and assign to the said   , assignee, as aforesaid, all the Estate, Real and Personal, of the said   , Bankrupt, aforesaid, including all the property, of whatever kind, of which he is possessed, or in which he was interested, or entitled to have on the day of   , A. D. 18 , with all his Deeds, Books, and Papers relating thereto, excepting such property as is Exempted from the operation of this Assignment by the provisions of said Fourteenth Section of said Act.

To HAVE AND TO HOLD all the forgoing premises to the said   , and his heirs forever, IN TRUST, NEVERTHELESS, for the use and purposes, with the powers, and subject to the conditions and limitations set forth in said Act.

IN WITNESS WHEREOF, I, the said Judge [*or*, the said Register] have hereunto set { L. S. of the Court. } my hand, and caused the seal of said Court to be affixed, this day of   , A. D. 18 .

_____ _____

District Judge, [*or, Register in Bankruptcy.*]

Form No. 19.

NOTICE OF ASSIGNEE OF HIS APPOINTMENT.

(In Bankruptcy.)

District of   , *ss:*
At   , the   day of   , A. D. 18 .
The undersigned hereby gives notice of his appointment as assignee of   , of   , in the County of   , and State of   , within said District, who has been adjudged a Bankrupt upon his own Petition, or on creditor's petition, [*or*, as the case may be] by the District Court of said District.

_____ _____, *Assignee, &c.*

To —————— —————————,

—————————————.

Form No. 20.

EXEMPTED PROPERTY.

In the District Court of the United States,
For the   District of

In the Matter of

                    } IN BANKRUPTCY.

          Bankrupt .

          } At , on the   day of , 18 .

District of   *ss:*

The following is a Schedule of property designated and set apart to be retained by the

Bankrupt aforesaid, as his own property, under the provisions of the 14th Section of the Act of Congress entitled "An Act to establish a Uniform System of Bankruptcy throughout the United States," approved March 2, 1867:

General Head.	Particular Description.	Value.	
		Do ll.	Cts.
Necessary household and kitchen furniture.....................			
Other articles and necessaries...			
Wearing apparel of Bankrupt and his family..................			
Equipments, if any, as a Soldier.			
Other Property Exempted by the laws of the United States.....			
Property Exempted by State Laws.			

District Judge [or, *Register.*]

Form No. 21.

PROOF OF DEBT, WITH SECURITY.

In the District Court of the United States,
For the   District of .

In the Matter of

}

⎱ IN BANKRUPTCY.

Bankrupt .

District of   , *ss :*
    On this   day of   , A. D 18   , before me   , a Register in Bankruptcy [*or*, United States Commissioner, or other proper officer] of said District, personally appeared   , of   , in the County of   , and State of   , and who, after being duly sworn [*or*, affirmed] and examined, at the time and place aforesaid, upon h   oath, says that   , the person by [*or*, against] whom a Petition for Adjudication of Bankruptcy is filed, w   at and before the filing of the said Petition and still   , justly and truly indebted to this Deponent, [*or*, the firm of   , composed of this deponent and   , transacting business at   ,] in the sum of   dollars and   cents, for which said sum of   dollars and   cents,   or any part thereof, this Deponent has not nor   any person by   order, or to this Deponent's knowledge or belief, for   use, received any security or satisfaction whatsoever, save and except the   , hereinafter mentioned; that the claim was not procured for the purpose of influencing the proceedings under the Act of Congress entitled "An Act to Establish a Uniform System of Bankruptcy throughout the United States," approved March 2, 1867; that no bargain or agreement, expressed or implied, has been made or

entered into by or on behalf of this Deponent to sell, transfer, or dispose of said claim, or any part thereof, against said Bankrupt, or to take or receive, directly or indirectly, any money, property, or consideration whatever, whereby the vote of this Deponent [*or*, the firm of which this Deponent is a member] for Assignee, or any action on the part of this Deponent, or any other person, in the proceedings under said act, has been, is, or shall be in any way affected, influenced, or controlled; [*Here insert a particular description of the debt, and also of the property held as security, and the estimated value of such property*.]

———— ————,
Deponent

Subscribed and sworn [*or*, affirmed] to, at , on the day of A. D. 18 .

Before me ———— ————,
District Judge, [*or*, *Register in Bankruptcy*.
Or, *U. S. Commissioner*.]

Received by me, at this day of , A. D. 18 .

———— ————,
Assignee.

Form No. 22.

DEPOSITION FOR PROOF OF DEBT WITHOUT SECURITY.

In the District Court of the United States,
For the District of .

In the Matter of

 IN BANKRUPTCY.

Bankrupt .

District of , *ss*:

At , in the County of , and State of , on the day of , A. D. 18 , before me came , of , in the County of , and State of , and made oath, [*or*, affirmation,] and says, that the said , the person whom a Petition for adjudication of Bankruptcy has been filed, at and before the filing of the said Petition, and still justly and truly indebted to this Deponent in the sum of, [*Here state the amount, and describe the consideration of the Debt, and whether any, and what, payments have been made thereon,*] for which said sum of dollars and cents, or any part thereof, this Deponent says that he has not, nor has any person by h order, or to.this Deponent's knowledge or belief, for use, had, or received any manner of satisfaction or security whatsoever.

And this Deponent further says that the said claim was not procured for the purpose of influencing the proceedings under the Act of Congress entitled " An act to Establish a Uniform System of Bankruptcy throughout the United States," approved March 2, 1867;

that no bargain or agreement, express or implied, has been made or entered into by or on behalf of this Deponent, to sell, transfer, or dispose of said claim, or any part thereof, against said Bankrupt, or to take or receive, directly or indirectly, any money, property, or consideration whatever, whereby the vote of this Deponent for Assignee, or any action on the part of this Deponent, or any other person in the proceedings under said Act, has been, is, or shall be in any way affected, influenced, or controlled.

————————— —————————,
Deposing Creditor.

Subscribed and sworn, [*or*, affirmed] to, before me,

————————— —————————,
Register in Bankruptcy.

—————————

Form No. 23.

DECLARATION FOR PROOF OF DEBT BY OFFICER OF CORPORATION.

In the District Court of the United States.
For the   District of   .

In the Matter of	
	} IN BANKRUPTCY.
Bankrupt .	

District of   , *ss :*
I,   , of   , in the County of   , and State of   , President [*or*, Cashier, *or*, Treasurer, *or*, as the case may be] of   , being a Corporation incorporated by and under the laws of the State of   and carrying on business at   , in the State of   , being duly sworn, do solemnly declare that I am such officer, and duly authorized to make this proof, and that the statement of the   , between the said Corporation and the said Bankrupt, hereunto annexed, is a full, true, and complete statement of account between the said Corporation and the said Bankrupt; and that it is within my own knowledge that the debt thereby appearing to be due from the estate of said Bankrupt to the said Corporation was incurred on, or before the   day of   , and for the consideration therein stated; and that to the best of my knowledge and belief the said debt still remains unpaid and unsatisfied.   And I do further declare that said claim was not procured for the purpose of influencing the proceedings under said Act, and that no bargain or agreement, express or implied, has been made or entered into by or on behalf of said Corporation to sell, transfer, or dispose of the said claim or any part thereof, against such Bankrupt, or to take or receive, directly or indirectly, any money, property, or consideration whatever, whereby the vote of such Corporation, or of any person in the proceedings under said Act, was, is, or shall be, in any way, affected, influenced, or controlled.

————————— —————————,
President [or, *as the case may be*]
of the Company, [or *Association.*]

Declared under oath at   , this   day of   , A. D. 18 .
Before me,

————————— —————————,
Register in Bankruptcy.

Form No. 24.

AFFIDAVIT FOR PROOF OF DEBT BY AGENT OR ATTORNEY.

In the District Court of the United States,
For the   District of

In the matter of

                          } IN BANKRUPTCY.

            Bankrupt .

District of   *, ss :*
On this   day of   , A. D. 18 , before me,   , Register in
Bankruptcy, [*or*, U. S. Commissioner, or other proper officer,] of said District, personally appeared   , of   , in the County of   and State
of   , Attorney, [*or*, Authorized Agent,] of   , in the County of
, and State of   , and after being by me duly sworn, [*or*,
affirmed,] says that the said   , the person by [*or*, against] whom a Petition
for Adjudication of Bankruptcy has been   filed,   , at and before
the filing of the said Petition, and still   justly and truly indebted to the said
, in the sum of   dollars and   cents, [*Here particularly describe the consideration of the debt, and whether any*, &c.,] for which said sum of
            dollars and   cents   , or any part thereof, this Deponent says
that he has not, nor has   any person by h   Order, or to this Deponent's
knowledge or belief, for   use had or received any manner of satisfaction or
security whatsoever. And this Deponent further says, that the claim was not procured
for the purpose of influencing the proceedings under the Act of Congress entitled " An
Act to Establish a Uniform System of Bankruptcy throughout the United States," approved March 2, 1867; that no bargain or agreement, express or implied, has been made,
or entered into, by, or on behalf of such creditor to sell, transfer, or dispose of said
claim, or any part thereof, against said Bankrupt, or to take or receive, directly or indirectly, any money, property, or consideration whatever, whereby the vote of such Creditor for assignee, or any action on the part of such Creditor, or any other person in the
proceedings under said Act, has been, is, or shall be, in any way affected, influenced, or
controlled. And this Deponent further says, that he is duly authorized by his principal to make this Affidavit, and that it is within his knowledge that the aforesaid debt
was incurred, as and for the consideration above stated, and that such debt, to the best
of his knowledge and belief, still remains unpaid and unsatisfied.
Subscribed and sworn [*or*, affirmed] to, this   day of   , A. D. 18 .
before me—

——————— ———————,
District Judge, [or, *Register in Bankruptcy :*
Or, *U. S. Commissioner.*]
Received by me, this   day of   , A. D. 18 .

——————— ——————.
Assignee.

Form No. 25.

PROOF OF DEBT WITH SECURITY BY AGENT.

In the District Court of the United States,
For the   District of

In the Matter of

           Bankrupt.

⎬ IN BANKRUPTCY.

At   , in said District, on the   day of   , A. D. 18 , Before Mr.   ,

Register in Bankruptcy.

District of   *ss :*

On the day above mentioned, personally came   , attorney [*or,* authorized agent] of   , who being duly   and examined at the time and place aforesaid, upon h   oath, says that   , the person   whom a Petition for Adjudication of Bankruptcy is filed, w   at and before the filing of the said Petition, and still   justly and truly indebted to the said   , in the sum of   dollars and   cents, for which said sum of   dollars and   cents, or any part thereof, this Deponent has not nor   any person by   order, to this Deponent's knowledge or belief for the use of said   , received any security or satisfaction whatsoever, save and except the   hereinafter mentioned. And this Deponent further says that he is duly authorized by his principal to make this deposition, and that it is within his knowledge that the aforesaid debt was incurred as and for the consideration above stated; and that such debt, to the best of his knowledge and belief, still remains unpaid and unsatisfied; that the claim was not procured for the purpose of influencing the proceedings under the Act of Congress entitled "An Act to Establish a Uniform System of Bankruptcy throughout the United States," approved March 2, 1867 ; that no bargain or agreement, expressed or implied, has been made, or entered into, by or on behalf of such Creditor to sell, transfer or dispose of said claim, or any part thereof, against said Bankrupt, or to take or receive, directly or indirectly, any money, property, or consideration whatever, whereby the vote of such Creditor for Assignee, or any action on the part of such Creditor, or any other person in the proceedings under said Act, has been, is, or shall be in any way affected, influenced, or controlled.

[*Here insert a description of the debt, and also of the property held as security, and the estimated value of such property.*]

Subscribed and   to, this   day of   , A. D. 18 .
Before me

————— —————,

Register in Bankruptcy.

Received by me, this   day of   A. D. 18 .

————— —————, *Assignee.*

Form No. 26.

LETTER OF ATTORNEY TO REPRESENT CREDITOR.

In the District Court of the United States,
For the   District of

In the Matter of . Bankrupt.	⎱ IN BANKRUPTCY. ⎰

To——— ——— ——— ———————,

                                    .

Sir, [Messrs., or Gentlemen :]—
   I,   , of the   of   , in the County of   , and State of   , do hereby
authorize you [*or*, either of you] to attend the meeting, or meetings of Creditors of the
Bankrupt aforesaid, advertised, or directed to be held at a Court of Bankruptcy at   ,
on the   day of   A. D. 18   , the day notified in the Warrant issued to the
Messenger by the said Court in said matter, or at such other place and time as may be
appointed by the Court for holding such meeting or meetings, or at which such meeting
or meetings, or any adjournment or adjournments thereof, may be held, and then and there,
from time to time, and as often as there may be occasion, for   , and in   name
to vote for or against any proposal or resolution that may be then submitted under the
12th, 13th, 14th, 18th, 19th, 21st, 22d, 23d, 27th, 28th, 33d, 36th, 37th, 42d, and 43d
Sections of the Act entitled " An Act to Establish a Uniform System of Bankruptcy
throughout the United States," approved March 2, 1867; and in the choice of assignee, or
assignees of the estate of the said Bankrupt, and for   [*or*, either of us] to accept such
appointment of assignee; and with like powers to attend and vote at any other meeting,
or meetings of Creditors, or sitting, or sittings of the Court, which may be held therein
for any of the purposes aforesaid, or the Declaration of Dividend, or for any other purpose
in   interest whatsoever.
   In witness whereof,   have hereunto signed   name , and affixed   seal
the   day of   , A. D. 18   .

Signed, Sealed, and Delivered in
      presence of—

——— ——— ———————, [L. S.]
——— ——— ———————, [L. S.]
——— ——— ———————, [L. S.]

[NOTE.—The party executing the above letter of attorney may acknowledge the same
before a Judge, Register, Clerk, or Commissioner of the Court, or any other officer authorized to take the acknowledgment of Deeds or other Instruments in Writing.]
   [N. B.—Upon the above letter of attorney should be endorsed the following Certificate
of the Register, to wit: " Exhibited to me, this   day of   , A. D. 18   , at   .]

——— ——— ———————,
Register in Bankruptcy."

Form No. 27.

AFFIDAVIT OF LOST BILL OR NOTE.

In the District Court of the United States,
For the   District of   .

```
                                         ⎫
        In the Matter of                 ⎬ IN BANKRUPTCY.
                                         ⎭
            Bankrupt .
```

District of   ss :

On this day of   , A. D. 18 , at   , comes before me   , of   , in the County of   , and State of   , and makes   and says that he has made a careful search for the Bill of Exchange, [or, note,] the particulars whereof are under written, and which ha been proved under this estate by   , but that he, this Deponent, has not been able to find the same, and verily believes that the same has been lost or mislaid; and this Deponent further says that he has not, nor has the said   , or any person or persons, to their use, to this Deponent's knowledge or belief, negotiated the said bill, [or, note,] nor in any manner parted with, or assigned, the legal or beneficial interest therein, or any part thereof; and that he, this Deponent, is the person now legally and beneficially interested in the same, and entitled to receive for his own use all dividends in respect thereof.

Bill or note above referred to.

Date.	Drawer or Maker.	Acceptor.	Sum.

Subscribed and to, before me,   on this day of   , A. D. 18 .

————— —————,
Register, or U. S. Commissioner [or, *other proper officer.*]

Upon the above named Deponent signing the annexed letter of indemnity, and giving security to the satisfaction of the official assignee, I direct the Dividend to be paid to him.

————— —————,
Register in Bankruptcy.

Form of notice of Indemnification to Register.

In the matter of   , of   , Bankrupt .

SIR: The Bill [*or*, Note] mentioned below, proved by   , under this estate, having been lost or mislaid, and the following dividend having been declared thereon, but not yet paid, viz:—   , in consideration of your paying to   or to   order the dividend   above mentioned   , hereby undertake to indemnify you against all claims ot any other person to the said dividend, or any part thereof ; and from all loss, damage, and expense, which you or your Executors or Administrators may sustain by reason of your making such payment to me ; and if it should hereafter appear that the said sum of $, or any part thereof, with the dividend already received or declared up to this day, exceed the amount of the Bill [*or*, Note] hereby engage to repay the same to you, or to the assignee, or assignees, of the above estate, with interest at the rate of   per cent. per annum from this day.

Dated at   , this   , A. D. 18 .

Bill or note above referred to.

Date.	Drawer or Maker	Acceptor.	Sum.

—————— ——————,
—————— ——————,
Sureties of Creditor receiving Dividend.
To Mr. ——————— ————————, *Register in Bankruptcy.*

—————————

Form No. 28.

NOTICE AND REQUEST OF ASSIGNEE.
(2d meeting of Creditors.)

In the District Court of the United States,
For the   District of   .

In the Matter of

    ⎫ IN BANKRUPTCY.

Bankrupt .⎭

To the Hon. ——————— ————————, *Judge of the District Court,*
'*or, Register in Bankruptcy*] *in the above District.*

SIR : I, [*or*, we,] the Assignee   of the estate of said Bankrupt   , respectfully represent

that   have accepted the appointment of Assignee   of said estate; that the period of
three months has elapsed since the date of the Adjudication of Bankruptcy in said case,
and request that the Court will order a General Meeting of the Creditors of said Bankrupt, to which   may make report of   proceedings in   **trust, according to**
the provisions of the Twenty-seventh Section **of the Bankrupt Act of March 2, 1867.**

—————————— ——————————,

Assignee.

Order Thereon—By the Court, or Register.

Under the foregoing application of   , Assignee of the estate of
Bankrupt, it is *Ordered* that a second General Meeting of the Creditors of said Bankrupt be held at   , in said District, on the   day of   , A. D.
18   , at   o'clock   m., at the office of   , one of the Registers in Bankruptcy in said District, for the purposes named in the twenty-seventh Section of the Bankrupt Act of March 2, 1867.

And it is further Ordered, That the Assignee give notice of said meeting by sending
written or printed notices by mail, post-paid, of the time and place of said meeting to all
known Creditors of said Bankrupt; and that   also notify the Bankrupt to be
present thereat; and   shall also publish notice of the time and place of said
meeting on two different days in the newspaper called the   , printed at   ,
at least   days prior to said meeting.

Witness the Honorable   , Judge of the said Court, and
{ Seal of }   the seal thereof, at   , in said District, on the
{ the Court. }   day of   , A. D. 18 .

—————— —————————,

Clerk of District Court, of said District.

Form No. 29.

FORM OF RETURN OF ASSIGNEE TO BE SUBMITTED TO THE REGISTER IN
BANKRUPTCY PRESIDING AT SAID MEETING.

In the Matter of

⎱
⎰ IN BANKRUPTCY.

Bankrupt.

—————————————— , *ss :*
District of

I, [or, we,] Assignee of the estate of   , a Bankrupt, do certify that
      have caused the notices required by the foregoing order to be published in the news-
paper called the   , printed at   , on the   day of   ,
A. D. 18   ; and that   have caused written or printed notices of the time and
place of said meeting to be sent by mail, post-paid, to all known Creditors of said Bankrupt. Said notices were mailed at the postoffice in   , on the   day of
      , A. D. 18   , at   days prior to the day appointed for the said meeting.

—————— —————————,

Assignee.

Subscribed and   to, at   , this   day of   , A. D. 18 .
Before me,

—————— —————————,

Register in Bankruptcy.

[N. B.—Like forms may be used for the third meeting of Creditors, and for subsequent
meetings, if such are ordered by the Court.]

Form No. 30.

DIVIDEND MEETINGS.

In the District Court of the United States,
For the   District of

In the Matter of

} IN BANKRUPTCY.

Bankrupt.

At   , in said District, on
the   day of   , A. D. 18 .
District of   , *ss:*

MEMORANDUM.—That at a meeting of the Bankrupt's Creditors duly called and held this day for the purpose set forth in the 27th Section of the Act entitled "An Act to Establish a Uniform System of Bankruptcy throughout the United States," approved March 2, 1867, we, the undersigned, being the majority in value of the Creditors of the said Bankrupt present, or represented at this meeting, seeing that it appears by the accounts of the Assignee   , now filed, that there is a balance of dollars, standing to the credit of this estate, in the Bank of   , and a balance of   dollars in the hands of the   , do *Resolve* that after payment of all proper costs, charges, and expenses, that after deducting and retaining a sum sufficient for all undetermined claims, which, by reason of the distant residence of the Creditors, or for other reasons satisfactory to us, have not been proved, and for other expenses and contingencies, the sum of   dollars remain for distribution among the Creditors of the above named Bankrupt, who have proved their debts against the said Bankrupt's estate. And it was further *Resolved* by the undersigned Creditors that the said sum be divided among the Creditors who have proved their claims against said estate, and that such proceedings be had for declaring and paying said dividend as are required by the 27th Section of said Act.

—————— ——————,
—————— ——————,
Creditors.

I hereby certify to the above.

—————— ——————,
Register in Bankruptcy.

[N. B.—In case one-half in value of the Creditors shall not be represented at such meeting, the fact shall be so stated in the Memorandum, and the amount to be divided, and the order for a dividend, shall be made and signed by the Assignee in accordance with the provisions of the 27th Section of said Act.]

[N. B.—Like forms may be used for the further proceedings provided for in the 28th Section of said Act.]

Form No. 31.

NOTICE OF DIVIDEND.

In the District Court of the United States,
For the   District of   .

> In the Matter of
>
>
>   Bankrupt .

} IN BANKRUPTCY.

At   , on the   day of   , A. D. 18 .
SIR : I hereby inform you that you may, on application at my office,   , on the   day of   , or on any day thereafter, between the hours of   , receive a Warrant for the   Dividend due to you out of the above estate. If you cannot personally attend, the Warrant will be delivered to your order on your filling up and signing the subjoined letter. The bills and securities, if any, exhibited at the time of the proof of your debt must be produced to me before the Warrant of Dividend can be received.

I am, sir, your obedient servant,

———— ————, *Assignee.*

To

Subjoined letter authorizing Assignee to give Warrant to party other than Creditor.

                               ,   , 18 .

To Mr.   ,
     Assignee in Bankruptcy of the estate of   , *Bankrupt.*
SIR : [*or,* Messrs.] Please to deliver to   the Dividend Warrant payable to me out of the above estate.

Yours, &c.,

———— ————, *Creditor.*

———

Form No. 32.

LIST OF PROOFS AND CLAIMS FOR DIVIDEND.

In the District Court of the United States,
For the   District of

> In the Matter of
>
>
>   Bankrupt .

} IN BANKRUPTCY.

At   , in said District, on the   day of   , A. D. 18 .

A list of debts proved and claimed under the Bankruptcy of   , of aforesaid,
with   Dividend at the rate of   per cent. this day declared thereon by
Mr.   , one of the Registers in Bankruptcy of said District Court.

No.	Creditors. To be placed alphabetically, and the names of all the parties to the proof to be carefully set forth.	Sum proved. The claims to be set forth in the same manner at the end of the whole of the profits.		Dividend.	
		Dollars.	Cents.	Dolls.	Cts.

Register in Bankruptcy.

Form No. 33.

LIST OF PROOFS OF DEBTS AND CLAIMS FOR ASSIGNEES TO PAY DIVIDENDS

In the District Court of the United States,
For the   District of

In the Matter of

              Bankrupt.   } Is BANKRUPTCY.

              , ss :

District of   At   , in said District, on the   day of   18 .

A list of Debts proved and claimed under the Bankruptcy of   Dividend at the rate of   per cent., this day declared thereon by Mr.
              , one of the Registers in Bankruptcy of said Court.

No.	Creditors. To be placed Alphabetically, and the names of all the parties to the proof to be carefully set forth.	Residence and Description.	Sums proved or claimed. Claims to be set forth in the same manner after the whole of the Proofs.		Dividend.		Bills and Securities exhibited.				
			Dolls	Cts.	Dolls.	Cts.	Date of Bill or Note.	Drawer or Maker.	Acceptor.	Indorser.	Sum.
											Doll. Cts.

, Register in Bankruptcy.

[N. B.—The Dividends will be paid from this List ; it is therefore required to be correctly extracted from the proceedings, signed by the register, and delivered to the Assignee.]

Form No. 34.

PETITION OF ASSIGNEE FOR POWER TO RELIEVE PROPERTY FROM LIEN.

In the District Court of the United States,
For the   District of   .

In the Matter of

Bankrupt.

} IN BANKRUPTCY.

To ———— ————,
, Assignee of the estate of said Bankrupt, respectfully represents
that a certain portion of said Bankrupt's estate, to wit: [*Here describe the estate or
property and its estimated value,*] is subject to a mortgage, [*Describe the mortgage,*] or to
a conditional contract, [*Describing it,*] or to a lien, [*Describe the origin and nature of
the lien,*] or, (if the property be personal property,) has been pledged or deposited and
is subject to a lien for, [*Describe the nature of the lien,*] and that according to the best
judgment of your Petitioner it would be for the interest of the Creditors of said estate
that said property should be redeemed and discharged from the lien thereon. Wherefore   pray that   may be empowered to pay out of the assets of said estate in
hands the sum of   , being the amount of said lien, in order to redeem said property
therefrom.
    Dated this   day of   , A. D. 18   .

                        ———— ————,
                            Assignee.

[N. B.—If the prayer is for a sale of the property, strike out all after the words
"*judgment of your Petitioner,*" and insert "it would be for the interest of the Creditors of said estate that said property should be sold, subject to said mortgage, lien, or
other encumbrance. Wherefore he prays that he may be authorized to make sale of
said property, subject to the encumbrance thereon, in the manner prescribed by the general order for the sale of property not encumbered."]

Form No. 35.

ASSIGNEES RETURN WHERE THERE ARE NO ASSETS.

In the District Court of the United States,
For the   District of   .

In the Matter of

Bankrupt.

} IN BANKRUPTCY.

                  At   , in said District, on
                  the   day of   , A. D. 18   .
District of   , *ss* :
On the day aforesiad, before me comes   , of   , in the County

of , and State of , and makes , and says that he, this
Deponent, as Assignee [or, one of the Assignees] of the estate and effects of the above
named Bankrupt , neither received nor paid any moneys on account of the estate.
Subscribed and to, at , this day of , A. D. 18 .
Before me,

Register in Bankruptcy.

Form No. 36.

ASSIGNEE'S NOTICE FOR SETTLEMENT OF HIS ACCOUNTS PREPARATORY TO FINAL DIVIDEND.

In the District Court of the United States,
For the District of .

In the Matter of

IN BANKRUPTCY.

Bankrupt .

At , on the day of , A. D. 18 .
To ,
SIR:
This is to give you notice that I have filled my final accounts as assignee of the estate
of , Bankrupt , in said Court, and that on the day of next,
I shall apply to said Court for the settlement of my said accounts, and for a discharge
from all liability as Assignee of said estate in accordance with the provisions of the twenty-
eighth section of the Bankrupt Act of March 2, 1867.
Yours, &c., , *Assignee.*

Form No. 37.

AFFIDAVIT TO BE MADE BY ASSIGNEE.

In the District Court of the United States,
For the District of ,

In the Matter of

IN BANKRUPTCY.

Bankrupt .

District of , *ss :*
On this day of , A. D. 18 , before me comes , of ,
in the county of , and State of , and makes , and says that he,
this Deponent, was, on the day of , A. D. 18 , appointed Assignee of
the estate and effects of the above-named Bankrupt, and that as such he has
151

conducted the settlement of the said estate. That the account hereto annexed containing   sheets of Paper, the first sheet whereof is marked with the letter

[*Reference may here also be made to any prior account filed by Deponent*] is true, and such account contains entries of every sum of money received by Deponent, on account of the estate and effects of the above-named Bankrupt , and that the payments purporting in such account to have been made by Deponent have been so made by him. And he asks to be allowed for said payments and for charges of settlement as set forth in said accounts.

——————— ——————, *Assignee.*

Sworn to and subscribed at   , in said   district of   , this day of   , A. D. 18 .

Before me,   ——————— ——————,

Register in Bankruptcy

Form No. 38.

ACCOUNT OF ASSIGNEE.

[To be annexed to affidavit of Assignee.]

The estate of   *Bankrupt , in connection with*   *Assignee.*

DR.

CR.

Dolls.	Cts.	Dolls.	Cts.		Dolls.	Cts.	Dolls.	Cts.

Form No. 39.

ORDER OF SETTLEMENT AND DISCHARGE OF ASSIGNEE.

In the District Court of the United States,
For the   District of   .

In the Matter of

     Bankrupt .

} IN BANKRUPTCY.

District of   , *ss:*

The foregoing account having been presented for allowance, and having been examined and found correct, it is *Ordered,* That the same be allowed, and that the said Assignee be discharged according to the provisions of the 28th Section of the Bankrupt Act of March 2, 1867.

—————— ——————,

District Judge, [or, *Register.*]

Form No. 40 .

PETITION FOR REMOVAL OF ASSIGNEE.

In the District Court of the United States,
For the   District of   .

In the Matter of

     Bankrupt.

} IN BANKRUPTCY.

To the Hon.   ,
     Judge of the District Court, for the   *District of*
         District of   , *ss:*

The petition of   , one of the parties interested in the settlement of said Bankrupt's estate, petitioning, respectfully represents, that   , heretofore appointed Assignee of said Bankrupt's estate, [*Here set forth the particular cause or causes for which such removal is requested.*]

Wherefore   pray that notice may be served upon said   , Assignee as aforesaid, to show cause, at such time as may be fixed by the Court, why an order should not be made removing him from said trust.

—————— ——————,

Subscribed and sworn [*or,* affirmed] to, this   day of   , A. D. 18 , at   , in said District.
Before me.

—————— ——————,

Register in Bankruptcy.

Form No. 41.

NOTICE OF MOTION FOR REMOVAL.

In the District Court of the United States,
For the   District of

In the Matter of

IN BANKRUPTCY.

Bankrupt.

At   , on the day of , A. D. 18 .

To——— ———,
          Assignee of the estate of   , *Bankrupt.*
. You are hereby notified to appear before this Court, at   , on the   day of   ,
A. D. 18 , at   o'clock   m., to show cause (if any you have) why you should not
be removed from your trust as Assignee as aforesaid, according to the Petition of   ,
one of the parties interested in said estate, filed in this Court on the   day of——, A.
D. 18 , in which it is alleged, [*Here insert the allegation of the Petition.*]
Hereof fail not.   ——————— ————————. *Clerk*, &c.
[N. B.—To be served by the Marshal, and return to be made in usual form.]

Form No. 42.

ORDER FOR MEETING OF CREDITORS TO CONSIDER QUESTION OF RE MOVAL OF ASSIGNEE AND APPOINTMENT OF HIS SUCCESSOR.

In the District Court of the United States,
For the   District of

In the Matter of

IN BANKRUPTCY.

Bankrupt .

At   , on the   day of   , 18 .

District of   , *ss :*
  WHEREAS   , of   , has filed his petition in this Court for the removal of   , heretofore appointed Assignee of the estate of said   , Bank
rupt , setting forth, [*Here insert the allegations of the Petition.*]
It is *Ordered*, that the Clerk of this Court give notice to the Creditors of   . by
letter to be mailed to each within   days after the date of this order, that a meeting of
said Creditors will be held at   , on the   day of   , A. D. 18 , at o'clock
    m., at which Mr.   , one of the Registers of this Court will preside, for the pur-
pose of considering the question of recommending such removal, and appointing a suc-
cessor in said trust.   ——— ———, *District Judge.*

[N. B.—If the meeting is called upon an application of a majority in number and value
of the Creditors of the Bankrupt, the Form may be varied accordingly.
[The vote for removal is substantially the same Form as that for the appointment of
Assignee in Form No. 15, substituting " removal" for " appointment;" and the Form of
vote for choice of new Assignee will be substantially the same as the Form referred to.]

Form No. 43.

ORDER FOR REMOVAL OF ASSIGNEE.

In the District Court of the United States,
For the   District of   .

In the Matter of

} IN BANKRUPTCY.

Bankrupt .

At   , on the   day of   , A. D. 18 .
District of   , *ss :*

Whereas   , of   , did, on the   day of   , A. D. 18 ,
present his Petition to this Court, stating as therein set forth, and praying that   ,
the Assignee of the estate of said   , Bankrupt, might be removed :

Now, THEREFORE, upon reading the said Petition of the said   , and the evidence submitted therewith, and upon hearing what was alleged by Mr.   , of counsel on behalf of said Petitoner, and by Mr.   , of counsel for   , Assignee as aforesaid, and upon the evidence submitted on behalf of said Assignee,

It is *Ordered,* That the said   be removed from the trust of Assignee of the estate of said Bankrupt, and that the costs of the said Petitioner incidental to said Petition be paid by said   , Assignee, [*or,* out of the estate of the said   , subject to prior charges.]

Witness the Honorable   , Judge of the said Court, and the seal thereof,
{ Seal of the Court. } at,   , in said District, on the   day of
A. D. 18 .

———— ————,
Clerk of District Court for said District.

Form No. 44.

FURTHER ORDER.

In the District Court of the United States,
For the   District of   .

In the Matter of

} IN BANKRUPTCY.

Bankrupt.

At   , on the   . day of   , A. D. 18 .
District of   , *ss :*

WHEREAS   , heretofore appointed Assignee of the estate of said Bankrupt ,
has upon the Petition of   , and after hearing thereon, been removed from said trust,

It is *Ordered,* That a meeting of the Creditors of said   , be held at   , in   , in said District, on the   day of   , A. D. 18 , at which Mr.   , one of the Registers of this Court, shall preside, for the choice of a new Assignee of said estate.

And it is further *Ordered*, That the Clerk of this Court give notice to said Creditors of the time, place, and purpose of said meeting, by letter to each, to be deposited in the mail within   days from the date of this order.

Witness the Honorable   , Judge of the said Court, and the seal

{ Seal of } thereof, at   , in said District, on the   day
{ the Court. }   of   , A. D. 18 .

_____   _____ ,

Clerk of District Court, for said District.

Form No. 45.

ORDER FOR BANKRUPT'S EXAMINATION.

In the District Court of the United States,
For the   District of   .

In the Matter of

⎱
⎰ IN BANKRUPTCY.

Bankrupt .

          At   , on the   day of   , A. D. 18 ,
District of   , *ss* :

On the application of   , Assignee of said Bankrupt, [*or*, Creditor of said Bankrupt, as the case may be,] it is *Ordered*, That said Bankrupt attend before   , one of the Registers in Bankruptcy of this Court, at his office, [*Describing the place*] on the   day of   , at   o'clock   M., to submit to the examination required by the 27th Section of the Bankrupt Act of March 2, 1867, and that a copy of this order be delivered to him, the said   , forthwith.

Witness the Honorable   , Judge of the said Court, and the seal

{ Seal of } thereof, at   , in said District, on the day
{ the Court. }   of   , A. D. 18 .

_____   _____ ,

Clerk of District Court, for said District.

[N. B.—Where the wife of the Bankrupt is to be examined the like form may be used, adding after the description of the application the words " and for good cause shown to this Court, she be required to attend before said-court, [*or*, before   , a Register in Bankruptcy."]

Form No. 46.

EXAMINATION OF BANKRUPT OR ANY WITNESS EXAMINED RELATIVE TO THE BANKRUPTCY.

In the District Court of the United States,
For the   District of

In the Matter of

|
> IN BANKRUPTCY.

          Bankrupt .
|

At   , in said District, on
     the   day of   , A. D. 18 .
Before Mr.   ,
One of the Registers in Bankruptcy of said Court.

District of   , *ss :*
     , of   , in the County of   , and State of   ,
being duly   and   examined at the time and place above mentioned, upon
h   oath says [*Here insert substance of examination of party.*]

————— —————. *Register.*

Form No. 47.

DECLARATION TO BE MADE BY BANKRUPT OR HIS WIFE.

In the District Court of the United States,
For the   District of   .

In the Matter of

|
> IN BANKRUPTCY.

          Bankrupt .
|

At   , in said District. on the
          day of   , A. D. 18 .
District of   , *ss :*
The person declared a Bankrupt under a Petition for Adjudication of Bankruptcy,
filed on the   day of   , in the year of our Lord one thousand eight
hundred and   , do solemnly   that I will make true answer to all such
questions as may be proposed to me respecting all the property of the said   ,
and all dealings and transactions relating thereto, and will make a full and true diselo-
sure of all that has been done with the said property, to the best of my knowledge, information, and belief.

—————— ——————,
     Bankrupt, [*Or,*   , *the wife of the said   , Bankrupt.*]
Subscribed and   to, this   day of   , A. D. 18 .
Before me,   —————— ——————,
          Register in Bankruptcy.

Form No. 48.

SUMMONS OF WITNESS AFTER ADJUDICATION.

In the District Court of the United States,
For the　　　　District of　　　　.

In the Matter of

Bankrupt .

}　IN BANKRUPTCY.

District of　　　　, ss :

Whereas,　　　　, of　　　　, in the County of　　　　, and State of　　　　, has been duly declared and adjudged Bankrupt, within the true intent and meaning of the Act entitled "An Act to Establish a Uniform System of Bankruptcy throughout the United States," approved March 2, 1867, and such Bankruptcy is in due course of prosecution in the District Court of the United States for the　　　　District of　　　　, at　　　　, in said District.

These are to require you, to whom this summons is directed, personally to be and appear before　　　　, Esquire, one of the Registers in Bankruptcy of the said Court, acting in the matter of the said Bankruptcy, on the　　　　day of　　　　, at　　　　o'clock m., precisely, [*Here insert the place of examination*]　　　　, then and there to be examined in relation to said Bankruptcy according to the provisions of said Act.

And hereof fail not.

Witness the Honorable　　　　, Judge of the said Court, and the seal

{ Seal of } thereof, at　　　　, in said District, on the
{ the Court. } day of　　　　, A. D. 18　.

_____,
Clerk of District Court, for said District.

Form No. 49.

RETURN OF THE ABOVE SUMMONS.

In the District Court of the United States,
For the　　　　District of　　　　.

In the Matter of

Bankrupt.

}　IN BANKRUPTCY.

District of　　　　, ss :

On this　　　　day of　　　　, A. D. 18　, before me came　　　　, of　　　　, in the County of　　　　, and State of　　　　, and makes　　　　, and says that he, this Deponent, did, on　　　　, the　　　　day of　　　　, one thousand, eight hundred and　　　　, personally serve　　　　, of　　　　, in the County of　　　　and State of　　　　. with a true copy of the Summons hereto annexed, by delivering

152

the same to   ; and he, this Deponent, further makes   , and says that he
is not interested in the proceedings in Bankruptcy named in said Summons.

   Subscribed and sworn to, this   day of   , A. D. 18   .
   Before me,

                               Register in Bankruptcy.

   N. B.—In case the witness is to be summoned before adjudication, the form may be
altered by substituting for the recital the following words: "*By virtue of the Petition
for Adjudication in Bankruptcy filed in said Court by   , against   , in
the District Court of the United States for the   District of   .*"]

Form No. 50.

FORM OF CERTIFICATE UNDER SECTION SIX.

In the District Court of the United States,
For the   District of

In the Matter of

                         } In Bankruptcy.

        Bankrupt .

District of   .   , *ss :*
   I,   , one of the Registers of said Court in Bankruptcy, do hereby certify that in the course of the proceedings in said cause before me the following question
arose pertinent to the said proceedings, and was stated and agreed to by the counsel for
the opposing parties, to wit : Mr.   , who appeared for the Bankrupt,
and Mr.   , who appeared for   , one of the Creditors of
said Bankrupt, [*Add other names if others are interested,*] and [*Here follows a summary
of the evidence upon the point or matter to be submitted to the Court, and the question of
law arising thereon as agreed to by the counsel.*]
   And the said parties requested that the same should be certified to the Judge for his
opinion thereon.
   Dated at   , the   day of   A. D. 18   .

                               Register in Bankruptcy.

Form No. 51.

PETITION OF BANKRUPT FOR HIS DISCHARGE.

In the Matter of

Bankrupt.

} IN BANKRUPTCY.

To the Hon. ———— ————, *Judge of the District*
Court·of the United States, for the *District of*
A. B., of , in the County of , and State of , in
said District, respectfully represents, that on the day of , last past, he
was duly declared a Bankrupt under the Act of Congress in that case made and provided;
that he hath duly surrendered all his property and rights of property, and fully complied with and obeyed all the orders and directions of the Court touching his Bankruptcy,
and is ready to submit himself to any other and further examinations, orders, and directions which the Court may require.

[N. B.—If this Petition is filed within less than six months after the filing of the original Petition, it should state that no debts have been proved against the Bankrupt, or that
no assets have come to the hands of the Assignee.]

WHEREFORE HE PRAYS that he may be decreed by the Court to have a full discharge
from all his debts provable under said Bankrupt Act, and a certificate thereof granted
according to the said Act of Congress.

Dated this day of , A. D. 18 .

———— ————, *Bankrupt* .

Order of Court thereon.

District of , *ss :*

On this day of , A. D. 18 , on reading the foregoing Petition, it
is *Ordered* by the Court, That a hearing be had upon the same on the day of
, A. D. 18 , before said Court, at , in said District, at
o'clock m.; and that notice thereof be published in newspapers printed in
said District for times once a week; and that all Creditors who have proved their
debts and other persons in interest, may appear at the said time and place, and show
cause, if any they have, why the prayer of the said Petition should not be granted.

And it is further ordered by the Court, That all such Creditors whose places of residence are known shall be entitled to a service of notice of the said Petition and order,
either personally or by letter addressed to them at their known usual place of residence,
attested by the Clerk of the Court, or served at their usual place of abode by the Marshal
or his deputy, or sent by mail, whereof due notice shall be given.

Witness the Honorable , Judge of the said Court, and the
{ Seal of } seal thereof, at , in said District, on the day of
{ the Court. } A.D. 18 .

———— ————,
Clerk of District Court, for said District.

Form No. 52.

NOTICE BY LETTER TO CREDITOR THAT BANKRUPT HAS PETITIONED
FOR DISCHARGE.

In the District Court of the United States,
For the   District of   .

In the Matter of

          Bankrupt .

}

IN BANKRUPTCY.

At   , in said District, on
the   day of   , A, D. 18 .

District of   , *ss:*

SIR : Take notice that a Petition has beeu filed in said court by   , of   ,
in said District, duly declared a Bankrupt under the Act of Congress of March 2, 1867,
for a discharge and certificate thereof, from all his debts, and other claims provable under said Act, and that the   day of   next, at   o'clock   m.,
is assigned for the hearing of the same, when and where you may attend and show
cause, if any you have, why the prayer of the said Petition should not be granted.

—————————————,
Clerk of the District Court.

To —————— ———————,

[N. B.—The certificate of the Clerk that these letters were duly mailed to each
Creditor, and that the proper postage stamps were placed thereon, will be evidence of the
fact of notice. If any are delivered to the Creditors or left at their usual place of residence, the persons so delivering or leaving them should make affidavit as follows :

Affidavit of Service of Notice.

District of   , *ss:*

I, *Marshal,* [*or, Deputy Marshal, as the case may be,*] make oath, that I delivered letters of which a copy is hereto annexed to the following named persons, at the times and
places stated in connection with the name of each, and that I left at the last and usual
place of abode in said District copies of the same letter, with the following named persons, on the day and hour mentioned in connection with the name of each. [*Here insert
names and other required particulars.*]

Served personally   day of   , A. D. 18 .

—————————————,

Marshal, [*or, Deputy.*]

[*Or,* left at last usual place of abode   day of   , A. D. 18 .

—————————————,

Marshal, [*or, Deputy.*]

This   day of——   A. D. 18 , subscribed and   to, before
me.

—————————————,
One of the Registers in Bankruptcy of said Court.

Form No. 53.

CREDITOR'S SPECIFICATION OF THE GROUNDS OF HIS OPPOSITION TO THE BANKRUPT'S DISCHARGE.

In the District Court of the United States,
For the   District of   .

In the Matter of

         } IN BANKRUPTCY.

         Bankrupt.

         , of   , in the County of   , and State of   .
Creditor, having proved   debt against the estate of said
       , Bankrupt, and having received notice of his Petition for a discharge from his debts, do hereby oppose the granting of said discharge and for the grounds of such opposition do file the following specification : [*Here insert one or more of the causes which should prevent the granting of the Bankrupt's discharge according to the provisions of Section Twenty-nine of said Act.*]

                                                  ————   , *Creditor, &c.*

To ———— ————— , *Dictrict Judge,*
           [or, *Register in Bankruptcy*] *of said District.*

Form No. 54.

CREDITOR'S PETITION.

To the Honorable   , Judge of the District Court of the United States
        for the   District of   .
THE PETITION of   , of the   ., of   , in the
County of   , and State of   , Respectfully shows :—That
he is a Creditor of   , who for a period of   , months next
preceding the date of the filing of this Petition, has resided at   , in County
of   , and State of   , and District aforesaid ;—That Your
Petitioner's demand is provable against the said   , in accordance with the
provisions of the Act of Congress entitled "An Act to Establish a Uniform System of Bankruptcy throughout the United States," approved March 2, 1867 ; That he believes that said   owes debts to an amount exceeding the sum of Three Hundred Dollars ; That Your Petitioner's demand exceeds the amount of Two Hundred and Fifty Dollars ; and that the nature of Your Petitioner's demand against the said is as follows :—

A certain promissory note signed by said   , payable to the order of Your Petitioner, [or, naming the party to whose order the said note is made payable,] of which the following is a Copy, to wit : [or, set forth evidence of indebtedness in any other form to a liquidated amount, exceeding Two Hundred and Fifty Dollars, to meet the case.]

And Your Petitioner further represents that within Six calendar Months next preceding the date of this Petition, the said   did commit an act of Bankruptcy within the meaning of said Act, to wit : In that the said did heretofore, to wit : on the   day of   , A. D. 18 , depart out of, and from the State of   of which he is an inhabitant as aforesaid, with intent to defraud his creditors, [or, being absent during said period, be has, with intent to de fraud his creditors, remained absent from said State:]—

[Or,

That the said   , within the period aforesaid, to wit : On the day of   A. D. 18   , within said District, did conceal himself, [or, did dis guise himself,] to avoid the service of Legal Process in an action for the recovery of a debt or demand, provable under said Act, to wit : To avoid the service of Legal Process in a suit   brought by   , in the   Court, of the State of   , [or, any other Court] in which such process had been issued, to be served upon the said   , by   , Marshal for said District, [or, Sheriff, Constable, or other Officer, or party, as the case may be,] at which time the said   did conceal himself, and remain secreted, to avoid the service of said Process, so that the said officer or party having the same to serve upon said Debtor was unable to find him, in order to make proper service of the same :—

[Or,

That the said   , within the period aforesaid, to wit : At   , in said District, on the   day of   , A. D. 18   , being possessed of cer tain Property, to wit : [Here describe the Property,] and he, being aware that Legal Pro cess had been issued, [or, was about to be issued,] to be levied thereon at the Suit of some one or more of his Creditors, did conceal [or, remove ; or, destroy the identity] of said Property to avoid its being Attached, Taken, or Sequestered on such Process :-

[Or,

That the said   , within the period aforesaid, to wit :—At   , in said District, on the   day of   , A. D. 18   , being possessed of cer tain Estate, Property, Rights or Credits, to wit : [Here describe the Property and where situated,] did make an Assignment [or, Gift, Sale, Conveyance, or Transfer, as the case may be] of the same [or, of any part thereof—mentioning the part] to   , of   , in the County of   , and State of   , with intent to delay [or, hinder ; or, defraud] the Creditors of him, the said   :—

[Or,

That the said   , within the period aforesaid, and within said District, to wit : At   , has been arrested and held in custody under and by virtue of mesne process, [or Execution ; or, as the case may be,] issued out of the   Court of the United States for the   District of   , [or, of any Court of any State, District, or Territory,] within which such debtor resides or has property, founded upon a demand, in its nature, provable against the Bankrupt's Estate under said Act, and for a sum exceeding One Hundred Dollars ; and that such Process is remaining in force, and not discharged by payment, or in any other manner provided by the Laws of such State applicable thereto, for a period of Seven days :—

[Or,

That the said   , within the period aforesaid, and within said District, to wit :—On the   day of   , A D. 18   , being Bankrupt, [or, insol vent ; or, in Contemplation of Bankruptcy, or Insolvency,] did make to   ,

of   , in the County of   , and State of   , a
payment [or, Gift, Grant, Sale, Conveyance, or Transfer] of money [or, of any other
Property, Estate, Rights or Credits,] [or, did give to   , of   ,
in the County of   , and State of   , a Warrant to Confess
Judgment, or, did procure, or Suffer his Property to be taken on Legal Process,] in
favor of   , of   , in the County of   , and State
of   ; the said judgment to be confessed, issuing out of the   Court
of   ; with the intent to give a preference to   , of
in the County of   , and State of   ; [or, to one or more of hi
Creditors; or, with the intent, thereby, to give preference to   ,. of   ,
in the County of   , and State of   , being a person, [or, persons,]
who were liable for him as Endorser, Bail, Sureties, or otherwise, [describing the particular relation,] or, with the intent by such disposition of his Property to Defeat, or Delay
the operation of said Act.]

[Or,

    That the said   , within the period aforesaid, and within said District,
to wit: On the   day of   , A. D. 18   , being a Banker, [or, Merchant;
or, Trader; or, as the case may be,] has fraudulently stopped, or, suspended (and has
not resumed) payment of his Commercial Paper within a period of fourteen days.

    [N. B.—Whichever of the acts is relied upon as the act of Bankruptcy of Debtor, the same
must be particularly described.]

    WHEREFORE YOUR PETITIONER PRAYS that he, the said   , may be de-
clared a Bankrupt, and that a Warrant may be issued to take possession of his Estate ;
that the same may be distributed according to law ; and that such further proceedings
may be had thereon as the law in such case prescribes.

————————————— ,   ————————— ————————— ,
    Solicitor [or *Attorney.*]   *Petitioner.*

Oath to Foregoing Petition.

UNITED STATES OF AMERICA,
        District of   , ss:
    I,   , the Petitioner above named, do hereby make solemn oath that the state-
ments contained in the foregoing Petition subscribed by me are true, so far as the same
are stated of my own knowledge, and that those matters which are stated therein on
information and belief, are true according to the best of my knowledge, information, and
belief.

                                          ————————— ————————— ,
                                                          Petitioner.

    Subscribed and sworn [or, affirmed] to, before me, this   day of   , A. D.
18   .

                                          ————————— ————————— ,
    District Judge,.[or, *Register in Bankruptcy,* or, *U. S. Commissioner.*]
    [N. B.—In case the parties proceeded against are a Copartnership, or a Corporation,
the above form may be varied accordingly.]

Form No. 55.

DEPOSITION AS TO PETITIONING CREDITOR'S CLAIM.

[To be filed with Creditor's Petition.]

In the District Court of the United States,
For the   District of   .

In the Matter of

Against whom a Petition for Adjudication } In Bankruptcy.
of Bankruptcy, was filed on the
day of   , A. D. 18   .

At   , in said District, on the   day
of   A. D, 18   .
Before   , one of the Registers of said
Court, in Bankruptcy.

District of   , *ss:*
, of   in the County of   , and State of   , being duly sworn [*or,*
affirmed] and Examined, at the Time and Place above mentioned, upon his Oath, [*or,*
affirmation, says that the said   was, [*or,* were,] on and before the   day of
, A. D. 18   , and still   justly and truly indebted unto this Deponent,—
[*Here give a particular description of the Debt.*]

———— ————, *Petitioning Creditor.*

On the   day of   , before me personally appeared   , the above named
Petitioning Creditor, and was duly sworn to the truth of the foregoing statement.

———— ————, *Register in Bankruptcy.*

———

Form No. 56.

DEPOSITION OF WITNESS TO ACT OF BANKRUPTCY.

[To be filed with Creditor's Petition.]

In the District Court of the United States,
For the   District of   .

In the Matter of

Against whom a Petition for Adjudication } In Bankruptcy.
of Bankruptcy was filed on the
day of   , A. D. 18   .

At   , in said District, on the
day of   , A. D. 18   .
Before   , one of the Registers of said
Court in Bankruptcy :—

District of   , *ss:*
being duly Sworn, [*or,* Affirmed,] and Examined, upon his Oath, [*or,* Affirmation,] says
that, [*Here set forth particularly the Witness's knowledge of the Act of Bankruptcy alleged
to have been committed by the party proceeded against.*]

On the   day of   , appeared personally   , the above named Witness,
and was duly sworn to the truth of the foregoing statement.

———— ————, *Register in Bankruptcy.*

Form No. 57.

ORDER TO SHOW CAUSE, UPON CREDITOR'S PETITION.

In the District Court of the United States,
For the   District of   .

> In the Matter of
>
> Against whom a Petition for Adjudication } In Bankruptcy.
> of Bankruptcy was filed on the
> day of   , A. D. 18   .

District of   , ss :

Upon filing proofs sustaining the allegations of the Petition aforesaid, it is *Ordered*, That the said   do appear at this Court, as a Court of Bankruptcy, to be holden at   , in the County of   , and State of   , and District aforesaid, on the   day of   at   o'clock,   m., and show cause, if any there be, why the Prayer of said Petition should not be granted; and—

It is further *Ordered*, That a copy of said Petition, together with a copy of this order, be served on said   , by delivering the same to him personally, or by leaving the same at his last usual place of abode, in said district, at least five days previous to the day herein required for his appearance.

Witness the Honorable   , Judge of the said Court, and the seal {Seal of the Court.} thereof, at   , in said District, on the   day of   , A. D. 18   .

————— —————,
Clerk of District Court, for said District.

Form No. 58.

ADJUDICATION OF BANKRUPTCY—CREDITOR'S PETITION.

In the District Court of the United States,
For the   District of   .

> In the matter of
>
>   } In Bankruptcy.
>
>   Bankrupt .

At   , in said district,
on the   day of   , A. D. 18   .
District of   , ss :

This cause came on to be heard at   , in said Court, and   ,
[*Here state the proceedings, whether there was no opposition, or, if opposition, what proceedings were had, and when and where, and what counsel appeared for the several parties.*]

And thereupon, and upon consideration of the proofs in said cause, (and the arguments of counsel thereon, if any,) it was found that the facts set forth in said Petition were true, and it is therefore adjudged that   became Bankrupt within the true intent and meaning of the Act entitled "An Act to Establish a Uniform System of Bank-

153

ruptcy throughout the United States," approved March 2, 1867, before the filing of the said Petition, and he is therefore declared and adjudged a Bankrupt accordingly. And it is further ordered that the said Bankrupt shall, within five days after the date of this order, make and deliver, or transmit by mail, post paid, to the Marshal, as Messenger, a Schedule of his Creditors, and Inventory of his estate, in the form, and verified in the manner required of the Petitioning debtor by the said Act.

Witness the Honorable   , Judge of the said Court, and the seal

{ Seal of } thereof, at   , in said District, on the   day of   ,
{ the Court. } A. D. 18 .

———————— ——————————,
Clerk of District Court, for said District.

————

Form No. 59.

WARRANT OF SEIZURE UPON ADJUDICATION OF BANKRUPTCY ON CREDITOR'S PETITION.

In the District Court of the United States,
For the   District of

In the Matter of

⎫
⎬ IN BANKRUPTCY.
⎭

Bankrupt .

District of   , *ss :*

To THE MARSHAL OF SAID DISTRICT, [OR, TO EITHER OF HIS DEPUTIES,] GREETING:

Whereas a Petition for Adjudication of Bankruptcy was, on the   day of   , A. D. 18   , filed against   , of the County of   , and State of   , in said District, under which he has been duly declared and adjudicated Bankrupt; you are therefore, by virtue of the said Petition and the adjudication thereon, according to the provisions of the Act entitled "An Act to Establish a Uniform System of Bankruptcy throughout the United States," approved March 2, 1867, required, authorized, and empowered, as Messenger, to take possession of all the estate, real and personal, of said   , the said Bankrupt, except such as may be by law exempt from the operation of said Act, and of all his deeds, books of account, and papers, and to keep the same safely until the appointment of an assignee.

And you are also directed to publish notice twice in the newspapers called and   , printed at   , in the County of   , the first publication to be made forthwith as follows:

District Court of the United States,
For the   District of

In the matter of

⎫
⎬ IN BANKRUPTCY.
⎭

Bankrupt .

A warrant in Bankruptcy has been issued by said Court against the estate of   , of the County of   , of the State of   , in said District, adjudged a Bankrupt upon the Petition of his Creditors, and the payment of any debts and the delivery of any property belonging to said Bankrupt, to him or to his use, and the transfer of any property by him, are forbidden by law. A meeting of the Creditors of said Bankrupt to prove their debts and choose one or more Assignees of his estate will be held at a Court of Bankruptcy to be holden at   , in said District, on the   day of   , A. D. 18 , at   o'clock   M., at the office of   , [giving the street and number,] one of the Registers in Bankruptcy of said Court.

——————— ———————,

Marshal, [or, *Deputy Marshal,*] *Messenger.*

And you will also serve written or printed notice by mail or personally on all Creditors whose names may be given to you by said Bankrupt within five days from the date of such adjudication, within   days after the date hereof, and also to said   , the Bankrupt, which notice shall be as follows :

In the District Court of the United States,
For the   District of   .

In the Matter of

      IN BANKRUPTCY.

Bankrupt.

District of   *ss :*
To   , one of the Creditors of said   , Bankrupt.
This is to give you notice :
1st. That a Warrant in Bankruptcy has been issued against the estate of   , Bankrupt aforesaid.
2d. That the payment of any debts, and the delivery of any property belonging to said Bankrupt, to him or to his use, and the transfer of any property by him, are forbidden by law.
3d. That a meeting of the Creditors of the debtor to prove their debts and choose one or more Assignees of the estate will be held at a Court of Bankruptcy to be holden at   , in said District, on the   day of   , at   o'clock m., at the office of   , [*giving the street and number,*] one of the Registers in Bankruptcy of said Court.

And the following are the names of the creditors of said Bankrupt and the amount of their debts as given to me by him.
[*E. g.*—A. B., (of Boston,)   dollars.)

——————— ———————,

Messenger.

And you have there this warrant, with your doings thereon.
IN TESTIMONY WHEREOF, I have hereunto set my hand and caused the seal of this Court to be affixed at   , this   day of   , in the year of our Lord 18 .

——————— ———————,

District Judge.

[L. S.]
Clerk of the Court.

Return by Marshal thereon.

District of   , *ss* :

By virtue of the within warrant, I have taken possession of the estate of the within named   , Bankrupt, except such as is by law excepted from the operation of said warrant by the Act of Congress, and of all his deeds, books of account, and papers which have come to my knowledge, and I have published notice by advertisement on two different days in the newspapers within mentioned, the first publication of which was on the   day of   , A. D. 18   . I also within   days after the date of the within warrant sent written or printed notice, as within directed, to the within named   , Bankrupt, and to the creditors named on the schedule delivered to me by him, and herewith returned. The notices sent by mail were deposited in the postoffice at   , on the   day of   , A. D. 18   , with the proper postage stamp affixed thereto, and those delivered personally by me to said creditors were delivered at the times and the places set opposite to the name of each, and all of said notices were according to the directions set out in this warrant.

—————— ——————,

Marshal, [*or, Deputy Marshal.*] *Messenger.*

Fees and Expenses.

1. Service of warrant.	$ 2	00
2. Necessary travel at the rate of 5 cents a mile each way		
3. Notice to creditors, 10 cents each...........................		
4. Actual expenses in publishing notices as follows..............		
5. Actual expenses in custody of property and other services as follows..		

[*Here render the particulars.*]

—————— ——————,

Marshal, [*or, Deputy Marshal,*] *Messenger.*

Affidavit as to Expenses.

District of   , A. D. 18   .

Personally appeared the said   , Messenger, and made oath that the above expenses returned by him under numbers four and five have been actually incurred and paid by him, and are just and reasonable.

—————— ——————,

One of the Registers in Bankruptcy in said District.

Form No. 60.

ADJUDICATION WHERE DEBTOR IS FOUND NOT BANKRUPT.

In the District Court of the United States.
For the   District of   .

In the Matter of

                 IN BANKRUPTCY.

       Bankrupt   .

District of   , *ss :*

At   , in said District,
            on   day of   , A. D. 18 .
Before Honorable ————— ————————, Judge of the   District of   .
       District of   , *ss :*

This cause came on to be heard at   , in said Court, and [Here state the proceedings, whether there was no opposition, or, if opposed, state what proceedings were had, and when and where, and what counsel appeared for the several parties.]

And thereupon, and upon consideration of the proofs in said cause, (*and the arguments of counsel thereon*, if any,) it was FOUND that the facts set forth in said Petition were not proved; and it is therefore *Ordered*, That said Petition be dismissed, and that all proceedings under the same be vacated and annulled.

Witness the Honorable   , Judge of the said Court, and the seal thereof
{ Seal of the Court. }   at   , in said District, on the   day of   , A. D. 18 .

Clerk of District Court for said District.

[N. B. 1. If default be made by the Debtor to appear pursuant to the order upon a Creditor's Petition, the subsequent order may be made by a Register in Bankruptcy.

N. B. 2. If no Schedule of Creditors shall be delivered to the Messenger by the Bankrupt, the Messenger shall prepare such Schedule from the best information he can obtain, and send notices accordingly.]

Form No. 61.

DENIAL OF BANKRUPTCY, AND DEMAND FOR JURY BY DEBTOR.

In the District Court of the United States,
For the   District of   .

In the Matter of the Petition
of   , Creditor,
         vs.   IN BANKRUPTCY.

       , Debtor.

At   , in said District,
         on the   day of   , A. D. 18 .
District of   , *ss :*

And now on this return day [*or*, adjourned return day] for the hearing of said Peti-

tion, the said appears and denies that he has committed the act of Bankruptcy set forth in said Petition, and avers that he should not be declared Bankrupt for
any cause in said Petition alleged, and this he prays may be inquired of by the Court,
[or, he demands that the same may be inquired of by a Jury.]

Witness the Honorable , Judge, of the said Court, and the seal thereof,
{ Seal of the Court. } at , in said District, on the day of , A. D. 18 .

——————— ———————,
Clerk of District Court, for said District.

Form No. 62.

ORDER OF COURT UPON DENIAL OF BANKRUPTCY AND DEMAND FOR JURY TRIAL.

(Involuntary Bankruptcy.)

In the District Court of the United States,
For the District of ,

In the Matter of the Petition
of , Creditor,

vs.

, Debtor.

At , in the said District,
on the day of , 18 .
District of , *ss* :
Upon the demand in writing filed by the Respondent to said Petition, that the fact of
the commission of an act of Bankruptcy may be inquired of by a Jury, it is *Ordered*,
That said issue be submitted to a Jury at the present term of this Court, (if a Jury be in
attendance,) *or*, if in vacation, at the next term of this Court.

Witness the Honorable , Judge of the said Court, and the seal thereof
{ Seal of the Court. } at . , in said District, on the day of , A. D. 18 .

——————— ———————,
Clerk of District Court, for said District.

Form No. 63.

APPOINTMENT OF TRUSTEES UNDER SECTION 43.

In the District Court of the United States,
For the District of

In the Matter of

Bankrupt.

IN BANKRUPTCY.

At this meeting of the Creditors of said Bankrupt, called specially by order of said
Court for the purpose of determining in what manner the estate of said Bankrupt shall be

settled, it was resolved by three fourths in value of the Creditors whose claims have been proved, as follows :

1st. That it is for the interest of the general body of the Creditors of said that the estate of said   , Bankrupt, should be wound up and settled, and distribution made among the Creditors by trustees under the inspection and direc-on of a Committee of Creditors.

2d. That this resolution be certified and reported to the Court.

3d. That   be nominated as trustee to take, hold, and distribute said estate.

4th. That   , of   , of   , be the Committee of the Creditors under whose direction the said Trustee shall act.

—————— ——————,

Creditors.	Amount of Debts.	
	Dolls.	Cts.

Affidavit of Bankrupt.

A. B., the said Bankrupt, being duly sworn, [or, affirmed,] says that the names of the persons affixed to the foregoing resolution represent three-fourths in value of all his creditors whose claims have been proven against his estate.

—————— ——————,

Subscribed and   to, before me, this   day of   , A. D. 18. .

—————— ——————,

Register, [or, *U. S. Commissioner.*]

Certificate of Register thereon.

In the District Court of the United States,
For the   District of   .

(In Bankruptcy.)

At   , the   day of   , A. D. 18 , I hereby certify that at a meeting of the Creditors of said   , held this day in pursuance of a notice regu-larly given according to the provisions of the Act of Congress entitled, &c., approved March 2, 1867, [or, *according to the order of the Court,* as the case may be,] the above resolutions were adopted and signed by three fourths in value of the Creditors of said Bankrupt, who were present or were represented at said meeting.

—————— ——————,

Register in Bankruptcy.

Order of the Court on above Proceedings.

In the District Court of the United States,
For the   District of

```
                                    ⎫
     In the Matter of                ⎪
                                     ⎬ IN BANKRUPTCY.
          Bankrupt  .                ⎪
                                    ⎭
```

The foregoing certificate having been filed and read, it is *Ordered,* That the said
shall convey, transfer, and deliver all his property or estate to   , as trustee
by deed, in the following form :
          District of   , *ss* :
          In the District Court of the United States, for said District.
     This indenture made this   day of   , A. D. 18 , between   ,
(the Debtor,) of   , in the County of   , and State of   ,
and   , on behalf and with the consent of   , Creditors of the said
          , WITNESSETH, that the said   *(the Debtor,)* hereby conveys,
transfers, and delivers all his estate and effects to   , absolutely, to have and
to hold the same in the same manner and with the same rights in all respects as the said
          would have had or held the same if no proceedings in bankruptcy had been
taken against him, to be applied and administered for the benefit of the Creditors of said
          , in like manner as if said   had been at the date hereof duly
adjudged Bankrupt, and the said *(trustees)* had been appointed assignee in bankruptcy
under said act.
     In testimony whereof, the said .   *(debtor,)* and the said   , *(trustees,)*
in acceptance of said trust, have hereunto set their hands and seals, this   day of
          , A. D. 18 .
     Executed in presence of—

                              ————— —————, [L. S.]
                              ————— —————, [L. S.]
                              ————— —————, [L. S.]

     This day appeared before me, a Register in Bankruptcy, the above-named   ,
(Bankrupt,) and acknowledged the foregoing instrument by him signed to be his free act
and deed.

                              ————— —————,
                                   Register in Bankruptcy.

We hereby give our assent to the execution of the above deed :

Names of Creditors.	Residence.	Amount.	
		Dolls.	Cts.

Oath of Bankrupt.

In the District Court of the United States,
For the   District of   .

In the Matter of

⎱ IN BANKRUPTCY.

Bankrupt.

     , the said Bankrupt, being duly sworn, doth depose and say that he has conveyed, transferred, and delivered all his property to the trustees in the above indenture named, and that the persons signing their consent to the above conveyance represent three-fourths in value of all his Creditors whose claims have been proved against his estate.

            —————— ——————,
                 Bankrupt.

 Subscribed and sworn, [*or,* affirmed,] this   day of   , A. D. 18
Before me,

            —————— ——————,
            Register in Bankruptcy.

 Witness the Honorable   , Judge of the said Court, and the seal thereof, at   , in said District, on the   day of   , A. D. 18
 { Seal of }
 { the Court. }   —————— ——————,
      Clerk of District Court, for said District.

Advertisement of Trustee.

In the District Court of the United States,
For the   District of   .
        (In Bankruptcy.)

 This is to give notice, that by an indenture bearing date the   day of   ,
A. D. 18 ,   , of   , has conveyed and assigned all his estate and effects whatsoever to   , as trustee, upon trust for the benefit of all the Creditors of   , and that said conveyance was duly executed according to the provisions of the 43d Section of the Bankrupt Act of March 2, 1867.
 Dated this   day of   , A. D. 18 .

           —————— ——————,
           —————— ——————,
           —————— ——————,
                Trustees.

Order of Court.

 The foregoing proceedings under the 43d Section of the Bankrupt Act of March 2, 1867, having been placed on file and read, it is
 Ordered, That all proceedings upon said Petition in Bankruptcy be stayed until the further order of the Court.
 Witness the Honorable   , Judge of the said Court, and the seal thereof, at   , in said District, on the   day of   , A. D. 18 .
 { Seal of }
 { the Court. }   *Clerk of District Court, for said District.*

Form No. 64.

ORDER CONCERNING SALE OF PROPERTY BY ASSIGNEE.

In the District Court of the United States,
For the　　　　　District of　　　.

In the Matter of
Bankrupt.

} IN BANKRUPTCY.

At　　　　　　　, in said District, on
　　　the　　　day of　　　, A. D. 18　.
District of　　　, ss :
Upon the representation of　　　, a Creditor of said　　　, and
upon the proofs filed therewith, it is *Ordered,* That the real estate of said Bankrupt,
when offered for sale by his Assignee, shall be sold in lots or parcels as follows, [*Here
follows the direction by reference to plat or any other specific description or order in which
the property shall be sold.*]
　Witness the Honorable　　　　　, Judge of the said Court, and the seal
{ Seal of the Court. } thereof, at　　　, in said District, on the　　　day of　　　,
　　　A. D. 18　.

――――――― ―――――――,
Clerk of District Court, for said District.

―――――――

Form No. 65.

ORDER CONCERNING SALE OF PROPERTY OF CORPORATION.

In the District Court of the United States,
For the　　　　　District of　　　.

In the Matter of the Bankruptcy of
A corporation formed under the laws of the State of

} IN BANKRUPTCY.

At　　　　　　　, in said District, on
　　　the　　　day of　　　, A. D. 18　.
District of　　　, ss :
Upon the representation of　　　, a Creditor, [*or,* the party in interest,]
and upon the proofs filed therewith, it is *Ordered,* That the franchise of said corporation
be sold in fractional parts according to the number of shares therein, as follows, [*If there
be one thousand shares of the corporation the order may require that the franchise be sold
in fractions of　　　, or, in any other proportion.*]
　Witness the Honorable　.　　　　, Judge of said Court, and the seal there-
{ Seal of the Court. } of, at　　　, in said District, on the　　　day of　　　,
　　　A. D. 18　.

――――――― ―――――――,
Clerk of District Court, for said District.

Form No. 66.

ORDER OF DIMINUTION OF CLAIM.

In the District Court of the United States,
For the   District of   .

In the Matter of

     IN BANKRUPTCY.

    Bankrupt .

At   , in said District, on
the   day of   , A. D. 18 .
District of   , *ss:*

Upon the evidence submitted to this Court upon the claim of   , against said estate, (*and,* if the fact be so, *upon hearing counsel thereon,*) it is *Ordered,* That the amount of said claim be reduced from the sum of   , as set forth in the affidavit in proof of claim filed by said Creditor, in said case, to the sum of   , and that the latter named sum be entered upon the books of the Assignee as the true sum upon which a dividend shall be computed, [if with interest, insert, "with interest thereon from the   day of   , A. D. 18 .

————— —————,
Clerk of District Court, for said District.

Form No. 67.

EXPUNGING OR ALLOWANCE OF CLAIM.

In the District Court of the United States,
For the   District of

In the Matter of

     IN BANKRUPTCY.

    Bankrupt.

At   , in said District, on
the   day of   , A. D. 18 .
District of   , *ss:*

Upon the evidence submitted to the Court, upon the claim of   against said estate, (*and,* if the fact be so, *upon hearing counsel thereon,*) it is *Ordered,* That said claim be disallowed and expunged from the list of claims upon the Assignee's record in said case.

Witness the Honorable   , Judge of said United States District Court.

————— —————,
Clerk of District Court, for said District.

[N. B.—If the claim is found to be good, say, "*It is Ordered, That said claim be established to the full amount thereof.*"]

Form No. 68.

IN CASE OF DISALLOWANCE THE CREDITOR MAY FILE THE FOLLOWING
NOTICE OR APPEAL.

In the District Court of the United States,
For the　　　　　　　District of　　　　.

In the Matter of

　　　　　　　　　　　　　　　　　IN BANKRUPTCY.

　　　　　Bankrupt.

　　　　　　　　At　　　　　, on the　　day of　　, A. D. 18　.
To ——————— —————————,
　　　　　　　Assignee of said estate :
　　You are hereby notified that I claim an appeal from the decision of the Judge of said
Court made on the　　　day of　　　　　A. D. 18　, refusing to allow my claim when
presented against the estate of　　　　　, Bankrupt, to the Circuit Court of the United
States next to be holden at　　　　, in said District, on the　　　day of　　　,
A. D. 18　.

　　　　　　　　　　　　——————— ————————.

　　[If the appeal is from a disallowance of part of the claim, instead of "*refusing to allow
my claim,*" say, "*reducing my claim.*"]

　　　　　　　　　　——————— ————————, *Creditor.*

OVERRULED CASES

UNITED STATES SUPREME COURT.

In re AIRD,
    ads. } *December Term,* 1867. *Appeal from District Court of Western Arkansas*
LUKINS,

2 *N. B. R.* 27. [*From 6th Wallace,* 78.]

DAVIS, J.

Decree reversed. District Court ordered to enter decree setting aside conveyance as fraudulent. Because debtor, in failing circumstances, cannot sell and convey his land, even for valuable consideration, by deed without reservation, and yet reserve to himself the right to possess and occupy, for even a limited time, for his own benefit.

In re J. E. BROMLEY & CO.,
    Territory of Utah. }

3 *N. B R.* 169.

HAWLEY, C. M. J.

  1. Defendant is liable to examination after due service, and

  2. Being before the court on his own behalf, is liable without notice, and

  3. He cannot claim protection of the court, on the ground that his answer will criminate himself.

In re THEIR CREDITORS,
    ads. } *Louisiana.*
MEEKINS, KELLY & CO.

Appeal from 3d District Court of New Orleans.—FELLOWES, J.
3 *N. B. R.* 126.

ISLEY, J.

Judgment *annulled, avoided* and *reversed,* and *rehearing refused.* Because the United States bankrupt law does not divest the State courts of the jurisdiction necessary to the final administration of the estate of an insolvent who had made a surrender previous to its passage.

In re FENTON,
    ads. } *Utah Territory.*
KENYON.

6 *N. B. R.* 238.

McKEAN, C. J. HAWLEY, J. STRICKLAND, J.

The publishers of a daily paper and proprietors of a book and job printing office are manufacturers within the meaning of the bankrupt act.

Payment of wages to employees, though made in the regular course of business, is an act of bankruptcy if done in contemplation of insolvency ; for, although the law prefers an employee to the amount of fifty dollars, this preference must be secured by and through the proceedings in bankruptcy, and not outside of them or independent of and in spite of the act. The negotiable paper of a firm of manufacturers is commercial paper within the meaning of the act, regardless of the purpose for which it was given.

Demurrer overruled.

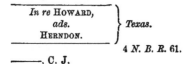

In re HOWARD,
ads.
HERNDON.

} *Texas.*

4 N. B. R. 61.

———, C. J.

Where an appellant in this court becomes bankrupt after his appeal is taken, his assignee in bankruptcy, upon the production of the deed of assignment of the register in bankruptcy, duly certified by the clerk of the proper court, may, on motion, be substituted as appellant in the case.

Order made accordingly. (9 Wallace, 664.)

In re HOWARD et al.
ads.
MASTERSON, *ass.*

} *Appeal from the U. S. Circuit Court for the Western District of Texas.*

5 N. B. R. 130.

MILLER, J.

When there has been a joint decree against two parties and one alone asks for an appeal, the appeal will be dismissed, unless it appears by the record that the other party had been notified in writing to appear; and that he had failed to appear, or, if appearing, had refused to join. Appeal dismissed.

In re HUNT, *Assignee of* KELLEY & GLADDING,
ads.
SECOND NATIONAL BANK OF LEAVENWORTH, *et al.*

} *Error to the Circuit Court of the U. S. for the District of Kansas.*

4 N. B. R. 198.

FIELD, J.

Where the mortgagor remains in possession of his stock of goods—the property mortgaged—and continues with consent of mortgagee to make sales therefrom, the mortgage does not constitute a lien. Judgment affirmed.

In re SAM'L D. BARDWELL, and others,
ads.
NATHANIEL C. DAY.

} *Worcester, Mass. Judicial.*

3 N. B. R. 115.

GRAY, J.

Bill in equity to set aside proceedings instituted under the insolvent laws of the commonwealth, March 18, 1867. General demurrer filed. Demurrer sustained.

In re BERRY,
ads.
MARTIN.

} *California, April Term,* 1869.

2 N. B. R. 188.

SANDERSON, J.

Judgment, rendered against debtor in State Court, claimed discharge by virtue of proceedings under insolvent law of the State, commenced May 1, 1867, and terminated by final decree, July 1, 1867. Appeal from court below denying motion to quash execution on such judgment.

Held—That the Bankruptcy Act did not take effect to supersede State laws until June 1, 1867. State insolvent court acquired jurisdiction of the case on issue, May 1, 1867, being prior to operation of Bankrupt Act; hence the proceedings are valid and unaffected by Bankrupt Act.

Semble—State insolvent laws were superseded by Bankrupt Act, June 1, 1867, and all proceedings commenced under said laws thereafter, are null and void.

In re DWIGHT FOSTER, *et al., ass.,*
      ads. } *Massachusetts. Judicial.*
JOHN Q. A. CLIFTON, *et al.*

3 *N. B. R.* 162.

GRAY, J.

Motion to dismiss petition to enforce mechanics' lien on the ground that petitioners on their own petition, had been subsequently adjudged bankrupt in the U. S. Bankruptcy Court.

The mechanics' lien was not dissolved thereby.

The State Court may entertain the petition without necessarily conflicting or interfering with the jurisdiction of the Bankruptcy Court.

Motion denied, and case to stand continued to await result of the action of that court.

In re GLIDDEN, *et al.,*
      ads. } *California.*
MERRITT.

5 *N. B. R.* 157.

When a complaint is defective in form, but not in substance, such defect can only be reached by demurrer, on the ground that the complaint is unintelligible or uncertain.

The filing in the Appellate Court of an adjudication of bankruptcy of the defendant, rendered by the register of the United States District Court, after the appeal is taken, will not have the effect to stay the proceedings on the appeal. A judgment of the court below, from which an appeal is pending, is a final judgment, in contemplation of section 21, of the United States Bankrupt Act.

Motion for nonsuit overruled.

In re HARMER,
      ads. } *Pennsylvania.*
PEIPER. •

5 *N. B. R.* 252.

SHARSWOOD, J.

Section 2, of the United States Bankrupt Act, does not preclude a State Court from jurisdiction of action by the assignee on a cause which accrued to the bankrupt.

Judgment for the defendant on the demurrer to the plea of the statute of limitations to the third court.

In re GEORGE A. HAWKINS,
      and others, } *Connecticut. Of Errors.*
APPEAL FROM PROBATE. *March,* 1868.

2 *N. B. R.* 122.

CARPENTER, J.

Voluntary assignment by debtor under insolvent law of the State held valid, although the U. S. Bankrupt Act was in existence and applicable to the case at the time of assignment.

Proceedings of Probate Court held good. Assignment good at common law without aid of statute.

| *In re* HOTCHKISS, ads. MALTBIE. | *Connecticut. Of Errors.* |

5 *N. B. R.* 485.

CARPENTER, J.

Debtor filed his deed of assignment under the insolvent law of Connecticut, and an assignee was appointed. The Supreme Court decided that the assignee was entitled to judgment against the deputy sheriff for property seized by virtue of a writ of attachment, holding that the distribution of a debtor's property, under the State insolvent laws, was not a violation of the provisions of the United States Bankrupt Act.

From the provisions of the 35th section of said Act, it is manifest that Congress intended that the various conveyances therein specified shall be valid, unless proceedings in bankruptcy are instituted within six months.

The Court of Common Pleas advised to render judgment for the plaintiff.

| *In re* MARTIN, ass., ads. TOOF, et al. | *December Term,* 1871. *Appeal from the U. S. Circuit Court for the District of Arkansas.* |

6 *N. B. R.* 49.

FIELD, J.

By insolvency, as used in the bankrupt act, when applied to traders and merchants, is meant inability of a party to pay his debts as they become due in the ordinary course of business.

The transfer by a debtor of a large portion of his property, while he is insolvent, to one creditor, without making provision for an equal distribution of its proceeds to all his creditors, necessarily operates as a preference to him, and must be taken as conclusive evidence that a preference was intended, unless the debtor can show that he was at the time ignorant of his insolvency, and that his affairs were such that he could reasonably expect to pay all his debts. The burden of proof is upon him in such a case, and not upon the assignee or contestant in bankruptcy.

A creditor has reasonable cause to believe a debtor, who is a trader, to be insolvent, when such a state of facts is brought to the creditor's notice respecting the affairs and pecuniary condition of the debtor as would lead a prudent business man to the conclusion that he is unable to meet his obligations as they mature in the ordinary course of business.

A transfer by an insolvent debtor with a view to secure his property, or any part of it to one creditor, and thus prevent an equal distribution among all his creditors, is a transfer in fraud of the bankrupt act. Decree affirmed.

| *In re* MASON, ass., ads. SMITH. | *December Term,* 1870. *Appeal from the Supreme Court of the District of Columbia.* |

6 *N. B. R.* 1.

CLIFFORD, J.

When a party lays claim to a certain fund, the possession of the depository is his possession, provided his claim is just and legal; therefore if the assignee in bankruptcy would divest him of the possession and control of the fund in question, he must do it by a suit at law or in equity, as provided in the third clause of the second section of the bankrupt act.

Strangers to the proceedings in bankruptcy not served with process and who have not voluntarily appeared and become parties to such a litigation, cannot be compelled to come into court under a petition for a rule to show cause, as the third clause of the second section of the said act affords the assignee a convenient, constitutional and sufficient remedy to contest every adverse claim made by any person to any property or rights of property transferable to or vested in such assignee.

Decree reversed and cause remanded for further proceedings.

In re SNEDAKER. } *Utah.*

4 N. B. R. 43.

HAWLEY, J.

Where a mortgagee fails to secure an equitable lien by bill and the appointment of a receiver on products or rents of mortgaged premises after a default, even though the premises sell for less than his claims, at a sale by the mortgagor's assignee in bankruptcy, he will only be entitled to a *pro rata* share on the deficiency of his claim out of the bankrupt's assets.

Motion of petitioning mortgagee *denied* and order issued directing assignee to distribute *pro rata*.

In re J. M. SNEDAKER,
 Territory of Utah. }

3 N. B. R. 155.

C. M. HAWLEY, J.

A creditor, whose debt is provable, cannot prosecute to judgment, either at law, or in equity. Holding security, he can be admitted as creditor only on the balance after sale thereof,—he must go into court.

In re STEWART & CO.,
 ads.
 LEVY. }

4 N. B. R. 193.

CLIFFORD, J.

A creditor's debts, due from belligerents, are not annulled, but only suspended during the war. When peace is restored they are revived, and the remedy in favor of the creditor is restored.

Judgment of court below *confirmed.*

In re WM. S. STRACHAN,
Territory of New Mexico. }

3 N. B. R. 148.

JOHNSON, A. J.

Discharge cannot be refused, simply for the reason that publication of notice of appointment of assignee was omitted. Petitioner having done and performed all matters and things required by law, and obeyed the orders of this court in the premises, his *final discharge,* as prayed for, *must be granted.*

In re KELSEY, *et al.,*
 ads.
 LEIGHTON. } *Maine.*

4 N. B. R. 155.

BARROWS, J.

The bankrupt certificate of discharge duly pleaded in an action against him in the Supreme Judicial Court, will not dissolve an attachment made by virtue of the writ in the action, more than four months prior to the defendant's commencement of proceedings in bankruptcy. The attachment thus made may be enforced by an execution issued upon a special judgment rendered by the court in which the action was entered and prosecuted.

The District Court of the United States does not have exclusive jurisdiction in such matters.

Exceptions overruled.

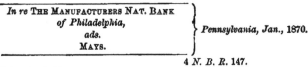

In re THE MANUFACTURERS NAT. BANK
of *Philadelphia*,
ads.
MAYS.

} *Pennsylvania, Jan.,* 1870.

4 *N. B. R.* 147.

SHARSWOOD, J.

The property of a bankrupt vests in his assignee as of the date of the commencement of proceedings, and no payment by or to him subsequent to that date is valid, even though made or received *bona fide*, or without notice. Judgment affirmed.

In re RIPLEY,
ads.
COREY, *et al.*

} *Maine.*

4 *N. B. R.* 163.

DICKERSON, J.

A discharge duly granted under the United States Bankrupt Act of 1867, when pleaded in bar to the further maintenance of an action for prior indebtedness, cannot be impeached in this court for any cause which would have prevented the granting of it under section 29, or been sufficient grounds for annulling it under sec. 24.

The authority to set aside and annul a discharge in bankruptcy, conferred upon the federal court by sec. 34, is incompatible with the exercises of the same power by a State Court; and the former is paramount.

Judgment for defendant for his costs in the law court only.

In re JOHN TAPPAN,
ads.
CARLTON BATES.

} *Suffolk, Mass.*

3 *N. B. R.* 159.

WELLS, J.

Assignment under the Bankrupt Act per c. 176, sec. 14, vests, in the assignee, title to all of the bankrupt property, " although the same is then attached on mesne process " and " shall dissolve any such attachment made within four months next preceding the commencement of such proceeding " in bankruptcy, does not prevent the enforcement of a judgment against the bankrupt on a portion of his property attached in an action more than four months before he commenced proceedings in bankruptcy.

The *judgment* therefore *affirmed.*

In re THOMPSON, GREENFIELD & ANOTHER,
ads.
L. W. GUNTHER & ANOTHER.

}

SAME, *ads.* MAX RAEDER—1st *District, New York.*

3 *N. B. R.* 179.

INGRAHAM, J.

Assignee must show right to property in controversy, in order to make himself a party.

Motion denied, with leave to renew upon other papers and paying costs of this motion.

In re THORNHILL, *et. al.*,
ads.
} *Louisiana.*
MORGAN, *et al.*

5 *N. B. R.* 1.

CLIFFORD, J.

Decrees in equity, in order that they may be re-examined in this court must be final decrees, rendered in term time, as contra-distinguished from mere interlocutory decrees or orders, which may be entered at chambers, or, if entered in court, are still subject to revision at the final hearing.

Appeal from decision of circuit dismissed for want of jurisdiction.

In re WOODS, *Ass., etc.*,
ads.
} *Missouri.*
FORSYTH.

5 *N. B. R.* 78.

STORY, J.

A joint request by the individual members of a firm soliciting B. to become a surety of one of them in an administration bond, does not create a liability of the firm. Hence upon the firm being subsequently declared bankrupt B. has no debt due therefrom, which is recoverable at law.

Judgment of Circuit Court affirmed.

OVERRULED CASES

IN THE

UNITED STATES CIRCUIT COURT.

In re ABLE, *et. al.,*
    ads. } *Kentucky.*
PAYNE & BROTHER.

4 *N. B. R.* 67.

LINDSAY, J.

Judgment reversed, because the discharge of one member from personal liability, does prevent enforcement of liens upon property fraudulently conveyed by a firm.

In re ALABAMA & CHATTANOOGA RAILROAD CO.,
    Vide 5 *N. B. R.* 97. } *S. .D., New York.*

6 *N. B. R.* 107.

WOODRUFF, C. J.

A railroad company incorporated by the laws of a State for constructing, maintaining and operating a railroad, cannot be proceeded against in bankruptcy in a district court without the State or States where its railroad is to be built, maintained and operated, on the petition of a creditor charging an act of bankruptcy. Allegation and proof that such company kept an office in said district for six months next preceding the filing of the petition, where its officers acted, its board of directors met, and where it contracted debts, made loans, purchases and payments, does not give such court jurisdiction.

In what districts proceedings against a debtor *in invitum* may be instituted, described.

"Carrying on business," within the meaning of the eleventh section of the bankrupt law, as applied to a railroad corporation, does not mean the conduct of such transactions as are merely collateral or incidental to the purpose for which the corporation is created, whether they are conducted by agents or officers, and although an office is continuously kept for the purpose.

The business of a railroad company, in the sense of the act, can only be carried on where the railroad is or is to be constructed, maintained and operated; hence, the district court of the United States for the southern district of New York, has no jurisdiction to adjudge an Alabama railroad corporation a bankrupt on such a petition by a creditor.

Adjudication of bankruptcy reversed.

In re ALEXANDER,
District of Virginia. }

3 *N. B. R.* 6.

CHASE, C. J.

A holder of a second lien on encumbered realty assets in the hands of the assignees in bankruptcy, and a tenant of the assignees in their name and with their approval, appeal from two orders of the District Court that the property be sold, and the first lien be received in part payment. The assignees withdrew permission for their names to be used in the proceedings on the appeal; whereupon application was made by the second lieu holder and the tenant to file bill in equity praying appropriate relief.

Held—That the special appellate jurisdiction of the Circuit Court is limited to controversies between assignees and claimants of adverse interests, and to controversies between assignees and creditor claimants.

Appeal would not lie from the orders in question, and would not lie in any case, unless made under the conditions prescribed by the 8th sec. of the bankruptcy act. Leave given to file bill, and *proceedings* in District Court *suspended*.

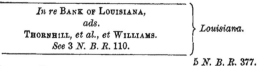

In re P. ADAMS AMES, *et al.,*
ads.
DWIGHT FOSTER, *et al., Ass., of* MCKAY & ALDUS. } *Massachusetts.*

2 *N. B. R.* 147.

LOWELL, J.

Bill in equity. Temporary injunction ordered. Leave to all parties to appear, with evidence, before register and to apply to court from time to time.

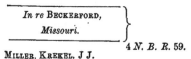

In re BANK OF LOUISIANA,
ads.
THORNHILL, *et al., et*
WILLIAMS, *et al. See* 3 *N. B. R.* 110. } *Louisiana.*

5 *N. B. R.* 367.

WOODS, J.

Petition to reverse and review adjudication of bankruptcy against defendant, commissioners having been appointed under State law for the purpose of liquidating the affairs of the bank. Defendants except on ground that the commissioners are not legal representatives.

Petition dismissed with costs. *Judgment* of abjudication *confirmed.*

In re BANK OF LOUISIANA,
ads.
THORNHILL, *et al., et* WILLIAMS.
See 3 *N. B. R.* 110. } *Louisiana.*

5 *N. B. R.* 377.

BRADLEY, J.

All orders in above entitled cause made by Circuit or District Court, since date of injunction, granted by circuit judge, *vacated* and *annulled*, and ordered that all things be restored to the condition at which they stood at date of injunction.

In re BECKERFORD,
Missouri. }

4 *N. B. R.* 59.

MILLER, KREKEL, J J.

Judgment confirmed, because setting apart the sum of $1,000 in lieu of a homestead was correct, according to provisions of Bankrupt Law, and not in violation of constitution of the United States.

In re S. R. BECKWITH, *et al.,*
ads.
J. C. NEAL, *on pet.* H. N. BILL, *ass.* } *N. D. Ohio.*

2 *N. B. R.* 82.

SWAYNE, J.

Decision reversed.

| In re J. B. BILLINGS, ads. ELIZA J. RUDDICK. | } Dist of Iowa. |

3 N. B. R. 14.

MILLER, P., J.

Writ of error dismissed at plaintiff's cost. Plaintiff remitted to such other proceedings as he may think advisable under Sec. 2, B. A.

| In re BININGER & Co., ads. HARDY, BLAKE & Co. | } S. D. N. Y. |

4 N. B. R. 77.

WOODRUFF, C., J.

Decree affirmed. *Held*, that the taking of property of insolvent traders, by a receiver appointed by a state court, is a taking under legal process within the meaning of Sec. 39 of the Bankruptcy Act.

And suspension of *commercial paper* without resumption, by a *solvent debtor* for a period of fourteen days, is *per se* fraudulent, and an act of bankruptcy.

| In re ABRAHAM BININGER, et al., (who are creditors of said Bininger and Abraham B. Clark,) for writ of prohibition. | } S. D. N. Y. |

3 N. B. R. 121.

WOODRUFF, J.

Clark commenced action in state court against his co-partner for an accounting, and receivers were appointed, who took possession of the firm property. Pending such proceedings the firm, with its members, was declared bankrupt on petition of firm creditors. Clark petitioned to the U. S. circuit court for a review of the decree adjudicating him a bankrupt, and commenced successively two actions in state court, and obtained injunctions restraining creditors from prosecuting proceedings in bankruptcy. Creditors thereupon moved the circuit court for a writ of prohibition under the judiciary act of 1789, directed to the state court, in the premises. Motion denied.

| In re BLOSS. Michigan. | } |

4 N. B. R. 37.

LONGYEAR, J.

Where a petition was filed, and an injunction allowed against C. E. B., a son of the bankrupt, to restrain the sale of certain real estate, etc., and C. E. B. moves to dissolve the injunction on affidavit of himself and the bankrupt, denying the collusion and connivance charged in the petition:

Held, 1. A secured debt is provable within the meaning of section 39 of the Bankrupt Act.

2. That a creditor who has a lien upon the property of his debtors by virtue of a judgment, etc., filing a petition for adjudication of bankruptcy without reference to such lien, therefore waives and relinquishes the same, and stands before the court as an unsecured creditor.

3. Allegations upon information, and being supported merely by other proof, are not sufficient to sustain an injunction.

Held,—C. E. B. had probable cause to believe that J. B. B., the alleged bankrupt, was insolvent, and that he suffered the said C. E. B. to obtain judgment execution and levy, with intent to give him a preference in violation of the bankruptcy act, and that this case ought to be retained and continued till the further order of the court.

Motion to dissolve denied.

In re BOATMEN'S SAVINGS INSTITUTION,
ads.
DARBY'S TRUSTEES. } *Missouri.*

4 *N. B. R.* 195.

DILLON, TREAT and KREKEL, J. J.

Bankrupt Act does not prohibit a person from loaning money at legal rates to one whom he has reason to believe to be insolvent, and taking security for such loan, provided it be made *bona fide*, and without any intent, or participation in any intent, to defraud creditors or defeat the bankrupt act.

General demurrer filed.

In re SAME. }

DILLON, C. J.

Bill in equity on questions arising. Demurrer overruled. Treat and Krekel, J. J., concur.

In re BOSTON, HARTFORD & ERIE
RAILROAD CO.* } *Connecticut.*

6 *N. B. R.* 209.

WOODRUFF, C. J.

All creditors have a direct interest in proceedings. A third party, seeking to intervene, must satisfy the court that his purpose is a meritorious one, although he may not prove his debt in the usual way, but must convince the court that he is in fact a creditor. Where two or more petitions are pending in different districts, only one adjudicature should be granted; proceedings in the other case to be stayed, but not dismissed.

In re BOSTON, HARTFORD & ERIE
RAILROAD CO.† } *S. D. New York.*

6 *N. B. R.* 222.

WOODRUFF, C. J.

Where the district judge for the southern district of New York privately signed the form of an adjudication in bankruptcy, on the first day of March, and endorsed on the same the words and figures "Filed March 1st, 1871, S. B.," and on the second day of March granted a re-argument of the application of the petitioning creditor in another district for leave to intervene and oppose an adjudication in this district, and at such re-argument on the third day of March, a certified copy of an adjudication made in such other district on the second day of March having been produced and read, the district judge produced the paper which had been signed by him on the first of March, but which, during the interval, had been in the sole knowledge and possession of the said judge, and had neither been entered with the clerk nor promulgated as an adjudication of the court, *Held*, that the said paper operated as an adjudication only as of the time when it was so produced in court, and promulgated, to wit, as of the third of March, and that the adjudication which was regularly made and entered in the other district on the second of March, took precedence as the earlier adjudication.

All proceedings subsequent to or founded upon adjudication of bankruptcy, *reversed;* and further proceedings in district court stayed.

*See 5 N. B. R. 230.   †See 5 N. B. R. 230, 232, 233.

In re BROOKMIRE & RANKIN,
        ads.
BEAN, *ass. of* KINTZING. } *Missouri.*

Writ of Error to Dist. Court for E. D. 4 *N. B. R.* 57.
———, J.

A payment, made by a debtor who is in insolvent circumstances more than four months before the filing of the petition in bankruptcy by or against him, although made to the creditor by way of preference, will be sustained as against the assignee under the provisions of the first clause of section 35 of the bankrupt act.

Declaration bad.

Demurrer properly sustained by the district court whose judgment is affirmed.

In re BUCHANAN, *et al.*,
        ads.
SMITH, *ass., &c.* } *N. D. New York.*

4 *N. B. R.* 132.
WOODRUFF, J.

A diligent creditor having obtained a judgment is entitled to hold it, except as against an assignee in bankruptcy; but upon adjudication being passed upon his debtor he must relinquish his preference and prove his debt under the provisions of section 23. If he does not, and the assignee is compelled to enforce his claim against the judgment by appeal to the Courts, then he is prevented from proving by the provisions of section 39.

Decree in accordance with prayer of the bill, with costs.

In re CITY BANK OF ST. PAUL,
        ads.
WILSON, *Ass.* } *Minnesota.*

5 *N. B. R.* 270.
DILLON, C. J.
    IN EQUITY:

A mercantile firm having no property but stock in trade, became insolvent, in accepted and sound definition of that term. When pressed for payment of debt, acknowledge its justness, give as reason for non-payment, their inability, and suffer judgment to be rendered against them.

Creditors have reasonable cause of knowledge of debtors' insolvency, and property taken on execution must be restored to assignee.

In re CHENEY,
        ads.
KNIGHT. } *Rhode Island.*

5 *N. B. R.* 305.
CLIFFORD, J.

Decision and decree of District Court *reversed.*

Because, under 25th section of Bankruptcy Act, it does not possess the power to order summarily the sale of an estate, though the same is claimed by assignee, and question existing whether title to same was derived from debtor before adjudication or from some former owner.

In re HUGH CLARK,
        ads.
UNITED STATES. } *Massachusetts.*

4 *N. B. R.* 14.
LOWELL, J.

Defendant indicted for disposing of goods and chattels, other than in usual way of trade, within three months of bankruptcy, obtained on credit.

Sentence, 15 months' imprisonment.

In re A. B. & C. L. CLASEN, } *District of Minnesota.*
ads.
A. J. PHELPS.

3 *N. B. R.* 22.

MILLER, P., J.

Judgment reversed; case remanded. Directions to set aside verdict and grant new trial.

In re COLE, *et al.,* } *Maine.*
ads.
SCAMMON, *Ass.*

5 *N. B. R.* 257.

CLIFFORD, J.

IN EQUITY:

A mortgage given to secure payment of promissory note, the consideration of which being pre-existing debt of bankrupt, is void when made within four months next preceding filing of petition, for express purpose of giving a preference.

Decree affirmed, with costs.

In re S. J. CORBIN, } *Michigan.*
ads.
H. POST, *Ass.*

5 *N. B. R.* 11.

LONGYEAR, J.

Bill filed to recover certain real estate and personal property, alleged to have been conveyed and transferred by bankrupt within four months next before filing petition against him for adjudication of bankruptcy in fraud.

Decree entered. Defendant must account to complainant for all property so conveyed.

In re ASA W. CRAFT. } *S. D. N. Y.*

2 *N. B. R.* 44.

NELSON, C. J.

Petition of creditors to amend 39th section of Act "*Nunc pro tunc.*" Amendment affirmed.

In re CRANE, } *N. D. Illinois.*
ads.
HARVEY, *Ass.*

5 *N. B. R.* 218.

DRUMMOND, J.

A chattel mortgage void as against creditors under the State law, and under which the mortgagee had taken possession, having at the time reasonable cause to believe his debtor insolvent, is also void as against the assignee in bankruptcy.

Motion for new trial overruled.

In re JOHN CRAWFORD, *et al.,* } *S. D. Ohio.*
ads.
THOMAS W. FARRIN.

2 *N. R. R.* 181.

SWAYNE, J.

A debtor, being and knowing himself insolvent, made a general assignment for benefit of creditors, under laws of Ohio, in December, 1868, before proceedings in bankruptcy.

Held—Such an assignment, when made in good faith, is not necessarily an act of bankruptcy, but it must be entirely clear from taint of fraud.

156

Where it appeared that the debtor did not turn over to the assignee money to an amount exceeding the limit of the authorized exemptions.

Held—That the assignment was fraudulent, and an act of bankruptcy.

Where the debtor, being insolvent, paid a freight debt in full by procuring an order from the railroad for and furnishing lumber.

Held—That the payment was a preference of a creditor, and an act of bankruptcy.

Creditors entitled to decree of bankruptcy. Costs of bill paid out of estate.

In re DEL. & HUD. CANAL CO.,
ads.
LITTLEFIELD.

Massachusetts—May, 1870.

4 *N. B. R.* 77.

CLIFFORD, J.

Demurrer sustained. Because petition to revise decision and judgment of District Court does not set forth the error, or nature of the error, for information of the Appellate Court, and as notice to the opposite party.

In re J. DOW. *Rhode Island.*

6 *N. B. R.* 10.

SHEPLEY, J.

In the absence of fraud the assignee takes only such rights and interests as the bankrupt himself had or could assert at the time of his bankruptcy, and consequently he is affected with all the equities which would affect the bankrupt himself if he were asserting those rights and interests.

A mortgage executed in a State having no statute on the subject of record, or if record is not required between the parties, will not be defeated by the proviso in the fourteenth section of the United States Bankrupt Act of 1867 in relation to recording.

When the revisory jurisdiction of the Circuit Court is invoked over the decision of the District Court upon a question of fact, the burden of proof is on the petitioner for review, to show cause in the decision; and he must also show that the evidence cannot support the finding.

Decree of District Judge affirmed, with costs.

In re WILLIAM DOURING. *Missouri—April Term,* 1870.

3 *N. B. R.* 182.

DILLON, J.

I. Where a partnership has been dissolved, and one of the co-partners purchases *all* of the assets of the firm, and agrees to pay all of the debts; and both partners subsequently become bankrupt, and are individually put into bankruptcy, so that there is no solvent partner and no firm property:

Held, under the Bankrupt Act of 1867, that the creditors of the firm, as well as the individual creditors of the partner who assumed to pay the firm debts, were entitled to share *pari passu* in the estate of such partner.

II. Under the Bankrupt Act (section 36), assets are to be marshaled between the firm creditors and the separate creditors of the partners only where there are firm and separate assets, and proceedings are instituted against the firm and the individual members, as provided in that section. Judgment reversed.

In re ELDRIDGE. *E. D. Wisconsin.*

4 *N. B. R.* 162.

DRUMMOND, J.

Mortgage of personal property being, under state law of Wisconsin, ineffectual to pass after acquired property, the assignee in bankruptcy is entitled to such property as against the mortgagee who had taken possession.

In re ELLIOTT,
ads.
SLAMMERS.

} *Eng.*

3 *Law Rep. ch. ap.* 188. 1 *N. B. R.* 204.

Appeal from vice-chancellor Malins. Decree reversed.

In re FILLEY,
ads.
WRIGHT.

} *Missouri.*

4 *N. B. R.* 197.

MILLER, J.

Mere honest inaction in a poor man, when a creditor seeks to make by law a just debt, is not in itself an act of bankruptcy.

Bill in chancery filed to obtain review and reversal of order of District Court. Order reversed.

In re SAMUEL GLASER.
Case pending in S. D. Ohio. Application for attachment for contempt aginst SIGUMUND ULLMAN, *et al.*

} *S. D. New York.*

2 *N. B. R.* 129.

BLATCHFORD, J.

Application refused, for the reason that no written interrogatories accompanied the commission, and no information furnished as to the particular inquiry.

In re GRAVES,
ads.
LAWRENCE, *ass.*

} *Missouri.*

5 *N. B. R.* 279.

TREAT, J. DILLON, J. concurring.

An action, substantially, of trespass "*de bonis asportatis.*"

Judgment of District Court confirmed.

In re HAFER & BROTHER,
ads.
CHAS. E. BECK.

} *E. D. Pennsylvania.*

1 *N. B. R.* 163, 164.

CADWALADER, J.

Referred back to Register. Adjudication of bankruptcy being made in District, during pendency of auxiliary proceedings in equity in Circuit, Court to restrain execution creditors, question arising as to their right of priority.

In re HACKLEY & SONS,
ads.
WILDER D. FOSTER, *ass. of* ALEXANDER BLAKE.

} *W. D. of Michigan. Action of Trover to recover value of Personal Property.*

2 *N. B. R.* 131.

WITHEY, J.

Trial by jury. Verdict for plaintiff.

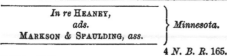

In re HEANEY,
ads.
MARKSON & SPAULDING, *ass.*
} *Minnesota.*

4 *N. B. R.* 165.

DILLON, C. J.

Bill in equity, praying for injunction and relief.

Debtor residing in Kansas adjudged a bankrupt and assignees appointed. After bankruptcy proceedings, mortgage creditor commenced suit to foreclose in *State Court of Indiana,* mortgagee being *resident and citizen of Minnesota,* making assignees defendants. Assignees file bill in Circuit Court of U. S. for District of Minnesota, against mortgagee, charging that the mortgage was fraudulent both in fact and under the bankrupt law, and ask for decree to have it declared void, and for injunction to restrain defendant from further prosecuting foreclosure suit in Indiana.

Injunction denied.

In re HUGHES,
ads.
IRVING.
} *E. D. Pennsylvania.*

2 *N. B. R.* 20.

GRIER AND CADWALADER, J J.

Jurisdiction established. Dissolution of injunction refused, but being modified, continues in force.

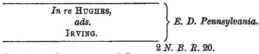

In re JONES,
ads.
ALABAMA & CHATANOOGA R. R. Co.
} *Alabama.*

5 *N. B. R.* 97.

WOODS, J.

The railroad company not being "a banker, broker," &c., and for other reasons, the decree of adjudication by the District Court is *reversed,* and petition *dismissed with costs*.

In re RICHARD P. RUNDLE,
and
FRED'K W. JONES.
} *S. D. N. Y.*

2 *N. B. R.* 49.

BLATCHFORD, J.

Where amount due creditor is in dispute in State Court, suit can proceed conditionally.

In re KARPER, *et al.,*
ads.
HOOD, *et al.*
} *E. D. Pennsylvania.*

5 *N. B. R.* 358.

CADWALADER, D. J. and McKENNAN, C. J.

Bill at suit of petitioning creditors of an involuntary bankrupt, merchant or trader, on behalf of themselves and others, to the intent that the assignee, when qualified, might be added or substituted as complainant. There can be no final decree until assignee in bankruptcy shall have become a party complainant.

In re KEEFER,
ads.
KEATING, *ass., &c.*
} *E. D. Michigan.*

5 *N. B. R.* 133.

LONGYEAR, J.

Decided, That if a married woman consents to the purchase of property with her means by her husband and in his own name, she cannot afterwards reclaim the property as against his creditors, whose debts accrued while the property was so held by him.

In re MORRIS KYLER.   } *S. D. N. Y.*

3 *N. B. R.* 11.

BLATCHFORD, J.

Appeals dismissed. Because they were not claimed and noticed within ten days after the entry of the decision.

In re LADY BRYAN MINING COMPANY. } *Nevada.*

4 *N. B. R.* 131.

SAWYER, C. J.

Petition to reverse order of District Court vacating the adjudication of a corporation as bankrupt, because the proceedings in which the petition was filed were informal and unauthorized, denied, and order of District Judge affirmed.

In re LATHROP,
    ads.
  VOGLE, *ass.* } *W. D. Pennsylvania.*

4 *N. B. R.* 146.

MCKENNAN, J.

Decree in favor of plaintiff's action, as falling within provisions of section 30 of Bankrupt Act.

In re ELIZA A. MASSEY, *et al.*
    ads.
  ALLEN, *ass., etc.* } *Missouri.*

4 *N. B. R.* 75.

DILLON, J.   KREKEL, J. concurs.

When a sale or conveyance by bankrupt before bankruptcy is void, as to creditors, under the statute of the State where he resides, the assignee of the bankrupt may impeach the same, and bring suit in respect to the property.

Order affirmed.

In re JOHN SEDGWICK, *ass.,* &c., WILLIAM MINCK, and CHARLES B. BOSTWICK,
    ads.
  JOHN SEDGWICK, *ass., &c.* } *S. D. N. Y.*

1 *N. B. R.* 204.

NELSON, J.

Motion to dissolve injunction granted. Bill filed by assignee in bankruptcy to compel receiver in creditor's bills against the bankrupt appointed before the proceedings in bankruptcy to deliver up the property in his hands as receiver.

In re MITTLEDORFER & Co., *Bankrupts,*
    ex parte,
  RUTHERGLEN, *ass.* } *Virginia.*

3 *N. B. R.* 9.

HON. SALMON P. CHASE, C. J.

Assignees in bankruptcy of a firm sent back to the Register for additional proof, a certain claim of M. proved by the oath of a member of the firm as trustee of the claimant. On application to the District Judge by the counsel of the trustee, it was ordered that dividend on the claim be paid. The assignee was not heard on the application, and petitioned the Circuit Court to review the case and reverse the said order.

Held—The District Court has power, upon petition of the contesting creditor, to reverse the decision of an assignee rejecting his claim, but the mode of proceeding must be regular, and the assignee should have opportunity to answer and contest the claim.

Semble—That a member of a bankrupt firm cannot represent claims against the estate

Orders reversed. Case remanded.

In re MOORE, FOOTE & CO.,
 ads,
FREDERICK E. DRIGGS, *ass. of* TON-
KINS & TREWARTHA, *Bankrupts.*
} *E. D. Michigan.*

3 *N. B. R.* 149.

WITHEY, J.

IN CHANCERY:

Mortgage in preference, creditors knowing it. Judgment for plaintiff.

In re MUNGER, *et al.,*
 ads.
CURRAN, *et al.*
} *W. D. Michigan.*

6 *N. B. R.* 33.

EMMONS, J.

When the petition for review under the rules in the Sixth Circuit is demurred to, its statements, like those of any other pleading, will be taken as true, and the appeal determined upon its averments. If the facts therein are sufficient, the demurrer will be overruled and the decree below reversed.

When an agent is sent by an insolvent debtor to compromise with creditors, and some of them, through him, return different terms than those submitted, such agent does not thereby become that of such creditors, but remains the agent of the debtor, and his knowledges, mistakes and acts are those of his principal—the insolvent. The same effect would be produced if he were deemed the *common* agent of both parties.

When a debtor and a preferred creditor know of the insolvency, but *erroneously* suppose all other creditors have compromised for thirty-five cents in time paper, a transfer so securing the creditor as to create a preference financially is an act of bankruptcy. If insolvency is once known all parties act at their peril, when such condition actually exists, whether known or unknown.

When proceedings were pending in bankruptcy, and ₐa preferred creditor and the insolvent settle the petitioning creditor's debt, and employ the attorney who conducts such proceedings to compromise with the other creditors, authorizing him to pay some one price and others another, and it appears that such discrimination was in fact made, such scheme is *prima facie* fraudulent, and the burden is upon the actors to show that all the creditors *consented* to such preferences. It will not be presumed. But if any one creditor does not consent it is a fraud upon him, although all the others are satisfied.

Decree below, dismissing petition, reversed, and adjudication of bankruptcy ordered. Vide 4 N. B. R. 90, for fuller facts.

NATIONAL BANK OF FAYETTEVILLE,
 et al., (right of banks to dividends
 against joint and separate estates
 of debtors),
  ads.
 CHAS. H. MEAD, *ass., &c.*
} *N. D. N. Y.*

2 *N. B. R.* 65.

HALL. J.

Decision dependent upon further research. Right valid conditionally. As *In re* Howard, Cole & Co., District of Maryland, 4 N. B. R. 185, Giles, J.

In re NEW YORK KEROSENE OIL CO. } *E. D. N. Y.*

3 *N. B. R.* 31.

NELSON, C. J.

Petition to District Court by assignee to be amended and filed as bill in equity. Proceedings stayed, and all orders and proceedings inconsistent set aside and vacated. *Because* proceedings by the assignee should have been by bill in equity and not by petition.

In re THE NEW YORK MAIL STEAMSHIP CO. } *S. D. N. Y.*

3 *N. B. R.* 155.

WOODRUFF, C. J.

Petitioner of creditors employs counsel. All others benefited. Counsel fees defrayed out of funds in hands of assignee. Decision. All reasonable expenses allowed.

In re MARY O'BRIEN. } *N. D. N. Y.*

N. B. R. Sup. 38.

NELSON, J.

Appeal from adjudication of bankruptcy. Dismissed for want of jurisdiction

---

In re PERRY,
ads.
LANGLEY. } *S. D. Ohio.*

2 *N. B. R.* 180.

SWAYNE, J.

Demurrer overruled. Judgment reversed. Cause remanded for the reason that the District Court erred in finding that the pleading and proofs substantiated commission of act of bankruptcy.

In re JAMES K. PLACE, et al.,
ads.
JOHN SEDGWICK, ass., &c. } *S. D. N. Y.*

1 *N. B. R.* 204.

NELSON, J.

To require assignee under State law to deliver property to assignee in bankruptcy. Motion denied. General assignment of insolvent debtor, under State law, untainted by fraud, as against any creditor, or the bankrupt act, is valid.

In re PLACE & SPARKMAN. } *S. D. N. Y.*

4 *N. B. R.* 178.

WOODRUFF, J.

Appeal dismissed, because creditor appealing failed to file statement of claim in writing within the ten days limited therefor.

In re RAPPLEE,
ads.
BALDWIN, ass. } *New York—June Term*, 1871.

5 *N. B. R.* 19.

WOODRUFF, J.

Decree entered in District Court in favor of complainant. Respondent files notice of appeal, giving requisite bonds. Citation issues within ten days and in due time, but the transmiss upon appeal not filed in Circuit Court till after two terms has gone over. Motion to dismiss appeal, because transmiss had not been filed at next term after the appeal, denied; because time to dismiss had been enlarged by agreement of counsel.

In re RICHTER'S ESTATE.	*Iowa.*

4 N. B. R. 67.

DILLON, J.

Orders to set aside judgment obtained against property fraudulently conveyed, confirmed.

In re WARD E. ROBINSON.	*S. D. N. Y.*

2 N. B. R. 108.

NELSON, J.

Petition for review denied, with costs. Bankrupt arrested and held to bail. Debt proved in bankruptcy shown by record of State Court to have been created in fraud. District Court refused to discharge bankrupt, or to direct satisfaction of judgment.

In re SCHOONER S. L. DAVIS and CARGO COTTON, *ads.* A. M. DOUGLAS.	*S. D. N. Y.—In Admiralty.*

2 N. B. R. 3.

NELSON, J.

Property of the United States is subject to contribution for salvage. Decree below, dismissing libel, reversed.

In re PATRICK SHEA and WILLIAM BOYLE, *ads.* J. H. HEINSHEIMER, *et al.*	*District of Indiana.*

3 N. B. R. 46.

McDONALD, G. J.

"*Prima facie*" evidence of commission of act of bankruptcy on "commercial paper."

In re LORING M. SMITH, *ads.* ALEX. R. LINN, *et al.*	*E. D. Michigan.*

4 N. B. R. 12.

EMMONS, J.

A creditor can file a petition against his debtor, even though his claim is not due.

If the debts are provable under the act, they are such as the act contemplates as sufficient on which to base a bankruptcy proceeding. Judgment affirmed.

In re SMITH, *et al.,* *ads.* MARTIN, *ass., etc.*	*Missouri.*

4 N. B. R. 83.

DILLON, C. J.

Decree reversed. Because, *in equity*, the statute of limitations is no bar to relief sought.

In re STANSELL.	*W. D. Michigan.*

6 N. B. R. 183.

EMMONS, J.

A debt wholly or in part secured, either by levy under an execution, by pledge of personal property or mortgage upon real estate, will sustain a petition for an adjudication of bankruptcy. The better practice is, when the debt is *fully* secured, to waive the security in the petition, but this is not necessary to its support.

Decree below reversed and adjudication ordered.

In re Trustees of University and C. Dewey, *ass. et al.,* ads. The State of N. Carolina.	*N. Carolina.*

5 *N. B. R.* 466.

Brooks, J.

Circuit Court of the United States have no jurisdiction of a case either at law or in equity, in which a state is plaintiff against its own citizens. *Bill dismissed.*

In re Jonathan W. Vickevy.	*W. D. Michigan.*

3 *N. B. R.* 171.

Withey, J.

Dissent from decision, *in re* Williams, 2 B. R. 79; and fully *concur*, in decision *in re* Brown, 3 B. R. 145.

In re Henry Vogel.	*S. D N. Y.*

3 *N. B. R.* 49.

Nelson, J..

Question of review. Goods of bankrupt *in State Court* after petition filed. Application to District Court, and goods ordered to be delivered. Appeal taken. Petition for review dismissed.

In re Wager & Fales, ads. Hall, *ass., etc.*	*W. D. Wisconsin.*

5 *N. B. R.* 181.

Hopkins, J.

Bill in equity to set aside mortgage given by bankrupt to defendants on the ground that it was void under the Bankrupt Act.

Mortgage declared void, and cancelment upon the records ordered.

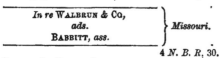

In re Walbrun & Co, ads. Babbitt, *ass.*	*Missouri.*

4 *N. B. R.* 30.

Dillon, J. Treat, J. concurs.

Judgment reversed. Case remanded, because a sale of property by bankrupt, out of the usual and ordinary course of business, is *prima facie* evidence of fraud.

In re Waller, ads. Bigler.	*Virginia.*

4 *N. B. R.* 86.

Chase, C. J.

Decree. Cessation of interest during civil war or hostilities.

In re Wilder, *et al.,* ads. Baldwin, *et al.*	*W. D. Michigan.*

6 *N. B. R.* 85.

Emmons, J.

A suspension of payment of commercial paper for fourteen days, under section thirty-nine, before the amendment of July fourteenth, eighteen hundred and seventy, was *per se* an act of bankruptcy.

The omission to pay such paper for fourteen days, subsequent to that amendment, is a suspension within its meaning, although the paper fell due and was dishonored before its passage.

Decree below, dismissing petition, reversed, and adjudication of bankruptcy ordered.

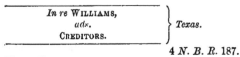

In re WILLIAMS, *ads.* CREDITORS.	} *Texas.*

4 *N. B. R.* 187.

WOODS, J.

Power of attorney, in accordance with Form No. 26, does not authorize filing of opposition to bankrupt's discharge.

Ruling of District Court correct. Case remanded at cost of petitioner. Ordered, that certificate of discharge issue.

In re FREDERICK A. WINSTON, *ads.* ROBERT A. KINSIE.	} *Illinois.*

4 *N. B. R.* 21.

WILLIAMS, J.

Plaintiff, immediately previous to his bankruptcy in March, 1842, had a fee simple title in Sand street, Chicago, subject to the public easement, which street then terminated in Lake Michigan, but more than 450 feet of accretion now exists between Sands street and the present lake shore.

Found for defendant.

In re CHAS. H. WYNNE—*Involuntary.* } *Virginia.*

4 *N. B. R.* 5.

CHASE, C. J.

A deed of trust, executed December 8, 1866, by a bankrupt who did not file his petition till June 8, 1867, was not recorded until March 2, 1867.

Decree of District Court reversed.

In re YORK & HOOVER. } *Louisiana.*

4 *N. B. R.* 156. *See* 3 *N. B. R.* 163.

WOODS, J

Appeal from District Court. Decision overruled and dismissed.

A proceeding in bankruptcy, from the filing of petition to distribution of bankrupt's estate and his discharge, is a single statutory proceeding.

OVERRULED CASES

COURT OF APPEALS.

In re ROBERT H. BARR, *et al.*,
      ads.
WILLIAM A. VAN NOSTRAND. } *Maryland. Appeal from Court of Common Pleas.*

2 N. B. R. 154.

BARTOE, C. J.

The Court of Appeals of Maryland has appellate jurisdiction from the Court of Common Pleas in insolvent cases, under a proper construction of section 28 of the 4th article of the State Constitution.

The United States Courts have exclusive jurisdiction in the case of an insolvent debtor, whether he can or cannot obtain a discharge in bankruptcy.

Order of the Court of Common Pleas, removing a trustee appointed under the State Insolvent Laws, and dismissing petition of insolvent debtor for want of jurisdiction, affirmed.

In re PHELPS, *et al.*,
      ads.
CASE. } *New York.*

5 N. B. R. 452

WOODRUFF, J.

A person about to engage in a new business may not, with a view thereto, and for the purpose of securing his property for the benefit of himself and his family, in the event of losses occurring in such new business, convey such property to his wife voluntarily, without consideration. Such a conveyance is fraudulent and void as to subsequent creditors.

It must be so declared, notwithstanding it be distinctly found that the conveyance was made without any intent to defraud creditors then existing.

Order appealed from reversed. Judgment of referee affirmed, with costs.

LIST

ABBREVIATIONS AND REFERENCES

IN VOLS. I AND II OF THIS DIGEST.

A.

A. & E............... Adolphus & Ellis.
Abb. D. C............ Abbott's United States District Court Reports.
Abb. U. S............ Abbott's United States Reports.
A. L. Reg............ American Law Register.
A. L. Rev............ American Law Review.
A. L. T.............. American Law Times.
Atk. Ch. R........... Atkinson's Chancery Reports.

B.

B. & A............... Barnewall & Anderson.
B. & Ad.............. Barnewall & Adolphus.
B. C. C.............. Lowndes & Maxwell's Bail Court Cases.
B. C. Rep............ Saunders & Cole's Bail Court Reports.
Barb................. Barbour's Reports.
Bayl. Bills.......... Bayley on Bills.
Beav................. Beavan.
B. & S............... Best & Smith.
Bell, C. C........... Bell's Criminal Cases.
Bing................. Bingham.
B. N. C.............. Bingham's New Cases or Series.
Bing., N. C.......... Bingham's New Cases or Series.
Bl. C. C............. Blatchford's Circuit Court Reports.
Bligh................ Bligh.
Bligh, N. S.......... Bligh's New Series.
B. & P............... Bosanquet & Puller.
Botts' P. L.......... Botts Poor Law.
B. & B.............. Broderip & Bingham.
Bro. C. C............ Brown's Chancery Cases.
Bro. P. C............ Brown's Cases in Parliament.
B. & L............... Browning & Lushington.
Buck .... Buck.
Bull., N. P.......... Buller's Law of Nisi Prius.
Burr .... Burrow.
Burr. S. C........... Burrow's Settlement Cases.
B.................... Benedict's Reports.

C.

C.................... Lord Chancellor.
C. C. A.............. County Court Appeals.
Cal................. California Reports.
Cald................ Caldecott's Settlement Cases.
Camp................ Campbell.
Car. C. L............ Carrington's Criminal Law.
Car. & M............ Carrington & Marshman.
Car. & K............ Carrington & Kirwan.

C. & P.............. Carrington & Payne.
C. & L. C. C...-.,.... Cave & Leigh's Crown Cases.
Chit .... Chitty.
C. & F.............. Clark & Finnelly.
Collyer C. C......... Collyer's Chancery Cases.
C. B............... Common Bench Reports, Old Series.
C. B. N. S........... Common Bench Reports, New Series (Scott's).
C. L. R.............. Common Law Reports of 1855-56.
Com............... Comstock's New York Reports.
Comr............... Commissioner.
Conn .... Connecticut Reports.
Cooper C. C......... Cooper's Chancery Cases.
Cowp..,..........,. Cowper.
Cox................ Cox.
Cox C. C............ Coxs' Criminal Cases.
C. L. N............. Chicago Legal News.
Cr.................. Cranchs' United States Reports.
Cr. & Ph........... Craig & Philip.
C. & J............. Crompton & Jervis.
C. & M............. Crompton & Meeson.
C. M. & R.......... Crompton, Meesen & Roscoe.
Cush.............. Cushing's Reports.
Curt.............. Curteis.

D.

Dall. Pa..........,... Dallas' Pennsylvania Reports.
Daniel.............. Daniel.
D. & M............. Davidson & Merivale.
Deacon............. Deacon.
Deac. & Chit........ Deacon & Chitty.
Deane Ecc. Rep..:... Deane's Ecclesiastical Reports.
Dears. C. C......... Dearsly & Bell's Crown Cases.
De G............... De Gex.
De G. F. & J........ De Gex, Fisher & Jones.
De G. J. & S........ De Gex, Jones & Smith.
De G. M. & G....... De Gex, Macnaughton & Gordon.
De G. & Sm.......... De Gex & Smale.
Den. C. C. .... Denison Exclr'r Cham. & Crim. Appeal.
D. & R............. Dowling & Ryland.
Drink.............. Drinkwater.
Drew.............. Drewry.
Drew. & Sm........ Drewry & Smale.

E.

East............... East.
Eden.............. Eden.
El. & Bl........ .... Ellis & Blackburn.
El. Bl. & El.......... Ellis, Blackburn & Ellis.
El. & El........... Ellis & Ellis.
Eq. R.............. Equity Reports of 1855-56.
Esp................ Espinasse.
Exch .... Exchequer Reports by Welsby, Hurlstone & Gordon.
Exch. Cham......... Exhecquer Chamber.

F.

Fonb. N. R.......... Fonblanque's New Reports.

G.

Ga................. Georgia Reports.
G. & D............. Gale & Davidson.
Giff .... Giffard.

Giff. & H............ Giffard & Hemning.
Glyn & J............ Glyn & Jameson.
Gow................ Gow.

H.

Hare .... Hare.
H. & R............ Harrison & Rutherford.
H. & W............ Harrison & Wollaster.
Holt............... Holt.
H. & H............ Horn & Hurlstone.
H. L............... House of Lords.
H. L. Cas........... House of Lords Cases (by Clark).'
How............... Howard's Reports (Sup. Ct. U. S.)
How. N. Y.......... Howard's New York Reports.

J.

Johns .... Johns.
Johns. (Eng.)........ Johnson (Chancery).
Johns. & H .... Johnson & Hemming.
Jur................ Jurist.
Jur. N. S............ Jurist, New Series.

K.

Kay .... Kay.
Kay & J.. .... Kay & Johnson.
K. & G.............. Keane & Grant.
Ker................ Kernan's New York Reports.
Ky................ Kentucky Reports.

L.

Ld. Kenyon.......... Lord Kenyon's Notes of Cases.
L. J................ Lord Justices' Court.
L. J. Adm.......... (Admiralty) Law Journal, New Series.
L. J. Bank.......... (Bankruptcy) Law Journal, New Series.
L. J. Chanc........ (Chancery) Law Journal, New Series.
L. J. C. P........... (Common Pleas) Law Journal, New Series.
L. J. Exch.......... (Exchequer) Law Journal, New Series.
L. J. M. C.......... (Magistrates' Cases) Law Journal, New Series.
L. J. Q B.......... (Queen's Bench) Law Journal, New Series.
L. J. Mat. Cas....... (Matrimonial Cases) Law Journal, New Series.
L. J. P. C.......... (Privy Council) Law Journal, New Series.
L. J. P. or Prob...... (Probate Court) Law Journal, New Series.
L. R Q. B............ Law Reports (Queen's Bench).
L. R. C. P.......... Law Reports (Common Pleas).
L. R. Exch.......... Law Reports (Exchequer).
L. R. Adm.......... Law Reports (Admiralty.)
L. R. P. or Prob..... Law Reports (Probate).
L. R. D............. Law Reports (Divorce and Matrimonial).
L. R. C. C.......... Law Reports (Crown Cases Reserved).
L. R. Eq........... Law Reports (Master of the Rolls and Vice-Chancellors)
L. R. Ch............ Law Reports (Lord Chancellor's and Appeal).
L. R. P. C.......... Law Reports (Privy Council).
L. R. H. L. Cas...... Law Reports (House of Lords Cases).
L. T. N. S.......... Law Times Reports, New Series.
L. M. & P.......... Lowndes, Maxwell & Pollock.

M.

Mac. & G .... Macnaughton & Gordon.
Macq. H. L .Cas...... Macqueen's Scotch Appeals.
Madd .... Maddock.

M. & G.	Manning & Granger.
M. R.	Master of the Rolls.
M C.	Magistrate Cases.
M. & W.	Meeson & Welsby.
M. & M.	Moody & Malkin.
M. & P.	Moore & Payne.
M. & Rob.	Moody & Robinson.
M. & R.	Manning & Ryland.
M. & S.	Maule & Selwyn.
M. & Scott.	Moore & Scott.
McCld	McCleland.
Marsh.	Marshall.
Mass.	Massachusetts Reports.
Mer.	Merivale.
Met.	Metcalf's Massachusetts Reports.
Min.	Minnesota Reports.
Mont.	Montagu.
Mont. & Ayr.	Montagu & Ayrton.
Mont. & Bligh.	Montagu & Bligh.
Mont. & Chit.	Montagu & Chitty.
Mont. D. & D.	Montagu, Deacon & De Gex.
Mont. & Mac.	Montagu & Macarthur.
Moore.	I. B. Moore.
Moore P. C. C.	Moore's Privy Council Cases.
Moore P. C. C. N. S.	Moore's Privy Council Cases, New Series.
Mylne & C.	Mylne & Craig.
Mylne & K	Mylne & Keene.

N.

N. B. R.	National Bankruptcy Register.
N. B. R. Sup.	National Bankruptcy Register, Supplement.
N. & M.	Neville & Manning.
N. & P.	Neville & Perry.
N. Y.	New York Reports.
N. Y. Leg. Obs.	New York Legal Observer.

P.

Pa. (or Penn.)	Pennsylvania Reports.
Pet.	Peters.
Peake.	Peake.
Peake's Add. Cas.	Peake's Additional Cases.
Ph	Phillips.
Pick.	Pickering's Massachusetts Reports.
Pitts. L. J.	Pittsburgh Legal Journal.
P. Wms.	Peere Williams.
P. & D.	Perry & Davison.

R.

Rob.	Robinson (House of Lords).
Robn.	Robinson on Bankruptcy.
Rob. Adm. Rep.	Dr. W. Robinson's Admiralty Reports.
Rose	Rose.
Russ.	Russell.
Russ. & Mylne.	Russell & Mylne.
Russ. C. & M.	Russell on Crimes and Misdemeanors.
R. & M.	Ryan & Moody.

S.

Scott.	Scott.
Scott N. R.	Scott's New Reports.
Selw. N. P.	Selwyn's Law of Nisi Prius.

Sim................	Simon.
Sim. N. S...........	Simon's New Series.
Sim. & Stu..........	Simon & Stuart.
Stark..............	Starkie.
Sm. & G............	Smale & Giffard.
Stock..............	Stocking's New Jersey Reports.

T.

Tiff................	Tiffany's New York Reports.
Tyr................	Tyrwhitt.
Tyr. & G...........	Tyrwhitt & Granger.

V.

Ves. jun...........	Vesey, Junior.
Ves. & B...........	Vesey & Beames.

W.

Wall...............	Wallace's Reports.
Wend..............	Wendell's Reports.
Wils...............	Wilson.
Wils. C. C..........	Wilson's Chancery Cases.
Wills Exch.........	Wills' Exchequer Reports.
W. Bl..............	Sir William Blackstone.
W. R..............	Weekly Reporter.
Wheat.............	Wheaton's Reports.
W. Jur............	Western Jurist.
W. & S. Pa. R.......	Watt's & Sargeant's Pennsylvania Reports.

Y.

Y. & J.............	Younge & Jervis.

TABLE OF CASES

159

C.

F.

G.

H.

N.

169

O

P.

Q.

R.

U

Lightning Source UK Ltd.
Milton Keynes UK
UKHW010944160119
335665UK00016B/1241/P